INTERNATIONAL BUSINESS AND
CENTRAL EUROPE, 1918–1939

International Business and Central Europe, 1918–1939

*Edited by Alice Teichova
and P. L. Cottrell*

Leicester University Press
St. Martin's Press, New York
1983

First published in 1983 by Leicester University Press

First published in the United States of America in 1983 by
St. Martin's Press, Inc., 175 Fifth Avenue, New York, NY 10010

Designed by Douglas Martin
Typeset in 10/12 pt Linotron 202 Plantin
printed and bound in Great Britain
at The Pitman Press, Bath

British Library Cataloguing in Publication Data

International business and Central Europe 1918–1939.
1. Central Europe–Foreign economic relations–History–Congresses
I. Cottrell, P.L.   II. Teichova, A.
338.1′0943   NC244

ISBN 0–7185–1206–5

Library of Congress Cataloging in Publication Data

Main Entry under Title:
International Business and Central Europe, 1918–1939
Includes index.
1. Corporations, Foreign–Europe, Eastern–History–Addresses,
Essays, Lectures. 2. International Business Enterprises–Europe,
Eastern–History–Addresses, Essays, Lectures. 3. Investments,
Foreign–Europe–Eastern–History–Addresses, Essays, Lectures.
I. Teichova, Alice. II. Cottrell, P.L.
HD2844.I57   1983   338.8′8843   83-13956

ISBN 0-312-41982-1

Contents

Part One Corporate Strategy and Structure: Substitution of the Market Mechanism?

Part Two German Concerns in Eastern Europe

Figures

Tables

Abbreviations

1. Abbreviations used in the text

AEG	Allgemeine Elektrizitäts-Gesellschaft-Union Elektrizitäts-Gesellschaft
AG	Aktiengesellschaft
ATiag	Lékařsko-technický průmysl akciová společnost, Prague
ATT	Associated Telephone and Telegraph Co., Chicago
BHO	Berg- und Hüttenwerkgesellschaft OstmbH
BUP	Banque de l'Union parisienne
CIA	Convention de l'Industrie de l'Azote
DAG	Dynamit-Actiengesellschaft vormals Alfred Nobel & Co., Hamburg
DN, Bratislava	Účastinná spoločnosť Dynamit Nobel, Bratislava
DN, Vienna	Österreichische Dynamit Nobel AG, Vienna
Emag	Akciová společnost pro výrobu elektrických zařízení a stavbu strojů, Müglitz (Mohelnice)
fr.	franc
GEC	General Electric Company
Hö	Höchst Works Archives
HTO	Haupttreuhandstelle Ost
IG	IG Farbenindustrie AG
Imco	International Match Corporation
ITT	International Telephone and Telegraph Corporation
K	crown
KA	commercial commission, IG Farben
Kč	Czechoslovak crown
KDK	Konwencja Dąbrowsko-Krakowska
KGS	Górnośląska Konwencja Węglowa
M	Mark
Monzap	Spolka Akcyjna do Eksploatacju Panstwowego Monopolu Zapalzcanego w Polsce
MW-Komotau	Mannesmannröhren-Werke AG, Komotau
MWT	Mitteleuropäischer Wirtschaftstag
ö. K	Austrian crown
ÖSSW	Österreichische Siemens-Schuckert Werke
Pg	Pengö
RM	Reichsmark
SaCO	Silesian-American Corporation
sch.	schilling

S & H	Siemens u. Halske Aktiengesellschaft
SEAG	Siemens akciová spol. pro výrobu elektrických zařízení, Prague
SIC	Standard Industrial Classification
SOA	Southeast European Commission, IG Farben
SOFINA	Société Financière des Transport et d'Enterprises Industrielles
Spolek	Spolek pro chemickou a hutní výrobu
SSW	Siemens-Schuckertwerke
TBs	technical bureaux, Siemens
Tiag	Siemens, technický průmysl akciová společnost. Prague
UEIF	Union Européenne industrielle et financière
Unal	Union Allumettière
VBs	distribution offices, Siemens
VIAG	Vereinigte Industrie-Unternehmungen Aktiengesellschaft
Vowi	Political Economy Department, IG Farben
VS	Vereinigte Stahlwerke
Wipo	Economic Policy Department, IG Farben
Zefi	Central Finance Department, IG Farben
Zendei	Zentralverband der deutschen elektrotechnischen Industrie e.V.
zł	złoty

2. Abbreviations used in the notes

ADAP	*Akten zur deutschen auswärtigen Politik*
APK	State Archive, Katowice
AVA	Österreichisches Staatsarchiv, Allgemeines Verwaltungsarchiv
AZ	*Arbeiter-Zeitung*, Vienna
BoE	Bank of England Papers, London
BWA	Bayer Works Archives
EcHR	*Economic History Review*
FA	Finanzarchiv, Vienna
Hö	Höchst Works Archives
MA	Mannesmann-Archiv
MAE	Ministry of Foreign Affairs Archive, Paris
ME	Ministry of the Economy – Ministry of the Budget, Economic and Financial Archives, Paris
NA	National Archives, Washington DC
NCA	*Nazi Conspiracy and Aggression*
NFP	*Neue Freie Presse*, Vienna
ÖVW	*Österreichischer Volkswirt*, Vienna

PRO	Public Record Office, London
SAA	Siemens Archiv Akte
TWC	*Trials of the War Criminals before the Nuremberg Military Tribunal*
USSBS	*United States Strategic Bombing Survey*
WPH	Urząd Wojewódzki Śląski Wydzial Przemyslu i Handlu

Note Places of publication are given only for works published outside the United Kingdom. Commonly accepted abbreviations such as *J.* for *Journal*, *Rev.* for *Review* have been used in addition to the abbreviations listed above.

Acknowledgments

This volume is the product of many hands and its publication has been greatly assisted by the generous support of the Social Science Research Council which has not only funded the research work of the editors but also financed the conference at which the papers contained in this volume were originally given. The organization of that conference was also supported financially by the University of East Anglia. The International Symposium ran smoothly because of a great deal of 'behind the scenes' work by Valerie Striker, Elizabeth Boross and Penny Ratcliffe. Dr Eva Kandler together with Maureen Cottrell assisted with the translation of some of the papers both for circulation at the conference and for the editorial stages in the preparation of this volume. Peter Teich and John Jillow aided in the process of producing legible diagrams while Irene Orgill, Gillian Austen and Margaret Christie have maintained a flow of typescript. The editors take this opportunity to thank the financial sponsors, the contributors, the discussants, and their technical supporters for their collaboration in what has been a truly multinational enterprise. Peter Boulton of Leicester University Press has encouraged the project of publishing this volume and has shown consistent interest and help.

December 1981 ALICE TEICHOVA
University of East Anglia and the Woodrow Wilson
International Center for Scholars, Washington
PHILIP COTTRELL
University of Leicester and Robinson College, Cambridge

Participants

International Business and Central Europe, 1918–39

Dr B. W. E. Alford, Bristol
M. C. Beaud, Paris
Prof. Dr I. T. Berend, Budapest
Ms E. Boross, UEA Norwich
Mr P. L. Boulton, Leicester
  University Press
M. E. Bussière, Paris
Prof. Dr F. Caron, Chatenay
  Malabry
Prof. A. D. Chandler, Jr, Boston
Prof. R. A. Church, UEA Norwich
Mrs M. Cottrell, Leicester
Dr P. L. Cottrell, Leicester
Prof. Dr E. Crouzet, Paris
Prof. Dr H. Daems, Brussels
Prof. Dr W. Długorborski, Bielefeld
Mr I. Farr, UEA Norwich
Dr P. G. Fischer, Vienna
Dr T. R. Gourvish, UEA Norwich
Mr W. Guttsman, UEA Norwich
Dr L. Hannah, London
Dr M. Hauner, London
Dr P. Hertner, Darmstadt
Dr B. A. Holderness, UEA Norwich
Mrs M. Holmes, UEA Norwich
Dr G. G. Jones, Cambridge
Dr E. M. Kandler, Oxford
Mr M. Kaser, Oxford
Dr P. Kennedy, UEA Norwich
Dr W. P. Kennedy, Essex
Dr W. R. Lee, Liverpool
Dr J. Leslie, London
Prof. Dr M. Lévy-Leboyer, Paris
Mr P. Lyth, UEA Norwich

Dr S. Marriner, Liverpool
Prof. Dr E. März, Vienna
Prof. Dr H. Matis, Vienna
Dr Malin, SSRC, London
Prof. Dr B. Michel, Paris-Poitiers
Mr M. Miller, UEA Norwich
Prof. A. Milward, Manchester
Dr R. Munting, UEA Norwich
Dr R. Nötel, Oxford/Geneva
Prof. U. Olsson, Sweden
Dr R. Overy, Cambridge
Prof. Dr A. Paulinyi, Darmstadt
Prof. Dr H. Pohl, Bonn
Prof. Dr G. Ránki, Budapest
Mr P. Salmon, London
Dr J. M. Sanderson, UEA Norwich
Dr H. J. Schröder, Mainz
Mr H. Schröter, Hamburg
Mrs V. Schröter, Hamburg
Dr D. Stiefel, Vienna
Dr N. Stone, Cambridge
Mr B. Supple, Oxford
Dr M. Teich, Cambridge
Prof. A. Teichova, UEA Norwich
Prof. J. Tomaszewski, Warsaw
Mr C. Trebilcock, Cambridge
Prof. Dr W. Treue, Göttingen
Dr M. Vogt, Darmstadt
Mr R. Waller, UEA Norwich
Dr F. Weber, Vienna
Prof. Dr B.-J. Wendt, Hamburg
Dr U. Wengeroth, Darmstadt
Dr U. Wikander, Stockholm
Dr R. G. Wilson, UEA Norwich

Introduction

Increasingly the attention of business historians has turned to the development of multi-unit and multi-national companies as is shown by the growing literature on these subjects.[1] This volume continues that trend but in terms of the yet unexplored relationships between companies and banks which had their head offices in Western Europe and their subsidiaries in East Central Europe during the inter-war period. Accordingly it is the first publication concerned specifically with international business interests in the successor states. These nations were established out of the Austro-Hungarian Empire in 1918 and their boundaries were delineated by the Versailles Peace Treaty system of 1919 to 1920. Although it is generally recognized in political history that the relations between the 'Great Powers' had a powerful influence upon the international position of the countries of the Danubian region, it is only recently that economic historians have become interested in the problems of Eastern Europe.[2] Despite the importance of this region in the power struggles on the eve of two world wars, research and the published literature is still not prolific. This is especially the case with regard to multi-national companies and direct foreign investment in Europe generally, and particularly with respect to the Danubian lands.

In order to make a start in filling this major gap in historical writing, the editors of this volume embarked upon a research project entitled 'Multi-national Companies in Interwar East Central Europe'. This has the aim of trying to establish greater insights into the significance and mechanisms of direct investment undertaken by British, French, and German concerns in Austrian, Czechoslovak and Hungarian industrial enterprises and financial institutions. During the course of this still ongoing research work, it was decided to offer some provisional results for discussion at a conference to be attended by others working in the same or related areas. The response to the invitations was much greater than had been expected and the papers given and remarks made at that conference both complemented the wider framework of our research endeavour and formed an integral part of it. The contributions published in this volume were prepared by scholars in the fields of economic, business and financial history and were discussed by 66 participants from nine countries at an International Symposium in Economic History held at the University of East Anglia, Norwich, between 20 and 22 September 1979.

The prepared papers have been somewhat rearranged for publication and are now divided into four parts as opposed to the original conference programme of three groups. Each individual study is based upon primary material and explores questions concerned with business and financial aspects of the complex economy of inter-war Europe. The comments made by discussants have been added after each relevant paper.

Part One, on 'Corporate Strategy and Structure – Substitution of the Market Mechanism?', looks at the process of concentration in the industrial sector and is concerned with comparisons between the highly advanced economies of Western Europe and the relatively backward countries of the Danubian region. Although there is evidence of the parallel development of multi-unit companies in similar branches of industry in all the economies examined during the first half of the twentieth century, the causes for this emergence of large enterprises differ. In the West, with the increasingly important mass consumption market, the self-adjusting market mechanism may have been complemented by the 'visible' hand of the managerial decision-making process, whereas in the smaller economies of the successor states with stagnant or even contracting markets, 'invisible' market forces[3] were largely regulated by cartels, mergers and state controls.

Part Two, on 'German Concerns and Eastern Europe 1919–1939', and Part Three, on 'German and Swedish Capital in East Central European Industry', consist of case studies of leading German-based industrial enterprises and a contribution on a Swedish-based multi-national concern. Part Four, 'Western Capital and the Commercial Banks of East Central Europe', examines the interests of West European banks in the successor states.

In particular the question of continuity and discontinuity in the development of the Danubian region is explored in Part One. On the one hand, the heritage of traditional market relations from the Habsburg economy continued until at least the crisis of 1929 to 1933, while on the other, the disintegrative features, which could be observed before 1914, had a major role in reshaping business structures during the 1920s. Some answers can be gleaned from an examination of what actually did disintegrate. If markets survived at least perfunctorily, industrial administration disintegrated because of the need to conform after 1918 to the different legal systems of the successor states and, above all, the structure of the ownership of capital changed substantially. As a result of the outcome of the war Austrian and German economic interests in the successor states were replaced largely by business and financial groups from the Entente Powers during the 1920s. This was partly due to Western businessmen and bankers regarding the Danubian region as something of a substitute area where investments could be made to replace those lost in Russia after the October Revolution of 1917.

The nature of change in the region in terms of continuity can be examined on the basis of whether either Austrian economic control was significantly eroded or if it was cloaked and so sustained by Western, mainly British and French, business. From the evidence gathered by the contributors to this volume, it is difficult to sustain the idea of the continuation of Austrian domination over banking and industry in East Central and South East Europe during the inter-war period. Rather it would appear that control over capital formation in this region slipped largely out of Austrian hands. However, in spite of nostrification (the legal repatriation) of capital by the governments of the successor states, this control did not pass over fully into the hands of national business but instead was assumed by West European business, the major post-1918 investor in the region.

Indeed if 'nostrification' did nationalize (in the sense of Czechoslovakize, Polonize, or Romanize) business, it did not prevent West European companies and institutions from operating in the successor states. Actually it came to be a legal token by which nationals of the successor states were engaged as directors or managers of local subsidiaries by foreign head offices. The loyalties of such officials were doubtless to their employers. The maxim of the Siemens concern seems to be an apt epitome of the strategy of Western multi-nationals: employ those local persons whose influence on the subsidiary company's general policy will be minimal but who have the greatest possible influence on the environment in which the company is operating, such as on market and government policy.[4] The complicated questions of conformity and divergence of 'national' and 'business' interests is discussed in this and other contexts.

A problem evident throughout the contributions to this volume is the question of the nationality of capital. First, no consensus could be reached over the meaning of the term 'multi-national company'. Individual authors have used and retained descriptions such as 'national', 'bi-national' and 'pre-multi-national'. The importance of clarity over concepts cannot be disputed but evidently further study is required to establish a thorough theoretical framework. In the interim the editors have adopted as a working hypothesis for their own research project the position that the terms 'international business', 'supranational or transnational corporation' and 'multi-national enterprise' are interchangeable;[5] and further, that a multi-national enterprise involves foreign direct participating investments which carry control in countries other than that in which the parent's head office is located. Second, the discussion in this volume, especially in Part Three, touches upon the national origin of capital investments in multi-national states where citizenship was not identical with nationality. It was often doubted in countries like Poland and Czechoslovakia, where citizens had German nationality, whether their capital should be regarded either as German or as belonging to the state of which such owners possessed citizenship. Differing points of view over where foreign capital ends and domestic begins were raised in the discussions over several of the papers at the conference. However, the need for judging each case on the basis of the historical evidence seems to point to a solution. The test in the case of multi-national concerns lies in determining whether its head offices and its subsidiary enterprises were scattered over several countries and where the seat of control was to be found.

As Parts Two and Three look at the strategy and structure of multi-national companies which had their headquarters in Germany, the impression – which is quite misleading – may be gained that German interests in Danubian Europe sprang mainly from industrial ties while French and British links with the real economy of the region arose indirectly via investments in financial institutions. This would be a distortion of the complex relationship of banks and industry and the contributions published in Parts Two to Four go some way towards lifting the veil masking the crosscurrents and mechanisms within this network of linkages.

The difficulties of separating industrial and banking interests is further demonstrated by the case of Mannesmannröhren-Werke AG which was entirely controlled by the Deutsche Bank but in which the industrial and technical decision-making process was based upon the expertise of a small but highly qualified General Management Board. This case study is included in Part Two and strictly speaking the two contributions concerned with Schneider et Cie should be placed with it. This major steel and engineering concern was the only French industrial company to operate through a financial holding company, L'Union Européenne industrielle et financière, during the inter-war period. It established this holding company with the Banque de l'Union parisienne to administer and finance its East Central and South-East European subsidiaries. The analysis of the formation of L'Union Européenne and its subsequent activities has been placed in Part Four so that it can be read in conjunction with the associated papers which deal with the Banque de l'Union parisienne and the Hungarian General Credit Bank in which Schneiders acquired an interest.

While the role of British and French banks in acting as important financing agents for a widely developed network of dependent commercial and industrial enterprises in East Central Europe in the 1920s and 1930s has until this volume received little attention, some aspects of the activities of West European industrial multi-national concerns in the Danubian region have been discussed as part of general histories of these concerns. There are major business histories of British Nobel Industries Ltd as a forerunner of Imperial Chemical Industries and of Unilever of London and Rotterdam.[6] Specialized work on the role of these companies in East Central Europe through their direct investments in Czechoslovakia has also been published[7] and this type of activity is being pursued further in ongoing research.

Dealing solely with German-based concerns has the advantage of giving Part Two greater cohesion as it produces evidence of the development of company strategies under changing, but common, political conditions. The case studies show the complexity of similarities and differences not only between industries such as iron, steel, and mechanical engineering on the one hand, and chemicals and the electro-technical industry on the other, but also in the differing policies developed in the individual successor states. Evidence of the striking interaction between economics and politics is provided by each paper analysing a particular concern. It should be pointed out that this interplay between political and economic forces was not peculiar to German-based economic interests. A grand strategy can also be discerned in French inter-war investments in East Central and Balkan Europe, and further political motivation was not absent in the attitudes taken by British concerns and institutions towards these regions. Yet the changed international position of Germany – a leading industrial and creditor nation before 1914 becoming a defeated and greatly indebted country after 1918 – is clearly reflected in the business strategies adopted by the large companies explored in Part Two. During the 1920s they concentrated on rebuilding their business connections with Central and South-East European countries through trade rather than investments, as unlike their Western counterparts they could not draw on substantial capital funds, but in the 1930s they intensified their trade drive and expanded their network of subsidiaries in parallel with German foreign policy aims, particularly after the Anschluss with Austria, the Munich Agreement of September 1938, and the subsequent dismemberment of Czechoslovakia. Only one case study, that of the Reichswerke Hermann Göring AG in Part Three, deals with the period beyond 1938 and provides a blatant and extreme example of the most intimate coordination of politics and economics. The multi-national expansion of the Göring concern into East Central and South-East Europe was closely identified with the political, economic, and military aims of the National Socialist régime in Germany.

Not surprisingly, the questions 'who benefited' and 'whether multi-national companies hampered or aided the industrialization process' emerge with concrete evidence as substantiated incidences in a number of the contributions and in terms of general viewpoints in the comments of several of the discussants. These problems have long been the subject of academic debate and the research results presented in this volume contribute to analysing their contradictory nature. There can be little doubt that export-orientated concerns such as IG Farbenindustrie and Siemens regarded the industrialization of South-East Europe as a process which was contrary to their own interests. However, as East Central and South-East European states during the inter-war period pursued policies of import substitution in order to reduce foreign commitments by encouraging domestic production, competing foreign concerns had necessarily to acquire shares in or completely take over local manufacturing enterprises or build new factories locally if they wished to penetrate the market of these areas. Only a large number of detailed case studies will eventually allow more general answers to these questions.

Part Four, on 'Western Capital and the Commercial Banks of East Central Europe', looks at the links between Britain and France and the leading joint stock banks of Budapest, Prague and Vienna and their networks of sub-sidiaries in Danubian and Balkan Europe. It is introduced by a survey paper which shows convincingly how the whole financial sector of East Central Europe was internationalized in the comparatively short period between 1919 and 1923 as a result of the penetration of Western capital into the great Viennese banks. The involvement of the West with Danubian banks continued through the 1920s and did not simply consist of providing short-term funds which local banks used to finance industry, but also of further equity investments and the creation in the West, particularly in London and New York, of trusts to hold portfolios of East Central European industrial shares. A detailed example is provided by a consideration of the development of the Hungarian General Credit Bank which provides a picture of both the acquisition of the bank's shares by Western interests and the bank's role in financing the state, local industrial enterprises, and the great landed estates. After a consideration of the activities of Schneiders and the Banque de L'Union parisienne through L'Union Européenne where the resilience of some local institutions, such as the Živnostenská banka, is shown, the effects of the crisis of 1929 to 1933 are examined in terms of the experience of the Credit-Anstalt and its Western creditors. There was a greater element of diplomatic involvement in the eastward flow of long-term funds after 1919. The motivations behind the export of capital to Danubian Europe are discussed and attention is paid to the often-stated generalization that 'British policy was economic whereas French aims were political'. Whatever the causes, the overall pattern in the financial sphere in the 1920s was a transition from banking in a multi-national empire to multi-national banks in a nationally fragmented area. From 1931 Western investments in local banks, both short-term and long-term, in the cases of Austria and Hungary were at first frozen and then slowly liquidated, usually as a consequence of direct negotiations between the state and Western creditors. As a result national commercial banks emerged which often had state shareholdings and which, in the case of the Credit-Anstalt, had a continuing degree of Western supervision in the form of a foreign general manager who was guiding the policy of the bank in the interests of foreign creditors, the state, local shareholders, and local customers.

Notes

1. Most recent and relevant to the problems discussed in this volume: A. D. Chandler, Jr, *The Visible Hand: The Managerial Revolution in American Business* (Cambridge, Mass., 1977); L. G. Franko, *The European Multinationals: A Renewed Challenge to American and British Big Business* (Washington DC, 1976); *Business History Rev.*, special issue (Autumn 1974); M. Wilkins, *The Maturing of Multinational Enterprises: American Business Abroad from 1914–1974* (Cambridge, Mass., 1974); idem, *The Emergence of Multinational Enterprise: American Business Abroad from*

the Colonial Era to 1914 (Cambridge, Mass., 1970).

2. Cf. I. T. Berend and Gy. Ránki, *Economic Development of East Central Europe in the 19th and 20th Centuries* (New York, 1974); idem, *Hungary A Century of Economic Development* (Newton Abbot and New York, 1974); A. Teichova, *An Economic Background to Munich: International Business and Czechoslovakia 1918–1938* (Cambridge, 1974); V. N. Bandera, *Foreign Capital as an Instrument of National Economic Policy* (The Hague, 1968).

3. Chandler, *op. cit.*

4. Cited in Harm Schröter's contribution to this volume, p. 185.

5. In the sense of a working hypothesis we agree with Mira Wilkins's opinion in her article 'Modern European economic history and the multinationals', *J. European Economic History*, VI (1977), 577.

6. W. J. Reader, *Imperial Chemical Industries. A History*, I (1970), II (1975); C. Wilson, *Unilever* (3 vols., New York, 1968).

7. Teichova, *op. cit.*

Part One

Corporate Strategy and Structure: Substitution of the Market Mechanism?

1. The Place of the Modern Industrial Enterprise in Three Economies*

Alfred D. Chandler, Jr

This paper does not attempt to answer the question posed by the Conference's organizers: 'Corporate strategy and structure – substitution for market mechanisms?' Rather, it provides information that might be used to attempt to answer that question. It examines the place of the large multi-unit enterprise in three leading industrial economies during the years up to the Second World War; and it does so by reviewing sets of statistical tables based on national censuses and lists of the largest industrial enterprises in the United States, the United Kingdom, and Germany. The information on Germany has been compiled from the German *Census of Manufacturers* of 1925 by Herman Daems and lists of companies from the *Handbücher der Deutscher A.G.* by Marc Vanheukelen; that on Britain from the 1935 *Census of Production* by Regina Pisa and from the *Stock Exchange Year Books* by Margaret Ackrill and Peter Grant; and that on the United States by Professor Daems, Regina Pisa and myself from the United States *Census of Manufactures* for 1935 and 1937 and from *Moody's Manuals*. These censuses were chosen because they were the first in each country to provide detailed information on the modern multi-unit industrial firm. Comparable information was not available for France and other large European economies until after the Second World War.

By any definition, the large modern industrial enterprise is multi-unit. Census-takers define the multi-unit enterprise as one that administers two or more establishments, and they define an establishment as a factory or processing plant which, as the American *Census* puts it, 'operates in one locality, and for which separate sets of records are kept'.[1] This is the definition generally accepted by economists. I have defined the unit more broadly. It is any unit administered by the enterprise – a factory, a commercial office (either for buying or for selling), a transportation facility, a mine, or even a research laboratory, having its own full-time manager or managers and its own set of books or accounts.[2]

As an analyst of the 1937 United States census data pointed out 40 years ago, 'The emergence of the large-scale, multi-unit enterprise was largely a phenomena [sic] of the last decade of the 19th and the 20th Century.'[3] By the 1930s, it had become a central institution in all advanced industrial market economies. Since the Second World War, its size and influence has continued to grow in national and world economies. For example, in 1973 there were

Table 1.1. COMPARATIVE: THE INDUSTRIAL COMPANIES IN
THE U.S.A. AND U.K. IN 1935, AND GERMANY IN 1925,
EMPLOYING +2,000 PERSONS.

	No.	Share in total industrial employment	Average employment	Average no. of establishments	Average employees per establishment
U.S.A.					
manufacturing	185–190*	24.6%	10,991–11,241	29	380
Germany					
manufacturing & mining	351	18.4	6,134	14	452
U.K.					
manufacturing firms†	238	17.6	4,397	n.a.	n.a.
U.K.					
manufacturing, mining & utilities – business units†	410	35.1	6,173	n.a.	n.a.

* See n. 6.
† For definition of firm and business unit see p. 17.

256 firms in the world that had more than 30,000 persons on their payrolls.
These 256 firms accounted for 40 per cent of the total world employment in
chemicals, 72 per cent in petroleum, 42 per cent in primary metals, 70 per
cent in electrical machinery and 62 per cent in transportation equipment.[4] On
the other hand, such large enterprises have never played a significant role in
the apparel, leather, furniture, or fabricated metals industries and, except in
an early period of an economy's industrial expansion, in textiles.

Let us begin by reviewing the statistical data for each of the three national
economies and then consider what the review tells us about the differences
between the large industrial enterprise in the U.S.,[4] the U.K. and Germany
which may reflect basic differences in the individual economies in which they
operated and about the similarities which may say much about the more
universal attributes of the multi-unit enterprise. The comparative review
should also contribute to an understanding of why this form of enterprise
appeared in some industries and not in others. And it can provide a useful
perspective for an investigation of the growth of big business in the less
industrially advanced nations of Europe.

THE AMERICAN EXPERIENCE

The 1935, supplemented by the 1937, *Census of Manufactures* emphasizes the
importance of the modern multi-unit enterprise in the American economy. In

Table 1.2. U.S.A. (1): AVERAGE NUMBER OF ESTABLISHMENTS PER ENTERPRISE AND PER MULTI-UNIT ENTERPRISE BY INDUSTRY GROUPS, 1937.

Group no.	Industry group	Multi-unit enterprises	Establishments operated by multi-unit enterprise	Average no. of establishments per multi-unit enterprise
1	Food & kindred products	1,600	9,546	5.8
2	Textiles & their products	810	2,671	3.3
3	Forest products	636	2,305	3.6
4	Paper & allied products	193	886	4.6
5	Printing, publishing & allied industries	232	817	3.5
6	Chemicals & allied products	380	2,229	5.7
7	Products of petroleum & coal	66	430	6.5
8	Rubber products	30	115	3.8
9	Leather & its manufactures	127	499	3.9
10	Stone, clay and glass products	343	1,316	3.8
11	Iron & steel & their products (not including machinery)	336	1,620	4.8
12	Nonferrous metals and their products	94	394	4.2
13	Machinery (not including transportation equipment)	393	1,429	3.6
14	Transportation equipment, air, land and water	91	561	6.2
16	Miscellaneous industries	225	881	3.9
	All industries	5,625	25,699	4.6

1937, the 5,625 firms with two or more establishments accounted for 51.1 per cent of the total number of wage earners (paid 53.5 per cent of the total wage bill) and 61.1 per cent of the value added.[5] In 1935, approximately 190 of the largest of these firms, those that employed more than 2,000 persons, accounted for 24.6 per cent of the total manpower in American manufacturing. These firms employed on average almost exactly 11,000 workers and managers and operated, on average, 29 establishments with an average of 380 employees per establishment.[6]

Tables 1.2 and 1.3, and fig. 1.1 indicate that multi-unit firms with the highest number of establishments and those of the largest size in terms of value added were in much the same industries. As table 1.2 shows, in 1937 the multi-unit firms with the largest average number of establishments were in petroleum with 6.5, transportation equipment (and here the automobile was the leading

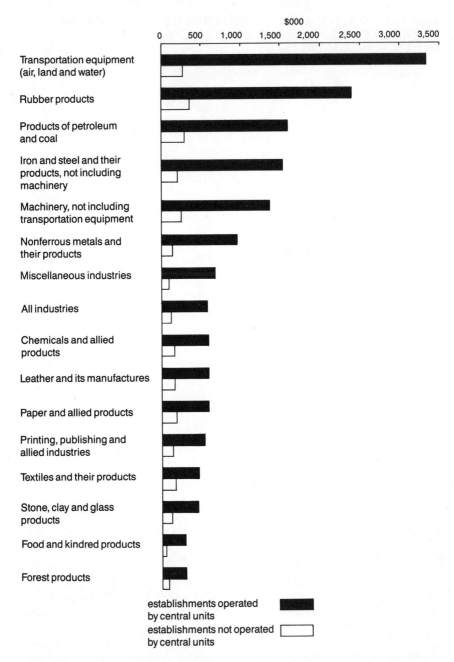

Figure 1.1. U.S.A.: average value added per establishment in single- and multi-unit enterprises by industry groups, 1937.

Table 1.3. U.S.A. (2): THE IMPORTANCE OF +2,000 COMPANIES BY INDUSTRIES.

	Estimated share of +2,000 companies' total employment	No. of companies	Average employment per company	Average no. of establishments	Average size of establishments
Typewriters	99.5	8	2,104	1.7	1,237
Cigarettes	90.3	4	5,689	2.2	2,667
Rayon & allied products	89.4	8	5,379	2.5	2,152
Motor vehicles (not motorcycles)	87.1	8	17,816	5.8	3,072
Agricultural implements	85.0	8	6,489	4.1	1,583
Photographic equipment	80.2	4	3,099	1.5	2,066
Rubber tyres	79.2	4	13,043	3.0	4,347
Boots & shoes, rubber	78.3	4	3,791	1.5	2,527
Aluminium	76.6	4	4,228	4.0	1,057
Tin cans	70.1	4	5,552	18.7	1,388
Motor vehicles, bodies & parts	70.5	8	23,027	6.8	3,386
Sugar	64.3	4	2,453	2.5	981
Cars, electric & steam	64.2	4	3,942	13.5	292
Ships & boat building	63.6	8	4,077	3.2	1,274
Soap	63.4	4	2,699	4.5	599
Steel works & rolling mill	58.7	8	28,582	11.8	2,422
Petroleum refining	58.0	8	6,672	11.7	570
Blast furnace products	57.6	4	2,406	7.5	320
Railroad repair shops	53.2	4	9,599	20.1	477
Carpets and rugs	52.2	4	4,308	2.0	2,154
Glass	48.9	8	4,484	6.1	735
Non-ferrous metal alloys	48.2	8	4,394	7.8	563
Chemicals	47.5	8	4,771	11.2	425
Meat packing	47.3	8	8,202	14.1	581
Clocks, watches	46.6	4	2,353	1.2	1,961
Electrical machinery	46.5	8	12,981	15.5	837
Refrigerators	44.8	4	4,790	1.7	2,817
Steam & hot water heating apparatus	41.1	4	3,298	3.7	824

industry) with 6.2, food with 5.8, chemicals with 5.7, and iron and steel with 4.8. Fig. 1.1 points out not only that the largest establishments in terms of value added were in much the same industries (with food being the major exception), but also indicates dramatically how much larger were the establishments in multi-unit enterprises than they were in single-unit ones.

Table 1.3 suggests the industries in which the large multi-unit enterprise had, by 1935, become the dominant form of organization. This table was computed by Professor Daems from compilations made by Gardner C. Means and his associates as to the shares of the total work-force employed by, respectively, the largest four and eight companies for all of the 275 industries listed in the 1935 *Census*. The data was used in order to determine the industries in which eight firms or less, each employing more than 2,000 employees, accounted for more than 40 per cent of the industry's total work-force. The figure of +2,000 employees was used here to make this data comparable with those in the German and British *Censuses*. The figure 40 per cent was used because it was assumed that if eight firms hired a percentage of the total work-force, the processes of production in that industry had become organized through the large multi-unit enterprise. Means's data was processed in the following manner. First, Professor Daems checked all industries in which the top eight employed more than 16,000 people. Second, in order to ensure that the eight firms employed over 2,000 he checked to see that employment by the eight largest companies was at least 8,000 persons more than the employment by the four largest companies. Third, he listed all industries in which the share of the eight largest companies in total employment for that industry was more than 40 per cent. When the second condition was not satisfied – that is, when the employment of the second four largest was less than 8,000 – he then listed the industry only if the total employment for the first four was over 40 per cent of the industry. The resulting table 1.3 provides a fairly reliable picture of the industries dominated by eight or fewer firms employing more than 2,000 persons. The major weakness of this procedure is that those small industries that are dominated by one or two big firms with a number of small competitors rarely meet the three conditions previously stated.

Nearly all the industries listed in table 1.3 are in those industry groups in which tables 1.2 and 1.3, and fig. 1.1 indicate that multi-industry enterprises as a group had the largest number of branches and the greatest value added per establishment. All industries in table 1.3 (except for railway repair shops and shipbuilding firms, both quite special cases) are those using new high-volume, larger-batch or continuous process techniques of production. Enterprises in cigarettes, petroleum and sugar refining, soap, rubber goods (both tyres and boots and shoes), plate glass, tin cans and chemicals were using continuous process techniques well before the turn of the century; while manufacturers of motor vehicles, agricultural implements, typewriters, cameras, refrigerators, clocks and electric machinery were using techniques based on mass-production by the fabrication and assembling of interchangeable parts. By the First World War they were beginning to do so on an assembly line basis. Meat packing was the classic example of a high-volume, disassembling line process. The last column of table 1.3 helps to suggest the extent of high-volume production. In typewriters, refrigerators, cigarettes, cameras, rayon, clocks, rubber tyres, rubber footwear and sugar, a small number of plants could meet the national and indeed the international demand. The marketing of such huge daily output required large sales forces and careful co-ordination between the sales and production units.

Volume production in all these industries required large investment in plant and machinery. As yet, Professor Daems and I have not worked out a solid indicator of capital intensity, but it seems fair to say that in all these industries the ratio of capital to worker per unit of output was high. For example, in table 1.3 there are no representatives of many industries that are among the largest employers of labour in the United States – industries such as leather, lumber, furniture, paper, printing and publishing and, except for rugs and carpets, textiles including apparel. (This one exception is the most capital-intensive industry in the textile group. Rayon is quite properly listed by the *Census* not as a textile but a chemical industry.) Significantly, in the 21 industries in the United States employing more than 100,000 workers, two-thirds are in these six industry groups. Finally, table 1.3 suggests that many of these concentrated industries produced new or greatly improved products as well as using new processes of production. The message from the *Census* appears to be that those industries organized through large multi-unit enterprises were those using high-volume, capital-intensive methods of production in new rather than traditional industries.

Data compiled from *Moody's Manuals* for the writing of *The Visible Hand* reinforce and sharpen the findings taken from the *Census*. Table 1.4 shows that of the 278 enterprises involved in all aspects of production in 1917 in the U.S.A. with assets of $20 million or over, 84.9 per cent were in manufacturing. Of these 171 (72.5 per cent) were clustered in five two-digit Standard Classification groups – metals, machinery, transportation equipment, food, chemicals and petroleum (this classification is the one used since the Second World War by the *Census*). Those in seven other groups belong to the subcategories (three- and four-digit industries) using capital-intensive, high-volume production facilities similar to those used in metals, food, machinery, transportation equipment, petroleum and chemicals. On the other hand, less than 10 per cent of the manufacturing firms with assets of $20 million or over operated in the seven remaining groups – textiles, apparel, lumber, furniture, leather, printing and publishing, and instruments. Of these, the first six were traditional industries and all were labour-intensive. Thus most of the largest firms that make up table 1.4 were in the industries listed in table 1.3 or in comparable capital-intensive, high-volume production industries. They include such well-known names as Remington Typewriter, American Tobacco, Du Pont, Ford, General Motors, International Harvester, John Deere, Eastman Kodak, U.S. Rubber, Goodrich, Aluminum Company of America, American Can, Continental Can, American Sugar, American Car and Foundry, Proctor & Gamble, the constituent companies of U.S. Steel, Standard Oil, Pittsburgh Plate Glass, the constituent companies of Allied Chemical and Union Carbon and Carbide, Armour & Swift, General Electric and Westinghouse, Babcock & Wilcox and American Radiator – all of whom

Table 1.4. U.S.A. (3): THE LOCATION OF THE LARGEST
INDUSTRIAL ENTERPRISES BASED ON ASSETS BY INDUSTRY
from *Moody's Manual*, 1917.

Of the 278 enterprises involved in the production of goods in the U.S.A. in 1917 with
assets of $20 million or over:

Mining	30
Crude oil	7
Agriculture	5
Construction	0
Manufacturing	236

Of the 236 manufacturing firms:

171 (72.5%) clustered in 6 two-digit SIC groups

Primary metals	39
Food	34
Transportation equipment	29
Machinery	24
Petroleum	24
Chemicals	21

23 (9.7%) scattered in 7 groups

Textiles	7
Lumber	5
Leather	4
Printing & publishing	3
Apparel	3
Instruments	1
Furniture	0

The remaining 42 were in continuous-process and large-batch four-digit industries
within the 7 remaining groups. In the paper group, the large firms were clustered in
the production of newsprint and craft paper; in stone, glass, and clay: in cement and
plate glass; in rubber: in tyres and footwear; in tobacco: in cigarettes; in fabricated
metals: in cans; in electrical machinery: in standardized machines; and in miscellaneous: in matches.

Source: A. D. Chandler, Jr, *The Visible Hand: The Managerial Revolution in American Business*
(Cambridge, Mass., 1977), 396–7.

had led their industries from almost the moment modern production
methods were invented.

Table 1.5 reveals that the pattern of 1917 remained relatively unchanged
for at least four more decades. The largest firms continued to cluster in about
the same numbers in metals, machinery and oil. They increased somewhat as
time passed in chemicals and decreased in food and tobacco. Further
investigation of the manufacturing firms on the 1917 list showed that about
85 per cent had integrated production with distribution and that 80 per cent
of these managed their manufacturing establishments, sales offices, mines

Table 1.5. U.S.A. (4): THE LARGEST INDUSTRIALS BASED ON
ASSETS BY INDUSTRY GROUPS, from *Moody's Manuals*, 1929, 1935, 1960
and 1978.

Groups		1929	1935	1948	1960
20	Food	8	8	9	6
21	Tobacco	4	3	3	2
22	Textiles	1	0	2	1
23	Apparel	0	0	0	0
24	Lumber	1	0	1	0
25	Furniture	0	0	0	0
26	Paper	2	5	1	3
27	Printing & publishing	0	1	0	0
28	Chemicals	5	5	10	9
29	Petroleum	19	16	17	18
30	Rubber	4	4	4	4
31	Leather	1	1	0	0
32	Stone, clay & glass	1	1	2	2
33	Primary metals	16	17	15	15
34	Fabricated metal	1	3	2	2
35	Machinery	4	7	6	6
36	Electrical machinery	3	3	3	4
37	Transportation machinery	8	6	5	7
38	Instruments	2	1	1	1
39	Miscellaneous manufactures	1	0	0	1
Totals		81	81	81	81

Source: A. D. Chandler, Jr, *The Visible Hand: The Managerial Revolution in American Business*
(Cambridge, Mass., 1977), 370.

and other raw material production units and transportation facilities through
a centralized structure consisting of functional departments for production,
marketing, purchasing, essential materials, research, and finance.[7] Thus, the
information derived from *Moody's Manuals* makes clear that the 236 biggest
multi-unit manufacturing enterprises clustered in the same industries in
which, according to the *Census*, the large multi-unit enterprise had become
the dominant form of organization, and in which multi-unit enterprises had
the largest number of factories, and in which the factories of multi-unit
enterprises added the greatest value in the production processes.[8]

THE GERMAN EXPERIENCE

The data from the German *Census* and the *Handbücher* are presented on
somewhat different lines from those of the U.S.A. – lines developed to make
the best use of the primary sources. Nevertheless, the comparisons are valid

and they show some striking similarities and also significant differences between the German and the American experiences. Tables 1.6 and 1.7 reveal that, as in the U.S.A., the larger firms employed an impressive portion of the labour force, although somewhat less than did the leading American enterprises. In 1925, the 351 enterprises in manufacturing and mining (the German *Census* does not separate the two sectors) which employed more than 2,000 workers accounted for 18.4 per cent of the total work-force in these two sectors. These firms employed on average 6,134 workers and operated an average of 14 establishments (factories), which in turn averaged 452 employees. Thus, although there were more firms employing 2,000 workers and managers in Germany than in the U.S.A. (the U.S.A. figure was just under 190), the American firms were much larger in terms of employment, with an

Table 1.6. GERMANY (1): SIZE DISTRIBUTION OF GERMAN INDUSTRIALS, 1925.

Size class in no. of workers	No. of firms in class	Employment in that class	Share in total employment
<10	886,891	2,695,850	23.0
11–50	85,965	1,859,026	15.9
51–200	22,034	2,068,569	17.7
201–500	4,434	1,335,273	11.4
501–1,000	1,250	860,268	7.3
1,001–2,000	539	745,140	6.4
2,001–5,000	240	723,700	6.2
+5,000	111	1,429,273	12.2
	1,001,464	11,717,099	100.0

Source: Calculated from German Census Data, 1925.

average of 11,000, and in terms of establishments, with an average of 29. Not surprisingly the German establishments were, however, larger (an average of 380 was the American figure).

Table 1.7, indicating the number of firms and the workers they employed by industry groups for the 351 firms employing more than 2,000 persons, reveals that the large firms clustered in much the same industries as they did in the U.S.A. (In that table the *Census* data has been presented so as to correspond as closely as possible to the United States Standard Industrial Classification two-digit categories.) As in the U.S.A., there were many large firms in metals, machinery, and chemicals, but unlike the U.S.A. there were more large firms in textiles and very few in petroleum, as might be expected, given the lack of Germany's petroleum resources and the historical importance of its textile industry. There are also more firms in stone, glass, and clay

Table 1.7. GERMANY (2): THE LARGEST INDUSTRIAL
ENTERPRISES BY INDUSTRY GROUPS from 1925 Census.

SIC-industries	111 largest (+5,000 employees)		351 largest (+,2000 employees)	
	No. of firms	Employment	No. of firms	Employment
Mining				
pure mining	18⎫	222,039⎫	50⎫	333,471⎫
with mining integrated	29⎭	559,896⎭	39⎭	594,788⎭
20 Food	1	6,798	16	47,614
21 Tobacco	★		★	
22 Textiles	5	33,064	40	129,123
23 Apparel			5	15,252
24 Lumber & wood				
25 Furniture	★		★	
26 Paper & printing	2	12,318	10	36,817
27 Printing	(see under SIC 26)			
28 Chemicals	6	76,765	18	113,356
29 Petroleum	★		★	
30 Rubber	3	27,819	5	32,663
31 Leather & linoleum	1	5,147	3	10,824
32 Stone & clay & building material	2	14,764	28	89,396
33 Primary metals				
pure works	1⎫	5,181⎫	11⎫	30,945⎫
with metal integrated	8⎭	84,528⎭	24⎭	134,216⎭
34 Fabricated metal production	1	8,105	9	30,926
35 Machinery & transport equipment	23	164,095	68	300,619
36 Electrical & optical	11	208,754	23	247,888
37 Transportation equipment	(see under SIC 35)			
38 Measuring & optical	(see under SIC 36)			
39 Miscellaneous (toys and musical instruments)			2	5,085
Totals	111	1,429,273	351	2,152,973
Average per firm		12,876		6,134

★ Not separately listed

than in the U.S.A. (about the significance of which I am uncertain) and
somewhat fewer in food. In neither country does the large firm appear in any
numbers in apparel, lumber, furniture, and leather, and only a small number
in paper and printing.

Table 1.8, based on data from the *Handbücher*, lists the location of the
largest (determined by capitalization) by industry groups. It reinforces the

Table 1.8. GERMANY (3): THE LARGEST INDUSTRIAL
ENTERPRISES BASED ON CAPITALIZATION BY INDUSTRY
GROUPS, 1913, from *Handbücher*.

SIC		1913	1929	
		Top 100	Top 100	Top 200
20	Food and allied products	4	6	28
21	Tobacco	1		
22	Textiles	2	4	15
23	Apparels & other products			
24	Lumber & wood		0	1
25	Furniture			
26	Paper & allied products	1	2	2
27	Printing & publishing		0	1
28	Chemicals	19	20	27
29	Petroleum & energy products	4	4	5
30	Rubber & allied products	1	1	1
31	Leather	1	0	3
32	Stone, clay & glass	4	4	9
33	Primary metals	32	29	47
34	Fabricated metal products	4	4	7
35	Non-electrical machinery	10	7	19
36	Electrical machinery	11	10	16
37	Transportation equipment	6	7	16
38	Instruments & allied products		1	2
39	Miscellaneous		1	1
		100	100	200

Census information on the largest companies where size was determined by employment. In 1931, 78, and in 1929, 73 of the largest 100 enterprises operated in three major industrial groups – metals, machinery, and chemicals. There were a sizeable number in food and textiles (but not in stone, glass, and clay). The difference in the criteria used for selection – capitalization for table 1.8 as compared to employment for table 1.7 – helps to explain the one major discrepancy in numbers between the two tables. In food there were 28 listed in the top 200 in table 1.7 but only 16 in the top 351 in table 1.8. A closer look at the 28 shows that they were nearly all either in brewing (11) or in processing of sugar and animal and vegetable fats – industries using the continuous processing methods that required large amounts of capital but little labour.

Table 1.9, which gives the share of the total work-force employed by the largest companies in each industrial group, indicates that in food and textiles the 351 with a work-force of over 2,000 accounted for only a small part of the total employment, 3.5 per cent in food and 11.8 per cent in textiles. However, in chemicals, rubber, primary metals, machinery and transporta-

Table 1.9. GERMANY (4): SHARE OF LARGEST ENTERPRISES IN TOTAL EMPLOYMENT BY INDUSTRIAL GROUPS, 1925.

		111 largest companies	351 largest companies
		%	%
	Mining (pure mining & with mining integrated)	73.5	87.2
20	Food	0.5	3.5
22	Textiles	3.0	11.8
23	Clothing		1.6
24	Lumber & wood		
26	Paper & printing	2.2	6.4
28	Chemicals	24.4	36.0
30	Rubber	41.1	48.3
31	Leather & linoleum	3.5	7.3
32	Stone, clay and building materials	0.7	4.2
33	Primary metals (pure works & with metal integrated)	20.1	37.1
34	Fabricated metal products	1	6.9
35	Machinery and transport equipment	13.7	25.1
36	Electrical & optical	34.9	41.4
39	Toys & musical instruments		5.3

tion equipment, and electrical and optical equipment (and also in mining), they account for a substantial share, ranging from 25.1 per cent to 48.3 per cent of total employment (in mining it was 87.2 per cent). In these five industries, the dominant form of organization had become the large, multi-unit enterprise.

The data in table 1.10 emphasize that, as in the U.S.A., the firms with the most establishments were in similar capital-intensive industries. Those with the greatest number of establishments were in electrical and optical, machinery and transportation equipment, metals, chemicals, rubber, food, and stone, glass and clay; except for the last two, these were the same industries in which, as table 1.9 shows, the large multi-unit firm had become the dominant form of organization. The large number of establishments in German food companies may be accounted for by the development of retailing chains of perishable products that had integrated backwards into production. Thus, the available data for the *Census* does underline similarities between the German and American experience. The one major difference indicated by the *Census* is that the biggest American firms were much larger in terms of employment and in number of establishments operated and therefore required more extensive and more carefully defined managerial hierarchies.

Table 1.10. GERMANY (5): AVERAGE NUMBER OF
ESTABLISHMENTS PER ENTERPRISE for all and for largest enterprises
(numbers of firms in brackets).

		All firms except those belonging to 351 largest group	111 largest* (+5,000 employees)	351 largest (+2,000 employees)
	Mining	1.22	24.7 (47)	16.4 (89)
20	Food	1.06	131　(1)	45.2 (16)
22	Textiles	1.14	12.6　(5)	5.2 (40)
23	Clothing	1.03		6.2　(5)
24	Lumber & wood	1.03		
26	Paper & printing	1.10	7.4　(2)	28.1 (10)
28	Chemicals	1.23	18.8　(6)	12.1 (18)
30	Rubber	1.35	24　(3)	18.6　(5)
31	Leather & linoleum	1.03	1　(1)	3.7　(3)
32	Stone, clay and building materials	1.04	42　(2)	15.0 (28)
33	Primary metals	1.28	14.2　(9)	8.1 (35)
34	Fabricated metal products	1.02	9　(1)	8.4　(9)
35	Machinery & transport equipment	1.12	25.4 (23)	13.4 (68)
36	Electrical & optical	1.09	43.3 (11)	25.5 (23)
39	Toys & musical instruments	1.10		21.5　(2)

* The mixed mining works with more than 5,000 people employed have 29.3 establishments on average; the mixed works with over 2,000 people employed have 24.1 establishments on average.

A closer look at the information provided by *Moody's Manual* and the *Handbücher* reveal differences that are only hinted at by the *Census*. A check of product lines indicates that, while in the U.S.A. large firms were operating in both consumer and in producer goods industries, in Germany they concentrated almost wholly in the manufacturing and processing of goods to be used by other manufacturers, rather than by the final consumer. In Germany nearly all the large enterprises producing consumer goods whose names appear on 1913 and 1929 lists were in the food industry and they were, as has been pointed out, nearly all brewers or processors of sugar and vegetable and animal oils. The brewers sold largely in local urban markets, while the producers of sugar and oil manufactured in bulk for wholesalers and large retailers who branded and packaged the product. In other words, German food firms apparently did not become involved with consumer marketing. It may be significant that food was the only industry group in Germany where subsidiaries of foreign enterprises were important. The leading food firms included the subsidiaries of Nestlé, Jurgens, and Van den Bergh (the latter two became part of Unilever in 1929). All three relied heavily on advertising to sell their packaged and branded products.

A great majority of the large German chemical companies also concentrated on producers' goods such as industrial inorganic products, and dyes, plastics, artificial fibres, pharmaceuticals and other products of organic chemistry. Of these, pharmaceuticals were the only ones used directly by consumers; and they appear to have been sold through wholesalers and other agents. In Germany there were no large producers of consumer chemicals such as soap, starch, toilet articles, proprietary or branded medicines and drugs (that is, those branded drugs that were not synthetically produced); or paints and varnishes comparable to Procter & Gamble, Sherwin-Williams, United Drug, and Parke, Davis in the United States. In other words, there were very few German firms which like the American ones and like Nestlé and Unilever sold advertised branded products directly to retailers.

Nor did the large German machinery firms mass-produce and mass-distribute such products as sewing machines, office machines (including typewriters, cash registers, adding, calculating and mimeograph machines), agricultural machines (reapers, harvesters, and ploughs), in whose production America excelled. Nor in 1928 did the Germans have any automobile enterprises close to the size of American ones. In fact, the largest, Adam Opel, had just become a subsidiary of General Motors. In machinery, the strength of the large German firms lay in the production of technically complex items, particularly in electrical machinery, built to precise specifications. The multi-unit enterprise thus appeared in Germany in capital-intensive, technologically advanced producers' goods industry where skills lay in science and its application; whereas in the United States, the skills were more in mass-production and mass-distribution. There more attention was paid to engineering than to science and more to quantity than to quality.

THE BRITISH EXPERIENCE

The British data, though somewhat less detailed than the American or German, does emphasize similarities or uniformities in the place of the large, multi-unit firm in all advanced industrial economies. At the same time, the differences revealed by the data help to explain the ways in which different economic environments affected the activities of these large enterprises.

Table 1.11, on the size distribution of British industrial enterprises in 1935, brings out a basic similarity – a minute number of large enterprises accounted for an impressive share of the total work-force. The original census acquired information on the firm which was defined as an 'aggregate of establishments trading under the same name'. By that definition 238 firms with over 2,000 employees accounted for 17.6 per cent of the total work-force in manufacturing – a figure that compares with 18.5 per cent accounted for by the 351 enterprises of comparable size in Germany (the German figure includes, it will be remembered, mining as well as manufacturing). However, as table 1.12 shows, the average number of workers was smaller, 4,397, about

Table 1.11. U.K. (1): SIZE DISTRIBUTION OF U.K. INDUSTRIALS, 1935.

Size class in no. of workers	No. of firms in class	Employment in that class	Share in total employment
<10	131,077	763,365	12.8
11–50	23,807	599,016	10.1
51–200	12,220	1,192,738	20.4
201–500	3,486	1,063,094	17.9
501–1,000	1,002	688,456	11.6
1,001–2,000	411	567,676	9.5
2,001–5,000	201	697,092	11.7
+5,000	37	349,515	5.9
	172,241	5,920,952	100.0

Source: Calculated from the *U.K. Census of Production*, 1935.

two-thirds as many as in German factories of enterprises in that size category and considerably less than half as many as the American ones.

In 1939 the British Census Office, in order to obtain more information on large enterprises, sent out a questionnaire to those employing more than 500 persons. This time the office defined the enterprise more accurately from a legal standpoint by calling it 'a business unit' which was a 'single firm or aggregate of firms owned or controlled by a single company employing 500 persons or more, control being defined as ownership of half the capital (or voting power) of each firm'.[9] Unfortunately for the purposes of this paper, the compilers in aggregating the results of the questionnaires included mining and utility as well as manufacturing companies. They provided no way to separate out the manufacturing firms from the totals given for each size category. Their data show that in manufacturing, mining, and utilities 410 firms employed more than 2,000 persons. These firms accounted for 35.1 per cent of the total work-force in these sectors and employed on average 6,173 employees.[10] Because these figures include railway companies, coal mines and tramways, which were among the most concentrated of the industries and those with the largest enterprises in terms of employees, the figures for the share of total employment and for the average employment of 'business units' in manufacturing employing over 2,000 persons, although larger than they were for the 238 manufacturing firms with over 2,000 employees, the average employment figure, at least, could not have been a great deal larger. Thus although the share of total employment of the biggest firms may have been larger than in the U.S.A. and Germany, the average employment was still smaller than those of the German firms and substantially smaller than those of the American ones.[11] Unfortunately, information

Table 1.12. U.K. (2): THE 238 LARGEST INDUSTRIAL
ENTERPRISES by industry groups from 1935 Census.

SIC-industries	(+5,000 employees)		(+2,000 employees)	
	No. of firms	Employment	No. of firms	Employment
20 Food	8*	55,738*	28	11,959
21 Tobacco	(included under SIC 20)			
22 Textiles	7	78,186	31	151,791
23 Apparel			8	38,061
24 Lumber & wood				
25 Furniture	(included under SIC 24)			
26 Paper	6*	33,442*	17	64,869
27 Printing	(included under SIC 26)			
28 Chemicals	7†	34,064†	15	53,539
29 Petroleum	(included under SIC 28)			
30 Rubber (linoleum under SIC 39)	(included under SIC 39)			
31 Leather & linoleum				
32 Stone, clay & building materials	3*	19,512*	6	28,228
33 Primary metals	7	54,594	37	146,974
34 Fabricated metal products	(included under SIC 33)			
35 Machine & transport equipment	23	216,735	87	415,171
36 Electrical & optical	(included under SIC 39)			
37 Transportation equipment	(included under SIC 35)			
38 Measuring & optical	(included under SIC 39)			
39 Miscellaneous			9	36,023
Total average per firm	‡	‡	238	1,046,605 4,397

* Data related to companies with over 4,000 persons employed.
† Data related to companies with over 3,000 persons employed.
‡ No details are reported because of the non-comparability of the data.
  Source: Calculated from *U.K. Census of Production*, 1935.

in the British *Census* does not permit a determination of the number of establishments operated by firms in either industry or size categories.

As table 1.12, which is based on information on the 238 'firms' employing over 2,000 employees, indicates, there was the same clustering of large companies in the machinery and metals industries, with a greater number of food companies than on the American lists and a larger number of textile firms than on the German lists. In Britain, these four categories contained 195 (or 81.9 per cent) of the largest 238. In a fifth, chemicals, there were somewhat fewer firms than there were on either the German or American lists and there were somewhat more in paper, printing and publishing. Finally, there were very few firms among these 238 in the apparel, leather, lumber, furniture and miscellaneous categories.

Again, information from financial handbooks tends to reinforce the *Census* data. In 1930, 145 (or 72.5 per cent) of the largest firms were in machinery, metals, textiles and food. As in the case of Germany, the only significant discrepancy between tables 1.12 and 1.13 came in food, and that discrepancy can also be explained by the different criterion used for determining size. In table 1.13, where size is based on market value of the company's securities, almost half of the food companies listed were breweries and all but one of these, Guinness, owned the public houses through which their products were sold. So their market value reflects this large investment in real estate.

Table 1.14, showing the share of large companies' total employment by industrial group, makes the same point that table 1.7 did for Germany. This table includes information based on the analysis of the 1939 information on 'business units' with more than 500 employed by H. Leak and A. Maizels as well as that from the 238 'firms' employing more than 2,000 persons. As in the case of the U.S.A. and Germany, large enterprises clustered in machinery (particularly electrical machinery, motors and cycles), in iron and steel, rubber, glass, cement and chemicals. In machinery, including transportation equipment, 87 'firms' employing more than 2,000 persons accounted for 34.4 per cent of the total work-force, an even larger percentage than that for the German electricity and optical group plus the German machinery and transportation industry groups. In metals, on the other hand, the percentage of the total work-force was substantially less than in Germany. In Britain, 37 'firms' employed 25.7 per cent of the total work-force and in Germany 35 companies accounted for 37.1 per cent. In chemicals the 15 largest 'firms' accounted for 26 per cent of the employees, substantially more than the 14.2 per cent in textiles and 17.7 per cent in food. However, as the Leak and Maizels data show, in the food group some industries such as biscuits and cocoa and sugar were highly concentrated. Moreover, 'firms' employing over 2,000 in food accounted for 17.7 per cent of the work-force, whereas in Germany enterprises of that size accounted only for 0.4 per cent. This information suggests that the British food firms sold their brand of consumer products in national and international markets, while the Germans still sold undifferentiated products to local markets. In addition, the Leak and Maizels data indicate that when legal control rather than trading names are used to define the enterprise, chemicals, machinery and metals had by the 1930s become organized in Britain, as they had in the U.S.A. and Germany, through large multi-unit enterprises. Moreover, in food and textiles this form

Table 1.13. U.K. (3): THE 200 LARGEST INDUSTRIAL
ENTERPRISES based on market values by industry groups, 1919, 1930, 1938,
from *Stock Exchange Year Books*.

SIC group	1919 No.	1919 %	1930 No.	1930 %	1948 No.	1948 %
0 Food & allied products	63	31.5	64	32	52	26
1 Tobacco products	3	1.5	4	2	8	4
2 Textile mill products	26	13	24	12	18	9
3 Apparel & allied products	1	0.5	3	1.5	3	1.5
4 Lumber & wood products						
5 Furniture & fixtures						
6 Paper & allied products	4	2	5	2.5	6	3
7 Printing & publishing	5	2.5	10	5	7	3.5
8 Chemical & allied products	11	5.5	9	4.5	15	7.5
9 Petroleum & energy products						
0 Rubber & allied products	3	1.5	3	1.5	2	1
1 Leather products						
2 Stone, clay & glass products	2	1	6	3	5	2.5
3 Primary metals	35	17.5	18	9	28	14
4 Fabricated metal products	2	1	7	3.5	8	4
5 Machinery (excluding electric)	8 ⎫	4 ⎫	7 ⎫	3.5 ⎫	7 ⎫	3.5 ⎫
6 Electrical machinery	11 ⎬39	5.8 ⎬19.8	18 ⎬39	9 ⎬19.5	13 ⎬42	6.5 ⎬21
7 Transportation equipment	20 ⎭	10 ⎭	14 ⎭	7 ⎭	22 ⎭	11 ⎭
8 Instruments & allied products			1	0.5	4	2
9 Miscellaneous	3	1.5	4	2	3	1.5
	200	100	200	100	200	100

Arranged in the categories of the U.S. Standard Industrial Classification.

Table 1.14. U.K. (4): SHARE OF LARGEST ENTERPRISES IN TOTAL
EMPLOYMENT by industrial groups, 1925.

	238 largest companies	
	(+5,000 employees)	(+2,000 employees)
	%	%
20 Food	8.8*	17.7
22 Textiles	7.3	14.2
23 Apparel		5.9
24 Lumber & wood		
26 Paper & printing	7.6*	14.7
28 Chemicals	16.5†	26.0
31 Leather		
32 Stone, clay & building materials	7.3*	10.5
33 Primary metals (nonferrous)	9.5	25.7
35 Machine & transportation equipment	17.9	34.3
39 Miscellaneous		18.3

* Data related to companies with over 4,000 persons employed.
† Data related to companies with over 3,000 persons employed.

of organization had become more widely used there than in either of the other two economies.

As with Germany, the *Census* brings out similarities in the role of the large enterprise in modern economies, but only begins to suggest the differences. Again, a close reading of product lines listed in the *Stock Exchange Year Books* brings out important differences. Nearly all the British food companies were makers of branded packaged goods sold through aggressive advertising and marketing. These large enterprises produced chocolates, jams, biscuits, canned meat, sparkling water, mustard and other condiments, whisky and gin, cigarettes and other tobacco products, as well as flour, sugar and margarine. In the production of the last three commodities, the manufacturers paid much closer attention to packaging, branding, and advertising than they appear to have done in Germany. In the chemical industries there were more companies in the list of the 200 largest in 1930 making consumer products – in soaps, starch, perfume, paints and varnishes, pills and other proprietary drugs, and even in briquettes – than there were in industrial chemicals. For the more technically complex industrial chemicals, especially dyes and synthetic drugs, Britain continued to rely on Germany until the 1930s.

In machinery, on the other hand, Britain lagged in the output of consumer products, such as automobiles and appliances, until the 1920s. In 1919, the two automobile companies listed among the top 200 were Ford and Rolls Royce (and by 1930 Ford's British subsidiary was the tenth largest manufacturing enterprise in the United Kingdom). Nor did large British machinery firms manufacture many technically advanced, volume-produced machines. American firms like Otis Elevator, Worthington Pump, Mergenthaler Linotype Company, American Radiator Company, John Deere, and International Harvester had as little competition from British firms in Britain as did Singer Sewing Machine, Remington Typewriter, and National Cash Register.[12] In fact, in 1919 three of the eight non-electrical machinery firms listed in the top 200 in Britain were or had been American subsidiaries – Babcock & Wilcox, Linotype and British Shoe Machinery. In electrical machinery, three of the four largest firms were subsidiaries of General Electric, Westinghouse and the German firm of Siemens, and in electrical consumer goods Gramophone, Columbia Gramophone, and Ever Ready Battery were American subsidiaries. The large British firm making machinery concentrated on supplying the more traditional industries – textiles, metals, mining and food. In electrical machinery the largest number were makers of cables. In transportation equipment they were builders of ships and locomotives, and other railway equipment.

THE DIFFERENCES

This brief review of the *Census* and Financial Handbook data suggests that, although in all three economies the large enterprises were clustered in much the same types of industries, those in each concentrated on manufacturing quite different types of products. In Britain the largest number of firms appeared in consumer goods industries, where they mass-produced by relatively simple technologies branded products which were sold through intensive advertising. In producers' goods they concentrated in making older products, iron and steel, explosives, alkalis, chlorines and acids, and machinery for the more traditional established industries. Very few produced the new chemicals made from organic synthesis and the new machines to generate and use electricity.

These product lines reflected Britain's history. As the first industrial nation, Britain had by 1900 the world's largest concentrated urban population which enjoyed a high *per capita* income and so provided a lucrative consumer market. At the same time Britain had become the machinery maker for the industries that fuelled the first industrial revolution – textiles, mining and transportation equipment at home and then abroad.

The product lines of the large German firms, on the other hand, reflect that nation's later industrialization and urbanization. This meant, for one thing, a less concentrated population with lower *per capita* income than Britain, and so a smaller consumer market. The need to compete with already-established British suppliers in European and world markets encouraged German industrialists to capitalize on an educational system that had long favoured the study of science. As a result, many of the largest German firms concentrated on producing new chemicals based on organic synthesis and new machinery – particularly electric – based on a knowledge of physics and metallurgy. With these they soon invaded foreign markets, including those of Britain and the U.S.A. Germany, therefore, quickly took the lead in what has been called the second industrial revolution – one which was based on the application of science to industry.

In the same manner the type of goods produced by the large American firms reflected the economic development of the U.S.A. As that nation was the world's largest producer of agricultural products and enjoyed the world's most rapidly growing domestic market – a market by which the new cities paced their growth – American processors of food products were assured of both a massive demand and a ready source of supply. The same was true for petroleum, for consumer chemicals, and to a lesser extent (because the raw materials came from abroad) for rubber. Expansive markets and abundant sources of supply also encouraged the mass production of machinery through the fabrication and assembly of standardized products – the American system of manufacturing as it had come to be called as early as the 1850s. It was in food and even more in light machinery that American firms made their reputation throughout the world.

If Germany's educational strengths lay in science, that of the U.S.A. came to be in engineering. The building of the railway and telegraph – the massive transportation and communications infrastructure required by this continental nation – had led to the blossoming of engineering schools. As industry boomed on the basis of the new infrastructure, these schools quickly added to their courses in civil engineering those in mechanical and then in electrical and chemical engineering. So it was in engineering rather than science that the Americans came to play a central role in the second industrial revolution. In Britain, where industry was still geared to the first industrial revolution, there was little demand for either industrial scientists or engineers, so that nation failed to exploit the potentials of the second revolution.

A further difference, and one indicated by the *Census* figures, may reflect geographical as well as economic and educational differences. Table 1.1 reminds us that in the U.S.A. the number of the largest enterprises – those employing more than 2,000 – were less than in Germany or Britain, but that the American enterprises employed much larger work-forces and operated many more establishments than did the German or British firms. So, too, the German firms had more employees than did the British. This information suggests that in administering the processes of production, the American firms were required to have more managers and to pay closer attention to overall co-ordination and control than were the German or British firms and that the German companies required more managerial strength than the British.

THE SIMILARITIES

If the differences in the goods produced by the large industrial enterprises reflect the environment in which they operated, the similarities, as indicated by the *Census* data, can help to explain why the large enterprises appeared in the industries that they did and what this clustering suggests about the role of the large multi-unit firm in modern advanced industrial economies.

Consider these similarities. A tiny number of enterprises, much less than 1 per cent, employed in the U.S.A. close to a quarter of the work-force in manufacturing and in the United Kingdom and Germany at least 17 per cent. These firms were concentrated in a relatively small number of in-dustries – metals, machinery, chemicals, food and textiles. All but the last have been at the core of all mature industrial economies. In Britain and Germany, and in the U.S.A., the large firm became the dominant form of organization in metals, machinery and chemicals, but not in textiles and food. The large firms in all five industries had more establishments than did firms in other industrial groups, and those factories of enterprises in the five were larger than those in other industries, and in the U.S.A. at least much larger than those of single-establishment firms.

What accounts for the clustering of large multi-unit enterprises in these five industrial groups? Clearly iron and steel and other metal-making enterprises appear on all lists because of the criteria used to determine size – that of capital or workers employed. Metal-making requires a heavy capital investment and a sizeable work-force. These characteristics are the same for railways – the largest business enterprise in all three economies before the coming of the multi-unit industrial firm. Indeed, both the all-weather, fast and regular transportation system provided by the railway and the new mass-production of metals through the Bessemer, open hearth, and other volume-producing technologies have been primary prerequisites for rapid industrialization. Textiles, on the other hand, have been in nearly all industrializing economies the first modern industry using machinery powered by water or steam and employing a massive work-force of relatively unskilled labour. Early in the industrializing process in the U.S.A., the U.K. and, I believe, Germany, textile firms accounted for the largest number of large enterprises. As industrialization continued, their number among the largest firms declined. Indeed, since the First World War in all three of the economies, textiles and metal-making have not been among the rapidly growing sectors.

On the other hand, chemicals, machinery and, to a lesser extent, food have been the most dynamic sectors in these economies. In these industry groups the criterion of capital investment or work-force seems to have been a less obvious determinant of size. Chocolate and biscuit factories, sugar, margarine and petroleum refineries, dye-works, plastic, rayon and other synthetic-producing plants, and most light machinery establishments required less capital than steel-making works and a smaller work-force than large textile mills. In these industry groups, size appears to have resulted more from integrating the processes of production and distribution.[13] In food, the large firm appeared as soon as enterprises adopted new continuous or large-batch technologies of production whose output was sold in large numbers in national and international markets. To assure a continuing use of high-volume, low-unit cost, methods of production required the food firms to take two moves. The first was the differentiation of product by packaging and branding, plus the maintenance of demand through forceful advertising of the branded goods. The second was to develop systems of careful scheduling in order to maintain the flow of thousands, often hundreds of thousands, of packaged items each month from the factory to the customers all over the world. Thus in Germany, where little attention was paid to marketing, very few of the large firms appeared in food and other consumer goods industries. In Britain and in the U.S.A., on the other hand, where advertising and scheduling of flows permitted enterprises to maintain a high volume of production, the portion of large enterprises in the consumer sector was much higher. In the refining of petroleum and the processing of rubber, the same type of high-volume, continuous process or large-batch techniques greatly reduced unit costs; and the same type of branding and advertising and the same careful scheduling of flows permitted a relatively few large firms to dominate in the production of kerosene and then gasoline and of rubber boots, shoes and outer clothing and then tyres.

In the chemical industries the large enterprises making consumer goods operated in much the same manner as did those in food, petroleum and rubber. The mass production of soaps, starch, paints, and proprietary drugs was maintained by branding, advertising, and a careful scheduling of flows. However, in the manufacturing of industrial chemicals where the basic methods of production were comparable to those in consumer goods, the methods of distribution and marketing differed in one critical aspect. The acquisition of distribution facilities and the provision of specialized services by marketing departments were much more important in maintaining output than was advertising. In production, the new processes were even more revolutionary than in consumer chemicals or food. As I. F. Haber points out in the beginning of his volume on the world's industrial chemical industry between 1900 and 1930: 'Continuous flow and pressure catalysis in combination gave chemical manufacturers of the 1910s and 1920s a totally different aspect from that of the 1880s or even the 1900s.'[14] Not only did this greatly expanded volume of production demand careful scheduling of materials into and out of the factory and then to the industrial customers, but also the shipment of products that were often toxic or otherwise dangerous required these enterprises to make or obtain their own storage, distribution and transportation facilities. Of even more importance, as German and then American enterprises developed synthetic products – dyestuffs, plastics, fibres, films, detergents, resins and the like – their salesmen had to explain and be prepared to see that the new product was properly used by the customer in the production of final products, for only they fully understood its properties.

Scheduling and specialized marketing services were also essential to the continuing profitability of large machinery firms. In the making of machinery, the fabrication and assembly of standardized products created a process similar to the large batch and, after the coming of the assembly line, to continuous processes in food and chemicals. The new processes permitted a tiny number of factories to meet the world-wide demand for sewing machines, agricultural equipment, typewriters and other office machinery, and then automobiles and trucks. To maintain the production of 10,000 machines a week, made up of dozens and even hundreds of parts, required an even more detailed scheduling than did the mass production of chemicals and food. To maintain the demand for products that went to tens of thousands of customers not only called for a steady pace of advertising but also such critical services as the demonstration, after-sales service and repair, and consumer credit. The sale of volume-produced machines purchased by other industrialists and businessmen for use in their establishments, such as elevators, printing presses, shoe machinery, and the like, required little advertising but close attention to installation, to assuring continuous after-sales service, and to providing both short- and long-term consumer credit. Where a new technology was involved, as in the case of electrical machinery, the sales force had to be made up of scientifically trained experts who came to know a great deal more about the technicalities of the power and light requirements of their customers than their customers could be expected to know unless they too had degrees in electrical engineering. Also, as in the case of chemicals, the constant interaction between the salesmen and scientific and engineering training, product designers, production managers, and research laboratories provided a powerful force to continuing innovation in these two technologically advanced industry groups.

Therefore, in food, chemicals and machinery, the ability of an enterprise to sell the product of its mass-producing factories required it to build a national and nearly always world-wide network of sales offices and, in addition, a somewhat smaller set of purchasing establishments. Indeed, in these industrial groups the large multi-unit enterprises often had more units and, therefore, more managers and a larger work-force involved in marketing than in manufacturing. In food and consumer chemical industries, the enterprises continued to use wholesalers and other middlemen to distribute their products physically, but their managers did the advertising and scheduled the flows. From the start the producers of perishable products requiring refrigerated distribution facilities, such as the large meat packers, replaced wholesalers with their own branch establishments. Then as producers of other branded products, particularly in petroleum and rubber, found economies in having their own distribution network, they too did away with the wholesaler. In industrial chemicals and in both consumer and industrial machinery, producers dispensed even more quickly with the services of middlemen. Wholesalers simply did not have the training in the fast-moving technologies to provide the necessary technical service, nor were they willing to invest the funds needed to provide consumer credit. The requirements of service and scheduling thus encouraged the large multi-unit enterprises to cluster in the food, chemical, and machinery industries and also in those with comparable characteristics, such as petroleum, rubber, and plate glass. In industries which were labour-intensive, with relatively simple production processes, with only a few items requiring systematic scheduling, and with products not complex or costly enough to call for specialized marketing services, the larger multi-unit enterprise had no special advantage. In those industries the small manufacturer who sold through the existing wholesaler continued to flourish. This review of the place of large-scale enterprise in the U.S.A., U.K., and Germany helps to explain why in the 1970s over 80 per cent of the 800 world's largest enterprises listed in *Fortune Magazine* were in the machinery, chemical, food, petroleum and rubber industries; why textiles had all but disappeared from the lists of the largest industrials; and why metals (which as part of the basic industrial infrastructure have, like transportation and communication, become increasingly nationalized) account for a smaller share of the larger firms than they did even a generation ago.

What relevance does this analysis of the place of the large multi-unit enterprise in Britain, Germany and the United States before the Second World War have for understanding business and industrial activities in the less-industrialized economies of Central and Eastern Europe? Not too much, I am afraid, except to provide a perspective. In those regions where in the inter-war years *per capita* income was still low and the rural population still large, the market for branded consumer goods must have remained small. The large food companies that did appear were probably processors of sugar, vegetable and animal fats, as was the case in Germany. These economies were still developing their basic transportation and communication infrastructure and expanding their textile industries. So enterprises in producers' goods industries undoubtedly concentrated in the production of iron, steel and other metals, of railway and communication equipment, and of machinery for the metals, textiles and mining industries. In other words, they were beginning to compete with the products of British industry. I suspect, however, that the Germans were providing the more sophisticated machinery, as well as electrical equipment and chemicals. If the Americans were involved at all, it would have been in the sale of light mass-produced agricultural and office machinery and possibly of electrical equipment, cigarettes, and canned food. As the number of producing establishments per firm was surely small and the number of sales offices even smaller, there cannot have been a strong demand for industrial managers. Corporate managers were not yet playing a major role in carrying out the processes of production and distribution. It would be interesting to learn how managers were recruited and large enterprises operated in what became the managerial-intensive industries in the West – in food, chemicals and machinery – after the Second World War in Central and Eastern Europe under very different economic and political systems.

Notes

*. I want to acknowledge with gratitude the valuable assistance received in the preparation of this article. Margaret Ackrill compiled the three lists of the largest 200 firms in Britain. Peter Grant categorized these lists into SIC categories and provided data on ownership, sales branches and factories. Regina Pisa, who compiled data from the British 1935 Census, also made lists of the largest American industrial corporations. Marc van Heukelen put together the lists of the large German companies. I am especially indebted to Herman Daems who developed the statistical data from the German Census and greatly improved the statistical information on the U.S.A. and U.K. This paper could not have been written without Professor Daems' constant help and his fine statistical and analytical abilities. I also wish to express my thanks for the financial support from the Alfred P. Sloan Foundation, the German Marshall Fund, and the Research Division of the Harvard Business School for the joint project that Professor Daems and I are undertaking on the history of large-scale business enterprises in the nineteenth and twentieth centuries of which this paper is a part.

1. U.S. Census Bureau, *Census of Manufactures*, 1937 (Washington, D.C., 1939), 4.

2. A. D. Chandler, Jr, *The Visible Hand: The Managerial Revolution in American Business* (Cambridge, Mass., 1977), 3.

3. U.S. Temporary National Economic Committee, *Investigation of Concentration of Economic Power* (Washington, 1941), 110.

4. Based on data collected by Herman Daems and Marc van Heukelen and calculated by combining *Fortune* lists of the largest companies with an estimate of world employment from the United Nations' *Statistical Year Book*.

5. U.S. Temporary National Economic Committee, *Investigation of Concentration of Economic Power*, 111.

6. The data were computed by Herman Daems from information compiled in U.S. National Resources Planning Board, *Structure of the American Economy*, Part I, 'Basic Characteristics: Report Prepared by the Industrial Section, Under the Direction of Gardner C. Means' (Washington, 1939), 271. The report gives information on the size distribution in terms of employment of the 200 largest U.S.A. corporations by value of sales. To protect the confidentiality of the data, the report gives the distribution by adding data for five corporations together. In this way 40 classes are obtained and they are ranked from the highest to the lowest employment. By dividing each of these classes by five, an estimate of average employment was derived. Class 37 has an average size slightly above 2,000, class 38, one that is slightly below. Since each class has five corporations, this means that between 185 and 190 companies had more than 2,000 employees.

7. Chandler, *op. cit.*, 347–8.

8. U.S. National Resources Planning Board, *Structure of the American Economy*, 271.

9. H. Leak and A. Maizels, 'The structure of British industry', *J. Roy. Statistical Soc.*, CVIII, pts. I–II (1945), 144.

10. Computed from tables 1 and 2, *ibid.*, 144–5.

11. Moreover, in Britain holding companies remained, as they did not in the U.S.A. and Germany, federations with almost no central office of salaried managers to co-ordinate, monitor and plan for the activities of the subsidiaries. If holding companies, which are defined by the British Census Office as 'aggregate(s) of two or more production firms controlled by a company not employed in production', are excluded, the total number of companies employing more than 2,000 was 373, the share of total employment 27.3 per cent and the average employment 5,848. The average employment for holding companies was 9.643: Leak and Maizels, *loc. cit.*, 144–7.

12. Chandler, *op. cit.*, 357–9.

13. Professor Herman Daems develops the more theoretical aspects of this relationship in a paper given at a conference in September 1979 at the Business History Unit at the London School of Economics.

14. L. F. Haber, *The Chemical Industry, 1900–1930* (1971), 4.

2. Industrial Structures in West and East Central Europe during the Inter-war Period

Alice Teichova and P. L. Cottrell

The large company now dominates the industrial sectors of most western capitalist economies. The importance of the largest manufacturing enterprises transcends national boundaries as many, particularly when their host country is small, have a majority of their operations abroad. As Prais has pointed out, over 80 per cent of the world employment of the four giants of Dutch industry (Royal Dutch-Shell, Unilever, Philips and Akzo) lies outside the Netherlands. All economically advanced countries provide the sites of headquarters of large, sometimes multi-national, companies no matter what the nation's physical size or resource base. Although Switzerland has a population only a tenth of that of the U.K., and while employment in her manufacturing sector is similarly only a tenth of that of the U.K., large manufacturing enterprises – namely those employing over 40,000 – play the same role relative to total population and manufacturing employment in Switzerland as in the U.K. There are differences in this respect between western economies with, for instance, giant companies being far less important relative to population and manufacturing employment in the case of Italy, but this is probably accounted for by that economy's more recent industrialization.[1] The commonplace nature of large industrial companies is a comparatively recent event, being in Britain's case a product of developments over the past eight or so decades.[2] Their rise has only been accurately observable since the publication of Censuses of Production and complementary financial data but the problem of concentration and its corollary of increased market power have been of concern to the statesman and his adviser since exchange economies emerged.

Various measures of concentration have been employed at both the aggregate level and the individual product market level. What is used depends upon available source material, but the share of the 100 largest enterprises in a country's net output in manufacturing is the starkest and clearest. However, alternative measures of aggregate concentration can be expected to move in much the same way over time, while there is an intimate connection between aggregate and market concentration. In Britain concentration has in the long term increased steadily and relentlessly with the share of the 100 largest enterprises in manufacturing output rising from 16 per cent in 1909 to 41 per cent in 1970.[3] By the early 1960s the 100 largest firms ranged over nearly all industrial groups, though they tended to predominate in either capital-intensive industries or where advertising and marketing economies were important.

Possibly, one of the main factors responsible for the rise in concentration would appear to be 'as simple and apparently innocuous a process as unconstrained variability in the growth rates of firms'. If unchecked then this produces a time trend of concentration sigmoid in shape, with initially a long-drawn-out rise, followed by a period of rapid acceleration but which then tails off. This process may have begun in the British economy as a result of the coming of the general availability of limited liability in the mid-1850s which upset the equilibrium of size distribution – incorporation provides for business enterprises a means to immortality. Concentration arising from variations in the annual growth rates of firms may be offset by the process of regression, but only if it is negative, that is if both dwarf and gigantic firms disappear. However, in recent decades, as far as Britain is concerned, it would appear that regression has actually been positive and therefore has accelerated concentration rather than checked it.[4]

Other factors, apart from what has been termed 'spontaneous drift', have been responsible for increasing concentration but they appear to have little to do with plant size, but are connected instead with the number of plants owned by large firms. The modern enterprise generally consists of a large number of plants, many of which are either medium or small in size. Statistics on multi-plant ownership are only readily available for the most recent decades. In Britain in 1968 the median manufacturing enterprise owned as many as 20 plants whereas the 100 largest firms had an average of 52 plants each.[5] Such multi-plant firms, in some numbers, have been a constituent of the modern industrial economy since the closing decades of the nineteenth century. Their appearance gave rise to new managerial problems, so much so that 'the economies of large-scale government rather than of large-scale techniques may have come to dictate the size of the modern business unit'.[6]

The extent of multi-plant business operations at least in the British case appears to have been determined more by the availability of industrial sites and the relative importance of transport costs of raw materials and finished goods than monopolistic motivations. The development of telecommunications has allowed the effective control of distant plants which has enabled firms, to whom transport costs are important, to reach markets by building dispersed plants. The increased speed and efficiency of transport and communications has played a major role in the spread of multi-plant working but only a marginal one in the growth of giant companies. Similarly Prais has concluded for Britain that marketing forces have played a detectable role in the rise of aggregate concentration but it has been a supporting rather than a leading force.[7]

II

Some may take exception to both classifying Austria-Hungary as an industrial economy and expecting it and its successor economies to display similar trends in industrial concentration to those of western modernized economies. Some normal tests of industrialization would support such an objection. The chief occupation of Austria-Hungary's labour force remained agriculture throughout the second half of the nineteenth century,[8] while in 1913 income per head was barely a third of that of Great Britain and little more than half that of France. But as Rudolph has recently stated, 'There is little doubt that poverty was widespread . . . and *per capita* consumption was low in most areas but it is also true that the "industrial" regions had a long history of industrial development and this development was perhaps, not inconsiderable'.[9] There is a major debate over the shape of the timescape of Austrian industrialization during the second half of the nineteenth century but some consensus is beginning to emerge which points to the rate of growth of Austrian industrial production being broadly comparable with that of other European countries.[10] Austria seems now to be another entry in the growing list of gradual industrializers but in her case this process may have been capped by a surge immediately prior to 1914.[11] However, the physical extent of Austrian industrialization was restricted to two regions in Cisleithania – non-Alpine Austria and the Czech Lands, with the centre of gravity of industrial output shifting to the latter by the 1880s – and in Transleithania to Budapest and Upper Hungary (Upper Slovakia). Such a process of highly restricted regional transformation, although not uncommon, resulted in a highly differentiated home market. Estimates indicate that in 1911–13 the share of the industrial regions accounted for over 76 per cent of national income while *per capita* income in these areas was more than twice that of the non-industrial and most populous regions.[12]

Certain major branches of Czechoslovak and Austrian industry were highly concentrated even before the end of the nineteenth century.[13] Changes in company law can in this instance have played little part in initiating a mechanism producing this concentration. The formation of joint stock companies was greatly hindered by fiscal and judicial discrimination and it was not until 1899 that company law was liberalized.[14] Although the number of companies then increased, most were not fully incorporated, there being only 1,914 limited companies in 1912. The fiscal penalties continued and in 1904 joint stock companies were subject to levels of taxation at least twice as heavy as that imposed upon unincorporated concerns.[15] However, there does appear to have been a stage in a firm's development when it was worth shouldering such costs in order to tap the potential wider sources of capital arising from conversion into an Aktiengesellschaft (joint stock company).

Concentration was apparent in mining and metallurgy by the 1880s. As early as the beginning of that decade, four large enterprises accounted for 86 per cent of all iron production in the Czech Crown Lands while ten years later the coal industry was dominated by six firms. This was paralleled by cartelization and vertical integration linking coal and iron. An agreement between the Vítkovice Mining and Foundry Works, the major producer of iron, and the Teplice mill with regard to rail production in 1877 was the foundation for a cartel for the whole monarchy established the following year.[16] The same process of consolidation and concentration occurred in sugar, although somewhat later, with the first sugar cartel for refiners being formed in 1891, followed in 1897 by an agreement between refiners and producers.[17] Of the major industries only metal fabrication proved to be resistant to some form of concentration. Two attempts to set up a cartel in successive years in the mid-1900s failed because although the firms concerned were specialized, they were not specialized enough to allow the non-specialized portions of their product ranges to fall into each other's hands.[18]

Austria-Hungary's industrial development during the 50 years before 1914 took place with increasing concentration in major branches of manufacturing.[19] This consisted of either cartelization or formal association, usually through vertical or horizontal integration.[20] The centralization of control, however, proceeded via a third channel – the industrial involvement of the banks. The major Austrian banks were generally of the 'mobilier' type but as recent research has stressed they remained aloof from industrial medium- and long-term business after the 1873 *krach* until the late 1880s. However, even during this period the banks kept in contact with the firms with which they had established links before 1873, these being mainly the major enterprises in mining, metallurgy and sugar. Further, the banks encouraged cartelization and consolidation, both by not founding rival producers and by assisting integration between established producers. In a number of industries, initially sugar but then subsequently coal, coke, petroleum, lumber and some agricultural products, the banks assumed marketing functions through commission sales arising from credits to the suppliers of the products.[21]

Connections between banks and industry became stronger from the late 1880s, and by the late 1890s had reached the stage of once more converting concerns into Aktiengesellschaften and sponsoring the consequent public issue of securities. Such ties were only with selected firms – 'the plump, juicy with favourable prospects'[22] – and began through the rolling-over of short-term credits. The next stage was directed mergers and the conversion of companies, some of which were concerns which had caused past embarrassments in the banks' balance sheets; often the banks retained a significant equity interest. Sometimes the resulting voice in the industrial concern's management councils had a forced presence, the result of private investors' general aversion to equity securities following 1873 and the consequent thinness of the market. The sum of these activities was that in 1914 the nine great Viennese banks held probably a majority interest in the share capital of all

Austrian Aktiengesellschaften.[23] Such holdings went in conjunction with sales bureaux and cartel supervision. This was coupled with interlocking bank-industry directorships, which at the very least provided information channels;[24] for example, in 1908 directors of the Österreichische Credit-Anstalt für Handel u. Gewerbe had seats on the board of 121 enterprises and banks in Austria and 39 in Hungary.

Such an industrial structure was the result of many shaping forces, not least a shortage of capital, but equally important was a highly differentiated market, splintered not only by wide variations in income levels but also by political animosity and high transport costs, while the export market could in the main only be reached through German middlemen. Stability and profitability could apparently only be contained by a combination of high external tariff barriers, cartelization and consolidation. A few foreign firms did jump these barriers. J. P. Coats, possibly the largest multi-national company in the world at the beginning of the twentieth century, had branch plants in the Czech Lands, Austria and Hungary.[25] However, it would appear that only one-eighth of Austrian industrial securities were in foreign, largely German, hands in 1901.

III

The successor states did not begin their separate economic lives in 1918 with blank sheets – they were the heirs of the industrial structure of the old monarchy. Broad macro-indicators in the late 1920s and early 1930s appear to show, as in the late nineteenth century, a considerable degree of unevenness in economic development. Agriculture's share of total employment was 26 per cent in the case of Austria and 34.2 per cent in Czechoslovakia but 53 per cent in Hungary. Average real income per head in East Central Europe was still only 50 per cent of that of Germany. Moreover, the consequences of the political settlements following the war had shattered the domestic market with tariffs cutting off the Czechoslovak and Austrian industrial regions from their previous most important market – Transleithania. Consequently local industrialists were faced with similar problems as they had confronted during the 'belle epoque' but now they were graver. The previously segmented domestic market was even more divided, tariff barriers internationally were higher, while the Entente powers and Germany became engaged in a fierce struggle for East European markets.

Industrialists responded by applying known strategies. Cartels had been dissolved at the end of the war, particularly those involving the Central powers. New political boundaries did split up what were previously constituent plants of industrial and financial groups. However, such groupings soon re-emerged, but perhaps in different guises and now often with substantial foreign participation. In Czechoslovakia at least 1,152 cartel arrangements were made during the inter-war period of which 212 were with foreign partners, chemicals alone accounting for 74 of the latter. As early as

1921 the Czechoslovak iron and steel industry was formally consolidated through the etablishment of the Prodejna sdružených československých železáren [Selling Agency of the United Czechoslovak Iron Works] dominated by the big producers led by the Vítkovice works, which collectively accounted for 90 per cent of steel output during the Republic's separate existence. Some of the major industries, as before the war, proved difficult to cartelize, the formation of such associations in the Czechoslovak mechanical and electrical engineering industry being a slower process than in iron and steel and chemicals. This, as previously, was due to the greater variety of products produced, the diversity of techniques employed, and the existence of small and medium-sized specialist producers. The A.s. dříve Škodovy závody [Škoda-Works] led attempts to form a general cartel but they were not successful until 1935.[26]

The aggregate effect on concentration of the rebuilding of cartels and consolidated enterprises may have been offset during the early years of the 1920s by the promotion of new companies and the opening of new concerns during the inflationary period. This resulted in a substantial increase in productive capacity in all the successor states but when the boom was halted by the 1921/2 crisis and subsequent stabilization policies, these new firms added to the burden of excess capacity. Consequently, in the medium term, they provided a further spur to the process of concentration.

Although exhaustive quantitative material cannot as yet be produced to be placed alongside the analysis made by Chandler of the place of large industrial enterprises in the three leading western inter-war economies, some comparable statistical material can be presented for the three main successor states – Czechoslovakia, Austria and Hungary. Czechoslovak sources are the most detailed and some outline indications can be given for Austria and Hungary. The Czechoslovak data has been drawn from the continuing graduate work of Božena Schröderova together with that of the authors of this paper. As with the Chandler/Daems enquiry, the concentration ratios presented here are based on official censuses of industrial enterprises made in the 1930s but unfortunately with varying criteria. Nevertheless, as with the Chandler analysis, valid inter-country comparisons can be made from which emerge striking similarities.

In the case of Czechoslovakia in 1930 the 115 largest enterprises, namely those with more than 1,001 employees, accounted for 16.6 per cent of the total labour force (cf. table 2.1), while the top 110 American firms had a share of 21.7 per cent in 1935, the largest 111 German enterprises a share of 18.4 per cent in 1925, and the largest 111 firms in Britain had a share of 13.4 per cent in 1935. From the Austrian industrial census of 1930 it appears that the largest 128 business units employing more than 500 persons accounted for 0.64 per cent of the total number of enterprises and employed 18.74 per cent of the total number of persons (cf. table 2.9). Hungarian data for 1937 indicate that the largest 98 firms – those employing more than) –

constituted no more than 3 per cent of the total number of industrial enterprises but accounted for 41 per cent of the Hungarian total industrial labour force (cf. table 2.7). Although the economies of the successor states were relatively small, these results point to a high incidence of concentration, certainly comparable with the advanced western economies.

Table 2.2, based on the Czechoslovak industrial census of 1930, shows concentration ratios for the 3, 8 and 20 largest enterprises by industry groups, arranged to conform as closely as possible with the tabulation employed by Chandler and Daems. Again, the results for Czechoslovakia show great similarities with the western economies as concentration, measured by share of employment, was substantial in a few often inter-related

Table 2.1. CZECHOSLOVAKIA (1): Size distribution of Czechoslovak industrials, 27 May 1930.

Size class in no. of workers	No. of firms in class		Employment in that class	Share in total employment
	No.	%	No.	%
6–20	28,612	69.0	262,326	15·6
21–50	7,020	17.0	223,358	13.3
51–100	2,905	7.0	202,617	12.2
101–250	1,833	4.4	281,144	16.8
251–500	622	1·5	213,667	12.7
501–1,000	331	0·8 ⎫	214,273	12.8 ⎫
1,001–2,500	102	0.3 ⎬ 1.15	174 097	10.4 ⎬ 29.4
2,501–5,000	8	0.35 { 0.03	33,481	2.0 } 16.6
5,001+	5	0.02 ⎭	70,309	4.2 ⎭
Total	41,438	100.05	1,675,272	100.0

Source: Calculated from Czechoslovak Census of Industrial Enterprises: *Československá statistika*, 114, Sčítání živnostenských závodů v Republice československé podle stavu dne 27.5.1930 (Prague, 1935).

industry groups – iron and steel (furnaces and rolling mills), motor car manufacture, railway carriage and wagon building, metal products, jute manufacture, shoe production, chemicals, vegetable and animal oils and fats (cf. table 2.2). The largest firms in Czechoslovakia were clustered in nearly the same small number of industry groups as the western economies analysed by Chandler. Moreover, if concentration ratios in Czechoslovak industry are compared with British, surprisingly large areas of conformity as well as certain significant differences can be observed (cf. table 2.6). High concentration ratios in Czechoslovak industry, unlike Hungary (cf. table 2.8), were not restricted to 'heavy' industry but can also be found in mass-production

Table 2.2. CZECHOSLOVAKIA (2):* The largest industrial enterprises by industry groups from 1930 Census (concentration ratio based on employment figures).

SIC group no.	Product group in industry	Concentration ratio 3 8 20 largest enterprises			Total no. of: Enterprises in product group	Employees
a. High concentrated industries						
22	Spinning & weaving mills (jute)	31.8	66.1	94.7	55	10,743
28	Fats & oils, cosmetics	47.0	56.1	66.5	184	7,537
	Heavy chemicals	35.7	56.0	84.7	99	14,691
31	Shoe industry	44.4	52.3	61.0	785	36,586
33	Furnaces & rolling mills	65.7	87.8	99.4	26	49,637
	Iron & steel foundries	36.4	65.4	84.4	52	4,866
34	Production of other metals	39.8	61.7	84.6	84	4,982
	Wire & wire products	43.0	72.7	86.0	65	6,968
35	Textile machinery	36.8	73.9	95.8	32	3,697
	Railway carriages & wagons	95.4			5	6,632
	Motor cars	96.2			7	6,435
36	Electrical wires and cables	68.3	88.4		18	2,689
b. Medium concentrated industries						
22	Spinning & weaving mills (silk)	17.8	37.3	67.8	95	22,933
26	Paper production	19.6	35.8	60.4	138	20,628
28	Dyes, pencils & inks	26.4	36.2	52.6	168	6,435
34	Tools & implements	18.4	34.3	55.4	124	3,231
35	Machine tools	21.9	35.1	78.7	59	3,286
	Agricultural machinery	25.7	43.4	53.7	199	10,256
36	Precision mechanics, optics	24.1	39.2	57.7	169	3,967
c. Low concentrated industries						
22	Spinning & weaving mills (cotton)	4.7	16.9	25.1	886	120,187
	Spinning & weaving mills (wool	13.8	30.1	45.7	267	62,140
	Spinning & weaving mills (flax)	13.6	31.8	58.6	121	23,294
	Cotton woven- & knitwear	12.0	23.7	45.5	281	20,448
	Woollen woven- & knitwear	13.3	26.9	50.7	177	8,345
	Textile finishing	10.8	21.2	38.7	265	20,687
	Other textile products	13.8	25.7	36.6	486	11,785
23	Clothing industry	3.8	7.7	11.5	3,567	42,690
26	Paper processing	12.2	19.7	29.8	533	14,178
34	Nails, screws, chains, etc.	17.5	30.9	48.6	256	13,462
	Coalmines	5.8	15.5	38.8	249	101,887

* Tables 2.2 and 2.3 are taken from B. Schöderova's prepared Ph.D. thesis. Data are rearranged to give a basis for comparison with A. Chandler's tables.

Table 2.3. CZECHOSLOVAKIA (3): Average number of establishments per multi-unit enterprise and share of multi-unit enterprises in total number of industrials and total number of persons employed by industry groups (1930).

SIC group no.	Industry group	Average no. of establishments per firm	No. of multi-unit firms*	% of total	No. employed in multi-unit firms	% of total employed
20	Food					
	a. Flour mills	2.04	839	8	5,331	18
	b. Sugar refineries	2.09	57	39	8,579	57
	c. Distilleries & yeast	2.40	112	12	2,527	57
	d. Breweries & malt-houses	2.17	425	70	18,060	84
	e. Other foods	2.05	5,671	12	33,948	20
22	Textiles	2.85	1,526	4	240,019	67
23	Clothing	2.08	2,050	3	24,593	12
24	Lumber – sawmills	2.18	414	11	13,455	33
25	Wood – furniture	2.16	746	2	18,863	14
26	Paper	2.12	926	33	24,062	61
27	Printing, arts, publishing	2.26	406	13	16,670	52
28	Chemicals	2.37	326	23	20,917	52
30	Rubber & asbestos	2.23	13	15	2,392	60
31	Shoes	2.13	356	0.9	17,154	19
32	Glass,	2.50	101	1	28,112	44
	quarries,	2.23	659	15	21,869	43
	stone & earth	2.20	1,020	14	45,564	40
33	Iron, steel & metallurgy	2.21	1,962	6	107,311	51
34	Metalworking industry	2.17	3,537	4	133,173	74
	Machine tools	2.26	65	5	1,893	27
39	Miscellaneous industries					
	Brushes	2.03	38	3	178	4
	Musical instruments	2.11	35	2	490	6
	Toys	2.10	22	4	501	18
	Furs	2.10	122	2	4,662	20
	Others	2.00	2	0.08	48	0.3
	Building and construction	2.02	2,312	8	31,258	11
	Waterworks	2.08	26	4	675	29
	Gasworks	2.19	58	70	1,802	67
	Power stations	2.45	268	19	10,225	72
	Mining – coal & peat	2.15	53	13	27,922	24
	Coke & brickets	2.00	6	24	1,830	37
	Totals	2.17	24,153	6.4	864,073	38

* Includes all firms which at the date of the Census (27.5.1930) registered subsidiary establishments, i.e. their number and persons employed in them. Unfortunately they are not divided into size classes.

Source: Calculated from Czechoslovak Census of Industrial Enterprises: *Československá statistika, 114,* Sčítání živnostenských závodů v Republice československé podle stavu dne 27.5.1930 (Prague, 1935).

Table 2.4. CZECHOSLOVAKIA (4): Multi-unit enterprises with largest share (above 50%) of total employment by industry groups (extracted from table 2.3).

SIC group no.	Industry group	Share of total employment in industry group %
20d	Breweries & malt-houses	84
34	Metalworking industry	74
	Power stations (electric)	72
	Gasworks	67
22	Textiles	67
25	Wood – furniture	61
30	Rubber & asbestos	60
20b	Sugar refineries	57
20c	Distilleries, yeast	57
27	Printing, arts & publishing	52
28	Chemicals	52
33	Iron, steel & metallurgy	51

Source: As for table 2.3.

consumer industries in which single large multi-unit firms were dominant. In shoes, Baťa of Zlin accounted for 85.7 per cent of Czechoslovak shoe production in 1937 and similarly there was Schicht-Unilever of Ústí nad Labem (Aussig on the Elbe) in the production of edible fats, oils, soap and cosmetics.

The strong similarities of the Czechoslovak and British industrial structures in the 1930s probably arise from the long-established export orientation of both economies. The stability of the Czechoslovak economy was highly dependent on exports, the latter accounting for 40 per cent of output. A survey of the industry groups with the greatest employment share in multi-unit as opposed to single-unit enterprises subtantiates such an interpretation and emphasizes the importance of the export industries in the field of both producer and consumer goods (cf. tables 2.3–2.5).

Unfortunately neither the Czechoslovak nor British censuses provide data on the number and size of establishments operated by the various size classes of multi-unit firms, but the average number of establishments and the share of the total number employed by multi-plant enterprises in each industry group can be determined (cf. table 2.3). In addition the average number of employees per multi-unit as opposed to single-unit firms can be ascertained and, as might be reasonably expected, it was substantially higher for multi-unit enterprises in all groups except gas (table 2.5). The industry groups in tables 2.4 and 2.5 correspond generally to those with the highest concentration ratios shown in Czechoslovakia (table 2.2). The only excep-

Table 2.5. CZECHOSLOVAKIA (5): Average number of persons employed per single-unit enterprise and per multi-unit enterprise by industry groups (27 May 1930).

Industry group	Average no. of employees in single-unit enterprise	Average no. of employees in multi-unit enterprise
Mining – coal & peat	255	526
coke & brickets	159	305
Glass	3	278
Rubber & asbestos	23	184
Textiles	3	157
Sugar refineries	71	151
Chemicals	19	64
Iron, steel & metallurgy	3	55
Shoes	2	48
Stone & earth	11	45
Breweries & malt-houses	23	42
Printing, arts, publishing	6	41
Metalworking industries	9	38
Electric power stations	4	38
Furs	3	38
Quarries	8	33
Lumber & sawmills	8	32
Gasworks	36	31
Machine tools	4	29
Waterworks	3	26
Paper	8	26
Wood – furniture	3	25
Miscellaneous industries	6	24
Toys	5	23
Distilleries & yeast	2	22
Building & construction	11	14
Musical instruments	3	14
Clothing	2	12
All industries	4	11
Flourmills	2	6
Brushes etc.	4	5

Sources: As for table 2.3.

tions are branches of brewing, sugar refining and distilling of the food group together with the glass industry where a large labour force was concentrated in multi-plant employment but where the share of the 3, 8 and 20 largest enterprises does not reveal a high concentration ratio. However, firms in these industries can be classified as large-scale enterprises as they reflect the specificity of Czechoslovak export-orientated production – beer based on rich hop and barley crops, sugar, the white gold of Czechoslovakia, together with textiles, glass and shoes.

Table 2.6. CONCENTRATION IN CZECHOSLOVAKIA (1930) AND GREAT BRITAIN (1935)

Czechoslovakia		*Great Britain*	
Industry	Concentration ratio	Industry	Concentration ratio
		Blast furnaces	35
Furnaces & rolling mills	65.7	Smelting & rolling	22
Iron & steel foundries	36.4	Iron & steel foundries	18
Wire & wire products	43.0	Wire	28
Motor cars	96.2	Private motor cars & chassis	48
Railway carriage, wagon building	95.4	Railway carriage & wagon building	38
Shoe production	44.4	Boot & shoe	9
Electrical wire & cables	68.3	Electrical wire & cables	52
Chemicals (without fats, oils, mineral oils	19.4	Chemicals, dyes & drugs	37
Agricultural machinery	25.7	Agricultural machinery	39
Dyes, dyestuffs, pencils, inks	26.4	Dyes, dyestuffs	82
Spinning & weaving mills (silk)	17.8	Silk & rayon	44
Textile finishing	10.8	Textile finishing	24
Spinning & weaving mills (cotton)	4.7	Cotton spinning & doubling	22
Spinning & weaving mills (flax)	13.6	Linen & hemp	25
Cotton weaving	7.2	Cotton weaving	4
Spinning & weaving mills (jute)	31.8	Jute	35
Clothing industry	3.8	Tailoring, dressmaking, millinery	6
Nails, screws, chain	17.5	Chain, nails, screws	19
Tools & implements	18.4	Tools & implements	10
Textile machinery	36.8	Textile machinery & accessories	35
Machine tools	21.9	Machine tools	26
Vegetable & animal oil, fats, & cosmetics	47.0	Soap, candle, perfume, oil & tallow	19
Precision mechanics & optics	24.1	Scientific instruments, appliances, apparatus	18
Paper production	19.6	Paper	20
Paper processing	12.2	Manufactured stationery	18
Coal mines	5.8	Coal mines	9
Electrical engineering	17.5	Electrical engineering	24

Table 2.7. HUNGARY (1): Size distribution of Hungarian industrials, 1933 and 1937.

Size class in no. of workers	No. of firms in class				Employment in that class		Share in total employment	
	No. 1933	%	No. 1937	%	No. 1933	No. 1937	% 1933	% 1937
0–20	1,864	58	2,028	53	16,207	19,315	8	7
21–50	662	20.5	897	24	21,651	28,921	11	11
51–100	303	9	404	10	21,372	28,172	11	10
101–500	340	10.5	403	10	73,640	86,567	38	31
501+	59	2	98	3	63,122	113,463	32	41
Total	3,228	100.0	3,830	100	195,992	276,438	100	100

Source: Calculated from *Annuaire statistique hongrois* (Nouveau cours), 43, 45.

Table 2.8. HUNGARY (2): The largest industrial enterprises by industry groups (1937) (share in employment).

SIC group no.*	Industry	Enterprises No. +500 employees	%†	Workers No.	%
20	Food	8	0.8	5,908	18
22	Textiles	37	9	37,054	55
23	Clothing	2	1	1,021	7
24	Wood	1	0.3	588	4
26	Paper	1	1	619	12
28	Chemicals	4	1	4,116	29
31	Leather, horsehair, fur, feathers, oilcloth	7	7	6,174	60
32	Stone, earth & glass	6	1	4,497	16
33	Iron, steel & metallurgy	13	4	27,668	62
34 & 35	Mechanical engineering	17	8	24,905	69
36	Electrical engineering & electricity	12	4	3,787	54
Misc.	Printing & arts products	2	2	1,313	18

* Industries against the SIC numbers have been approximately arranged to give a basis for comparison – very tentatively – with A. D. Chandler's tables.
† Percentages refer to total number of enterprises and total number of workers in each branch of industry.

Source: Calculated from *Annuaire statistique Hongrois* (Nouveau cours), 45.

Note: Rank order of largest industrial enterprises by industry groups based on above table:

34 & 35	Mechanical engineering	69% of total workers employed
33	Iron, steel & metallurgy	62% of total workers employed
31	Leather etc.	60% of total workers employed
22	Textiles	55% of total workers employed
36	Electrical engineering	54% of total workers employed

Table 2.9. AUSTRIA (1): Size distribution of Austrian industrial enterprises.

Size class in no. of workers	No. of enterprises in class		Employment Share in	
			in class	total
	No.	%	No.	%
6–20	14,478	72.96	141,497	23.07
21–50	3,238	16.32	101,525	16.56
51–100	1,128	5.69	78,414	12.79
101–300	728	3.67	122,099	19.91
301–500	143	0.72	54,784	8.93
501–1,000	98	0.49 } 0.64 } 1.36	65,797	10.73 } 18.74 } 27.67
1,001+	30	0.15	49,134	8.01
Total	19,843	100.00	613,250	100.00

Source: Calculated from *Gewerbliche Betriebszählung in der Republik Österreich vom 14. Juni 1930*, Bundesamt für Statistik (Vienna, 1932).

Since in table 2.2 (Czechoslovakia) concentration ratios are calculated and in table 2.10 (Austria) straightforward census figures of employment are used, percentages of concentration can be compared only in a general sense, i.e. to ascertain trends rather than precise figures. However, in almost every aspect the Austrian pattern of concentration in large enterprises, measured by employment according to product groups, roughly resembles that of Czechoslovakia. The Austrian census of business enterprises divided industry into 12 branches and 349 product groups. Out of the 349 product groups only 60 included enterprises employing more than 500 persons and their share in employment is calculated in table 2.11. Amongst those groups 24 employed more than 50 per cent of the total number of employees in their respective product groups. Like the western economies and Czechoslovakia, employment was most highly concentrated in Austria's producer goods industries (iron and steel, machines and transport equipment, electrical industry and chemicals). In addition 7 out of the 24 product groups showed large clusters of employment in consumer goods industries, such as rayon, tobacco, jute, sugar, cellulose, glass, which played a significant role in Austria's exports.

Although generally the structure of large-scale enterprise together with the concentration of production in multi-plant enterprises in the successor states resembles the pattern of western economic development, and although as far as heavy industry is concerned Austrian and Hungarian experience is similar, there are significant differences with regard to Czechoslovakia. These arise not only from the export orientation of the Czechoslovak economy but also were the result of the pattern of its long-term modernization. As elsewhere, industrialization in Bohemia and Moravia began with the transformation of the textile industries but then spread to primary processing (brewing, sugar, distilling) followed by the emergence of capital goods production – iron, steel, coal and agricultural and textile machinery manufacture.

However, there is a further important difference discernible between the largest multi-unit enterprises operating in the economies of the successor states during the inter-war period and those of the western economies, which is of particular relevance to the themes being addressed here. It was the result of the constant scarcity of capital in this region during the inter-war period. The largest companies in the mostly highly concentrated industries of East Central Europe were generally either wholly or partially owned subsidiaries of Western European multi-national enterprises. Quantitative analysis of the incidence of foreign equity investment in East Central and South-Eastern European industry reveals that the highest proportion of non-domestic involvement was in the largest companies of the mining and metallurgical industries, followed by, in descending order, chemicals, engineering, stone, glass, ceramics, wood, textiles, and the paper and printing industries. So, by either penetrating the comparatively strongest and to a large extent already concentrated industries or playing some formative role in the foundation of multi-unit companies, direct foreign investment placed by Western European multi-national companies emphasized and accelerated the existing tendencies towards the growth of concentration in the receiving countries' economies.

This raises the question of whether there existed a sizeable demand for managers in the large industrial enterprises of the successor states. The history of industrial development in Austria-Hungary contains a long tradition of technical education and professionally managed enterprises. The problem cannot be thoroughly examined here but at least certain aspects can be indicated. Institutions of higher technical education (*Technische Hochschulen*) were founded earlier in the Habsburg Monarchy than in the neighbouring German states – in Prague in 1806 on the basis of the first technical school opened in Europe in 1717/8, in Vienna in 1815, and in Brno in 1849, followed by a management-technical school in Budapest in 1860. These institutions produced formally trained technical managers for the following industries – chemicals, glass, iron, tanning, dyeing – through the study of applied chemistry together with mathematics, mechanics, hydraulics and building construction. Traditionally all large companies' production processes were supervised and controlled by technical managers from at least the 1850s. By the inter-war period the largest multi-unit companies in every branch of industry were professionally managed. As is evident from some of the other papers in this volume, the management functions were divided into technical and business administrative (*kaufmännische*) operations, similar to the divisions of the corporate manager's role as portrayed by Chandler. They were in charge of the processes of production and distribution.

Table 2.10. AUSTRIA (2): Share of large enterprises in total employment by industrial groups.*

SIC group no.	Product group	% share in largest enterprises			Total no. of enterprises with +6 employees in product group	
		3	8	20	*Enterprises*	*No. employed*
20	Food	5.6	12.3	20.2	2,909	60,197
	incl. sugar	69.1			7	3,402
	dairies	53.8			103	3,783
	cocoa & chocolates	40.0			71	6,353
	beer brewing	24.7			105	8,943
21	Tobacco	48.7	94.5		10	8,031
22	Textiles	7.5	14.8	25.2	985	71,712
	incl. rayon	2/100†			2	2,374
	wool spinning	71.5	98.7		10	2,292
	wool weaving	41.9	66.3	92.2	33	4,522
	cotton spinning	19.4	41.0	72.4	42	11,286
	cotton weaving	30.0	50.2	82.6	53	8,512
	hemp spinning & weaving	99.1			5	1,121
	jute spinning	2/100†			2	1,320
	jute weaving	100			3	1,666
	bleaching & dyeing	23.1	41.2	84.8	54	5,317
	tricotage	27.1	49.3	68.0	93	4,066
	ribbons, belts, etc.	57.9	82.9	99.3	24	1,425
	knitted material	11.8	20.9	42.7	248	10,017
23	Apparel	1.2	3.2	8.0	3,248	56,450
	incl. shoe manufacture	22.7	37.6	64.1	81	6,205
26	Paper	9.5	21.4	32.9	505	29,356
	incl. cellulose	55.3	96.8		10	3,631
	paper goods	24.8	43.4			
27	Graphic industry	3.6	9.5	23.8	561	19,679
	incl. printing	10.8	17.6	30.0		
28	Chemical industry	12.9	19.1	25.3	443	19,456
	incl. gas for lighting & heating	69.4	90.9	99.0	22	2,467
	gas supply	2/100†			2	1,184
	explosives	62.4	97.6	12/100†	12	1,442
30	Rubber	79.7	89.0	95.5	50	5,936
31	Leather	7.8	20.7	51.8	288	8,253
	incl. tanneries	55.5	76.3	91.1	47	2,432
32	Stone, earth, clay, glass, building	9.7	18.3	36.1	980	39,438
	incl. cement	35.6	76.9	16/100†	16	4,078
	bricks	17.8	23.6	34.4	292	12,580
	potteries	53.0	71.7	83.6	55	2,006
	glass	67.5	81.7	92.9	27	1,105

building firms	9.3	14.3	19.3	886	36,566
construction engineering	21.6	34.9	66.8	86	6,523
bridge construction	96.3	5/100[†]		5	1,242
hydraulic construction	50.3	72.3	97.0	25	1,887
builders' bureaux	17.6	24.9	42.7	235	12,298
33 Iron, steel & metallurgy	50.8	72.4	86.2	38	16,026
incl. pig iron	100			3	4,269
iron & steel	100			3	4,446
iron & steel rolling mills	65.0	89.5	13/100[†]	13	4,555
34 Fabricated metal products	7.3	11.2	15.6	2,280	61,136
incl. ironware	58.1	98.4	12/100[†]	12	1,959
toolmaking	32.9	44.9	55.3	203	3,586
lamps	89.2	99.1		9	871
wire, nails, chains	41.7	70.3	91.9	32	4,615
alpaca ware	96.6	99.7		9	3,060
35 Machines & transport equipment	10.1	21.1	37.3	1,050	44,022
incl. lifts	76.5	96.4		12	1,191
locomotives	100			3	984
waggons	100			3	3,172
automobiles	27.8	47.9	68.0	251	11,027
shipbuilding, docks	99.0			4	904
agricultural machines	52.3	77.0	92.8	53	3,237
machinery (general)	21.9	32.5	49.6	327	9,236
weapons	78.8	91.5	98.0	23	1,470
36 Electrical industry	30.1	48.3	64.9	184	21,742
incl. cables	76.1	95.7		12	3,092
bulbs	56.8	90.1	100	20	2,422
electric motors	61.5	89.5	97.6	31	5,810
telegraph & telephone industry	68.8	93.7	16/100[†]	16	4,539
radio industry	69.9	82.2	95.6	28	1,507

* All product groups in which there were enterprises with 500+ employed persons.
[†] Figure denotes under 20 enterprises.

Source: As for table 2.9

Table 2.11. AUSTRIA (3): Share of enterprises with +500 employed persons in total employment according to product groups.*

SIC group no.	Product group	% share of enterprises	
		+500 employed	+1,000 employed
20	Food		
	incl. sugar	69	
	dairies	53	
	cocoa, chocolates	40	
	brewing	25	13
	bakeries		10
21	Tobacco	94	48
22	Textiles		
	incl. rayon		98
	jute weaving		95
	hemp weaving		92
	jute spinning	63	
	wool spinning		44
	cotton spinning	38	10
	ribbons, belts, etc.	38	
	wool weaving		32
	cotton weaving	30	15
	bleaching, dyeing	19	
	tricotage	18	
	knitted material	8	
23	Apparel		
	incl. shoe manufacture	20	
26	Paper		
	incl. cellulose	55	
	paper goods	38	12
27	Graphic industry		
	incl. printing	11	7
28	Chemical industry		
	incl. gas supply	81	
	gas for lighting & heating	63	
	explosives	37	
30	Rubber	79	50
31	Leather		
	incl. tanneries	39	
	Stone, earth, clay, glass		
	incl. glass	50	
	potteries	35	
	cement	27	
	bricks	18	8
	Building		
	bridge construction	84	
	hydraulic construction	27	

	construction engineering	19	
	builders' bureaux	17	
	building firms	13	6
33	Iron, steel & metallurgy		
	incl. pig iron		97
	iron & steel		90
	other metals	88	
	iron & steel rolling mills	64	
34	Fabricated metal products		
	incl. alpaca ware		85
	lamps	82	
	wire, nails, chains	36	24
	iron ware	36	
	toolmaking	17	
35	Machines & transport equipment		
	incl. wagons		99
	shipbuilding, docks	69	
	locomotives	68	
	lifts	61	
	weapons	51	
	automobiles	47	21
	agricultural machinery		31
	machinery (general)	20	14
36	Electrical industry		
	incl. electric motors	85	49
	telegraph & telephone industry	81	44
	cables	76	
	radio industry	46	
	bulbs	37	

* Percentages obtained from total in table 2.10.

Source: As for table 2.9.

Note: Rank order of largest industrial enterprises by product groups based on above table:

SIC no.	Product group	% share of employment in the group	SIC no.	Product group	% share of employment in the group
35	wagons	99	28	gas supply	81
22	rayon	98	30	rubber	79
33	pig iron	97	36	cables	76
22	jute weaving	95	20	sugar refining	69
21	tobacco	94	35	shipbuilding	69
33	iron & steel	90	33	iron & steel rolling mills	64
33	other metals	88	28	gas for lighting & heating	63
36	electric motors	85	22	jute spinning	63
34	alpaca ware	85	35	lifts	61
32	bridge construction	84	26	cellulose	55
34	lamps	82	35	weapons	51
36	telephone & telegraph	81	32	glass	50

Table 2.12. NUMBER AND CAPITAL OF COMPANIES DEPENDENT UPON THE FOUR LARGEST JOINT-STOCK BANKS IN AUSTRIA, CZECHOSLOVAKIA AND HUNGARY BY INDUSTRY (preliminary incomplete table to show range of industries involved with banks). Roman figures show no. of banks, *italic figures show nominal capital (in 000s Pg)*

Total no. of dependent companies	Name of bank	Banking & finance	Breweries & beverages	Building	Chemicals	Engineering: electrical	Engineering: mechanical
	AUSTRIA (1929)						
215	Österreichische Creditanstalt für Handel & Gewerbe	35	10	3	8	8	25
133	Niederösterreichische Escompte-Gesellschaft	24	4	7	6	25	16
128	Anglo-Austrian Bank	19	3	5	10	2	24
98	Zentral-Europäische Länderbank	18	1	2	8	5	11
	CZECHOSLOVAKIA (1937)						
90	Živnostenská banka	9	3	5	12	2	11
88	Česká Eskomptní banka	6	3	2	10	3	9
33	Anglo-Czechoslovak Bank	1	2	2	2	4	4
49	Czech Bank Union	5	1	1	2	1	–
18	Bank for Commerce & Industry formerly Länderbank	–	–	–	2	1	4
	HUNGARY (1929)						
75	Hungarian General Creditbank	–	–	–	5 *2,655*	18 *51,007*	6 *33,800*
79	Hungarian Commercial Bank of Pest	–	–	–	11 *12,835*	7 *20,535*	10 *44,097*
19	British & Hungarian Bank	–	–	–	3 *792.4*	–	5 *6,244*
19	First National Savings Bank Corporation of Pest	–	–	–	– *400*	1	4 *1,320*

Notes:
* Including sugar refining and distilleries.
† Including hotel companies.
‡ Including paper (paper and printing make up the majority).

Sources: For Austria: *Compass* and Finanzarchiv, Vienna; for Hungary: I. T. Berend and Ránki, G., *Magyarországa gasdasága az elsö világhaború után 1919–1929* (Budapest, 1966), 222–8; for Czechoslovakia: A. Teichova, *An Economic Background to Munich* (1974), 346–7, 352–5, 358–65.

Food	Glass, china, clay, stone	Miscellaneous companies	Insurance	Mining & metallurgy	Mineral oil	Shoes & leather	Store- & warehouses	Textile	Transport	Wood & paper & print
19*	3	18†	5	23	6	2	1	16	23	10‡
3*	3	7	2	9	7	1	–	4	8	7‡
15*	2	10	–	6	6	5	2	3	4	12‡
15*	–	4	3	6	4	4	–	4	8	5‡
24*	–	–	3	7	–	–	–	5	4	5‡
17*	7	–	1	11	–	–	–	13	–	6‡
4*	5	–	1	1	–	2	–	2	2	1
4*	8	1	1	11	–	–	–	10	–	4‡
5*	1	–	–	–	–	–	–	5	–	–
10	9	–	–	4	–	–	–	17	–	6‡
50,426	9,534			77,520				27,496.8		2,003.72
18	7	–	–	10	–	–	–	10	–	6‡
59,606	14,150			30,630				10,590		6,310
–	4	–	–	–	–	1	–	1	–	5‡
	4,060					400		1,000		1,477.5
9	4	–	–	–	–	–	–	–	–	1
26,286.5	938									750

Although there existed an identity of interest, there was not usually an identity of ownership and management. As little attention has so far been paid to this aspect of East Central European business history, no further details regarding the functions of managers in this area can be given. However – given that local managers with training were available – why did Western European companies generally prefer to appoint members of their own staff to leading positions in their East Central European subsidiaries, while leaving the ranks of middle management to be filled by locals? In the case of Austria and Czechoslovakia, and with regard to the large Hungarian industrial works, this was due less to the inability of indigenous technicians and administrators than to the desire for and necessity of control by head offices abroad – an essential ingredient of personnel policy in multi-national companies.

As before the First World War, industrial concentration was mirrored by financial concentration through bank-industry links. At the same time there was substantial western investment in the banking systems of East Central Europe which was attracted by such ties and which augmented concurrent equity participations in industrial enterprises. Occasionally some such placements were actually twinned, with investments by the same Western European group taking place in both the industrial concern and the local bank which serviced it financially.

The capital shortage experienced by the region was exacerbated by the effects of the severe post-war inflations which destroyed financial capital. Consequently the banks were faced in the early 1920s with the continuing need to enlarge their equity bases in order to keep pace with the march of inflation. Consequent new issues of equity capital provided the opportunity for western participation and exactly the same process occurred with regard to industrial concerns. Then the general collapse of the domestic new issue market in the mid-1920s, especially in Austria, reinforced the already existing ties between the local banks and industrial enterprises which dated from the late 1880s through forcing firms to rely for financial resources upon their bankers. Generally accommodation was now only available from the banks but this resulted in a substantial immobilization of banks' assets and acted as an added spur to the banks to further enlarge their own capital basis. This set in motion another cycle of western equity participation in the financial sectors of the successor states.

One consequence was that the major banks now became more than ever in effect industrial holding companies as a result of involuntary investment banking. Their substantial industrial interests are listed in table 2.12. The exact significance of these ties, as before the war, is difficult to discern. The balance is difficult to strike, but certainly in the case of Austria it was from the mid-1920s a problem of 'disaster' banking. Client firms had to be sustained through long-term credits and, if possible, security issues in order to stave off bankruptcy which would further endanger the position of the bank. Although the banks' investment portfolios were diversified, the firms whose shares they contained had strong general associations through facing similar market pressures. Consequently, the banks, as before the war, supported and favoured cartelization and concentration as a way of ensuring at least market stability, thereby reducing to a degree the risks that they faced through their investments. The banks continued to make product sales, were the physical homes of cartel bureaux, and managed mergers. By fulfilling these roles, they acted as the corporate financing departments of their client firms and often the marketing department too.

However, the banks did not replace the capital market as far as industrial issues were concerned, since a domestic securities market had never developed as an independent entity in East Central Europe. In the 1920s, if a firm's internal sources of finance were meagre, then the only readily available dispensers of funds were either a western concern, often a multi-national eager to expand in East Central Europe, or a local bank with whom the firm had established ties but which now in the post-war period was itself reliant to some degree or another on western financial resources.

IV

The nations of East Central Europe have had little experience of development under the conditions of a free market. Their industrialization had involved substantial state intervention. As follower economies, their industrial enterprises in the producer goods industries often began as relatively large-scale units. Consequently tendencies towards concentration were well established before 1914. Further, the unprecedented needs of the war economy of 1914–18 brought about an even closer alignment of the state and private business which augmented industrial concentration through mergers and integration. After the war the international situation favoured the expansion of the business of the strongest industrial companies and financial institutions of the Entente on the one hand, but also of defeated Germany on the other. The victors aimed at penetrating a comparatively new market, more so in the case of Britain than of France, while Germany regarded East Central Europe as its traditional market (*angestammtes Absatzgebiet*) and viewed its own efforts to hold or gain markets in the Danube region as reconstruction (*Wiederaufbau*).

But what was the nature of this market? Shattered, broken up by the end of the war, split into small new national entities, although still regarded by many as an entity for practical business purposes, it was viewed by many western companies as a substitute for opportunities now lost further to the east as well as being a potential area for trade in its own right. Other reasons for developing the East Central European market were not only economic but also political, as the Danubian region constituted an area of competition for both economic and political influence. Britain and France, to varying degrees, aimed at eliminating Germany as a major trading competitor. There existed a community of interests between policy makers at the Foreign Offices, economic ministries and business circles in the desire to penetrate into former German and Austrian markets in order to prevent a resurgence of German economic, financial and political power.

The largest combines within this process aimed at creating and shaping markets by manipulating and regulating supply and demand – they attempted by various methods and strategies to replace the market mechanism. Here they were able to build upon a foundation established by local firms and financial interests.

Notes

1. S. J. Prais, *The Evolution of Giant Firms in Britain* (1976), 155–8.
2. L. Davis, 'The capital markets and industrial concentration: the U.S. and the U.K., a comparative study', *EcHR*, 2nd ser., XIX (1966). P. L. Payne, 'The emergence of the large scale company in Great Britain, 1870–1913', *ibid.*, 2nd ser. XX (1967).
3. Prais, *op. cit.*, 2–10.
4. *Ibid.*, 25–40. The role of what has been termed 'spontaneous drift' is still not clear and other scholars have put forward a forceful case that with respect to Britain, mergers have been the main cause of concentration. See L. Hannah and J. A. Kay, *Concentration in Modern Industry* (1977), but also P. E. Hart 'On bias and concentration', *J. Industrial Economics*, XXVII (1979).
5. Prais, *op. cit.*, 60–9.
6. D. H. Robertson, *Control of Industry* (1923), 25.
7. Prais, *op. cit.*, 69–86.
8. H. Matis, *Österreichs Wirtschaft 1848– 1913. Konjunkturelle Dynamik und gesellschaftlicher Wandel im Zeitalter Franz Josephs I* (Berlin, 1972), 422–3; I. T. Berend and G. Ránki, *Underdevelopment and Economic Growth* (Budapest, 1979), 77.
9. R. Rudolph, *Banking and Industrialization in Austria-Hungary* (1976), 40.
10. D. F. Good, 'Stagnation and "take-off" in Austria, 1873–1913', *EcHR*, 2nd ser., XXVII (1974); J. Komlos, 'Is the Depression in Austria after 1873 a "myth"?', *ibid.*, XXXI (1978); D. F. Good, 'The Great Depression and Austrian growth after 1873', *ibid.* See also E. März, *Österreichische Industrie und*

Bankpolitik in der Zeit Franz Josephs I (Vienna, 1968); N. Gross, 'Economic growth and the consumption of coal in Austria and Hungary, 1831–1913', *J. Economic History*, XXXI (1971), and Rudolph, 'The pattern of Austrian industrial growth from the eighteenth to the early twentieth century', *Austrian History Yearbook*, XI (1975).
11. W. Ashworth, 'Typologies and evidence: has nineteenth-century Europe a guide to economic growth?', *EcHR*, 2nd ser., XXX (1977); Matis, *op. cit.*, 434–40; Berend and Ránki, *op. cit.*, 78–9.
12. Rudolph, *op. cit.*, 19; Matis, *op. cit.*
13. J. Křížek, *Die wirtschaftlichen Grundzüge des österreich-ungarischen Imperialismus in der Vorkriegszeit 1900–1914* (Rozpravy Československé akademie věd, 14/37, Prague, 1963); H. Matis and K. Bachinger, 'Österreichs industrielle Entwicklung' in *Die Habsburgermonarchie 1858–1918*, I (Vienna, 1973), 134–40.
14. *Ibid.*, 216; Rudolph, *op. cit.*, 193–4.
15. *Ibid.*, 77, 159–60.
16. *Ibid.*, 51–2, 97–9; I. T. Berend and G. Ránki, *Economic Development in East Central Europe in the 19th and 20th Centuries* (1974), 158.
17. Rudolph, *op. cit.*, 108–9; Berend and Ránki, *Economic Development*, 160.
18. Rudolph, *op. cit.*, 116–17.
19. A. Mosser, 'Raumabhängigkeit und Kozentrationsinteresse in der industriellen Entwicklung Österreichs bis 1914', *Bohemia*, XVII (1976), 136–208: I. T. Berend and G. Ránki, *Hungary: A Century of Economic Development* (New York, 1974), 75–6.
20. Z. Jindra, 'Průmyslové monopoly v Rakousko-Uhersku' (Industrial

monopolies in Austria–Hungary),
Československý časopis historický, IV
(1956), 231–70, and A. Mosser,
'Konzentrationserscheinungen in der
Österreichischen Industrie bis 1914',
*Bericht über den elften österreichischen
Historikertag in Innsbruck, veranstaltet vom
Verband Österreichischer Geschichtsrereine
in der Zeit vom 4. bis 8. Oktober 1971*
(Vienna, 1972), 198.
21. März, *op. cit.*, 370; Rudolph, *op. cit.*,
105; Behrend and Ránki, *Hungary*, 76.

22. Rudolph, *op. cit.*, 118.
23. *Ibid.*, 120.
24. *Ibid.*, 159; A. Teichova, 'Versailles and
the expansion of the Bank of England into
Central Europe', in *Law and the
Formation of the Big Enterprises in the 19th
and Early 20th Centuries*, ed. N. Horn and
J. Kocka (Göttingen, 1979), 372.
25. PRO, FO 120 987 526/21.
26. A. Teichova, *An Economic Background
to Munich* (1974), 58, 71–5, 221–53,
312–35.

3. Concentration and the Finance of Austrian Industrial Combines, 1880–1914

A. Mosser

Concentration is a characteristic feature of modern economic growth. From the Austrian point of view, from the last third of the nineteenth century it can be called a constant regulator of economic development. A clear understanding of this process is assisted if some of the aspects of the tendency for concentration to take place are distinguished. There are several different kinds of concentration: establishment and enterprise concentration, concentration of income, concentration of authority. A certain number of indices have been developed for measurement: absolute and relative or horizontal, vertical, and diagonal concentration, etc.

In spite of the variety and strength of the processes of economic concentration which have taken place during the past 100 years, their importance has often been over-estimated, first, as far as their general effect on all branches of economic life is concerned, and second, in the reliance placed upon them as indicators and even as causes of economic growth. The location of enterprises, as determined by the proximity to markets, labour pools and supplies of capital, can weaken the concentration process even in growth phases or indeed reverse it. This is evident particularly during a war economy when changed market interrelations bring about contrasting developments within various branches of industry and even within enterprises. It is often unrecognized that state regulations are also able to affect concentration, e.g. by tax law.

An attempt will here be made to show some of the principal features of the process of concentration in the period before the First World War and to trace, if possible, the phenomenon at the level of the individual business establishment on the one hand and the enterprise on the other. These features will be compared with the typical parallel trends in finance. References to the successful development of enterprises represent a kind of control for assessing the success or failure of a given enterprise strategy.

First, the question of the connection between industrial growth and the concentration of places of production will be considered. Table 3.1 shows the production indices for some typical branches of the raw material and food supply industries. In the case of sugar, the amount of processed sugar beet has been taken as the basis for calculation. Contrary to what might have been expected from the distinct growth trend, the concentration movements show

Table 3.1. INDEX OF PRODUCTION 1870–1913 (CISLEITHANIA).

Year	Hard coal	Brown coal	Iron ore	Pig iron	Petroleum	Beer	Sugar
1870	42	23	56	36		61	24
1873	50	38	70	47		78	35
1875	51	45	47	39		76	19
1880	66	56	47	41		69	54
1885	82	70	62	64		82	91
1890	100	104	91	85	13	89	126
1895	109	122	93	100	26	113	170
1900	123	143	127	128	48	131	151
1905	141	150	128	143	111	125	114
1910	154	167	176	192	245	137	132
1913	184	182	203	225	155	138	183

Average = 100

Table 3.2. INDEX OF ABSOLUTE ENTERPRISE CONCENTRATION 1870–1913 (CISLEITHANIA).

Year	Hard coal	Brown coal	Iron ore	Pig iron	Petroleum	Beer	Sugar
1870	66	61				73	130
1873						75	87
1875	70	64	54	55		77	97
1880	98	85	75	65		85	97
1885	110	101	69	73		92	94
1890	112	106	88	83	134	100	96
1895	113	113	128	99	136	110	96
1900	107	117	132	126	117	123	98
1905	115	141	152	173	97	137	101
1910	130	162	173	276	89	148	106
1913	128	166	218	319	67	164	109

Average = 100

no uniform picture but instead present a picture full of contrasts. Table 3.2 shows the indices of absolute concentration of enterprises in these branches.

The highest concentration is to be found in pig iron and iron ore production where between 1875 and the outbreak of the First World War output had increased six-fold and four-fold respectively. Coal-mining was characterized by a considerably slower concentration process. In this period concentration in the production of brown coal increased only 2.6 times and in hard coal only 1.8 times. Between 1890 and 1913 the number of enterprises in the oil industry doubled and concentration dropped by half as a consequence. Traditionally the brewing industry had always been dispersed – in 1870 the number of firms in Cisleithania alone amounted to 2,420 – and as a result concentration was a very slow process, increasing by only 2.25 times between 1870 and 1913. The sugar industry experienced sometimes very large fluctuations in the concentration of production centres. By 1913 there had occurred an increase of only 25 per cent over the 1873 level. It is evident therefore that the absolute concentration of enterprises does not correlate with the growth indices for the various branches of industry. Rather, a complex series of causes came into play. It consisted of wide-ranging government intervention, economic and technical factors, and even included national consumer habits.

The slower progression of concentration in hard coal and brown coal mining reflected the inadequate domestic supply of higher grade coal for industry. Enterprises in need of considerable amounts of energy and heat supplies acquired mining claims and established small operations for their own requirements. A considerable number of small and medium-sized businesses were able to retain their independence because of their mutually advantageous contacts with near-by industry. This tendency was also reflected in the average growth of enterprises. Between 1875 and 1913 this increased 10.5 times in the field of brown coal mining, whereas in hard coal mining the increase was only a factor of 6.6.

As far as the sugar industry is concerned, the extremely weak trend of concentration was caused by dependence on the availability of the basic raw material – sugar beet. The distribution of cultivation determined, by and large, the location of manufacturing establishments as the transport of beet over long distances was impossible due to insufficient infrastructure and high local railway freight costs. Many processing plants received their entire sugar beet supply from within a radius of 20km. A supplementary supply from more distant sources – even from company-owned businesses – proved to be uneconomic.

The position in the oil industry was entirely different. In this relatively young branch of production, which only began to grow rapidly in the 1890s, the number of suppliers doubled between 1890 and 1913, while at the same time the average establishment size increased six-fold. If the highly capital-intensive nature of this branch of industry is taken into account, which is most evident when a change occurred from small to middle-sized and large firms, at first glance this development seems to be not very plausible. But what it does demonstrate is that in industries whose products can be sold rapidly and profitably despite substantial increases of output, deconcentration occurs in the initial phase of their growth. However, as a consequence of overproduction there did occur in the case of the Austrian oil industry a decline in prices in 1910 and structural developments then reversed. In the course of the next four years the number of firms fell by 10 per cent as a result of amalgamation.

Ancient rights of authority still existed in the brewing industry. These rights, together with a certain orientation towards raw materials, were evidently two essential factors which hindered concentration in this branch of industry.

The relative concentration of Austrian industry, characterized as disparity, cannot be fully explained by the situation in the capital market, or the internal financing problems of firms, or the growth of branches.

It is only in the cases of the iron ore and pig iron industries that there was a high degree of development before the outbreak of the First World War in terms of both relative and absolute concentration. With regard to pig iron, in 1911 two companies were the major producers, responsible for 55 per cent of Austrian output: the Pražská železářská společnost [Prague Iron Industry Company] which produced 21 per cent and the Österreichisch Alpine Montangesellschaft [Austrian Alpine Montan Company] with 34 per cent. In the same year the Brüxer Kohlen-Bergbau-Gesellschaft [Brüxer Mining Company] and its affiliated business units, the largest enterprise in the field, produced 15 per cent of the entire Austrian brown coal output. The other major producers of brown coal were the Nördböhmische Kohlenwerks-Gesellschaft in Brüx [North Bohemian Mining Company in Brüx] with 8 per cent and the Trifailer Kohlenwerks-Gesellschaft [Trifailer Coal Mining Company] with 5 per cent, together with some other firms such as the Austrian Alpine Montan Company. The most important plant producing hard coal was the Kladno factory, part of the Prague Iron Industry Company. It was responsible for 10.5 per cent of the total production of hard coal in 1911. The next largest producers accounted for between 3.5 and 5 per cent of coal production.

The extremely slight concentration movement in the Austrian sugar industry has been mentioned already. In 1914 each company accounted for an average of only 0.56 per cent of production in Cisleithania, as opposed to 0.48 per cent in 1876. No clear process of relative concentration lay behind this slight change but there was generally a marked growth in the size of establishments. In 1911 40 per cent of Austrian production came from the 10 most important establishments.

There are many obstacles in the way of establishing the changing business structure of industrial enterprises. The accessible sources are few. Although there is quite a considerable amount of statistical material for the period since 1867 in official and semi-official investigations and questionnaires, the resulting material is not very satisfactory and the data are of little use for comparison. Accordingly the official statistics on which the values for concentration here are based do not reflect accurately developments at the level of either the individual business unit or the large enterprise. These not very satisfactory results arise from the way in which the investigations were conducted; e.g. in the field of mining the survey was based on the regional mining offices with the result that the same enterprise, depending on the number of coal and steel districts in which its constituent firms were situated, was recorded several different times on the lists resulting from the survey. It

Table 3.3. THE STRUCTURE OF BUSINESSES AND ENTERPRISES OF INDUSTRIAL JOINT STOCK COMPANIES (transformation procedure).

Process regulator	1880	1901–2	1913
Concentration as far as business is concerned	Heterogenous structure of business, predominance of medium-sized business	⇒	Increasing concentration, predominance of big business
Concentration as far as enterprise is concerned	Distinctly marked concentration process, predominance of big enterprise	⇒	Receding of the concentration process, predominance of big enterprise
Strategy of enterprise	Starting position: high functional integration (= vertical concentration), development in the direction of horizontal concentration	⇒	Renewed vertical, but also diagonal concentration
	Starting position: product differentiation on a higher scale, development in the direction of a unification of products	⇒	Renewed differentiation of products
Cartels	Assimilation of the heterogeneous business structure and protection of medium-sized enterprises	⇒	Substitutional function for a slower concentration process
Neutral funds of enterprises	Priority financial function	⇒	No financial function
Depreciation allowances	Loss anticipation	⇒	Basis of important part of finance
Investment motives	Rationalization	⇒	Capacity extension and substitutional supply

is to be expected, therefore, that the figures for enterprise concentration are somewhat lower than they should be. Fortunately, however, such deviations are not serious.

As a correct basis of reference for the period being discussed there is only the industrial business census of 1902, the results of which will be used for the subsequent discussion. Furthermore, an attempt will be made to place concentration problems within the context of the most important financial events. The analysis will be concerned with Austrian industrial joint stock companies in order to maintain an approximately equally broad and similarly structured data base. The conclusions drawn in connection with financial aspects are the result of a business and balance analysis of 70 enterprises covering the following industries: raw materials, investment goods, consumer goods, and food (table 3.3; figs. 3.1–3.6).

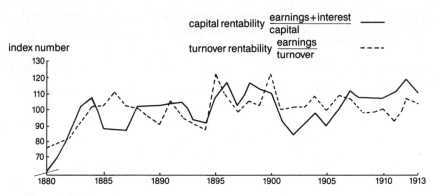

Figure 3.1. Enterprise success.

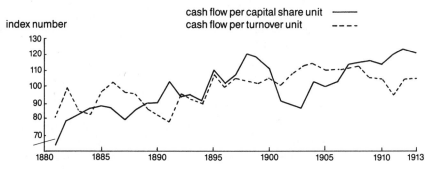

Figure 3.2. Financial power.

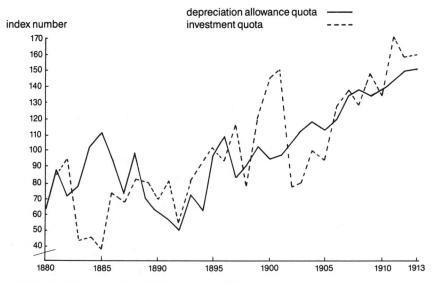

Figure 3.3. Depreciation of allowances and investments.

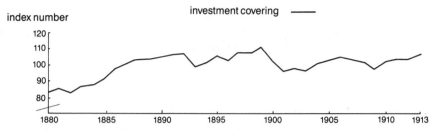

Figure 3.4. Financial relations.

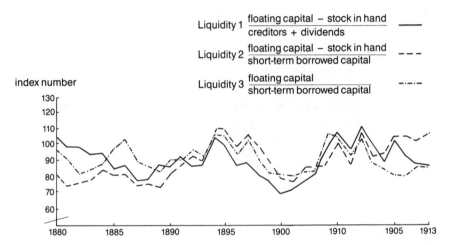

Figure 3.5. Readiness of payment.

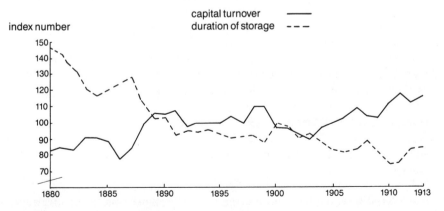

Figure 3.6. Turnover frequency.

First, what part did joint stock companies play in the course of the development of the enterprise as well as the business structure?

In 1902 the proportion of joint stock companies relative to the total number of firms, the number of employees and output differed quite considerably between the various branches of production. In the electricity industry, joint stock companies accounted for 21 per cent of businesses, 48 per cent of the labour force, and 43 per cent of output. Joint stock companies were also well represented in some branches of the raw material industry, in machinery and metals, and paper. It is noteworthy, as far as the last three industries are concerned, that in each one only a small number of businesses were joint stock companies but that these were responsible for a high proportion of both the labour force and output. The situation was similar in the chemical industry. The comparison of the data makes it apparent that in these branches of industrial production the joint stock company, as a form of enterprise, was not yet widespread in terms of numbers, but that with its organizational techniques and volume of production, it had nevertheless reached a leading position.

Further insights can be gained by analysing the size structure of businesses. If the average size (based on the number of employees) of businesses owned by joint stock companies is charted, using a scale which is valid for the whole branch of production (see table 3.4), then a picture emerges which is typical for the period but surprising. In all sectors except the textile industry, these businesses fall into the medium size range. The median number of employees for joint stock company-owned businesses in the chemical industry is 73, although 42 per cent of all employees of businesses having 100 workers (average 255) are included in the data. In the electro-technical industry the median is 173 which is still within the range of a medium-sized business. Even in the machinery and paper industries the figures are far from the average for large businesses.

The following has to be added to the picture already drawn. In table 3.4 the number of employees has been distributed according to the average size of the business. A completely different view arises, however, if the whole enterprise, not the business, is chosen as the point of reference (table 3.5). The census data for 1902 reveal that the 360 firms in the machinery and metal manufacturing industries belonged to only 80 enterprises. Each business employed on average 204 workers and employees, but the total for each enterprise amounted to over 1,042. The ratio between the average value per enterprise and per business are 918 as against 155 for the paper industry and 733 as opposed to 249 in textiles. This situation will be considered again in connection with the investment strategies which were developed by the enterprises.

Financial analysis shows that the boom periods of 1888–91, 1896–1900, and 1906–13, which have been given various designations in the literature, are also significant from the point of view of the microeconomy of the enterprise. There is one deviation, however – 1896 did not mark a turning point but was rather simply part of the widening of industrial development. But the 1880s were the foundation decade of the period of Austrian large-scale industrial development which continued until 1913.

From varying perspectives, an important development turning-point can be distinguished around 1901 and 1902. These years show distinct signs of marking a break in trend and divide the overall period into two. The two sub-periods are characterized both by differences in the underlying trend and contrary trend processes. Further, 1901 and 1902 stand out as a significant turning-point with respect to long-term changes in business and establishment structures through the development of new schemes of organization and management techniques, as well as with regard to the concentration processes taking place in the secondary sector. To illustrate these structural changes and the shifts which took place in the effect of individual factors, it is necessary to make a few brief points about the crisis of 1901–2 which arise from this analysis.

A weak market and falling prices had already reduced revenue and gains in 1900 and led in the following two years to an average reduction of profits of 25 per cent. Similarly great losses in financial capacity occurred. The ability to pay was for many firms most uncertain in 1901. The low degree of liquidity proved to be primarily a consequence of the capital expenditures of the preceding years. Falls in turnover and revenue aggravated the already tense situation. The crisis struck industry at a critical moment – at the height of investment activity. Hoping for a quick resumption of boom conditions, most companies clung to their capital expenditure programmes in 1901. But industry was forced by the continuing depression to cancel many current financial plans in 1902, when 50 per cent less was spent on investment. Mechanization in factories fell back by 15 per cent, capital turnover slowed by 20 per cent and the period for holding raw materials and finished goods rose by the same amount.

The degree and nature of this crisis have to be kept in mind throughout the following discussion which deals with the course of development trends over the entire period, as well as with its details.

Without doubt when a comparison is made of business indicators between 1880 and 1913 an impressive picture of progress emerges. Measured by the supply of capital, the profitability of enterprises rose by more than 50 per cent, while the average period for holding stocks seems to have been reduced by nearly a half. The floating speed of capital rose by 40 per cent. The financial vigour and viability of industrial companies can be estimated to be 60 per cent higher in 1914 than in the early 1880s. These indices and briefly outlined trends illustrate the result of a profound change which took place in the area of business and enterprise.

It has been indicated earlier that the periods 1888–91, 1896–1900, and 1906–13 have been considered generally in the literature to be phases of boom

Table 3.4. THE POSITION OF JOINT STOCK COMPANIES IN AUSTRIAN INDUSTRY: Comparison of the extent of businesses based on the number of employees in 1902.

Metal industry

Businesses with nos. of employees from	No. of businesses*	Employees	Employees per business
1–5	46,485	93,540	2
6–20	3,423	31,351	9
21–100	796	35,216	44
More than 100	282	85,136	302
Total businesses	50,986	245,243	5
No. belonging to joint stock companies	210	35,740	170

Machine industry

Business with nos. of employees from	No. of businesses*	Employees	Employees per business
1–5	22,382	38,878	2
6–20	1,278	12,431	10
21–100	605	27,071	45
More than 100	220	83,408	379
Total businesses	24,485	161,788	7
No. belonging to joint stock companies	150	39,818	265

Chemical industry[†]

Businesses with nos. of employees from	No. of businesses*	Employees	Employees per business
1–5	5,543	10,559	2
6–20	724	7,190	10
21–100	323	14,609	45
More than 100	91	23,197	255
Total businesses	6,681	55,555	8
No. belonging to joint stock companies	145	10,656	73

Petrol industry

Businesses with nos. of employees from	No. of businesses*	Employees	Employees per business
1–5	34	101	3
6–20	49	496	10
21–100	27	1,452	54
More than 100	12	2,836	236
Total businesses	122	4,885	40
No. belonging to joint stock companies	13	1,698	131

Electrical engineering

Businesses with nos. of employees from	No. of businesses*	Employees	Employees per business
1–5	205	535	3
6–20	91	921	10
21–100	48	1,976	41
More than 100	20	7,969	398
Total businesses	364	11,401	31
No. belonging to joint stock companies	38	6,559	173

Paper industry

Businesses with nos. of employees from	No. of businesses*	Employees	Employees per business
1–5	2,654	6,016	2
6–20	691	7,389	11
21–100	333	14,192	43
More than 100	111	26,285	237
Total businesses	3,789	53,882	14
No. belonging to joint stock companies	62	9,629	155

* Exclusive of those not working.
† Including gasworks, and the dye, rubber, petrol and soap industries.

Sources: *Österreichische Statistik*, 75 (Vienna, 1905), Heft 1; F. Somary, *Die Aktiengesellschaften in Österreich* (Vienna, 1902), 45–56; *Compass* (1914), chapter on 'Industriestatistik'.

Table 3.5. BUSINESS AND ENTERPRISE STRUCTURE of the industrial joint stock companies in Austria, 1902

Types	No. of businesses*	No. of enterprises*	No. of employees in business	No. of employees in enterprises	No. of employees per business (average)	No. of employees per enterprise (average)
Original production	216	38	72,745	62,165	337	1,636
Blast-furnace plants	12	2	1,778	3,769	148	1,885
Industrial stones, glass	211	39	23,744	22,008	113	564
Metalworking industry	210	31	35,740	46,015	170	1,484
Machine industry	150	49	39,818	37,378	265	763
Wood, wicker-work	127	12	7,639	4,578	60	382
Rubber industry	8	7	3,213	3,434	402	491
Leather industry	10	5	680	697	68	139
Textile industry	104	38	25,893	27,841	249	733
Wallpaper trade	1	—	45	—	45	—
Clothing industry	5	2	895	515	179	258
Paper industry	62	12	9,629	11,021	155	918
Foodprocessing industry	284	172	19,214	284	172	19,214
Restaurant and retail trade	186	12	1,712	1,041	9	87
Chemical industry	145	50	10,656	9,676	73	194
Building trade	74	15	6,885	7,054	93	470
Graphic arts trade	27	6	2,773	754	103	126
Lighting and power plants	67	18	2,023	1,800	30	100
Industry	1,899	508	265,082	259,727	140	511

* Exclusive of those not working.

Source: *Besteuerung und Entwicklung der Industrie-Aktiengesellschaften in Österreich* (Vienna, 1904), table 81/I a.III.

Note: The number of employees differs between businesses and enterprises because the individual businesses were sometimes assigned to multiple trade categories and their employees were hence counted more than once.

and that from the point of view of the present investigation they must also be seen as periods of growth in business. These years mark exactly the periods of considerable capital investment. This shows, once again, that capital investment on the part of enterprises is a true reflection of the prevailing situation in the business cycle. The liquidity figures correspond with this: companies quickly paid their debts at the beginning of each of the three capital investment periods. Although the payment capability of companies appears to have been solid in the first period, it seems to have been doubtful around the turn of the century at the end of the second period. Difficulties in meeting payments during the third period beginning in 1906 then eased and were not comparable with the alarming experience of 1900–1.

These changes can be explained mainly by the changing function of the depreciation allowance. Until the turn of the century, companies only allowed an extremely low rate of depreciation which did not guarantee the maintenance of capital, even with complete re-investment. Although these procedures were in accord with the companies' statutes, the majority of enterprises changed their policies in the depression of 1901 and 1902. Setting aside considerations of dividend policy, higher depreciation allowances were made and internal financing capacity was thereby strengthened. This new policy continued during the following phase of prosperity so that the financing function of the depreciation allowance became more and more prominent. In this way, during the years preceding the First World War and despite considerable capital expenditure, the liquidity of companies suffered less than in 1900. The crisis had brought about this change of course. It made it obvious that past depreciation allowance policies were no longer appropriate, considering the rate of technical development, because they fostered an over-long utilization of production equipment which in turn led to an over-estimation of a company's assets.

But how can one explain why the capital investment period 1888–91 actually led to an improvement in the liquidity situation, given that depreciation allowances during this period were an insignificant factor in financing? This situation had its origins in the process of the regrouping of funds which appears to have been completed, by and large, at the turn of the century. The Austrian industrial joint stock company was still marked in the 1880s by a most heterogeneous establishment structure. Many enterprises were, when they were founded, important conglomerations which had to be structured and amalgamated to form single units under newly formulated planning goals. It was typical of the prevailing situation at the beginning of the development of big industry that many medium-sized and larger establishments possessed considerable funds arising from non-industrial sources which had been acquired gradually in the step-by-step expansion of the firm. They were the result of resource accumulation and, for example, many industrial firms had extensive agricultural estates among their basic possessions, an occurrence which enables their origins to be traced.

The fusion of such firms into a new enterprise brought about an accumulation of reserve funds. As a rule rationalization measures and the centralization of production usually introduced soon after the founding of a large enterprise released certain assets of a neutral disposition. The sales proceeds from these often covered the current cost of investment for many years. This regrouping process resulted in the balance of the effective capital gain or loss on the balance sheet. Therefore the actual extent of the re-investment of such neutral capital funds cannot be estimated by an analysis of the balance sheet. That it took place can be established from other sources and explains why capital expenditures from 1888 to 1891 led to no narrowing of the payment margin.

During the second, far more extensive, investment period between 1896 and 1901 the possibilities of using reserve funds to finance capital projects seem to have been exhausted. In the decade-long boom before the First World War neutral capital funds played no role in the finance of capital projects by companies. This also means that the rates of investment, as calculated to 1900, were in part considerably under the extent of actual asset-purchasing.

This corresponds to the change of prevailing investment motives: rationalization measures were stressed until the turn of the century but the extension of capacity and substitutional funds formed the primary aims after 1900.

Such a view fits the picture of changes in the business and entrepreneurial structure of industrial companies. Until 1900 the company-managed firms in almost all branches of industry were medium-sized. However, when an enterprise not an individual firm is taken as the point of reference a different picture emerges, as has already been mentioned. The industrial joint stock company in fact represents a trust; it may be called elitist. On the one hand the industrial company was distinguished until 1900 by a low concentration of firms (predominance of small production units); on the other hand it represented the outcome of an important tendency to merge in the field of enterprise (high business concentration). From the financial viewpoint the industrial company was a trust, but as far as production techniques were concerned it still had, by and large, the traditional business structure in consisting of a multitude of units. The ultimate development phase of large industry before the First World War reduced the elitist character of joint stock companies in respect of both the form and size of enterprise but accelerated quite considerably the concentration of businesses.

Parallel to this another process was taking place. During the initial phase of the period being discussed – the 1870s – the predominant tendency was for vertical concentration, i.e. uniting several production stages into one enterprise, including obtaining raw materials (= high functional integration). At the same time a wide range of products was offered on the market. Then with the business upswing of the 1880s many companies changed to a policy of uniting firms at the same stage of production (= horizontal concentration). A unification of stock went hand in hand with this. International competition in various markets, especially strong in the crisis years 1901 and 1902, led to a new management attitude in the immediate pre-war period. Entrepreneurs tried harder to cover themselves in different, independent markets by vertical and diagonal concentration. As a result product differentiation rose again. Therefore functional integration and a high degree of product differentiation are not only indicators of technical-economic progress. They can also be features of a relatively backward situation and appear in precisely those countries which have a traditionally highly developed industrial production. These goals are only renounced with progressive development and then they determine, again in the late phase, the position of the entrepreneur.

Against this background of structural changes in the fields of business and enterprise, the significance of the cartel organization for Austria becomes evident. The heterogeneous varieties of business and production structures stood in the way of a large-scale merger movement. Consequently the tendency to merge and the possibility of forming large enterprises at all was limited. The Austrian cartel, in such a situation, took on an important substitute function. It exerted a unifying influence on the various business forms, production programmes, and interests. This process was at least responsible for the degree of large-scale industrial development reached by the time of the First World War.

Concentration and the finance of industry are related in manifold and complex ways. The outlines of developments presented here need consequently to be further discussed and supplemented.

4. Disintegration and Multi-national Enterprises in Central Europe during the Post-war Years (1918–23)

Herbert Matis

Interest in questions of economic and political integration of regions with varying socio-economic levels and different ethnic-historical development, understandable as a consequence of the creation of the Common Market, has drawn attention to the specific historical example of the multi-national Habsburg Monarchy. So Krisztine Maria Fink[1] stresses the parallel between the 'melting pot' of the ancient Empire with its population of 53m and the E.E.C., and as early as 1952 the Rockefeller Foundation intended to carry out an international research project aiming at a closer examination of the problems concerning the functioning of supranational state organizations, 'whereby the experience of the history of the Danubian Monarchy as to creation and dissolution, achievements and failure of the multinational Hapsburg Empire . . . should be rendered accessible and serviceable. The Monarchy's history should serve as a model case, both in its positive and negative aspects.'[2] The dissolution of this multi-national state body can serve as an example for the consequences of political and economic disintegration – for the disruption of maintenance of economic links under different political conditions. The fall of the Empire was – and is still – judged differently by the various nationalities which formerly were embodied in it. Some had to face painful losses of influence and territories, others gained their long-desired national sovereignty and political self-determination. In the economic sphere, the creation of the successor states meant the disruption of a centuries-old inter-regional division of labour and the splitting-up of a large, fairly autarkic domestic market.

The new borders delimited in the post-war peace treaties neither took into account the above-mentioned division of labour between regions nor that which existed between the various branches and sectors of the economy. The customs policies of the newly emerged states and their subsequent efforts to achieve economic self-sufficiency further intensified the effects of disintegration, brought about by the area's new frontiers. The vast inland market of the Austro-Hungarian Monarchy, previously autarkic, was divided into a number of small national markets, where, in order to secure autonomous development, it was necessary to use tariff protection and trade restrictions of the severest kind.[3] But one particular feature of the new frontiers, which were primarily political and in disregard of the basic economic conditions in the area, partly made up for the disadvantages of disintegration – many companies, which had been purely national (in the sense of the Monarchy as a whole) until 1918, were now forced to turn into 'multi-nationals', if they wished to retain their markets, now belonging to the successor states.

In the course of this short study three main topics will be considered:

1. Functional effects of disintegration beginning after 1918, as seen from the Austrian point of view. Here, the purely negative picture of the consequences of the Empire's dissolution for the new Austrian Republic, drawn in the contemporary and subsequent literature, will be disputed.
2. The question whether Austrian financial capital after 1918 lost or conserved its previous influence in the successor states.
3. Whether foreign capital could gain considerable influence in East Central Europe in the immediate post-war period.

The First World War drastically changed the map of Central Europe. The fall of the ancient Habsburg Empire did create an entirely new situation not only in geopolitical respects, changing basically the strategic and political balance of power in Europe, but also economically. Economic disintegration in Central Europe in the immediate post-war period, i.e. in 1918–23, has been viewed up to now by historians and economists mainly in terms of which successor state grabbed the largest part of the 'Austro-Hungarian cake'. Consequently the two leading 'historic' nationalities, the Germans and Magyars, thought themselves to have suffered the greatest loss, in territorial terms as well as in their until then unchallenged economic supremacy. It was mainly in the part of the Habsburg Monarchy which now formed the Republic of Austria, after the loss of German-Bohemia and the Sudetenland, that there was a widespread feeling of having been deprived of the most valuable resources and parts of the economic potential of the former 'im Reichsrat vertretene Königreiche und Länder'.[4] A rational and realistic judgment of German-Austria's economic situation was prevented by the country's political leadership – bearing in mind its tactical position in the St Germain peace negotiations – making the theory that Austria was unable to exist in her present form an official doctrine. This, in turn, contributed to the perpetuation of a negative socio-physological effect. As Karl Bachinger has said, 'Public opinion, being in a state of neurosis, sometimes gave the impression of a "malade imaginaire" who, deeply convinced of his suffering, reacts offendedly or even aggressively to statements to the contrary.'[5] This basic attitude of a large part of the Austrian population was characterized by Walré de Bordes as follows:

> The Allied Powers had compelled them, for the present, to dwell in this little state; but it was plainly impossible that this artificial creation should continue to exist – the official propaganda had supplied plenty of

arguments in this sense. For the time being they had to conform to the will of the Entente, but in one way or another salvation would finally come. The sooner it was recognized that the state was unable to exist, the quicker the hour of deliverance would arrive . . .[6]

In judging their own economic situation, German Austrians, under the impression of the lost war and the break-up of the Dual Monarchy that seemed to bring an end to their political and economic viability, erred in an understandable way: they overlooked the fact that none of the newly created or enlarged national states of the Danubian region would be able to afford the luxury of pursuing a policy of complete autarky. Furthermore, they thought that the no doubt painful economic isolation of their country, created by the Allied Powers and even more by the latter's Central European associates, would endure for a long time to come.

In such a situation, the Alpine Republic would have been absolutely, as well as in comparison with the other successor states, in a desperate position, 'for industry was not based upon great natural resources and rich agriculture, but mainly upon trained labour and free intercourse with the country's natural markets.'[7] But it was exactly this free intercourse that re-established itself within a few years, partly as a consequence of the western industrialized nations' (and Czechoslovakia's) over-production crisis of 1920–21, partly with the general worsening of the successor states' own currency situations. So many of the structural problems that an isolated national economy would have had to struggle with became potential assets which, properly exploited, could secure for Austria a considerable advantage over even the other most developed country of the area, the Czechoslovak Republic.

An inquiry into the division of the national product among the successor states was published in Austria only in 1929, more than a decade after the Empire's division and six years after the appearance of a similar study for Hungary. Starting from Friedrich Fellner's[8] work published during the war, and taking into consideration the adjustments later made by Alfred Gürtler, Ernst Waizner estimated the average yearly national income in Cisleithania for the period of 1911–13 at 15,300m crowns. Thereof 4,400m or 29.7 per cent was accounted for by the Republic of Austria, while her share of Cisleithania's total population was 22 per cent. The figures for Czechoslovakia were 6,700m crowns (44 per cent) and 34 per cent of the population, and for the territories ceded to Poland, Italy, Yugoslavia and Romania 4,100m crowns (25.6 per cent) against their share of 44 per cent of 'historic' Austria's population.[9] A new evaluation by the Austrian Institute for Economic Research shows a division of the national income slightly different, and even more favourable as regards the position of Austria. The new study – contrary to those of Waizner and Hertz – emphasizes the income gradient inside Cisleithania with the Alpine countries possessing a higher average wage level than the other areas.[10]

Table 4.1. AUSTRIAN, CZECHOSLOVAK AND HUNGARIAN
SHARES OF THE HABSBURG MONARCHY'S NATIONAL
INCOME.

	Austro-Hungarian Empire	Austria	Czecho-slovakia	Hungary
Population (1910)				
(000)	40,137	6,646	13,636	7,605
%	100	13.5	27.6	15.4
Net proceeds of production				
(000 crowns)	19,522,520	3,594,446	7,022,366	2,961,802
%	100	18.4	35.9	15.1
per capita in crowns	396	541	515	389
Produced national income				
(000 crowns)	23,392,720	4,610,379	8,080,794	3,422,437
%	100	19.7	34.5	14.6
per capita in crowns	176	694	593	450
Available national income				
(000 crowns)	23,289,504	4,607,527	8,096,051	3,120,829
%	100	19.8	34.8	13.4
per capita in crowns	474	693	594	410

Sources: F. Fellner, *Die Verteilung des Volksvermögens und Volkseinkommens der Länder der Ungarischen Heiligen Krone*, 77f; E. Waizner, *Das Volkseinkommen Alt-Österreichs und seine Verteilung auf die Nachfolgestaaten*, 82f; *Wirtschaft und Statistik*, I (1921), 199; *Das Handbuch für die Republik Österreich*, VIII (1926), 1f.

That the new Republic of Austria – contrary to traditional and widespread opinion – had taken over highly developed parts of the ancient economic territory, is proved clearly by the data on *per capita* income: this was, according to Waizner as well as the Institute of Economic Research, not only higher in Austria than in Cisleithania as a whole, but also than in the Czech Crown Lands.[11] Moreover, one has to assume that relations shifted further in favour of Austria during the war, as the region immediately around Vienna benefited most from the wartime measures of centralization and state investment activities. Austria's disintegrational advantages become even more apparent when her statistical data are compared to those of the Monarchy as a whole and not just those of economically advanced Cisleithania.

Austria's share of the overall population was 13.5 per cent but nearly one-fifth of the national income was generated within the Austrian Republic. This gives a *per capita* income of 694 crowns (against Austria-Hungary 476 crowns, Czechoslovakia 593, and Hungary 450 crowns). Although the incorporation of the Burgenland (former West Hungary) did not gravely affect the Austrian *per capita* quota, the integration of underdeveloped former

Table 4.2. NATIONAL INCOME IN CISLEITHANIA 1911–13.

	Percentage of region	Crowns per capita	Percentage of region	Crowns per capita
	A		B	
Alpine countries	29.7	695	33.9	790
Bohemia, Moravia, Silesia	44.7	660	42.8	630
Galicia	15.1	274	13.7	250
Southern Tyrol, Trieste, Istria	5.2	485	4.8	450
Slovenia, Dalmatia	3.6	326	3.3	300
Bukowina	1.7	327	1.6	300
Totals	100	520	100	520

A Figures of E. Waizner, *Das Volkseinkommen Alt-Österreichs und seine Verteilung auf die Nachfolgestaaten.*
B Figures of the Institute of Economic Research.

Hungarian territories constituted a heavy burden for Czechoslovakia's national economy.

The phenomenon of economic disintegration can also be seen from another point of view. If it is true, as has been so often stated, that the regionally imbalanced structure of the Habsburg Empire (it remained an agrarian state until the very end, due to its vast underdeveloped territories) constituted a major obstacle for economic growth, then consequently the loss of such backward areas as the eastern agrarian provinces must be defined as an advantage. The much higher national income in Austria as compared with all other successor states stresses the point that disintegration was in fact a 'leap forward' for the Alpine Republic. The same conclusion can be made when examining the sectoral division of national income and labour force.[12]

Julius Deutsch, too, in connection with the 1921 census, pointed out the positive aspects of the changes in Austrian structure of production. From the

Table 4.3. SECTORAL DIVISION OF NATIONAL INCOME AND LABOUR FORCE: Austria and Cisleithania.

	Percentage of the overall national income		Percentage of the overall labour force	
	Cisleithania	Austria	Cisleithania	Austria
Agriculture, forestry, mining	30.4	20.5	59.8	41.0
Industry	36.1	37.8	25.4	35.6
Trade, transportation, services	33.5	41.7	14.8	23.4

Source: E. Waizner. *Des Volkseinkommen Alt-Österreichs und seine Verteilung auf die Nachfolgestaaten,* 84; *Wirtschaft und Statistik,* I (1921), 47.

latter he expected – according to his ideological background – a rapid transition to socialist society. ('We are moving towards the workers' state!'[13]) In Europe, only the highly industrialized countries of Great Britain and Belgium had a larger number of employees in the trade and services sectors than Austria, which was approximately on the same level as Germany, France or Switzerland. However, as a consequence of the widespread opinion that 'small country' meant at the same time 'inability to exist', Deutsch's view was dismissed almost unanimously as sophisticated, statistical casuistry.

This question has been explored in depth because even today it is the dominant opinion that the Austrian Republic which emerged from St Germain could, as a consequence of post-war economic disintegration, certainly not have survived all on her own. But there is sufficient statistical evidence that the actual endowment of Austria, with economic resources inherited from the Habsburg Monarchy, did not justify this pessimistic view, fostered by post-war Austrian leaders' 'tactical thinking'. With the only really serious weakness of Austria's post-war economic structure, i.e. fuel shortage,[14] having been surmounted at a very early date, the Alpine Republic's industrial upswing quite easily kept pace with development in Czechoslovakia, widely considered the then leading economic power in the area. For both countries, the index of industrial production shows an increase of 146 per cent over the period 1920–29.[15] Taking into account Vienna's still dominant position in the field of East Central European commerce, traffic and banking, comparison should produce a result even more favourable to Austria. Another proof of the Alpine Republic's viability (given the possibilities of using her economic potential) is furnished by her encouraging development after 1945 which, although so much different from that immediately following the First World War, was still based upon exactly the same resources.

Examining disintegration as a whole, one cannot look at the dismemberment of a naturally-grown economic organism in a merely quantitative way. The further development of specific interdependences is of great importance too. Here the question of disintegration's functional aspects arises: have the traditional economic and financial links been maintained or disrupted?

The economic structure of the Habsburg Empire was characterized by regional division of labour, varying in extent from branch to branch but generally strongly developed.[16] In heavy industry, connections existed between Styrian iron ore and Bohemian coal mines. Regional division within the same branch of industry existed in iron production: while pig iron was made in the Alpine Countries, cast iron production dominated in Bohemia. A similar situation had developed in the chemical sector, where primary production, being overwhelmingly oriented towards the domestic market, was concentrated in the Northern Provinces, while the finishing was done in Austria.[17]

The most radical changes brought about by disintegration were in the textile industry. Although Austria had a considerable percentage of Cisleithania's cotton-spinning mills (25 per cent), located in Vorarlberg and the Vienna Basin, her weaving capacity was insignificant (9 per cent), in contrast to Bohemia and Moravia. On the other hand Austria possessed a great variety of textile processing and printing industries, based upon the Northern Provinces' raw manufacture, the main outlet for which was the important Vienna market. Just as in the case of heavy industry, the exchange of textile manufactures was hampered by the new borders; the wool and cotton industries both suffered from similar problems. Both distortions in production and structural imbalances were the consequences for the new national economies.[18]

Table 4.4. REGIONAL STRUCTURE OF THE TEXTILE INDUSTRY (at 30 June 1914).

Successor state	No. of cotton spindles	No. of cotton looms	No. of wool spindles	No. of woollen looms
Austria	1,171,000	11,000	181,000	1,280
Czechoslovakia	3,583,000	136,000	1,950,000	37,000
Hungary	31,000	5,000	15,000	500
Yugoslavia	100,000	3,000	15,000	300
Poland	1,600,000	32,000	700,000	29,000

Source: H. Bayer, *Strukturwandlungen der Österreichischen Volkswirtschaft nach dem Kriege* (Vienna, 1929) 97f.

But this can be considered a grave setback only from a neo-mercantilistic point of view. Once the immediate post-war chaos was surmounted, the exchange of goods quickly re-established itself. Austrian industry continued to obtain its coal from the north, particularly because Czechoslovakia and Poland could not sell all their production on the domestic market and therefore became strongly interested in coal exports. On the other hand, Styrian iron ore remained an important raw material for Czechoslovak heavy industry.[19]

Not only was the exchange of raw materials scarcely affected by the new political constellation in the long term but also in other fields of industrial activity traditional links were maintained by efficient measures of reorganization. A strategy widely used to outflank the successors states' nostrification laws consisted of founding holding companies, mostly based in an Entente or neutral country. Consequently a series of multi-national corporations came into being, which easily kept considerable influence in East Central Europe, being no longer Austrian, i.e. Vienna-based, but Swiss, British, French, etc., instead. An example of such a holding in the textile industry is the Färbereien und Druckereien Trust AG, established in Chur in 1921, which controlled all the successor-state branches of the former Vereinigte Färbereien AG

Vienna. Another holding company of this kind was the Tarbouches Trust AG of Zurich, which held the whole capital stock of both the Aktiengesellschaft der österreichischen Fezfabriken and the Elsö magyar nemez-posztó és fezgyár részvénytársaság [First Hungarian Felt-Cloth and Fez Factories, Köszeg].[20]

The largest Austrian industrial firm, the Österreichisch-Alpine Montangesellschaft [Austrian Alpine Montan Company], strongly linked with the Bohemian mining industry and connected especially with the Pražská železářská společnost [Prague Iron Industry Company] before the war, at first tried to preserve its influence by founding affiliated companies in the successor states. In 1923 the Austrian Alpine Montan Company set up the Ferro AG in Budapest and the Montansyndikat in Zagreb as footholds in Eastern Europe. In the same year, when the Austrian Alpine Montan Company was already under the influence of German capital, it participated in the Polish-Silesian Bismarckhütte and the Kattowitzer AG für Bergbau und Eisenhüttenbetrieb in Katowice, in order to secure its coke supplies. (In this transaction the Niederösterreichische Escompte-Gesellschaft acted as intermediary.) As early as 1921, however, the majority of the Austrian Alpine Montan Company had been transferred to a Swiss holding company, Promontana AG, Zug.[21]

The Böhler factories also founded a Zurich-based holding company, combining a series of independent, national affiliate companies: Gebrüder Böhler AG (Berlin, Düsseldorf and Vienna); Bratří Böhlerové a spol, akc. spol. (Prague, Moravská Ostrava); Böhler Testvérek és Társa (Budapest) Otelul Boehler Societate Anonimâ Romanâ (Bucharest) Bohler Keitei Goshi Kaisha (Tokyo); Bohler Bros & Co. Ltd (Shanghai); Gualterio Denk (Buenos Aires); and finally St Egydyer Eisen- und Stahl-Industrie-Gesellschaft (Vienna).[22] Holding companies were also established in the timber industry. Furniture manufacturers united under the name of Mundus Allgemeine Handels- und Industrie-Aktien Gesellschaft (a Zurich firm), and so were able to continue running their successor-state companies under a centralized administration. Another form of co-operation was found in the mineral oil industry in order to secure the Austrian refineries' raw material base after the loss of the Galician oilfields. Early in the 1920s, the Erdöl-Industrie Bank AG was set up in Vienna with the help of the Österreichische Credit-Anstalt für Handel und Gewerbe [Credit-Anstalt]. This new bank was meant to organize the imports of Polish crude oil and oil products as well as the equipment of Polish and Romanian drilling sites with Austrian machinery.[23]

In contrast, some other functional interdependences were minimized. Austria sought to overcome her chemical industry's shortages of unprocessed materials by expanding domestic production. In this way the loss of primary industries was to be compensated. In the textile sector efforts were made to alleviate the burden of structure imbalance by both investing in weaving and reducing the number of spindles.

More serious economic difficulties arose mainly in those branches of industry which until now 'had devoted themselves calmly to the untroubled domestic market protected by high customs tariffs, and – unchallenged by foreign competitors – never had been compelled to keep up with technical progress.' However, those branches that had already before the war reached a high standard of performance and, partly, a considerable degree of concentration, in general easily maintained their market position and even secured themselves new export outlets.[24]

In Austria-Hungary more than 200 cartels existed before the war and cartelization continued after 1918 across the national frontiers. Austrian and Czechoslovak firms were combined in nine bilateral cartels in 1926, not to speak of multilateral cartels in which several successor states participated. The Alpine Montan Company, mentioned above, in 1924 drew up a cartel with Czechoslovak steel producers, aiming at the division of the Central European market for pig iron, unprocessed goods, rails, iron sleepers, and plate among its members. The Alpine Montan Company's domestic market share was fixed at 82 per cent for bar iron and 50 per cent for cast iron; its share outside Austria was 35 per cent in total.[25] Other expanding sectors with a high pre-war level of concentration were the electric and rubber industries, which occupied a strong market position in East and Central Europe. Interlocking arrangements of production were maintained in the paper industry too; here the Austrian-based trusts controlled most of the manufacturing in the successor states.

The regional distribution of production and of markets which developed during the Habsburg Empire's industrialization did not, it can be concluded, undergo such drastic changes after 1918 as have often been described by historians and economists, both at the time and subsequently. The repeatedly cited standard view of the Monarchy's dissolution and the successor states' tariff policy having deprived Austrian industry of its natural outlets and forced it into a permanent state of recession for all the inter-war period must be regarded as being incorrect in these general terms, though historical research seems to take this opinion as fact.[26]

A trade balance covering the flow of goods between the lands of the Habsburg Crown has of course never been drawn up. However, the extent of their economic relations after the break-up of 1918 justifies the conclusion that there were no serious restrictions. Had the impact of both protectionism and efforts towards self-sufficiency by the successor states really been as great as was complained of in Austria, then exports of the latter to Czechoslovakia ought to have diminished during the 1920s. But, on the contrary, total Austrian exports to this neighbouring country rose between 1923 and 1929 from 167.4m to 294.6m sch. (current prices), i.e. by approximately 76 per cent. As a percentage of Austrian overall exports, Czechoslovakia's share increased from 10.2 to 12.0 per cent.[27] From the standpoint of trade policy, the main difference between the Austrias of 1913 and after 1918 was that the latter no longer formed part of an economically autarkic, almost completely self-sufficient territory. The abrupt switch for Austrian industry from supplying a protected inland market to entering into the competition-ridden field of external trade constituted the main problem. It has been estimated that the Austrian Republic had to export 50 to 80 per cent of her overall industrial production, just to be able to make a living.[28]

Nevertheless, disintegration meant difficulties, but only in the field of technically and commercially backward branches. Here, strictly speaking, nothing more occurred than the emergence of latent structural problems, which until 1918 had been masked by the system of protective tariffs and which would have had to have been tackled anyway, even if the Empire had survived. However, disintegration did not mean disruption of the ancient functional interdependences for the advanced sectors of Austrian industry. These only came to an end because of the political changes in the course of and following the Second World War. But at that time no one paid much attention – in contrast to the situation after 1918, when debate was strongly emotional.

Another question arising in this context is if, as a consequence of the various successor states' nostrifications, there really took place a major distintegration of capital. To put it another way: did Vienna-based capital lose or conserve its position in Central Europe in the early post-war years? Did the nationalization laws in the successor states have real consequences or did they only (and perhaps deliberately) constitute *pro forma* acts, easily outmanoeuvred and therefore having no effect?

Quantitative evaluation of a sample of 50 Austrian enterprises (taken from the *Compass* volumes of 1920–25) will serve as a beginning to discover developments in the field of sub-companies and capital participations and how the new political and economic conditions were actually coped with. The sample contains only firms that existed before November 1918, which both had their head offices on the territory of the future Austrian Republic and capital participations in the successor states. It includes 10 banks, 10 mines, 6 companies in the machine-building and metal industries, 2 distilleries, 2 chemical and 3 mineral oil plants, 3 electrochemical plants, 3 enterprises in the timber industry and 3 in the paper and printing sector, 4 textile factories and 3 sugar refineries. When examining the results of this inquiry the restricted size of the sample has to be borne in mind which permits only conclusions as to the actual strategies chosen by the companies' financial managements in the respective branches. Overall, however, the range of 50 enterprises should provide enough evidence of any general trend.

In the mining industry head offices were in four cases (40 per cent of the sample) transferred to successor states (two to Czechoslovakia, one each to Poland and Hungary). Only two of these four companies moving out of Austria had production sites on the latter country's territory. In the case of the Železárny Rotava-Nýdek, akciová společnost [Rothau-Neudek Ironworks Company] the Austrian plant was incorporated into a newly founded Eisenwerke-Aktiengesellschaft Krieglach, which remained under control of the now Czechoslovak management.[29] The *Compass* does not give clear evidence to what extent Austrian influence prevailed when a firm moved out of the country. In the case of the Silesia Bergbau Aktiengesellschaft set up by the City of Vienna and the Allgemeine Depositenbank with the aim of securing the capital's coal supply, and which moved in 1922 to Poland, continuing Austrian predominance is almost certain. Regarding the Západočeský báňský akciový spolek transferred to Prague in 1920, it seems likely.[30]

Four out of the six firms which remained in the Austrian Republic had run factories or offices in the successor states before 1918. In two cases these had to be abandoned; the Bleiberger Bergwerks-Union sold its foreign agency to a British company (Central European Mines Ltd) and only in the other instance was there a real loss suffered from nationalization.[31] The two companies not interested in successor state business before the war took up capital participations in this area after 1919, as did two of the companies already established in the East Central European market. Altogether the influence of the Austrian mining companies within the sample in the successor states after 1918 can be rated at 60 per cent of its pre-war extent.

In the metal and machine industries only one out of six companies transferred its headquarters [První brněnská strojírenská společnost – First Brno Engineering Company], but as this firm was controlled by the Länderbank, Austrian capital influence continued.[32] The First Brno Engineering Company had run a plant in Austria, which was now transformed into an independent joint stock company. Three of the remaining five companies had possessed local branches in the successor states before the war. 1918 brought almost no changes for these, as they either took over the majority of shares of the 'nationalized' Hungarian and Czechoslovak successor firms or, as happened in one case, everything continued without any change.[33] New capital participations in East Central Europe were taken by the two companies which until then had not been interested in the area and by two of the already-established firms.[34] So Austrian metal industry was able to conserve its pre-war position to the full extent in all observed cases.

In the cases of the sample's two distilleries, the Jungbunzlauer transferred its head office to Czechoslovakia, while the other avoided the nostrification of a Polish branch by acquiring the majority of shares of a national holding company into which it had been incorporated.[35]

None of the mineral oil plants moved into a successor state, although all had local branches or affiliated companies in the area. 'Schodnica' Actien-Gesellschaft für Petroleum-Industrie and Fanto AG took over shares of the newly founded national companies and thereby preserved their former influence.

The electro-technical plants also remained in Austria. The only company which had facilities in the successor states before the war – Elin Aktiengesellschaft für elektrische Industrie – had to abandon them all. But after 1918 Elin, together with Felten & Guilleaume Fabrik elektrischer Kabel, Stahl- und Kupferwerke Aktiengesellschaft and AEG-Union Elektrizitäts-Gesellschaft all participated in successor state companies and so their influence in East Central Europe can be considered to have increased rather than diminished.[36]

In the timber industry, one company (Holzhandels AG) moved to Zurich and so succeeded in outflanking the successor states' nostrifications. Another Austrian company remained in charge of its Romanian branch via a capital participation but the third lost its Polish affiliate.[37]

All the three paper firms examined continued to be Austrian-based; all had local branches in the successor states but nostrification was a nominal process – the Austrian companies taking over shares of the successor state national firms.[38]

Three out of the four textile factories transferred their head offices to foreign countries, one of them, Aktiengesellschaft der Vöslauer Kammgarnfabrik, to Zurich, so that in its case East Central European influence can be considered undiminished, even if one Czechoslovak plant was lost to a 'friendly trust'. The two other companies moved to Czechoslovakia, the Austrian plant being in one case taken over by a separate Austrian management while in the other instance the Austrian factory was sold. Both firms' transfers ended Austrian capital's decisive role in the respective field of the successor states' economies.[39]

In the sugar industry two of our sample's factories moved (Österreichische Zuckerfabriks AG and Chropiner). In one case management was split up into two autonomous regional branches. In spite of its transfer the other firm's management remained under Austrian influence due to the capital participation of the Länderbank. The headquarters of the Leipnik-Lundenburger Zuckerfabriken-Actien-Gesellschaft remained in Austria and it purchased shares of the local company now running its former Czechoslovak plant.[40]

The above attempt to try and evaluate the influence of Austrian industrial capital in the successor states is only a first step towards obtaining the necessary information. The sample is of course much too small to permit firm conclusions. But for the purpose of summarizing the above analysis an attempt will be made to quantify continuing Austrian influence in East Central Europe. In order to do this the assumption has to be made that Austrian influence on a firm's policy was significant if there existed at least an Austrian blocking minority in a succeeding national company. Taking into account both the estimated percentages of Austrian influence in the various branches of the economy and the number of companies examined per branch (an evaluation according to the respective importance of each sector for the overall economy would be more appropriate, however), the conclusion emerges that in the field of industrial joint stock companies nearly 70 per cent of pre-war Austrian capital influence continued to prevail. It is true that in several instances companies' head offices were transferred to the areas of production but this almost never meant the abandonment of the Austrian establishments. Even if a joint company's administration was shifted to a successor state, the Viennese branch continued to be of vital importance. The influence of established Viennese capitalist groups survived in this way at least during the immediate post-war years: 'Austrian capital was invested in the mining and metallurgy industry, sugar refining, textiles, and the food industry, that is, those branches of industry where links had existed between the later successor states before World War One'.[41] Of course an approach to the problem of capital connections between the private economies of Austria and the other successor states like the one above can only produce superficial results. The statement that 70 per cent of the companies, having turned into 'multi-nationals' after the breakup of 1918 in an undefined way, were still under the influence of Vienna is of no significant value. It can for the moment only be viewed as a general hypothesis which requires verification through further detailed research.

Austrian participation in successor state enterprises was not restricted to a vaguely defined right of co-determination in the firms' management (even if this was of great importance in view of the continuation of pre-war industrial division of labour), but had a strong impact on the Alpine Republic's international accounts. This point was stressed by A. Basch and F. Hertz before 1925. The former recalled that Austria in 1924 succeeded in increasing her holdings of gold and foreign exchange by 16.2m schillings in spite of both an adverse trade balance amounting to as much as 1.132m gold crowns and the adverse effects of local unsuccessful speculation against the franc upon the National Bank's reserves. This was only made possible, according to Basch, by the still very considerable inflow of royalties and dividends (from Czechoslovakia alone 200m Kč were remitted to Vienna) and of gains made by Austrian-owned foreign companies.[42] Friedrich Hertz estimated the Alpine provinces' pre-war income from fixed dividends on capital participations abroad, profits of Austrian-owned firms operating outside Austria, yields of Austrian agricultural undertakings abroad, and salaries of Austrian members in successor state companies' boards of management at 822m gold crowns.[43] He conceded that the war and consequent disruption of Austria-Hungary had serious repercussions in this area but when allowing for this the First Republic would at best be able to count on 400m gold crowns as the annual income from foreign invisible activities. But even this reduced amount can be considered sufficient to serve as proof of the East Central European investments' continuing importance for Austria's balance of payments. It represented approximately 7.5 per cent of total Austrian national income and almost 20 per cent of the income from possessions and undertakings.[44]

In both respects, considering simply the quantity of Austrian capital holdings in the successor states as well as their impact upon the flow of income to Vienna, one can therefore agree with Pasvolsky at least as far as the first inter-war decade is concerned: 'Austrian participation in industrial, commercial and banking enterprises in the other Danubian states is still considerable'.[45] No doubt the dissolution of the Monarchy had shaken Vienna's position as the financial and economic centre and as the home of most Central European large companies' head offices. But decentralization did not reach its initially feared degree. Vienna on the one hand lost its previous importance as the administrative centre of a large Empire but on the other hand retained 'its ancient function of intermediary in the exchange of goods between the industrialized Sudeten countries and the agrarian regions of the Danube Basin', as noted by Otto Bauer, the spiritual leader of the Austrian Social Democrats.[46]

Legal difficulties in connection with nostrifications also contributed to the subsequent revaluation of Vienna's position as the location for a company's head office. Moving a company to the 'Neuausland' (former parts of the Empire) in terms of the law meant its total liquidation in Austria and the founding of an entirely new company abroad. As such a manoeuvre was subject to heavy Austrian taxation, most managements preferred to leave their registered offices where they were and to search for other possibilities to retain control of what were now foreign interests.[47]

An important reason for big industrial enterprises to leave at least part of their administration in Vienna was the necessity of retaining their traditional links with the city's large banks. The close relationship between banking and industry had been a characteristic feature of the Austrian economy since the beginning of its industrialization. Sometimes it is even said that Austria's economic history is to a large extent the history of her banks.[48] Vienna-based capital participated in nearly all important industrial corporations and in many cases played a dominant role. Vienna's position as a financial centre – its specific function as the economic heart of the Habsburg Monarchy – was primarily a consequence of the status of its banks.[49]

> Any somewhat more important financial operation serving the economic needs of the countries, no matter if it was an issue of securities, the creation of a syndicate, the raising of a loan or just a larger industrial credit, was undertaken, supervised, and often completely carried through by the Viennese banks. Relations with the international 'haute finance' were concentrated in Vienna. In Vienna, foreign credits for the whole of the Empire were fixed by quotas and partitioned. It was the Vienna banks that directed East and Southeast Europe's penetration with Austrian capital.[50]

The extent of the Viennese big banks' financial interest in the successor states was calculated at approximately 3,500m gold crowns with regard to

Table 4.5. THE POSITION OF VIENNA IN HISTORIC AUSTRIA'S
BANKING SYSTEM (1913).

	Share capital	Reserves	Creditors	Deposits
	in m crowns			
Historic Austria's joint stock banks (74)	1,351.6	521.3	4,669	1,156.3
Thereof Vienna banks (22)	888.7	436.8	3,391	642.5
Thereof Vienna large banks (10)	834	410.6	3,258.7	635.3
Share of the Vienna large banks in % of historic Austrian total	61.7	78.8	69.8	54.9

Source: W. Huth, *Die wirtschaftlichen Kräfte Deutschösterreichs*, 70.

only the most important branches of industry. The estimated figures for the different sectors are: petrochemical industry 800m gold crowns, leather industry 70m, machine building 320m, glass industry 70m, electrical industry over 100m, chemical industry 250m, textile industry 1,000m, and sugar industry 300m. Added to this, there were capital investments in commerce and services.[51]

Given the above, it is of the utmost importance to examine the question of whether Vienna succeeded in retaining its strategic position after the dissolution of its former economic territory. The successor states after 1918 did undertake efforts to reduce their dependence upon Austrian financial capital. These ambitions, however, were in most cases bound to failure because as a rule the capacities of their new domestic banks were not sufficient to satisfy the industrial companies' demand for credit. As before, it was inevitable that they should call on the Viennese banking world. Max Sokal, Austrian banking expert and director of the Wiener Giro- und Kassen-Verein, noted in 1925:

All that went for the companies on the soil of the Austro-Hungarian Monarchy before 1918 applies to nowadays' successor state enterprises too. Austrian banks' participation in industry and trade still today not only is far beyond the usual in Austria herself, but in the whole of Central Europe, above all in Czechoslovakia, Yugoslavia and Poland.[52]

Most of the Vienna banks had a network of local branches extending over the whole Empire. Immediately after the fall of the Habsburg Monarchy, negotiations concerning reorganization of the banking system were started. These did not only arise from the intentions of the successor states but also those of the Viennese banks, as it became more and more difficult to provide customers with credits directly from Vienna due to state exchange control and other restrictions of money transfer after the separation of currencies.

Thus, for instance, the Credit-Anstalt in 1920 transferred all its Czechoslovak branches and liaison offices to the Böhmische Escomptebank [Bohemian Discount Bank]. Large parts of the latter's share capital were already in the hands of the Niederösterreichische Escompte-Gesellschaft, which had in 1918 sold a block of shares to a Czechoslovak group but re-established its former position after 1920. After having taken over the Credit-Anstalt's local branches, the Bohemian Discount Bank changed its name to Česká eskomptní banka a úvěrní ústav. The Viennese Credit-Anstalt was represented in the board of directors by three delegates and it held 22 per cent of the total share capital. In 1922 the Credit-Anstalt together with the Magyar Általános Hitelbank [Hungarian General Credit Bank] set up the Slovenská všeobecná úvěrná banka [Slovak General Credit Bank] in Bratislava, gaining an additional foothold in the Slovak economic area.[53]

Similarly the Credit-Anstalt was eager to conserve its sphere of influence in the other successor states. The Kreditni zavod za trgovino in industrijo was set up in Yugoslavia in 1920 to take over the Ljubljana Credit-Anstalt branch. Vienna participated in the newly established bank by subscribing part of the share capital. Further, close relations were established with the Agrarna i industrijska banka a.d. of Belgrade, the Hravtska sveopéa kreditna banka dioničarsko društvo [Croatian General Credit Bank], Zagreb, and the Trgovačka i obrtna banka d.d. Novisad. Credit-Anstalt branches in Trieste, Gorizia and Pula were ceded to an Italian syndicate under the leadership of the Banca Commerciale Triestine. The Lemberg branch was taken over by the Warsaw Discount Bank, one of the Credit-Anstalt's Polish affiliates. In addition the Credit-Anstalt purchased shares of the Akcyjny Bank hypoteczny (Lwów) and the Silesian Credit-Anstalt.

The Wiener Bank-Verein, like the Credit-Anstalt, had local branches and affiliated banks in all successor states. Its Polish establishments were run from 1921 on by the newly founded and largely Vienna-owned Powszechny Bank Związkowy w Polsce SA. Nostrification of the Bank-Verein's Czechoslovak branches led to the establishment of the Všeobecná ceská bankovní jednota, which remained under strong Austrian influence, although another Czechoslovak bank (Moravská agrární a průmyslová banka, Brno), and two Brussels banks (Société Générale de Belgique and Banque Belge pour l'Étranger) had taken part in its foundation. In Hungary (Budapest), Romania (Cernăuti) and Italy (Bolzano, Merano) the Bank-Verein was able to continue running its local branches without disturbance. In Yugoslavia it even set up new local branches: a Croatian office opened in Zagreb, a new Belgrade establishment was formed in 1921. The Wiener Bank-Verein kept its capital participation in the Zemaljska banka za Bosnu i Hercegovinu which it had formed in 1895 in conjunction with the Magyar ipari és kereskedelmi bank.[54]

The Mercurbank also succeeded in efficiently regrouping and stabilizing its Neuausland capital participations. The Czechoslovak Mercur branches were taken over by the Česká komerčni banka [Bohemian Commercial Bank] created for this purpose in 1920. The Polish branches (Kraków, Lwów) went to the Commercial Bank AG Kraków, and the Cernăuti office became part of the Banca Comercială Natională.[55]

It is true that some of the above cited transactions implied a certain restriction of direct Viennese influence on the successor states' industrial and transportation companies, but only in very few cases did they involve a financial loss for the Austrian big banks. Some medium-size banks, however, did come off worse: as they had only limited financial reserves, their bargaining position in the post-war negotiations concerning reorganization of their foreign investments was a weaker one. So, for instance, the Unionbank, which had been mainly interested in the region of Trieste, suffered considerable losses when it sold its Neuausland capital participations.[56]

The settlement of pre-war debts constituted a far more serious problem for the banks than the reorganization of their branch networks. The Articles of the St Germain Treaty concerning the valorization of foreign debts forced two major Austrian banks (the Anglobank and the Länderbank), which had branches in Great Britain and France, to transfer their headquarters to London and Paris respectively in order to cover their huge foreign exchange liabilities. The Anglobank was taken over by the Anglo-Austrian Bank Ltd, established in London in March 1922. The Austrian authorities agreed to the bank moving to London, provided that its domestic business activities should not be restricted, Austrian deposits should be invested at home, and the actual relations with Austrian creditors and debtors should remain unchanged as far as possible (Anglobank-Bill of October 1921).

In the case of the Länderbank a similar solution was found by agreement with the bank's foreign creditors. In January 1920 a contract was signed with a French banking syndicate under the leadership of the Banque de Paris et des Pays Bas, arranging for the bank's transfer to Paris and at the same time changing its name to the Banque des Pays de l'Europe Centrale (Zentraleuropäische Länderbank). The capital stock was converted into francs and increased by the issue of additional preferential shares. Debentures were issued to settle the debts of a London branch. With the Länderbank-Bill of autumn 1921 the migration of this important bank was finalized.

Apart from those mentioned above, Austrian banks generally were spared the initially feared serious consequences of their pre-war indebtedness.[57] An examination of the ten leading Austrian Banks shows that none of them moved its headquarters to a successor state. The Anglobank's and Länderbank's respective 'anglicization' and 'francization' made control of their East Central European network of branches easier. The British Anglobank took over all the former Austrian headquarters' branches except the one in Prague, which was incorporated into the newly founded Anglo-československá banka [Anglo-Czechoslovak Bank] in 1923. The Anglobank's industrial participations in the successor states remained fully intact; in

Austria itself they even increased due to large investments in the machine-building and metal industries.[58] The Czechoslovak Länderbank branches were taken over in 1921 by the Prague Banka pro obchod a průmysl [Bank for Commerce and Industry], but the majority of the latter's shares remained with the new, Paris-based Banque des Pays de l'Europe Centrale.[59]

The Wiener Bank-Verein retained its branches in Hungary, Yugoslavia and Italy. It participated in establishing domestic successor banks in Poland and Czechoslovakia. The extent of the Bank-Verein's investments in Hungary and Austria increased, while in the other successor states it remained fairly stable.[60] The Credit-Anstalt für Handel und Gewerbe, which had run local branches in Poland, Czechoslovakia, Yugoslavia and Italy before 1918, sold its Trieste establishments, cartelized with the Magyar Általános Hitelbank, and secured itself capital participations in its Polish and Czechoslovak successor banks of 30 per cent and 22 per cent respectively. Capital participations also took place in Romania and Yugoslavia.[61] Although the Allgemeine Depositenbank lost its branch in Romania, it increased investment activities in the successor states. There existed close relations with the Banca Commerciale Italiana as well as with Czechoslovak and Austrian banks in the field of industrial financing.[62] The Niederösterreichische Escompte-Gesellschaft was able to maintain its influence on the Česká eskomptní banká's management, although its participation in the latter's share capital decreased.[63] The Mercurbank (former Bank- und Wechselstuben AG) had an affiliated bank in Budapest and held shares of its now nationalized branches in other successor states.[64] But the Verkehrsbank was deprived of its Hungarian and Yugoslavian connections and from 1920 had no more influence in these areas. In Austria, however, the Verkehrsbank's participations in industrial corporations increased.[65] The Unionbank, having been interested primarily in the Galician oil business before the war, now acquired shares of its Polish successor bank.[66] The Österreichische Industrie- und Handelsbank, which before 1918 had been controlled by the German Raiffeisen Cooperative of Berlin, had prior to the war only one local branch, in Bohemia. The Vienna bank in 1924 merged with the Centralbank der deutschen Sparkassen, the latter taking over the Czechoslovak office and participating in the Magyar Német Bank of Budapest.[67]

Summarizing the above, it can be concluded that nationalization in the field of banking also brought no radical changes. Although 80 per cent of all Austrian banks previously interested in the successor states had – nominally – lost their local branches, Viennese influence in the area prevailed, mostly through capital participation in domestic banks set up in the course of nostrifications. Of the 'affiliated banks', as they were called, 70 per cent remained closely linked with the former Austrian parent companies.

Not all successor states pursued an equally aggressive policy of nationalization, which of course helped Austrian capital influence to survive in the area. While Romania must be considered the hard-liner in this respect, Polish and

Table 4.6. AUSTRIAN BANKS, THEIR INDUSTRIAL CLIENTS, AND FOREIGN CAPITAL, 1920–5.

Name of bank	Foreign capital influence	Main fields of investment *branches*	*country*
Anglo-Austrian Bank	Great Britain	Banks, machine-building, paper	Austria, Hungary, Czechoslovakia
Wiener-Bank-Verein	Belgium, Switzerland	Machine-building, banks, textiles, mining, transport	Austria Hungary, Bulgaria
Credit-Anstalt	Great Britain, Netherlands, U.S.A.	Machine-building, textiles, sugar, chemicals, banks, timber	Austria, Czechoslovakia, Poland, Hungary, Yugoslavia
Allgemeine Depositenbank	Poland, Italy, Czechoslovakia	Construction, machine-building, oil	Austria, Czechoslovakia, Germany, Poland
'Nö' Escompte-gesellschaft	Great Britain, Switzerland, France, Belgium	Machine-building, banks, construction, textiles	Austria, Poland, Czechoslovakia, Yugoslavia, Hungary
Länderbank	France	Sugar, chemicals, machine-building, banks, leather	Austria, Czechoslovakia, Hungary
Mercurbank	Germany, Switzerland	Timber, machine-building, metal, construction, banks	Austria, Hungary, Poland, Czechoslovakia, Yugoslavia
Verkehrsbank		Machine-building, leather, shoes, paper, textiles	Austria
Unionbank	France	Banks, paper, timber, metallurgy	Austria, Hungary, Yugoslavia, Poland
Österreichische Industrie- und Handelsbank	Germany	Paper, construction, tourism	Austria, Hungary, Czechoslovakia, Germany

Source: *Compass* (1920–5).

Czechoslovak nostrification measures had hardly any effect on their respective countries' economic structure. Often in Italy, Yugoslavia and Hungary not even a purely formal nationalization took place.

The thesis of continuing Austrian capital influence in East Central Europe is underlined by the results of more detailed research. So Alice Teichova notes with regard to the situation as late as 1937: 'The relatively high share of Austrian investments is somewhat surprising, even though the historical roots of Austrian economic influence cannot be overlooked'.[68] But she also raises the decisive question of the role that foreign capital played in the Austrian economy. Here, too, the evaluation of our small sample clearly indicates a certain trend: in 90 per cent of the Viennese banks examined, foreign capital participation existed, and in six out of nine cases it was acquired only after the war. The Anglobank and Länderbank were under British and French influence before 1918, but now their Viennese head offices became local branches. Anglo-American capital infiltrated the most important Austrian bank, the Credit-Anstalt, which controlled 60 per cent of the country's industry. The Anglo-International Bank and the New York International Acceptance Bank were the Credit-Anstalt's major participants.[69] French capitalists, for their part, could not afford to stand back: they secured their influence via participations in the Unionbank (Crédit Mobilier Français) and the Länderbank (Banque de Paris et des Pays Bas). The latter had shown German participation before the war (Deutsche Effekten- und Wechselbank).[70]

It was mainly the Entente powers, Great Britain and France, and then the neutral Benelux countries and Switzerland that entered into the field of Austrian financial capital. Foreign investors moreover benefited from the Alpine Republic's post-war inflation, which led to a 'sell-out' of Austrian stock.[71] German capital participation in the country's economy dated from before the war; immediately after 1918 the German economic 'eastward expansion' had not yet started. The successor states themselves also took part in the foreign penetration of Austrian banking, acquiring shares of the Depositenbank.

The increasing importance of foreign capital can be noted also in the field of industrial joint stock companies. A characteristic example is provided by the Alpine Montan Company, Austria's largest industrial firm in the inter-war period. In 1919–20 a block of shares was transferred to an Italian group comprising the Banca Commerciale Italiana, Societa Italiana di Credito Milano, and the Torino Fiat Works, with the Viennese banker R. Kola acting as intermediary. This transaction constituted the first major inroad of foreign capital into Austrian industry. An adequate speculative gain having been secured, the notorious Viennese tycoon Camillo Castiglioni arranged for the transfer of the Italian shares to the German Rhein-Elbe-Union, which belonged to the Hugo Stinnes trust. From then Austria's largest company remained under German influence. When in 1926 the Stinnes group ran into financial difficulties, 56 per cent of the Alpine Montan Company's shares were passed to the Vereinigte Stahlwerke AG, Düsseldorf. So while Britain and France secured their influence on the Austrian economy via participations in Vienna banks, Germany chose the method of direct industrial investment. In this way, she succeeded in subsequently strengthening her – already favourable – pre-war capital position.[72]

In conclusion:

1. Functional effects of post-war disintegration are usually overestimated. Mutual structural dependences led to the maintenance of traditional forms of co-operation across the new borders (only for such branches of industry which already lacked competitiveness as a consequence of an unsatisfactory structure of production did the loss of a large, protected domestic market constitute a real disadvantage). Only the Second World War finally destroyed Austria's close contacts with North-East and East European countries and shifted the Austrian economy from its former central position to the periphery of its historic sphere of influence.

2. Viennese banking capital at first succeeded in preserving its previous influence in the area. By applying various strategies (foundation of holding companies in neutral countries, participations in new successor state companies) nostrification laws were easily and efficiently outmanoeuvred. Further, it must not be overlooked that only Viennese banking and trade had the indispensable experience in dealing with the East Central European business partners who had been fellow-countrymen of the Austrians until most recently. On the one hand almost no other economic territory was as complex and inaccessible as the area of the successor states (considering the variety of languages, alone, spoken in the former Monarchy), while on the other few potential intermediaries held the key to it.

   Not only did Western investors and businessmen realize and make use of Austria's particular position; that it was almost impossible to do without Vienna's services had to be acknowledged even by the successor states themselves. A large part of their foreign transactions continued to be effected through Viennese banking and commercial channels.

3. However, more and more foreign capital penetrated into Austria, not only by means of direct industrial participation, but also indirectly by gaining influence through Viennese banks. Mostly it was the international financial syndicates that tried to benefit from the traditional Viennese commercial relations with the successor states.[73] This implies that Austrian capital in East Central Europe was not initially replaced by the successor states' own domestic sources after 1918, but by Anglo-American, French, Swiss, Dutch, etc. investing combines. In this way the 'financial gap' caused by the fall of the ancient Habsburg Empire was closed by the nations of the world both politically and economically.

Notes

1. K. M. Fink, *Die österreichisch-ungarische Monarchie als Wirtschaftsgemeinschaft* (Munich, 1968).
2. A. Wandruszka and P. Urbanitsch (eds.), *Die Habsburger-Monarchie 1848–1918*, I: *Die wirtschaftliche Entwicklung* (Vienna, 1973), xii.
3. W. Goldinger, *Geschichte der Republik Österreich* (Vienna, 1962), 118–20.
4. K. Wessely, 'Die Pariser Vororte-Friedensverträge in ihrer wirtschaftlichen Auswirkung', in *Europa vor fünfzig Jahren* (Munich, Vienna, 1971), 143–65; cf. also *Die Volkswirtschaft der Nationalstaaten* (Überreicht von der Allgemeinen Depositenbank: Vienna, 1921) 12–15; J. Gruntzel, 'Die wirtschaftliche Wirkung des Selbstbestimmungsrechtes', *Das Handelsmuseum*, XXXIII (Vienna, 1918), 330; R. Juooviz, *Ueber die wirtschaftliche Kraft Deutschösterreichs* (Graz, 1919), 3; *Bericht über die Tätigkeit der deutsch-österreichischen Friedensdelegation*, I, 75f.
5. K. Bachinger, 'Umbruch und Desintegration nach dem Ersten Weltkrieg. Österreichs wirtschaftliche und soziale Ausgangssituation in ihren Folgewirkungen auf die Erste Republik' (unpublished MS: Vienna, 1979), 65.
6. J. van Walré de Bordes, *The Austrian Crown. Its depreciation and stabilization* (1924), 15.
7. F. Hertz, *Ist Österreich wirtschaftlich lebensfähig?* (Vienna, 1921), 23f.
8. F. Fellner, 'Das Volkseinkommen Österreichs und Ungarns', *Statistische Monatsschrift*, XXI (1971); A. Gürtler, 'Das Volkseinkommen Österreichs und Ungarns. Kritische Ergänzungen zu dem gleichnamigen Buche von Friedrich von Fellner', *Weltwirtschaftliches Archiv*, XIII/2 (1918).
9. E. Waizner, 'Das Volkseinkommen Alt-Österreichs und seine Verteilung auf die Nachfolgestaaten', *Metron*, VII/4 (Rome, 1929), and F. Fellner, 'Die Verteilung des Volksvermögens und Volkseinkommens der Länder der Ungarischen Heiligen Krone zwischen dem heutigen Ungarn und den Successions-Staaten', *Metron*, III/2 (Rome, 1923).
10. 'Österreichs Volkseinkommen 1913 bis 1963', *Monatsberichte des Österreichischen Instituts für Wirtschaftsforschung*, XIV (1965) 30f.
11. E. Waiziner's income figure of 695 crowns *per capita* differs from his basic data; it seems to be a miscalculation: Waizner, *op. cit.*, 85.
12. H. Matis, *Österreichs Wirtschaft 1848–1913. Konjunkturelle Dynamik und gesellschaftlicher Wandel im Zeitalter Franz Josephs I* (Berlin, 1972), 394f. Cf. also S. Koren, 'Die Industrialisierung Österreichs. Vom Protektionismus zur Integration', in *Österreichs Wirtschaftsstruktur gestern – heute – morgen*, ed. W. Weber (Berlin, 1961), I, 265.
13. J. Deutsch, 'Deutschösterreich – ein Industriestaat', *Der Betriebsrat*, I (1921/2), 65–8. See also W. Schiff, 'Beweist die ausserordentliche Volkszählung eine zunehmende Industrialisierung Deutschösterreichs?', *Der Betriebsrat*, I (1921/2), 114–16.
14. See D. F. Strong, *Austria (October 1918–March 1919); Transition from Empire to Republic* (New York, 1974), 185ff.
15. I. Svennilson, *Growth and Stagnation in European Economy* (Geneva, 1954), 304f.
16. H. Bayer, 'Strukturwandlungen der österreichischen Volkswirtschaft nach dem Kriege. Ein Beitrag zur Theorie der Strukturwandlungen', in *Wiener Staats- und Rechtswissenschaftliche Studien*, ed. Hans Kelsenn, XIV (Vienna, 1929), 91.
17. J. Jellinek, 'Die Industrie Deutschösterreichs', in *Zehn Jahre Nachfolgestaaten* (Vienna, 1928), 85f. Cf. also *Österreichisches Statistisches Handbuch*, XXXV (1916/17), 101; *Statistisches Handbuch für die Republik Österreich*, I (1920); *Das Handelsmuseum*, XXXIV (1919), 241 and 120f.; K. Hudeczek, *Die Wirtschaftskräfte Österreichs* (Vienna, 1920), 25f.
18. O. Kende, 'Die volkswirtschaftlichen Grundlagen von Deutsch-Donauland und seine Abhängigkeit vom Weltmarkt', *Weltwirtschaftliches Archiv*, XIV (1919), 123f.; A. Kuffler, 'Die Baumwollindustrie in den Nachfolgestaaten', in *Zehn Jahre Nachfolgestaaten*, *op. cit.*, 28f.; A. Katz-Foerstner (ed.), *Handbuch der österreichischen Wirtschaft* (Berlin, 1924/5), 101f.

19. 'Der Aussenhandel Österreichs in der Zeit zwischen den beiden Weltkriegen', *Beiträge zur österreichischen Statistik*, I (1946), 75.

20. *Ein Jahrhundert Creditanstalt-Bankverein* (Vienna, 1957), 339–41.

21. *Die Österreichisch-Alpine Montangesellschaft 1881–1931* (Vienna, 1931).

22. G. Otruba, 'Die Entwicklung des Böhler-Konzerns. Vom ersten Weltkrieg bis zur Gegenwart', in *100 Jahre Böhler Edelstahl* (Vienna, 1970), 53–6.

23. *Ein Jahrhundert Creditanstalt-Bankverein*, *op. cit.*, 340.

24. Koren, *op. cit.*, 309f.

25. M. von Allmayer-Beck, *Materialien zum österreichischen Kartellwesen* (Vienna, 1910), 31f., and J. Křížek, 'Beitrag zur Geschichte der Entstehung und des Einflusses des Finanzkapitals in der Habsburgermonarchie in den Jahren 1900–1914', in *Die Frage des Finanzkapitals in der Österreich-ungarischen Monarchie 1900–1918* (Bukarest, 1965), 16–18. Cf. also G. Erlacher, 'Kartelle in Österreich in der Zeit zwischen 1848 and 1938' (unpublished doctoral dissertation, Graz, 1970), and Robert Liefman, *Cartels, Concerns and Trusts* (1932).

26. Jellinek, *op. cit.*, 86; E. Herz, 'Eisenindustrie', in *Handbuch der österreichischen Wirtschaft*, ed. A. Katz-Foerstner, 45. O. Berl, *Die chinesische Mauer. Österreichische Betrachungen zur Absperrungspolitik der Nachfolgestaaten* (Vienna, 1923), 5. W. Anreiter, 'Industrie', in Bundesministerium für Handel und Wiederaufbau, *100 Jahre im Dienste der Wirtschaft*, II (Vienna, 1961), 48f.

27. 'Der Aussenhandel Österreichs', *op. cit.*, 76; see also *Statistische Nachrichten* (Bundesamt f. Statistik, Vienna). For percentage shares of various countries in Austrian exports see L. Pasvolsky, *Economic Nationalism of the Danubian States* (1928).

28. F. Hertz, *op. cit.*, 13. See also E. Heinl (ed.), *Bericht des Obmanns des Ausschusses für Handel und Gerwerbe, Industrie und Bauten über die in der Zeit vom 29. Jänner bis 30 April 1926 abgehaltene Wirtschaftsenquete* (Vienna, 1926), 3.

29. *Compass* (1920), 480; (1921), 546; (1922), 595; (1923), 617.

30. *Ibid.* (1920), 495; (1921), 561.

31. *Ibid.* (1920), 502; (1921), 569; (1922), 615; (1923), 642; (1924), 732; (1925), 784.

32. *Ibid.* (1920), 507; (1921), 578; (1922), 624; (1923), 655.

33. *Ibid.* (1920), 568; (1921), 651; (1922), 712; (1923), 760; (1924), 881; (1925), 945.

34. *Ibid.* (1920, 583, 588, 591; (1921), 669, 674, 677; (1922), 739, 733, 736; (1923), 783, 786, 789; (1924), 910, 914, 917; (1925), 978, 983, 986. M. Bouvier, 'Die Entwicklung der chemischen Industrie in Österreich', in *Zehn Jahre Nachfolgestaaten*, *op. cit.*, 115–18. For the history of the Nobel Trust see W. J. Reader, *Imperial Chemical Industries* (London, New York & Toronto, 1970).

35. *Compass* (1920), 604, 610; (1921), 697, 703; (1922), 760, 766; (1923), 819, 825, (1924), 951, 958; (1925), 1024–26.

36. *Ibid.* (1920), 261; (1921), 268; (1922), 298; (1923), 308; (1924), 994; (1925), 1073. E. Futter, 'Elektro-Industrie', in *Handbuch der österreichischen Wirtschaft*, *op. cit.*, 98.

37. *Compass* (1920), 646; (1921), 757.

38. F. Haber, *Österreichs Wirtschaftsbilanz. Ein Vergleich mit der Vorkriegszeit* (Munich, 1927), 66. Cf. C. R. Morstedt, 'Papierindustrie', in *Handbuch der österreichischen Wirtschaft*, *op. cit.*, 114–16, and R. Schwarz, 'Die Zelluloseindustrie Deutsch-Österreichs', *Das Handelsmuseum*, XXXIV (1919), 201f.

39. *Compass* (1920), 702; (1921), 833; (1922), 904; (1923), 1000; (1924), 1182; (1925), 1287.

40. *Ibid.* (1921), 855; (1925), 1322.

41. A. Teichova, *An Economic Background to Munich. International Business and Czechoslovakia 1918–1938* (1974), 50.

42. A. Basch and J. Dvořáček, *L'Autriche et son existence economique* (Prague, 1925), 125f.

43. F. Hertz, *Zahlungsbilanz und Lebensfähigkeit Österreichs* (Munich, 1925), 46f.

44. *Österreichs Volkseinkommen 1913–1963* (Monatsberichte des österr. Inst. f. Wirtschaftsforschung, 14 Sonderheft), 39.

45. Pasvolsky, *op. cit.* 584.

46. Quoted by C. Supplanz, *Die österreichische*

Inflation 1918–1922 (Institute for Advanced Studies, III Vienna, 1976), 91.

47. *Neue Freie Presse*, 4 May 1919, 15f.

48. E. März, *Österreichische Industrie- und Bankpolitik in der Zeit Franz Josephs I. am Beispiel der k.k. priv. Österreichischen Credit-Anstalt für Handel und Gewerbe* (Vienna, 1968), 11.

49. According to Waizner, *op. cit.*, 69, the net income of Cisleithanian joint-stock banks 1911–13 was estimated at approximately 143m crowns. The share of Austria was 74.3 per cent, that of the later Czechoslovak Republic was only 19.9 per cent.

50. W. T. Layton and C. Rist, *Die Wirtschaftslage Österreichs. Bericht der vom Völkerbund bestellten Wirtschaftsexperten* (Vienna, 1925), 86

51. *Neue Freie Presse*, 26 June 1919, 11.

52. M. Sokal, 'Banken', in *Handbuch der österreichischen Wirtschaft, op. cit.*, 12; idem, 'Vom österreichischen Bankenwesen in Deutsch-Österreich', *Schriften des Vereins für Socialpolitik*, ed. Gustav Stolper CLXII (Berlin, Leipzig, 1921), 31.

53. *Ein Jahrhundert Creditanstalt-Bankverein, op. cit.*, 165.

54. Bayer, *op. cit.*, 160.

55. *Compass* (1924), 383.

56. W. Federn, 'Die österreichischen Banken', in *Zehn Jahre Nachfolgestaaten, op. cit.*, 55.

57. Bayer, *op. cit.*, 163f.

58. *Compass* (1920), 245; (1921), 270; (1922), 279; (1923), 288; (1924), 289; (1925), 335.

59. *Ibid.* (1920), 285; (1921), 32a; (1922), 333; (1923), 347; (1924), 364; (1925), 411.

60. *Ibid.* (1920), 252; (1921), 278; (1922), 288; (1923), 298; (1924), 300; (1925), 346.

61. *Ibid.* (1920), 261; (1921), 268; (1922), 298; (1923), 308; (1924), 319; (1925), 368; *Ein Jahrhundert Creditanstalt-Bankverein* (Vienna, 1957), 165–7.

62. *Compass* (1920), 270; (1921), 296; (1922), 307; (1923), 319; (1924), 333; (1925), 381.

63. *Ibid.* (1920), 274; (1921), 303; (1922), 343; (1923), 358; (1924), 343; (1925), 388.

64. *Ibid.* (1920), 294; (1921), 330; (1922), 343; (1923), 358; (1924), 380; (1925), 426.

65. *Ibid.* (1920), 305; (1921), 342; (1922), 355; (1923), 370; (1924), 397; (1925), 444.

66. *Ibid.* (1920), 300; (1921), 335; (1922), 349; (1923), 366; (1924), 390; (1925), 437.

67. *Ibid.* (1920), 283; (1921), 312; (1922), 325; (1923), 338; (1924), 356; (1925), 403.

68. Teichova, *op. cit.*, 379.

69. *Ein Jahrhundert Creditanstalt-Bankverein, op. cit.*, 167f.

70. *Compass* (1922), 333.

71. *Monatsberichte des Österreichischen Instituts für Konjunktur-forschung* (Vienna, 1936), 270.

72. *Die Österreichisch-Alpine Montangesellschaft, op. cit.*, 50f.; H. Strakele, 'Die österreichische Alpine-Montangesellschaft. Ihre Entstehung, Entwicklung und Bedeutung', *Das Wirtschaftsarchiv*, I (1946), 13. Cf. also Layton and Rist, *op. cit.*, 33.

73. See also Teichova, *op. cit.*, 345.

COMMENTARY on chapters 3 and 4

C. Trebilcock

Professor Matis argues convincingly, like Kurt Rothschild[1] before him, but not like many others, that the Austria of the Versailles settlement was a viable economic unit and that the 'size pessimism' which afflicted the industrial community of the new state was an ill-founded assessment of its prevailing economic circumstances. In this revisionist contention, however, there are surely ambiguities as to exactly which areas of the economy enjoyed immunity from disintegrative effects. In fact, three kinds of disintegration became somewhat conflated in this analysis: the disintegration of market relationships; the disintegration of industrial administration; and the disintegration of capital ownership. What is true of any one of these need not be true of the others.

With regard to markets, the position is clear and Professor Matis – and, indeed Dr Rothschild – wholly correct: the custom available to Austrian-based firms in the former Habsburg provinces kept up after 1919 and supplied an entirely adequate foundation of demand for Austrian manufacturing. But markets were not the only economic variables affected by the redrawing of political frontiers. With regard to the organization and ownership of industrial assets, the settlement clearly provoked more substantial changes. It is not obvious that pessimism was an inappropriate reaction to *these* alterations.

By Matis's own account, the Austrian industrial structure underwent substantial adjustments after 1919. Frequently, it proved necessary to switch the administrative control of large organizations to Zurich, Paris or London. Yet devices of this type raise important questions to which the paper does not give exact answers. Did these transfers leave effective control in Austrian hands, even if directed extra-territorially? Were they genuinely Austrian devices for overcoming Austro-Hungarian disintegration? When the locus of the holding organization shifted, did the distribution of the holding also shift? When the Länderbank transferred to Paris, were not large capital shares assumed by French interests? One notes that among the sample of 50 companies, no less than 15 are forced to transfer or extinguish important sections of their pre-war administrative systems. Sifting the instances with a somewhat more jaundiced eye, it is not difficult to obtain substantial percentage losses even in that inexact measure, 'Austrian influence against its 1914 level' – perhaps 50 per cent in distilling and textiles, 30 per cent in chemicals and timber. Such forfeits might be thought sufficiently large to excite real worries about centrifugal pressures within Austrian industrial management. Certainly it is not clear how the conclusion is reached 'that in the field of industrial joint stock companies nearly 70 per cent of pre-war Austrian capital influence prevailed.' Leaving aside the true measure of insignificance which should be attributed to the other 30 per cent, the crucial feature here is precisely the size of the 'Austrian blocking minority in succeeding national companies'. But that is not defined.

By Matis's own account, indeed, the third matter – capital ownership – is not successfully resolved. It is rightly, and freely, admitted that the sample of firms is restricted. And the methodology ensures that the designation of firms as Austrian-controlled or other-controlled is fairly arbitrary, and often appears impressionistic. Ideally, of course, the measure of foreign infiltration within an industrial economy should not be approached by a sample of individual firms. The counsel of perfection – and the only convincing answer to the problem – lies in a *sectoral* analysis providing percentage shares of total sectoral assets held by foreign capitalists for pre- and post-war dates. If such an analysis were available, it is by no means unlikely that it would display significant increases in the foreign ownership share – and thus solid grounds for concern about the measure of industrial initiative remaining to indigenous interests.

In some fields this analysis itself reveals marked advances in foreign capital participation: in 90 per cent of the Viennese banks surveyed foreign capital was present and in two-thirds of cases it had been present only since 1918. Even the mighty Credit-Anstalt 'which controlled 60 per cent of the country's industry' passed under strong foreign influences. This must surely devalue the residual power of Viennese *bankinitiative* within the regional economy since its autonomy is obviously deeply compromised.

There are more ways than one to suffer economic disintegration. It need not appear only in the loss of satellite markets, nor even in the surrender of valuable industrial out-stations. Here, it is perhaps most marked in the fragmentation of control at the *centre* of major industrial and financial concerns. This in turn implies that a substantial leverage over the capital formation of East Central Europe did slip out of Austrian hands. It merely failed to pass into those of the successor states. Only in this sense is disintegration avoided. But there were other beneficiaries: in the greatly increased powers of the major investing nations there is surely a fracture of Austrian industrial control – and a genuine reason for pessimism about the country's ability to determine its own economic fortunes.

The paper demonstrates that the new Austria suffered no market deprivation and that the Viennese financial ligatures remained an essential part of the regional economic body. But the changed proportionate influence of Austrian-owned capital *vis à vis* other types does not emerge clearly. And nor does the shifting balance of power within the industrial nerve centres. Organizations Austrian in location or in title might preserve the form of existing connections, but they did little to guarantee that the *control* or the *content* of those connections remained genuinely Austrian.

By contrast Dr Mosser deals with an area free from size pessimism, but not, interestingly, one free of doubts concerning the integrity or coherence of the Austrian business structure. His picture of company organization within the Empire prior to 1914 sketches three dominant features. First, when viewed at the level of the production unit, the business structure is characterized by a multiplicity of small-to-medium concerns. The units managed predominantly by joint stock companies turn out to be not the largest ventures but, most unusually, firms of intermediate size. Such polycentricity is perhaps most suited to economies of a highly regionalized type where demand is organized in a parochial or fractionalized pattern. Second, and quite distinctly, when the viewpoint is placed not at the level of the production unit but at the level of the enterprise, the measure of concentration becomes very much more marked. Third, the entire structure – the extensive array of manufacturing points controlled by a much smaller array of organizational centres – entered the late nineteenth-century Austrian growth phase with considerable, if highly traditional, reserves of investable capital. These were clawed into industry as provincial capitalists, attracted by manufacturing profits, brought their estate or farmstead profits with them. As industrial rationalization proceeded between 1880 and 1900 – whether by the sinister 'spontaneous drift' or not – and the traditional capital streams became depleted, so more modern methods of capital management became increasingly necessary. The economic crisis of 1901–2 initiated a much-needed learning process in up-to-date methods of capital depreciation. But at no point before 1914 did the tactics of business diplomacy or of capital mobilization become sufficiently adept to sustain any determined merger movement.

There is here an interesting amalgam of modern and archaic methods. The joint stock company assumes an 'élitist', trust-like structure, but its component parts retain the parochial and miniature forms of primitive industrialism. The economy can generate a genuine industrial investment boom in the 1890s, but it is substantially financed by estate assets drawn into business by conglomerations of rural capitalists.

Some arresting implications emerge from these findings; and two of them deserve special attention. To begin with, one of Alexander Gerschenkron's masterly but deliberately broad-brushed generalizations about backwardness – that backward economies will favour *large-scale* business organizations – encounters an Austrian reality that is a good deal more intricate than the theory can readily handle. Here theory is both right and wrong; it is incorrect at the level of the firm, broadly accurate at the level of the enterprise. Interestingly, it is much more accurate for chronically backward Hungary than for moderately backward Austria. In Hungary, industry did contain a disproportionate number of very large concerns, primarily in milling and electro-technicals. One might tie these differences to the structure of markets: Austria was at least sufficiently advanced to have developed pockets of provincial demand for industrial products, together with the local manufacturing resources to service them, while Hungary had to rely primarily on an export market for its grain and capital goods. Or one might tie the variations, in the Chandler style, to the characteristics of industrial process. Both milling and electro-technicals involved continuous or standardized processes which were well fitted to large-scale operation. But meeting the internal demand of metropolitan Austria was as variegated in process as it was diffuse in geographical location.

In the second place, there is finance. As Mosser rightly says, 'concentration and financing are related in manifold and complex ways'. One of those ways lies through the bank system. It, too, has played a central part in the economic historian's reflections on backwardness, primarily as the leading sponsor of growth – technological and organizational – within economies of *medium* backwardness. In recent research, however, the financial sector has been allocated a much less dynamic role within the Austrian version of medium backwardness. Richard Rudolf has castigated Austrian bankers for their attachment to 'plump, juicy firms of sound prospects', to a determined policy of risk minimization, that is, to a distinctly inferior style of *bankinitiative*.[2] Obviously, a cast in the eye of investment banking, producing a fixation upon the secure minority of large ventures, would create particular distortions in a business structure of the type described here. If financiers held generally aloof from industry – or traded, when they did so at all, only with industrialists of the most impeccable standing – there could be deficiences in both the quantity and quality of bank services. One might wonder how far the early Austrian reliance on very traditional capital streams, the retained array of small production units, or the absence of a large scale merger movement could each be traced back to the bank vaults, to a financial community which displayed a greater variety of tactics than Germanic or Gerschenkronian best practice requires, interpreting its function less in terms of entrepreneurial risk-taking than in those of bureaucratic risk-evasion.

It seems that the gangling business system of imperial Austria was not well defended from disintegrative tendencies even before the Allied diplomatists of 1919 reached for their long pens.

Notes

1. K. W. Rothschild, 'Size and viability: the lesson of Austria', in *The Economic Consequences of the Size of Nations*, ed. E. A. G. Robinson (1963).

2. R. Rudolf, 'Austrian banking, 1800–1914', in *Banking and Economic Development*, ed. R. E. Cameron (New York, 1972), 47ff.

Part Two

German Concerns in Eastern Europe

5. The Mannesmann Concern in East Central Europe in the Inter-war Period*

Alice Teichova

THE PLACE OF THE AUSTRIAN SUBSIDIARY COMPANY IN THE PRE-1914 PERIOD

Although the invention for producing seamless rolled tubes was the brain-child of the brothers Reinhard and Max Mannesmann, the business of making manufacture economically viable was launched by the Deutsche Bank. Production, according to the Mannesmann patents, had begun in the mid-1880s at three separate works on the Continent – Remscheid and Bous/Saar in Germany and Komotau (Chomutov) in the Bohemian Land of the Austro-Hungarian Empire. These were under the management of the Mannesmann brothers, amongst whose most prominent financial backers were the brothers Werner and Friedrich von Siemens. At the same time a further venture in manufacturing Mannesmann seamless tubes under licence was started by Werner von Siemens at Landore in Britain.

When, as a result both of technical difficulties in the embryonic stages of manufacture and business inefficiency, capital requirements grew constantly and returns on the initial investments were delayed, the Siemens brothers persuaded the leading director of the Deutsche Bank – their cousin Dr Georg Siemens – to take the financial reorganization of the Mannesmann works in Germany and Austria into his hands. Subsequently the continental rolling mills were brought together by the Deutsche Bank who founded the Aktiengesellschaft Deutsch-Österreichische Mannesmannröhren-Werke with a capital of M 35m. on 16 July 1908 and established the works' common head-quarters, first in Berlin and later (1893) in Düsseldorf, which was nearer to its German production plant.[1]

While both the Mannesmann and Siemens families had played a decisive part in the first phase of the works' existence, after 1890 the business developed into a professionally managed company dominated by the Deuts-che Bank. Representatives of the Deutsche Bank occupied a large number of seats on the German-based company's board of directors, and, most impor-tant, the office of the board's chairman remained continually in their hands. They had the decisive voice in the appointment of the general manager of the Düsseldorf parent company who acted as chairman of a managing board (Vorstand), which consisted of a small number of technicians and administrators. In the case of the Mannesmannröhren-Werke's German headquarters a remarkable continuity of the bank-industry connection was maintained in the person of Max Steinthal who, as director of the Deutsche Bank, remained at the helm of the company and devoted himself to its business from its reorganization in the 1890s to his retirement in 1936.[2] As chairman of the board of directors, Max Steinthal formulated the company's policy in consultation with the chairman of the managing board – a co-operation which developed into a particularly close liaison with Nicolaus Eich from 1900 to his death in 1919.[3]

Their long-term strategy aimed at vertical integration by providing the seamless tube rolling mills with their own raw material sources and supplies of semi-finished products on the one hand, and securing a market for their finished goods through a network of warehouses, sales companies and export agencies on the other. By the eve of the First World War considerable steps had been taken towards establishing a multi-unit company structure within Germany. The supplies of semi-finished materials for the seamless tube manufacture at the Bous works were secured by the acquisition of the Saarbrücken Cast Steel Works in 1906. The welded tube production at the works in Rath from 1911 onwards obtained its plates from the sheet-iron works Gewerkschaft Grillo, Funke & Co., now part of Mannesmann, and the steel and sheet rolling mills in Huckingen, the location of which on the banks of the Rhine brought the company within reach of erecting its own blast furnaces. At the same time coal mines were bought (Königin Elisabeth in 1912, and 'Unser Fritz' in 1918), while negotiations for the acquisition of iron ore deposits in the area of the Siegerland and the River Lahn were completed during the war.[4] On the sales side, merger activity progressed at a somewhat slower pace as Mannesmann products were marketed though established trading firms. Only gradually, beginning in the immediate pre-war years, did the Düsseldorf head office send out representatives, pairing a technician with a salesman (*Kaufmann*) to found the company's own sales agencies in and outside Germany.[5]

Throughout its existence the Mannesmannröhren-Werke's central management pursued a course of concentration and consolidation by purposefully strengthening forward and backward linkages (*Verschachtelung* – pyramiding – was the term used internally)[6] at home and abroad. Whenever circumstances allowed, they made complete take-overs; if this proved to be unattainable at once, then 100 per cent ownership of formerly independent firms was obtained in stages. This was followed by merging these enterprises with the parent company and transforming them into departments with at the same time incorporating their accounts into the head office's balance sheets. In this essentially piecemeal way a multi-unit organizational pattern emerged which was adapted and perfected according to the demands arising out of tighter concentration within a growing combine rather than through following a preconceived organizational-administrative design. However, in any decision-making process, the question of exercising the maximum possible control over subsidiary enterprises, acquired either partially or wholly by direct participating investments, remained a paramount requirement.

A similar policy was adopted by the Mannesmann management in its endeavours to gain a foothold on the world market where, at the turn of the century, potential demand for the company's products – such as bicycle tubes, water-, gas- and oilpipes, all types of tubes and their accessories for engineering constructions and machinery – undoubtedly existed. From its origin, production was export-orientated and where difficulties in conventional trade relations seemed insurmountable, it was the headquarter's strategy to break into protected foreign markets by initiating the manufacture of Mannesmann products abroad through direct investments which carried control.

Production outside Germany was first limited to the Bohemian works in Komotau. As the Austrian part of the Deutsch-Österreichische Mannesmannröhren-Werke, its consistently German technical and commercial management was entrusted with the expansion into East Central and South-East Europe. Although a 100 per cent German-owned subsidiary, it was able under a separate registration in the Habsburg Monarchy to conduct its business in the Danubian region as a legally recognized domestic undertaking. Within the first few years of commencing the production of seamless tubes, the Komotau works not only survived competition from the four existing Austrian tube manufacturing companies, among whom the mightiest rival was the Witkowitz [Vítkovice] works, but also achieved a market share of 35 per cent in the Austro-Hungarian tube cartel. In 1905 the Mannesmann works purchased the majority of shares of the tube factory Röhrenwerke AG Schönbrunn in Austrian Silesia, where butt-welded tubes and flange-pipes were produced, and within three years its entire capital was brought into the combine. As a result of this acquisition the Austrian company was formally severed from the German parent and reconstituted in 1908 as Österreichische Mannesmannröhrenwerke GmbH with its head office in Vienna and its production plants in Komotau and Schönbrunn.[7] Through being the focus of output and sales in the Central and South-East European market, the Austrian branch remained the most important foreign subsidiary, the business volume of which reached about one-third of the Mannesmann combine's total turnover in the last pre-war year.[8]

According to the same year's balance sheet (1912–13) all non-German subsidiary companies accounted for 45 per cent of the combine's total turnover.[9] This was the result of carrying the manufacture of seamless tubes into other countries since the end of the nineteenth century. In 1899 the works at Llandore in Britain were taken over by the Düsseldorf parent firm and the British Mannesmann Tube Co. was established as a fully-owned subsidiary. Sales in Britain and Ireland were thereby secured and further, an entry into the Empire markets, since products of Llandore were delivered as

British goods. By 1909 the British company had achieved profitability and in 1913 the decision was taken at the head office to expand production with a plant at Newport; however, this undertaking had not progressed very far by the outbreak of war. Manufacture was also started in Italy where demand for Mannesmann products was known to exist but high tariff walls hampered imports. The management envisaged correctly that a company formed under Italian law would be able to obtain state orders. In order to tap this market the Società Tubi Mannesmann at Dalmine was founded in 1906 by the Deutsche Bank and the Düsseldorf headquarters jointly with the Società Metallurgica Italiana and the Banca Commerciale Italiana of Milan.[10] This company had also begun to make a profit by the eve of the First World War. In the field of foreign trade, various plans for the founding of a specialized export organization had been considered by the Düsseldorf management, but only one venture was embarked upon – the establishment of the Sociedad Tubos Mannesmann Ltda in Buenos Aires in 1908.[11]

The commercial success of the finished products of the Mannesmann works had won the German combine an exceptionally favourable position on the world market and had boosted the management's confidence to such an extent that in its report, surveying the last year of peace and presented to the board of directors in September 1913, it mapped out 'the forceful conquest of production and markets for all its finished goods'.[12]

Until the First World War these foreign subsidiary enterprises were directed and controlled financially, technically and administratively by their German parent company and thus, historically, they constitute the origin of the Mannesmannröhren-Werke's multi-national character. While concentration inside Germany moved along lines of vertical integration, foreign expansion moved horizontally, because constraints to diversification were too great to be overcome and in this direction control by the German-headquartered company could not be achieved.

Against this historical background the relations between the German-based head office and the East Central European subsidiary companies, in particular the question of control during the inter-war period, will now be explored.

THE AFTERMATH OF WAR AND THE RECONSTRUCTION OF THE EAST CENTRAL EUROPEAN MANNESMANN INTERESTS

The outcome of the war put an end to the confident expectations of the Mannesmannröhren-Werke's central management of reaching an unrivalled domination of the world market in their specialized products. In the general confusion of defeat the whole combine's structure had been upset, ranging from a decimated sales organization to a disrupted production pattern. Yet paradoxically, in spite of the break-up of the Austro-Hungarian Empire, the weight of the East Central European part of the combine increased relatively as potentially its only viable foreign possession. This statement needs to be explained and substantiated.

After the Armistice, output in the Rhenish-Westphalian Mannesmann tube, steel and plate rolling mills fell between December 1918 and June 1919 to less than a third compared with the monthly average output of the period from 1 July 1913 to 30 June 1914, but production in the cast-steel works in Saarbrücken and the seamless tube rolling mill in Bous dropped to 19 per cent.[13] In the summer of 1919 usual business intercourse between the occupied and unoccupied German regions became more difficult. At the same time the French occupation authority under its raw material allocation scheme starved the German works in the Saar region of coal supplies and these conditions caused their temporary closure.[14] As a result the Mannesmannröhren-Werke's management agreed to release both works from their Düsseldorf headquarters in order to reach a settlement with a French group of tube manufacturers damaged by the war. The outcome was the establishment of a new company, the Société anonyme des Aciéries et Usines à Tubes de la Sarre, with its head office in Paris and a capital of 50m. fr. of which the French group took up 60 per cent and Mannesmann of Düsseldorf retained a participation of 40 per cent. Until the end of the League of Nation administration of the Saar in 1935 German control was greatly curtailed, although dividends transferred from the Paris head office soon began to appear in the Mannesmannröhren-Werke's balance sheets.[15]

Although part of the formerly German Saar works remained in the possession of the Düsseldorf parent company, the British Mannesmann Tube Co. Ltd was sequestrated by the British government as enemy property and sold to an English industrial group. Gradually, from 1926 onwards, the German headquarters managed to repurchase the British company's shares. However, problems connected with raw material supplies and management control were too great and, therefore, the effort to re-activate German-controlled production in Britain was finally abandoned in 1936. Only a trading firm was maintained in London.[16] Similarly, the Dalmine works were put under compulsory administration after Italy had entered the war on the side of the Entente. Later, in the autumn of 1916, the Mannesmann parent company in Düsseldorf was able to sell its Italian subsidiary on favourable terms to an Italian group led by one of the Dalmine company's local shareholders, the Banca Commerciale Italiana.[17]

The Mannesmann interests in the Danubian area developed quite differently. There – as it subsequently turned out – neither assets, nor productive capacity, nor effective control had to be relinquished, which left a nucleus for reconstruction and potential expansion under altered conditions in that region. In comparison with the disruption of the manufacturing programme at the parent company's works in Germany, the flow of production in the rolling mills at Komotau and Schönbrunn was, in spite of uncertainties, at no time seriously interrupted during the political change-over from the Habsburg Monarchy's reign in Vienna to an independent Czechoslovak Republic governed from Prague. Indeed, significant economic advantages eventually accrued to the whole Mannesmann combine from its Austrian subsidiary's production works finding itself overnight on the territory of a successor state which belonged to the victorious camp of the Entente powers.

With rather remarkable business acumen the German manager of the Austrian daughter company – Otto Klesper[18] – realized the necessity to abandon Vienna as quickly as possible and opt for Czechoslovakia as the seat of the Mannesmannröhren-Werke in East Central Europe. Therefore this strategy was adopted by the Düsseldorf headquarters and the works in Komotau, together with their coalmines and their sister-plant in Schön-brunn, were registered as a Czechoslovak firm, backdated to 28 October 1918, the day of the establishment of the new state.[19] A skeleton staff remained at the Vienna office to act as the Czechoslovak firm's future sales agency. The whole transformation was completed by August 1920.

Although the attitude of the leading personalities of the Mannesmann combine in Düsseldorf and Berlin was – to put it mildly – not wholly sympathetic to the new state, they accepted the economic expediency of this move. In the same spirit and in consideration of the existing political atmosphere, it was decided that the management of the Komotau company should join the Association of Czechoslovak Industrialists and should not become a member of the Association of German Industrialists in Czecho-slovakia.[20] In this way the Mannesmann works in Czechoslovakia could not formally be regarded as German or Austrian (real or potential) armament producers and was able to avoid sequestration or liquidation under the terms of the Versailles Peace Treaties.[21] Consequently, they were not only sheltered from demands to contribute to reparation deliveries but also as a Czecho-slovak enterprise could and did register a claim with the Prague govern-ment – to be passed on for recognition by the Reparation Commission – for payment of war materials delivered to the former K. u. K. Heeresverwaltung (i.e. the administration of the former Austro-Hungarian Imperial and Royal Forces) amounting to Kč 8,355,525.97 at a rate of 1:1 (1 Kč to 1 ö.K.).[22]

Similarly, the altered nationality of the former Vienna-based Mannesmann firm sheltered it from the storm of the Austrian hyper-inflation because of the Czechoslovak government's swift and incisive separation of the Czechoslovak currency from the Austrian and the stabilization of the Czechoslovak crown at the turn of 1918–19. Its opening balance sheet as a Czechoslovak joint stock company under the name of Mannesmannröhren-Werke A.G. Komo-tau showed considerable general and hidden reserves which were not whittled away by galloping inflation. Under these circumstances the Komotau man-agement was able to extend important services to the German parent company.

Since the Komotau company had obtained export permits for tubes from the Czechoslovak government, it was in a position to execute not only its own export orders but also those which the Düsseldorf head office redirected from the partially incapacitated German works to Komotau. Thus deliveries to the German and Czechoslovak home markets and to foreign markets could be met during 1919 and 1920. Indeed, demand from Düsseldorf rose to such an extent that by the end of 1919 the management in Komotau asked the head office to discontinue further orders as the works were fully employed and unable to obtain the necessary raw materials for expansion.[23] The reality of this post-war boom is reflected on the one hand in the high dividends of the Czechoslovak works, amounting to 25–30 per cent, which were transferred together with a 10 per cent provision on Komotau's turnover to Düsseldorf, and on the other in the large superdividends shown in the profit and loss accounts of the Mannesmannröhren-Werke Düsseldorf.[24] There can be little doubt that this relationship between the centre and the foreign subsidiary facilitated the transition from war to peace production for the Mannesman combine as a whole.

Further, the violent class struggles in post-war industry were generally fraught with relatively less danger for the Mannesmann works' interests in Czechoslovakia than in either Germany or Austria. The highly industrialized areas of Czechoslovakia such as north-west Bohemia, where the Komotau works were situated, and northern Moravia, the location of the Schönbrunn works, were, like the Ruhr, Rhine and Saar industrial conglomerations, affected by the social upheavals and revolutionary outbreaks which swept throughout Europe at the end of the war. However, the national solution of the Czechs' political claim to independent statehood had taken the edge off the social struggle and the Czechoslovak government's social legislation before the end of 1918 had contributed towards reducing strife in industrial relations, particularly by the introduction of the eight-hour working day and the promise of works councils. Nevertheless, confrontations and negotiations between workers and employers were a common feature at all plants in Czechoslovak industry including those of the Mannesmann tube works. How to meet the workers' demands for wage increases, clothing allowances and the shortening of the working day was closely and constantly debated within the Mannesmann combine either by correspondence or by personal emissaries between Komotau, Vienna and Düsseldorf from autumn 1918 to spring 1919.[25] The general manager at the head office, Nicolaus Eich, regarded industrial relations at the Czechoslovak works as rather harmonious compared with the situation on the Ruhr, and at the beginning of 1919 instructed the Komotau management to make concessions to workers and employees only if there were sufficient orders and raw material reserves to continue production profitably, but otherwise not to shrink from an open clash.[26] Since the state of orders was satisfactory and supplies of raw materials had been left over from the works' considerable engagement in the Austro-

Hungarian war effort, differences with the work-force were smoothed over and capacity was fully employed throughout 1919–20.[27]

Although the Mannesmann possessions in Czechoslovakia had not shared the ill fortune that had befallen the British and Italian subsidiaries, there remained the threat of socialization of heavy industry contained in the initial Czechoslovak government programme on the one hand, and of nationalization in the sense of Czechoslovakization (i.e. replacing German with Czechoslovak ownership and management) on the other.[28]

With regard to socialization, fears were based not only on strikes and social unrest in the country but also on the order of the Czechoslovak government requiring all firms to produce a 'liquidation balance sheet' for 1918–19, which alarmed the management of the Mannesmann combine. Businessmen were apprehensive and reluctant to provide the Czechoslovak state with the basic information which they thought was needed for socializing large industrial enterprises. However, these fears were soon dispelled as the real motivation of the government was to obtain an estimate of the Czechoslovak national wealth in preparation for applying to the Entente for a loan. At the same time as it was accepted in the Mannesmann management that the Czechoslovak government did not intend any general socialization, it was viewed with little sympathy that the government would extend its social welfare measures from mining to other industries, such as the legal enforcement of establishing welfare funds in companies by annually committing 10 per cent of net profits to reserves for that purpose.[29]

In the case of nationalization, however, tactics had to be devised by the Mannesmann headquarters together with an internal strategy to adapt to new conditions without losing control. In order to secure the ownership and control of the Komotau company, certain concessions had to be made by the Düsseldorf concern in order to comply with the requirements of the Czechoslovak nationalization legislation – above all, those obligations connected with the Nostrification Act and regulations concerning domestic joint stock companies.[30] These stipulated that the head offices of companies must be transferred to the new state if their plants were situated on its territory and that the majority of the members of a domestic company's board of directors and its audit committee had to be Czechoslovak citizens and domiciled in Czechoslovakia.[31]

Accordingly, the composition of the board of directors of the newly constituted Mannesmannröhren-Werke AG Komotau was carefully constructed to reflect on the one hand the decisive influence of the parent company on its business policy and on the other hand its new capital structure, but at the same time satisfying the laws of the host country. The company started out with a capital of Kč 30m. divided into 30,000 shares of Kč 1,000 each and in 1928 its nominal capital was increased to Kč 60m. by doubling the value of each share but leaving their number unchanged. From its foundation until the end of the independent existence of the Czechoslovak

Republic 85 per cent of the shares belonged to the Mannesmann-röhren-Werke AG of Düsseldorf. The remaining 15 per cent were, for political reasons, ceded in equal shares of 5 per cent to three of the largest Czechoslovak banks – the Živnostenská banka, the Česká eskomptní banka a úvěrní ústav [Bohemian Escompte Bank and Credit Institute] and the Česká banka Union [Bohemian Bank Union]. This was to give the company a certain Czechoslovak façade. Although the banks' shareholdings entitled them to one seat each on the board of directors, this was regarded by the Mannesmann headquarters as purely formal. By a syndicate agreement amongst the shareholders signed in 1921 the banks were bound to sell their shares only to the Mannesmannröhren-Werke and the same agreement contained a contractual declaration by the banks that they would never use their representation on the board of directors to influence the company politically.[32]

There were 11 seats on the MW-Komotau's board of directors, which were occupied with a notable continuity by the same persons representing in fixed proportions clearly defined interests. A minimum of six had to be filled by Czechoslovak citizens and this minimum was never exceeded during the company's existence. In addition to the three leading bankers (J. Bělohříbek of the Živnostenská banka, O. Feilchenfeld of the Bohemian Escompte Bank and Credit Institute and V. Schuster of the Bohemian Bank Union) a further Czech industrialist, Z. Hořovský, joined the board to represent the Komotau works' main raw materials supplier, the Pražská železářská společnost [Prague Iron Company], in which both the MW-Komotau and the banks were themselves shareholders.[33] The two remaining places were filled with the Mannesmann works' own candidates: J. Matys from the ranks of the company's executive staff and J. Scherb, a Czechoslovak citizen of German nationality who was the president of the Chamber of Commerce and Industry in Eger (Cheb) and chairman of the Mining and Foundries Employers Association in the region where the Komotau works were situated, which had a German-speaking majority. Yet, business policy and decision-making power actually lay in the hands of the five directors on the board who represented the Deutsche Bank and the German-based Mannesmann combine. They held the offices of chairman (Max Steinthal) and first deputy chairman (Heinrich Bierwes); a further two seats were taken up by Hugo von Gahlen, a joint director of the Deutsche Bank and the Düsseldorf company and H. Marcus, also a director of the Düsseldorf board and of the Wiener Bank-Verein; and lastly, one seat was reserved for the central manager of the Komotau company – Otto Klesper – who was appointed to this post by the Düsseldorf headquarters and who, as a German citizen, became domiciled in Czechoslovakia to manage the company until his retirement in 1939.

The former manager in Komotau, Fritz Rosdeck, had been recalled to join the managing board in Düsseldorf. Otto Klesper was moved from Vienna to Komotau and began, in close collaboration with the general manager at

Düsseldorf – in the early months of 1919 Nicolaus Eich, and after his death Heinrich Bierwes – to re-organize production, finance and sales, in order to equip the MW-Komotau as the combine's focus for the East Central and South-East European market. Management staff – especially tech-nicians – for the Czechoslovak company were drawn from the German headquarters, but it was also necessary to engage at least one leading Czech-speaking engineer and a certain number of Czech-speaking foremen at each of the works in Komotau and Schönbrunn. Further appointments of executives were needed to head newly established sales, accounts and legal departments at Komotau as well as to staff the secretariat which was moved from Vienna. The whole organizational plan of the Czechoslovak undertak-ing followed, as far as local conditions permitted, the management practice of the parent company. All these changes were discussed with and decided by the Düsseldorf general management – above all, managerial appointments and staffing problems generally, since personnel policy was a jealously guarded prerogative of the centre and used as one of the principal tools of influence and control over all parts of the concern.[34]

The period of reconstruction of the Czechoslovak works raised a whole complex of managerial questions regarding internal organization, administra-tion and, especially, financial control of a foreign subsidiary. During the war years prime costs in the Austrian daughter company had been calculated and reported to the head office only quarterly, which had made it difficult to ascertain the precise financial situation at short notice, or to intervene in time to reduce wastage in production, or to curtail rising administrative over-heads. As profits had soared between 1914 and 1918, uncertainties about costs did not prove to be as disturbing as at the end of the war when the possibilities of profitable employment of the works became limited. For these reasons Klesper had suggested in January 1919 that cost accounting should be simplified and systematized throughout the concern and that monthly standardized reports should be sent to the head office in Düsseldorf. Klesper's initiative was taken up by the general manager[35] and eventually a conference of works representatives (one technical manager and a head clerk from each subsidiary enterprise) was convened both to get their agreement and to instruct them before introducing a unified system of cost calculations and regular reporting. This administrative improvement facilitated compara-tive cost analyses in the head office's finance department and contributed to the strengthening of links between the central management and the subsidi-ary enterprises. Since the Komotau undertaking functioned outwardly as an independent company, internal financial reports reached Düsseldorf through personnel travelling regularly to Komotau on business. But the Düsseldorf headquarters could not carry out its own internal audit at the MW-Komotau as the Czechoslovak authorities insisted that only officially recognized Czechoslovak auditors perform this legal duty. Whilst the MW-Komotau complied with this requirement, its internal balance sheet was annually analysed with each item commented upon in minute detail by a Berlin firm of auditors who was engaged to produce full audit reports for the head office of the Mannesmann concern in Düsseldorf.[36] Vital information was thus available to the central management about all aspects of its Czechoslovak subsidiary enterprises and on this basis policy decisions were taken concerning their role in the overall business strategy of the combine. In the course of time the MW-Komotau emerged from the process of reconstruction with an organizational pattern closely resembling the multi-unit structure of the Düsseldorf parent company (cf. figs. 5.1 and 5.2).

THE GROWTH OF THE EAST CENTRAL EUROPEAN 'CONCERN WITHIN THE CONCERN'

Due to the reconstitution of the Mannesmann subsidiary in East Central Europe, part of its former international interests had been rescued by the German-headquartered company, a foothold had been maintained in the two most industrialized successor states, Czechoslovakia and Austria, and a nucleus for future multi-national expansion had once more been established. No fundamental change had taken place in the concern's long-term business policy which continued to be backward integration to secure raw material supplies for its manufacturing plants and a strategy of forward linkages to secure markets for its finished products.[37] But under the new balance of economic power prevailing in Europe, the Düsseldorf parent company in the early 1920s was restricted to realizing these aims within Germany. Conditions for expansion across national borders were, therefore, more favourable for the MW-Komotau. Hence the task of extending the multi-national activities of the combine into the Danubian economies fell to the Czechoslovak subsidiary.

At the time of changing its balance sheet from Austrian crowns to Czechoslovak crowns with an accounting year ending on 30 June 1920, the MW-Komotau consisted of two coal mines ('Julius' and 'Gottes Segen' Schacht) in the vicinity of the Komotau works, the rolling mills in Komotau and Schönbrunn and the trading company in Vienna. On that date it employed altogether 3,487 blue and white collar workers in Czechoslovakia, i.e. about 17 per cent of the total employed at the German works (20,477) of the parent company. However, its gross profits of M 37,087,300 amounted to 36 per cent of the total gross profits of M 104,228,357 shown in the Düsseldorf company's balance sheet.[38] Its importance to the centre of the German concern can hardly be doubted, as the Czechoslovak company was the largest east of Germany in the rank order of tube manufacturers in the inter-war period. When the Prodejna sdružených československých železáren [Selling Agency of the United Czechoslovak Iron Works][39] founded a national tube cartel on 1 January 1921 to replace the defunct Austro-Hungarian cartel, the position of the MW-Komotau as the leading tube

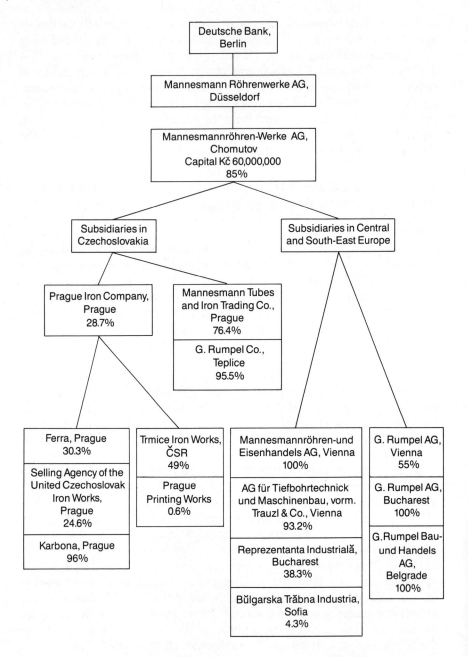

Figure 5.1. The East Central European concern of Mannesmannröhren-Werke AG, Düsseldorf, 1937. (*Sources* A. Teichova, *An Economic Background to Munich. International Business and Czechoslovakia 1918–1938*, 1974, 126; Mannesmann-Archiv, Düsseldorf.)

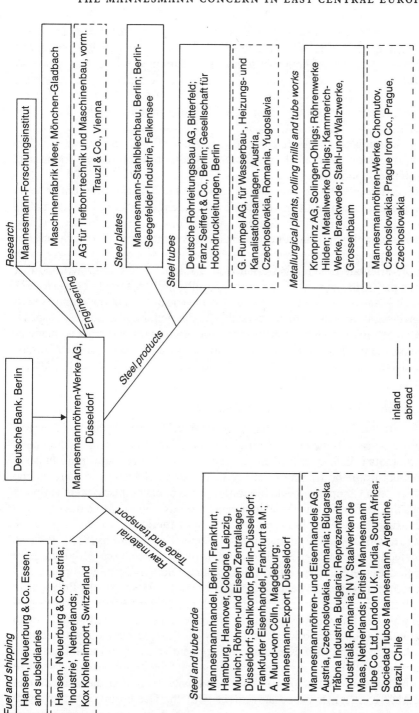

Figure 5.2. The Mannesmannröhren-Werke combine, 1937. (*Sources* A. Teichova, *An Economic Background to Munich. International Business and Czechoslovakia 1918–1938* (1974), 126; Mannesmann-Archiv, Düsseldorf; H. Koch, *75 Jahre Mannesmann 1890–1965*, Düsseldorf, 1965.)

producer was reaffirmed and its proportionate market share fixed at 48.347 per cent as against 33.548 per cent of the Witkowitz and 19.105 per cent of the Hahn works.[40] Although in terms of absolute percentages this meant an increase compared with its pre-war quota, domestic demand in the new state had shrunk to about 20–25 per cent of the former Austro-Hungarian market, while 100 per cent of the former Empire's tube production was situated on Czechoslovak territory.[41] Consequently, it became necessary to export the overwhelming part – about 70 to 80 per cent – of total output and to try to recapture under generally less favourable conditions the so-called 'traditional' markets of South-East Europe.

In order to achieve this aim, the Komotau management under Otto Klesper implemented the main lines of the parent company's business policy and set out to build a 'concern within the concern', in the process emphasizing the multi-national character of the enterprise as a whole (cf. fig. 5.1). Expansion was based on an investment strategy which was both supply-orientated and market-orientated. Table 5.1 shows the growth of direct participating investment both chronologically and territorially between 1921 and 1938 and at the same time highlights the endeavours of the Mannesmann management to gain a majority stake in the acquired companies' capital, preferably 100 per cent, to ensure control. An attempt will now be made to analyse the mechanism and to assess the measure of success of the Mannesmann enterprise's supply-orientated and market-orientated multi-national strategies.

a. Supply-orientated direct foreign investment

From the beginning the Mannesmann tube works in Bohemia and Moravia did not possess its own raw material supplies. Traditionally, the rolling mills at Komotau had drawn their requirements of steel and semi-finished products from the leading steel producer of the Habsburg Monarchy, the Prague Iron Company at Kladno, and the Schönbrunn plants were supplied from the nearby Witkowitz Mining and Foundry Works at Ostrava.

During the war the business connection of the Komotau works with the Prague Iron Co. had been uneasy after claims for damages in 1911 – because of defective steel deliveries – had led to prolonged litigation. Although these differences were finally settled out of court, relations between supplier and consumer continued to be troubled after the war.[42] However, the Prague Iron Co. lost a great deal of its former strength in the immediate post-war years[43] and was therefore willing to come to a long-term understanding with its main customer in the Czechoslovak home market. There was even more eagerness on the side of the MW-Komotau management to clear up the uncertainties connected with steel deliveries, because it had long desired to gain a stake in its chief raw material supplier. This was finally realized at the same time as the MW-Komotau reached agreement with the Czechoslovak banks about their participation in its capital. Actually MW-Komotau's agreements with the Živnostenská banka and the Bohemian Escompte Bank and Credit Institute and with the Prague Iron Co. were signed on the same day, 5 June 1921.[44] This solved the Komotau works' raw material supply problem for the whole inter-war period.

With the approval of the Czechoslovak government, the MW-Komotau bought 35,000 out of the total of 144,000 shares of the Prague Iron Co. (cf. table 5.1), but the real purchasers were the Deutsche Bank, Berlin, and the Mannesmannröhren-Werke AG, Düsseldorf.[45] In this way the Mannesmann concern took the first step in its post-war foreign expansion by acquiring a direct participating investment of 24.3 per cent in the capital of the Prague Iron Co., the third largest iron and steel producer in the Czechoslovak economy. As a result it became entitled to a quarter of the seats on the Czech company's board of directors which were taken up by Max Steinthal (Deutsche Bank), Heinrich Bierwes (MW-Düsseldorf and Deutsche Bank) and Otto Klesper (MW-Komotau).[46] In the following years until the end of the inter-war period the Mannesmann participation gradually increased to 28.7 per cent (cf. table 5.1).

Most important, the Mannesmann combine's acquisition of a quarter of the share capital of the Prague Iron Co. was linked to a long-term delivery agreement valid until 1941, the conditions of which enabled it to influence strongly the Prague enterprise's production programme and commercial policy. Under the terms of the 20-year contract, the Prague Iron Co. undertook to meet the entire raw material demands of the Komotau works which amounted to roughly a quarter of its total output of ingot and semi-finished products. Although this provided a guaranteed market for a substantial part of the Prague Iron Co.'s production, the price levels fixed in the agreement were generally lower than prime costs because they were based on the principle of 'indirect export' prices.[47] There existed, of course, the possibility of recovery on other business but the unequal association with the Mannesmann works was reflected in the Prague Iron Co.'s continuously poor economic performance. The extraordinarily favourable delivery conditions and low prices enjoyed by the MW-Komotau constituted a mechanism of profit transfers between two subsidiary enterprises of the Mannesmann concern. As a result the MW-Komotau showed steady profits during the inter-war period, in contrast to the Prague Iron Co. Its net profits in the 1920s were relatively low and in the early 1930s it did not distribute any dividends. From 1932 the Prague Iron Co. made substantial losses which persisted until the rearmament boom began in 1936.[48] Although this seemingly unsatisfactory situation might have aroused objections from the Czech bank consortium, as the other shareholders of the Prague Iron Co., these Czech banks had the company's account and as creditors they received more returns in form of interest on loans than in dividends for their shares.[49]

In 1936 when orders became plentiful and world steel prices were rising, the Prague Iron Co.'s management found its obligations to the Mannesmann

Table 5.1. DIRECT PARTICIPATING INVESTMENTS OF THE
MANNESMANNRÖHREN-WERKE AG KOMOTAU, IN
SUBSIDIARY ENTERPRISES
(percentages of subsidiaries' total capitals).

Name of subsidiary company	1921	1922	1923	June 1926
Prague Iron Co., Prague	24.3	25.7	25.7	25.7
Freistädter Stahl- und Eisenwerke AG, Freistadt	75.1	75.1	75.1	–
Mannesmannröhren- und Eisenhandelsgesellschaft, Vienna	46.0	46.0	74.0	100
Mannesmannröhren- und Eisenhandelsgesellschaft, Budapest	46.0	100	100	100
Mannesmannröhren- und Eisenhandelsgesellschaft, Brno	46.0	46.0	100	100
Mannesmannröhren- und Eisenhandelsgesellschaft, Prague	–	–	70.0	73.0
G Rumpel AG, Teplitz-Schönau	–	–	–	72.0
G Rumpel AG, Vienna	–	–	–	–
Reprezentanta Industriala SAR, Bucharest	–	–	–	–
AG für Tiefbohrtechnik und Maschinenbau, Trauzl & Co., Vienna	–	–	–	–
NV Staalverken de Maas	–	–	–	–
G Rumpel, SAR, Bucharest	–	–	–	–
G Rumpel, AG, Belgrade	–	–	–	–
Bŭlgarska Trăbna Industria, Sofia	–	–	–	–
British Mannesmann Tube Co. Ltd, London	–	–	–	–
Čapek & Reichel, Prague	–	–	–	–

Note: the number of subsidiary enterprises and the percentages of participating investments in them remained unchanged until 30 September 1938.

December 1926	1927	1929	1930	1934	Nominal capital 15 April 1935
25.7	25.7	25.7	27.52	28.7	72,000,000 Kč
–	–	–	–	–	sold
100	100	100	100	100	1,500,000 Ö sch.
100	100	100	–	–	liquidated
–	–	–	–	–	merged with Prague Co.
73.0	73.0	76.4	76.4	76.4	10,000,000 Kč
75.2	75.2	93.6	93.6	95.5	5,000,000 Kč
–	55.0	55.0	55.0	55.0	100,000 ö.Sch.
–	25.9	36.7	38.3	38.3	10,000,000 Lei
–	–	42.9	42.96	93.2	2,100,100 Ö sch.
–	–	16.7	16.7	5.8	1,000,000 hfl.
–	–	–	18.5	100	10,000,000 Lei
–	–	–	100	100	1,000,000 Dinar
–	–	–	–	4.3	10,000,000 Leva
–	–	–	–	1.775	£1,000,000
–	–	–	–	100	310,000 Kč

Source: Calculated from balance sheets of the Mannesmannröhren-Werke AG, Komotau, 1920–1938 (Mannesmann-Archiv, Düsseldorf).

works onerous and wanted to renegotiate the price clauses of the delivery agreement. But the MW-Komotau insisted on retaining its privileged rates. In order to support its Czechoslovak subsidiary the general manager of the Düsseldorf head office (since 1934, Wilhelm Zengen)[50] let it be known to the Prague Iron Co.'s manager, for tactical reasons only, that should prices increase Kladno steel could be replaced by steel from the German sister works.[51] By that time Hitler's National Socialist government had been in power in Germany for three years during which Czechoslovak-German relations had steadily deteriorated. They were particularly strained in the areas bordering Germany, including the location of the Komotau works, where the aggressiveness of the German nationalist movement – encouraged by the German Nazi Party – inside Czechoslovakia was growing. Partly because of the political situation, but mainly as a result of the difficulties which had arisen about prices, the three Czech banks which participated in the capital of the MW-Komotau made an attempt to extricate the Prague Iron Co. from its contractual commitments. They offered to exchange their Mannesmann-Komotau shares for an equivalent amount of Prague Iron Co. shares in the possession of the MW-Komotau. This would have reduced the Mannesmann concern's holding in the Prague Iron Co. and automatically cancelled the 1921 syndicate and delivery agreements.

The offer was rejected at the Mannesmann concern's headquarters because of the following considerations. First, since the Prague Iron Co. was the raw material supplier for the Komotau works, the Mannesmann participation of over 25 per cent in its capital protected tube production from either withdrawal or increasing prices of supplies. Second, the fate of the Czechoslovak subsidiary would be uncertain should either the whole or part of the Prague Iron Co. shares be exchanged for the MW-Komotau's own shares. Third, it was therefore considered vitally necessary to leave the 15 per cent participation in the hands of the Czechoslovak banks so that the enterprise in Komotau could formally continue to be regarded as not fully German-owned.[52] Following these moves, negotiations took place early in 1937 between W. Zangen of the Mannesmann head office in Düsseldorf and J. Dvořáček of the Živnostenská banka, representing the three Czechoslovak banks, which resulted in the renewal and restatement of the original agreements for a further 10 years. The renewed delivery agreement bound the Prague Iron Co. not only for a longer period than had been originally fixed, i.e. until 1947, but it tied the company even more firmly to the Mannesmann concern because by concluding a shareholding syndicate with the Živnostenská banka, the influence of the Mannesmann representatives on the board of directors of the Prague Iron Co. was strengthened.

Efforts to secure control over raw material supplies for the Schönbrunn works of the Mannesmann concern were less successful. Until 1921 the Vitkovice Iron Works had been the main supplier of steel to the Schönbrunn plants. In order to end its dependence on outside deliveries the MW-

Komotau, through a loan from its German headquarters, acquired 17.1 per cent of the capital of the Freistädter Stahl- und Eisenwerke AG (cf. table 5.1), situated in Freistadt (Frýštat) within easy reach of the Schönbrunn rolling mill.[53] The iron and steel works consisted of modern well-equipped plant with an annual capacity of 100,000 tons of steel, 60,000 tons of semi-finished material and 10,000 tons of steel plate. In addition, it brought into the MW-Komotau three trading companies situated in Brno, Vienna and Budapest. All these firms were given the name Mannesmannröhren- und Eisenhandels-Aktiengesellschaft.[54]

However, the Freistadt iron and steel works could not survive competition from the powerful Czechoslovak iron and steel producers. They fell victim to the systematic drive of 'The Big Three', of which the Vitkovice Works was the strongest, to dominate the domestic cartel – the Selling Agency of the United Czechoslovak Iron Works.[55] By 1923 the MW-Komotau was forced to sell its participation in the Freistädter Stahl- und Eisenwerke-AG to the cartel, which shut down its plants. Steel deliveries to the Schönbrunn works had thereafter to be secured by a delivery agreement with the Vitkovice Iron Works valid for 10 years in the first instance.[56] This arrangement lasted throughout the inter-war period. Only the trading firms of the Freistadt company remained in the possession of the Mannesmann concern.

In pursuing a supply-orientated investment strategy in Czechoslovakia, the Mannesmann combine succeeded in securing a raw material base for its chief works in Komotau by participating directly in the supplier's company capital and by integrating it contractually and commercially into its business structure. However, in the case of its smaller plants in Moravia, it had to abandon this strategy and satisfy itself with a long-term delivery agreement.

b. Market-orientated direct foreign investment

Even under the unstable economic conditions of the post-war period in Central and South-East Europe, the Mannesmann products gave the company an advantage in pursuing a market-orientated investment strategy at home and abroad. The initial post-war investment, apart from the reconstruction of the subsidiary MW-Komotau itself, was designed to secure raw material supplies for the manufacture of finished tube products in Czechoslovakia and was made by the Düsseldorf parent company. However, further business expansion across national frontiers in the East Central and South-East European area was financed wholly from earnings of the Czechoslovak subsidiary.[57]

The MW-Komotau's investment strategy to hold and gain markets can be divided into three interconnected parts: first, to modernize and extend plant – the introduction of new machinery, the rationalization of production and the broadening of the product range of its main works; second, to expand the manufacture of certain product groups in newly-acquired enterprises to enable it to serve a wider market; and third, to extend its sales organizations.

The first line of expansion through investment in new technology can only be referred to in general terms from the present point of view which is concerned with the relationship between the head office and the East Central European subsidiary of the Mannesmann concern. However, it needs to be emphasized that any extensions of plant or office buildings, technological improvements or innovations anywhere in the concern needed the head-quarters' approval, because there the framework of the entire concern's production programme as well as the sources and methods of financing were decided. The head office did not, as a rule, provide funds for new technology or buildings; at most, equipment was shifted between sister works at cost price.[58] But the MW-Komotau was granted resources for both building projects and new machinery out of its own gross profits. Its most effective investment in technical innovation during the inter-war period was the construction of a tube reaming mill in Komotau in 1928 which made the production of light seamless tubes up to a diameter of 500mm, and later up to 800mm, possible. So far this particular size had been produced only by welding: seamless tubes had been manufactured up to a diameter of only 300mm.[59] With the success of the tube reaming mill at Komotau, the Düsseldorf management decided to build a similar rolling mill at the Mannesmann works, Rath on the Ruhr, which began production in 1933.[60] This example shows that experiences were not only communicated from the centre downwards but that the reverse mechanism also existed.

As the largest of the Danubian countries' producers, the Komotau works manufactured a wide range of tubes and related products (seamless tubes from 5 to 800mm, welded tubes of smaller dimensions, cold-drawn tubes, masts of all kinds, drilling tubes, steel bottles and other special tube products). Production at the Schönbrunn works amounted to about one-third of the volume of output in Komotau and it specialized mainly in manufacturing gas pipes. In the early 1920s the two original works in Czechoslovakia experienced two periods of rapid growth interrupted by a deflationary slump in 1921 when the Czechoslovak crown was over-valued, which hampered exports. The first period, referred to earlier, was when the works were involved in the post-war reconstruction and renewal boom. In addition their output was augmented as they gave a helping hand to their German parent company in evading the Versailles Treaty restrictions.[61] In the second period they fulfilled orders for the German concern when its works were shut down in 1923 during the French occupation of the Ruhr.[62] This is evident from the pattern of their exports in which deliveries to Germany figure prominently (cf. table 5.2). In the mid-1920s the MW-Komotau began to expand production beyond its original works.

The second line of expansion pursued by the MW-Komotau was aided by the generally rising rate of investment and production in the Czechoslovak economy from about 1923/24. The company broadened its production programme to capture a greater share of the market in the successor states by investing directly in manufacturing enterprises. Accordingly in 1925 a 72 per cent participation was acquired in the old-established and reputable firm of G. Rumpel A.G. für Wasserbau-, Heizungs- und Kanalisationsanlagen in Teplitz-Schönau (Teplice-Šanov) in Bohemia, which specialized in laying water supply systems. It was mainly employed in executing water supply projects for towns.[63] In 1927 a 55 per cent share in the firm of the same name in Vienna was obtained[64] and later its branches in Bucharest and Belgrade were brought into the MW-Komotau concern as well. All the Rumpel companies were directed to extend their product range from water pipes to radiators, tanks and welded pipes. The Belgrade company became the leading supplier of these products in the Yugoslav market. A further investment brought the production of oil pipes within the orbit of the Mannesmann combine, when in 1928 shares amounting to 42.9 per cent of the capital of the AG für Tiefbohrtechnik und Maschinenbau, vormals Trauzl & Co., in Vienna, were bought. Its works in Strebersdorf manufactured seamless drilling and conducting tubes.[65] Although the world economic crisis dramatically interrupted Czechoslovakia's economic advance, the MW-Komotau continued with its market-orientated investments. In 1931 the manufacture of cold-drawn tubes was expanded by taking over 100 per cent of the firm Čapek & Reichel in Prague, whose capacity was later (in 1937) used to fulfil defence orders for aircraft tubes.[66] Step by step the MW-Komotau increased its direct participating investments until it held a majority of shares and thus undisputed control of each manufacturing enterprise in its possession (cf. table 5.1).

To complete the picture of building 'a concern within the concern', the third line of expansion into market-orientated investment needs to be discussed; this is connected with the acquisition of trading companies. However, the whole problem of the inter-war European market, particularly in iron and steel products, was influenced decisively by cartels. So in the case of the Mannesmann concern, the functioning or breakdowns of the tube cartel shaped its sales policy and, therefore, also that of its Central European subsidiary. Indeed, the Mannesmann-Werke AG, Düsseldorf, played a leading role in the German and the Continental Tube Cartel of the inter-war period.

Before 1918 all exports of the Austrian Mannesmann works were managed through Düsseldorf. This practice was carried over into the inter-war period. Only sales on their formerly domestic market – the so-called 'original territory' (angestammtes Absatzgebiet') – were left as before in the hands of the MW-Komotau and their Viennese agency. As a member of the reconstructed tube cartel of Czechoslovak producers the MW-Komotau did not originally have its own sales organization but observed the cartel's ruling to use the services of wholesalers favoured by the cartel to cover demand in both the home market of Czechoslovakia and the markets of the successor states.[67] Since, however, the formerly compact market of the Austro-Hungarian

Empire was split up into individual states surrounded by tariff walls and divided by antagonistic national economic policies, a fierce competitive struggle broke out with foreign producers who had until 1918 respected the tube cartel's rules on mutual market protection. In particular the German tube manufacturers penetrated into the former Austro-Hungarian as well as the Yugoslav and Polish markets, where they rapidly established their own sales agencies in the new capital cities.[68] The German cartel had collapsed and, unlike the Czechoslovak manufacturers, the German producers had not reconstituted it. There was thus no partner with whom the Czechoslovak cartel could negotiate a market agreement until 1925 when the Continental Tube Cartel began to function.

In order to hold on to their old market and to intensify selling activity in the successor states, the MW-Komotau management reacted to this situation by establishing its own sales organization. Its network of trading companies was built up during the first decade of the inter-war period. It arose out of firms in Vienna and Budapest which had remained in the possession of the MW-Komotau as a legacy from its abortive supply-orientated investment in the Freistädter iron and steel works, thus leaving it with a market-orientated direct foreign investment in 1921. Two further companies in Prague and Brno were added to these foreign subsidiaries between 1921 and 1923 which were later merged. In due course the Vienna company expanded its selling activity through further branches in Graz and Salzburg. All of these trading firms were reorganized as joint stock companies under a common name, the Mannesmannröhren-und Eisenhandels AG. Table 5.1 shows the progressive acquisition of their capital as they were fully absorbed into the Mannesmann concern.[69] The MW-Komotau was allocated a certain share of the important Romanian market by the parent company and participated with it in the Reprezentanta Industrială Societata Romana, Bucharest (cf. table 5.1). All other exports from the MW-Komotau were administered and distributed through the office of the Mannesmannröhren-Werke in Düsseldorf, where until 1935 the headquarters of the German and Continental Tube Cartel was also situated.

Exports were all-important for the MW-Komotau's business activity because of the narrowness of the Czechoslovak home market. Table 5.2 shows the territorial distribution of the company's sales in percentages and reveals that 70 per cent of its output was regularly exported. While deliveries to the domestic market vacillated around 30 per cent, the composition of export markets changed fundamentally between 1929 and 1937 (cf. table 5.2). This reflected the fall in exports from Czechoslovakia to the South-East European states generally, but this was compensated by a rise in exports to other more distant markets. The causes for this shift in the direction of Czechoslovak foreign trade can be found mainly in the impact of the world economic crisis and the subsequent policy of bilateral trade agreements between National Socialist Germany and the South-East European states.

In the case of the Mannesmann concern, yet another factor impinged on the Czechoslovak business operations connected with the breakdown of the Continental Tube Cartel in 1935. Although many cartels fell apart during the crisis, the Tube Cartel survived. It only broke up after the Saar plebiscite in 1935 when the Bous works were re-incorporated into Germany and became part (indeed, like all its other German works, a department) of the Mannesmann concern in Düsseldorf. As a result the French and German tube producers failed to reach agreement about the re-division of quotas.[70] The MW-Komotau was affected through the subsequent refusal of the

Table 5.2. DELIVERIES TO HOME MARKET AS COMPARED WITH DESTINATION OF EXPORTS of the Mannesmannröhren-Werke AG Komotau (Czechoslovakia), in percentages.

Destination of deliveries	1923*	1926	1929	1937	Value of turnover 1923 in Kč
Home market		29.6	30	28	
Export:	47				75,321,034.70
Successor states		18.5	16	4	
Romania		22.1	11	2	
Poland		4.5			
Other countries	41	25.3	36	66	65,615,134.58
Export:					
Düsseldorf	12		7		19,546,282.35
Total	100	100	100	100	160,482,451.63

* No separate item for Czechoslovak home market given.

Source: Calculated from financial reports of MW-Komotau to the head office in Düsseldorf (Mannesmann-Archiv, Düsseldorf).

German Tube Cartel to administer the sale of tube products from Czechoslovakia. Accordingly the head office in Düsseldorf had also to abandon the administration of exports on behalf of their own subsidiary. For a short period, paradoxically, the parent and daughter companies competed on the world market until the direction of MW-Komotau's trading companies and sales agents was channelled into the countries of North-West Europe (Holland, Britain, Denmark, Norway and Sweden) and to more distant overseas markets (Argentina, India, China, South Africa). Freed from cartel restrictions, the Czechoslovak company was able to increase its exports from a quota of 20,000 tons in the last year of the cartel to more than double this amount within barely two years.[71] Due to increased production, its costs fell and sales activity became substantially cheaper than under the cartel, although export prices had to be reduced considerably to be competitive. In this period without quotas or market regulations of an international cartel – the domestic cartel remained intact – the Czechoslovak company reached its

Table 5.3. DELIVERIES OF THE MANNESMANNRÖHREN-WERKE AG, KOMOTAU (1937 compared with 1929), in tons.

	1937 Total turnover into:	1937 Total turnover (monthly average) into:	Highest monthly total (December 1937)	1929 Total turnover into:
Inland	19,851.2	1,654.3	1,499.7	21,691.7
Export:				
Successor states	2,869.6	239.1	278.5	11,372.5
Romania	1,413.5	117.8	118.5	8,046.0
Other countries	45,964.5	3,830.4	6,180.5	25,347.9
	50,247.6	4,187.3	6,577.5	44,766.4
Export: Düsseldorf				5,119.6
Total	70,098.8	5,841.6	8,077.2	71,577.7

Source: Financial reports of MW-Komotau to head office in Düsseldorf (Mannesmann-Archiv, Düsseldorf).

highest output and delivery figures of the inter-war period, comparable only with the other peak year of 1929 (cf. table 5.3).

In the second half of the 1930s the market-orientated direct investments of the MW-Komotau paid off not only for the East Central European section of the concern but also for the whole Mannesmann concern. Ironically, the German headquarters, as an export-orientated business, was apprehensive about the autarkic policy of the Hitler Government but had integrated its domestic works into recovery and rearmament at home. However, through its Czechoslovak subsidiary it was able to participate in defence orders at its Komotau works[72] and to benefit from international trade in the clearing area, so bypassing the foreign exchange restrictions imposed in Germany on the eve of the Second World War.

Surveying the methods and mechanisms of 'building a concern within a concern' it can be concluded that they resulted in a considerably larger multi-national structure in the East Central and South-East European region at the end of the inter-war period than at its beginning. Yet, the question of profit transfers needs to be investigated in order to define the multi-national nature of the concern more closely.

THE MECHANISM OF PROFIT TRANSFERS

As mentioned in another context, the post-1918 reconstruction of the Mannesmann interests in East Central Europe began with two types of direct investment by the Düsseldorf parent company.[73] In the first instance funds were provided to finance the transfer of its subsidiary's head office from Vienna to Komotau and change its legal status from a private to a public joint stock company. At the end of these transactions the German concern became the reorganized firm's majority shareholder. In the second instance, investments were made to penetrate the iron and steel industry of Czechoslovakia and gain a stake in the companies supplying raw material to its daughter works. The sums involved in these investments were debited by the head office in Düsseldorf to the MW-Komotau at an annual rate of interest of 7 per cent.[74] From the point of view of the subsidiary company, the headquarters in Germany acted as its banker, providing it with long-term credits. Therefore, as an investor the parent company was legally entitled to receive dividends, and as a creditor it could claim regular interest payments. From the point of view of business strategy the participating investments were made in Czechoslovak crowns and paid at a comparatively favourable exchange rate in rapidly depreciating German Marks.[75] Accordingly the Mannesmann concern expanded its assets, as well as claims to future returns, in one of the relatively stable European currencies.

The performance of the MW-Komotau between 1920 and 1937 is recorded in table 5.4. It shows a constantly growing volume of business, reflected in both the mounting totals of annual balance and the rising number and value of participating investments (cf. tables 5.1 and 5.4). Throughout the inter-war period no losses were incurred, although at the trough of the world economic crisis in 1932 and 1933 net profits fell drastically and no dividends were declared. In those years the parent company registered losses on manufacturing which were partially made good by income from participating investments.[76] Dividends of the MW-Komotau were distributed on the basis of net profits. They consisted of a basic dividend of 4 per cent and, as can be seen from table 5.4, were in every case augmented by a superdividend payment varying between 2 and 26 per cent. Of the total dividend distributed 85 per cent was transferred regularly to the head office in Düsseldorf, after deducting Czechoslovak taxes. From 1921 Czechoslovakia imposed a 10 per cent tax on exported dividend payments which did not exceed 15 per cent of the nominal value of shares, but progressive taxation was applied to exported dividends above this level. Consequently it was the policy of the Düsseldorf management not to transfer to Germany more than 15 per cent in officially declared dividends so as to avoid higher taxation, but to apply alternative mechanisms of profit transfers within the concern. Since profits were rising steeply between 1923 and 1929 (cf. gross and net profits in table 5.4) the heads of both managements (O. Klesper for Komotau and H. Bierwes for Düsseldorf) deliberated in 1926 about the most favourable way of transferring higher dividends to the head office but at the same time staying within the basic tax band. In order to achieve this, it was decided to double the value of shares of MW-Komotau by releasing funds from the company's own

Table 5.4. GROWTH OF THE 'CONCERN WITHIN THE CONCERN': indicators of the economic performance of the Mannesmannröhren-Werke AG, Komotau,* based on internal balance sheets, 1920–37 (in Kč).

Closing date of balance sheet	Total balance	Income from sales[†]	Gross profit[†]
30 June 1920[‡]	111,897,587.05	31,563,570.69	
1921	208,317,834.68	52,906,384.79	37,087,300.00
1922	165,007,774.93		16,810,728.57
1923	140,421,545.57		15,885,607.30
1924	164,753,711.63		11,496,742.12
1925	147,561,528.59		
1926	133,425,879.77	42,367,816.70	27,981,482.63
31 Dec. 1926	197,336,097.57		21,158,431.56
1927	238,288,236.87		34,117,326.19
1928	247,386,254.70	55,004,885.95	43,290,678.45
1929	262,109,490.10	69,875,811.15	44,653,665.65
1930	260,486,964.55	48,029,239.40	37,404,535.75
1931	267,677,871.65	43,484,759.20	24,730,917.70
1932	271,977,175.25		19,577,647.20
1933	274,138,428.95		18,578,995.75
1934	273,220,823.05		20,073,962.95
1935[‖]	216,650,857.15		13,118,669.50
1936	214,823,106.60		25,110,460.55
1937	247,684,570.75		38,320,031.50

* Nominal capital of the MW-Komotau until 31 Dec. 1926 = 30,000,000 Kč; from 1927 to 1937 = 60,000,000 Kč.
† Intermittant information because of incomplete material in the Mannesmann-Archiv, Düsseldorf.
‡ Opening balance sheet in Kč.
§ Includes 36,048,000 Kč, the value of the Freistädter iron and steel works which were sold to the Vitkovice Iron Works in July 1921, according to cartel agreement.
¶ Note in balance sheet of 1932 that accumulated dividends from participating investment amounting to 12,624,000 Kč were booked under reserves. Until 1932 dividends from participating investments were transferred to 'Reserves'.
‖ Restabilization balance sheet after devaluation of the Czechoslovak crown by 30%.
Source: Compiled from balance sheets of the Mannesmannröhren-Werke AG, Komotau (Mannesmann-Archiv, Düsseldorf).

accumulated reserves.[77] In the following years larger sums could legally be transferred to Germany without exceeding the limit of 15 per cent of MW-Komotau's capital in dividends. The mechanism of dividend payments was the least problematical way of transferring profits across national borders.

Among the methods of profit transfers within the multi-national concern, several other channels were used to employ the earnings of the MW-Komotau. One important channel led through the utilization of gross profits.

Net profit	Dividends in %	Book value of participating investment[†]	Dividends from participating investment[†]	Net profits in % of gross profit
5,161,120.30	20			
8,374,369.33	30	87,081,699.57[§]	2,558,290.00	23
2,537,374.54		45,457,655.00	2,584,610.00	15
2,439,283.62		50,644,251.40		15
6,266,592.23	10	40,979,589.85		54
9,095,905.58	10	40,620,090.55		
11,585,795.47	15	39,506,540.75		41
11,554,256.33	7.5	57,697,118.55		
7,021,409.01	10	58,496,876.57		20
11,612,172.06	15		3,748,082.55	27
14,782,951.15	15	63,767,249.70	4,132,570.00	33
8,391,751.40	15	70,004,004.40	4,921,529.65	22
4,363,335.60	6	77,015,244.55	6,066,500.00	18
200,191.20		77,226,839.50	1,429,757.00[¶]	1
211,393.45		77,265,646.00		1
4,118,762.90	6	77,612,024.20		20
630,808.55		37,055,477.35		5
4,025,382.45	6	36,826,317.35		16
11,853,711.10	10	35,354,515.40		31

One can hardly fail to notice the striking gap between gross and net profits, when surveying the company's financial results in table 5.4. Only in four out of 18 years did net profits amount to over 30 per cent of gross profits (1924, 1926, 1929 and 1937); otherwise net profits, as a percentage of gross profits, varied between 15 and 27 per cent and fell to 1 per cent and 5 per cent in the dividendless years of 1932, 1933 and 1935. Even in those meagre years the company's gross profits were relatively considerable (cf. table 5.4). The reason for the discrepancy between net and gross profits lies in the headquarters' policy of utilizing gross profits within the framework of the concern. A part of gross profits was transferred annually to the head office as either a contribution of Kč 10m. or as a commission of 10 per cent on MW-Komotau's total turnover.[78] Another part of gross profits represented the source of MW-Komotau's further direct investments in Czechoslovakia and in South-East Europe (cf. table 5.1).[79] For, barring the initial outlay of the Mannesmann centre at Düsseldorf, all other subsequent investments in East Central and South-East Europe were financed out of the Czechoslovak subsidiary's earnings, except for the joint investment in the Reprezentanta Industrială SAR, Bucharest, placed in Romania in 1927 (cf. table 5.1).[80]

Further parts of gross profits, together with returns from the acquired participating investments, were ploughed back into the reserves of the MW-Komotau.[81]

Capital thus accumulated in reserves played a crucial role in inter-concern profit transfers. On the one hand, such reserves were directed to finance the subsidiary manufacturing and trading enterprises of the MW-Komotau who acted as their banker and guarantor.[82] On the other hand, accumulated capital of the MW-Komotau was directed into investments on behalf of the parent company, such as for example the purchase out of MW-Komotau funds of RM 2.5m. worth of shares of the Kronprinz AG für Metallindustrie, Solingen-Ohligs, in 1935. The sole purpose of this transaction was to transfer earnings from Komotau to Düsseldorf, as the acquired shares remained in the hands of the German headquarters and the voting right they carried was exercised by the Mannesmannröhren-Werke AG, Düsseldorf. Actually the Kronprinz shares did not appear in any of the MW-Komotau's participation accounts but were accounted for as a direct participating investment of the parent company (cf. fig. 5.1).[83] Similarly, MW-Komotau reserves contributed to the loans and investments of the German headquarter's venture in Britain.[84]

A memorandum of the Düsseldorf head office on the advantages of the MW-Komotau for the purposes of the German concern written at the turn of 1937 and 1938 by the head of the Düsseldorf finance department, von der Tann, states that between 1924 and 1935 the concern's headquarters received c. Kč 102m. from dividends and other forms of financial transfers.[85]

Between 1935 and 1938 National Socialist Germany constituted an ever-increasing threat to Czechoslovakia's national security and independence. In the economic sphere suspicion and distrust was fostered through the NSDAP's foreign organization, particularly amongst Germans living in the border areas of Czechoslovakia, and through the Henlein movement among the so-called Sudeten Germans. As a result of Hjalmar Schacht's 'New Plan', Czechoslovak claims in Germany had been turned into frozen accounts (Sperrmark), although Czechoslovakia belonged to the multi-clearing states. Yet, during the world economic crisis the Czechoslovak government had also introduced exchange controls administered by the Czechoslovak National Bank. In the case of profit transfers to Germany the Czechoslovak National Bank stipulated that dividends should be paid to German owners of Czechoslovak shares in Sperrmarks released from Czechoslovakia's frozen accounts in Berlin and not in free exchange from Prague. These regulations referred also to profit transfers from the MW-Komotau. However, through interventions and special applications to the Exchange Control Office in Prague half of the 1934 dividends were transferred in free exchange and in the next years the full amount of dividends was transferred to the head office in Düsseldorf in free exchange through the good offices of the Živnostenská banka.[86] It was received with great satisfaction at the parent company's head office that dividends had passed normally through clearing for, on the one hand, this gave them negotiable foreign exchange which was very scarce in Germany, and on the other hand, saved the Düsseldorf company a 30 per cent loss which it would have suffered had the dividend payments gone through compensatory channels.[87] Under the prevailing strict exchange controls in National Socialist Germany the concern's headquarters was able to use its Czechoslovak subsidiary as a means of acquiring scarce foreign exchange.

Political tensions continued to rise. During 1936 the anti-Czechoslovak propaganda campaign in Germany got under way, accompanied by rising militancy on the part of nationalistic Germans living in the border areas of Bohemia and Moravia. Under these pressures more comprehensive national defence legislation was introduced by the Czechoslovak parliament. It empowered the Czechoslovak military authorities to draw up a list of enterprises designated as vital for the defence of the Czechoslovak state. The MW-Komotau was included in this list and this caused irritation in Düsseldorf as well as fears of more stringent Czechoslovak government controls. These were to a certain extent justified because in accordance with the National Defence Law, the military administration were to issue passes to personnel employed in undertakings of national importance, official permission had to be granted to employ foreign nationals, and special approval had to be sought for the appointment of foreign members to the boards of directors of such listed companies.[88] It had been the Mannesmann headquarters' consistent policy to keep its staff in Czechoslovakia overwhelmingly German and to place control exclusively in the hands of German managers and directors appointed from Düsseldorf. With the advent of the Hitler government in Germany, policies of this kind were used as a political instrument in pursuing its nationalistic and racialist aims. This was also reflected in pressures from government institutions and NSDAP offices on the Mannesmann concern. From 1934, when Wilhelm Zangen replaced the retiring Heinrich Bierwes as general manager at the Düsseldorf headquarters, the company's German-orientated policy in Komotau became increasingly political and thus was pursued – intentionally or unintentionally – as part of Germany's general National Socialist foreign policy towards Czechoslovakia, particularly in the areas of the Czechoslovak state inhabited by a German-speaking population. In reality the new Czechoslovak defence legislation did not present any special problems for the MW-Komotau's management, as permits were granted for German nationals working in the enterprise and official approval was given to the new appointments of German directors to the company's board in 1937.[89] However, it was thought in the Mannesmann concern's headquarters that, among other unwelcome interferences, the Czechoslovak authorities kept a more stringent watch on profit transfers and that under the growing strain of political tensions there existed a potential danger of nationalization.

The unsettled political developments coincided with preparations by the Czechoslovak Ministry of Finance to impose a special tax of 15 per cent on dividend payments abroad exceeding 5 per cent of a joint stock company's nominal capital.[90] A similar situation had occurred 10 years earlier, in 1926, which had been met by the concern's headquarters' decision to double the MW-Komotau's capital out of its own reserves.[91] This had made it possible to remit higher dividends to Germany at the basic level of Czechoslovak taxation. By 1937 the MW-Komotau had again accumulated comparatively large reserves of which Kč 40m. could freely be dispensed. At that time the question debated by the general management in Düsseldorf was 'How to transfer a higher rate of return on the Czechoslovak subsidiary's capital to Germany without overtly increasing the percentage of dividends declared for distribution?' Since the new Czechoslovak tax law exempted dividend payments out of company reserves, Wilhelm Zangen decided to offer the free reserve of Kč 40m to the MW-Komotau's shareholders, but to convert the thus officially declared dividends into a long-term loan to the MW-Komotau at an annual rate of interest of $7\frac{1}{2}$ per cent. By this mechanism the shareholders became creditors and were, therefore, entitled – in addition to a dividend within the lowest tax limits – to receive regular interest payments on a total capital of Kč 100m (e.g. total nominal capital = Kč 60m. + credit = Kč 40m)[92]. Consequently, the Mannesmannröhren-Werke AG, Düsseldorf, could draw higher returns from its Czechoslovak subsidiary and transfer them to Germany in urgently needed free foreign currency. In addition, Wilhelm Zangen argued that as a large creditor the parent company's claims on its subsidiary could be maintained even if the Czechoslovak authorities were to nationalize the MW-Komotau by enforced purchase of its shares.[93]

In the event the German-Czechoslovak dispute in the border regions of Bohemia and Moravia was settled unexpectedly in National Socialist Germany's favour by the Munich Agreement of 30 September 1938. The Düsseldorf headquarters acted quickly and made forceful and successful representations to the German Foreign Office and the military authorities that its works at Komotau and Schönbrunn should be included in the section of territories ceded to Germany which were to be immediately occupied by German troops.[94] When this was accomplished the relationship and, above all, the control mechanisms between the Mannesmann concern's headquarters and the subsidiary concern in East Central Europe changed fundamentally, because its multi-national character disappeared at the same time as the national boundaries between them were erased.

CONCLUSION

An attempt has been made to show and analyse the development of the East Central and South-East European multi-national expansion within the Mannesmann German-headquartered concern during the inter-war period.

The extension of the MW-Komotau's participating investments across national borders is quantitatively recorded in table 5.1, while the rising value and, in certain years, also the returns from subsidiary manufacturing and trading enterprises can be seen from table 5.4. Starting in 1920–1 with one sales office in Vienna, at the time of the last full accounting year as a joint stock company in the independent Czechoslovak state, i.e. 1937, the Mannesmannröhren-Werke AG, Komotau, participated – in addition to its original works and mines – in the capital of seven manufacturing and eight trading companies in Czechoslovakia, Austria, Hungary, Romania, Bulgaria, Holland and Britain. Employment figures rose from an average of 3,000 in the works and mines in Czechoslovakia between 1921 and 1937 to a total – for the whole group of the MW-Komotau – of 5,248 in 1937 (cf. table 5.5). Thus 30–40 per cent of the total number employed between 1933 and

Table 5.5. GROWTH OF THE 'CONCERN WITHIN THE CONCERN': figures of employment, turnover and output of the Mannesmannröhren-Werke AG Komotau, 1921–37.*

| Closing date of balance sheet | No. of employees (white and blue collar workers) | | | Total turnover (value in Kč) | Total output (in tons) |
	(a) Works & mines	(b) Subsidiary trading and manufacturing companies	(a) + (b)		
30 June 1921	3558				
1922	3312				
1923	3332			160,482,451.63	
1924			3527		
1925	2483				
1926				177,491,375.31	44,659.4
31 Dec. 1927	3000	347	3347		
1928	3368				
1929	3496				71,577.7
1930	2936			181,384,497.65	45,000
1931	2811			137,387,197.10	33,000
1932				83,500,000.00	20,500
1933	2656	754	3410		
1934	2613	726	3339		31,000
1935	2612	836	3448		48,000
1936	2921	971	3892		
1937			5248		70,098.8

* Intermittent information because of incomplete material in the Mannesmann-Archiv, Düsseldorf.

Source: As for table 5.4, and *Compass*, Čechoslovakei, relevant years for figures of employment in works and mines.

1937 consisted of blue and white collar workers in the subsidiary companies (cf. also table 5.5). In order to give some provisional quantitative indication of the proportions between the parent company's magnitude and that of the East Central European subsidiary, table 5.6 was constructed from certain balance sheet items. It shows that on the basis of a very small percentage of nominal capital in terms of the parent company's nominal joint stock capital, the MW-Komotau remained on average at about 15–17 per cent of its headquarters' employment figures, net profits and total balances. However, in comparison with the Düsseldorf parent company, its proportionate share of participating investments rose from nil in 1921 (i.e. 30 June 1921) to 30 per

Table 5.6. MANNESMANNRÖHREN-WERKE AG, KOMOTAU, in percentages of its parent company, the Mannesmannröhren-Werke AG, Düsseldorf, on the basis of selected balance sheet items for 1921, 1925, 1930 and 1937.*

Balance sheet item	1921	1925	1930	1937
	%	%	%	%
Total balance		10	13	
Gross profit	36		12	
Net profit	12	41	13	18
Book value of participating investment		21	$27\frac{1}{2}$	30
Total no. of employees	17	9	15	17.4
Nominal capital		3	4	

* Uncompleted sample.

Source: Comparative calculations from balance sheets of both companies; rate of exchange of Kč according to quotations on Berlin Stock Exchange (Mannesmann-Archiv, Düsseldorf), and *Statistická ročenka Protektorátu Čechy a Marava* (Prague, 1941), 'Doplněk za bývalou Československou republiku', 212–13.

cent of the total book value of participations shown in the MW-Düsseldorf's balance sheet at the closing date of 31 December 1937 (cf. table 5.6). This only emphasizes the multi-national structure of the concern extending into East Central and South-East Europe, as the parent company's investments in the inter-war period were mainly placed inside Germany (cf. fig. 5.2). The majority of the acquired German firms did not remain on the company accounts as share investments for long, because they were, as a rule, incorporated as departments into the multi-unit structure of the German concern. Thus, although the strategy of expansion in the parent company's home country proceeded essentially on multi-unit lines, it was conducted on multi-national lines mainly through the subsidiary company in Czecho- slovakia until the Munich Agreement and the dismemberment of the inter-war Czechoslovak Republic.

Notes

* This paper represents a case study based upon material collected during a research project on 'Multi-national companies in East Central Europe in the inter-war period' supported by the Social Science Research Council, which is gratefully acknowledged here. At the same time I should like to thank the archivist of the Mannesmann-Archiv in Düsseldorf, Dr Lutz Hatzfeld, for the help he extended to me and the many interesting discussions we had during my work there.

1. H. Koch, *75 Jahre Mannesmann 1890–1965* (Düsseldorf, 1965), 46.
2. *Ibid.*, 225.
3. P. von Strandmann, *Unternehmenspolitik und Unternehmensführung. Der Dialog zwischen Aufsichtsrat und Vorstand bei Mannesmann 1900 bis 1919* (Düsseldorf-Vienna, 1978).
4. Mannesmann-Archiv (MA), MA-M13001, Bericht der Mannesmannröhren-Werke, Düsseldorf, über das Geschäftsjahr 1912/13.
5. Koch, *op. cit.*, 85.
6. MA-M16019, Elaborat Beteiligungen Komotau.
7. MA-M16010, Geschichte-Klesper.
8. Estimated from balance sheet of the Mannesmannröhren-Werke (MW), Düsseldorf, for the year ending 30 June 1913: MA-M13001.
9. *Ibid.*
10. P. Hertner, 'Deutsches Kapital in Italien: die "Società Tubi Mannesmann" in Dalmine bei Bergamo, 1906–1916', *Zeitschrift für Unternehmensgeschichte* (1977), 190–1.
11. Koch, *op. cit.*, 86.
12. MA-M13001, Bericht . . . 1912/13.
13. MA-M13001, Bericht der MW-Düsseldorf über das Geschäftsjahr 1918/19.
14. G. D. Feldman and H. Homburg, *Industrie und Inflation* (Hamburg, 1977), 78, 130.
15. MA-M13001, Bericht der MW-Düsseldorf über das Geschäftsjahr 1919/20.
16. Koch, *op. cit.*, 116.
17. P. Hertner, 'Deutsches Kapital in Italien: die "Società Tubi Mannesmann" in Dalmine bei Bergamo, 1906–1916'

(2. Teil), *Zeitschrift für Unternehmensgeschichte* (1978), 67.
18. Otto Klesper began his career at the works in Remscheid in 1890 and worked his way through various departments of the concern until he was appointed business manager in the Società Tubi Mannesmann in Dalmine. In 1917 he was moved to Vienna as director. From there he was entrusted with the management of the MW-Komotau, promoted to central director in 1924 and general director in 1937, retired in 1939. Thus he was a man who came up from the ranks of the company to hold managerial positions.
19. MA-M16053, Prüfungsbericht der Deutschen Treuhand-Gesellschaft, Berlin, 1919/20. Also MA-M16053, Bericht der MW-Komotau über das Geschäftsjahr 1919/20.
20. MA-M16063, f. 293f.
21. A. Teichova, *An Economic Background to Munich. International Business and Czechoslovakia 1918–1938* (1974), 102.
22. MA-M16053, Prüfungsbericht . . . 1919/20.
23. MA-M16063, Brief Rosdecks an Vorstand in Düsseldorf, 5 Dec. 1919.
24. MA-M16053, Prüfungsbericht der Deutschen Treuhand-Gesellschaft, Berlin, and General-Bilanz der MW-Komotau, 1919/20 and 1920/21; MA-M13001, General-Bilanz der MW-Düsseldorf, 30 June 1920 and 30 June 1921.
25. MA-M16063, MW-Komotau's reports to and correspondence with headquarters in Düsseldorf, 1918–19.
26. MA-M16063, Eich to Rosdeck, 10 June 1919.
27. MA-M16063, Niederschrift von Besprechung in Komotau, 9–14 Jan. 1920.
28. Teichova, *op. cit.*, 98.
29. MA-M16063, fos. 145/6-Aktennotiz verfasst von Rosdeck.
30. Teichova, *op. cit.*, 98–99. The Nostrification Act was passed on 11 Dec. 1919.
31. MA-M16053, Bericht der Deutschen Treuhand-Gesellschaft, Berlin, über das Geschäftsjahr 1920/21.
32. MA-M16017, Komotauer Abkommen, 5 July 1921.
33. Teichova, *op. cit.*, 119–37.

34. MA-M16017, Bericht von Zangen, 2 June 1937, betrifft MW-Komotau.
35. MA-M16063, fos. 52, 54–65, 20 Feb. 1919.
36. MA-M16019, Notiz 12 Dec 1935: on audit of MW-Komotau by Deutsche Treuhand-Gesellschaft, Berlin, which was paid until then by the Czechoslovak company, but costs would have to be met by MW-Düsseldorf and booked under a different heading to MW-Komotau because of objections to foreign audit by the Czechoslovak National Bank.
37. See p. 104 of this present article.
38. MA-M16053, Prüfungsbericht der Deutsche Treuhand-Gesellschaft, 1919/21, and MA-M13001, Gewinn-und Verlust Rechnung der MW-Düsseldorf, 30 June 1920.
39. The Czechoslovak iron and steel industry organized in the Selling Agency of the United Czechoslovak Iron Works was the most tightly knit cartel in the world's steel industry during the inter-war period: Teichova, *op. cit.*, 70–5.
40. MA-M16053, Bericht der MW-Komotau über das Geschäftsjahr 1920/21.
41. MA-M16010, Geschichte-Klesper.
42. MA-M16063, f. 308.
43. Teichova, *op. cit.*, 119.
44. MA-M16017, Lieferungsabkommen, 5 July 1921.
45. MA-M16053, Bericht der MW-Komotau . . . 1920/21.
46. Cf. *Compass, Čechoslovakei* (1924).
47. Teichova, *op. cit.*, 192 n. 3.
48. *Ibid.*, 124.
49. *Ibid.*, 123.
50. Wilhelm Zangen was appointed chairman of the management board (Vorsitzender des Vorstandes) by the 'king makers' of the Mannesmann concern – the directors of the Deutsche Bank, Max Steinthal and Oskar Schlitter – and then approved by the full board of directors (Aufsichtsrat) of the Mannesmannröhren-Werke AG, Düsseldorf: Commonwealth and Foreign Office Library, *Report on the Investigation of the Deutsche Bank*, in Nuremberg Subsequent Trials (Case XI, Box 461, especially Exhibits 69 and 70).
51. MA-M16019, Zangen an die Herren Winkhaus, Meier und von der Tann im Hause, August 1936.
52. MA-M16019, Aktennotiz v. der Tann, 29 Aug. 1936.
53. MA-M16053, Bericht . . . 1920/21.
54. MA-M16010, Geschichte-Klesper.
55. Teichova, *op. cit.*, 75.
56. MA-M16010, Geschichte-Klesper.
57. MA-M16016, M16053, M16054, Reports to board of directors and balance sheets of the MW-Komotau, 1919–38.
58. MA-M16036, 229.232.
59. MA-M1607, Niederschrift über die Besprechung in Berlin am 12.5.1927, Niederschrift über die Verwaltungsratssitzung der Mannesmannröhren-Werke A.G., Komotau, 21 June 1927.
60. Koch, *op. cit.*, 26.
61. Similar tactics were employed by Krupp through their direct participating investment in Aktiebolaget Bofors in Sweden. Cf. Mira Wilkins, 'Multinational enterprise', in *The Rise of Managerial Capitalism*, ed. H. Daems and H. van der Wee (Louvain, The Hague, 1974), 225.
62. MA-M16010, Geschichte-Klesper.
63. *Ibid.*; also *Compass, Čechoslovakei*, relevant years.
64. The firm of G. Rumpel AG, Vienna, was originally a public company. Until 1936 the state-owned Österreichisches Credit-Institut für öffentliche Unternehmungen held 45 per cent of its shares. These were bought by the MW-Komotau in 1936 to secure 100 per cent possession: MA-M16019, Elaborat Beteiligungen Komotau, vom 4.4.1936.
65. MA-M16010, Geschichte-Klesper.
66. MA-M16013, Niederschrift über die Verwaltungsratssitzung der MW-Komotau, 25 May 1937.
67. MA-M16063, Correspondence between Vienna office and Düsseldorf head office, April 1920.
68. MA-M16053, Bericht . . . 1920/1.
69. MA-M16010 Geschichte-Klesper, also M16018 Bericht vorbereitet von Mader für die wirtschafts-politische Arbeit des Gauwirtschaftsbearbeiters Ing. Richter in Oktober 1942 – an Zangen zur Begutachtung.
70. MA-M16017, Niederschrift über die Besprechung in Berlin (Mannesmann-haus) 15 Feb 1935; also M16011, Bericht des Verwaltungsrates der MW-Komotau über das Geschäftsjahr 1934.

71. MA-M1603, Situationsbericht zur 39. Verwaltungsratssitzung der MW-Komotau am 19 Juni 1935 über die abgelaufene Periode des Geschäftsjahres 1935.

72. From 1936 the MW-Komotau was listed as an enterprise of national importance for the defence of the Czechoslovak state. On the reaction of the Mannesmann concern see M16019 Brief der Mannesmann-röhren-Werke-Verwaltungsstelle Berlin vom 15.7.1936, and its representations to the Reichswirtschaftsministerium and Auswärtiges Amt in Berlin.

73. See pp. 110–17 of this present article.

74. MA-M16053, Balance sheets of the MW-Komotau 1920–1924 and Konto separato 1924.

75. MA-M16053, General-Bilanz der MW-Komotau, and Prüfungsbericht der Deutschen Treuhand-Gesellschaft, Berlin, 1920/21.

76. See balance sheets of both companies: M16016 and M16011 for the MW-Komotau, and M13002 for the MW-Düsseldorf, for 1932 and 1933.

77. MA-M16054, General-Bilanz der MW-Komotau und Prüfungsbericht der Deutschen Treuhand-Gesellschaft, Berlin, für das Geschäftsjahr 1927; also correspondence Bierwes-Klesper 1926–8.

78. MA-M16016, M16053, M16054.

79. Especially MA-M16016, Prüfungsbericht der Deutschen Treuhand-Gesellschaft, Berlin, für das Geschäftsjahr 1929, also 1930.

80. MA-M13002, Bericht der MW-Düsseldorf über das Geschäftsjahr 1938.

81. MA-M16016, M16053, M16054, Summarizing this financial policy, the auditors state in their report for 1930 that accumulated resources are reflected in a) higher bank deposits, b) further financing of participations and c) in reserves to cover new investments (cf. M16016). During the crisis years the above strategy was pursued rather than distributing dividends.

82. MA-M16019, Elaborat Beteiligungen Komotau.

83. MA-M16017, Bericht von Zangen, 2 June 1937.

84. MA-M16011, Bericht des Verwaltungs-rates der MW-Komotau über das Ges-chäftsjahr 1934, also 1936. References to loan and purchase of shares of the British Mannesmann Tube Co. Ltd, London, for which items are booked in the relevant balance sheets.

85. MA-M16019, Aktennotiz v. der Tann in Sache Komotau und Abkommen mit den 3 Banken (Feb. 1938).

86. MA-M16019, Correspondence between Klesper Mader (MW-Komotau), and v. der Tann, Zangen (MW-Düsseldorf) in the period from 22 June 1936 to 21 Oct. 1937.

87. Ibid.

88. MA-M16017, Klesper's report to Zangen, 21 Apr. 1937.

89. MA-M16017; during 1937 the directors representing the Deutsche Bank and MW-Düsseldorf on the Board of the MW-Komotau either retired (like Steinthal and Bierwes) or were pressurized to resign. Max Steinthal was replaced by Wilhelm Zangen as chairman of the board of directors. In these changes the racial criteria of Nazi Germany were employed in the personnel policy of the Düsseldorf headquarters, the full impact of which emerged after the Munich Agreement.

90. MA-M16017. Brief Zangens an v. der Tann (im Hause)-Sekt, 10 Sept. 1937.

91. See p. 110 of this present article.

92. MA-M16017, also MA-M16011, Draft of protocol for the annual general meeting of the MW-Komotau in 1937; also Protocol of annual general meeting of the MW-Komotau, 19 March 1938.

93. MA-M16017, Brief Zangens an v. der Tann (im Hause)-Sekt, 10 Sept. 1937.

94. MA-M16017, Brief Zangens an den Vortragenden Legationsrat Altenburg des Auswärtiges Amtes in Berlin. 1 Oct. 1938. This refers to urgent personal representations, in order to impress upon the occupying authorities the importance of the Komotau works as one of the most modern industrial complexes of the 'Sudetendeutschland' [sic] and to prevail upon them to occupy the area earlier than planned, i.e. not between 7 and 10 October but between 3 and 5 October 1938.

6. The IG Farbenindustrie AG in Central and South-East Europe, 1926–38

Verena Schröter

IG Farbenindustrie AG, founded in December 1925 through the merger of six major chemical enterprises, was the largest company in inter-war Germany,[1] and was estimated by one contemporary to represent 2 per cent of all German property values.[2] Although the concern possessed a worldwide network of economic interests, it was still far from being a multi-national company in any strict sense of the word. A quantitative assessment of its foreign economic interest is very difficult as the value of its patent rights, licence agreements and trademarks are hard to estimate. Moreover, the explicit policy of IG Farben was that of camouflaging its foreign participations as 'national enterprises' in overseas countries[3] in view of growing nationalism. Taking the former factor at least into account, it was estimated that the total value of IG Farben's foreign assets amounted to one milliard Reichmark on the eve of the Second World War.[4] The character of these foreign interests, however (table 6.1), shows clearly that the combine was still mainly concerned with the sale of exports.[5] The bulk of these interests consisted of sales agencies all over the world but there were also some administrative and finance companies and research institutes. Even the vast majority of the 70 foreign producing companies in which IG Farben held shares and which constituted less than 10 per cent of all its foreign engagements, had often only taken over the packing and finishing of pharmaceuticals and dyestuffs for local markets.[6]

Table 6.1. FOREIGN SUBSIDIARIES AND PARTICIPATIONS OF IG FARBENINDUSTRIE AG before the Second World War.

Direct and indirect participations in foreign companies (in 42 countries)		268
of these: producing companies	70	
IG branches and agencies		458
	Total	726

Sources: BWA 4c 31.13, Die Abwicklung des Auslandsvermögens der IG Farbenindustrie AG; 'Im Auftrage der Rechtsabteilung der FF Bayer bearb. v. K. Timm', unpublished MS (Leverkusen, 1951), 11f.; H. W. Knauff, 'Bayer im Ausland', unpublished MS (Leverkusen, 1971), 3, BWA without file no.

It is the purpose of this article, using the countries of Central and South-East Europe as examples, to show how this system of primarily export-orientated interests of IG Farben developed and gradually changed during the inter-war period. These interests included – besides exports and foreign investments – cartel and licence agreements, together with political efforts involved to secure them. The world economic crisis of the early 1930s provided the main trigger for the development of production abroad. However, the strategy and structure of an important economic and political concern like IG Farbenindustrie cannot be discussed without taking into account German penetration into Central and South-East Europe, especially in the 1930s through foreign economic and trade policy.[7]

The size of IG Farbenindustrie AG and the diversification of its production and sales interests were reflected clearly in the complex and highly sophisticated organizational structure of the concern which was finally shaped between 1926 and 1930 according to Carl Duisberg's principle of 'decentralized centralization'.[8] It consisted of several closely interconnected patterns and a variety of committees and commissions dealing with production, technology and sales. The production and technical sides were covered by the co-operation of regional Betriebsgemeinschaften (works communities)[9] which had developed on a traditional basis. Their units were, at the same time, assigned to one of three Sparten[10] and vertically to a number of scientific and technical committees, of which the Technischer Ausschuss (Tea, Technical commission) was the final arbiter. The commercial sphere was similarly organized into four Verkaufsgemeinschaften (sales communities),[11] originally divided according to markets and distributed amongst the major works. They became centralized only at the end of the 1920s in Frankfurt, Leverkusen and Berlin.[12] The highest commission in the sales field, analogous to the Tea Commission, was the Kaufmännischer Ausschuss (KA, commercial commission) which dealt with all the basic questions concerning sales, prices, export interests, cartels, agencies, advertising, etc.[13] There were, in addition, several committees – the dyestuffs, chemicals and pharmaceuticals commissions[14] – which co-ordinated the technical and commercial fields. Internal communications were also assisted by various experts attending the meetings of commissions outside their field when matters of common interest arose.

The work of all these commissions provided the necessary basis of information and decisions for the business policy of the concern. Although, in the last resort, decisions were made in the meetings of the Vorstand (management board) – or rather its Arbeitsausschuss (working commission) and Zentralausschuss (central commission) respectively[15] – this decision-making process tended to confirm the recommendation of the special commissions.[16] In addition, the active members of the board each held personally a number of organizational functions simultaneously.[17] Therefore it can justifiably be assumed that the leading commissions, namely the Tea and KA, played a crucial role in the managerial decision-making process of IG Farben and were involved fundamentally in the investment, export, cartel and licence policies of the concern with regard to Central and South-East European countries.

Besides this, there existed a central organizational structure within the IG Farben concern, the importance of which grew especially during the 1930s. In part, this consisted of several offices in Frankfurt and Ludwigshafen which dealt with accountancy, taxes, insurance, contracts, propaganda and traffic questions.[18] The various IG Farben offices in Berlin NW7, however, are of special interest in the determination of the economic policy of IG Farben and its activities in the countries of South-East Europe. From 1926, this organization had been built up in Berlin in order to keep in contact with the German ministries and government, and the central offices of industrial organizations.[19] After 1933 it became a widely extended apparatus, of which the most important and influential departments in its final state (in 1937) were the Zentrale Finanzverwaltung (Zefi, Central Finance Department), the Wirtschaftspolitische Abteilung (Wipo, Economic Policy Department) and the Volkswirtschaftliche Abteilung (Vowi, Political Economy Department).[20] In the second half of the 1930s, the Berlin NW7 administration, under the management of Max Ilgner, developed widespread and growing activities in South-East Europe, which reflected the mounting interest of the concern as a whole in this area. One main task of NW7, especially its Vowi Department, was to compile and handle all kinds of information available on foreign economies, export markets, competitors, raw material resources, etc. For this purpose the Vowi Department co-operated closely with the Statistisches Reichsamt (German Central Statistical Office) and economic research institutes such as the Institut für Konjunkturforschung, Berlin, and the Institut für Weltwirtschaft, Kiel.[21] It also depended on a multitude of reports from employees of IG Farben sales agencies all over the world, which had been appointed 'Zefi-Vertrauensmänner' (or after 1937, 'Zefi-Verbindungsmänner'). According to Max Ilgner, these confidants had been introduced in the early 1930s when the collapse of the Austrian Credit-Anstalt and the devaluation of the pound sterling generated a need for immediate information about resulting foreign exchange and export problems.[22] Besides other things, they had to observe closely any industrializing tendencies and the activities of other foreign firms in their respective countries. From the early 1930s, the head of the Austrian sales organization was the Zefi-Vertrauensmann for Austria and all other Central and South-East European countries.[23] Following this, a worldwide information service developed, and from the late 1930s an intelligence service evolved which also co-operated with the German state bureaucracy and army.[24] The Zefi-confidants were immediately subordinated to the central Berlin organization. In 1936 the KA confirmed a statement which compared the relationship between the Zefi-Vertrauensmänner and the NW7 organization to that of the head of a sales agency abroad with the respective Verkaufsgemeinschaft.[25] On this basis the Vowi Department produced numerous reports which were circulated within the IG Farben concern and which provided a factual basis for managerial decisions. On Central and South-East Europe alone, 547 reports could be traced by H. Radandt, the bulk of which were written during the years 1938 to 1941 (table 6.2). Until

Table 6.2. VOWI-REPORTS ON CENTRAL AND SOUTH-EAST EUROPE, 1933–44.

	No. per year												Total 1933–44
	1933	34	35	36	37	38	39	40	41	42	43	44	
Albania							1						1
Bulgaria			2	1	4	4	7	8	8	5	8		47
Greece			5	3	2	6	8	7	2	2			35
Yugoslavia		1	2	1	7	6	8	8	8	3	5		49
Austria	1		3	5	6	18	5	7	2	3	1	1	52
Romania			5		7	12	12	24	18	5	11	2	96
Czechoslovakia	1	4	3	8	5	27	21	14	6	9	4	1	103
Hungary		4	9	3	6	8	6	9	23	11	6		85
South-East Europe in general			3	2	4	14	18	20	6	6	3	2	79
	3	9	32	23	41	95	86	97	73	44	38	6	547

Source: H. Radandt, 'Berichte der Volkswirtschaftlichen Abteilung der IG Farbenindustrie AG über Südosteuropa', in *Jahrbuch für Wirtschaftsgeschichte*, IV (1966), 289–314, table on p. 292.

1938 these Vowi-reports dealt mainly with foreign trade and export questions, except for several reports on South-East European metal ore deposits and firms in 1935. It was only from 1938 onwards that foreign trade became less important than the analysis of political and economic conditions, chemical industries and concerns in Central and South-East European countries. This interest, of course, reached its height at the time of the annexation of Austria and Czechoslovakia.[26] The number and contents of the Vowi reports thus reflect quite clearly the varying phases of the prevailing interests which can be distinguished in the business policy of IG Farben during the 1930s.

The Vowi reports were also considered to be an attractive and reliable source of information by the ministerial bureaucracy. It was not least through its business experience and these information channels that IG Farben could influence, according to its interests, the trade negotiations in 1935 between Germany on the one side, and Hungary, Romania, Greece, Czechoslovakia, Bulgaria and Yugoslavia respectively, on the other.[27] As well as this, IG Farben proved on the one hand to be always helpful to the state administration – for example, with regard to the complicated system of foreign trade regulation after 1933[28] – while on the other hand, the concern profited greatly from German state intervention in favour of its business policy. In the foreign economic field, the close collaboration between the state and the IG became particularly evident when IG Farbenindustrie carried out a number of private barter transactions and the investigation of metal ore deposits in South-East Europe. The activities were widely supported by German diplomacy in the respective countries.[29] At the same time, IG Farben experienced similarly cordial support from the South-East European governments and state administrations,[30] which proved the usefulness of constant contacts – of the policy of friendly relations maintained by the IG's Berlin organization – as well as, in some cases, more or less direct 'private gratuities'.[31] For the same purpose of knitting together business and more general connections, prominent members of the IG Berlin organization undertook a number of journeys to Central and South-East European countries from 1932 onwards,[32] while, vice versa, industrialists and politicians of these countries were invited to visit the IG Farben enterprises in Germany.[33]

From 1935–6 Max Ilgner also became a very active member and vice-president of the Mitteleuropäischer Wirtschaftstag (MWT), an institution reorganized in 1931 by the most prominent German industrial enterprises in order to promote their interests with regard to Central and South-East Europe. Among these, IG Farben was in a prominent position to subsidize and co-operate with the MWT, both in the matter of stipends to young South-East European scientists and businessmen and, for example, in prospecting for metal ore deposits and the cultivation of soya beans.[34]

Organizationally all these activities were carried out by the central IG Farben organization in Berlin, whose structure had been built up mainly between 1929 and 1934 to meet the effects of the development of the crisis, especially its impact on exports. Only after the annexation of Austria, when IG Farben interests in Central and South-East Europe became much stronger and oriented towards direct participation in the chemical industries and the industrialization process of those countries, were the new requirements satisfied by organizational extensions. At a board meeting in October 1938 a Südosteuropa-Ausschuss (SOA, South-East European Commission) was founded in order to deal with all IG Farben matters concerning the area.[35] The new commission, to which 12 directors of IG Farben and Dynamit AG (see below) and, besides Ilgner, several officials of the Berlin organization belonged,[36] was affiliated to the KA.[37] But in the following years conflicts arose between the merely consultative role intended for the SOA on the one side, and Ilgner's widespread and ambitious activities within the commission and his Berlin organization aimed at a 'New Order' of the Central and South-East European chemical industries on the other. This went far beyond his authority to make decisions and was met by a rather sharp reaction from Georg von Schnitzler, the chairman of the KA.[38]

Another major organizational response to IG Farben's extended activities in Central and South-East Europe was the establishment in 1938 of a Vowi Department branch in Vienna which was, actually, the only one ever to be founded[39] under the leadership of Hermann Gross.[40] This Vowi Vienna branch, with its economic research and activities concentrated on Central and South-East Europe, provides one more indication of the extent to which the business policy of IG Farben had become directed towards this area.[41]

In accordance with its export interests and its internal organization, IG Farben developed a worldwide network of sales agencies. In Central and South-East Europe, as in most other countries, the future constituent firms of IG Farben had been able to resume their old business relations shortly after the First World War, so that from its beginning the new company had the use of an extensive sales organization.[42] One of the main rationalizing aims of the merger was to combine all these separate sales organizations, with their various inventories and relatively large number of employees, into one efficient and less costly apparatus.[43] This task was performed very quickly, in some cases even before the merger of the main companies in 1925,[44] and actually resulted in rising sales figures.[45] In the field of pharmaceuticals, famous trade-marks like the 'Bayercross' were preserved for advertising reasons and, after 1929, the 'Behring' Serum Institutes and their production were also incorporated within the IG Farben sales organization.[46] The sales agencies were organizationally subordinated to one of the four Verkaufs-gemeinschaften,[47] to which their heads respectively belonged. Consequently, each major product group was represented by a sales agency of its own in many countries, although numerous agencies had to take over the sales of several Verkaufsgemeinschaften.[48]

After the First World War, and even during the first years after the merger, IG Farben was often represented by indigenous agent firms which worked on a commission basis. These were replaced only gradually by companies founded by IG Farben under the laws of the respective country and worked on a sole importer basis.[49] On occasion, however, either the former agents were taken into the new firm or foreign participations in IG Farben firms continued and, where required by legislation, trustees were appointed to represent part of the capital.[50]

With a reliance on its main sales companies in each country, IG Farben developed a widespread and well-organized sales apparatus, especially in markets where it was particularly strong. In Austria, for example, the IG Farben sales agencies[51] delivered their products to several hundred independent retail traders all over the country, who then sold them on their own account. Nevertheless, the leadership of the whole organization remained with IG Farben.[52] The bulk of the sales in the dyestuffs trade went to the local textiles and leather industries.[53] With the special economic conditions of the less industrialized South-East European countries, there existed subagencies which specialized in sales to home dyers and small business establishments.[54]

In Austria another main agency of IG Farben, the Anilinchemie Aktiengesellschaft Vienna, played a very interesting role, going beyond the tasks of a simple sales agency. The capital ties between IG Farben and Anilinchemie, however, were not direct. Assessments of IG Farben's position in Austria produced by the Vowi Department in 1938 show an indirect IG Farben participation, via the Carbidwerk Deutsch-Matrei Actiengesellschaft, Vienna (a 100 per cent subsidiary of Účastinná spoločnosť Dynamit Nobel (Bratislava), see below) of 83.3 per cent.[55] Further, Anilinchemie was not only a sales agency for IG Farben, but also sold chemicals for five major Austrian firms, thereby establishing 'close co-operation' between them.[56] The firms were Skodawerke Wetzler AG, Vienna;[57] Chemische Fabrik Wagemann, Seibel & Co. Aktiengesellschaft, Vienna; Carbidwerk Deutsch-Matrei Aktiengesellschaft, Vienna;[58] Österreichische HIAG-Werke GmbH, Vienna (acetic ether);[59] and Bleiberger Bergwerks-Union, Klagenfurt (Lithopon).

This co-operation, which covered not only sales in Austria but also in the South-East European markets,[60] has to be placed in the perspective of the cartel agreements between IG Farbenindustrie and the Austrian chemicals manufacturers, particularly the biggest producer of heavy chemicals, Skoda-werke Wetzler AG. Before the First World War, whereas basic chemicals had either been manufactured mainly by plants on the territory of what was later to become Czechoslovakia or had been imported from Germany, the Austrian plants had produced only some special chemical products.[61] Immediately after the war, however, the Austrian chemical industry started the production of a variety of chemicals. It was soon able to supply its relatively small home market and, as a consequence of economies of scale, even started to export to Germany and France. This situation was very soon regulated by cartel agreements.[62] From 1927 onwards, these agreements resulted in a strict division of markets between Austrian, German, French and Swiss manufacturers. The Austrian producers agreed to keep out of Germany, France and Switzerland, while reciprocally the French Kuhlmann group and IG Farben would not sell those chemicals in Austria which were also produced by the Austrian industry.[63] As far as the relationship between IG Farben and the Austrian chemical industry was concerned, however, the mutual agreement went far beyond a mere guarantee of the respective home markets. With the exception of mineral acids and salts, which had become one of the most important branches of the Austrian chemical production after the war,[64] the IG Farben organization took over the sales of all Austrian heavy chemicals under this agreement. This applied to the Austrian market, where the IG then sold mainly Austrian products, as well as to the South-East European countries, where IG Farben's sales organization marketed a certain quota of Austrian chemicals besides German products.[65] The Czechoslovak market was reserved to IG Farben, but this was already very restrictive

Table 6.3. FOREIGN SALES OF IG FARBENINDUSTRIE for main export products, 1926–40.

(a) Total foreign sales of product group (mill. RM)
(b) Percentage of total sales of product group (%)
(c) Percentage of total foreign sales of IG (%)
    (including nitrogen)

Year	Dyestuffs			Chemicals		
	(a)	(b)	(c)	(a)	(b)	(c)
1926	268.0	77.0	46.6	53.7	37.3	9.3
1927	293.2	72.4	43.0	74.2	36.3	10.9
1928	334.2	77.0	41.1	83.9	36.0	10.3
1929	300.3	75.0	38.4	106.6	40.6	13.6
1930	269.8	74.2	46.7	87.8	39.0	15.2
1931	263.0	74.3	49.2	78.9	42.4	14.8
1932	234.4	74.0	49.5	63.1	42.4	13.3
1933	230.2	70.0	50.9	68.4	40.5	15.1
1934	225.9	66.6	54.0	58.1	28.5	13.9
1935	232.4	68.4	51.5	66.5	24.7	14.7
1936	219.2	62.6	48.7	70.1	21.2	15.6
1937	243.0	63.0	49.8	75.7	18.1	15.5
1938	209.0	57.4	49.6★	74.2	15.4	17.6★
1939	208.9	55.0	46.3★	79.2	12.0	17.6★
1940	162.8	46.0	43.7★	77.1	9.4	20.7★

★ Figures of total foreign sales of IG for the years 1938–40 exclude nitrogen exports.

Source: Grundlegendes Material (der Verteidigung) über die IG Farbenindustrie Aktiengesellschaft aus dem Nürnberger IG Prozess 1947/48, (Nuremberg, 1948).

because of highly protective tariffs and the competition of the Spolek pro chemickou a hutní výrobú (Spolek) Ustí n.L.

By this sales agreement, IG Farbenindustrie consolidated what was obviously a predominant position in the Austrian and South-East European markets. Additionally, it must also be taken into account that Austria produced neither synthetic nitrogen[66] nor considerable quantities of dyestuffs and pharmaceuticals; for the latter situation an agreement between IG Farben and the Austrian chemical industry was suggested[67] (these products were mostly imported from Germany in any case[68]). Thus IG Farben and its sales organization played an important role in the marketing of chemical products in Austria and, via Austria, in South-East Europe. In this context Anilinchemie must be considered the company which played a decisive role in securing IG Farben's position.

Following the world economic crisis of the early 1930s, Anilinchemie took over tasks which went beyond the mere marketing of the products of IG

Pharmaceuticals			Photographic			Total foreign sales (mill. RM)	% of total sales
(a)	(b)	(c)	(a)	(b)	(c)		
69.9	78.7	12.1	23.9	58.0	4.2	575.5	56.0
44.4	68.3	6.5	35.5	57.3	5.2	681.7	53.7
51.0	68.0	6.3	47.1	55.4	5.8	813.5	57.2
51.9	65.7	6.6	57.5	57.5	7.4	781.6	55.0
51.8	66.4	9.0	43.7	52.2	7.6	577.9	50.0
70.4	73.3	13.2	44.9	55.4	8.4	534.6	52.6
61.8	72.0	13.1	35.8	49.7	7.6	473.2	54.0
62.5	71.0	13.8	33.3	51.6	7.4	452.0	50.6
60.4	68.6	14.4	32.6	50.0	7.8	418.2	42.5
66.5	69.3	14.7	36.1	47.0	8.0	451.1	41.0
71.1	69.0	15.8	37.1	44.7	8.2	450.0	34.7
83.9	70.0	17.2	40.2	40.6	8.2	488.4	32.3
90.3	67.4	21.4*	42.8	39.3	10.2*	421.5*	25.5*
90.2	59.3	20.0*	39.7	29.0	8.8*	451.0*	23.0*
75.5	49.0	20.2*	41.7	27.6	11.2*	372.4*	17.0*

Farben and its cartel partners. The managing director of Anilinchemie until 1937 – Wilhelm Roth – was IG Farben's Zefi-Vertrauensmann for Austria and the whole of South-East Europe and so was responsible for the establishment of economic, political and social relations with those countries. Further, Anilinchemie was also the organizational centre from which IG Farben's South-East European export remittances were transferred to Germany to evade exchange controls.[69] Moreover, after 1933 the IG organized transactions via Anilinchemie to secure its supply of raw materials from abroad. In 1934 the managing director of Anilinchemie procured credits of £1,300,000 from Hambro's Bank in order to buy raw materials in Britain which were then sent to Germany. The finished products were sent by IG Farben to Anilinchemie, which sold them in Austria and South-East Europe, thereby making it possible to obtain sterling to repay the credits of the British bank.[70] When IG Farben acquired Chemosan-Union and Pezoldt AG in Vienna in 1932, this transaction was also settled through Anilinchemie.[71] Similarly, IG Farben intended to raise the capital for a planned Austrian synthetic nitrogen factory in 1936 via Anilinchemie and the Österreichische Dynamit Nobel Aktiengesellschaft, in which IG Farben also held an indirect capital participation.[72] On all these issues Anilinchemie was clearly used by IG Farben to pursue its policy in Austria and South-East Europe, though the capital ties between the two companies were only indirect ones.

IG Farben's well-established sales organization is indicative of the strong market position held by the concern in Central and South-East European countries. As table 6.4 shows, the German chemical industry, of which IG Farben was by far the largest exporter,[73] supplied a quarter of all world chemical exports during the inter war period,[74] but had a considerably higher

Table 6.4. GERMANY'S SHARE OF THE CHEMICAL IMPORTS
of Central and South-East European countries (in %).

	1929	1934	1935	1936	1937
Austria	50.2	50.9	45.4	45.3	42.4
Czechoslovakia	43.3	39.5	38.9	44.3	*
Hungary	39.7	36.4	40.0	46.7	47.0
Bulgaria	55.0	59.9	60.8	73.6	*
Romania	*	35.7	46.1	57.7	51.6
Yugoslavia	40.0	35.2	34.0	47.4	49.8
for comparison: Germany's share of world chemical exports (%)	23.4	25.2	25.4	26.0	25.3

* Data not available.

Source: C. Ungewitter, *Chemie und Außenhandel* (Hamburg, 1939), 34f. and 32.

share of the chemical imports of Central and South-East Europe. Germany was the most important supplier of chemical products for the successor states, especially chemicals, dyestuffs and pharmaceuticals.[75] The Central and South-East European area as a whole provided considerable markets for the German chemical industry, and IG Farben in particular.[76] The main customer was Czechoslovakia, followed by Austria, Hungary and Romania (see table 6.5).[77] In the 1920s the successor states alone constituted the third largest market for the German chemical industry.[78] From the figures it becomes evident why the German producers were so vitally interested to maintain their market position in this area.

This development has to be placed within the context of the contraction of the world market for chemical products and the existence of structural surplus capacities during the whole inter-war period, especially in the 1930s, which was caused by the building up of national chemical industries in many countries. These new industries were protected by high tariff barriers and various import restrictions.[79] Due to technological superiority, however, which was maintained after the First World War, the German chemical industry, especially IG Farbenindustrie, regained its pre-war world market position[80] by producing commodities of both a high technological level and high quality and value. This strategy was applied most successfully in the export-intensive sectors of dyestuffs and pharmaceuticals,[81] whereas the heavy investments in the technology of synthetic nitrogen were frustrated by a dramatic breakdown of this market after 1929.[82] As a result of the structural changes of the world market after the war, the German chemical industry shifted its exports to overseas markets and, within Europe, towards the less

Table 6.5. SALES OF THE IG FARBENINDUSTRIE AG in Central and South-East Europe (including nitrogen).

	1931 mill. RM	%	1932 mill. RM	%	1933 mill. RM	%
Total foreign sales of IG	534.6	100	473.2	100	452.0	100
Czechoslovakia	27.1	5.1	27.5	5.8	21.1	4.7
Austria	13.0	2.4	14.7	3.1	16.3	3.6
Hungary	8.0	1.5	8.5	1.8	10.6	2.3
Romania	8.2	1.5	8.7	1.8	9.9	2.2
Yugoslavia	6.0	1.1	5.2	1.3	5.7	1.3
Bulgaria	2.5	0.5	2.8	0.5	3.1	0.7
Greece	2.2	0.4	1.6	0.5	1.9	0.4
Total sales in Central and South-East Europe	67.1	12.5	69.0	14.6	68.5	15.2

Sources: Hö 1086, Branchenumsätze 1931–1933; table 6.3.

developed agrarian economies, e.g. South-East Europe.[83] Although – Czechoslovakia and Austria excluded – this area purchased still a rather small percentage of IG Farben's foreign sales,[84] it was considered by leading IG Farben managers, like Carl Bosch and Carl Duisberg, to possess the potential to become a prosperous and important market in the long run,[85] which was even more important in view of the contracting world market.

For these reasons, IG Farbenindustrie attempted to secure and develop the Central and South-East European markets using a variety of strategies. Given the conditions of strong regulation and cartelization of the markets for almost all major chemical product groups in the inter-war period,[86] cartels provided an important framework for IG's marketing strategies. In many international agreements IG Farben, due to its technological superiority and intensive research, its effective selling organization and high market shares, was strong enough to secure as the dominant partner high exports quotas, thus largely restricting the other cartel members to their home countries.[87] Therefore, Central and South-East Europe was secured internationally as a sphere of interest for IG Farben, especially in agreements between the dominant world concerns.[88] The emergence of national chemical industries in these formerly 'safe' markets has also to be taken into account, and they became an increasing crucial feature in international cartel relations and IG Farben's marketing strategies. In some cases, as for example the previously mentioned heavy chemicals arrangement between IG Farben and the Austrian producers, IG Farben was able to solve the emerging problems on the whole according to its own interests. Nevertheless, Spolek had begun to seriously threaten IG Farben's position in the Czechoslovak and South-East European dyestuffs markets by the end of the 1920s[89] and, with regard to synthetic nitrogen, Czechoslovakia and Hungary had become self-suppliers by this time.[90] As this development coincided with, and was accelerated by, the world economic crisis of the early 1930s, the regulation of market conditions became an even more crucial instrument for IG Farben.

All these factors can, for example, be demonstrated clearly in the International Dyestuffs and Nitrogen Cartels, of which IG Farben was the dominant member.[91] The German-French dyestuffs agreement of 1927 granted the home market to the French producers but reserved a number of countries totally to IG Farben, among them Austria, Hungary, and the 'Balkan' countries. Other markets were to be covered jointly according to the agreed sales quotas. In a third group of countries, among them Czechoslovakia, the IG Farben organization also took over the selling of French products under their own trade-marks.[92] The Three-Party Dyestuffs Cartel of April 1929, which now included the Swiss producers, again covered the entire world, except the U.S.A., and included a statement by the French group to keep out of Austria as well as other countries.

Though generally the international dyestuffs cartel worked successfully even during the crisis years, the repercussions of the world economic crisis – tariff barriers, import restrictions and a reinforced movement towards autarky – posed a long-term structural threat to IG Farben's export interests.[93] In view of constant surplus capacity and the competition of outsiders, however, the IG attached an overall importance to the continuance of the cartel and subordinated its crisis strategies to this framework.[94] The Swiss producers and IG Farben agreed repeatedly that neither bilateral clearing agreements nor IG Farben's private barter transactions with Romania would change the division of market quotas between the respective cartel members in these countries.[95] When German dyestuffs exports to Czechoslovakia were severely disturbed, not only by competition from Spolek but also by prohibitive import restrictions,[96] the development of this important market became a frequent subject of discussion in the various IG Farben commissions,[97] as well as during the cartel meetings.[98] The IG pursued a strategy of including Spolek within the international dyestuffs agreements.[99] But as Spolek's demands – to reserve its home market and to obtain preferential treatment in the other successor states – were considered to be unacceptable,[100] IG Farben made serious preparations at the end of 1932 to open a dyestuffs plant in Czechoslovakia.[101] These included a thorough market analysis,[102] the storage of a large amount of intermediary products in Czechoslovakia and the securing of the appropriate production facilities in connection with Účastinná spoločnosť Dynamit Nobel (Bratislava), a closely affiliated company.[103] The measures were not only aimed at counteracting possible new import restrictions, but also 'to keep the tactical position in view of Spolek'.[104] Apparently IG Farben's position was strong enough to convince Spolek, in view of the costs of a potential fight with the cartel, of the advantages of an agreement,[105] and by July 1933 contacts over this matter had been made.[106] Finally, in April 1934, the so-called 'Zurich Agreement' was concluded between the Three-Party Dyestuffs Cartel and Spolek, which was to last for five years.[107] This agreement granted a sales quota to Spolek consisting of its 1933 sales volume plus a certain extension of its business which the enterprise could not even fulfil during the first year of the agreement.[108] It was for this reason that in 1935 the agreement was extended until 1940. The rise in Spolek's sales was organized by means of business transfers from the cartel to Spolek and for a transition period dyestuffs deliveries of the cartel to Spolek. These were cheap enough to be 'economically interesting' for this concern, and therefore a deterrent to any production of its own.[109] In addition, some prices were also fixed in the agreement. Though there were no explicit territorial restrictions, it was agreed that Spolek would extend its business mainly in Czechoslovakia and South-East Europe (which of course meant in reality a restriction), and that the cartel would not start with the production of dyestuffs or intermediary products in Czechoslovakia without Spolek's consent.[110] Although in the short run the Three-Party Cartel, especially IG Farben, had to give up part of its Czechoslovak dyestuffs sales and also regretted the further 'dissipation' of the market, the agreement with Spolek was viewed very favourably in 1935. With import restrictions and state intervention, the expansion of Spolek on its home market was considered to be inevitable. By means of the agreement, this development had been controlled according to IG Farben's interests,[111] which were concerned with safeguarding a maximum share of exports to this particular market. In view of worldwide surplus capacity, production abroad was not really accepted by IG Farben as an alternative strategy of busines expansion but served only as either a means of pressure to gain a regulation of markets, as with Spolek, or as an ultimate solution where a market would otherwise have been lost completely.

The considerations guiding IG Farben's role in the International Nitrogen Cartel were similar. This cartel, the so-called CIA agreement (Convention de l'Industrie de l'Azote), was concluded in August 1930 for one year. After one year of fighting, it was renewed and extended from July 1932 until the Second World War. The cartel developed from June 1929 when the main European nitrogen producers – ICI, IG Farben, and the Norwegian Norsk

Hydro Elektrisk Kvaelstof-aktieselkab – formed the so-called DEN- group. This agreement was actually a bilateral arrangement between ICI and IG, as Norsk Hydro was connected with IG Farben while its sales were handled by the German Stickstoff-Syndikat dominated by IG Farben. The DEN-group decided not only sales quotas, but also a division of markets, reserving Empire markets to ICI and most European markets to the IG.[112] This group became the core of the CIA, with IG Farben again playing a dominant role.[113] The main purpose of the CIA was the regulation of the international nitrogen market, which had been greatly disturbed by worldwide surplus capacity, through granting export quotas according to capacity figures.[114] For political and military reasons, however, the home markets were guaranteed to each producer group and as the building up of new capacity could not be prevented, this cartel neither solved the structural problems of the market, nor provided the means to insure even a dominant member like IG Farben against a long-term loss of its export markets. As Vowi reported in 1937, the only important markets left for IG Farben's nitrogen fertilizers in the near future would be developing agrarian economies in East Asia and East and South-East Europe.[115]

In the short run, however, the DEN-group attempted to retain for itself as many exports as possible. The other European CIA members[116] were encouraged to reduce their production by compensation payments out of a common fund and conclude special agreements with the DEN-group aimed at further reducing their exports. With the Czechoslovak producers, for example, who were organized in the Sdružení pro prodej dusíkatých látek, s.s r.o., Prague, the DEN-group agreed to pay RM 75,000 against a transfer of their export quota.[117] ICI and IG Farben could also control the European nitrogen exports effectively because these were sold mainly via a cartel agency called Internationale Gesellschaft der Stickstoff-Industrie AG, Basle. This agency, however, had no selling organization of its own – sales being left to the Stickstoff-Syndikat and ICI respectively.[118]

Even during the year of contest – 1931–2 – the DEN-group, which continued to co-operate, negotiated separate agreements with the French, Italian and Czechoslovak nitrogen producers, who then ceased to export. IG Farben's export sales, however, were 16 per cent higher than in the previous year, whereas its home market sales had dropped by 13 per cent. The DEN-group was also allowed by special agreements to deliver such nitrogen products to Poland, Belgium and Czechoslovakia as were not produced there.[119] With the new CIA agreement in 1932 IG Farben obtained priority to deliver those products to the Czechoslovak Republic.[120] In a special agreement annexed to the CIA extension in 1935, the Czechoslovak group transferred its export quota of 0.6 per cent to the DEN-group, which agreed to produce and deliver the respective quantities to the International company in Basle for the Czechoslovak group, against a payment of 18.52 Swiss centimes per kilo nitrogen to the DEN-group.[121] From these examples it becomes clearly apparent how much the Czechoslovak nitrogen producers in particular subordinated their own business policy to the cartel aims of the DEN-group, which sought to keep as large a share of the remaining export markets as possible. The cartel, however, faced considerable difficulties with newly-built production plants in many countries, e.g. Hungary.[122] In long and difficult negotiations between 1932 and 1936, the new Hungarian producers, protected by the policy of their government,[123] refused to join the nitrogen cartel.[124]

Government protection was an important item, especially for military reasons, in the nitrogen field. Where national production became inevitable, IG Farben tried to take the initiative to save at least part of the export market. Accordingly, within this context, IG Farben planned to start the production of nitrogen chemicals in Yugoslavia, Romania and Austria during the later 1930s.[125] Nonetheless, these plans were still the result of a 'defensive' strategy of safeguarding home production and export outlets. It was only after 1938, when most of Central and South-East Europe could be considered to be politically and economically a safe part of the German war economy and *Grossraumwirtschaft*, that IG Farben's attitude towards production in this area changed.[126] Direct investments in chemical production facilities in South-East Europe became an accepted strategy of expansion, though even then the priority of export interests remained the most important feature in IG Farben's foreign business policy. Thus new industrial projects or participations in South-East Europe were neither to curtail export facilities and IG monopoly positions, nor were they to become a basis for further industrialization.[127] One main purpose of direct foreign investment was to fight competitors in their respective markets, but either a regulation of these markets via agreements or other means to obtain influence – like an exchange of patents and licences – was always preferred.[128]

The changes of the world market for chemical products were, from many aspects, long-term structural ones, but as this development accelerated during the world economic crisis, production abroad became an even more pressing demand after 1930. IG Farbenindustrie developed a variety of strategies by which to adapt itself to crisis conditions. Falling prices were met, apart from by cartel regulation, by intensified technological research, rationalization and cutting of costs, in the concern itself as well as in the sales organization.[129] Where tariff barriers became prohibitive and could not be overcome by cartel agreements, production abroad became inevitable. By the end of 1932, IG Farben started the manufacture of basic dyestuffs in Hungary. This production, however, was based on highly concentrated intermediate products delivered by IG Farben, which could be imported under much lower customs tariffs than the finished dyestuffs.[130]

Particularly in the field of pharmaceuticals, where specialities faced high tariff barriers, strict legislation, and national industries or the strong competition of foreign producers,[131] small final-stage finishing plants became a common feature of IG Farben's export policy. In Central and South-East Europe, these were set up in Czechoslovakia, Hungary and Romania, where they existed mostly in connection with local sales agencies. The necessary pharmaceutical substances and partly also the packing materials were supplied by the German IG plants. Only in Hungary were some products fully manufactured.[132]

The only company to produce a variety of pharmaceuticals, was Chemosan-Union und Pezoldt AG, Vienna, which became affiliated to IG in 1932.[133] Even though the firm seemed financially sound and provided through its subsidiaries and agencies a solid basis for further expansion into Central and South-East Europe, the acquisition of Chemosan was only justified by the argument of import restrictions.[134] In this production field, once again, IG Farben's foreign investment policy was merely a response to try to avoid production abroad as far as possible.

After 1931, IG Farben's exports to Central and South-East Europe, as to many other countries, were also severely hampered by exchange controls and currency devaluations. IG Farben pursued a rather cautious financial policy at home as well with respect to its sales to the crisis-shaken countries of Central and South-East Europe. With the exception of Czechoslovakia, which was considered to be economically stable,[135] all the countries of this area were the object of special measures by which IG Farben undertook to secure its export receipts. Financial transactions were carried out as quickly as possible. Customers received very short terms of payment (Romania), had to pay in cash (Hungary), or even in advance (Austria), and in any case in gold currencies[136] – though the IG risked with these rigid methods losing customers to outsiders in these markets.[137]

The situation became further complicated with the introduction of exchange controls in 1931. By this time IG Farben had considerable frozen accounts in Central and South-East Europe which somehow had to be liquidated. During the following years, the Central and South-East European states, as well as Germany after 1933, settled a growing part of their foreign trade by means of bilateral clearing and compensation agreements.[138] For this reason, the business expansion of Spolek into South-East Europe, for example, was greatly hampered by Czechoslovakia buying only a limited amount of South-East European agricultural products.[139] In contrast, the IG Farben concern, with its organizational and economic potential, was able to meet the new requirements very quickly, by-passing state agreements through private barter transactions.[140] In August 1932 Max Ilgner visited Czechoslovakia, Hungary, Romania and Yugoslavia in order to promote the new business methods.[141] In these compensation agreements, IG Farben undertook to sell agrarian products, mainly from Hungary and Romania, to third markets[142] in return for a comparable amount of sales of IG products to these South-East European countries. The difference between the South-East European prices for agrarian products and the much lower world market prices was met by German export subsidies and could mostly be covered by financial transactions of IG Farben and price increases on the respective markets.[143]

Though in 1932 and 1933 state compensation agreements were concluded between Germany on one side, and Hungary and Romania respectively on the other, IG Farben was very eager and successful in ensuring through its contacts with German ministries that it could continue its private clearing policy.[144] The official clearing agreements were considered to work much too slowly, with the Hungarian frozen account of IG Farben having a six months' turnover.[145] The private barter transactions, however, worked very successfully.[146] Their number and the variety of products and business partners they included increased greatly during 1932 and 1933.[147] In spite of the crisis and the serious fall of dyestuffs sales on the Czechoslovak market, IG Farben maintained its turnover figures in Central and South-East Europe and raised their share of total IG exports to 15 per cent in 1933.[148] From 1933 the IG Farben policy of private compensation agreements gradually changed its character. The early transactions of 1931 and 1932 had been a short-term reaction to the crisis and had served mainly to liquidate frozen accounts. With the development of a whole system of private compensation, and within the framework of the German trade policy after 1933, these transactions became an integral part of IG Farben's business policy of securing and expanding its market position in South-East Europe. From 1933–4, IG Farben, in close co-operation with MWT,[149] promoted a programme to develop export-intensive sectors in the South-East European agrarian economies, mainly the cultivation of linseeds in Hungary[150] and soya in Romania and Bulgaria.[151] Although these products (vegetable oils) were badly needed by the German autarkic economy after 1933, IG Farben also pursued this programme for reasons of private business policy. The marketing of these products was expected to facilitate the compensation transactions and was considered to be part of the firm's trade policy.[152] It was not simply the immediate opportunity of unrestricted exports, the maintenance of high market shares and the preparation of a future expansion[153] that was attractive for IG Farben. The policy of raising purchasing power through 'organic' agrarian and industrial development in South-East Europe but complementary to the needs of the German economy, played, for prominent IG Farben directors like Max Ilgner, an increasingly important part. In these changes, therefore, IG Farben decided to play an active and shaping role.[154]

Compared with the manifold export and market-orientated activities of IG Farbenindustrie, foreign capital investments were of only secondary importance within the business policy of the concern. IG Farben's main stake in production companies in Central and South-East Europe was a rather indirect one. After the First World War, the former Nobel concern fell apart, leaving as separate entities, besides others, British Nobel Industries Ltd, which later became part of ICI, and the German Dynamit-Actiengesellschaft vormals Alfred Nobel & Co., Hamburg (DAG). In August 1926, DAG became closely connected with the newly founded IG Farbenindustrie, though keeping its legal independence, when the two firms concluded a 98-year *Interessengemeinschaftsvertrag* (community of interest treaty) and IG Farben took over DAG shares.[155] By this association, IG Farben became indirectly engaged in DAG's Central and South-East European interests.

These interests consisted partially of pre-war links, especially the Öster-reichische Dynamit Nobel AG, Vienna (DN Vienna), but to a considerable extent the inter-war structure was the result of the export pressure to which DAG, together with other German explosives manufacturers, was exposed due to the restricted home market in the early 1920s. This resulted in considerable export successes – regaining old markets and acquiring new ones, e.g. in South America – and in the acquisition of monopoly concessions for making and selling explosives in Hungary and Romania by the Austrian Dynamit Nobel subsidiary.[156] At the same time, arrangements between the main competitors in the explosives field – DuPont, Nobel Industries, DAG, and the German Köln-Rottweil AG[157] – were negotiated, leading finally to a series of bilateral gentlemen's agreements early in 1926. Besides regulating the important South American market, these agreements involved technical co-operation, an exchange of patents and knowhow, the granting of mutually exclusive licences and effectively a division of markets.[158] According to this division, DuPont obtained exclusive licences for the U.S.A. and most of Central America, Nobel Industries for the British Empire, and DAG for certain continental European countries – Germany, Holland, Poland, Aus-tria, Denmark and Bulgaria. With certain exceptions,[159] the other European markets were to be supplied jointly by Nobel Industries and DAG.[160] In Central and South-East Europe this applied to Czechoslovakia, Yugoslavia, Hungary and Romania.

Another major feature of these arrangements was the participation of DuPont and Nobel Industries in the stock of the two German companies – DAG and Köln-Rottweil – which increased their capital by RM 7,500,000 each. These shares were taken over by DuPont and Nobel Industries equally as 'permanent property'.[161] Following both the take-over of Köln-Rottweil by IG Farben and the formation of the DAG–IG Farben 'community of interest', the role of DuPont and Nobel as major shareholders in the German explosives industry shrank to negligible proportions.[162] But the main purpose of this investment, the establishment of a 'binding community of interests'[163] in the context of a worldwide arrangement in the explosives field, remained.

It is within the framework of these international agreements that the interests of DAG in Central and South-East Europe must be viewed. In this area, however, the division of markets between DAG and Nobel Industries confirmed the status quo established in 1923. After the war, Nobel Industries had expanded into Central and South-East Europe, mainly by participations in the Czechoslovak Explosia a.s. together with the French Société Centrale de Dynamite, which received favourable assistance from the Czechoslovak state.[164] Both the Czechoslovak state monopoly for explosives granted to Explosia and the export expansion which Nobel Industries had expected with regard to the South-East European market were severely disturbed, however, by the activities of Österreichische Dynamit Nobel AG which had maintained its links with the German DAG. As has been mentioned, the Österreichische Dynamit Nobel AG had secured a production and selling monopoly for explosives in Romania and Hungary and it had kept a production factory in Bratislava. The outcome of the negotiations that followed was a 16 per cent participation by Österreichische Dynamit Nobel AG in Explosia, a.s. pro průmysl výbušnin.[165] This was paid for with the machinery of the Bratislava explosives factory that was closed down and a 'community of interests' agreement between Nobel Industries and the Austrian Nobel company regarding Hungary and Romania.[166] As a precondition – even though it was greatly disliked in Czechoslovakia – of its participation in Explosia, Öster-reichische Dynamit Nobel had to register as a Czechoslovak company and in 1923 was converted into Účastinná spoločnosť Dynamit Nobel Bratislava (DN Bratislava).[167]

Part of the arrangement of the early 1920s between Nobel Industries and the Austrian DN seems to have been the joint ownership of the Nobel-Bickford Company, of which Nobel Industries bought a 25 per cent share by supplying its fuse factory at Trenčín with machinery from an Austrian Nobel Industries subsidiary, Bickford & Co., AG, Vienna.[168] By the end of the 1930s, Nobel-Bickford AG was still owned by ICI (25 per cent) and DN Bratislava (75 per cent).[169]

With regard to the British-German Nobel relationship, the balance of power finally reached was rather more than a mere restoration 'broadly on pre-war lines',[170] for in contrast to pre-1914, Nobel Industries had established itself in Central and South-East Europe, especially in Czechoslovakia. Nevertheless, and in spite of the restrictions of the Versailles Treaty,[171] DAG succeeded in regaining a respectable market position, based on both the survival of at least part of its pre-war investments in Central Europe and an aggressive export policy in the years of the German post-war inflation.

It seems that the Central and South-East European structure of the German DAG interests remained largely unchanged until 1938. Dynamit AG, Hamburg (later Troisdorf), being closely affiliated to IG Farben, owned 51 per cent of the joint stock of Účastinná spoločnosť Dynamit Nobel, Bratislava.[172] This company for its part already possessed production sub-sidiaries in the 1920s, including sub-participations, in each country of the area, except Bulgaria, which was considered only as an export market (see fig. 6.1).[173]

Whereas the Bratislava works, due to the Explosia arrangement, were converted to the production of basic chemicals – such as sulphuric acid, superphosphate, later also carbon disulphide – the subsidiaries produced and

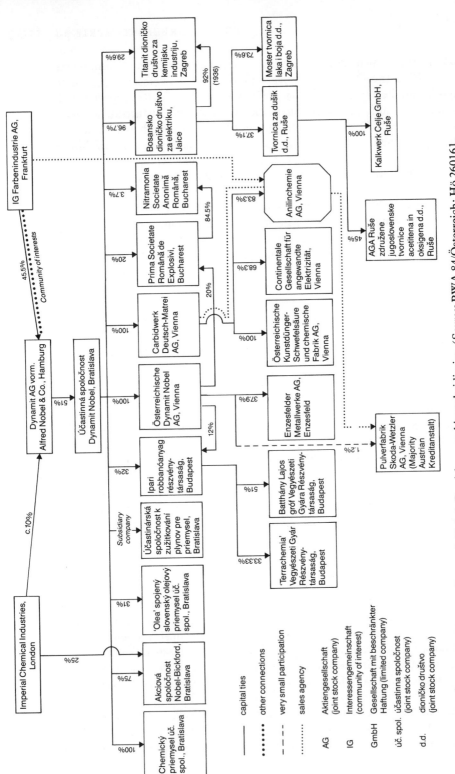

Figure 6.1. Účastinná spoločnost Dynamit Nobel, Bratislava, and its subsidiaries. (*Sources* BWA 84/Österreich; Hö 260161, Auslandslizenzen; H. Radandt, 'Die IG Farbenindustrie AG und Südosteuropa bis 1938', *Jahrbuch für Wirtschaftsgeschichte*, III, 1966, 146–95.)

sold a rather wider range of heavy chemicals, explosives, nitrogen, electro-chemical and electro-metallurgic products.[174] The high dividends paid suggests not only the prosperity of the business, but also indicates that this was an important way to channel profits back to the mother company, DAG:[175] DN Bratislava paid 30 per cent from 1929 to 1934, 33 per cent in 1935 and 19 per cent in 1936 and 1937,[176] though for 1932, for example, DN Bratislava was reported to have balanced '+ nought'.[177] The DN Bratislava subsidiaries were also, of course, affected by the world economic crisis. The Bosansko dioničko društvo za elektrinu Jaice, the main subsidiary in Yugoslavia, paid a dividend of 8 per cent in 1929–31 and again in 1935–6, but none in the period 1931–4.[178] The balance sheet of the Austrian Dynamit Nobel group in 1931 showed profits which, as the minute of a Tea meeting reports, merely resulted from the run-down of reserves.[179] This procedure – notably in the year of the collapse of the Austrian Credit-Anstalt – suggests the rather sound financial background of these firms. In 1934, most DN companies showed again a considerable increase of turnover.[180]

It was not only capital, but also personal ties, which inter-linked the various Central and South-East European DN subsidiaries. Erwin Philipp was not only president (Generaldirektor) of DN Bratislava, but also of DN Vienna, and belonged, as a vice-president, to the board of directors (Verwaltungsrat) of the Bosansko dioničko društvo za elektrinu.[181] Out of six members of the managing board (Direktion) of this Yugoslav subsidiary, four were at the same time directors of the Austrian DN subsidiary Carbidwerk Deutsch-Matrei AG in Vienna.[182]

The question arises, however, as to whether and, if so, how, the IG Farben concern could either influence or make use of its rather indirect capital interests in the DAG/DN Bratislava combine during the inter-war period.

Based on reports of the IG Vowi department and other internal assessments in 1938–40, it has been argued widely by historians that, despite its capital participation, the IG concern was able to influence neither the composition of boards nor the business policy of the DN Bratislava enterprises. Due to the nationalist economic policy of the Czechoslovak state, DN Bratislava was a Czechoslovak firm and had to work 'on the whole independently' ('weitgehend selbständig'), as Max Ilgner put it.[183]

Even though the available evidence is scarce, a number of links between IG Farben and DN Bratislava or Vienna can be traced. These were partly on rather conventional lines, e.g. the grant of licences, or the deliveries of basic chemicals from IG Farben to the DN enterprises.[184] The enterprises of the Austrian and Czechoslovak DN company also belonged to the most important suppliers of Anilinchemie in Vienna.[185] In 1932–3, when IG Farben planned the manufacture of dyestuffs in Czechoslovakia, an arrangement was made with the DN Bratislava factories to store intermediate products there and to use offices and production equipment. In spite of its unfavourable location, DN Bratislava was judged to be a suitable supplier of intermediate products for future IG Farben manufacture because first, it was registered as a Czechoslovak joint stock company possessing a concession for the production of chemicals, and second, DAG had a 51 per cent capital interest in this enterprise.[186]

With respect to long-term considerations, DN Bratislava was used by IG Farben, too, as in October 1933 when the IG Farben chemicals commission discussed an offer of the former Kreuger concern to DN Vienna, to take over Kreuger's majority of 86 per cent in the stock of Radocha, Chemische Fabrik AG, Warsaw. It was stated that a manufacturing base in Poland would be 'desirable for DN Vienna', and that 'also from the view of IG such a base could gain importance' ('könnte ein solcher Stützpunkt Bedeutung erlangen'). Finally the chemicals commission 'authorized' ('ermächtigte') Philipp, the president of DN Bratislava and Vienna, to negotiate an offer with the Polish firm.[187] Apparently the deal between Kreuger and Dynamit Nobel was not completed, but the negotiations show that the IG chemicals commission[188] had the authority to include the business policy of Dynamit Nobel in its considerations.

The relationship between IG Farbenindustrie, DAG, and the DN Bratislava combine requires further research. The foregoing examples show that there were capital links as well as business connections between the IG organization and this concern. Immediate interests and long-term considerations of IG Farben were met by co-operation. Notwithstanding this, the DN Bratislava combine undoubtedly possessed an independent organization and management of its own, though this seems to have been on the basis of a smoothly maintained identity of interests and friendly relations between IG Farben and DN Bratislava.

It was only after the annexation of Austria in March 1938, which was followed by a phase of immediate and direct expansion into the chemical industries of Central and South-East Europe, that the attitude of IG Farben towards DN Bratislava changed, with the interests of the IG becoming very direct. As a part of the 'reorganization' of the Austrian chemical industry,[189] IG and DAG took over directly the Austrian subsidiaries of DN Bratislava, Carbidwerk Deutsch-Matrei AG and DN Vienna, and their respective sub-participations. The purchase price was not paid in cash, but compensated through the annual dividend payments of DN Bratislava to DAG,[190] which meant actually that DN Bratislava granted a long-term credit to IG.

The remaining DN Bratislava combine with its numerous South-East European participations became the centre of IG Farben's expansion in this area after 1938, which was now almost as much oriented towards direct investment as to exports. In addition to the old capital ties, the management and supervisory boards of DN Bratislava were largely taken over by IG Farben officials in June 1939. This indicates the importance attached to DN Bratislava with regards to the 'New Economic Order' to come. From 1939 to 1943 the DN Bratislava combine founded seven new subsidiaries and obtained participations in another six companies in Central and South-East Europe.[191]

From its foundation until 1938, however, the IG Farbenindustrie remained, regarding its investment policy as well as its market strategies, mainly orientated towards home production and commodity exports. Three phases can be distinguished in the inter-war development of the IG. The first years, until 1930, were a period of consolidation, characterized by rationalization and centralization, the recovery of foreign markets, and the construction of the first important international cartels. Following the world economic crisis, IG Farbenindustrie tried to adjust to the structural and political changes of world market conditions through establishing final production processes abroad, compensation agreements, and increasing political activities. Nevertheless, it continued, on the whole, to pursue its former business principles: a reluctance towards direct foreign investment, cutting of costs, and the regulation of markets by means of cartels, and licence and patent agreements. After 1938, IG Farben reinforced its penetration into the Central and South-East European markets by either direct participations in local chemical industries, or the foundation of new companies. During most of the inter-war period, however, direct foreign investments and capital ties played only a minor role; though, if they existed, as in the case of Účastinná spoločnost Dynamit Nobel Bratislava, the resulting relations were instrumentalized according to IG Farben's business policy. This policy had to be pursued necessarily by more or less indirect or informal means, given the political circumstances of growing nationalism and the Little Entente, as well as the relative lack of capital in inter-war Germany.

The possibilities of German foreign trade policy towards South-East Europe from the 1920s also provided the framework for IG Farben's strategies; and vice versa, this policy was influenced by the IG: hence the parallel between the extended interests of the state bureaucracy and IG Farben towards this area. The political conditions in Central and South-East Europe, however, did not simply promote co-operation between IG Farben and the German state, or with the state administrations of the respective countries. After all, IG Farben was also encouraged to use cartel agreements as a means of market regulation because, in many cases, these went beyond the aims and measures of the policies of Central and South-East European governments.

Generally cartels developed as a strategy of IG Farben's policy mainly in the industrially developed markets, especially in Czechoslovakia, where the competition of Spolek had to be taken into account. In this case, the development of the domestic chemical industry was influenced in so far as further expansion via exports and the diversification of product lines were discouraged. However, the priority of exports and, later, Max Ilgner's strategy of an active and dominating engagement in the industrialization of less developed countries, hampered the development of independent domestic chemical industries in South-East Europe in various and more basic ways. Consequently the latter of these two strategies was carried through by IG Farben only after 1938, though various industrial projects had paved the way towards this policy during the 1930s.

Both strategies of the firm, co-operation with state bureaucracies as well as measures reaching beyond state policies – such as cartels and partly compensation agreements – could only be undertaken successfully because IG Farben possessed an extensive organizational structure, the elements of which reacted flexibly and efficiently to the requirements of IG's business aims.

Notes

1. In 1926 IG Farben's shares had a value of RM 1,100m whereas the second largest German company, the Vereinigte Stahlwerke AG (United Steelworks), had only RM 800m.: see Ter Meer, *Die I.G. Farbenindustrie Aktiengesellschaft. Ihre Entstehung, Entwicklung und Bedeutung* (Düsseldorf, 1953), 27; *Der Farbenkonzern 1927, Die I.G. Farbenindustrie A.-G., ihre Tochtergesellschaften und Beteiligungen. Aufbau, Statistik, Finanzen* (Berlin, 1927; special print from *Das 'Spezial-Archiv'*), 11. Of the remaining German chemical enterprises, none had a capital stock larger than 10 per cent of IG Farben: see table in H. Tammen, *Die I.G. Farbenindustrie Aktiengesellschaft (1925–1933). Ein Chemikonzern in der Weimarer Republik* (Ph.D. thesis, Berlin (W), 1978), 19.

2. A. Marcus, *Die grossen Chemiekonzerne* (Leipzig, 1929), 32.

3. As an example, see Bayer Works Archives (BWA) 9/A1, Vertrauliche Niederschrift der Amerika-Besprechung vom 22.12.1927; also Extract of the Documentary Evidence of the US-American Kilgore Committee, printed in R. Sasuly, *IG Farben* (Berlin, 1952), Appendix 3, 317–22.

4. BWA 4c 31.13, K. Timm, 'Die Abwicklung des Auslandsvermögens der I.G. Farbenindustrie AG. Im Auftrage der Rechtsabteilung der Farbenfabriken Bayer bearbeitet' (unpublished MS, no place and year of publication given [Leverkusen, 1951]), 13.

5. See the figures given in table 6.3. Until 1933 IG exported 50 to 57 per cent of its production, in some fields up to 75 per cent.

6. B. W. Knauff, 'Bayer im Ausland' (unpublished MS, no place of publication given [Leverkusen, 1971]), BWA without file no. Nevertheless, IG Farben held major direct investments, above all in the dyestuffs, pharmaceuticals and photographics fields in the U.S.A., and also in the dyestuffs industries of Italy, Spain and Switzerland.

7. Recent publications, e.g. H.-J. Schröder, 'Deutsche Südosteuropapolitik 1929–1936. Zur Kontinuität deutscher Aussenpolitik in der Weltwirtschaftskrise', *Geschichte und Gesellschaft*, II (1976), 5–32; idem, 'Südosteuropa als "Informal Empire" Deutschlands 1933–1939. Das Beispiel Jugoslawiens', *Jahrbücher für Geschichte Osteuropas*, XXIII (1975), 70–96; D. Stegmann, '"Mitteleuropa" 1925–1934: Zum Problem der Kontinuität deutscher Aussenhandelspolitik von Stresemann bis Hitler', in D. Stegmann, B.-J. Wendt and P. Witt (eds.), *Industrielle Gesellschaft und politisches System, Beiträge zur politischen Sozialgeschichte, Fs. F. Fischer zum 70. Geb.* (Bonn, 1978), 203–21; H. Sundhaussen, 'Die Weltwirtschaftskrise im Donau-Balkan-Raum und ihre Bedeutung für den Wandel der deutschen Aussenpolitik unter Brüning', in W. Benz and H. Graml (eds.), *Aspekte deutscher Aussenpolitik im 20. Jahrhundert* (Stuttgart, 1976), 121–64.

8. See in detail, e.g. Tannen, *op. cit.*, 15f., 21ff.; Ter Meer, *op. cit.*, 29f.

9. See H. Schreyer, 'Der IG-
Farbenkonzern, seine Vorgänger und
Nachfolger. Ein Beitrag zur
Organisationsgeschichte der deutschen
Chemieindustrie', *Archivmitteilungen*,
XVI (1966), pt 1, 101–6, pt 2, 148–58,
here esp. 105; Marcus, *op. cit.*, 47ff.
10. The *Sparten* comprised interrelated
chemical fields:
   Sparte I: e.g. nitrogen, hydrogenation
   fuels, nickel, coal.
   Sparte II: e.g. heavy chemicals,
   magnesium, organic
   intermediary products,
   dyestuffs, pharmaceuticals,
   artificial materials, artificial
   rubber.
   Sparte III: e.g. photographics, cellulose,
   artificial silk and fibres and
   their processing.
The *Sparten* co-ordinated and controlled
technical developments, research, etc.,
but did not interfere with the
management of the individual works.
They were organized in 1929. See Ter
Meer, *op. cit.*, 32; Tammen, *op. cit.*, 23;
Schreyer, *loc. cit.*, 151f.
11. Verkaufsgemeinschaft Chemikalien
(heavy chemicals, intermediary
products, metals, etc.)
Verkaufsgemeinschaft Photo und
Kunstseide (photographic articles,
artificial silk and fibres, etc.)
The sale of nitrogen fertilizers and
technical nitrogen had been taken over
by the Stickstoff-Syndikat GmbH in
Berlin, founded in 1919, a very tight
cartel and common sales agency of
German nitrogen producers. Synthetic
fuels were sold by the Deutsche Gasolin-
AG, Berlin, an IG subsidiary. See Ter
Meer, *op. cit.*, 45f.; Tammen, *op. cit.*,
22f. and 40ff.; *Activities of I.G.
Farbenindustrie AG in the Nitrogen
Industry*, ed. Economics Division,
Decartelization Branch, Control Office
I.G. Farbenindustrie AG, U.S. Zone
(1946), Höchst Works Archives (Hö),
without file no., 7–28.
12. Annual Reports of IG Farbenindustrie
AG, 1928, 1929, 1930.
13. Ter Meer, *op. cit.*, 46. The commercial
commission was called 'Kaufmännische
Kommission' from 1926 to 1928,
thereafter 'Kaufmännischer Ausschuss'.

In the years 1933 to mid-1937 it did not
hold regular meetings. Commercial
questions were then dealt with in the
Arbeits-Ausschuss and Technischer
Ausschuss respectively. BWA 13/8 and
13/9; see also Tammen, *op. cit.*, 24f.
14. Farbenausschuss, Chemikalien-
ausschuss, Pharmazeutische Hauptkon-
ferenz: Ter Meer, *op. cit.*, 46.
15. As with the merger in 1925 all directors,
then 83, had been incorporated into the
new board of directors: the
Arbeitsausschuss and, from 1931
onwards, the more informal Zentralausschuss were established as executive
committees. The board of directors as a
whole did not even meet before 1937.
Both AA and ZA can be considered as
rather temporary institutions derived
from the special situation after the
merger. The Arbeitsausschuss was
dissolved in 1938 and the
Zentralausschuss lost its function as a
place for top decision-making after 1935.
By this time, the *Vorstand* – greatly
reduced by retirements and deaths –
took over top management functions.
Similarly the supervisory board
(*Aufsichtsrat*) elected a working
commission (*Verwaltungsrat*): see Ter
Meer, *op. cit.*, 51–7; Tammen, *op. cit.*,
27f.; Schreyer, *loc. cit.*, 148f.
16. Ter Meer, *op. cit.*, 53.
17. To give one example: F. Ter Meer was:
   1926–45 member of the board of
   directors (1926–38 also of the
   Arbeitsausschuss, 1933–45 of
   the Zentralausschuss)
   1925–45 member of the Tea (1933–45
   chairman of this commission)
   1929–45 leader of the Sparte II
   1936–45 representative of the Tea
   (Technical field) in the
   Farbenausschuss (dystuffs
   commission)
Besides that he held seats on numerous
supervisory or managerial boards of IG
subsidiaries: see 'Aus dem Urteil des IG-
Farben-Prozesses', in *Fall 6. Ausgewählte
Dokumente und Urteil des IG-Farben-
Prozesses*, edited and introduced by H.
Radandt (Berlin (GDR), 1970), 183; Hö
110, meetings of the Farbenausschuss;
Tammen, *op. cit.*, 24; Schreyer, *loc. cit.*,
149.

18. Ter Meer, *op. cit.*, 47.
19. *Ibid.*, also Schreyer, *loc. cit.*, 106.
20. See in detail Schreyer, *loc. cit.*, 153–6; Tammen, *op. cit.*, 155–61.
21. *Ibid.*
22. Max Ilgner, IG-Konzern-Bericht über meine Ibero-Amerika-Reise August/ Dezember 1936. Allgemmeiner Teil und Beobachtungen in den einzelnen Ländern (unpublished MS No. 177, no place and year of publication given [1937]), 40 and 42ff.
23. Hö 1306, Österreich-Bericht für die Vorstandssitzung am 21. Oktober 1938; see Tammen, *op. cit.*, 252f.; H. Radandt, 'Die IG Farbenindustrie AG und Südosteuropa bis 1938', *Jahrbuch für Wirtschaftsgeschichte*, III (1966), 146–95, here 178f.
24. See e.g. MI 6646, Eidesstattliche Erklärungen von Justus Saxer vom 20.3.47 und 18.4.47, in *Fall 6, op. cit.*, 100f.
25. Ilgner, IG-Konzern-Bericht, 41.
26. See table 6.2. H. Radandt, 'Berichte der Volkswirtschaftlichen Abteilung der IG Farbenindustrie AG über Südosteuropa. Bibliographie', *Jahrbuch für Wirtschaftsgeschichte*, IV (1966), 289–314, esp. 291ff.
27. See J. Schmelzer, *Unternehmen 'Südost'. Südosteuropapläne der IG-Farben* (Wolfen, 1966) (Aus der Geschichte der Filmfabrik Wolfen 11), 13f.; with regard to the German–Hungarian commercial treaty of June 1933: Radandt, *loc. cit.* (1966), 155.
28. Ilgner, IG-Konzern-Bericht, 53.
29. *Akten zur deutschen auswärtigen Politik* (ADAP), Series C. Vol. 1, 2, Doc. No. 414; Aufzeichnung des Gesandtschaftsrats Benzler, Aktenvermerk v. 5.9.33, 768–770; Radandt, *loc. cit.* (1966), 160f., 172.
30. See Ilgner, quoted in *ibid.*, 157f., 172: also *ADAP*, C, 1, 2, Doc. 414.
31. *ADAP*, Series C. Vol. 1, 2, Doc No. 415: Ergänzung zu der Aufzeichnung über ein deutsch-rumänisches Kompensationsgeschäft vom heutigen Tage, 5.9.33, 770.
32. Radandt, *loc. cit.* (1966), 154f.
33. *Ibid.*, 174–7.
34. With regard to the MWT, see: T. v. Wilmowsky, 'Entstehung, Entwicklung und Arbeit des Mitteleuropäischen Wirtschaftstages. Referat, gehalten auf der Mitgliederversammlung des MWT am 22.11.38', BWA 62/40; H. Barche, 'Der "Mitteleuropäische Wirtschaftstag". Zur Ostund Süd-osteuropa-Politik des deutschen Imperialismus in Vorbereitung des Münchener Abkommens', *Deutsche Aussenpolitik*, v (1960), 1294–1302; R. Berndt, 'Wirtschaftliche Mitteleuropapläne des deutschen Imperialismus (1926 bis 1931)'. *Wissenschaftliche Zeitschrift der Martin-Luther-Universität Halle*, XIV (1965), 227–36, esp. 233ff.; W. Schumann (ed.), *Griff nach Südosteuropa. Neue Dokumente über die Politik des deutschen Imperialismus und Militarismus gegenüber Südosteuropa im Zweiten Weltkrieg* (Berlin (DDR), 1973), 51 and numerous documents; Tammen, *op. cit.*, 248ff.; T. v. Wilmowsky, *Rückblickend möchte ich sagen . . . An der Schwelle des 150 jährigen Krupp-Jubiläums* (Oldenburg/ Hamburg, 1961), 188ff., esp. 192, 204f., 212.
35. Minutes and papers of the Südosteuropa-Ausschuss in BWA 13/25 and Hö 191a. See also for details Radandt, 'Die IG-Farbenindustrie AG und Südosteuropa 1938 bis zum Ende des Zweiten Weltkrieges', *Jahrbuch für Wirtschaftsgeschichte*, I (1967), 77–146, esp. 77ff.; Ter Meer, *op. cit.*, 46; Schumann, *op. cit.*, 45f. and numerous documents. In 1936 an analogous East Asian Commission (Ostasien-Ausschuss, OAA) had been founded.
36. BWA 13/25, note 'Mitglieder des Südosteuropa-Ausschusses', undated. The SOA was led by Director Dr Hans Kühne.
37. Ter Meer, *op. cit.*, 46; Schreyer, *loc. cit.*, 150.
38. BWA 13/25, Minute of a meeting under the leadership of Max Ilgner in Berlin of 28 Aug. 1940; *ibid.*, letter v. Schnitzler to Ilgner, 11 Sept. 1940.
39. Radandt, *loc. cit.* (1966), 178 (quotation of Hermann Gross).
40. For H. Gross, see R. Vogel, 'Hermann Gross-Forschung, Lehre, Leben', in *Wirtschaftswissenschaftliche Südosteuropa-Forschung* (Munich, 1963), 1–8, esp. 3f.

41. NI 7987, Aktennotiz von Hermann Gross (IG-Farben) vom 28.3.1939: 'Die Wiener Zweigstelle der Volkswirtschaftlichen Abteilung der IG Farbenindustrie Aktiengesellschaft'. Printed in *Fall 6*, *op. cit.*, 92f.

42. See e.g. for Austria, BWA 84/ Österreich, Vowi-report: 'Die IG in Österreich', 19 March 1938.

43. See e.g. Tammen, *op. cit.*, ch. 1.

44. E.g. in Czechoslovakia, BWA 1/ 6.6.18.2. 'Verkauf Pharma Länderübersicht' (unpublished MS, no place and year of publication given [Leverkusen, after 1953]), 384.

45. *Ibid.*, with regards to Romania, 347f.

46. *Ibid.*, 9. The German Behring works, which produced sera and vaccines, co-operated closely with Höchst and later IG, and in 1929 became affiliated to IG Farben (*ibid*. 117). 'Behring'-Institutes existed in Yugoslavia, founded in 1920, and in Hungary and Bulgaria.

47. See above, n. 11.

48. See Ilgner, IG-Konzern-Bericht, 49. In Central Europe, dyestuffs and chemicals were often sold by the same firm:
Austria: Detag, Deutsche Teerwaren- und Chemikalien-Handels-gesellschaft
Czechoslovakia: Tefa, Teerfarben- und Chemikalien-Handels-AG
Hungary: Budanil, Farben- und Chemikalien-Verkaufsgesellschaft
Romania: Romanil, Aktiengesellschaft für Teerfarben und Chemikalienhandel
– compiled from: 'Activities of IG Farbenindustrie AG in the Dyestuffs Industry' (unpublished MS), ed. Economics Division, Decartelization Branch, Control Office IG Farbenindustrie AG, U.S. Zone (1946), Hö without file no., Annex X, e.a.

49. The development in Central and South-East Europe in the pharmaceuticals field provides a good example for this development. In each country IG products were represented by foreign agents after the war. IG-owner companies were founded as follows:
Austria: Vedepha GmbH, Verkaufsorganisation für Pharmazeutika und Pflanzenschutz (founded 1925)

Hungary: Magyar Pharma Gyógyráu R.T. (1929)
Romania: Romigefa SAR (1936)
Yugoslavia: Jugefa 'Bayer'-Pharma K.D. W. R. Mann (1929)
Bulgaria: 'Bayer' Pharma A.D. (1936)
In Czechoslovakia an agent firm continued to exist: 1925–1930 Sperk & Prochaska o.H.G., afterwards with other associates.
– compiled from: 'Activities of the former "Bayer" IG Farbenindustrie AG in the Pharmaceuticals Industry', ed. Economic Division, Decartelization Branch, Control Office IG Farbenindustrie AG, U.S. Zone (1946), Hö without file no., *passim*.

50. *Ibid.*, 11; BWA 1/6.6.18.2, 'Verkauf Pharma', *passim*.

51. Besides the Detag and Vedepha (see nn. 48 and 49), these were the Agfa Photo GmbH (founded in 1931), and Kalle & Co. (for Cellophane, Ozalid, and other synthetic foils): BWA 84/Österreich, Vowi-report, 19 March 1938.

52. *Ibid.*, 2.

53. BWA 84, Annual sales reports from various countries.

54. These were: Bagrilo A.G., Sofia; Anilin a.d., Belgrade; Ceramil S.A. Czernovice; Coloranil S.A., Bucharest; Timanil S.A., Temesvar – 'Activities of I.G. . . . in the Dyestuffs Industry', Annex X.

55. BWA 84/Österreich, Vowi-report, 19 March 1938; *ibid.*, Figure AG Dynamit Nobel Bratislava, 1938.

56. BWA 84/Österreich, Vowi-report 19 March 1938, 1f.

57. IG Farben held indirectly, via the Austrian Dynamit Nobel Company (see below), a small share of 1.2 per cent of the Skodawerke Wetzler AG, Vienna (SWW) but did not succeed until 1938 in gaining a major participation in the firm, whose majority was held by the Austrian Credit-Anstalt: *ibid.*, 3f.

58. See below and fig. 6.1.

59. The Austrian Hiag-Werke, founded in 1930, was a 100 per cent subsidiary of the Deutsche Gold- und Silberscheideanstalt, Frankfurt/M: see *Das Land Österreich im deutschen Wirtschaftsraum*, ed. Deutsche Bank, printed MS (Berlin, 1938), 21; F.

Birkenkamp, *Deutsche Industrie-Anlagen im Ausland* (Würzburg, 1935), 47.

60. BWA 84/Österreich, Report on IG activities in Austria in 1938, 9f.

61. Wirtschaftsbericht Österreich, IG Farbenindustrie AG, Volkswirtschaftliche Abteilung, author: Bernd Wegmann, 31 March 1938, Fl–F3; O. Deutsch, Vienna, 'Europäische Chemieabkommen. Die Verflechtung der I.G. Farbenindustrie mit der österreichischen chemischen Industrie', in *Industrie- und Handelszeitung*, no. 126, (Berlin), 2 June 1929.

62. *Ibid.*

63. *Ibid.*

64. Wirtschaftsbericht Österreich, 31 March 1938, F2f.

65. See 'Österreichisch-deutsche Chemiebeziehungen', *Frankfurter Zeitung*, no. 749 (8 Oct. 1927); 'Die I.G. Farbenindustrie und Österreich', in *Berliner Börsen-Courier*, no. 20 (12 Jan. 1928); Industrie- und Handelszeitung, *op. cit.*, 2 June 1929; also 'Ausschuss zur Untersuchung der Erzeugungs- und Absatzbedingungen der deutschen Wirtschaft (Enquete-Ausschuss)', in *Die deutsche chemische Industrie* (Berlin, 1930), 123.

66. Wirtschaftsbericht Österreich, 31 March 1938, F3.

67. *Industrie- und Handelszeitung, op. cit.*, 2 June 1929.

68. Wirtschaftsbericht Österreich, 31 March 1938, H21 and H22.

69. Radandt, *loc. cit.* (1966), 183.

70. Public Record Office, FO 371 17686, C 5368 and C 5369, Reports of the British Embassy in Berlin, 26 July 1934 and 2 Aug. 1934, about conversations between the Commercial Counsellor of the Embassy and Messrs Krüger, Fahle (directors of IG Farben) and Roth (managing director of the Anilinchemie, Vienna).

71. See *Hamburger Fremdenblatt*, no. 325 (22 Nov. 1932); BWA 13/12, minutes of the 68th meeting of the AA, 15 Apr. 1932, and of the 73rd meeting of the AA, 12 Dec. 1932, 5.

72. Hö 86, Stickstoffbesprechung, 17 Dec. 1936, 14f.

73. IG Farben's foreign sales in % of German chemical exports:

1929	81.7%
1930	66.7%
1931	70.8%
1932	83.8%
1933	80.7%

Sources: table 6.3, *Wirtschaft und Statistik* (Berlin), issues 1930–4.

74. Germany's share in the European market for chemical products was higher: about one-third of all chemical imports into European countries was supplied by the German industry (1931): *Die Chemische Industrie*, no. 45 (5 Nov. 1932), 864.

75. See Vowi-reports: B. Wegmann, Wirtschaftsbericht Österreich, 31 March 1938, H21 and H22; *idem*, Wirtschaftsbericht Ungarn, 30 June 1939, H7, H8, H9; *idem*, Wirtschaftsbericht Tschechoslowakei, 1 Sept. 1938, Vowi No. 2960, H4.

76. The shares of IG Farben tended to be higher than those of the total German chemical exports:

| | 1931 | | 1932 | | 1933 | |
	a	b	a	b	a	b
Czechoslovakia	4.8	5.1	5.5	5.8	3.4	4.7
Austria	2.6	2.4	2.9	3.1	2.4	3.6
Hungary	1.4	1.5	1.4	1.8	1.7	2.3
Total	8.8	9.0	9.8	10.7	7.5	10.6

Sources: Table 6.5; *Wirtschaft und Statistik*.

77. *Statistisches Jahrbuch für das Deutsche Reich* (Berlin), resp. issues.

78. With the U.S.A. taking up first and the Netherlands second place: Enquete-Ausschuss, *Die deutsche chemische Industrie*, 13.

79. For an assessment of the inter-war situation, see e.g. Enquete-Ausschuss, *Der deutsche Aussenhandel unter der Einwirkung weltwirtschaftlicher Strukturwandlungen*, xx, 2; (Berlin, 1932), 196–208; Enquete-Ausschuss, *Die deutsche chemische Industrie*, 8–13; *ibid.*, statement of Carl Bosch (chairman of the board of IG), 121–5; L. F. Haber, *The Chemical Industry, 1900–1930. International Growth and Technological Change* (1971), 325ff.

80. Chemical exports of certain countries (in mill. M/RM and percentage of world chemical exports):

| | 1913 mill. M | 1925 mill. RM | 1929 mill. RM |
	%	%	%
Germany	853 27.1	922 22.9	1,330 27.7
U.K.	500 15.9	593 14.8	650 13.5
U.S.A.	310 9.9	649 16.1	752 15.7

Enquete-Ausschuss, *Der deutsche Aussenhandel*, XX, 2; 200, table 110.

81. Though in 1929 Germany supplied only 61.7 per cent of the world's dyestuffs exports, compared with 88.7 per cent in 1913: *Ibid.*, 204f.; see also table 6.3.

82. See in detail Tammen, *op. cit.*, 42ff., 112ff.

83. Enquete-Ausschuss, *Der deutsche Aussenhandel*, 208.

84. See table 6.5.

85. See Tammen, *op. cit.*, 253. Numerous statements in C. Duisberg, *Abhandlungen, Vorträge und Reden aus den Jahren* 1922–1933 (Berlin, 1933); also C. Bosch, *Handelspolitische Notwendigkeiten*, e.a.

86. See e.g. Stocking, G. Ward and M. W. Watkins, *Cartels in Action: Case Studies in International Business Diplomacy* (New York, 1947), 418ff., with regard to IG 466ff.; also statement of C. Bosch in Enquete-Ausschuss, *Die deutsche chemische Industrie*, 131–3.

87. Stocking, Ward and Watkins, *op. cit.*, 510.

88. A. Teichova, *An Economic Background to Munich. International Business and Czechoslovakia 1918–1938* (1974), esp. 320–35, gives several examples for this kind of agreement. See also BWA 19/ Verträge, including Aussig: Ameisensäure 1926, 1931; Chlorbarium 1926; Schwefelsäure 1934.

89. With regards to the Aussiger Verein, see Teichova, *op. cit.*, 279–94.

90. The Czechoslovak producers held an export quota of 0.62 per cent in the International Nitrogen Cartel. The production of synthetic nitrogen started in 1928; in 1933–4 the capacity amounted to 15,000 tons. In this year 83 per cent of consumption was provided by home production (1929–30: 57 per cent); After the CIA agreement of 1930, no nitrogen products were imported into Czechoslovakia without the previous consent of the Czechoslovak producers. See Wirtschaftsbericht Tschechoslowakei 1 Sept. 1938, H4; Tammen, *op. cit.*, 129; Teichova, *op. cit.*, 319; BWA 19/Stickstoff 1. Hungary's synthetic nitrogen production exceeded its consumption considerably after 1932/3:

1932–3 3,500 tons nitrogen production
– 885 tons consumption
1936–7 6,000 tons nitrogen production
– 1,801 tons consumption
See Vowi-reports: Wirtschaftsbericht Ungarn, 30 June 1938, F5; Die chemische Industrie Ungarns, Vowi No. 3036, 1 Aug. 1938, 5f. (BWA 91/3, Ausarbeitungen III).

91. Indicated by the agreed sales quotas:
German–French dyestuffs cartel 1927
IG 88.5%
CMG 11.5%
Three-Party Dyestuffs cartel 1929
IG 71.67%
Swiss IG 19.0%
CMG 9.33%
Four-Party Dyestuffs cartel 1931
IG 65.602%
Swiss IG 17.391%
CMC 8.54%
ICI 8.467%
DEN agreement 1930
IG (including Norsk H.) 80.5%
ICI 19.5%
CIA agreement 1930
DEN-group 75.86%
CIA agreement 1934
DEN-group 71.5%
Sources: Activities of IG in the Dyestuffs Industry, 44, 52, 56, 33; BWA 19/Stickstoff 1; Hö 85, Stickstoffbesprechung, 7 Feb. 1934, 11; W. J. Reader, *Imperial Chemical Industries*, II (1975), 114.

92. BWA 13/19 and Hö 305, Deutschfranzösischer Kartellvertrag 15.11.27, bestätigt 27.4.29.

93. A thorough and comprehensive analysis of the situation in the dyestuffs field, esp. the impact of the crisis development on cartel and export conditions, was written by the IG director Georg v. Schnitzler for a meeting of the *Arbeits-Ausschuss* on 26 Jan. 1933: Hö 110, Farbenausschuss 1931–33.

94. *Ibid.*, 16 e.a.

95. BWA 13/18, minutes of the meetings of the Deutsch-Schweizerische Geschäftsführung (des Kartells), 10 Dec. 1931, 6; *ibid.*, 13 Dec. 1932, 2f; *ibid.*, 11 Sept. 1933, 5f.

96. Hö 2508, Vorträge Dr Loehr: Zum Farbengeschäft in der Tschechoslowakei, 25 Jan. 1935, esp. 4f. The

market shares of the Czechoslovak market were as follows. In the average of the years 1924–8, the Three-Party cartel supplied 90 per cent of the sales volumes; of these IG alone 72 per cent, Aussig 8 per cent; values: cartel 95 per cent, IG alone 77 per cent. In 1931, the cartel supplied 85 per cent of the volume, 92 per cent value. Aussig supplied 14 per cent of the volumes, 6.5 per cent value. In 1933, Aussig's percentages rose to 21 per cent of the volume and a share of 10 per cent of the value of the Czechoslovak dyestuffs market. The cartel then supplied 86 per cent of the values.

These figures show that Aussig's position was not too strong, but growing fast. Moreover, the firm disturbed the cartel's financial and production potential to become a severe competitor in the dyestuffs field (*ibid.*, 8, 9, 12–15).

97. BWA 13/8, 1. Sitzung der Kaufmännischen Kommission, 25 Feb. 1926, 10; Hö 110, Farbenausschuss, Sitzungen, 13 Feb. 1931, 5; *ibid.*, 14 Sept. 1932, 8, 15f.; *ibid.*, 11 Oct. 1932, 4, 10; *ibid.*, 8 Nov. 1932, 6, 30; *ibid.*, 30 Nov. 1932, 3. BWA 13/12, Arbeits-Ausschuss, 18 Oct. 1932, 2; *ibid.*, 12 Dec. 1932, 4; Hö 81, Tea, 26 Sept. 1932, 2.

98. E.g. BWA 13/21, Minutes of the meetings of the Board of Directors of the Four-Party Cartel, 14 Dec. 1932, 2; *ibid.*, 23 March 1933, 8.

99. Hö 110, Minutes of the Farben-ausschuss, 14 Sept. 1932, 8; *ibid.*, 30 Nov. 1932, 3.

100. *Ibid.*, 30 Nov. 1932, 3; see the market shares, n. 96.

101. Since 1930, the firm Englert & Becker, Prague, had already produced certain dyestuffs for IG against payment (Lohn-Fabrikation). Hö 81, 23. Montags-besprechung des Tea, 23 Jan. 1933, 1.

102. E.g. Hö 1227, Azofarben-Fabrikation in der Tschechoslowakei, *c.* second half of 1932.

103. Hö 2508, Vortrage Löhr, 6; also Hö 110, 14 Sept. 1932, 15f.; *ibid.*, 10–11 Oct. 1932, 4 and 10. With regard to Dynamit Nobel Bratislava, see below.

104. 'um die taktische Position gegenüber

Aussig zu wahren', Hö 110, meetings of the Farbenausschuss, 30 Nov. 1932.

105. Hö 2508, Löhr, 6.

106. BWA 13/12, 79. AA-Sitzung 18 July 1933, 2.

107. Activities of IG in the dyestuffs industry, 67–9; Hö 2508, Löhr, 7ff.; Hö 304, Besprechung zwischen dem 'Verein' und der Dreiergruppe in Dresden am 24 Mai 1935.

108. The sales quota consisted of the:

1933 sales volume	mill. RM 3.3
plus 'Outlet' 1935–6	mill. RM 1
1935–6	mill. RM 2
1936–7	mill. RM 3

109. Hö 304, Besprechung 24 May 1935, 3.

110. Activities of IG in the dyestuffs industry, 67–9; Hö 2508, Löhr, 11, 15, 7.

111. *Ibid.*

112. Reader, *op. cit.*, 113.

113. See the export quotas, n. 91. With regard to the nitrogen agreements, see in detail Activities of IG in the Nitrogen Industry, *passim*; BWA 19/Verträge: Stickstoff.

114. BWA 19/Stickstoff 1.

115. Untersuchung über den Stand und die Entwicklungstendenzen der Weltlandwirtschaft und deren Einfluss auf den Absatz von Stickstoffdüngemitteln, written by W. Klatt, Vowi-report (Berlin, 1937), 1 Apr. 1937, 129f.

116. Belgium, Netherlands, Italy, Poland, Switzerland, ČSR.

117. BWA 19/Stickstoff 1, CIA agreement 1 Aug. 1930, Annex.

118. Activities of IG Farben in the nitrogen industry, 32; Hö 86, Stickstoffbesprechung, 23 Oct. 1935, 28, 30, 39. With regards to Czechoslovakia, see also Teichova, *op. cit.*, 315–30.

119. Hö 85 and 86, Stickstoffbesprechungen, 10 June 1932, 2, 5.

120. *Ibid.*, 1 Sept. 1932, 6f.

121. *Ibid.*, 23 Oct. 1935, 39.

122. See n. 90.

123. The Hungarian Nobel factory, a subsidiary of Dynamit Nobel Bratislava which had indirect capital ties to IG Farben, was forced, for example, to purchase its basic chemicals from the new Hungarian factories instead from IG. Hö 85, 10 June 1932, 2.

124. Hö 85 and 86. Stickstoffbesprechungen,

10 June 1932, 2; 7 Dec. 1932, 3; 24 Feb. 1944, 5; 28 March 1933, 5; 26 Sept. 1933, 11; 20 Feb. 1936, 12f.

125. *Ibid.*, 17 Dec. 1936, 14f., 18; 22 Dec. 1937, 43f., 46; 25 March 1938, 40f.; Hö 331, Schreiben der Verkaufsgemeinschaft Chemikalien vom 25 Nov. 1937; BWA 84/Österreich, Vowi-report 19 March 1938, 3.

126. *Ibid.*, 4f.; also Hö 191a, SOA, Exposé 'Unterlagen für eine Stellungnahme der IG zur Frage der Entwicklung der chemischen Industrie in Südosteurope' of February 1942.

127. *Ibid.*, 6f. (Hö 191a).

128. *Ibid.* See also the speeches and articles of Max Ilgner on industrialization problems: M. Ilgner, Deutschland und die wirtschaftliche Intensivierung der südosteuropäischen Länder (Vortrag, gehalten auf der Hauptversammlung des MWT am 2.9 1940 in Wien, BWA 62/40); *idem*, 'Exportförderung im Rahmen des Vierjahresplanes' (unpublished MS, 1937), 4–7; *idem*, 'Exportsteigerung durch Einschaltung in die Industrialisierung der Welt' (Jena, 1938).

129. See in detail Tammen, *op. cit.*, 72–144.

130. BWA 84/Ungarn, annual sales reports, 1932, 1933; Hö 350, Bericht Dr Thiel über ausländische Fabrikationsstätten, 6; Hö 81, 23. Montagsbesprechung des Tea, 23 Jan. 1933, 2.

131. See a survey of market conditions in various countries in Activities of IG in the pharmaceuticals industry, 68–93. In Central and South-East Europe, competition of national producers was strong in Czechoslovakia and, partly, in Hungary. See also an article in *Kronstädter Zeitung*, no. 215 (22 Sept. 1934), 'IG Farben und Beiersdorf erzeugen ihre Produkte in Ungarn'.

132. *Ibid.*, Activities, 56; also BWA 13/15 meeting of the Tea, 27 Apr. 1933, 3; Verkauf Pharma 348, 385, 395.

133. Verkauf Pharma, 313; BWA 13/12, 68. AA-Sitzung 15 Apr. 1932, 4 and 73. Sitzung 12 Dec. 1932, 5.
     The Hellco AG, Prague, with a factory in Opava (Troppau), also belonged to this enterprise. Verkauf Pharma, 384; *Volk und Wirtschaft im Sudenland. Eine volkswirtschaftliche Studie*, überreicht

von der Dresdner Bank (Berlin, 1938), 29f.; see also the article in *Hamburger Fremdenblatt*, no. 325 (22 Nov. 1932), 'Erweiterung der IG Farben-Interessen in Österreich'.

134. BWA 13/12, *ibid.*

135. BWA 13/9, meeting of the KA, 23 Oct. 1931, 2; 19 Nov. 1931, 2.

136. BWA 13/9, KA, 19 Nov. 1931, 1–3 and 16 Feb. 1932, 3; Hö 110, Farbenausschuss 9 Oct. 1931, 2 and 28 Aug. 1931, 3; BWA 84, Annual and monthly reports from various countries 1931, *passim*.

137. BWA 84/Ungarn, Annual and monthly reports 1931.

138. See A. Basch, *The Danube Basin and the German Economic Sphere* (1944), 87f.

139. Activities of IG in the dyestuffs industry, 69.

140. IG Farbenindustrie Aktiengesellschaft, Annual Report 1932.

141. BWA 13/9, KA, 6.9.32, 5; Radandt, *loc. cit.* (1966), 154.

142. In this way the highly protectionist agrarian policy of the German government was evaded.

143. Radandt, *loc. cit.* (1966), Annex 187f.; BWA 84/Ungarn, monthly report 7/33, annual report for 1933; see also Basch, *op. cit.* 179; *ADAP*, C, Bd. 1.2, 768–70, Doc. 414, 415.

144. Hö 110, FA, 2 Feb. 1932, 8; also PRO, FO 371 16824, C 8024, C 8025, C 8166, embassy reports from Berlin and Romania; Hö 110, FA, 5 Apr. 1932, 2.

145. BWA 84/Ungarn, monthly report 4/32, also 10/32: 'Wir konnten im Clearing-Verkehr mit Ungarn bisher praktisch keine Auszahlungen erhalten und sind nach wie vor auf Privatclearing angewiesen'.

146. BWA 84/Ungarn, monthly reports 6/32 and 7/32.

147. *Ibid.*, monthly reports 1932, *passim*. Also IG Farbenindustrie AG, Annual report 1933, 1; Radandt, *loc. cit.* (1966), Expose Ilgner (Annex), 189.

148. See table 6.5. In 1928 IG had sold 11.3 per cent of its exports to Central and South-East Europe: Radandt, *loc. cit.* (1966), 190.

149. Wilmowsky, *op. cit.*, 204f.; Schumann, *op. cit.*, doc. 13, 89; Siemens archives, SAA 49/Ls 74, Präsidial- und

Vorstandssitzung des MWT, 28 Jan. 1935, 1–3 and other minutes and papers, *ibid.*

150. Historical Archives Krupp, FAH IV E 181, RDI, Wochenbericht 14/33, 30 Sept. 1933, 9; Radandt, *loc. cit.* (1966), 191. The IG signed the (secret) German–Hungarian linseed-treaty in September 1933 as a trustee for the Reich.

151. Basch, *op. cit.*, 189; BWA 13/11, ZA: 'Übersicht über die von der I.G. Farbenindustrie AG in letzter Zeit durchgeführten Auslandsgeschäfte' (*c.* 1937).

152. BWA 13/11, *ibid*; Verkauf Pharma, 115; BWA 62/40, Referat *v.* Wilmowsky auf det Tagung des MWT, 22 Nov. 1938; BWA 84/Rumänien, annual report 1937 and 1938, 2; Radandt, *loc. cit.* (1966), 162; Von Werk zu Werk, Monatsschrift der Werksgemeinschaft der IG Farbenindustrie Aktiengesellschaft, Mai 1938. In 1937, 16,283ha in Bulgaria, and 110,000ha in Romania were cultivated with soya beans, with a value of 400 mill. Lei (in Romania), of which 50 per cent were at IG's disposal. 1938 the Romanian soya exports amounted to a compensation value of RM 10.5 mill.

The cultivation and sales of soya beans were supervised by an organization called Oelsaatverwertungsgesellschaft GmbH, which was founded by IG and the Reichsverband der Deutschen Ölmühlen in 1935. This company owned subsidiaries in Romania and Bulgaria, the Soia, Rumänische AG für den Anbau und Export von Ölsaaten, Bucharest, and Soja, Bulgarische AG für den Anbau und Export von Ölsaaten, Sofia.

153. See Radandt, *loc. cit.* (1966), 160.

154. See nn. 128 and 126.

155. The treaty contained a guarantee of dividends by IG, the possibility of merger and exchange of DAG against IG shares. Besides this 'community of interests', IG held about 20 per cent of the DAG capital, including preference shares; in later years IG held 45.65 per cent. See *Der Farbenkonzern* 1927, 15, 17, 53; Ter Meer, *op. cit.*, 27f.; IG Farbenindustrie Aktiengesellschaft, Abwicklungsbericht und Nachfolge-gesellschaften (no place and year of publication given [Berlin, Essen, 1952])

(Das Spezialarchiv der deutschen Wirtschaft).

An important factor was the dependency of DAG on the delivery of nitrogen from IG factories, and the prices charged for this basic product. See Ter Meer, *op. cit.*, 28; NI 8313, Eidesstattliche Erkärung Ernst Struss, 3 June 1947, printed in: *Fall 6*, 109.

Besides, IG had four of its directors in the DAG supervisory board, and the TEA decided also on DAG's investment and business policy (*ibid.*).

156. For details of the development of the Nobel concern and its foreign interests after the First World War, see Reader, *op. cit.*, I, 404–13; Stocking, Ward and Watkins (eds.), *op. cit.*, 438–48; Teichova, *op. cit.*, 284–94; H. Possin, 'Die ökonomischen, militärischen und politischen Ergebnisse aus Mono-polvereinbarungen der IG-Farben-industrie AG mit amerikanischen Mono-polen und deren Bedeutung für die Vor-bereitung und Durchführung des Zweiten Weltkrieges' (Ph.D. thesis, Halle, 1965), 120–3.

157. This former explosives firm was merged into IG Farben on 1 September 1926 by exchange of shares: Ter Meer, *op. cit.*, 28; *Der Farbenkonzern* 1927, 11.

158. *Der Farbenkonzern* 1927, 53; Stocking, Ward and Watkins (eds.), *op. cit.*, 442–4; Reader, *op. cit.*, I, 411f.

159. Spain, France, Belgium, Italy.

160. Stocking, Ward and Watkins (eds.), *op. cit.*, 443f., and Reader, *op. cit.*, I, 411f.

161. *Der Farbenkonzern* 1927, 53. This meant an investment of £375,000 for each company. For the history of this investment from the Nobel side, see Reader, *op. cit.*, I, 410f.

162. In September 1926, Nobel Industries held RM 2,625,000 of IG's nominal capital, i.e. 0.24 per cent (Reader, *op. cit.*, I, 413). The RM 3.75 mill. which Nobel Industries and DuPont respectively held in the DAG, meant a nominal capital participation of each about 10 per cent in this company (*Der Farbenkonzern* 1927, 53). In 1934, the DAG participation was given as 8 per cent by DuPont and 12.5 per cent by ICI (Stocking, Ward and Watkins (eds.), *op. cit.*, 442, n. 44).

163. See the remark of the chairman of Nobel Industries, Sir Harry McGowan, quoted in Reader, *op. cit.*, I, 410; Stocking, Ward and Watkins (eds.), *op. cit.*, 442, n. 46.

164. See in detail Teichova, *op. cit.*, 284ff.; Reader, *op. cit.*, I, 405f. The Explosia was founded in 1921.

165. Nobel Industries and the French Nobel company also held 16 per cent each in 1923, the rest of 52 per cent was held by Czechoslovak banks: see Teichova, *op. cit.*, 284, 286; Reader, *op. cit.*, I, 405. The DN Bratislava shares were taken over by ICI only in 1931 (Teichova, *op. cit.*, 287).

166. Reader, *op. cit.*, I, 405.

167. Teichova, *op. cit.*, 286f.

168. Reader, *op. cit.*, I, 406.

169. BWA 91/2, Vowi-report No. 3068, *c.* 1938, 'Die Organisation der Imperial Chemical Industries Ltd.', 24. *Ibid.*, also about Bickford & Co. Vienna. It could not be traced whether other minority holdings of Nobel Industries, 20 per cent in a Romanian and 12 per cent in a Hungarian company (Reader, *op. cit.*, I, 406) were also invested in the respective subsidiaries of DN Vienna (Bratislava resp.) as part of the agreed 'community of interests'.

170. See McGowan's views in Dec. 1925, in Reader, *op. cit.*, I, 411.

171. See Possin, *op. cit.*, Stocking, Ward and Watkins (eds.).

172. See, e.g., Hö 1227, 'Aufnahme einer Farbstoff-Produktion in der Tschechoslowakei' (undated, *c.* second half of 1932), 3. Another 30 per cent were owned, or represented, by the Pester Ungarische Commercialbank, at least in the 1930s: Radandt, *loc. cit.* (1967), 85, 89ff.

173. Hö 43, Tea meeting of 22 Nov. 1926, 33f. This minute, noting that semi-annual reports on the works of the former explosives concern have been given, mentions the following subsidiaries:
AG Dynamit Nobel, Vienna
AG Dynamit Nobel, Bratislava
AG für industrielle Sprengstoffe, Budapest
Prima Societate Romana Explozivi, Bucharest
Titanit AG für chemische Industrie, Agram
Nobel-Bickford AG, Trencin
Bosnische Elektricitäts AG, Jaice
Carbidwerk Deutsch-Matrei AG, Vienna
Olea, Vereinigte slowakische Oel-Industrie AG, Bratislava
See also fig. 6.1. above.

174. 'Übersicht über die Interessen der IG in Südosteuropa', in *Weltherrschaft im Visier. Dokumente zu den Europa- und Weltherrschaftsplänen* (Berlin, 1975), 360; Radandt, *loc. cit.* (1967), 84, n. 35.

175. BWA 12/19, Notiz for the meeting of the ZA, 28 July 1938.

176. BWA 91/2, Vowi-report No. 3025, 27.9.38: 'Die wichtigsten Firmen der chemischen Industrie in der Tschechoslowakei', 1. For comparison: IG Farben paid dividends of: 1926 – 10 per cent; 1927 and 1928 – 12 per cent; 1929 – 14 per cent; 1930 – 12 per cent; 1931–6 – 7 per cent: H. Gross, *Material zur Aufteilung der I.G. Farbenindustrie Aktiengesellschaft* (Kiel, 1950), table Ia.

177. Hö 108a, Sitzung des Chemikalien-Ausschusses, 14 Oct. 1933, 2. Report of director Weber-Andreae about a meeting with Generaldirektor Phillipp, DN Vienna.

178. Hö 260–261. Auslandslizensen, Bosn. Elektricitäts AG.

179. Hö 81, 23. Montagsbesprechung des Tea, 23 Jan. 1933.

180. Hö 1086, turnover figures of DN Bratislava firms in RM:

	1934	1933	1934 in % of 33
DN Bratislava	2,233,872	2,715,422	82
DN Vienna	648.039	540,716	120
Carbidwerk Deutsch-Matrei	1,207,989	1,238,406	98
Bosnische-Elektricitats	1,492,770	1,112,794	134
Continentale Ges.	979,344	823,900	119
Stickstoffwerke Ruše	2,562,449	1,487,962	172

181. Hö 260–261; Hö 108a, Meeting of the Chemikalienausschus, 14.10.33, 2; Radandt, *loc. cit.* (1967), 86, n. 47.

182. These were: Dir. Ludwig Hopfgartner, Dir. Siegfried Kann, Zentraldir, Ing.

Karl Platzer, Wilhelm Ehrenstein (Dir.-Stellvertreter in Vienna and Jaice). The remaining two members were managing directors of the Jaice works. Of these, Ing. Fedor Slajener was also a member of the supervisory board of the Moster Lack- und Farbenwerke (Hö 260–261).

183. Unterlagen zum Bericht von Herrn Dr Ilgner, 11 Nov. 1940 (BWA 13/25); see Radandt, *loc. cit.* (1967), 84f.; Schumann, *op. cit.*, 27; Tammen, *op. cit.*, 422f.; n.410.

184. BWA 13/15 meeting of the Tea, 24 Feb. 1931, 7; Hö 256, Auslandslizensen; Hö 85, Stickstoffbesprechung, 10 June, 1931, 5.

185. See the quotation in Radandt, *loc. cit.* (1966), 183.

186. Hö 110, Sitzung des erweiterten Farbenausschusses, 8 Nov. 1932, 6; *ibid.*, 27 Feb. 1933, 2f.; Reports of Fritz Ter Meer on his journeys to Vienna and Bratislava concerning the manufacture of dyestuffs in Czechoslovakia.

187. Hö 108a, Sitzung des Chemikalien-Ausschusses, 14 Oct. 1933, 2.

188. The Chemikalien-Ausschuss consisted of commercial and technical directors and staff and was designed to discuss basic questions regarding the sale of chemicals; see above.

189. BWA 84/Österreich, Vowi-report, 19 March 1938.

190. BWA 12/19, Notiz der Direktions-Abteilung Chemikalien vom 28.7.38 zu Top 5e) der Vorstandssitzung am 30.7.38, betr. Österreich. See Radandt, *loc. cit.* (1967), 85.

191. For development after 1938, see in detail Radandt, *loc. cit.*, (1967), esp. 86f., 91, Annex; *idem*, 'Die wirtschaftliche Expansion des IG-Farben-Konzerns in Südosteuropa', in *Actes du Premier Congrès International Des Etudes Balkaniques et Sud-Est Européennes, Sofia* (Sofia, 1970), 273–6, esp. 275; NI 5196, Testimony of Georg v. Schnitzler, 18 March 1947, printed in *Fall 6*, 81–90, esp. 85f. See also Hö 191a, SOA, Memorandum by Gattineau and Meyer on 'Die chemische Industrie in Südost-Europa unter Berücksichtigung des Verhältnisses der A.G. Dynamit Nobel Pressburg zum Prager Verein', 9 Feb. 1942.

7. Siemens and Central and South-East Europe between the two World Wars

Harm Schröter

Siemens was one of the biggest German enterprises in the inter-war period. Manufacturing both high and low voltage electrical equipment, the company was part of export-orientated industry but was not very typical of this branch of industry. Its overall business policy was very cautious and conservative and several main decisions, e.g. about concessions, were forced upon Siemens by its more aggressive rivals. This rather passive than active attitude also characterized one of the most important elements of its industrial policy, namely the structure of the internal organization of the firm. It was kept largely as it had been immediately before the First World War.[1] This prompts some questions: to what extent did these elements hinder Siemens in Central and South-East Europe? Or, perhaps, were they even part of its success? Furthermore, it should be established whether Siemens could be labelled as a 'multi-national enterprise'. There is no generally accepted definition of a 'multi-national', but obviously there are several characteristics which should be traced. For example, did production take place where the highest profit margin could be expected? Did an offensive strategy for foreign markets exist? Was co-operation to be pursued with several foreign governments or merely with its own national one? And did the company subordinate its strategy to national policy or did it go beyond it?

Shortly after the First World War Siemens prospered (see table 7.1) but during the inflation it was forced to retrench. After 1923 Siemens consolidated its position in order to fight for the world market again. This was done primarily by exporting from Germany because investments of any kind abroad were not favoured. Central and South-East Europe was an important market in this struggle but it had always the character of a complementary economy.[2] Central and South-East Europe fitted into the overall trend in selling policies of the European electro-technical industry of concentrating on Europe rather than on the world market. Siemens-Schuckertwerke (SSW) sent to this region in 1924–5 7.7 per cent, and in 1929–30 10 per cent, of all its exports,[3] whereas Siemens as a whole sold in 1936 11 per cent of its exports there. These amounts and the fact that they were neighbouring markets made them important for Siemens.

Besides its own organization, Siemens had two major subsidiaries, the ownership of which was shared with the Allgemeine Elektrizitäts-Gesell-

Table 7.1. SIEMENS AND ITS SUBSIDIARIES IN CENTRAL AND SOUTH-EAST EUROPE: capital and labour

	1919	20	21	22	23	24	25
Share capital of S & H Berlin (mill. RM)	63	63	130	130	130	130	97.5
Dividends of S & H, Berlin, %	12	12	20	80		0	6
Share capital of SSW (mill. RM)							120
Dividends of SSW %							
Employees of S & H plus SSW (000)				79			95
Share capital of ÖSSW (mill. K/sch.)	50	75	200	3500	3500	3500	26.25
Dividends of ÖSSW %	5	8	20	50	100	200	6
Shown profits of ÖSSW (mill. K/sch.)	3	8	40.8	2071	4501	7853	1.8
Shown reserves of ÖSSW (mill. K/sch.)	12.6	80.2	375	3877	4000	4550	23.75
Employees of ÖSSW (000)	5.8	5.2	5.5	5.9	6.3	6.5	6.1
Share capital of USSW (mill. K/Pg)	8	8	8	8	8	8	2
Dividends of USSW %	0	6	10	20	25	500	4
Shown profits of USSW (mill. K/Pg)	0.02	0.06	1.1	2.6	7.0	63.9	0.09
Shown reserves of USSW (mill. K/Pg)	0.24	0.24	0.27	0.32	0.6	4.0	2.0
Workers of USSW (000)							

Sources: SAA 4/Lf 711; Deutsche Bank (ed.), *Das Protektorat Böhmen und Mähren im deutschen Wirtschaftsraum* (Berlin, 1939); Deutsche Bank (ed.), *Das Land Österreich im deutschen Wirtschaftsraum* (Berlin, 1938); Hafeneder, *op. cit.*; Nehring, *op. cit.*; Das Spezialarchiv der deutschen Wirtschaft S & H und SSW, Ausgaben 1928–1935; Waller, *op. cit.*

schaft-Union Elektrizitäts-Gesellschaft (AEG). The subsidiaries – Telefunken and Osram – operated without being managed directly by Siemens. Telefunken concentrated on the radio field and Osram on the production of bulbs. Telefunken held between 17 and 74 per cent of the domestic markets in Central and South-East Europe,[4] while Osram had factories in Czechoslovakia, Greece and Poland.[5] As Osram was allocated Central and South-East Europe (except Greece) as a protected market in a cartel agreement with the General Electric Company (GEC) and NV Gemeenschappelijk Bezit van Aandeelen Philips' Gloeilampenfabrieken (Philips' Incadescent Lamp Works Holding Co. Eindhoven – 'Philips'), it was the main supplier of bulbs to this region.[6]

The organizational structure of Siemens was complicated as the enterprise covered the whole range of electro-technical equipment. Essentially it was divided into a high voltage section, covered by Siemens-Schuckertwerke (SSW), and a low voltage, covered by Siemens u. Halske Aktiengesellschaft (S & H), but both spheres gradually coalesced as a result of technological progress. Several departments, e.g. the Zentral Finanzabteilung (central

26	27	28	29	30	31	32	33	34	35	36	37	38	39	40
97.5	97.5	97.5						107	107	107	107			
10	12	14	14	14	9	7	7	7						
120	120	120	120	120	120	120	120	120	120	120	120			
8.5	9	10	10	7.5	0	0	0	0						
94	116	130	138	113	99	75						183		
26.25	26.25	35	35	35	35	35	35	35	32	32	32	21.35		
6	6	6	8	8	0	0	0	0	0	0				
1.9	2.0	2.6	3.5	3.3	0.2	0	0	0	0	0	0.4	0.7		
23.75	23.75	15.0	15.0	15.0	15.0	11.9	9.0	7.1	7.1	7.1	7.1	4.7		
5.7	7.0	8.2	7.9								4.8	6.0	7.0	
2	2	2	2	2	2	2	2	2	4	4	4	4	4	4
8	10	12	12	12	8	6	5	5	5	7	8		0	8
0.2		0.4	0.4	0.3	0.2	0.2	0.2	0.3	0.4	0.5			0.5	0.5
2.0		2.1	2.2	2.3	2.3	2.4	2.4	0.5	0.6	0.6		0.8	1.7	1.9
		0.3					0.2					0.5		

finance department), the Zentrale Verkehrsverwaltung (central sales department) and the Wirtschaftspolitische Abteilung (department for economic policy), served both companies. But the main linking element was the personal one of Carl-Friedrich von Siemens, a member of the owning family, who directed the companies himself. Decisions were made at board meetings by von Siemens, who as chairman decided any issues personally at the end of the discussion.[7] Although the chairmen of the management boards (Vorstandsvorsitzende) of S & H – Dr Franke and Dr von Buol – and Dr Köttgen and Dr Biugel of SSW, took part in decision-making, to apply the terminology of Chandler and Daems, Siemens was a classic 'entrepreneurial enterprise'.[8]

All Siemens' exports to Europe were managed from Berlin, except those to Central and South-East Europe for which Vienna remained the centre responsible. Sales were pursued by 'technical bureaux' (TBs) which were usually headed by a technical and commercial manager (*Kaufmann*). It was typical of Siemens that the technician was often the leading figure in the team.[9] Though Siemens had a large worldwide network (62 producing and 200 selling companies in total),[10] the firm was primarily German and aimed at exporting.

During the decade after the First World War reparations became significant for German industry. A certain amount of reparations was paid in commodities and these goods, received without payment, opened up foreign markets for German merchandise. In this way reparations turned out to be a drawback for the industry of the former Entente powers in third markets. Deliveries on reparation account were quite important for Siemens, especially to Yugoslavia and Romania. Because of the lack of capital in these countries a large share of the electro-technical exports was imported via reparations,[11] in the case of Yugoslavia 23–70 per cent (1927–31).[12]

The peace treaty of Trianon forced Siemens, like other German enterprises, to reorganize its connections with Central and South-East Europe, but the overall policy seems to have been to make as few changes as possible. Because of the high investments there and its continuing substantial connections[13] with the area, Vienna was chosen as the centre of operations: 'the business in South-East Europe could better be directed from Austria, because in this area the old relations made it unnecessary to knit new threads.'[14] Political considerations, such as French influence in the region and the greater suitability of Vienna than Berlin as a base for exports, might also have played a role.[15] The Österreichische Siemens-Schuckert-Werke (ÖSSW) remained as a foreign-based subsidiary, in charge of all high voltage business. It was the biggest electro-technical enterprise in Central and South-East Europe (except Germany). In an agreement signed in 1922, the markets were formally divided between ÖSSW and SSW, with the former concentrating on that area.[16]

Low voltage production was organized differently. The 'Wiener Werk' factory (Siemens & Halske AG, Vienna) was not an independent company, because in spite of being situated in a foreign country, it was run according to German law and was included into the balance sheet of S & H Berlin.[17] Despite this, the Wiener Werk was looked upon as a genuine Austrian enterprise, which was important with regard to Austrian state orders.[18]

Austria was the most important country for Siemens in Central and South-East Europe. The biggest factories were situated there and Vienna was a stepping stone to the whole region (see fig. 7.1). The Austrian subsidiaries concentrated on this area and the various Siemens' sales companies in those countries were organized from Vienna. The formation of these companies took place soon after the Treaty of Trianon: Czechoslovakia in 1920, Romania in 1922, Yugoslavia in 1922, and Bulgaria in 1923. As usual, operations were divided between high and low voltage, with the ÖSSW directing all activities in the field of high voltage, including the plants in Czechoslovakia and Hungary, while the Wiener Werk controlled only the sales organizations. Bigger assets, such as factories and concessions, were directed from S & H in Berlin.

The Wiener Werk, a factory with more than 1,000 workers, produced nearly the same product range as S & H in Berlin.[19] But its capacity could not meet demand and up to 60 per cent of all its sales consisted of re-exported goods of German origin.[20]

During the post-war inflation in Austria things went quite well for the ÖSSW. Though profitability is difficult to measure, there were plenty of orders and the employment situation was good. Between 1921 and 1924, an additional 1,000 workers were employed, raising the total work-force to 6,500 (see table 7.1). However, on the financial side it was not quite so rosy. Though the inflation gave Siemens a unique chance to buy up 75 per cent of ÖSSW shares, the relatively small sum of 700,000 Gold marks needed for this purpose was not available.[21] After the conversion from the crown to the schilling in 1925, ÖSSW had a capital of 26.25m sch. with an additional 23.75m sch. in the reserve fund. This financial picture clearly illustrates a strong characteristic of the Siemens concern, namely its appreciation of a high degree of security in finance. It was laid down in the renewed foundation agreement that each year ÖSSW had above all to transfer a portion of profits amounting to 5 per cent of the share capital to the reserve fund, before it could issue a dividend.[22]

In Hungary, Siemens had inherited a factory from the Habsburg 'K.u.K.' régime. After the war it was set up as the Ungarische Siemens-Schuckert-Werke (USSW), Budapest and organized as a subsidiary of ÖSSW. Immediately after the Treaty of Trianon it had to be reduced in size. The well-known problem caused by the territorial shrinkage of Hungary forced USSW to sell all its eight power stations.[23] During the post-war disturbances hardly any work was done,[24] but after the victory of Admiral Horthy the employment situation remained good as long as inflation continued. After the currency stabilization in 1924 a lack of orders caused great problems.

The new frontiers laid down by the Treaty of Trianon were favourable for Siemens, as it had an established factory in each of the main successor states. In Czechoslovakia the ÖSSW-branch in Prague was set up as a subsidiary of ÖSSW. This was done only in 1920, because immediately after independence, Czechoslovakia imposed a tax on newly founded foreign-owned companies of up to 1.5 per cent of the respective capital of the parent company,[25] though this policy was abandoned later. Siemens & Co KG, Prague, was established with distribution offices (VBs) in 10 different towns. A factory in Bratislava which was owned by USSW was 'saved' by leasing it as early as 1918.[26]

It was only after the various inflations ended that Siemens was able to pursue an active policy of its own. Its overall aim was to regain the world-wide position it had held before the First World War. In this struggle Central and South-East Europe was looked upon as a minor part of further expansion. Industrial strategies had to be adapted to the prevailing economic and political conditions in the various countries and required elaborate policy and organization. The question is, whether the policy and the organization of Siemens were equal or superior to those of their competitors.

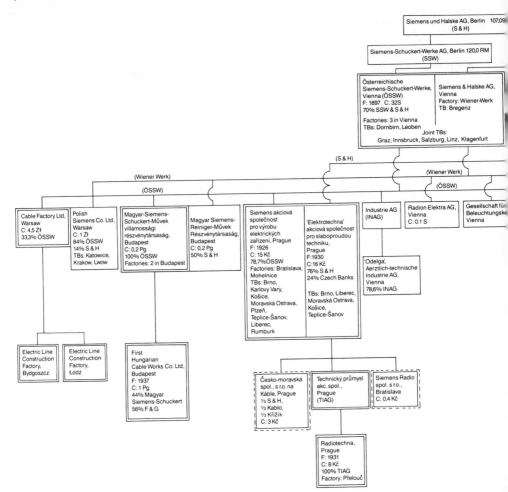

Figure 7.1. Siemens' Central and South-East European organization scheme, 1937.
(*Sources* SAA 4/1f 711 (Organisationsplan des Wiener Werkes); Deutsche Bank
(ed.), *Das Protektorat Böhmen und Mähren im deutschen Wirtschaftsraum*, Berlin,
1939; *idem* (ed.), *Das Land Österreich im deutschen Wirtschaftsraum*, Berlin, 1938;
T. Hafeneder, 'Das Haus Siemens von der Weltwirtschaftskrise bis zum

Siemens' attitude towards industrialization in other countries was very important. The Central and South-East European countries pressed for industrialization by various means, like protective tariffs and favouring domestic production.[27] Pursuing these policies, the three most advanced countries of the former Habsburg Empire (Austria, Czechoslovakia and Hungary) made substantial progress in the electro-technical industry.

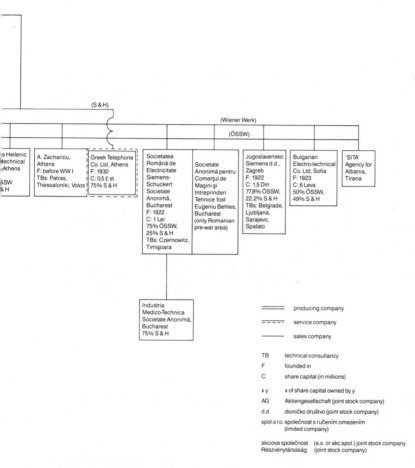

(S & H)

(Wiener Werk)

(ÖSSW)

| s Hellenic technical Athens SW H | A. Zachariou, Athens F: before WW I TBs: Patras, Thessaloniki, Volos | Greek Telephone Co. Ltd, Athens F: 1930 C: 0,5 £ st. 75% S & H | Societatea Română de Electricitate Siemens-Schuckert Societate Anonimă, Bucharest F: 1922 C: 1 Lei 75% ÖSSW, 25% S & H TBs: Czernowitz, Timişoara | Societate Anonimă pentru Comerţul de Maşini şi Intreprinderi Tehnice fost Eugeniu Behles, Bucharest (only Romanian pre-war area) | Jugoslavensko Siemens d.d., Zagreb F: 1922 C: 1,5 Din 77,8% ÖSSW, 22,2% S & H TBs: Belgrade, Ljubljana, Sarajevo, Spalato | Bulgarian Electro-technical Co. Ltd, Sofia F: 1923 C: 6 Leva 50% ÖSSW, 49% S & H | 'SITA' Agency for Albania, Tirana |

Industria Medico-Technica Societate Anonimă, Bucharest 75% S & H

═══════ producing company

╌╌╌╌╌ service company

───── sales company

TB   technical consultancy
F   founded in
C   share capital (in millions)
x y   x of share capital owned by y
AG   Aktiengesellschaft (joint stock company)
d.d. dioničko društvo (joint stock company)
spol.s r.o. společnost s ručením omezením
        (limited company)
akciova společnost   (a.s. or akc.spol.) joint stock company
Részvénytársaság   (joint stock company)

Zusammenbruch des Deutschen Reiches', II. Bd II. Fassung: unpublished MS, SAA 49/La 581 [Munich, 1972]; K. Nehring, 'Siemens in Ungarn', *Südost-Europa Mitteilungen* III.16 1976, 69; Das Spezial-Archiv der deutschen Wirtschaft S + H und SSW 1929–35; E. Waller, 'Studien zur Finanzgeschichte des Hauses Siemens, V. Teil (1960/61), unpublished MS, 280, SAA 20/Ld 366.)

Whereas the pre-war monarchy had a share of 1.5 per cent of world exports in 1913, these countries together exported 4.3 per cent in the crisis year of 1933, with Hungary the leader.[28]

Industrialization was not in Siemens' interests, as it was aimed at import substitution and, whenever possible, Siemens avoided foreign industrial investments in order to maintain its exports from Germany. But if an important market like Czechoslovakia was in danger of being lost to competitors through lack of investment, Siemens was ready to start domestic production very quickly. Furthermore, once established, subsidiaries of Siemens were backed up to the hilt by credits and other means.[29]

The ÖSSW was the biggest investment Siemens held in Central and South-East Europe, with a share capital of 35m sch. It had three factories in Vienna, two for electro-technical equipment and one for cables, and several subsidiaries and TBs within Austria.[30] It produced nearly all the electrical equipment for power stations, factories, transport systems, and even the household. No other Siemens plant outside Germany had as wide a variety of products as ÖSSW. A special 'Vermittlungsstelle' (mediation bureau) guaranteed close contacts between SSW and its Austrian subsidiary. The ÖSSW flourished in the 1920s, but during the crisis and subsequently development was very sluggish and by 1936 its share capital was reduced to 32m sch. Fortunately its reserves were high enough to sustain the firm during these years. From 1936 onwards the ÖSSW recovered, and this is reflected directly in the trend of employment figures and, with a lag of a year, in dividends (see table 7.1).

The ÖSSW and the Wiener Werk were the management centres for Siemens in Central and South-East Europe. But though the Wiener Werk was not an independent company and the spheres of high and low voltage were separated, they appeared together on the various markets, often using the same office. This picture becomes further complicated, if the occasional sales of subsidiaries for political reasons are taken into account.[31] Therefore the table given is valid only for 1937 (but with minor changes only from 1934 to 1938).

Siemens' Hungarian enterprise, the USSW, was small but quite prosperous, and earned the highest dividends in Central and South-East Europe. When the Pengö currency was established, its capital was fixed at 2m Pg, with a reserve of another 2m Pg.[32] Benefiting from extensive state orders from 1926 onwards, the firm expanded its capacity and further investments were made in a cable factory. In 1934, despite surrounding economic calamities, the USSW doubled its share capital to 4m Pg by using its reserve fund. In 1941 the capital was raised again to 6m Pg, this time with the aid of a 0.848m Pg investment directly from SSW.[33] Though USSW was designed only for high voltage production, it started manufacturing low voltage equipment in 1930, in response to the government's policy of protection. This broke Siemens' basic organizational principle of keeping the spheres of S & H and SSW apart. This new line of production increased quickly and in 1940 275 workers were employed, producing mainly radio and military equipment.[34]

In 1937 Siemens, together with Felton & Guilleaume Fabrik elektrischer Kabel, Stahl- und Kupferwerke Aktiengesellschaft[35] bought from the Czech Moravská banka the 'Elsö Magyar Kábelgyár Reszvénytársaság' (Budapest) [First Hungarian Cable Works Co. Ltd] which employed 500 workers.[36]

The Czechoslovak authorities pursued a policy of restricting imports so as to favour local production and from the early 1920s Siemens had been hampered by high tariffs[37] and other administrative obstacles.[38] Consequently it expanded production in the high voltage sphere quite early. In 1925 ÖSSW founded a community of interests with the banks behind the Akciová společnost pro výrobu elektrických zařízení a stavbu strojů (Emag) in Müglitz (Mohelnice), which led in the following year to the merger of Siemens & Co. KG with the Mohelnice enterprise to form Siemens akciová spol. pro výrobu elektrických zařízení, Prague (SEAG).[39] ÖSSW owned 78.7 per cent of the share capital of 15m Kč. As well as its factories in Mohelnice and Bratislava and its headquarters in Prague, SEAG was represented in eight other Czechoslovak towns.

During the 1920s Siemens, in the area of low voltage production, was only represented by the Lékařsko-technický průmysl akciová společnost, Prague (ATiag). This firm, working in the field of electro-medicine, was sold by S & H to the Wiener Werk in 1926 and thereafter was directed from Austria.[40]

Though the world economic crisis of the early 1930s had a very severe impact on Siemens,[41] the concern was strong enough to continue to pursue overall long-term expansion and other aims in that period. Furthermore, Siemens' abundance of capital, a function of its cautious financial policy, contrasted sharply with the troubles of its main international competitors. Accordingly Siemens was able to expand and win several structurally important victories over its competitors inside and outside Europe. This behaviour was by no means seen as 'aggressive', because the steps taken were meant as a defensive strategy to secure long-term access to important markets. This applies especially to S & H, because the main battle fought during the crisis was for the expanding telephone market and this mainly involved the International Telephone and Telegraph Corporation (ITT, U.S.A.), L. M. Ericsson (Sweden), and S & H, although affecting all telephone-producing enterprises.

In this context, and reacting to Czechoslovak government pressure, S & H founded the Elektrotechna a.s. pro slaboproudou techniku, Prague, in 1930, with the object of producing equipment required by the state. For this reason it was convenient to have Czechoslovak capital participating in the total capital of 16m Kč. Officially 51 per cent of the share capital was held by the Moravská agrární a průmyslová banka, but in reality S & H owned 76 per cent to the bank's 24 per cent. An additional 27 per cent was handed over by S & H to be kept by the bank with the latter acting as trustee for S & H.[42] The bank received from S & H a guaranteed dividend of 9 per cent over the next five years for the 24 per cent of the shares. Among other reasons these actions were necessary to become a member of the Czechoslovak armament federation.[43]

In 1931 Siemens managed to extend its holdings in Czechoslovakia, and ATiag was sold to Elektrotechna akciová společnost pro slaboproudou techniku (Elektrotechna). Its name was altered to Siemens, technický průmysl a.s., Prague (Tiag) and its share capital was raised from 1m to 10m Kč.[44] The reason for this was a change in its sphere of business as it now switched from electro-medicine to military production. It supplied mainly Czechoslovakia, Romania and Yugoslavia, states of the Little Entente, in product ranges not open to a German manufacturer.[45] Therefore it was especially necessary for Tiag to be regarded as a Czechoslovak enterprise.

The capital of 'Radiotechna', another subsidiary which produced wireless sets in close connection with Telefunken, was increased in the same year to 8m Kč.[46] The radios were sold entirely by Telefunken. Here again it was thought necessary to change the external appearance of the company. Although Tiag owned 100 per cent of its capital, only 76 per cent of this was shown publicly with the other 24 per cent being formally held by a Telefunken director.[47] All these three new subsidiaries were important, especially in the competition between S & H and ITT.[48]

Another possibility of growth, besides production, was to establish generating companies. Before the First World War the German concerns AEG and Siemens had built up such enterprises, mainly for electricity supply,[49] but after the war they lacked the necessary large amounts of capital.[50]

S & H succeeded in sharing the capital (3m Kč) of the 'Böhmisch-Märische Fernkabel GmbH', Prague, on equal terms together with Křižík-Chaudoir and the Kablo akciová továrna na káble a drátěna lana Prague.[51] By this Siemens acquired another connection with domestic Czechoslovak capital, but as Kablo was a subsidiary of Škoda,[52] and Škoda in its turn was to a great extent owned by the French Schneider group,[53] it was in reality a connection with French capital as well.[54] This was a result of a policy of approaching the Schneider group for cable business in France[55] and Czechoslovakia, suggested by C. F. von Siemens as early as 1929.[56]

During the crisis considerable world wide competition developed between Ericsson, ITT and S & H, mainly due to the expansion of ITT, which belonged to the Morgan Group; and Central and South-East Europe became one of the most important 'battle grounds'.[57] For this struggle a huge amount of capital was needed and in 1930 S & H borrowed $14m in the U.S.A. The loan was negotiated by Dillon & Read and most of the non-voting debentures were bought by GEC.[58] Siemens appreciated the purchase by GEC, despite it being another Morgan Group member, as it helped S & H indirectly in its competition against ITT, and gave the possibilty of developing a 'friendly relationship' between the two concerns.[59] Therefore it is wrong to interpret, as Schacher did, the advance of ITT in Europe as a general attack by the Morgan group on the European electro-technical market.[60]

The main field of contest was telephone concessions. Most countries were not advanced enough financially and technically to install a telephone network themselves, so concessions for construction and maintenance of such networks were invariably granted to foreign enterprises. For the firms this meant a structural change in the market, with large, long-term orders which allowed more rationalized production. Consequently 'an organized production was faced with an organized consumption, and by joining supply and demand, the basic economic law that production is determined by demand, was annulled.'[61]

At first Siemens did not intend to enter the business of concessions, because it was too costly, but it was soon forced to do so, by the great advance of ITT in this particular field.[62] The case of Romania will be discussed here, but there were similar negotiations with Yugoslavia and Greece. Romania was considered to be one of the most important countries in South-East Europe and therefore Siemens made the greatest effort to get the concession there in its competition with ITT.[63] In this world-wide contest Siemens saw that the decision would come soon: 'I believe that Romania will perhaps play the decisive role, as it surely has the greatest capacity for development and it is the biggest country in Europe, in which concessions are obtainable!'[64]

It was the aim of S & H, after a period of contest, to conclude an agreement of friendship with ITT.[65] Since 1926 the three main companies on the world market, ITT, Ericsson and S & H, had competed for the Romanian concession. In 1929 S & H tied its bid to the German credit offer to Romania made by a German group headed by the trade firm Otto Wolff which offered a credit of RM 125m in commodities.[66] But this project failed because of the veto of the French side of the international stabilization loan represented by Rist.[67]

Thereafter Siemens tried to advance with the aid of its international connections. Co-operation with Siemens Brothers Ltd, London (SB) and Autelco, Chicago, was increased. Furthermore, co-operation was begun with the Bancamerica Blair Corporation, a bank which became an important partner for S & H during the following years. The connection with Blair was appreciated by S & H, because this bank specialized in telephone business, could provide capital for concessions, and – equally important for S & H in Central and South-East Europe – it had excellent contacts with the French state and administration. A good offer by the Siemens group, an offer by Blair to provide an agricultural credit of $8m, and the interventions of the German, British and French embassies, made Siemens optimistic about winning the concession.[68] S & H was in close contact with the Romanian Prime Minister, the Finance Minister, and the Minister of Traffic and the General Director of the Post.[69] But ironically it was these contacts which may have prevented S & H from gaining the concession, for following Prince Carol's *coup d'état* in 1930 the new government which came into power gave the concession to ITT, this company being less 'compromised' in their eyes. As this decision had a political character, neither the co-operation of the Siemens group with Ericsson (Kreuger group) nor the increased credit offer of Blair could have changed anything.[70]

But Siemens was successful in Greece. In co-operation with Ericsson,

Siemens received the telephone concession for the whole country, though the British electro-technical industry dominated the Greek market. In this case, an agreement that SB would leave Greece to S & H was useful.[71] Though the concession needed a large amount of money, it yielded high profits.[72] Greece soon became important as an export market and even in the first year of the concession exports of telephone equipment rose tenfold.[73] The negotiations for the Greek concession were, like all others, conducted directly from Berlin.

Agreements between electro-technical companies played an essential role in Central and South-East Europe. American firms were the most important both as partners and as opponents for Siemens. Both Siemens firms were technically and financially advanced and independent and there was no risk of their subordination to one of the big American electro-technical groups, e.g. Westinghouse.[74] SSW had had an agreement since 1924 with Westinghouse for the exchange of patents and allocations of markets, but on equal terms. In this treaty SSW received Germany, Austria and Hungary as exclusive markets. In the production of high voltage equipment, the Agreement of Ouchy between the big European companies and the Seba Agreement, the latter limited to Austria, should be mentioned.[75] In the area of low voltage articles agreements were much more numerous. In June 1929 S & H, SB and Associated Telephone and Telegraph Co., Chicago (ATT), signed the so-called 'Zurich Treaties' as a comprehensive world-wide patent and quota agreement.[76] For S & H, the purpose of this treaty was to align the other companies against ITT, which replied by gaining control of Ericsson in mid-1931.[77] With the end of the world economic crisis S & H finally achieved its aims because the struggle was ended and a comprehensive agreement worked out. A characteristic of this agreement was the decisive nature of the territorial allocation of the respective firms in the various countries.[78] In Central and South-East Europe it was determined which group had a concession or a factory in a respective country. Though apparently the agreement was never signed, it indicated the end of the time of contest. However instead of the one comprehensive pact, several smaller agreements came into force, which shaped the relations between the groups of ITT and S & H in a 'friendly' way, but included competition.

There are two other agreements covering Central and South-East Europe which should be mentioned. In the Bulb Cartel this area was allocated to Osram; but in the Cable Cartel (ICDC), Germany obtained only Austria as exclusive market.[79]

An important reason for the success of Siemens was its cautious, even conservative financial policy, a factor which became distinctive during the crisis. Like AEG, Siemens had to borrow capital several times in the U.S.A., but it managed to receive loans without succumbing to foreign influence.[80]

Though Siemens looked for a good return on capital invested in Central and South-East Europe, the overall aim was a steady, long-term return of dividends rather than immediate profits. The subsidiaries were financed on the one hand by their own resources, and on the other hand by direct investment of the parent companies. But the overall aim was to avoid direct investment. This policy was successful in the case of Emag, which was merged with Siemens & Co. KG in 1926 (see above). Once subsidiaries were established, capital increases could be financed by the liquidation of reserves. It was suggested that this method be adopted for the capital increases for Radiotechna, so not draining German capital.[81] A balance sheet analysis shows that the capital increases for ÖSSW in 1928 and USSW in 1935 were undertaken in the same way (see table 7.1). However, to help cope with temporary difficulties, Siemens had to give substantial credits to its subsidiaries.[82] These credits were formulated in terms of strategy rather than mere business practice. A 'reasonable' rate of interest should be paid, but if the situation of the subsidiary was not good, it was possible to abandon interest payments.

Though substantial profits were reinvested, some were remitted to the centre in Germany. For this purpose the normal way of dividend payments was available (see table 7.1). Of course, a highly efficient economy was the ultimate aim: for example, the Romanian telephone concession aimed at a minimum profit margin of 9 per cent, and in the case of Greece it amounted only to 8 per cent.[83] For the success of a subsidiary operation, besides the dividends, the patent duties payable to Siemens were essential too. It was hoped in 1931 that Elektrotechna could yield RM 1m of patent duties on a turnover of RM 15m.[84]

As in most big businesses, personalities played a great role in the field of the electro-technical production. C. F. von Siemens realized this and initiated a long-term policy of personnel development.[85] The importance of personal relationships applied to an even greater extent in the case of state orders. For success, the support of local people was often indispensable. Accordingly, in the case of the Romanian concession SB offered S & H the help of Jonesco, who was said to have influence with King Carol; but S & H believed it had sufficient support in local circles.[86] Furthermore, it was thought to be useful to keep contacts with important people, even when no orders were in sight.

Several states had introduced laws to ensure that important posts on the supervisory board and directorate of a foreign subsidiary were held by their own nationals.[87] In choosing these people, Siemens paid attention to several points: the person's influence on the firms should be minimized, while his influence beyond it should be at a maximum. This could be achieved by employing personalities either with significant influence in the political sphere or in relation to the market concerned.[88] It was often difficult to find such people. Siemens wanted representation by electro-technical specialists of high quality[89] and for this reason there were only two individuals in Central and South-East Europe – Dimitrijević in Yugoslavia and Zachariou in Greece – who represented Siemens firms independently in the manner used in other countries like Sweden. In 1930 SSW dismissed Zachariou, who had been operating as a representative for both SSW and S & H, without informing S & H. This occurred during the negotiations over the Greek telephone concession. C. F. von Siemens criticized this as a mistake of *régie* (direction) and it was soon reversed.[90]

Siemens' economic policy towards Central and South-East Europe was contradictory. On several occasions Siemens' economic interests were opposed to those of German industry in general, but Siemens loyally supported the majority. For economic reasons the company was against the projected German–Austrian Customs Union in 1931, because it was bound to affect ÖSSW seriously, mainly because of its exports to South-East Europe. Again, for economic reasons, Siemens favoured a Danubian tariff union (Tardieu-Plan), as a way of increasing Austrian exports.[91] Because Siemens, in contrast to most other German enterprises, had several fully equipped plants in Central and South-East Europe, its position was different, but these opposing interests of Siemens were not pursued openly. No inter-industrial clash in public of this kind can be traced and Siemens remained loyal to the policy pursued by the majority of German companies. Both S & H and SSW were members of the Mitteleuropäischer Wirtschaftstag (MWT). The director of the Siemens economic policy department, Fellinger, was a member of its management board (Vorstand) (replaced by von Buxhoeveden in 1935) and von Winterfeld was a member of its presidential council (Präsidium). As most federations, the membership of MWT was regarded in a strictly pragmatic way and Siemens checked regularly the usefulness of their association with it.[92]

In the case of trade policy, Siemens and the 'Zendei' (Zentralverband der deutschen elektrotechnischen Industrie e.V.) were basically orientated towards free trade,[93] but high German tariffs were found to be not totally incompatible with an export trade for German industry. Even agricultural tariff protection could be useful as a weapon in negotiations.[94] Only exceptionally, as in the case of extremely high agrarian tariffs (e.g. butter) and the Hugenberg economic policy during the first half of 1933, were counter-actions started. Though bilateralism in trade policy (clearing agreements, etc.) was not appreciated, once it was established Siemens took part as a matter of course. Compensation agreements (barter) were concluded not only with South-East Europe, but also with Iran and South America.[95] The exchange policy pursued by the Nazi Government was detrimental to Siemens and from 1934 Siemens had difficulties in obtaining adequate exchange allocations to purchase raw materials like copper and lead. Here the international network of Siemens helped the parent company to cope with the problem. In this, the ÖSSW played a major role (though Austria also had strict foreign exchange laws) together with a Swiss subsidiary and the British bank Messrs Henry Schröder, London.[96] Compared with other industries, e.g. iron and steel, the trade policy of Siemens was reactive rather than active. However, Siemens was in a better position to cope with pressure on a national as well as on an international level because of its organizational structure.

Because Siemens had connections and was producing in both the Little Entente states and in those which had lost the war, it was able to overcome many difficulties better than other enterprises. It was possible to cope with the problems arising for its Polish subsidiary in 1934 by shifting its centre of direction from Berlin to Vienna.[97] Siemens succeeded in getting British and French contracts, especially for Central and South-East Europe.[98] On the French side too, closer connections with Siemens were appreciated, sometimes even in the field of politics.[99]

In the case of problems in foreign countries, caused by political circumstances, German diplomacy often intervened at Siemens' request. But in special cases, C. F. von Siemens himself influenced personalities in respective governments. Immediately after the Dollfuss Affair and the preceding disturbances in Austria, ÖSSW was threatened with the installation of a State Commissioner. However, after negotiating with the government von Siemens managed to settle the differences by suggesting a 'minor change' in the Verwaltungsrat (board of directors).[100] But a planned meeting with the Czechoslovak Prime Minister Hodža in 1937 did not take place when it became clear that the Czechoslovak Government was taking a hard line towards Elektrotechna. Here again the overall importance of the Munich Agreement is clearly shown,[101] because only after 'Munich' was Elektrotechna allowed to produce for the Czechoslovak state again.[102] This reflects the comparatively 'soft line' pursued by the reduced state – avoiding anything which could be interpreted by the Nazis as 'provocation'. 'Munich' was also decisive for the organizational structure of Siemens in Central and South-East Europe. In December 1938 changes were prepared in both low and high voltage production to switch the centre of all business from Vienna to Berlin from January 1939 onwards.[103]

Siemens cannot be looked at entirely as a multi-national company because of its aims and organizational structure in the inter-war period. Due to its Austrian connections, Siemens' attitude towards Central and South-East Europe was close to 'bi-national', but generally the Siemens organization in this area was exceptional. Taking into account the previously mentioned characteristics of a 'multi-national' there is again a conflicting picture. Within its cartel policy, Siemens went beyond German national economic policies, but it subordinated its overall strategies to those of German industry and the German state. In fact genuine co-operation with government was pursued only in the German case, as is illustrated during the economic conflict between Austria and Germany in 1933, when German policy was supported without question.[104] The majority of characteristics indicate that Siemens was in a 'pre-multi' stage and the whole enterprise was undoubtedly rooted in

Germany. Only as a reaction to pressure from both foreign governments and competitors was production moved to other countries.

The organizational structure for the export markets remained on the whole unchanged during that period. This was more due to passive adjustment to necessities than to an active policy. Only in 1940 were unequivocal areas of responsibility established and overlaps removed within the framework of an overall general discussion on export organization. As Winterfeld has pointed out, such overlaps had caused trade losses in South-East Europe.[105]

Surveying the reasons for the obvious success of Siemens in this area, the management structure seems to be one of the weaker factors. As early as 1932 overlapping problems which had harmed business in foreign countries were discovered,[106] whereas the long-term personnel policy turned out to be very successful. The strategy of directing business from Vienna and co-operation with West European partners was especially effective and successful.

Siemens' interests were not focussed primarily on Central and South-East Europe. The major new investments there – Elektrotechna and the Greek telephone concession – were made not merely as a limited territorial strategy, but as a global one of securing markets against international competitors. In the late 1930s an ever-growing interest of German industry and its organizations, like MWT, can be traced in this area; but this trend is shared only to a minor extent by Siemens. Again this is indicated by the characteristic attitude of Siemens towards MWT. Though MWT focussed attention on Central and South-East Europe at the same time as Siemens made its major investments there, this occurred in parallel, without any particular mutual agreement.

Siemens always acted loyally in concert with the foreign policy of the German government, and industry as a whole, during both the Weimar Republic and the Third Reich. But the concept of a far-reaching economic domination over other European nations by means of a trade policy to be implemented after a victorious war was not adopted by Siemens at the end of 1940. Even then, Siemens accepted a long-term 'normalization' of business in foreign countries. This would force German industry to work under 'normal' conditions of competition, and Siemens tried to prepare itself for this.[107]

Siemens hesitated in the late 1930s and 1940s to act like other German enterprises; it was very reluctant to become involved in the trend of backward integration of raw material supplies. It seems possible that Siemens preferred to safeguard the status quo, because it was an old-established firm. Even the First World War did not seriously threaten the company, so that later there was no need to be as aggressive as some of the newcomers. A cautious, conserving policy, avoiding major clashes, was generally followed. This applies to both internal policy, where Siemens favoured both the Zentrale Arbeitsgemeinschaft[108] and later the attitude of Brüning-Hindenburg in preference to that of Hitler, and external policy, where co-operation with the Entente Power groups was sought to the extent that Siemens could reconcile such collaboration with loyalty to Germany. The concession policy shows a reluctance to step into new market spheres and cartel policy, maintaining the company's existing position, was preferred to fierce competition. This very long-term and conservative economic policy, typical of the 'House of Siemens', was one of the main reasons for its success in business during the economically and politically difficult years of the inter-war period.

Notes

1. J. Kocka, *Unternehmensverwaltung und Angestelltenschaft am Beispiel Siemens 1847–1914* (Stuttgart, 1963), 457.

2. *Viz.* B.-J. Wendt, 'England und der deutsche Drang nach Südosten', in Geiss and Wendt (eds.), *Deutschland in der Weltpolitik des 19. und 20. Jahrhunderts* (Düsseldorf, 1973), 483.

3. Siemens Archiv Akte (SAA) 11/Le 570 (Graupe) SW-exports 1922–31. Central and South-East Europe for the purposes of this article include Albania, Austria, Bulgaria, Czechoslovakia, Greece, Hungary, Poland, Romania, Yugoslavia.

4. Market shares of Telefunken in Europe 1927/28: Austria 74 per cent, Czechoslovakia 65 per cent, Hungary 43 per cent, Poland 37 per cent, Yugoslavia 17 per cent (SAA 4/Lf 690).

5. E. Waller, 'Studien zur Finanzgeschichte des Hauses Siemens, V. Teil (o.O 1960/61)' (unpublished MS, 280 [SAA 20/Ld 366]).

6. Aktennotiz betr. Besprechung GEC, Philips (SAA 4/Lt 398, VI).

7. As example: Aktennotiz über eine Beteiligung an einer Kabelfabrik in Polen und Zusammengehen mit F & G und AEG, 4 July 1929, 10 (SAA 4/Lt 398, III).

8. A. D. Chandler and H. Daems, 'The rise of managerial capitalism and its impact on investment strategy in the Western World and Japan', in H. Daems and H. van der Wee (eds.), *The Rise of Managerial Capitalism* (The Hague, 1974), 6.

9. 'Kabelfabrik', 5 (SAA 4/Lt 398, III).

10. DWI-Bericht Nr. 7 (Berlin (DDR), 1955), 5.

11. Zentralverband der deutschen elektrotechnischen Industrie [Zendei] (eds.), *Deutscher Elektro-Aussenhandel, Statistischer Bericht 1932* (Berlin, 1932) (printed only for members), 14 (SAA 29/Lg 476).

12. Romanian imports via reparations were concentrated on electro-, medical-, lighting equipment and power stations up to RM 8.21m. (1927–31): *ibid.*, 71; Yugoslavian imports via reparations were concentrated on electrotechnical machinery and telephones up to RM 8.116m. (1927–31): *ibid.*, 71.

13. A. Basch, *The Danubian Basin and the German Economic Sphere* (1944), 51.

14. Waller, *op. cit.*, 192.

15. *Viz.* A. Glardon, *Die deutsche Elektroindustrie und der Absatz ihrer Erzeugnisse in der Nachkriegszeit* (Hamburg, 1933), 90.

16. Waller, *op. cit.*, 204.

17. T. Hafeneder, 'Das Haus Siemens von der Weltwirtschaftskrise bis zum Zusammenbruch des Deutschen Reiches', II.Bd II.Fassung, (unpublished MS, SAA 49/La 581 [Munich, 1972]).

18. Letter of Dir. Krauss, Vienna to Dir. Schwenn, Berlin, 24 March 1933, (SAA 49/Ls 137).

19. Künftige Fertigung im Wiener Werk, 24 Oct. 1938 (SAA 4/Lf 711).

20. Besprechung mit Lammers, 18 June 1932 (SAA 44/Lt 398, IVa).

21. Waller, *op. cit.*, 205. This was later than the heavy investments Siemens made in the Alpine Montangesellschaft on the demand of Stinnes in the period of the Siemens-Rhein-Elbe-Schuckert Union, amounting to more than 1.8m sch. (*viz.* Letter of C. F. von Siemens to Stinnes, 13 Feb. 1923 (SAA 4/Lf 537).

22. *Das Spezialarchiv der deutschen Wirtschaft, Die Siemens Schuckert Werke AG* (1928), 19.

23. K. Nehring, 'Siemens in Ungarn', in *Südost-Europa Mitteilungen* 3, XVI (1976), 69; Waller, *op. cit.*, 213.

24. *Viz.* I. Berend and G. Ránki, *Economic Development in East-Central Europe in the 19th and 20th Centuries* (1974), 171.

25. Waller, *op. cit.*, 219.

26. *Ibid.*, 213. VBs were established in Bratislava, Brno, Karlovy Vary, Moravská Ostrava. Plzeň, Prague, Liberec, Rumburk, Teplice, Opava.
27. *Viz.* Basch, *op. cit.*, 17, 80; I. Berend 'Investment strategy in East-Central Europe', in Daems and van der Wee (eds.), *op. cit.*, 178.
28. (Enquete-) Ausschuss zur Untersuchung der Erzeugungs- und Absatzbedingungen der deutschen Wirtschaft, *Der deutsche Aussenhandel Bd*, 20 Feb. 187; P. Czada, *Die Berliner Elektroindustrie in der Weimarer Zeit* (Berlin (West), 1969), 317.
29. For example the credits given to the Elektrotechna AG für Schwachstromtechnik, Prague, exceeded its share capital of 16m. Kč: Waller, *op. cit.*, 221.
30. TBs were established in Dornbirn, Graz, Innsbruck, Klagenfurt, Leoben, Salzburg, Vienna.
31. For example the factories in Poland were sold from SSW to ÖSSW in 1934: Hafeneder, *op. cit.*, 171.
32. Nehring, *op. cit.*, 57.
33. *Ibid.*, 57.
34. *Ibid.*, 59.
35. Felton & Guilleaume (F & G) was dominated by ARBED, which in its turn was dominated by the Schneider group. This co-operation with French capital, counteracting the overall trend of the French/British-German contest for influence in Central and South-East Europe, was the last one that could be traced.
36. Nehring, *op. cit.*, 59.
37. Beantwortung des Enquete-Fragebogens, 4 March 1927 (SAA 4/Lf 729).
38. For example, telephones of foreign origin were not allowed to be connected to the official network run by the post: *ibid.*
39. Waller, *op. cit.*, 219.
40. *Ibid.*, 208.
41. *Viz.* Czada, *op. cit.*, 194.
42. Besprechung bez. 'Elektrotechna', 8 Apr. 1931 (SAA 4/Lt 398 V).
43. *Frankfurter Zeitung*, no. 558 (29 June 1930).
44. *Spezialarchiv, S & H* (1920), 20; Waller, *op. cit.*, annexed paper no. 6, 1.
45. 'Elektrotechna'.
46. Waller, *op. cit.*, annexed paper no 6, 1.
47. Siemens was not a participant, minor to the participating ITT, in the Telegrafia,

as it is assumed in A. Teichova, *An Economic Background to Munich* (1974). 220. Telegrafia, a subsidiary of ITT – the Czech state had a minor shareholding too – was the biggest and most important competitor of Siemens in Czechoslovakia (*viz.* 'Elektrotechna'; *viz.* Bericht über die Stockholmer Besprechung zwischen Ericsson, ITT und S & H, 16–17 Aug. 1934 (SAA 4/Lf 701).
48. Glardon, *op. cit.*, 48; 'Elektrotechna' (SAA 4/Lf 709).
49. Glardon, *op. cit.*, 54.
50. Waller, *op. cit.*, 213.
51. *Spezialarchiv* (1932), 17; Walter, *op. cit.*, 223.
52. Teichova, *op. cit.*, 268.
53. *Ibid.*, 100, 263.
54. 'Kabelfabrik', 10 (SAA 4/Lt 398, III).
55. Waller, *op. cit.*, 223.
56. Only genuine investment, not share capital (in mill. Kč). SEAG: 11.76; 'Elektrotechna': 12.16, Tiag: 10; 'Radiotechna': 8; B.-M. Fernkabel: 1; Siemens Rundfunk: 0.4; all together 43.32; total amount of share capital: 50.4. If we count in investments (share capital) made by Osram (20.0) and AEG (11.0), the holdings of the two biggest German electrical companies alone total 81.4. This exceeds by far the 44.4m. Kč investment of all German electro-technical enterprises traced by Teichova, *op. cit.*, 218, relying on Czech material.
57. *Viz. Bohemia* (Prague), no. 146 (22 June 1930).
58. *Spezialarchiv S & H* (1932), 28; *Deutsche Bergwerkszeitung*, no. 28, (2 Feb. 1930).
59. G. von Siemens, *Geschichte des Hauses Siemens*, III. *Die Dämonie des Staates 1922–1945* (Freiburg/Munich, 1951). 258.
60. G. Schacher, *Der Balkan und seine wirtschaftlichen Kräfte* (Stuttgart, 1930), 166.
61. E. Brandstetter, *Finanzierungsmethoden der deutschen elekrtotechnischen Industrie* (Giessen, 1930), 170.
62. Beantwortung des Enquete-Fragebogens, 4 March 1927, 7 (SAA 4/Lf 729).
63. Letter C. F. von Siemens to Haller and Franke, 12 Apr, 1930 (SAA 4/Lf 703).
64. *Ibid.*
65. *Ibid.*
66. Similar to the credits for the Soviet

Union, the German state should guarantee the credit. The group, aiming at railway materials, consisted of AEG, Borsig, Demag, Eisenbahn-Verkehrsmittel AG Bislig, GHH, Krupp, Linke-Hofmann-Busch, Löwe, Otto Wolff, Schiess-Defries, SSW, Vereinigte Eisenbahn-Signal-Werke AG, Vestag, Vereinigte Westdeutsche Waggonfabriken, and Vögele AG (SAA 4/Lf 703, Zentrale Verkehrsverwaltung an Fessel, 30 July 1929).

67. Zusammenfassung über das rumänische Telefongeschäft (Grabe), 26 July 1929 (SAA 4/Lf 703).

68. Besprechung über Rumanien, 24 March 1930 (*ibid*.): Lage in Rumänien (Grabe), 27 March 1930 (*ibid*.); Vorschlag Esterer nach Rücksprache mit Blair, 31 March 1930 (*ibid*.).

69. Stand des Rumäniengeschäftes, 24 July 1929 (*ibid*.).

70. Schacher, *op. cit.*, 166.

71. Besprechung mit Wright (Chairman of SB), 7 Jan. 1929 (SAA 4/Lf 677).

72. Waller, *op. cit.*, 200.

73. Glardon, *op. cit.*, 218.

74. Teichova, *op. cit.*, 218.

75. The Seba agreement allocated the Austrian market in the following way: (Ö)SSW: 41 per cent; AEG: 25 per cent; Elin (Vienna): 16 per cent; BBC: 15 per cent (Aktennotiz: Zusammengehen AEG und SSW bez. Tauern- und Donauprojekte, 4 March 1931, 2; SAA 4/Lf 529).

76. As it was valid for all subsidiaries, too, ATT included its British subsidiary International Automatic Telephone Co. Ltd, London (IAT). Quotas: S & H 46 per cent; ATT and IAT: 38 per cent; SB: 16 per cent (Hafeneder, *op. cit.*, 38). It was valid until it was suspended for the time of the war (letter from ATT to S & H, 15 Sept. 1939) (SAA 4/Lf 690).

77. Letter Grabe to Wright, 19 Nov. 1932 (SAA 4/Lf 690).

78. The allocation was the following: Austria: S & H, ITT; Bulgaria: S & H, ITT; Czechoslovakia: S & H, ITT; Greece: S & H; Hungary: ITT; Poland: ATT/IAT; Romania: ITT; Yugoslavia: S & H, Ericsson (Mitteilung an C. V. von Siemens betr. Weltverständigung, 28 Aug. 1934; SAA 4/Lf 701).

79. Bulbs: Besprechung GEC/Osram, 29 June 1929 (SAA 4/Lt 398, III); Political and Economic Planning (PEP), *Report on International Trade* (1937), 106. ICDC: *Viz*. Teichova, *op. cit.*, 266; Aussprache über Verlängerung der Kabelkartelle, 4 July 1929, 2 (SAA 4/Lt 398, III).

80. In 1932 loans amounted to:

S & H   26,961,500 S + 22,500,000 RM
SSW   6,590,750 S + 12,500,000 RM
_____
33,552,250 S + 35,000,000 RM

(*Spezialarchiv* [1932]. 27; [1935], 37.)

81. 'Elektrotechna' (SAA 4/Lf 709).

82. Examples for credits: SWW Romania borrowed (in mill. RM)

	1927	1928	1929
from ÖSSW	1.46	2.233	2.12
from SSW	—	—	0.08

(Betr. Rumänien, 30 July 1929; SAA 4/Lf 703.) In 1931 'Elektrotechna' owed S & H 50m Kč ('Elektrotechna'; SAA 4/Lf 701). In 1938 the Greek telephone concession owed S & H 161,100 Kč (Waller, *op. cit.*, 202).

83. Besprechung über das rumänische Telefongeschäft, 28 Apr, 1930 (SAA 3/Lt 398, III).

84. 'Elektrotechna' (SAA 4/Lf 701).

85. S. von Weiher and H. Goetzeler, *Weg und Wirken der Siemens-Werke im Fortschritt der Elektrotechnik 1847–1972* (Munich, 1972) (*Tradition*, Beiheft nr. 8), 90.

86. Wright's letter to Witzleben, 19 March 1930, and Witzleben's letter to Wright, 23 June 1930 (SAA 4/Lf 677).

87. Teichova, *op. cit.*, 98.

88. 'Elektrotechna' (SAA 4/Lf 701).

89. Überlegungen bez. des *Exportgeschäfts* (Diercks), 31 Oct. 1940 (SAA 4/Lf 690).

90. Besprechung über Griechenland, 29 Nov. 1930 (SAA 4/Lt 398, III).

91. Besprechung mit Lammers, 18 June 1932 (SAA 4/Lt 398, III).

92. Siemens' estimation of the usefulness of the Deutsch-österreich-ungarische Wirtschaftsverband was very positive in 1927, less positive in 1929; finally in 1932 Siemens seceded (7 Oct. 1927, 10 Aug. 1929, 20 Feb. 1931, 30 May 1931, 21 Sept. 1931, 29 June 1932) (all SAA 49/Ls 77).

93. Sitzung des Vorstandsrates des Zendei, 15 Jan 1932, 2 (SAA 4/Lf 812); Aktennotiz; Sicherung des Rohstoffbedards, 25 Sept. 1934, 1 (SAA 11/Lb 366, Jessen).
94. Vorstandssitzung des Zendei, 15 Dec. 1932, 8 (SAA 4/Lf 812).
95. Hafeneder, *op. cit.*, 23.
96. Letter to Messrs Schröder, 10 Aug. 1934 (SAA 4/Li 336); Aktennotiz vom 8 Aug. 1934 (*ibid.*).
97. Hafeneder, *op. cit.*, 171.
98. *Viz.* above-mentioned examples (Czechoslovakia, Greece, Romania) and the negotiations with a French group for operations in Yugoslavia, consisting of Tréfileries & Laminoires du Havre, L'Electro-Cable, Société des Telephones Grammont, (Bericht Deibel, 23 Dec 1929; letter of Robard (Tréfileries) to Deibel, 11 Jan. 1930, letter Deibel to Robard, 21 Jan. 1930, (SAA 4/Lf 703).
99. Unterredung mit F. Marsal, 14 Jan. 1923 (SAA 4/Lf 543).
100. Hafeneder, *op. cit.*, 171.
101. *Viz.* Teichova, *op. cit.*, esp. 381.
102. Schreiben Diercks, 30 Jan. 1939 (SAA 4/Lf 703).
103. Mitteilung vom 17 Dec. 1938; Rundschreiben nr. 90, 22 Dec. 1938 (SAA 4/Lf 703).
104. Germany took diplomatic steps against a further restriction of Austrian imports of electro-technical equipment in 1933. The Wiener Werk co-operated with the German mission in Vienna by supplying it with the relevant material. It asked von Broich of the mission not to mention this co-operation, because in that case the Wiener Werk would lose its image as an 'Austrian' firm, which would cause trouble in receiving state orders (letter of chairman Kraus, Wiener Werk, to S & H, Berlin (von Schwenn), 24 Apr. 1933 (SAA 49/Ls 137).
105. 'Also the insufficient [this word is marked with an '?', presumably by C. F. von Siemens] share of the market of the House of Siemens of the Balkan business is not at least caused by the division of central direction between Wiener Werk and ÖSSW. We did not succeed in creating viable selling agencies with capable management, but two on both sides insufficient parallel organizations emerged!' (Überlegungen zur Ausfuhr [Winterfeld], 27 Nov. 1940, 9); (SAA 4/Lf 690).
106. Bespr. bez. auswärtiger Fabriken, 15, 23 Dec. 1932 (SAA 4/Lt 398, V).
107. 'Exportgeschäft', 2 (SAA 4/Lf 690).
108. This was a co-operation scheme between the unions and the employers.

COMMENTARY *L. Hannah*

I would like to compliment all three of the authors of the papers in this section on excellent empirical business history studies. Without such studies we cannot hope to understand the economic issues posed by multi-national investment. My brief is to put these in a wider framework, discussing one or two general issues which occur to a non-specialist in German multi-nationals and Central Europe.

I would like to start by considering an issue which was raised by Mr Kaser when he was making a contribution to the discussion of nostrification. He defined nostrification as the opposite of multi-nationalism. As a British business historian I find that a very stange definition, because most of the recent Anglo-Saxon-American and British-literature of multi-national companies stresses that one of their most important strategies is to appoint people in the localities to run their enterprises in order to gain local confidence and political support. One of the major themes of comparative international business history has been that the Americans have been rather more successful at doing this, and indeed that this is one reason why their corporations dominate the multi-national field. Gaining local support, and 'nostrification', in the sense of setting up local head offices, giving local people positions and prestige within the enterprise etc., are very important aspects of their strategy. When we look at the case studies which have been presented to us by Alice Teichova and the Schröters I think we find exactly the same thing. The legal requirements in the successor states may have been the motive for these firms either appointing local directors or setting up their head offices in local cities, but it is quite clear that these are legal 'tokenisms'. The real control, surely, rests with the people who hold the shares, who need not be nationals of the countries. From the point of view of a government strategy of maximizing local economic welfare, the successor states appear, in a broader international perspective of possible strategies, to deal with multi-nationals in a relatively unsophisticated way. In trying to develop legal principles of dividend control (see ch. 5, p. 110) none of the countries whose policies are investigated in these papers appear to have any idea how to share the rents of entrepreneurship. It appears strange, for example, that there is no idea of insisting on 50 per cent participation, a common stipulation the post-Second World War period in under-developed nations (see, for example, D. K. Fieldhouse, *Unilever Overseas*, 1978). Another Balkan state, Romania, was developing extremely tight control over foreign capital in her oil industry from the early twentieth century, and it would be instructive to know if any early lessons were learnt from that.

In management personnel also, it is strange that the successor states attached so much importance to nationality. The sort of nationals appointed as directors, as representatives, presumably of the 'national interest', are upper-middle-class people who have a certain cosmopolitanism, who have certain financial interests which they share very clearly with their companies and the capital-exporting country to whose multi-national capital they are host. The view that if you appoint your own nationals to positions of power within a multi-national organization, you automatically provide any protection to your country, seems to me to work only under rather special conditions. There may be a national benefit and I draw my example from the British case which I know best. We had, of course, a great deal of American investment in Britain in the 1920s and 1930s and although there was no legal requirement to appoint British directors, the American multi-nationals quite sensibly saw that it would be good for their public image. They behaved very much as did the German multi-nationals in Central Europe (under more direct host government pressure). For example, they appointed ex-Conservative cabinet ministers to be members of the board and if they had also been viceroys of India or something of the kind, so much the better. These people pursued generally the interest of their paymasters, the Americans. They perhaps cared slightly about the specific national interests of the British Empire once they got into this different role. Yet their basic allegiance appeared often to be to the prosperity of capitalism, in which they thought the Americans had a legitimate part. Then in the mid-1930s the Americans, afflicted by the depression at home, started declaring dividends on some of the British companies they owned at an excessive level. In one company, the Greater London & Counties Trust (which owned public utility companies), the dividends the American parent requested were as high as 50 per cent. The British directors saw that this was against the British national interest and, with the support of the Bank of England and City institutions, they managed to repatriate the capital in order to prevent this exploitation by the capital-exporting country.

One sees from this comparison that the problem of acting in the Czechoslovak or Hungarian national interest in the later 1930s is of a completely different order of magnitude. When there are political and military overtones, it is arguable that having national directors simply cannot help the successor states to preserve their national interest. Was the 'tokenism' of the host governments simply a reflection of their inherently powerless state, or was it, more simply, a rather uncritical patriotism which led to these regulations, involving no serious attempt by the host country to share prosperity? The fact that the nostrification laws go back to the 1920s – when the external political and military constraints were not overwhelming – suggests that uncritical patriotism, or some other cause of failure to view the problem critically, may be at the root of the government's ineptitude on this field.

The second matter I would like to raise is the economic welfare question. Is it true that what is good for Škoda is good for Czechoslovakia, as Beaud claims (see p. 375), in terms of the companies with which we are now describing? I think that one of the strengths of these papers is that they bring together a great deal of statistical information of a kind which only emerges from a great deal of digging in archives. The authors provide data not only on dividends and percentage returns, but also on the other transfers of a capital nature which were occurring, which are so often the most important transfers within international corporations. The rich data could provide the basis for a longer series of the overall rate of return. One could then come to some difficult comparisons and judgments. If one finds out in the end that the real internal rate of return to the multi-national parent on a discounted cash flow analysis is 7 per cent, is that high or low? Guidelines might be sought in the average rate of return in capitalist enterprises in the host countries or of the same companies at home and in other host countries.

I do not know what the answer would be, but I presume that in some of these cases we would judge that the profit was high. There may have been many advantages in having an international company in the successor republics and a higher than average rate of return may indicate simply that the companies were receiving the just rewards of innovation and efficiency: post-war studies have often indicated (e.g. in Britain) that the multi-nationals are more profitable than home companies quite simply because they have better management, better labour relations, etc., and can draw on the technical and marketing expertise of the parent at less cost than creating it themselves.

Yet there are some areas covered by these papers where there are clearly some disadvantages to having the international companies with their cartel-backed monopoly profits. The cartel in bulbs cited by Harm Schröter (p. 184) was a very clear monopoly restriction, I would guess without very great benefit. As mentioned in chapter 5, when the relevant cartel was abolished, the local Mannesmann company did very well and increased its export share. This suggests that the cartel was holding back the local company. On the other hand, it does not necessarily always follow that it would have been good for the local company to expand. Verena Schröter suggests (p. 152) that nitrogen production in one of the Central European states was held back by being involved in an international cartel. That seems to me a great advantage: it was a terrible thing to be in nitrogen production in the 1930s (ICI in Britain lost £20m in the process). It seems excellent in such cases, both from a national and a world point of view, to hold back production.

The overall welfare assessment is obviously going to be difficult. There was a problem for all these countries: it seems that they had less developed economies and they faced what seems at times to have been a monopoly of technical knowledge or a monopoly of expertise in management integration. The classical way in which small countries can benefit from foreign technology is to play off foreign companies against each other. This is certainly what technically weak Western European economies at the time, like Britain, did. (It is important to realize that in the new industries considered here, Britain was almost as backward as the Central European economies.) However, I see little sign from the cases discussed above that any of the South-East European countries did this. Romania intervened in the telephone industry, but then perhaps lost the advantage of this by making a purely political decision rather than playing competitors off to maximize the economic benefits to the host country.

I wonder also why this does not happen elsewhere, for example in the steel tube manufacturing industry. It is true that Mannesmann had the patents; but when Britain wanted to import this technology, it discussed with the U.S. steel consultants Brasserts how to do it. Then it discussed with Mannesmann how to do it, but Mannesmann had to withdraw in 1936 and the U.S. technology was chosen instead because it was a better deal. Why was this not possible in some of these Central European cases? The answer may be political and the comparison with Britain unfair. But one should not under-estimate the extent to which Britain was a backward nation and faced almost exactly the same problems. Britain did have, for example, foreign companies as the major source of technology in electrical engineering. This had been true before the First World War when the industry was inadequately developed. In the 1920s and 1930s it became even more obvious. The biggest expansion in the electrical industry came with American capital: two of the three best manufacturing firms were subsidiaries of the U.S. companies, General Electric and Westinghouse. It is true that in the long run, in the 1950s, British capital bought back those firms. Yet the earlier experience suggests that it may be no bad thing to be subject to multi-national domination. If you look at the statistics of Britain's share in the world market in electrical engineering products, you find that before the First World War (except in cables) it was low; as soon as the Americans took over and dominated the British industry and ran it – that is between the late 1920s and early 1950s – the market share went up to over 25 per cent; and when the British took over again, it went down to about 5 per cent (which is what it is now), a much faster decline than the general post-war decline in Britain's share of world exports.

Any discussion of the impact of multinationals, must, then, assess realistically the weaknesses of the host economy and the contribution of the multi-nationals to solving those weaknesses. Only then will an adequate picture of the balance of gains and losses emerge.

COMMENTARY *Bernd-Jürgen Wendt*

1. THE TERM 'MULTI-NATIONAL ENTERPRISE' AND ITS CHARACTERISTICS

The term 'multi-national enterprise' apparently implies such a wide range of aspects, company structures and stages of company development that it cannot be defined precisely. As Harm Schröter illustrates, there is obviously 'no generally accepted definition of a "multi-national"', but there are 'several characteristics which should be traced' in the context of individual concern history. Alice Teichova takes Mannesmann as an example to describe 'the methods and mechanisms of building a concern (i.e. in Central East and South-East Europe) within a concern'. By this she clearly shows the administrative and capital structures within the concern as well as the mechanisms of control and dependency between the German-based head office in Düsseldorf on the one hand, and the foreign subsidiary enterprises in Czechoslovakia and in the Danubian area on the other hand. In her interpretation, which seems to emphasize more the structural and organizational aspects than the political ones, the concept of the long-term strategy of a 'multi-national combine' and its investment and commercial policies means the following:

More vertical integration inside Germany and more horizontal foreign expansion.

Concentration and consolidation.

Supply – as well as market-orientated direct foreign investment to gain foreign bases and stepping stones for further future multi-national expansion into protected markets of the Danubian area and the Balkans.

The maximum possible control over the decisions taken in the daughter company by the parent firm in Düsseldorf and by the Deutsche Bank.

Verena and Harm Schröter take the examples of IG Farben and Siemens in order to extend the signification of the term 'multi-national enterprise' and its characteristics; thus they are able to include the political component, i.e. the aspect of power politics, besides the structural component and the pure business or industrial strategies. In their papers they focus their attention on the following problems:

The existence of an offensive and homogeneous concern strategy for foreign markets.

The co-operation of the parent as well as the daughter firms with foreign governments and/or with their own national one.

Personal relationships and contacts with national bureaucracies, ministries and the central offices of industrial organizations as well as with the ruling national elites.

The foreign trade policy of the government as a framework for concern strategies and vice versa.

The influence of given political circumstances of growing nationalism and state intervention and of the Little Entente upon concern strategies.

The grade of subordination of company strategy to national policy.

The adaptation of industrial strategies to the prevailing economic and political conditions in the various countries.

In evaluating the importance of the political and social consequences of multi-national combine strategies, besides the economic ones, we must take into account the whole range of foreign as well as domestic policies, the social and political environments of 'multi-nationals' in different countries, their influence upon the labour market and upon the growth of national products etc. Seen in this light, there are undoubtedly various stages of development a 'national combine' has to pass through in order to become a 'multi-national one', with different business strategies and certain forms of intertwining between parent and daughter firms.

With the example of Mannesmann, Alice Teichova describes a 'multi-national enterprise' in the strict sense of the word – at least until the Munich Agreement when the multi-national character disappeared with the dismemberment of the Czechoslovak Republic.

Harm Schröter, basing his argument on the example of Siemens, draws the following conclusion: with regard to the aspect of combine strategy, Siemens' attitude towards East Central and South-East Europe was, due to its Austrian connections, not 'multi-national' but rather 'bi-national'; and in this way it greatly differed from the structure of the Mannesmann concern. 'The majority of characteristics indicate that Siemens was in a "pre-multi" stage and the whole enterprise was undoubtedly focused on Germany.' Verena Schröter underlines that till 1938 the activities of IG Farben in East Central and South-East Europe were, compared with those of Mannesmann, primarily export- and market-orientated, while 'foreign capital investments were only of secondary importance within the business policy of the concern.' From this she concludes that IG Farben 'was still far from being a multi-national company in any strict sense of the word.'

Emphasizing the more political aspect of the national environment in which the parent firm of a 'multi-national' is operating, Dieter Stiefel in chapter 16 points out that only at the time of the Habsburg Monarchy were the Viennese banks 'multi-national' in a 'multi-national monarchy'; with the fall of the Monarchy in 1918 'multi-national' became 'international' and in the 1930s under the impact of the world economic crisis 'the still international Austrian banking system was reduced more and more to a national basis.'

I wonder if these different terms – 'multi-national', 'international', 'bi-national', 'pre-multi', etc. – and their different characteristics are primarily due to different combine structures and stages of concern development themselves or if they are rather a consequence of different viewpoints and different theoretical and methodological approaches.

2. THE PROBLEM OF CONTINUITY AND DISCONTINUITY

Against the historical background 1890–1914/18 Alice Teichova clearly stresses the continuity between the pre-war and inter-war period, and she does this by taking the structural aspect into account. To my mind, however, Harm and Verena Schröter put stronger emphasis on the elements of discontinuity between the wars with regard to the industrial and business strategy. The three authors together distinguish between certain phases of concern policy in the inter-war development.

There was a period of reconstruction, consolidation, rationalization, modernization and expansion with the construction of the first important international cartels (1925 Continental Tube Cartel) in the 1920s.

Following the shock of the world economic crisis (1929–32) with growing state intervention, with the contraction of the world market and the intensification of a fierce world-wide competition, with tariffs and strict foreign exchange controls, there appeared a policy of readjustment to the political as well as the structural changes on the world market with the aim to pursue overall long-term expansion.

Since 1933, but already prepared in the late 1920s, there was a forceful political and economic German penetration into the 'Grosswirtschaftsraum Südosteuropa' as an important step in the National Socialist concept of *Wehrwirtschaft* (war economy) and *Lebensraum* (living space).

Then in the late 1930s after the 'Anschluss' and the Munich Conference, but already beginning in the mid-1930s, there came a reinforcement of the German offensive and a far-reaching economic and political German domination over Central East and South-East Europe by means of direct investments and of trade policy, i.e. clearing agreements and compensation trade.

This tough policy was much more intensively adopted by Mannesmann (personnel policy and control 'as a political instrument in pursuing the nationalistic and racialist aims of the German government' [p. 131] and by IG Farben ('either by direct participation in the chemical industries, or by the foundation of new companies' [p. 143] than by Siemens, whose economic interests on several occasions 'were opposed to those of German industry in general' and even to the German government's 'concept of a far-reaching economic domination over other European nations by means of a trade policy' (H. Schröter, pp. 186, 188).

I would like to ask Alice Teichova to what extent can this tough line of nationalistic expansion in 'Mitteleuropa', which she impressively illustrates after the advent of the Hitler government, be traced in the concern strategy of Mannesmann before 1933? Did the multi-national strategy of the combine also threaten the independence of the other successor states apart from Czechoslovakia? What role did Mannesmann play in a German banking and business policy which endeavoured 'to undermine the political ties between the states of the Little Entente and their alliance with France, as well as their economic relations with Great Britain, in order to create more favourable conditions for intensifying its economic penetration of Central and South-eastern Europe?'[1] To what degree was the business strategy of the head office in Düsseldorf under Wilhelm Zangen, who in 1934 was entrusted with the general management of the Mannesmann combine by the Deutsche Bank and who in October 1938 became leader of the 'Reichsgruppe Industrie', 'intentionally' integrated into the National Socialist foreign policy towards Central and South-East Europe and to what extent was it, like Siemens, beyond this conception? Did Zangen, who 'played an active part in the economic preparations of Fascist Germany for the Second World War'[2] and who 'was determined to expand German economic influence in Central and South-East Europe',[3] emphasize new features in the concern policy, and did he possibly synchronize concern and national strategies towards the South-East more intensively? Was the 'unequal association' between Mannesmann and the Prague Iron Co. in Kladno[4] just part of highly aggressive concern strategy in order to subordinate 'the production as well as commercial and financial policy of the Prague Iron Co. to the interests of the Mannesmann combine in Germany'[5] or was it, especially in the crucial year 1936–37

(*Vierjahresplan!*), already part of a national power policy that had carefully been agreed upon with Berlin, as Král points out?[6]

3. THE 'MULTI-NATIONAL ENTERPRISE' AND THE PROGRESS OF INDUSTRIALIZATION IN THE LESS-DEVELOPED COUNTRIES OF SOUTH-EAST EUROPE

The following question is of immense political and economic importance and relevance, even for the inter-war period, especially with respect to post-war development in South-East Europe as well as in the Third World: to what extent do or did 'multi-nationals' promote or hamper the progress of industrialization and the transfer of technology and of technical know-how in the underdeveloped economies with the aid of their world-wide concern policy and mechanisms of controlling their foreign daughter companies by direct investments? To what degree can the fact that foreign subsidiary companies in the less-developed economies depend on the control of the common head office of a 'multi-national' in a highly industrialized country influence the processes of industrialization in a way that does not create political and economic autonomy and independence, but, on the contrary, new dependencies? The answer will certainly be different, if you consider such an industrialized country as Czechoslovakia, that occupied a special position in the inter-war period, compared with the underdeveloped countries, in South-East Europe. So one should distinguish between the forms and consequences of investment and business strategies in Czechoslovakia and in Yugoslavia or Bulgaria, for instance.

My question is: When Mannesmann and the Deutsche Bank constructed a 'concern within a concern', did the general management in Düsseldorf intentionally consider the consequences that such a policy of industrialization by means of direct investments and of subsidiary companies would have in the less developed areas? Let us suppose that there were such intentional and far-reaching concern strategies which aimed at an 'organic' and only 'complementary' development of the South-East and thereby deliberately blocked a process of autonomous industrialization and diversification of product lines, how were they brought into effect?

Harm and Verena Schröter have, in this case, given clear answers. They dispel the popular legend which even nowadays tells us of the great support the industrialization in South-East Europe generally received from the Third Reich in the inter-war period to its real nucleus. Harm Schröter's conclusion leaves no doubt when he says: 'Industrialization was not in the interest of Siemens, as it was aimed at import substitution, and whenever possible, Siemens avoided foreign industrial investments in order to maintain its exports from Germany.' Only when important markets like Czechoslovakia were in danger of being lost to competitors through lack of German investment, 'Siemens was ready to start production there very quickly.' Verena Schröter's argument follows the same line, when she underlines that investments and industrialization were to have only complementary (i.e. complementary to German needs), but not substitutive (i.e. substitution of imports) character: 'The argument of rising purchasing power through an "organic" agrarian and industrial development in South-East Europe above all, which was, of course, complementary to the needs of the German economy, played for prominent IG Farben directors like Max Ilgner an increasingly important role. In these changes, therefore, IG Farben should play an active and determining role.' Therefore Max Ilgner's famous words of 'Exportsteigerung durch Einschaltung in die Industrialisierung der Welt' (i.e. to increase German exports by getting involved with the world-wide processes of industrialization), uttered in 1938, must be taken in the more restricted sense of 'organic' and complementary' industrialization and development, i.e. in the sense of subordinating the changes in the South-East European 'periphery' to the needs of the highly industrialized and swiftly rearming 'core'. J. Tomaszewski, in chapter 9, also stresses the consequences of German investment policy in the Upper Silesian industry between the wars for 'the economic retardation of the Polish Republic'.

Alice Teichova mentions the 'tendencies towards stagnation' in the Bohemian works in Kladno and the 'long-term effect of the technical backwardness of the Prague Iron Co.' which 'became fully apparent only between the two world wars, because in that period no basic technical improvements were undertaken.'[7] Does this development, as well as the 'unequal contract' between Düsseldorf and Kladno so strongly emphasized by the author, mean that the general management in the headquarters in Germany intentionally tried to hamper a stronger modernization and indus- trialization in Czechoslovakia or at least wanted to subordinate this develop- ment to the German needs? Was the dependency of the Prague Iron Co. on imported German coke, which you could also observe elsewhere in South- East Europe at that time, also a way of influencing their progress of modernization?

In Chapter 10, P. G. Fischer gives an impressive example of how a dependent daughter (the Alpine Montangesellschaft) was exploited by the German mother company (Vereinigte Stahlwerke AG) 'who insisted on the supply of higher price coke from the Ruhr as against coke from Ostrau; a factor which must have affected production costs unfavourably.'

4. SOUTH-EAST EUROPE AS AN INTEGRAL PART OF A GLOBAL CONCERN STRATEGY

Harm Schröter stresses the point that 'Siemens' interests were not focused primarily on Central and South-East Europe' [p. 188] and that the concern's investments there 'were made not merely as a limited territorial strategy, but as a global one of securing markets against international competitors' [p. 188]. Barter agreements were concluded by the concern 'not only with South-East Europe, but with Iran and South America as well' [p. 186]. In a similar way it must be said that the interests and activities of IG Farben by no means pointed only to South-East Europe, but also to South America.

Alice Teichova distinguishes between two phases in the export policy of MW-Komotau: in the 1920s, there was a major task for the daughter company, 'to export the overwhelming part – about 70 to 80 per cent – of her total output and to try and recapture under generally less favourable conditions [i.e. than in the pre-war period] the so-called 'traditional' markets of South-East Europe' [p. 109]. In the mid-1930s there occurred a fundamental change in the composition of export markets (as shown in tables 5.2 and 5.3 above); whilst deliveries to the domestic market vacillated around 30 per cent, the exports to the successor states and Romania shrank from 27 per cent (1929) to 6 per cent (1937). In the same period – and this was mainly due to the impact of the world economic crisis and of the subsequent policy of 'bilateralization' of German foreign trade with the South-East European states – exports to more distant and overseas markets doubled from 36 per cent (1929) to 66 per cent (1937).

From this I derive three conclusions:

1. Apparently the South-East European market, which was in the end rather limited, in spite of National Socialist tendencies towards autarky within a 'Grosswirtschaftsraum Südosteuropa' in reality played a very different role in the global export and investment strategies of all three concerns; it was less dominant with Siemens than with Mannesmann and IG Farben. Surely it is necessary to examine closely what importance the three combines attributed to South-East Europe in their global strategies of expansion. I think we must always distinguish between investment and capital interests on the one hand and (as the British example shows, sometimes quite disproportionate and differently orientated) trading interests on the other hand. Investment and capital interests are only one indicator of 'penetration économique'; in order to evaluate the economic influence in less-developed countries we must also take into consideration the trade relations as the reverse side of the coin called 'business expansion' or 'political-economic domination.'

2. Alice Teichova and I agree on the following point: despite economic recovery and the rearmament boom at home, such export-orientated combines as Mannesmann, Siemens and IG Farben in the long term made more profit by channelling their exports of semi-finished and finished products into the highly industrialized and traditional markets of Western Europe than they did before the First World War than by sending them to under-developed countries of the clearing area. The tendency to shift exports from the 'Reichsmarkbloc' to the countries without exchange controls, as men-

tioned by all three authors, in order to get foreign exchange for the purpose of raw materials in the world market increased as the pressure of Hitler's autarkic policy intensified. National Socialist foreign trade policy, which was only partly dictated by the consequences of the world economic crisis, was a rather unsound deviation from the long-term patterns of German foreign trade.

3. This important conclusion, that can be deduced from Alice Teichova's paper on Mannesmann, from Harm Schröter's paper on Siemens, and perhaps even from the export and foreign investment policy of IG Farben, forces us to consider a general problem more intensively than research work on the German 'Drang nach Südosten' has done so far. It deals with a certain lack of harmony or even with the contradictiveness between world-wide export-orientated business and investment interests of 'multi-national enterprises' with a wide range of products such as Mannesmann, Siemens or IG Farben on the one side and the geographically rather restricted aim of the Hitler government to build up a self-sufficient 'Grossraumwirtschaft' in Central East and South-East Europe as a base for further expansion to the East on the other side.

Notes

1. A. Teichova, *An Economic Background to Munich. International Business and Czechoslovakia 1918–1938.* (1974), 55.
2. *Ibid.*, 127.
3. *Ibid.*, 132.
4. *Ibid.*, 119–37.
5. *Ibid.*, 125.
6. *Ibid.*, 132 n.4, *re* V. Král.
7. *Ibid.*, 119.

COMMENTARY   *Hans Pohl*

I have not specialized in South-East European affairs, but as an economic historian I would like to make some comments on the papers of Alice Teichova and Harm and Verena Schröter. Let me begin with two more general remarks which concern not only these papers.

1. If we talk of economic and political influence or of founding so-called empires by capitalistic enterprises, we must first of all define what the words mean and we must develop indicators that help to measure the kind of influence exercised. First of all, capitalistic enterprises have the obligation to make as large a profit as possible. At the end of the year the board of directors has to reveal whether a company has been working successfully or not. Only a few entrepreneurs or managers are able to pursue a general long-term policy; more often, they need economic success within a short time. Looking at the

companies considered in chapters 5, 6 and 7, we must keep in mind that these do not stand for the whole German industry.

2. Siemens and IG Farben were not multi-national units. Therefore their policy had to be different from that of multi-nationals like Unilever, Nobel, and Mannesmann. The organization and policy of both Siemens and IG Farben were built upon traditional sales agencies that were kept under tight control by the concern headquarters in Germany. Both Siemens and IG Farben displayed an enormous reluctance to make direct foreign investments. I received the impression that this policy was not only typical of Siemens but also of the entire electrotechnical industry. Felten & Guilleaume of Cologne followed the same policy.

Taking the example of Nobel Industries Ltd, Alice Teichova has, elsewhere, explained the expansion investment strategy of British industry and banks in the post-war years. Returning from the United States in 1903, Carl Duisberg had already stated what the chairman of the Nobel Industries Trust was to say in 1915: in case of a war, the German chemical industry was bound to lose its leading position, and the chemical industry in other European countries and in the U.S.A. would compete successfully with Germany. Nobel's Explosive Company in Glasgow is only one example of how international trade relations were destroyed by the war.

As Teichova has made evident, British Nobel Industries and the American DuPont Company divided their market interests, which led to the foundation of chemical industry companies in the successor states of the Austro-Hungarian monarchy with British and French participation, knowhow, and capital. Teichova referred to a Czechoslovak example. I would like to ask her and our colleagues from the successor states: Has this been the only example? How did things develop in the other states? Teichova has only mentioned that it did not work in other states. Were there any attempts and why did they possibly fail?

In her paper Teichova refers to the policy of the top executives with regard to concentration and amalgamation before 1914. I think that Mannesmann was not exceptional but rather typical, as it was common in many big combines at that time to exercise the utmost control over subsidiary enterprises. In that respect Mannesmann was certainly not exceptional in the iron and steel industry. However, the policy of the Mannesmann company to conquer foreign markets was outstanding, as there were only a few firms starting to produce by investment abroad. As Teichova has pointed out, this policy proved to be very effective in the case of Komotau and Schönbrunn.

I would like to agree with Teichova's statement that the expansion outside Germany was horizontal, but I have to add that within Germany concentration was horizontal and vertical. As the paper made clear, the situation in the iron and steel industry was different from that in other branches.

With reference to Verena Schröter's paper on the IG Farben, I agree with her that IG Farben was not a multi-national company; that IG Farben was export-orientated and reluctant to make direct foreign investments; and that one must distinguish three phases in the development of exports (recovery, cartels, direct participation).

Verena Schröter has clearly shown the importance of international cartels for conquering markets. However, I am not fully convinced of her statement that German foreign trade policy towards South-East Europe was strongly influenced by IG Farben. The examples of collaboration she mentioned only prove that co-operation existed concerning information and economic negotiations. But these contacts were common in the old Reich, in the Weimar Republic, in the Third Reich, and take place even in the Federal Republic nowadays. More details on the kind and the degree of the so-called influence of IG Farben bureaucracy on the state bureaucracy and on politicians seem to be necessary to provide evidence of the strong industrial influence on politics which, according to Mrs Schröter, existed.

It is a hard reproach indeed to say that IG Farben hampered the development of independent national chemical industries in South-East Europe. Is Verena Schröter sure that all foreign investments and foreign sales policies are obstacles to national industrialization? I think the industrialization of many less developed countries – remember Germany in the nineteenth century, the United States, Russia, Japan, Mexico, etc. – provide evidence which conflict with this hypothesis.

Concerning Harm Schröter's paper, I want to mention three points.

1. Harm Schröter states: that Siemens began to reconquer the world market after 1923 not by investment abroad but by exporting from Germany; that the financial policy of Siemens was cautious, even conservative, and its strategy was steady, defensive and planned for long terms; and that Siemens always adhered to the policies of the majority of the big German enterprises and the German government.

I think that these have been traditions not only of Siemens but of all electrotechnical firms. They obtained many orders from the public utilities and in some branches they were dependent on them. Therefore they had to be cautious and be content with small but sure profits. I would like to prove this policy by referring to Felten & Guilleaume, a company I have already mentioned. Since they had to co-operate with the state bureaucracy they were obliged to co-operate among themselves too. Therefore the cultivation of the *Verbandsbewusstsein* (perception of the group) must have been important in the electrotechnical industry. This would explain Harm Schröter's statement that Siemens supported the majority.

2. The policy of founding trading companies in South-East Europe had also been followed by Felton & Guilleaume at the end of the 19th century. The Guilleaume brothers founded two sales companies in Vienna and

Budapest by buying national firms in 1893. They converted them into manufacturing firms which produced until 1901–2. Later on these two companies founded a cable factory (Kabelfabrik) in Novisad, Yugoslavia. In 1928, when great investments were necessary, the headquarters of Felten & Guilleaume in Cologne participated directly. Because of the shortage of raw materials, especially after 1937, F & G and other German companies shared research and mining companies, looking for metals such as lead in Yugoslavia and lead and zinc in Bulgaria.

3. Early in his paper, Harm Schröter only mentions briefly the Kabelfabrik in Budapest founded in collaboration with Felton & Guilleaume. I should like to use this reference to the international collaboration of German electrotechnical firms to point out that this collaboration for sharing in a foreign market went back to the beginning of this century. In 1900 Felton & Guilleaume established a subsidiary company in Russia which was taken over by Siemens and Halske, AEG and F & G in 1906. It was called Vereinigte Kabelwerke St Petersburg. This policy of founding a German electrotechnical enterprise with the participation of the German big three (Siemens, AEG and F & G) was renewed in 1927, when Poland increased its import taxes. In 1930 the Kabelwerk Ozarow near Warsaw commenced production. Each of the three German firms participated with a one-third share.

Part Three

German and Swedish Capital in East Central European Industry

8. The Swedish Match Company in Central Europe between the Wars*

'Internal power struggle' between former competitors – Solo v. Swedish Match

Ulla Wikander

INTRODUCTION

Matches became a mass-consumption commodity in Western Europe and the United States after 1850. Rapidly they also became a common source of state income. Matches were frequently taxed and governments often intervened in the match industry, e.g. by regulating production quotas and/or prices or by introducing match monopolies. This paper deals with an aspect of the worldwide expansion of Swedish match interests during the inter-war period.[1] The Swedish Match Company expanded its sphere of influence at the expense of a former competitor, the Austrian Solo group. The main participants in the struggle for markets and export opportunities in Eastern and Central Europe were the Swedish Match Company and the Austrian and Czechoslovak Solo Companies and, to a limited extent, new and independent match producers. The governments in question also played an important role in this power contest because they received revenues from the match industry. The states' activities were further influenced by the policies of domestic protection which gradually developed in Eastern Europe.[2]

1. MARKET CONDITIONS

Conditions on the match market during the first four decades of the 1900s may be briefly summarized. The gradual development of a high degree of mechanization in match production, combined with state regulations against the poisonous phosphorus match – which caused difficulties particularly for small producers – paved the way for rationalization and mergers in the non-monopolized match industry. At the turn of the century the market for matches was moving towards an oligopolistic structure. Large, horizontally integrated groups had already developed before the First World War, including Diamond Match in the U.S.A., Bryant & May in Great Britain, Solo in Austria/Hungary, Union Allumettière (Unal) in Belgium, and Jönköping & Vulcan and AB Förenade Tändsticksfabriker in Sweden.

As soon as the war ended Ivar Kreuger of the Swedish Match Company was determined either to gain control of, or enter into agreements with, the largest competitors in the match industry. He was rapidly able to reach market and price agreements in the United States and Great Britain, although the British market continued to be a weak spot, being a 'free' and lucrative match market between the wars, and acting as a source of re-exports to all corners of the world.[3] On the European continent, his plans for control were endangered mainly by extensive match production in Belgium, Austria and Czechoslovakia. Export traditions in these countries were as long and well established as those in Sweden.

Eastern and Central Europe had been outside the scope of influence or even the interest of the Swedish match industry before the war. The only contact consisted of regular purchases of aspen wood from Russia. The South-Eastern area had been dominated by Austrian and Czechoslovak match manufacturers, who had a long-established tradition of producing matches and had turned to safety matches at an early stage in their development.[4] The countries in Eastern and Central Europe were divided clearly into either producers and exporters, or importers, of matches. Before the war the area which later became Poland imported matches, since only one-third of its needs were manufactured domestically. (At that time imports came from the three large producing countries of Germany, Russia and Austria-Hungary). The Romanian and Bulgarian match monopolies were also importers to a large degree, as were the Serbian and Greek monopolies. These had all been Solo markets.[5]

A quite new structure developed after the war due to the new frontiers and the industrial protectionism that emerged with the new economic nationalism in Eastern Europe. The new countries created out of the former Austro–Hungarian Empire all had ambitions to become match producers, at least to satisfy demand on their home markets. Match manufacturing did not require substantial capital investment. Very sophisticated automatic match-making machines, called continuous machines, handled almost the whole process of producing matches in modern factories; but at the same time, simpler machines could function with the same results.[6] Many of the countries in North-Eastern Europe also had their own supplies of high-quality aspen wood, the best raw material for matches. These factors, combined with the very special currency situation of inflation, even hyperinflation,[7] accounts for the establishment of many new producers of matches in Eastern Europe after 1921–2, with consequent overproduction.

1924 was a difficult year for the match industry in general. The problems stemmed from overproduction, with the result that markets were congested. The Swedish Match Company experienced heavy attacks from different quarters against its market position, which in 1920 had seemed rather secure. Now the world market for matches was shaken by excessive overproduction leading to severe price competition. The problem centred on Britain, because it was a free trade market and better prices could be obtained there. Countries on the Continent often adhered to protective policies, including tariffs and other restrictive measures. Rather lucrative match markets were also to be found in the Near East and the United States, less so in East Asia and Africa south of the Sahara.[8]

The control of exports from Eastern Europe became urgent for Swedish Match after 1923, when they entered into a cartel agreement regarding the British market with Bryant & May, Belgian Unal and Norwegian Nitedal. Under this agreement, Swedish Match undertook to include in their own quota all imports by outsiders exceeding 25,000 cases per year. For imports above their own quota, Swedish Match would pay damages to the other members of the cartel. In 1923 these damages amounted to £40,000.[9] Imports by outsiders to London lowered the price level for matches on the best market. The period of keen competition reached its peak between 1924 and 1926 and resulted in the annihilation of most of the independent match manufacturers.

The market for matches stabilized after 1926–7 and prices could be maintained at a higher level. But soon the depression, in conjunction with a steadily rising tax burden on matches, led to drastic cuts in match consumption. Electrification and lighters also played their part in this development. According to estimates made by Håkan Lindgren, total world export sales of matches fell from 1,600,000 cases (of 50 gross) in 1913 to 519,000 cases in 1938. Matches from Sweden accounted for 27 per cent of the international match market in 1913, whereas Solo accounted for 6 per cent (but had an enormous home market as well). In 1938 Swedish Match dominated the international market with 60 per cent and Solo Zündwaren- und Wichse-Fabriken AG (Solo Vienna) and Solo akciové sirkárny a lučební továrny (Solo Prague) combined had only 2.3 per cent of the world export market (and much smaller home markets).[10]

Swedish Match v. Solo: an outline

During the First World War the Swedish match industry had profited both from Sweden's neutral status and the scarcity of matches throughout the world. The industry consolidated its activities and in 1917 it merged into one large firm, Svenska Tändsticks Aktiebolaget (Swedish Match Company). Swedish Match became the main firm in a holding company called Kreuger & Toll. Ivar Kreuger was the managing director of Swedish Match and had a controlling influence in Kreuger & Toll. From the outset he had extensive plans for the international expansion of Swedish Match.

Prior to the war, the Austro-Hungarian match industry consisted of two concerns: Solo (Solo Zündwaren- und Wichse-Fabriken AG) and Helios (Zündwaren AG Helios). In 1913 they created a joint sales organization, Ignis (Ignis Zündhölzchen-Verkaufs-GmbH), with Bernard Fürth as manager. The government took control of further entry into the industry. When the Habsburg Empire was divided after the war the group split into two national companies known as Solo Vienna and Solo Prague ('Solo' Zündwaren- und

Wichse-Fabriken AG, Vienna, and Solo akciové sirkárny a lučební továrny, Prague). But there was a mutual exchange of shares and only one managing director, Dr Ernst Fürth, who had headed Solo before the war; he and his brother came from a family that had been in match production for three generations. The Solo factories' natural markets outside the former imperial home market were the Balkans, Turkey, the Levant and Egypt. Despite the division into two national companies, the two Solos acted as one body outwardly – all the agreements with e.g. Swedish Match were signed by both of them.[11]

The structure of the conflict[12]

A complicated structure of intertwined interests evolved in Central Europe. The Swedish Match Company was in an early 'ethnocentric' stage of its expansion as an international corporation, favouring production in Sweden and regarding the rest of the world as a potential export market. Even in countries where the company bought match factories, thereby producing at lower costs than in Swedish factories, the decision was to curb exports from such plants and if possible, production for the home market as well. The overall aim was to secure export markets for matches from Sweden. This made Swedish Match and Solo competitors. If a firm (in this case Swedish Match) bought a minority or even a majority share in a competing firm of another nationality (here Solo), a situation was bound to arise in which the 'bought' firm tried to safeguard the interests of its domestic shareholders in an 'internal power struggle' with the new shareholder. This is a natural reaction in the sense that a reduction in the range of activity in favour of the former competitor – now the new foreign shareholder – would decrease the profits of the firm, at least in the long run, and thus threaten the dividends to the shareholder. Contrary to this, the natural course of the new shareholder (especially if the firm is in an ethnocentric stage) was to support the activities of the main company, which was the purpose of buying into the competing firm in the first place.

In the special case of relations between the Swedish Match Company and the Solos, the various governments played an important role. Both in Austria and Czechoslovakia there were home market cartels supported by the government and state interests in the match industry in the form of a special match tax. Ivar Kreuger as well as the Fürth brothers took this protectionism into consideration and deemed it dangerous to reveal the foreign influence in local industry. As a result the Swedish Match majority shareholding was kept secret throughout the 1920s and well into the 1930s. Solo was thus able to 'take cover' behind this circumstance and use the threat of state intervention in the struggle with Swedish Match for influence and markets.

The newly-established, smaller factories constituted another factor. They had mainly a 'nuisance value';[13] their production capacity was often insignificant, although they could disturb the price structure in an otherwise regulated market and divert the profits obtained through cartels or agreements. Accordingly they were often in conflict with all three of the other parties, but could eventually be used to favour the interests of one of them against the other(s). They were regularly bought out in the end, mostly at high prices.[14]

The Swedish Match Company applied different methods in their attempts to take over markets and gain control of exports in Central Europe. These attempts can be divided into two periods, the *pre-monopoly period* (up to 1925) and the *monopoly period*. Of course these 'periods' overlap to some extent and the monopoly period could be said to have begun as early as 1924. The vague expression 'Central Europe' is applied in a broad sense, excluding Germany but including all of Eastern Europe from the Baltic states in the north to Balkan Greece in the south. This choice is due to the structure of Swedish Match's activities in the area. A division has also to be made between the so-called 'Solo-area', equivalent to the former Solo home market and export markets in the Balkan area, the northern part of Poland and the Baltic states. The developments in this northern area are touched upon only in passing in so far as they are related to the conflict between Solo and Swedish Match and the methods applied by Swedish Match to solve it.

2. THE PRE-MONOPOLY PERIOD

Solo area

The Solo group was the most important link in the chain of Swedish Match's efforts to control the match market in Central Europe. As early as 1918 Ivar Kreuger had discussed with Bernard Fürth market agreements for the Balkan area and Turkey. Kreuger's talks resulted in a transaction in February 1920 which gave the Swedes slightly more than a 50 per cent majority in Solo Vienna. Lack of capital and the post-war depression prevented Ivar Kreuger from using an option which would have given him a direct majority share interest in what became Solo Prague in 1921. By relying on the close co-operation that existed between the two Solos through a common manager as well as price and market agreements, it was hoped that influence could be exerted on Czechoslovak sales policy abroad, even without a direct majority share.

After 1921, Ivar Kreuger also held 19 per cent of the shares in Solo Prague. But the Czechoslovaks did not know of his larger stake in Solo Vienna, which in turn held so many shares in Solo Prague and, combined with Kreuger's 19 per cent, constituted a majority.[15] Ivar Kreuger's majority in Solo Vienna and in Solo Prague was kept entirely secret from everyone except the three top directors, including the two brothers, Bernard and Ernst Fürth. The Fürth brothers explained the situation in a letter in 1932 as follows:

it was mutually agreed to keep these transactions secret, as it was already at that time considered inadvisable, in view of the close relationship existing between the two companies and their respective governments, to disclose the passing into foreign hands of the controlling interest in the two companies, public opinion being especially sensitive on this point. Although it has from time to time been rumoured that Swedish Match had acquired a certain number of shares in Solo Vienna and Solo Prague, on the whole the fact that the majority of shares is held by Swedish Match has up to the present moment remained unknown, especially in political and Government circles . . .[16]

It seems evident that the very narrow limits Swedish Match soon tried to impose on Solo exports came as somewhat of an unpleasant surprise to the Solo management. The Fürth brothers had been looking forward with some confidence to co-operating with Swedish Match in order to regulate export markets, mainly because they were eager to keep prices high. But if their share of the markets became too small, they would be losers in the long run. Bernard Fürth, who was also the export adviser to the Czechoslovak Solo, was so upset about these export limitations that he wrote a long memorandum to Ivar Kreuger in 1921. He tried to convince Kreuger that if the Czechoslovaks were kept out of the good export markets, a total 'Lahmlegung' of the match industry would result. He threatened that 'die czechoslovakische Regierung, auf deren Wohlwollen wir angewiesen sind, ganz energische Massregeln gegen die Erzeugungsgesellschaften ergreifen würde, wenn der Verdacht einer künstlichen Drosselung des Verkaufes aufkommen würde.' Fürth now wanted to revise the market division that had been verbally agreed upon some years earlier, because it had been based on war-time conditions, which he thought was no longer fair.[17]

The export problem had not become apparent until Solo Prague was established. Solo Vienna had almost no export capacity. As a sign that they were earnest in their intentions to export, the Czechoslovaks launched a campaign to recapture their former traditional markets in the Levant, Egypt and Turkey, through fierce price competition between 1920 and 1922. This was highly disturbing to Swedish Match which was selling to the same markets. In 1923 Solo Prague even sold matches to the United States and undercut the Swedish prices there. Solo Prague also insisted on exporting matches to Poland, one of their former markets – more than 6,000 cases during 1924. This clashed with Swedish interests. Ivar Kreuger found it 'perfectly absurd' that the Solo Fürths could not exercise their influence (which in this case meant Kreuger's will), but the two brothers simply made excuses, referring to the political situation without intervening. In 1924, Solo also entered into competition with matches from Sweden on the Chinese market in Hong Kong. On this very crowded and weak market (where the

Japanese were also seeking an outlet for matches) Solo underbid Swedish Match. When Swedish Match requested that he put a stop to this, Bernard Fürth replied that the quantities were comparatively small and that he could not go against the wishes of the Czechoslovaks.[18]

Many independent producers were established inside Austria between 1922 and 1924. Solo Vienna ran into serious difficulties. Swedish Match secretly bought some outsider factories and competed with Solo in order to 'soften' them to co-operate more faithfully, preferably on the export markets. In 1925, Solo Vienna showed a loss of 53,000 sch. Through pressures on Solo Vienna, Swedish Match wanted to exert influence on exports from Czechoslovakia.

At last, in 1926, the competitors were able to agree and the Austrian home market was again regulated by a cartel. It was approved by the government, which introduced production quotas along with an increased match tax. The result was lower consumption in the country, less production for Solo Vienna (74 per cent of the home market), but a good and secure profit rate. During 1926 the cartel agreement was in force for nine months and Solo's profits amounted to 710,000 sch.

In Czechoslovakia there was a dual home market cartel, for political reasons. Solo Prague was the main producer for the home market (about 80 per cent) and had obtained sole export rights by paying the other producers to abstain from exporting. Even in this cartel Ivar Kreuger tried to gain some influence, acting behind a domestic front through non-Solo factories.[19]

Poland and the Baltic States

There was no single large competitor in the north, but an ever-increasing number of newly-established independent producers in countries without any match-exporting tradition. As early as 1921 enough Polish and Baltic matches – manufactured in small units – were produced to supply the home markets. They soon threatened Swedish Match Company's exports, particularly to Great Britain. The threat was quite serious. A small country such as Estonia began by exporting a mere 48 cases (of 50 gross) to Great Britain in 1921 but reached as many as 9,000 cases in 1924, more than 7 per cent of the total match imports to Great Britain. Poland, which imported about 34,000 cases in 1920 (60 per cent of these from Austria and Czechoslovakia), exported 12,000 cases by 1922.

In the midst of this chaotic competition in the northern area, Swedish Match tried in vain to secure market or price agreements in 1922 and 1923, in a desperate attempt to achieve some kind of control over this sudden expansion. Then Swedish Match applied a somewhat different tactic. Secretly it bought one or more factories in each exporting country and tried to unite producers in a joint sales or export organization, often explicitly said to be directed against 'the Swedish trust'. But the method did not accomplish much as long as export sales flourished. The purchase of import agencies in

London – which were the sole agents for their competitors' matches – proved to be somewhat more satisfactory but did not result in any overall control. Swedish Match also felt compelled to initiate tough price competition campaigns in Great Britain, Poland, and the Baltic countries, but this was a costly method.[20]

At the same time Czechoslovakia continued to export matches to southern Poland. This of course led to a rise in the exports from Poland, which was annoying to Swedish Match.

Agreements

The outcome of attempts to gain control through owner-influence in Eastern and Central Europe was not satisfactory for Swedish Match until 1924. In Austria and Czechoslovakia, where they ought to have had control, the situation had developed instead into a competitive one. On Solo's home markets, Swedish Match had to buy outsider factories and compete in order to have a voice in developments. The situation was the same on the export markets; competition instead of co-operation. Obviously this state of affairs was not advantageous to either of the protagonists in the long run. But Solo had made a serious, and threatening, attempt to reconquer some export markets and verbal orders from Swedish Match were not sufficient to stop them. Solo's export drive was also prompted to some extent by the secrecy that was judged necessary to protect the Swedish holding in the company. The state favoured export industries.

A further step entailed market agreements. These could not be made in the north so long as owner-influence was too small and profitable exports were possible. Agreements had to be made in the south, despite the fact that Swedish Match had a majority – although with limited influence. The first formal market and price agreements between Swedish Match and the 'Solos' concerned the Levant market. They were signed in 1922 and 1923. The first Levant agreement split the market shares between the two competitors on a 50–50 basis. Later Solo was slowly manoeuvred to accept even smaller shares of that market.[21]

An agreement – in many instances not really adhered to – was made with the 'Solos' in March 1922 to cover worldwide exports. Later on, negotiations for improving this agreement were held during the years until 1925. Swedish Match was inclined to leave Balkan and Central Europe to Solo (except the Greek monopoly and Albania), but otherwise to restrict Czechoslovak matches more and more; whereas Solo tried to assert the right to regain their pre-war export markets. Poland was a constant problem in the negotiations – the Czechoslovaks refused stubbornly to cease exporting there. The result was a global agreement, concluded in 1925, according to which the markets were divided. Solo got 10 per cent of the British market, 15 per cent of the French, and was otherwise restricted to Eastern and Central Europe, except for permission to sell smaller quantities to low-price areas in Asia and Africa.

Romania remained more or less an open question. It was further stipulated that the Czechoslovaks could not export more than 1,250 cases of matches per year to Poland and only 'solange ein Import nach Polen generell möglich ist'.[22] Swedish Match was preparing a new strategy.

THE MONOPOLY PERIOD

Monopolies

In 1924 Swedish Match started to take resolute counteraction against overproduction. This was the year when Ivar Kreuger began negotiating for leases of match monopolies on a large scale. After some years these efforts resulted in a total of 15 monopolies, primarily in Central Europe and Latin America. Match monopolies have a history as long as the mass production of matches, due to their popularity as an object for taxation. The French Match Monopoly, which gave revenues to the treasury, was founded as early as 1872. Other European match monopolies were established in Spain and Portugal, and in Eastern Europe in Greece, Bulgaria, Romania and Serbia at the end of the nineteenth century. Some of these monopolies were leased to private firms, others were run by the state; some produced matches, others were sales monopolies with regular imports. In all instances part of the sale proceeds went to the state.

Early in 1924 Swedish Match made contacts for a Polish match monopoly. During the spring and summer, serious negotiations were conducted for monopolies in Hungary and Germany. Rumours about a lease of the Romanian monopoly caused Swedish Match to send a preliminary negotiator to Bucharest. During the autumn, there were negotiations at high level in Estonia and elaborate plans for a monopoly in Yugoslavia. Some of these plans were connected with small loan offers, but none higher than $2–3m.

After 1924, Ivar Kreuger's interest in monopolies in Eastern Europe to some extent diminished. For a period he had to devote more time to acute competition, but the idea of obtaining monopolies was never discarded. Up until 1927 monopoly plans were pursued most eagerly in industrialized western countries such as France, Belgium and Germany,[23] initially without result. In 1926 Kreuger even made a serious attempt to achieve a match monopoly in Austria – in return for a $10m loan. The government chose to uphold the home market cartel instead, with the intention of supporting Austrian capital against foreign influence.[24]

For some reason it was considered to be a loss of prestige for a state to lease out a monopoly. In western countries such as France and Belgium, attempts by Swedish Match to obtain monopolies were unsuccessful. But in Central Europe different kinds of state revenues or state monopolies were frequently given as collateral for foreign loans. Well-known examples of this are the League of Nations loans to Austria in 1922 and Hungary in 1924. The Monopolies Institute of Yugoslavia is another example.[25]

Poland and the Baltic States

Among the monopoly negotiations started by Swedish Match in 1924 the Polish transactions were the only ones that gave immediate success; the others were postponed and not resumed until later, under different conditions. As soon as the Polish Minister, President Grabski, had stabilized the Polish currency in 1924, Ivar Kreuger found the economic situation in Poland favourable, and was prepared to grant a loan, up to $8m in exchange for a match concession. A larger loan, floated for the Poles in March 1925 by Dillon, Read and Company, was a failure. Not more than $35m could be placed on the New York market against an expected $50m.[26] The Polish government now appreciated Kreuger's offer.

In July 1925, Parliament granted an exclusive concession for the manufacture and sale of matches to a Polish monopoly company called 'Monzap' (Spolka Akcyjna do Eksploatacju Panstwowego Monopolu Zapalzcanego w Polsce). This company was under the control of Swedish Match and its American subsidiary, the International Match Corporation (Imco), founded in 1923, for the explicit purpose of handling foreign match interests bought by the Kreuger group. The group granted the Polish government a $6m loan at 7 per cent, to be amortised in 20 years. The Polish monopoly company had to buy the outsider factories and pay the state a minimum annual sum of 5m złoty. Exports were not only allowed but obligatory, amounting to about 10,000 cases in the first year and later to one-third of the match sales inside Poland (about 30,000 cases for exports). However, Swedish Match could choose to pay damages instead of exporting and, above all, they were permitted to export to other, less profitable markets than the British, which was reserved for Swedish matches. Match imports were totally forbidden.

After the start of the monopoly régime on 1 October 1925, only 10 factories were kept busy (as opposed to 19 in 1923) and production was lowered. Exports went mainly to the Romanian match monopoly, thus combating the Solo concern in the Balkan area, or to low-price Asian countries.[27]

The method of legal monopolization was also applied in the small, match-exporting Baltic states. Swedish Match began by purchasing all existing factories, but could not control future new establishments, which was deemed a necessity. Previous experience in Belgium between 1920 and 1923 had taught Swedish Match that *de facto* (but not *de jure*) control of the match industry in a country could very quickly turn into dangerous competition. The Swedes had been preparing these monopoly dealings for years in advance, through continuous contacts in high political circles and by paying for information and assistance. The Estonian monopoly went into effect in July 1928, in return for a loan of 7.6m Swedish Crowns (about $2m); the Latvian in January 1929, in return for a loan of $6m; and the Lithuanian in April 1930, also in return for a loan of $6m. This led to cuts in match exports and diverted the necessary (according to the contracts) exports away from the British to other less lucrative markets.[28]

Solo area

In a market agreement with the Swedish Match Company in 1925,[29] the Solo group had accepted export restrictions. But in this agreement it had also been made quite clear that the markets of Bulgaria, Hungary, Yugoslavia, Czechoslovakia and Austria were reserved for Solo and would remain outside the agreement. In January 1927 a new kind of export agreement was made with the Solo companies. During the next 10 years their exports were to pass through a Swedish subsidiary, the Alsing Trading Company Ltd, and not amount to more than 6,100,000 kg of matches (= 50,000 cases of 50 gross of boxes, an allotment equal to roughly 15 per cent of the export business of the Swedish factories). Solo's entire sales organization abroad was thus annihilated. As compensation Solo would receive comparatively high prices for their matches and thus a secured profit, even from the export trade. But Yugoslavia, Hungary, Bulgaria, Czechoslovakia and Austria were still kept outside the agreement, as was Romania, which was subject to special arrangements. (Romania, in 1927, as in 1925, continued to be a more or less open question. From an order in 1927 to deliver 50,000 cases to the Romanian match monopoly, Solo had to give one-third to the Swedish-owned Polish monopoly factories).[30] The earlier disputes over Solo exports to Poland had been settled through a monopoly concession. This solution would be used further to strengthen the position of Swedish Match.

Early in the 1920s, Swedish Match had forced Solo to refrain from trying to regain its former pre-war market in Greece, which Swedish Match had taken over during the war. There had been some disagreement over this.[31] In 1926 Greece gave the Alsing Trading Co. (the Swedish Match subsidiary) the sole right to import matches to the Greek monopoly, which had no production of its own. This monopoly thus provided total control and excluded Solo. From 1928 to 1930 the Swedish Match group managed to obtain legal monopolies more or less directly in all of the countries belonging to the former Solo area in Europe, except in Solo's home countries Austria and Czechoslovakia. In 1928 monopoly contracts were signed with Hungary and Yugoslavia. Romania's state monopoly was leased to the Swedes in 1929. Finally, in 1930, the Swedish Match group acquired monopolies in Danzig, Germany and Turkey, new monopoly conditions in Poland, and bought the majority share of the Belgian company which leased the Bulgarian state monopoly.[32]

The structure of the match industry in Hungary and Yugoslavia had developed along similar lines after the First World War. There were factories producing for the home market in both countries. The respective states had an interest in the industry because matches were taxed. Sales cartels, initiated by the Fürth brothers, fixed common prices and production quotas. Solo-controlled factories dominated the industry, which gave good profits, at least in Hungary. The sales organization in Yugoslavia was a state monopoly, while in the case of Hungary there were still some small outsiders on the market. Ivar Kreuger bought factories in both countries – an outsider in Hungary and a large Solo factory in Yugoslavia – before he started monopoly negotiations. The latter purchase was not appreciated by Solo's Ernst Fürth.

The Hungarian government introduced a law which gave it total control over the production of matches. This right was transferred to Swedish Match for 50 years in return for an annual lease-tax and a $36m loan. Management of the state monopoly in Yugoslavia was transferred to the Swedish Match group – along with an obligatory lease of the private factories – in exchange for a $22m loan for 30 years. Solo Vienna retained shares in the producing units but of course lost its controlling influence in the area to the Swedish Match group.[33] The match monopolies in Yugoslavia and Romania were leased in close connection with stabilization of the currencies, large international loans from bank syndicates and the backing of autonomous monopolies institutes which were to constitute the security for the foreign loans obtained. An Autonomous Monopolies Institute had existed in Yugoslavia since before the war. It had two purposes: to administer the monopolies (tobacco, salt, petroleum, matches, cigarette paper and alcohol were the most important) and to serve as a guarantee for the repayment of foreign loans.[34] In Romania the match trade had consisted of a state monopoly and some imports. For several years Swedish Match and the Solos had been either competing or, after negotiations, sharing orders from it; the Swedes had wished to use it as a market for the obligatory exports from the Polish monopoly.

Beginning in 1927, the Swedes negotiated eagerly with the Romanians to take over the management of the match monopoly, but this did not lead to any results until 1929 and then in connection with a larger stabilization and development loan. This loan of $101m was issued by an international group of banking houses, primarily French and American. The revenue of the Kingdom of Romania Monopolies Institute was to be reserved as collateral. This Institute – relying on the income from tobacco, cigarette paper, playing cards, dynamite, salt and match monopolies – was founded in 1929 with the explicit aim of serving as a security guarantee for foreign creditors. Swedish Match took over $30m of the stabilization bonds on special conditions. The Swedes promised to pay the Monopolies Institute $3m annually as a specified royalty for match sales (thus contributing to the guarantee for the loan service) and they also promised to keep their part of the bond issue out of the market for three years. The reward for Swedish Match was total control of the Romanian match monopoly for 30 years. Matches to meet home demand had to be produced inside the country.[35]

The loans

The last monopoly loan granted by Ivar Kreuger was a new one to Poland – the former 1925 loan of $6m was increased to $32.4m in exchange for better conditions. These included a longer monopoly period (40 years from 1925, instead of 20), an extension of the monopoly to cover lighters, and deletion of the obligatory export clause. Between 1925 and 1930 the direct monopoly loans given by the Kreuger group amounted to a total of $280.41m (excluding the $75m loan to France in 1927). Of this sum $125m went to Germany, $7.97m to four Latin-American countries and $147.44m to states in Eastern Europe including Turkey. Poland, Hungary, Yugoslavia and Romania received a total of $120.4m.[36] In 1927, Kreuger & Toll had lent France $75m in connection not with an entire match monopoly but preferential treatment with regard to deliveries to the state match monopoly. This significant transaction attracted attention throughout Europe and contributed to Ivar Kreuger's reputation as an international financier.

In order to obtain public monopolies, Swedish Match had to wait for a 'good opportunity', that is until a government was in need of credits and had difficulties in raising them. This was the case in most Central and Eastern European countries at the end of the 1920s. These small and new countries needed a mediator in order to gain the confidence of the money markets in New York and London.[37] Ivar Kreuger was well known as a financier and was considered reliable by banking houses in the United States and Europe. The fact that the issues he made were based on match monopolies (although not always in a strictly formal way) made them look highly attractive and secure.

When the Austrian home market cartel – on which the good profits of the industry depended – expired on 31 December 1931, Ivar Kreuger tried to prevent its renewal through two cartel factories (Sirius and Bibi) he had bought many years earlier. He wanted total export prohibition for these factories in return for heavy compensation from Solo Vienna. In other words, he demanded damages for not exporting, in accordance with his own benefit. This last attempt to get a monopoly in Austria, but without a loan offer, can be seen as additional pressure on Solo. Solo had either to agree to the compensation or be subjected to a new period of cut-throat competition. But Solo claimed that Swedish Match had failed to live up to their export obligations and thus never paid this compensation. The cartel was renewed and business resumed, but the 'co-operative spirit' had once again been put to a severe test.[38]

4. THE END OF THE 'INTERNAL POWER STRUGGLE' BETWEEN SWEDISH MATCH AND SOLO

In March 1932, Ivar Kreuger shot himself and soon afterwards the Kreuger & Toll Company went bankrupt. By 1932 the export obligations agreed by Alsing Trading Co. with Solo and guaranteed by Swedish Match in 1927 had not been met for some years, despite a reduction in the quantities to approximately half the initial ones. The Czechoslovakian currency embargo enforced the public disclosure of the foreign interest in Solo. The shares had meanwhile gone to an European subsidiary of the International Match

Corporation, the Continental Investment Company. All of these companies, as well as Swedish Match, had belonged to the so-called Kreuger group but met with different fates after the Kreuger & Toll bankruptcy. Imco was liquidated, along with Continental. The Swedish Match Company was reconstructed after several years of investigations, revisions, negotiations and new owner responsibilities.

In 1933 Imco/Continental sold its share in Solo Prague (23 per cent) to a Czechoslovak consortium consisting of other shareholders in the two Solo Companies, against the will of Swedish Match. But co-operation continued and renewed export agreements were made between the two Solos and Swedish Match in 1933 – the Solos were granted exports equal to 10 per cent of all match exports from Sweden.

After a series of mutual exchanges and agreements Swedish Match acquired the shares in Solo Vienna from Imco/Continental in 1935 (slightly more than 53 per cent of the total share capital). In 1936, these Solo shares were sold to an Austro-Czechoslovak consortium headed by Dr Ernst Fürth, in exchange for $700,000 and three match factories in Hungary and Yugoslavia. This ended Swedish owner interests in the Solos (until the 1970s), but the outcome was forced. The Solo group now had the upper hand owing to the previous sale of shares in Solo Prague – and Solo Prague provoked the sale of Solo Vienna by threatening not to adhere to export restrictions, since Swedish Match had not fulfilled their export obligations. The threat of price competition and government intervention forced Swedish Match to sell its Solo Vienna majority back to the indigenous Solo group. In connection with the sale of the Solo Vienna shares, a new export agreement was drawn up, aimed at gradually diminishing Solo exports to 5 per cent of Swedish match exports.[39]

A short period of export competition with Swedish Match after 1938 may be regarded as an interlude in the history of Solo. After the Anschluss of Austria to Germany, Solo Vienna was completely cut off from Solo Prague, came under the control of the Nazi party and cancelled the export agreement with Swedish Match. Solo Vienna then began exporting to Great Britain with government subsidies, but the war put an end to this.[40]

5. CONCLUSIONS

In order to keep profits from the home market cartel, the managing director of Solo, Ernst Fürth – even if unwillingly and after a competitive struggle on the export markets – agreed to Ivar Kreuger's demands for both real and formal export restrictions. Ivar Kreuger's majority share in Solo Vienna was of little use to him in achieving this result. He had been forced to buy outsider factories in both Austria and Czechoslovakia and because of either competition or the threat of competition there as well as abroad, he was able to carry out his intentions. The toughest 'internal power struggle' was over by 1926, but the Solos still resisted. Toward the end of the 1920s Kreuger also shut Solo off from control on their former 'home' markets in the successor states through the lease of public monopolies, despite the fact that these areas were reserved for Solo in the common market agreements.

Solo Vienna and Solo Prague gave good dividends of around or above 20 per cent each year after 1926. Ernst Fürth apparently had an extra interest in the 'welfare' of his Solos, because he was paid partly in relation to the profits. He received 10 per cent of the profits in Solo Vienna and 4.5 per cent of the profits in Solo Prague.[41]

Throughout the years of 'co-operation' relations between Ivar Kreuger and the Fürth brothers were obviously strained. In a report about Solo Vienna in connection with liquidation of the International Match Corporation in 1932, the situation was described as follows:

> the business of Solo-Vienna has been conducted shrewdly and profitably. The relations between Dr Fürth and the late Ivar Kreuger were not cordial and Dr Fürth's attitude was manifestly of great benefit to the shareholders. . . . the Solo Vienna organization . . . is efficient and highly individualistic. It has kept down the influence of the Swedish Match Company to a minimum and has never paid anything in the way of administration and similar charges to Stockholm.[42]

Despite this praise, it is evident that the Fürth brothers had the impression that they and 'their' companies received unfair treatment. They were eager to buy back the majority from Swedish Match as soon as a possibility presented itself. But the period 'under the Swedes' had definitely curbed the Solos' leverage for free action and their expansion possibilities. In the market agreement of 1936, Swedish Match promised to keep out of only two countries: Austria and Czechoslovakia.[43]

Notes

* I would like to thank Jan Glete, Karl Gustaf Hildebrand, Ragnhild Lundström, Lars Hassbring, Bo Gustafsson and György Péteri for having read and commented on an earlier draft of this paper.

1. At Uppsala University in Sweden, a research project led by K. G. Hildebrand has studied different aspects of 'The Swedish Match Company, 1917–1939'. So far this project has resulted in four books: H. Modig, *Swedish Match Interests in British India during the Interwar Years*; H. Lindgren, *The Swedish Match Industry in Its Global Setting*; L. Hassbring, *The International Development of the Swedish Match Company, 1917–1924*; U.

Wikander, *Kreuger's Match Monopolies, 1925–1930* (Case Studies in Market Control through Public Monopolies, Stockholm, 1979). Forthcoming within this project is a book by K. G. Hildebrand. Further research about the Kreuger group has been undertaken by J. Glete, *Kreugerkoncernen och Boliden* (Stockholm, 1975) and *Kreugerkoncernen och krisen på svensk aktiemarknad* (mimeo, 1977) and by B. Gäfvert, *Kreuger, riksbanken och regeringen* (Falköping, 1979). These books will provide the interested reader with further information on the international Swedish match group and the Kreuger concern. My book about the monopolies contains case studies including Estonia and Hungary in Eastern Europe (Turkey, Belgium and Germany are also treated), but no analyses of the special 'internal power struggle' between Swedish Match and the two Solos. This paper is a result of further research.

2. I. T. Berend & G. Ránki, *Economic Development in East-Central Europe in the 19th and 20th Centuries* (1974), ch. 10.

3. Lindgren, *op. cit.*, gives a view of the development of the world market for matches as well as a special study of the British market.

4. *The History and Development of Solo* (mimeo, author unknown (c. 1950), from the files of Diamond SA, Nyon, Switzerland, 7 pp (this short paper does not contain any reference at all to Swedish interests in Solo).

5. *Frankfurter Zeitung*, 21 Dec. 1924, 'Über die polnische Zündholzindustrie . . .'; *Swedish Match's Archive* (Jönköping); K. E. Hedborg, 'Report on the Subsidiary Companies of the Belgian Group', Jan. 1934.

6. Lindgren, *op. cit.*

7. F. Zweig, *Poland between Two Wars. A Critical Study of Social and Economic Changes* (1944).

8. Lindgren, *op. cit.* pt I, ch. 7.

9. *Ibid.*, pt I, ch. 7.

10. *Ibid.*, table 32.

11. Swedish Match Archive (Jkp); 'Report on "Solo" Czechoslovak United Match and Chemical Works, Ltd.' (Czechoslovakia, 29 Oct. 1932, probably S. Carlberg); The Hotchkiss-Fisk report on Austria, 'Report on "Solo" Match and Chemical Works, Ltd.' (Austria, 10 Oct. 1932).

12. Thanks to Lennart Brynhoff for sharing his insights on this topic with me.

13. 'Nuisance value' was the term used for this kind of factory in the Swedish Match company's internal correspondence, e.g. in letter S. Carlberg to the Swedish Minister in Vienna, Torsten Unden, 21 Aug. 1934 (Corr. F Lj 29 Swedish Match Archive (Jkp)).

14. Hassbring, *op. cit.*, gives examples of this, as does Wikander, *op. cit.*

15. For a detailed study of investments in the Solos, see Hassbring, unpublished mimeo from 1975 (in Swedish).

16. Swedish Match Archive (Jkp); letter B. &

17. *Ibid.* (Jkp); 'Report on Solo . . .', 29 Oct. 1932; letter and memo, B. Fürth to I. Kreuger, 8 Oct. 1921 (Corr. K-002).

18. *Ibid.* (Jkp); telegram I. Kreuger to B. Fürth, 24 Nov. 1924 (Corr. K- 'K. Littorin . . . Mossige-Norheim'; letter I. Kreuger to K. Littorin, 22 Mar. 1922 (Corr. K-005); telegram K. Littorin to I. Kreuger, Nov. 1923 (Corr. K-007); letter S. Carlberg to I. Kreuger, 19 Dec. 1924 (Corr. SC 067 col. 353); Swedish Match Archive of Agreements (Sthlm); Minutes from a conference about price agreements, S M – Silos, 16 June 1922.

19. As in n. 11. Letter S. Carlberg to I. Kreuger, 19 Dec. 1924 (Corr. SC 067 col. 353); Protokoll, aufgenommen in Wien, 9 May 1925 (Corr. SC 059); letter I. Kreuger to B. Fürth, 15 July 1925 (Corr. K-011).

20. Wikander, *op. cit.*, ch. IV, Swedish Match Archive (Jkp); memo, unsigned, Warschawa, 18 Apr. 1922, along with other letters of information during 1922, 1923, e.g. 'Prospects of agreements with Polish Manufacturers', 14 Nov. 1923, unsigned (Corr. SC 065 col. 341); letter I. Kreuger to G. Cederschiöld, 14 Jan. 1924 etc. (Corr. K-009).

21. Swedish Match Archive of Agreements (Sthlm); Protocol 16 June 1922. Deed of Agreement, 1 Oct. 1922. Appendix to Deed of Agreement, 7 Nov. 1923.

22. Swedish Match Archive of Agreements (Sthlm); Protocol, Berlin, 11 Mar. 1922. Uebereinkommen, Prag, 29 May 1925.

23. Wikander, *op. cit.*, chs. III and V. Swedish Match Archive (Jkp); Mémoire, before Oct. 1924 (Corr. SC 064 col. 329).

24. Swedish Match Archive (Jkp); letter B. Fürth to I. Kreuger, 10 Sept. 1926 (Corr. K-013). Memorandum, 13 Oct. 1926 (Corr. SC 058 A).

25. League of Nations, *Reconstruction Schemes in the Inter-War Period* (Geneva, 1945). H. Gross, 'Die Entwicklung der europäischen Finanzmonopole in der Nachkriegzeit', *Weltwirtschaftliches Archiv*, XXXIII (1931).

26. Zweig, *op. cit.*, 36 etc. Swedish Match Archive (Jkp); letter I. Kreuger to T. Kreuger, 18 Apr. 1924 and memo, unsigned, summer 1924. Telegram I.

E. Fürth to K. Littorin (trans. from the German), 23 Apr. 1932 (Corr. K-203).

Kreuger to T. Kreuger, 19 Nov. 1924 (Corr. H-9).

27. Swedish Archive (Jkp); 'Kontrakt' Poland, 19 Sept. 1925, signed Grabski – T. Kreuger/G. Widell (Corr. W. Ahlström – 3). 'Report regarding International Match Corporation for the period Jan.–Sept. 1925, Poland', 7–9, probably written by I. Kreuger.

28. Wikander, *op. cit.*, chs. III and IV and Appendix VIII.

29. Swedish Match Archive of Agreements (Sthlm); Austria, Contract nr Ö II-2, Uebereinkommen, Prag, 29 May 1926. Swedish Match Archive (Jkp); PM about Solo's memo, 27 Mar. 1925 concerning a general agreement (in Swedish) (Corr. SC 067 col. 353).

30. Swedish Match Archive of Agreements (Sthlm); Austria, Contract Ö II-2, Protocol, Berlin, 13 Jan. 1927. Swedish Match Archive (Jkp); 'Report on Solo . . . Prague', 29 Oct. 1932 (see n. 11).

31. Swedish Match Archive of Agreements (Sthlm); Austria, Contract nr Ö II-2. Protocol, Berlin, 11 Mar. 1922. Wikander, *op. cit.*, Appendix VIII.

32. *Ibid.*

33. For Hungary, see *ibid.*, ch. VI. For Yugoslavia, see Swedish Match Archive (Jkp); Mémoire before Oct. 1924, and a lot of letters (especially W. Ahlström to I. Kreuger, 1 May 1927) in Corr. SC 064 col. 329. See also Corr. K-015 and K-018.

34. *Compass, Finanzielles Jahrbuch Jugoslawien*, 1933, 389 etc.

35. Swedish Match Archive (Jkp); e.g. Corr. SC 065 col. 341–342, K-009, K-013, K-015 (reports from Ermolin), K-017 and K-021. See also Wikander, *op. cit.*, Appendix VIII.

36. *Ibid.*

37. Berend and Ránki, *op. cit.*, chp. 9. Wikander, *op. cit.*, chs. IV, V and VI.

38. Swedish Match Archive (Jkp); Hotchkiss-Fisk report on Austria, 10 Oct. 1932 (see n. 11). Letter I. Kreuger to Paul G. Courtney, Lee, Higginson & Cie, Paris, 4 Apr. 1931, and other letters in K-051.

39. Swedish Match Archive of Agreements (Jkp); Austria–Czechoslovakia, Contract nr Ö LL-10 (470), 14 Dec. 1932. Swedish Match Archive (Jkp); 'Report on Solo . . . Prague', 29 Oct. 1932 (see n. 11). PM . . . about the selling of the majority in Solo (in Swedish), 20 Apr. 1936 and Heads of agreement, 11 and 12 May 1936 and translation of 'Utkast', 30 and 31 Mar. 1936 (Corr. F Lj 21). 'Berätelse', Apr. 1936 (Corr. F Lj 29).

40. Lindgren, *op. cit.*, pt III, last chapter.

41. See n. 11. 'Solo Prague, Gewinn 1913–1931' (Corr. K-023).

42. Swedish Match Archive (Jkp); ' Report on Solo . . . Prague', 29 Oct. 1932 (see n. 11).

43. Swedish Match Archive of Agreements (Sthlm); Austria/Czechoslovakia, Contract nr Ö II-7 (469) and Contract nr Ö II-14. Memorandum of Agreement, 10 Sept. 1936.

9. German Capital in Silesian Industry in Poland between the two World Wars

Jerzy Tomaszewski

Defining the term 'foreign capital' is not so easy a task as it is considered in some historical studies. I do not agree with the opinion shared by some of even the leading historians that all capital either coming from abroad or owned by businessmen of foreign descent is foreign in the economic sense of the word. Many industrialists or craftsmen migrated from one country to another in the nineteenth century with all their money and property. They established new enterprises and developed them for the benefit of their new homeland. All profits were invested locally. From all points of view these emigré businessmen belonged to the local bourgeoisie. They were members of the professional corporations, cartels or other organizations and co-operated with the 'native' industrialists. Together they influenced the authorities and fought against foreign, in its geographical sense, competitors. The only difference was their origin, their national consciousness, though very often immigrants were sooner or later assimilated. In the case of such newcomers who became a part of their new homeland's bourgeoisie it is therefore difficult to define it as 'foreign capital'. Such was the case for instance, with the German immigrants to Lódź in the first half of the nineteenth century: the newcomers soon became closely connected with the Polish Kingdom, then under Russian rule, and together with other financial groups formed the reservoir of the native capital of this area.[1] Another example can be seen in the life of the famous Italian banker Giuseppe Töplitz, the head of the Banca Commerciale Italiana. Born in Warsaw, he belonged to a well-known family and married a Polish woman. He was personally connected with Poland during the whole of his life, being – with his brothers and kinsmen – deeply involved in Polish economic and political life. But his professional activity as the head of a big Italian bank had nothing in common with Polish capital and was influenced by Italian policy and Italian economic interests.

Frequently other criteria, of a formal character, are used in making this definition which are connected with the requirements and limitations of statistical investigation. Statistical data concerning foreign capital – if available – are in most cases based on the criterion of citizenship. The capital belonging to foreign citizens of foreign corporate bodies, i.e. companies with central boards registered in other countries, is considered to be foreign.[2] This is a very simple criterion and can be useful in many investigations due to its preciseness. However, a historian cannot consider it to be sufficient. Citizenship is a legal matter and the real financial or political links can differ from it. The example of big Silesian companies in Poland, discussed here, is a convincing proof.

In every historical analysis, and not only in historical analysis, the most important question is: what are the economic and political consequences of the activity of foreign capital? From this point of view the origin, nationality, etc. of a shareholder is not so significant. Therefore I use the words 'foreign capital' when the investigated company is subordinated to, or closely connected with, an economic or political centre abroad whose interests are decisive in all fundamental questions, such as the area and policies of activity, the investment of profits, international agreements and so on.[3]

To explain the real character of capital it is necessary to make a thorough and detailed investigation concerning every financial group or every company, such as Alice Teichova has done for Czechoslovakia.[4] There is no such study covering either the whole Polish economy or even industry, although there are numerous articles and books concerning particular companies, branches of industry or regions. In this paper an attempt will be made to discuss some questions concerning the role of German capital in inter-war Poland. The most important German financial and industrial groups were involved in Upper Silesian industry, and some had connections with companies in Czechoslovakia. It is rather difficult to present the role of foreign capital, especially German capital, in the whole Polish economy. The most comprehensive figures were given in the statistical yearbooks covering the period from 1929 until 1937 (table 9.1). However, the figures given in table 9.1 give only fragmentary information. As well as joint stock companies there were enterprises with foreign participation organized in other legal forms. And although in most cases big business was organized as joint stock companies, there were some important exceptions, especially in Upper Silesia. Even in the case of joint stock companies the figures in table 9.1 have only an approximate value, for they were based on information given by the companies themselves. It is generally known that a company could not keep track of all its shares held abroad; besides, there are aspects of intermediate influence which cannot be explained in all cases. Sometimes a minority shareholding in a company allows the owner to decide its policy: the case of Bank Handlowy w Warszawie SA is to the point here.[5] Therefore I consider data in table 9.1 to understate the actual share of foreign capital in Polish joint stock companies; that is, the influence of foreign financial groups, being hard to describe in index numbers, was more significant than the data imply. It is probable, though, that in the companies other than joint stock concerns foreign investment was not so great. The only figure which can be quoted here is the foreign shareholding in limited liability companies in 1936: 32.7 per cent in the total capital of 317m zł.[6] (It is worth noting that the

Table 9.1. FOREIGN CAPITAL IN POLISH JOINT STOCK
COMPANIES, 1929-36.

	1929	1930	1931	1932	1933	1934	1935	1936
No. of joint stock companies registered in Poland	1,552	1,580	1,609	1,266	1,130	1,123	1,118	1,110
of which those with foreign shares	368	407	454	463	466	481	446	427
Total stock and reserve capital in zł.m	5,497	4,242	4,300	4,273	4,070	3,926	3,880	3,910
including foreign shares in zł.m	1,831	1,741	1,712	1,845	1,849	1,850	1,715	1,503
Foreign share in % of the capital of companies registered in Poland	33.3	41.0	39.8	43.2	45.4	47.1	44.2	38.4
Foreign share in % of the capital of all companies acting in Poland	39.4	49.0	44.7	46.9	49.5	51.0	48.2	42.6

Source: Z. Landau and J. Tomaszewski, *Kapitały obce w Polsce 1918-1939. Materiały i dokumenty* (Warsaw, 1964), 15.

Note: The figures published in *Mały Rocznik Statystyczny 1939* covering the period 1935-7 are somewhat different and it is impossible to compare them with the ones published in the previous volumes of this edition.

investigation by Andrzej Grodek, based on other sources and methods, gave a very similar result.[7])

It is even more difficult to investigate the 'nationality' of foreign capital engaged in Poland, that is the country of its origin, or of its centre of direction. Very complicated inter-relations among various financial groups cause all the available data to be of an approximate value only and therefore the possibility of error is significant. The most probable estimate seems to be that which was made by Leopold Wellisz (table 9.2). However, here the share of German capital was under-estimated, for it is generally known that after 1918 some German companies used the protective shield of other countries to hide their real origin.[8] In some cases such protection was given by Swiss companies, sometimes by Dutch or others.

Even from the quoted figures it is obvious that the role of German capital in inter-war Poland was significant. Though the German financial groups were not involved in the credits given to the Polish state or local governments, they held very considerable shares of the capital of private companies

Table 9.2. FOREIGN CAPITAL IN POLAND ACCORDING TO THE COUNTRY OF ORIGIN, 1933 (zlm).

Country of origin	State debt	Communal debt	Credit for companies	Share in the capital of companies	Total	%
Total	4,764	261	2,455	2,077	9,557	100.0
Austria		2	41	69	112	1.2
Belgium	36		18	194	248	2.6
Czechoslovakia	29	3	10	26	68	0.7
Denmark	1		2		3	0.0
France	970	19	225	646	1,860	19.5
Germany		4	113	437	554	5.8
Great Britain	205	28	120	113	466	4.8
Italy	184		8	4	196	2.1
Netherlands	73		33	49	155	1.6
Norway	26		1		27	0.3
Sweden	294	14	65	40	413	4.3
Switzerland	54	9	21	49	133	1.4
U.S.A.	2,557	179	48	418	3,212	33.6
Not known	325	3	1,750	32	2,110	22.1

Source: L. Wellisz, *Foreign Capital in Poland* (1938), Appendix A.

and the credits granted to them. Of these, the shares and credits in the Upper Silesian industry were the most important. Upper Silesia was the main industrial region in Poland. In 1936 it supplied 75 per cent of the coal, 100 per cent of the coke, 75 per cent of the pig iron and steel, 100 per cent of the zinc, 99 per cent of the lead, and 45 per cent of the calcium nitrate produced in Poland, not to mention many other products. In 1931 nearly 55 per cent of the population of the region earned their income in mining and industry while the average for Poland was 19.4 per cent.[9] The Silesian companies ranked among the most important and biggest in the country and the majority were in the hands of German proprietors.

One of the most important groups in Silesian industry was the Ballestrem family. The core of it was organized at the end of the eighteenth century on the basis of the family's estate.[10] In 1871 the Oberschlesische Eisenbahn-Bedarfs AG (Oberbedarf) was established: in 1922 this was divided after the political partition of Upper Silesia between Poland and Germany. The following companies in Poland belonged to this group: 'Huta Pokój' SA, Friedenshütte, and Śląskie Zakłady Górniczo-Hutnicze SA. In 1922 the majority of shares belonged to Oberbedarf, the rest were held directly by the Ballestrem family and by the large German credit banks (Deutsche, Disconto-gesellschaft and Dresdner). In 1929 the group headed by SA 'Ferrum' produced 2.2m tons of coal, 183,000 tons of pig iron and 106,600 tons of steel. The majority of SA 'Ferrum's' shares belonged to Huta Pokój and Oberbedarf. The company supplied various iron products and in 1929 employed 1,300 workers. Similarly, the Zarzad Zakładow Przemysłowych Mikołaja hr. Ballestrema (Nikolaus Graf von Ballestrem'sche Industrie Verwaltung), the property of Nikolaus Ballestrem, produced 1.2m tons of coal in 1929. The Rudzkie Gwarectwo Węglowe, which was established in 1931 with 85 per cent of its shares owned by Ballestrem and the rest by Oberbedarf, took over some mines from other companies of this group.

In the case of Dampfkesselfabrik W. Fitzner in Laurahütte AG, shortly after 1922 nearly 50 per cent of its shares were taken over by the old Cracow company L. Zieleniewski. The two companies were amalgamated and renamed Zjednoczone Fabryki Maszyn, Kotłów i Wagonów L. Zieleniewski i Fitzner-Gamper SA. In 1929 about 50 per cent of its shares belonged to SA 'Ferrum'. The company supplied various machines, tools, iron constructions and railway cars, and employed 4,900 workers in its plants situated in Kraków, Lwów, Sosnowiec and other towns. With regard to Suchedniowska Fabryka Odlewów i Huta 'Ludwików' SA in 1929 50 per cent of shares belonged to SA 'Ferrum'. The Ballestrem group possessed some shares of other companies but it is difficult to discern fully all the connections.

The next big business family in Upper Silesia was the Donnersmarcks, divided into two lines, one Catholic. This group owned the Generalna Dyrekcja hr. Henckel von Donnersmarck, Beuthen [The Henckel von Donnersmarck-Beuthen Estates Ltd], which produced 715 tons of coal in 1929. Another subsidiary was Angielska SA [the Hugohütte Chemical Works Ltd], a producer of sulphur, barium, boron and other compounds. This group held some shares of 'Wirek' Kopalnie SA (the company produced in 1929 1.4m tons of coal). Other shares of 'Wirek' belonged to the Ballestrem group and to the Protestant Donnersmarck group.

The Protestant line of Donnersmarck owned, as a family estate, the enterprise Dyrekcja Kopalń i Hut Księcia Donnersmarcka (Fürst von Donnersmarck'sche Bergwerks- und Hüttendirektion). Its output in 1929 was 7m tons of coal and some quantity of zinc, and it employed about 10,000 workers. The group held a minority of the shares of Śląskie Kopalnie ie Cynkownie SA (in which French capital was dominant), Górnośląskie Zjednoczone Huty Królewska i Laura SA, 'Huta Pokój', and Katowicka SA dla Górnictwa i Hutnictwa.

The coal merchant for the Ballestrem and Donnersmarck (Protestant line) groups was the company Związek Kopalń Górnóśląskich 'Robur' sp. z o. o. It was established in 1922 by Emanuel Friedländer Co., a well-known Berlin company, with the sole aim of selling Silesian coal. 'Robur' was also the agent for the following other companies: first, the 'Godulla' SA, established in 1922 from the eastern part of Gräflich Schaffgotsch'sche Werke; the best part of the estate remained in Germany. 'Godulla' raised 1.7m tons of coal in 1929 and held some 'Wirek' shares. Second, Rybnickie Gwarectwo Węglowe, formed by Frederic von Friedländer-Fould and in the inter-war years owned by his daughter Anna Marie von Goldschmidt-Rothschild. It produced 2.4m tons of coal in 1929. Lastly, the Gwarectwo Węglowe 'Charlotte', which in about 1930 was bought by Rybnickie Gwaretctwo Węglowe, was the smallest, with an output of 0.8m tons of coal in 1929.

All the companies mentioned above (excluding those of the Catholic Donnersmarcks) produced together 16.7m tons of coal in 1929, about half of the total Silesian output. This made 'Robur' the most important coal trading company in Poland. Later on 'Robur' invested in some harbour improvements at Gdynia and established a shipping company to transport coal.

The next important company was the Vereinigte Königs-und Laurahütte AG für Bergbau und Eisenhüttenbetrieb, founded in Berlin in 1871 by a group of the larger German credit banks with a minority of shares held by Hugo Henckel von Donnersmarck. After 1922 the majority of shares were bought from these banks by Frederic Weinmann (Czechoslovakia), who sold some part to Sigismund Bosel (Austria).[11] The company had an output of 3.1m tons of coal, 157,000 tons of pig iron and 322,000 tons of steel, together with many other products, and employed 17,000 workers in 1929. It owned all the shares of the Częstochowskie Towarzystwo Górniczo-Hutnicze SA and some other companies.

In 1889 two of the German D-Banks (Discontogesellschaft with the Dresdner Bank) established in Katowice the Kattowitzer AG für Bergbau und Eisenhüttenbetrieb, the next big Silesian company. It was based on the Thiele-Wincklers' family estates. At the end of 1921, the majority of shares of this company passed into the hands of Frederic Flick, whose influence on German economic life was at that time developing rapidly. Somewhat later Flick sold 80 per cent of his shares in the Kattowitzer AG to another of his companies – the Bismarckhütte AG.[12]

The Bismarckhütte AG had been formed in 1882 by two banks. Flick bought its shares in 1920 and used them for some very lucrative ventures in Silesia and West Germany. In 1927 Bismarckhütte bought the shares of Huta 'Silesia' SA. In 1923 Flick sold the shares of his Silesian companies. Bosel tried to buy them with the help of a well-known Polish politician, Wojciech Korfanty, who was involved in some Silesian companies. Hugo Stinnes had more luck but after his death in 1924 Flick regained, in 1926, his former property. Bosel and Weinmann did, however, arrange to acquire some minor shares. In 1929 the Bismarckhütte AG, Huta 'Silesia' SA and the Kattowitzer AG were amalgamated under the name of Katowicka SA dla Górnictwa i Hutnictwa. The company then produced 2.4m tons of coal, 109,000 tons of pig iron, 349,000 tons of steel and other products. All its plants, together, employed 20,800 workers.

The seller of coal raised by the companies of the Flick group was Cäsar Wollheim in Berlin. He had a branch in Katowice, which in 1924 was reorganized as 'Progress' Zjednoczone Kopalnie Górnośląskie sp. z o. o.

'Progress' was the agent of the Donnersmarcks (Catholic) as well as of Śląskie Kopalnie i Cynkownie SA (Donnersmarck, Protestant). The capital of 'Progress' was in the hands of the four companies which supplied the coal, but the links with Cäsar Wollheim in Berlin continued.

In 1905 the industrial plants and mines belonging to the family of Hohenlohe-Oehringen were organized in the Hohenlohe Werke AG. In 1921 the company was divided. Oehringen Bergbau AG developed from the western part, while the eastern part remained in Poland as Zakłady Hohenlohego SA. An important group from Ústi n. L. (Czechoslovakia) – the Petschek family – was interested in the company.[13] Zakłady Hohenlohego produced 2.2m tons of coal in 1929, together with some quantity of zinc ore, raw zinc and lead. Connected with Zkałady Hohenlohego was the Czernickie Towarzystwo Węglowe SA, which had an output of 0.6m tons of coal in 1929. Both companies had the same coal dealer – Górnośląski Handel Węglem 'Fulmen' sp. z o. o. – which between 1919 and 1924 went under the name Ostkohlen-Handelsgesellschaft.

The next big Silesian family were the Giesches. Their origins can be traced as far back as 1704, when a merchant, Georg von Giesche, received the concession to mine zinc ore in Upper Silesia. At the beginning of the twentieth century the group was organized as Georg von Giesche's Erben AG. In 1922 the eastern part of the company's estates and plants was converted into a subordinate company, 'Giesche' SA. ' Giesche' produced coal, zinc and zinc derivatives, employing in 1929 more than 17,000 workers. 'Giesche' SA held the shares of two companies: 'Giesche' Fabryka Porcelany SA and Fabryka Chemiczna dawniej Carl Scharff and Co. SA. The majority of the shares of Belgijska Górnicza i Przemysłowa SA (SA Minière et Industrielle) belonged to Giesche too. It is worth noting that 'Giesche' SA and Georg von Giesche's Erben AG ranked among the main suppliers of zinc and zinc derivatives in the world.

The last family enterprise to mention here is Dyrekcja Kopalń Księcia Pszczyńskiego (Bergwerkdirektion des Fürsten von Pless). In 1929 it produced 2.6m tons of coal.

All the above-mentioned companies possessed vast landed estates and forests – their reserves for future exploitation of coal and ore. They held shares in many other companies of minor importance in Upper Silesia and other regions of Poland as well. The Protestant line of the Donnersmarcks owned, for example, the shares of Grodzieckie Towarzystwo Kopalń Węgla SA (0.6m tons of coal in 1929), Górnośląski Bank Związkowy SA (a company of local importance only), Polskie Towarzystwo Handlowe SA and 'Lignoza' SA.

At the end of 1929 the Upper Silesian coal mines employed 94,600 workers, its metallurgical plants 21,600 workers, and its zinc and lead plants 10,600 workers. Polish coal production in the same year was 46.2m tons (including Upper Silesia, 34.4m tons), pig iron 704,000 tons, and steel

1,377,000 tons.[14] These figures can be compared with the data concerning the above-mentioned companies. In 1929 they produced more than 29m tons of coal (more than 85 per cent of Upper Silesian output and more than 64 per cent of total Polish output). They had a monopoly in zinc and lead production and were the most important producers of iron and steel. They also played a significant role as the suppliers of machines, tools, etc.

The partition of Upper Silesia in 1922 raised important questions connected with the activity of Silesian companies. It was generally known that some shareholders and managers were involved in the elaboration and fulfilment of the political plans of German imperialism in Central Europe. The union of Upper Silesian businessmen – Oberschlesicher Berg- und Hüttenmännischer Verein – was very active in this field, preparing memoranda and projects, especially during the First World War. Its spokesmen were Gustav Williger and Paul Geisenheimer,[15] both from the Katowicka SA dla Górnictwa i Hutnictwa. Some of the declarations against the unification of Upper Silesia with Poland carried the signatures of Ballestrem, Henckel von Donnersmarck and other coal barons,[16] some of whom were active in implementing a chauvinist policy, aiming to germanize the Polish population.

The reorganization of the Silesian companies as a result of the partition of the whole territory did not change the political and economic ties of these men and corporations. The citizenship of the Polish Republic, which many of them acquired on the basis of international agreements, could not influence their opinions and loyalty to the German fatherland. The question was complicated because of the specific social and national structure of the Silesian population. Though the majority were Polish, the businessmen, managers, technical staff, white collar workers and in most cases even the upper strata of other workers were German. Under German rule professional and social promotion had almost been impossible for people who declared themselves to be Poles.

After 1922 the German civil servants, policemen, etc. were in most cases dismissed and replaced by Poles. Polish schools were organized (the German ones – necessary for the German sector of the population – remained). However, changes in the national structure of private companies were rather insignificant. The German language remained in use in documents, in current business affairs, in plants and mines, even in official letters to the Polish authorities.[17] German staff favoured workers who declared their loyalty to Germany and whose children attended German schools. Thus in independent Poland important factors remained that encouraged a continuation of the germanization policy of the former German authorities, and often a Polish worker's job was dependent on the goodwill of German managers. The matter of schools, which has been analysed in some historical studies, was especially important.[18]

All these facts were politically significant and capable of influencing the future of Upper Silesia. The German government promoted a policy of frontier revision and the secret fight for the soul and loyalty of the Upper Silesian workers was part of it. In such a situation the Polish government tried to change the financial ties existing in Silesia and to gain influence in industrial companies. Some possibilities were contained in the stipulations of the Treaty of Versailles. The allied countries (Poland was considered to be an ally) could expropriate (with compensation) German property on the basis of Section 92 and Section 297 of the Treaty. These and other provisions were used in Czechoslovakia in order to implement the so-called nostrification of capital. Poland was in a much more difficult situation because of the damages suffered by the native financial groups during the war. For these and other reasons there was not sufficient capital available in Poland for the purchase of Silesian shares.[19] The only important change in ownership after 1922 was the take-over of the former Prussian state estates by the Polish government. On the basis of this property the following companies were founded: Polskie Kopalnie Skarbowe na Górnym Śląsku Spółka Dzierzawna SA (Société Fermière des Mines Fiscales de L'Etat Polonais en Haute Silésie SA), generally known as Skarboferm, which produced 3.4m tons of coal in 1929 and some other products; Polska Huta Skarbowa Ołowiu i Srebra w Strzybnicy Spółka Dzierzawna Tarnowskie Góry SA, which supplied lead, silver and some other products. In both companies the government retained 50 per cent of the shares, the rest being in French hands.[20]

The Polish government tried to draw the attention of Allied – mainly French – capital to possibilities for investment in Silesia. The effect of these efforts was minimal because businessmen did not want to involve their money in this region which was generally unknown to them. As well as the above-mentioned companies (founded with some political help from the French government) only in the case of Zakłady Hohenlohego was 15 per cent of shares bought by a Polish-French group. The Polish 7.5 per cent was held by the state while the French group involved – as became evident later – began to collaborate with the German shareholders against the interests of the Polish authorities.[21]

The attitude of the Silesian companies towards the new-born Polish Republic was hostile, combined with some fear concerning the future of German property and mistrust in the stability of the new frontiers. The anxiety was somewhat dispelled when a Polish-German Upper Silesian convention was signed in May 1922 in Geneva. By this Poland relinquished some of her rights concerning German property.[22] The lack of capital in Poland had some importance too because the German businessmen realized that it was impossible to find a Polish financial group capable of paying for shares.

It is interesting to note that the Polish government decided not to apply compulsory methods. In the case of Zakłady Hohenlohego the German shareholders agreed to sell a part of their shares on the condition that the state would waive its right to expropriate the company and grant some tax reductions.[23]

These factors allowed the Silesian companies to adapt their activity to the new conditions created with the rebirth of the Polish Republic. After the division of property and the establishment of formal independence of German and Polish companies (though in reality strictly connected owing to the possession of shares), the reconstruction of mining and industry began. The proprietors were mainly developing their plants located on the western side of the state frontier. As a result of the delimitation (i.e. drawing of new frontiers) the bulk of mines and industrial plants were situated in Poland, whereas mainly unexploited mining endowments and some mills remained in Germany which did not constitute fully independent factories. The German businessmen wanted to develop these estates and to change them into an important component of the German national economy.[24]

It would be interesting to investigate the impact of German economic policy on the Silesian companies and their investment policy. The Polish-German convention guaranteed free trade between both parts of Upper Silesia from 1922 till the middle of June 1925. The temporary quotas for imports from the eastern part of Silesia introduced in Germany in Spring 1924 were of no importance, but in June 1925 Germany declared an economic war against Poland. In both countries several orders severely restricting mutual trade were introduced, concerning especially the Polish export of coal.[25] This meant a serious blow to the East Silesian mines. Was this expected by the German businessmen? When they invested in West Silesian plants had they been aware of the preparations for economic war which stopped exports from East Silesia, and did they want to retain their position on the German market in spite of competition from other companies?[26] Maybe, at the same time, they considered Poland to be a *Saisonstaat* and did not want to risk their money there. Such an investment policy had some importance to the economic retardation of the Polish Republic.

In 1924 the Polish authorities discovered that some Silesian companies were behaving contrary to law. A full description of their corrupt practices is not necessary here. It is sufficient to say that Zakłady Hohenlohego were financing investments of Oehringen Bergbau in Germany by entering the expenses on their own accounts. The company in Poland was deprived of its funds, the State received diminished taxes, but from the point of view of the proprietors of both companies it was a mere formality where the cost of investments was accounted. The same or similar practices were discovered in Vereinigte Königs- und Laurahütten, 'Giesche', the Cäsar Wollheim branch in Katowice, and companies belonging to the Ballestrem and Henckel von Donnersmarck groups. Besides these illegal practices, there existed some others which were in accordance with the letter of the law. When the property of Silesian companies was divided and the Polish companies were established, the legal procedure in most cases involved the formal purchase of the mines, plants and estates by the new companies from the old ones. Most of the East Upper Silesian companies were deeply indebted to their German sisters, because the purchases were made on credit. The interest payments burdened the companies established in Poland and were an illegal means of transferring money to Germany. At the same time some companies imported the necessary raw materials or equipment from German partners at very high prices, or exported their own products at relatively low prices. These procedures allowed not only profits but even capital to be transferred discreetly.[27]

The Polish authorities could only stop illegal practices, whilst other means of exploiting the East Upper Silesian companies in order to develop the West Upper Silesian enterprises remained. Therefore the Polish government tried to influence the Silesian companies by various methods. Some Polish members were appointed under pressure to the central boards of directors and some Poles received managing posts. In some cases minority shareholdings were bought by Polish businessmen.[28] All this did not alter the real position of German capital, and indeed many Polish members of the boards of directors were called *Strohmänner* (puppets) because of the way they permitted their names to be used to give countenance to the old practices.

More significant changes occurred in 1926 and 1927. The Berlin company Vereinigte Königs- und Laurahütten was heavily burdened with unpaid taxes and proposed – against the remission of them – an agreement with the Polish government. In July 1926 a new company was established in Katowice: Górnośląskie Zjednoczone Huty Królewska i Laura SA Górniczo-Hutnicza. The company took over all the Silesian property of its Berlin founder, which possessed 82.5 per cent of shares and became a holding company. The other shares were taken up by the Polish government, who had three delegates on the central board of Królewska i Laura and nominated the general director (the former minister Józef Kiedroń was appointed to this post). The Weinmann-Bosel group promised to maintain till 1929 the former German credits given to the Berlin company.

Some months later Bosel and Weinmann suffered heavy losses on the Paris Stock Exchange and sold most of their shares of Vereinigte Königs- und Laurahütten to Vereinigte Stahlwerke AG, the stronghold of Flick.[29] Approximately at the same time Flick regained his former position in other Silesian companies and became one of the leading persons in the eastern part of Upper Silesia, taking this region into his industrial and financial realm. It seems that the Polish businessmen and politicians, who observed with great anxiety Stinnes' conquests, perceived Flick's progress too late to undertake any counteractions. Katowicka SA dla Górnictwa i Hutnictwa (including Bismarckhütte and Huta 'Silesia') and Huty Królewska i Laura established in 1929 a so-called Wspólnota Interesów (community of interests).[30] They remained independent legal bodies but had a common management and in both it was Flick who dominated.

U.S. capital was also interested in both companies. In 1929 the New York Consolidated Silesian Steel Corporation (CSSC) with William Averell Harriman and others was established. Harriman agreed to co-operate with Flick. The shares of CSSC were divided; Flick received about 66 per cent, the rest went to Harriman and his group. The U.S. company acquired 83 per cent of the shares of Vereinigte Königs- und Laurahütten AG, the rest was in the hands of Weinmann and German banks. CSSC also received 97 per cent of the shares of Katowicka SA dla Górnictwa i Hutnictwa.[31] From the formal point of view, U.S. influence – personified in CSSC – dominated in both Silesian companies. In reality Flick was the main shareholder. The co-operation with Harriman was a strong argument in all disputes with the Polish government and facilitated the procurement of credit in the U.S.A. Wspólnota Interesów placed itself in a special position in Polish mining and industry. According to data from 1937 it produced 22.4 per cent of the iron ore extracted in Poland, 27.3 per cent of the coke, 33.2 per cent of the pig iron, 42.1 per cent of the steel, 42.1 per cent of the rolling-mill products, 45.3 per cent of the wrought iron wares and some other products.[32]

The same Harriman group acquired the shares of 'Giesche' SA. In 1926 in New York the Silesian-American Corporation (SACO) was established, which received 100 per cent of 'Giesche' shares. The German group (mainly the Giesche family) possessed 49 per cent of SACO shares, the rest was retained by the Harriman group. The whole matter was settled with the active co-operation of the Polish government. 'Giesche' was burdened with vast sums of unpaid taxes and the Polish government agreed to cancel them and to grant some other privileges on condition that SACO should invest $10m in Poland.[33]

At the same time two agreements were signed. The first provided that the sale of all 'Giesche' products abroad would be monopolized by SACO. The second stipulated that the sole trading rights in zinc, lead and other metals which SACO would have for sale in Europe (except Poland) would be in the hands of the Bergwerksprodukte GmbH in Berlin – the company connected with Georg von Giesche's Erben AG.[34] As a result of these agreements Georg von Giesche's Erben could dispose of the bulk of the Polish zinc exports.

Some other documents suggest that U.S. domination was only superficial. In June 1938 an interesting memorandum of Georg von Giesche's Erben was prepared, whose authors stressed that the aims of the agreement with Harriman were 'the maintaining and guarantee of the future prosperity of the company in Poland under the U.S. banner' and 'the obtaining of the floating capital for the German 'Giesche' company with the support of credit'. The whole agreement was constructed so as to hide the real German share in 'Giesche' SA.[35]

It is difficult to explain the reasons which led the Harriman group to invest in Silesian companies. It may be that it was Harriman's personal sympathy for Poland. The Polish government helped him to acquire the shares from the hands of German financial groups in the hope that this would influence investment and undermine the importance of the German managers and clerks. It is true that the number of Poles employed in the offices of these companies grew; but there is not sufficient documentary evidence to show whether the real influence of the Germans diminished.

The German shareholders considered the deal with Harriman to be a convenient way of defence against the Polish authorities and of gaining some money for investments in the western part of Upper Silesia. Harriman paid $4m for the shares of 'Giesche', granted $8.5m credit for Georg von Giesche's Erben, and paid the debt of 'Giesche' to the German company. At the same time he did not diminish the role of the German group in the European market.

The co-operation of Harriman with Flick and Giesche awakened the anxiety of the Polish military authorities. When the U.S. group tried to obtain a vast concession for the production and sale of electricity in Poland which included the most important industrial regions of the state, the project was strongly criticized and at last rejected in 1936.[36] Possibly this explains why Harriman resigned from the other projects concerning Poland and later on did not interest himself in Silesian shares. However, the most important reason was the Great Depression which influenced the possibilities of all U.S. financial groups. The Silesian companies declared losses but SACO duly received its interest payments. The total sum transferred to the U.S.A. from 'Giesche' (not counting Georg von Giesche's Erben) reached about 150m zł, whereas the Harriman group invested in both (Polish and German) companies about 200m. zł.[37]

The Silesian companies belonged to several Polish and international cartels which played an important economic role. These questions have not yet been thoroughly investigated. Here I shall mention only the coal agreement and zinc cartel.

Almost the whole supply of coal in Poland was organized in two agreements: Górnośląska Konwencja Węglowa (in most cases abbreviated KGS) and Konwencja Dąbrowsko-Krakowska (KDK). They signed a general agreement called Ogólnopolska Konwencja Węglowa (KOP). The original agreement divided the production quotas thus: KGS 74 per cent, KDK 25.5 per cent, the state-owned coal mine Brzeszcze 0.5 per cent. In the following years only insignificant changes were introduced. In 1931 both regional agreements were dissolved and the coal producers and traders organized a new one – Polska Konwencja Węglowa.[38] The share of every company in the production quotas was relatively stable because it depended on their economic strength and their possibilities of coal output. To illustrate the role played by the Silesian groups it is sufficient therefore to quote figures from 1929 (table 9.3) only.

The zinc-producing companies in Germany were organized in the Zinkwalzverband GmbH in Berlin, to which all Silesian companies belonged. In

Table 9.3. THE SHARE OF THE SILESIAN COAL COMPANIES IN
THE POLISH COAL CARTEL IN 1929 (in %).

Company	Share	
	KGS	KOP
'Robur'	36.7	27.3
'Progress'	21.2	15.8
Skarboferm	11.1	8.3
'Fulmen'	10.8	8.0
'Giesche'	9.0	6.7
'Unitas' (von Pless)	8.8	6.6
'Silesia' SA	1.3	0.9
'Waleska' SA	1.1	0.8
Silesian companies (together)	100.0	74.4
KDK		25.6

Source: Letter to George Sage Brooks ('Giesche'), 26 Feb. 1929: APK, 'Giesche' SA 5325, 46–8.

March 1928 the producers from Poland organized their own cartel, Biuro Rozdzielcze Zjednoczonych Polskich Walcowni Cynku, which had a close association with the German partner, who retained the exclusive right for the export of German and Polish zinc.[39] In 1931 the International Zinc Cartel was established (without U.S.A. companies which were bound by the anti-trust laws, but which unofficially co-operated with the European producers). The cartel allocated quotas of production (table 9.4). Czechoslovakia and Yugoslavia remained outside this cartel producing only small quantities of zinc.[40] The figures concerning both cartels (coal and zinc) illustrate the domination of the Silesian companies in some branches of Polish mining and industry. It facilitated the international influence of those German financial groups which played the main role in Upper Silesia.

The economic role of the Silesian companies was so strong that the Polish government had to take their interest into account though their political position in Poland was weak. The traditional organization of Silesian big business – Oberschlesischer Berg- und Hüttenmännischer Verein (which changed its name into Górnóśląski Związek Przemysłowców Górniczych i Hutniczych) – ceased to exist in 1932 under the pressure of the Polish authorities and a new union, Unia Polskiego Przemysłu Górniczo-Hutnicze-go, was established.[41] Among the members of its Presidial Committee Polish names prevailed though these men represented in most cases the big Silesian companies. Some former German managers were pensioned off, others remained employed in Unia.

The Silesian companies tried to gain the adherence of some Polish politicians for their aims. A well-known member of the National Democratic Party, Zygmunt Seyda, accepted the lucrative post of a delegate of Górnóśląs-

Table 9.4. THE SHARE OF PARTICULAR COUNTRIES IN THE INTERNATIONAL ZINC CARTEL IN 1931 (in %).

Country or company	Share
Belgium	27.6
Poland	18.3
Including:	
Slaskie Kopalnie i Cynkownie SA	7.3
'Giesche' SA	7.0
Zakłady Hohenlohego SA	2.5
Dyrekcja Kopalń i Hut Kzięcia Donnersmarcka	1.3
Franko-Polskie Towarzystwo Górnicze SA	0.2
Great Britain (including Australia)	11.5
Canada	12.7
Germany	10.1
Mexico	5.7
France, Italy and Spain	14.1
Total	100.0

Source: Letter, probably of George Sage Brooks, 30 Dec. 1931: APK, WPH 1497.

ki Związek Przemyslowców Górniczych i Hutniczych in Warsaw. His political opponents stated that the conduct of another right-wing politician, Wojciech Korfanty, towards the Silesian companies was not correct.[42] All these questions have not yet been investigated, though it seems that at least part of these accusations are groundless.

At the end of the 1920s the system of the main financial groups in Upper Silesia seemed to be established. However, the Great Depression changed the situation significantly. In the great industrial and mining empires of Flick, Harriman and others the shares in the companies established in Poland were of minor importance. It seems that the proprietors of the companies situated on both sides of the frontier were interested – as in previous years – mainly in the maintenance and development of their western plants situated in Germany. During the Great Depression they received, in various forms, profits from Poland but used them in Germany. There were numerous legal reasons. Many companies were indebted in Germany as a consequence of taking over mines and plants from their former legal proprietors (e.g. Zjednoczone Huty Królewska i Laura in Katowice was indebted to Vereiningte Königs und Laurahütten in Berlin) and duly paid interest. The companies of Wspólnota Interesów paid regular interest to Cäsar Wollheim, apparently for commercial goodwill. Sometimes the companies paid for licences from abroad.[43] These were the major reasons why Silesian companies suffered losses and why some of them collapsed financially.

On 18 December 1931, 'Huta Pokój' SA was declared insolvent and closed a part of its rolling mills. Some weeks earlier the newly organized Ballestrem company, Rudzkie Gwarectwo Węglowe, bought all the coal mines from the defunct 'Huta Pokój', not with cash but against the cancellation of old debts. Ballestrem retained the most important mines for himself. 'Huta Pokój' was put in the hands of an Official Receiver.[44] The balance sheet made on 31 December 1931 revealed that the value of the whole property equalled 156m zł, the losses were 46m zł and the liabilities totalled 82m zł (including 20m zł to Oberbedarf and 12m zł to the American and Continental Corporation, New York). In addition, the debt secured on the mortgage was 17m zł. The insolvency of such a big company had an important impact on the economic and political situation of Poland. The closure of the mills increased unemployment, which was very high during the hard times of the Great Depression. This threatened to increase social disorder and encouraged unfriendly comments towards Poland and comparisons with conditions behind the German frontier. Therefore the Polish government engaged itself in the financial reform of the company. The task was difficult because there was no Polish financial group able to take over the shares and secure the necessary credit. At last an agreement with the German credit banks was signed. They granted a credit on rather hard conditions (guaranteed by the Polish state); the government took over 52 per cent of the shares, the rest was retained by the Ballestrem group. In the following years the Polish government had to pay back the debts to the German credit banks and the former owners of the shares.

Much more dangerous was the insolvency of Wspólnota Interesów.[45] It was caused by some unsuccessful financial ventures of Flick which were made at the two companies' expense. The losses burdened them heavily, totalling approximately 170m zł. In March 1934 both companies constituting Wspólnota Interesów were handed over to the Official Receiver. The debt secured on the mortgaged totalled 156m zł, the unpaid state taxes and other public liabilities 112m zł. Compulsory state management and credit granted by the state-owned bank allowed the companies to continue their existence and averted the dismissal of their workers. In 1936 an agreement concerning both companies was signed. The government took over the shares and German liabilities against state securities which were to be paid partly in cash, partly in coal and other goods exported to Germany. The Polish government – as it is clear from the documents – did not want to take over the companies of Wspólnota Interesów but had to intervene in order to prevent the disastrous social and political consequences of their insolvency.[46] Attempts to find a private group able to purchase the shares ended without result. Wspólnota Interesów became state property but it was an undesired turn of events.

Not so spectacular as the two insolvencies described above was the case of Zakłady Hohenlohego. The company suffered some losses, but more important was the gradually diminishing value of its mines and plants. Some of them were closed. New investments did not equal the depreciation of old installations. After 14 March 1939 – when the Petschek family was hit by the Nazi rule in the Czech Lands – the Polish authorities appointed a receiver to the company because of unpaid taxes (15m zł).[47]

The activity of German banks in the eastern part of Upper Silesia was of minor importance from the economic point of view, though it had some significant political implications. Polish law excluded banks whose head offices were situated abroad from activity in Poland. Therefore after 1918 Austrian, German and Russian banks had either to close their branches or to change them into legally independent companies registered in Poland. An important exception was made in the Polish-German convention signed in May 1922 which allowed the branches of the four German D-banks to continue their activity till May 1937.

This question was connected with the general attitude of Silesian companies towards the Polish Republic. The German D-banks facilitated the separation of the Silesian economy from the rest of the state, discriminated against Polish companies, and helped German economic intelligence. The local Silesian authorities tried to draw the attention of the Polish government to these facts, arguing in 1927 that it was necessary to close the branches of the German D-banks. A significant argument was that the credits granted by these branches were based on local savings and not on the money received from their central offices. Therefore, it was possible to replace the German banks with Polish ones.[48]

However, political reasons made it impossible to solve this question in accordance with the proposals of the Silesian authorities. Probably the real financial significance of the German D-banks was not so negligible. An investigation in 1931 revealed that some Silesian mining and industrial companies ('Godulla', 'Robur', Katowicka SA dla Górnictwa i Hutnictwa) received important short-term credits from these branches. Even more important was that the German credit banks acted as intermediaries in relation to French and British banks.[49] It seemed that their role diminished later with the impact of the Great Depression.[50] The Polish diplomats tried to gain French financial and political help in order to fight the German banks.[51] Though it seems that the French diplomats were at first interested in the project there are no traces that their interest was implemented. Anyway, we have to note that the bulk of short-term as well as long-term credits was negotiated not in the Katowice branches but in the central offices of the German D-banks in Berlin.

It is possible that the German D-banks' branches played a much more important role for the middle- and small-sized German companies, craftsmen and landowners. In this field the co-operative German banks were active too.

In 1925 the formally independent society Deutsche Stiftung in Berlin (in fact subordinated to the Auswärtiges Amt) began to implement a vast financial programme in Poland. Their instruments in the eastern part of Upper Silesia were the Agrar und Commerzbank AG in Katowice (dependent on German co-operatives) and the Oberschlesische Bankverein AG in Chorzów (established in 1920 by the German D-banks). They received money from the Deutsche Stiftung through banks in Switzerland and Gdańsk.[52] These channels were sufficient for little enterprises but too small for big business; and in any case the Polish government had to decide the questions connected with the large mining, industrial and credit companies not only from a purely economic but also from a political point of view.

On the eve of the Second World War German capital lost some important companies which were taken over by the Polish state. This was achieved not as a result of a systematic policy but mainly owing to the Great Depression and the insolvency of some enterprises. Whatever the causes, these changes diminished the influence of hostile German financial groups in Poland.

The activity of German companies in Upper Silesia caused – as we have seen – an outflow of capital from Poland. This was not only an outflow of profits which was then invested in Germany, but in some cases an outflow of formerly invested capital. This trend constituted a heavy burden on the Polish economy.[53] Some part of the sums paid abroad was included in the statistical estimates concerning the Polish balance of payments. Another part was hidden in various legal or illegal forms of transfer and could not be estimated. The undesired nationalization in the 1930s was connected with the continued outflow of capital, though it was more orderly and under the supervision of the Polish authorities.[54]

It is interesting to note that the outflow of German capital from Poland differed from the trends observed in some other countries of Central and South-East Europe where in the 1930s the role of German companies was growing. These differences were connected with the political aims of the Third Reich and with the policy of particular countries in which German capital was invested.

Notes

1. Another opinion is that expressed by Wladyslaw Rusiński, who considered this immigration to be equal to an inflow of foreign capital: W. Rusiński, *Rozwój gospodarczy ziem polskich w zarysie* (Warsaw, 1963), 314.

2. See, e.g., S. Wykretowicz, *Przemysł cukrowniczy w zachodniej Polsce w latach 1918–1939* (Poznań, 1962), 65.

3. For more detailed arguments, see J. Tomaszewski, '"Fremdes Kapital". Ein Versuch zur näheren Bestimmung', *Jahrbuch für Wirtschaftsgeschichte*, II (1978), 29ff.

4. A. Teichova, *An Economic Background to Munich. International Business and Czechoslovakia 1918–1939* (1974).

5. See Z. Landau and J. Tomaszewski, *Bank Handlowy w Warszawie S.A. History and Development* (Bank Handlowy w Warszawie SA) (Warsaw, 1970), 56ff. This bank was influenced by the Banca

Commerciale Italiana owing to the personal and financial ties of some Polish shareholders with Giuseppe Töplitz.

6. *Mały Rocznik Statystyczny 1939*, 114.
7. A. Grodek, *Wybór pism w dwóch tomach. II. Studia nad rozwojem kapitalizmu oraz inne prace* (Warsaw, 1963), 261ff.
8. *Ibid.*, 276f.
9. A. Landau and J. Tomaszewski, *Zarys historii gospodarczej Polski 1918–1939* (Warsaw, 1971), 41f.; *Mały Rocznik Statystyczna* (1938), 32, 34.
10. The basic data concerning the Silesian companies, if not otherwise stated, are from: Grodek, *op. cit.*, II, 285ff.; J. Jaros, *Historia górnictwa węglowego w Zagłebiu Górnośląskim w latach 1914–1945* (Kraków, 1969); J. Jaros, *Słownik historyczny kopalń węgla na ziemiach polskich* (Katowice, 1972); J. Popkiewicz and F. Ryszka, *Przemysł ciężki Górnego Sląska w gospodarce Polski międzywojennej, 1922–1939* (Opole, 1959); R. Schmidt, *Die Entwicklung der Oberschlesischen Grossindustrie und ihrer Besitzverhältnisse von 1700–1942* (Katowice, 1942; mimeographed), and *Rocznik informacyjny o spółkach akcyjnych w Polsce 1930.*
11. Weimann was interested in Czechoslovakia in Weinmann-Werke, Teplice-Šanov, the zinc producer: Teichova, *op. cit.*, 255, 258.
12. About this company see also A. Loch and G. Szendzielorz, *Kartki z dziejow Huty "Batory"* (Stalingrad, 1956), 61, 88f.
13. Petscheks were interested in the Anglo-československá banka in Prague too: Teichova, *op. cit.*, 350, 356.
14. *Rocznik Statystyki Rzeczypospolitej Polskiej 1930*, 85, 89, 90; *Mały Rocznik Statystyczny 1939*, 128f.
15. It is interesting to note that both Geisenheimer and Williger were in the Polish delegation during the conference of Polish and German businessmen in December 1927. They met there the member of the German delegation E. Jacob, the former director of Hohenlohe Werke AG, who had to escape from Poland because of his unpleasant role in tax-offences and other illegal practices. Some other managers of Silesian companies were in the German delegation too. The conference was connected with Polish-German official talks concerning the preparations of a trade agreement. See the documents in Archiwum Panstwowe w Katowicach (The State Archive in Katowice, hereafter cited as APK), Zakłady Hohenlohego 2805.
16. Jaros, *Historia . . .*, 161f.; F. Baiły, *Górnosląski Związek Przemysłowcow Górniczo-Hutniczych 1914–1932* (Wrocław, 1967), *passim.*
17. Often meetings of boards of directors of East Silesian companies were held in Berlin, not in Poland, e.g., the conferences of the proprietors and managers of Zakłady Hohenlohego in the years 1922–30. See APK, Zakłady Hohenlohego 394.
18. R. Staniewicz, *Mniejszość niemiecka w województwie śląskim w latach 1922–1933* (Katowice, 1965, Biuletyn nr 26); S. Mauersberg, *Szkolnictwo powszechne dla mniejszości narodowych w Polsce w latach 1918–1939* (Wrocław, 1968), 131ff.
19. See J. Tomaszewski, 'Akumulacja kapitału w Polsce. Tendencje generalné', *Badania nad historia gospodarczo-społeczna w Polsce (problemy i metody)* (Warsaw – Poznań, 1978), 101f.
20. *Rocznik informacyjny o spółkach akcyjnych w Polsce 1930.* The documents of both companies are held in APK.
21. Documents were published in Z. Landau and J. Tomaszewski, 'Misja profesora Artura Benisá', *Teki Archiwalne*, VI (1959).
22. Z. Landau and J. Tomaszewski, *Gospodarka Polski międzywojennej 1918–1939*, I, *W dobie inflacji 1918–1923* (Warsaw, 1967), 26f.
23. About the reasons for the agreement with the French group, see 'Niederschrift über die Ausschussitzung des Aufsichtsrates der Hohenlohe Werke Spolka Akcyjna vom 31. August 1923', in Hohenlohehütte, APK, Zakłady Hohenlohego 394. The company received some tax privileges. Some stipulations of the agreement were slow in being implemented. This allowed the Polish government to find arguments against the company in 1938 and to cancel its tax privileges: see 'Sprawozdanie z konferencji odbytej 20 paźdz.1938 r. u p.' Dyrektora Martiná, APK, Skarboferm 458.

24. Such tendencies can be seen in some formulations in 'Niederschrift über die Sitzung des Ausschusses am 2. Dezember 1922 in Berlin', APK, Zakłady Hohenlohego 394.

25. The motives were political as well as economic. Germany wanted to obtain some important political concessions from Poland. At the same time the West German industrialists voted against the competition of East Upper Silesian companies. B. Puchert, *Der Wirtschaftskrieg des deutschen Imperialismus gegen Polen 1925–1934* (Berlin, 1963), 43ff., 61ff.; H. Mottek, W. Becker and A. Schröter, *Wirtschaftsgeschichte Deutschlands. Ein Grundriss*, III, *Von der Zeit der Bismarckschen Reichsgründung bis zur Niederlage des faschistischen deutschen Imperialismus 1945* (Berlin, 1975), 255f., 262, 267.

26. About the competition between the Upper Silesian and Lower Silesian coal mines in the Czechoslovak market see the letter of the Górnośląska Konwencja Węglowa, 23 June 1924, APK, Urząd Wojewódzki Śląski Wydział Przemysłu i Handlu (hereafter cited as WPH), 280, 40ff.

27. Some documents are in Z. Landau and J. Tomaszewski, *Kapitały obce w Polsce 1918–1939. Dokumenty i materiały* (Warsaw, 1964), 261ff. See Jaros, *Historia . . .*, 163f., 175, 179ff., 186, 188.

28. Popkiewicz and Ryszka, *op. cit.*, 190ff.

29. *Ibid.*, 203f.

30. For the text of the agreement, see R. Piotrowski, *Wspólnota interesów w świetle praktyki Sądu kartelowego* (Warsaw, n.d.), 84–91.

31. Popkiewicz and Ryszka, *op. cit.*, 206ff.; Jaros, *Historia . . .*, 171f.

32. *Księga gospodarcza Polski. Informator przemysłowo-handlowy 1939* (Warsaw, 1939), 20.

33. Popkiewicz and Ryszka, *op. cit.*, 206ff.; Landau and Tomaszewski, *Kapitały*, 299ff. According to the letter of 'Giesche' SA to the Ministry of Finance dated 13 July 1929, SACO had lent $12.2m including $4.5m in order to pay back some old debts: APK, WPH 1773.

34. For documents, see Landau and Tomaszewski, *Kapitały*, 307f. The most important point of the agreement between SACO and Bergwerksprodukte was: 'The German company shall act as commission merchant for the sale in all of Europe, except Poland, of zinc, lead and other metal products which the American company may have for sale, for the period of the duration of this agreement.' The Polish government knew about this stipulation and suspected some other fully secret co-operation between SACO and Georg von Giesche's Erben. It is not clear if the sale in the USSR was included in this agreement. See documents in APK, WPH, 1497.

35. L. Grosfeld, *Polska w latach kryzysu gospodarczego 1929–1933* (Warsaw, 1952), 89. In a letter of Georg von Giesche's Erben of 4 Apr. 1934 we read: 'Für die Loyalität der Amerikaner in der Deutschtumsfrage verbürgen wir uns.', *ibid.*, 95.

36. Z. Landau and J. Tomaszewski, *Anonimowi Wladcy. Z dziejów kapitału obcego w Polsce (1918–1939)* (Warsaw 1968), 171ff. The whole question is not yet fully clear. Some critics were personally engaged in the electric companies and were afraid of the financial strength of Harriman.

37. Jaros, *Historia . . .*, 186; Landau and Tomaszewski, *Kapitały*, 301f.

38. Jaros, *Historia . . .*, 61–3; circular letter of KGS from 17 Feb. 1925, APK, Konwencja Górnośląska 13.

39. Teichova, *op. cit.*, 253f.

40. It is necessary to note that in the years 1927–30 the average Polish share in the zinc output of the countries named in table 9.4 (excluding Mexico and Canada) reached 24.3 per cent: letters, probably by G. S. Brooks, dated 31 July, 21 Aug., 30 Dec. 1931, APK, WPH 1497. According to Teichova the small quantity of zinc supplied by Czechoslovakia and Hungary was administered by the German group in the international cartel: Teichova, *op. cit.*, 255.

41. Baily, *op. cit.*, 210–15; APK, Unia Przemysłu Górniczo-Hutniczego 3.

42. For some documents, see Z. Landau and B. Skrzeszewska, *Wojciech Korfanty przed Sądem Marszałkowskim. Dokumenty* (Katowice, 1964).

43. Jaros, *Historia . . .*, 69, 224–8.

44. Popkiewicz and Ryszka, *op. cit.*, 352ff.;
Jaros, *Historia* . . ., 175f.
45. Popkiewicz and Ryszka, *op. cit.*, 355ff.,
425ff.; Landau and Tomaszewski,
Kapitały, 317ff.; F. Ryszka and S.
Ziemba, *Dwa dziesięcil ęcia Huty
Kościuiszko* (Warsaw, 1955), 38ff.; Jaros,
Historia . . ., 171ff.; T. Rasimowicz (T.
Borkowski), *Szkice o węglu* (Warsaw,
1936), 137ff.
46. Landau and Tomaszewski, *Kapitały*,
317ff.
47. Jaros, *Historia* . . ., 189f.
48. Letter dated June 1927, APK, WPH 131.
49. See the documents in Landau and
Tomaszewski, *Kapitały*, 312ff.
50. Letter dated 17 July 1931, APK, WPH
131.
51. The counsellor of the Polish Embassy in
Paris, Anatol Mühlstein, discussed this
question with the French diplomat
Phillipe Berthelot and said that 'as long as
the German credit monopoly in Upper
Silesia exists and the possibility of
German pressure over this extremely
important region for the Polish state, we
shall have incidents and political
difficulties.' Therefore he argued that 'as

long as there was a normal situation the
fight against the German banks was a very
difficult one but now, when the German
collapse impaired their authority, it would
be simply a political sin not to try to
replace German with French capital.':
letter of Mühlstein, 8 Aug. 1931,
Archiwum Akt Nowych w Warszawie
(Archive of Contemporary Documents in
Warsaw), Ministerstwo Spraw
Zagranicznych 3764, 39f.
52. T. Kowalak, *Zagraniczne kredyty dla
Niemców w Polsce 1919–1939* (Warsaw,
1972), 141ff.
53. Z. Landau and J. Tomaszewski, *Druga
Rzeczpospolita. Gospodarka,
społeczeństwo, miejsce w świecie (sporne
problemy badań)* (Warsaw, 1977), 325ff. It
would be interesting – though I doubt if it
is possible now – to estimate the share of
the German and associated capital in the
capital outflow from Poland. Maybe it was
the most important component.
54. See J. Jaros, 'Koncentracja przemysłu
górniczo-hutniczego (1918–1939)',
*Uprezemysłowienie ziem polskich w XIX i
XX wieku. Studia i materiały* (Wrocław,
1970), 357.

COMMENTARY *Waclaw Długoborski*

After 1921 in the parts of Upper Silesia that had returned to Poland, German capital found itself in a new position, somewhat different from the pre-war state. Considering the situation up to 1918 it is ambiguous to call this 'foreign', 'external' or even *nichteinheimisches* capital since in the majority of the mining-metallurgical concerns the founders, owners and other principal shareholders were Silesian landlord families which had been domiciled there for centuries.[1] They saw themselves as the masters of this land, in the political sense as well, controlling as they did most of the official posts in local government, the normal custom in the eastern parts of the Prussian state.

Certainly, in 1857 one of the Paris banks bought a percentage of the shares of the 'Schlesag' works in Lipiny, but there were no more deals of this kind up to 1922. I cannot agree with Tomaszewski that for French capitalists this was an 'unknown' region, since at the end of the nineteenth century they made appreciable investments in the neighbouring Dąbrowa Basin and in the

Częstochowa textile industry.[2] However, new capital did make an entry here: beginning in the 1870s the share acquired by large Berlin and west German banks grew steadily. And this was the *nichteinheimisches* capital in the region. In the pre-1914 period there was also a growing rivalry between Upper Silesian capitalists and those from Rhineland-Westphalia who had received privileged treatment from the state in the allocation of armaments contracts and in tariff policy.[3] Hence for the Upper Silesian capitalists, squeezed out of the central German market, the potential markets of the Russian possessions (Great Poland, Pomerania) and of the Russian and Austrian sectors of partitioned Poland became particularly attractive.

After 1921 the part of Upper Silesia that returned to Poland (which included two-thirds of its production potential) found itself, together with Great Poland and Pomerania, within the boundaries of a single state. And hence the customs barriers between Upper Silesia and those important markets were removed. At the same time the vigorous efforts of the reunited Polish state to rebuild after the destruction of war and to integrate the three former partitioned sectors, especially by extension of the communications network, had the effect of increasing the demand for investment goods. It might have been expected that economic considerations would prompt the Upper Silesian capitalists to make the most of this market opportunity, thus hastening the integration of Upper Silesia with the other Polish territories, and also to undertake capital investment geared to the needs of the Polish market. However, as has been convincingly demonstrated by Tomaszewski, they pursued a completely opposite policy. Not only did they maintain their links with the German sector of Upper Silesia but sent there the bulk of their profits, undertaking investment projects on that side of the border; Giesche's Erben even constructed a zinc electrolysis plant in faraway Magdeburg. Could it be then that national-political considerations triumphed over economic calculations? This would appear to be confirmed by the social and nationality policies of the German capitalists and their managers, who 'favoured workers who declared their loyalty to Germany and whose children attended German schools' and even exerted pressure to make the workers switch their children from Polish to German schools under threat of dismissal. Workers who were known to be active in Polish matters or belonged to Polish political, social and cultural organisations were also often the victims of this policy. It was also aided by the fact that some of the Upper Silesian workers, of undoubtedly Polish origin, did not have any clearly formed idea of national allegiance and gave in fairly easily to economic pressure of every kind. Thus the German industrialists continued the germanization policy of the former German authorities, although before 1918 not all of them were so ardent in carrying out this policy. With the object of reducing social tensions in their plants they had curbed the activities of the nationalist Ostmarkenverein, whereas in the inter-war period they financed the Volksbund, and after 1933 other German organizations from the Polish part of Upper Silesia seeking *gleichgeschaltete* in the Nazi interpretation.[4] Again, before the First World War the Upper Silesian industrialists tried to get round Bismarck's 1886 Act (dictated by national-political considerations) ordering all Russian and Austrian citizens of Polish nationality, including workers, to quit Prussian territory. A few years later these industrialists again applied for permission to recruit workers from this source, for the obvious reason that they accepted lower wages and made less demands than the local workers. As a result, in 1913 migrants from the Congress Kingdom of Poland and Galicia represented 10 per cent of the total number of workers in Upper Silesian industry, while their employers were criticized by the more chauvinist sectors of the Prussian bureaucracy for lack of 'patriotism'.[5]

Hence clearly in this period economic arguments could sometimes outweigh national-political considerations. Why then did the situation change after 1921? Tomaszewski points out that the leading representatives of Upper Silesian capital had been involved first of all in the political plans of German imperialism in Central Europe from the years of the First World War, and next in the struggle to keep the whole of Upper Silesia in Germany in the years 1919–21, and he also stresses that 'most of the East [i.e. Polish/Upper Silesian] companies were deeply indebted to their German sisters'. The Upper Silesian industrialists, in common with the majority sector of German public opinion and not merely the propertied classes, treated Poland as a *Saisonstaat*, professing disbelief 'in the stability of the frontiers'. But when this state had been in existence for ten years and its economy had successfully coped with the first and most difficult period of the 'customs war' waged by the Germans, should not pragmatic reasoning – political and economic – have prompted them to seek a *modus vivendi* with the Poles?

Of course there were psychological-social factors exerting an influence here, such as the loss of status of the German establishment (landlords, industrialists and their managerial staff) who had hitherto played the leading political, as well as economic, role in Upper Silesia; then again the feeling of superiority to the Poles and consequent disdain of Polish administrative and organizational abilities; and also the conviction of the German-ness of Upper Silesia and the injustice of the Versailles Treaty. Hence it was considered in these circles, as was recently recalled by W. Rohland who held a number of managerial posts in German heavy industry, that accepting an appointment in Upper Silesia was a kind of patriotic duty.[6]

Nevertheless, I believe that in spite of all this the policies of German capital in the Polish parts of Upper Silesia were governed primarily by economic considerations. This concept should be treated in the broadest sense, not limited to matters of current markets and their structure, which the Germans thought of as only temporary. German capitalists, including those from Upper Silesia, never gave up their plans for eventual economic hegemony in Eastern Central and South-Eastern Europe. After the 1918 defeat they were resurrected in the latter years of the Weimar Republic (as recently noted by R. Frommelt),[7] making use of more 'peaceful' methods, not quite so drastic as during the First World War, such as the known ploy of customs unions. This was aimed at ensuring a privileged position in the less developed part of Europe for German industry, especially heavy industry, whose potentates were the chief promoters of the scheme which covered both supply of raw materials and a market for manufactured products. This scheme was partially realized immediately after 1933 by means of bilateral clearing agreements with economically weaker partners.

It appears to be obvious that for long-term implementation of this programme it was essential to control the production potential of the whole of Upper Silesia, the region later to be described by Nazi propaganda as the 'Ruhrgebiet des Ostens', or 'Hüttenkombinat Ost'. It may also be taken that such plans would be particularly attractive for Upper Silesian industrialists (further research in depth is required here), ensuring for them both political dominance of eastern Upper Silesia together with the Dąbrowa Basin, whose annexation had been postulated in 1915–18, and also opportunities for further expansion to the east and south-east. These latter hopes were partially fulfilled during the First World War.[8] Nevertheless, in the Polish parts of Upper Silesia annexed in 1939, German capital did not manage to regain its former position. During the wartime years considerable influence in economic management was wielded by particular branches of Reichsgruppe Industrie which is well known to have been associated with the Nazi governing elite and the most powerful groups of German industrial capital, mainly from Rhineland-Westphalia. Thus in the allocation by Haupt-treuhandstelle-Ost of the assets of the Polish state and of English and French capitalists, the key plants went to the new state-monopoly concerns Berghütte and Reichswerke Hermann Göring.

Notes

1. Cf. J. Tomaszewski, '"Fremdes Kapital". Ein Versuch zur näheren Bestimmung', *Jahrbuch für Wirtschaftsgeschichte*, II (1978), 36–7.

2. Cf. S. Jasiczek, 'Kapitał francuski w przemyśle górniczo-hutniczym Zagłębia Dąbrowskiego 1870–1914', *Zeszyty Naukowe Szkoły Głównej Planowania i Statystyki*, XV (1959), 84ff.

3. T. Pierenkemper, 'Struktur und Entwicklung der Schwerindustrie in Oberschlesien und im Westfälischen Ruhrgebiet 1852–1913', *Zeitschrift für Unternehmensgeschichte*, XXIV (1979), 7, 13–14.

4. J. Chałasiński, *Antagonizm polsko-niemiecki w osadzie fabrycznej "Kopalnia" na Górnym Śląsku. Studium socjologiczne* (Warsaw, 1935).

5. A. Brozek, *Robotnicy z poza zaboru pruskiego w przemyśle w Górnym Śląsku 1870–1914* (Wrocław-Warsaw-Cracow, 1966), 56ff., 99ff.

6. Cf. W. Rohland, *Bewegte Zeiten. Erinnerungen eines Eisenhüttenmannes* (Stuttgart, 1979), 60.

7. R. Frommelt, *Paneuropa oder Mitteleuropa. Einigungsbvestrebungen im Kalkül deutscher Wirtschaft und Politik 1925–1933* (Stuttgart, 1979), 90ff.

8. C. Łuczak, *Polityka ludnościowa i ekonomiczna hitlerowskie Niemiec w okupowanej Polsce* (Poznań, 1979), 356ff.

COMMENTARY *I. Berend*

I wish to make only two critical remarks on this excellent paper.

First, although I fully agree with the definition of foreign capital made in the introduction, I have difficulties when applying it to the interpretation of the nature of Upper Silesian German capital. The problem arises when considering Silesia, and elsewhere in Eastern Europe, from the peculiarity of families which had amassed wealth in the eighteenth century and established large firms in the 1870s remaining *in situ* despite substantial territorial and political changes. It is a common East Central European phenomenon – a mixed population – but one which has particular and special complexities. Consequently German capital in inter-war Poland has to be treated on its own, apart from foreign capital *per se*. Further, the role of German capital in Poland has its own explanation. There appears to be a conflict between the Polish experience during the Nazi period – German influence declining in the 1930s – as opposed to the countries of South-East Europe, where a contrary trend was taking place. I cannot entirely agree with Tomaszewski's interpretation here, which sees the outflow of German capital from Poland in the 1930s as a conscious or deliberate German political decision, for the Nazis certainly thought that Silesia was a part of Germany. It was a region which was to be incorporated into the Reich in the future. I would argue that the reason for the withdrawal of German capital stemmed from the economic problems which came with the Great Depression. After 1929 there was a certain outflow of capital from all the debtor countries of Europe, including Poland. The politics of Hitler's Germany did not influence that process.

Second, and an old problem: foreign capital is often considered to be either a devil or a helping angel. In the case of Poland the role of German capital is fairly clear but there may be a degree of bias in the interpretation. Silesian German capital, by wishing to separate Silesia from Poland, was very harmful to the Polish economy in a number of ways. However, this capital did play a role in the performance of Polish foreign trade and so contributed, to some extent, to avoiding a serious decline in production. But it must not be overlooked that the German industrial base in Silesia pursued politically a revisionist policy which was the basis of Nazi Germany's aim in Poland.

10. The Österreichisch-Alpine Montangesellschaft, 1918–38

P. G. Fischer

The Österreichisch-Alpine Montangesellschaft (hereafter referred to as the Alpine) was founded in 1881 by the merger of the most important iron works in the Alpine region which, in part, had themselves arisen from previous amalgamations of smaller wheel and hammer works. After 1890 new works, which met the technical standards of the time, were set up in Donawitz, Eisenerz and some other places in Styria, and existing plants were extended. With the Erzberg the Alpine owned one of the most significant European iron ore deposits.[1] After the break-up of the Habsburg Monarchy the Alpine acquired a monopoly position in the new Austria which endowed it with great economic and political power; at the same time, however, it was cut off from a large part of its former consumers by continually rising tariff walls.[2] A few years after the war the majority of shares in the enterprise was taken over by German capital and this made the Alpine a part of the efforts towards expansion of the German economy and political development in the German Reich.[3] The following study – based on the limited source material accessible – will devote itself to following four problems.[4]

1. THE DEVELOPMENT OF OWNERSHIP

During the last years of the Habsburg Monarchy the Alpine belonged to the industrial division of one of the Austrian big banks, the Niederösterreichische Escompte-Gesellschaft. As well as the Alpine, two other mining and metallurgic enterprises belonged to this concern, the Poldina huť (Kladno) and the Pražská železářská společnost (Prague). It seems that with regard to the ownership of shares a method was chosen whereby the Pražská železářská společnost and not the Niederösterreichische Escompte-Gesellschaft was the main shareholder in the Alpine.[5]

During 1919 ownership of the Alpine changed rapidly. For one thing, this largest mining and metallurgical enterprise of the new Austria headed the list of companies chosen for socialization.[6] In order to carry this out drafts of two bills were presented to the National Assembly in April 1919, one on the expropriation of business enterprises, the other on public institutions.[7] While the spontaneous take-over of the main works at Donawitz by its workers in April 1919 was short-lived,[8] Parliament procrastinated in passing the bills –

apparently due to sectionalist interests – to such an extent that the intended acquisition of the Alpine by the state became increasingly difficult.[9] In any case, with a coalition government, expropriation without compensation was not politically feasible.

Furthermore, the market quotation of the shares of the Alpine had become unstable during the second third of 1919. While the market price of the shares had risen 18 times their nominal value of 200 K by 1913 and had fallen only insignificantly during the war, in May 1919 they then fell to their lowest level.[10] The state did not use this favourable situation for purchase and after June 1919 the price of Alpine shares rose rapidly again.[11] This was caused by the acquisition of shares by the banking house Kola & Co. on behalf of an Italian client, the Fiat concern. As the Secretary of State for Finance, Joseph A. Schumpeter, did not prevent this transaction, it resulted in the Social Democrats making vigorous protests.[12] The Secretary of State, however, regarded the obvious interest of foreign businessmen in Austrian ordinary shares as advantageous for the value of the Austrian crown and justified his co-operation with the notorious speculator Kola by saying that it was necessary for the state to use the services of this experienced stockbroker in order to support the foreign exchange value of the currency.[13] In November 1919 the state nevertheless claimed 500,000 shares of the Alpine's new issue on the basis of the law concerning public enterprises.[14] But after very strong protests by the Italian shareholders, backed by diplomatic *démarches*,[15] 20,000 of these shares were soon sold into private hands.[16] Thereafter until March 1921 the capital of the Alpine was increased step by step from the original nominal 72m K to 100m K (= 500,000 shares), in order to repay above all the large bank debts of the enterprise. At this point a further significant change took place in the ownership of the Alpine. After negotiations with other interested parties – among them Schneider-Creusot – had evidently broken down,[17] 200,000 shares out of the Fiat concern's (Credito Italiano) holding were bought up by the Stinnes group[18] through Camillo Castiglione, one of the most elusive personalities in the economic life of the First Austrian Republic, who himself, with the Milan Banca Commerciale, had acquired 50,000 Alpine shares at the end of 1919. The Hugo Stinnes group – which essentially consisted of the Deutsch-Luxemburgische Bergwerks- und Hütten AG and the Gelsenkirchner Bergwerks AG as well as the Bochumer Verein für Bergbau und Gusstahlfabrikation – used for the transaction the services of Promontana AG, Zug (Switzerland), which also acted as trust company for the successors of the Stinnes concern up to the Anschluss.[19]

In fact in 1926, after the collapse of the Stinnes concern, its interest in the Alpine was transferred to the Vereinigte Stahlwerke AG,[20] which in the end had 56.66 per cent of the capital at its disposal, evidently after it had taken over some shares from Castiglione. In 1936 the Vereinigte Stahlwerke founded the Stahlverein GmbH as a holding company which took over the

Alpine shares and in February 1939 the shares were transferred to the Reichswerke Hermann Göring.[21]

In a manner which cannot be fully described here, the Niederösterreichische-Escompte Gesellschaft became the second strongest partner in the Alpine with a capital participation of 13.57 per cent, while the remaining 30 per cent was widely scattered.[22] Displeasure with the management of the Alpine increased steadily at the beginning of the 1930s and Austrian circles explored possibilities for obtaining decisive influence over the enterprise not only for domestic but also for Italian or French capital.[23] It still remains to be seen how seriously these efforts should be taken; in any case, they did not meet with success. The Alpine itself had a series of subsidiaries and participations at its disposal. Among these the most significant company was the Graz-Köflacher Eisenbahn- und Bergbau Gesellschaft, the most important Austrian lignite mining enterprise, which was acquired in 1928.[24]

2. THE DEVELOPMENT OF PRODUCTION AND BUSINESS[25]

The iron and steel industry naturally played a central role in the First World War. However, after the peak of the war production had been reached in 1916 the Alpine, as well as other enterprises, experienced increasing operating difficulties. There was a shortage of labour, coal output was insufficient, and the railways broke down. At the beginning of 1918 work in the plants had to be stopped several times, and after a temporary improvement in the summer of 1918 a stage was reached in the autumn when the blast furnaces, the steel works and the rolling mills were not working for most of the time.[26] Considerable wage increases, with rising prices, caused the profit situation to become worse from 1917 to 1918 and it proved possible only to distribute a dividend of 10 per cent (in comparison with 13 per cent in 1917 and 25 per cent in 1916). More serious were the increasing bank debts, above all to the Niederösterreichische-Escompte Gesellschaft,[27] a pattern that was repeated during the world economic crisis of the early 1930s.

Output did not improve very much during 1920 because of the limited supplies of coke delivered from Czechoslovakia. The transfer of a large part of the Alpine shares to the Stinnes group brought about a considerable increase in coke deliveries in 1921. However, the supply of labour with transport problems as well as restricted markets unfavourably affected the situation, particularly since price levels were to be maintained.[28] In 1921 only half the capacity of the Martin furnaces were in operation in the steel works, but in 1922 an improvement in production can be ascertained.[29] Obviously, this progress was very uneven; from time to time supplies of coke from the Ruhr were not available, the temporary stabilization of the crown and the fall of the Reichsmark brought sales to a halt, and finally a careless financial agreement of the company through its Rhenish shareholder led to a large increase of debts in Czechoslovak crowns for coke deliveries.[30]

As a result of the occupation of the Ruhr the works were almost fully employed from January 1923, to meet increasing demand.[31] From the end of 1923, however, the state of orders deteriorated. Thus 1924 was a year of crisis for the Alpine.[32] Ore mining had to be brought to a standstill, a position which had not occurred for decades, and also the blast furnaces and the Martin works were closed for a time.[33] From the beginning to the end of the inflation it is difficult to assess accurately the profit and asset situation of the Alpine. With the conversion to the schilling currency it becomes clear that the enterprise was burdened with debts at high interest rates which exceeded by more than half the company's own assets. Employment of the works improved only slowly after the depth of the crisis in 1924. Prices, however, were still worse in 1926.[34] At the same time 1926 can be regarded as the year of consolidation because it was then possible to liquidate the irresponsible financial actions of the Castiglione-Stinnes era through the sale of the Bismarckhütte shares.[35]

The formation of the International Steel Cartel as well as the increase in Austrian iron tariffs seemed to further improve business conditions for the development of the Alpine. Turnover and profits appreciated somewhat in 1927 in comparison with the previous year. Investment in plant and installations increased, while in the immediate post-war years funds had been used to house workers and to improve their social amenities.[36] In 1928 the Alpine was able to pay dividends again after an interval of four years, but at a modest rate of 4 per cent in comparison with the war and pre-war years.[37] A big investment programme was started which was intended to last for the next five years but which soon had to be abandoned because of the outbreak of the world economic crisis. The turn came in August 1929. First the ability of foreign markets to absorb products slackened and export prices fell. In the course of the autumn conditions on the domestic market became worse.[38]

While the accounts for 1929 – with a 4 per cent dividend – were still good, 1930 was a bad year. The sharp decline of state investments exacerbated the situation, in particular in railways which were left without effective management for almost threequarters of the year.[39] The Alpine's balance sheets for 1930 and 1931 were calculated in such a way that profits and losses cancelled each other out precisely. Production of the rolling mills was reduced from 65 to 43 per cent in 1931, while a loss of one-third was registered in the sale of iron goods and workshop products. Iron ore exports were brought to a complete halt and the sale of pig iron fell by half. In the middle of May 1932 the last blast furnace went out.[40] That year as well as 1933 ended with considerable losses and the number of employees fell to one-third of the 1929 workforce. At the same time a slight revival took place in the course of 1933 which continued during 1934 so that the year ended with reduced losses.[41]

In 1935 the Alpine was able to produce balanced accounts after three years of losses. On 9 July a second blast furnace was fired again after all the furnaces had been cold between December 1932 and May 1933. This second furnace remained in action for the whole of 1936,[42] in spite of the temporary recession at the end of the year.[43] In 1937 the Alpine almost reached its 1929 level of output and, for the first time after seven years without dividends, it was able to distribute a dividend of 4 per cent again. Even net profits were not insignificantly lower than in 1929. At the end of 1937, however, serious crisis conditions hit sales.[44]

With the Anschluss of Austria to Hitler's Germany and with the subsequent transfer of tasks within the framework of the Four Year Plan, production expanded with a third blast furnace started up in 1937 and a fourth on 20 April.[45] In this way the Alpine Montangesellschaft became integrated into the war production of the expansionist National Socialist régime. The end of this phase came with the considerable destruction of the plants of this enterprise.

3. THE POSITION OF THE ALPINE IN BOTH THE INTERNATIONAL AND AUSTRIAN ECONOMY

Section 2 above endeavoured to sketch the economic development of the Alpine during the period between the two wars in a descriptive-quantitative way. This section will devote its attention to some aspects of the international economy which were of decisive significance for the Alpine, and it will also strive to assess the company's position in the Austrian economy.

As has been mentioned already, a large part of the regions to which the Alpine traditionally exported became foreign territory in 1918. It was, therefore, highly unfavourable when Austria's neighbours – above all Czechoslovakia – introduced high tariffs at the beginning of the 1920s in order to protect their domestic production.[46] In 1924 the Alpine succeeded in securing the sale of a certain quantity of pig iron in a cartel agreement with the Prodejna sdružených československých železáren [Selling Agency of the United Czechoslovak Iron Works], but in return it had to concede an 18 per cent share of the Austrian market in other iron products, while the Czechoslovak market in these products remained closed to the Alpine.[47] In due course an Austrian-Czechoslovak export cartel was concluded which contained agreements about market quotas of rolled products in neighbouring export countries (Albania, Bulgaria, Greece, Italy, Yugoslavia and European Turkey) and which was joined later by the most important Hungarian iron works through the so-called Rima Agreement.[48] At the turn of 1926 and 1927 the international cartel contacts of the Alpine were further extended when the company, together with the Czechoslovak and Hungarian works, joined the International Steel Cartel. The member works thereby secured territorial protection of their domestic markets and a quota of over 2m tons per year was allocated to them, out of which 70 per cent went to Czechoslovakia, 20 per cent to Austria and 10 per cent to Hungary.[49] Although the International Steel Cartel was dissolved in 1929, the Alpine concluded other agreements with foreign works and international cartels which basically aimed at territorial protection against other iron-producing countries and at export regulation to the most important consumer countries.[50]

A specific form of foreign dependency was imposed on the Alpine by its German mother company, who insisted on the supply of higher-priced coke from the Ruhr as against coke from Ostrava; a factor which must have unfavourably affected production costs.[51] Similar problems of dependency must have arisen for Austrian inter-war industry generally, which were diagnosed as a 'simplification' (*Primitivisierung*) of foreign trade and thus of production.[52] In the case of the Alpine this was reflected in that, against the general trend, output of fully-finished products did not develop into mass production,[53] but output of iron and steel products fell in comparison with the production and export of pig iron and crude steel.[54]

The fact that, as mentioned before, the Alpine had a virtual monopoly position in the Austrian iron and steel production presented a permanent threat to domestic metalworking industries. When the Alpine called for the introduction of a special protective tariff on iron imports at the beginning of the 1920s after the iron tariffs were lifted in 1919,[55] the affected industrial groups and their political representatives charged into the attack against it.[56] The introduction of the new autonomous tariff in 1924 produced only a modest tariff rate,[57] since neither the government nor the Central Association of Industrialists in Austria could agree on a common tariff policy.[58] However, in the period up to 1926 the Alpine succeeded in persuading the bourgeois majority in Parliament to agree to increases of iron tariffs after threats of, or at times actual, dismissals of workers as well as other measures.[59]

Earlier an agreement with the metalworking industries had been reached by which the Alpine supplied iron at lower than export prices for iron products destined for export.[60] This so-called AVI Agreement, which was to last during the high tariff period, was revised many times and gave the Alpine reason to complain about the disadvantages that it suffered from in consequence of it. However, it remained in force for the whole duration of the First Republic.[61] At the beginning of the 1930s the Alpine again took up the fight for a further increase of tariffs on products in which it was interested. This campaign was conducted by conditions of additional price security stemming from the conclusion of the international territorial protection cartel.[62] Efforts of this kind necessarily led to tensions with parts of Austrian industry, to which we shall return in the next section.

4. THE POSITION OF THE ALPINE IN AUSTRIAN POLITICS

The position which the Österreichisch-Alpine Montangesellschaft had as the greatest provider of work and the single largest industrial producer in Austria had also a political dimension. It came into effect at various levels: first, at the management level – above all with regard to the attitude towards organizations representing the interests of the workers – then as a factor of economic and socio-political influence on opinion and decision-making at a communal level (in all places where there was an Alpine works) as well as at provincial (Styria) and federal levels. Finally, the Alpine itself played a part in the struggle for the maintenance of the political system as well as for Austria's independence.

In the first phase of the Republic a number of socio-political laws had led to the curtailment of entrepreneurial power in the Alpine – in particular through the establishment of works councils and workers' representatives on the board of directors, the legal recognition of collective agreements and the introduction of the eight-hour day. The management of the Alpine turned its attention specifically to these areas. At this stage, under the threat of socialization, state intervention was tolerated in the area of unemployment benefits during periods of reduced working, and it was not as yet regarded as 'the root of all evil'.[63] A certain willingness to co-operate also existed towards the Austrian Metal Workers Union, which was within the Social Democratic trade union organization.[64] Workers' representatives on the board of directors were elected from this organization.[65] However, in 1921 works councils were already being warned[66] and the Alpine began rapidly to get rid of politically undesirable workers through dismissals. When labour was needed again these workers were not reinstated and were partly replaced by foreign workers.[67] The politically undesirable workers were put on the so-called Black List which made it very difficult, if not impossible, for them to get work elsewhere.[68]

In the case of the white-collar workers, who had conducted a major strike in 1921,[69] the management was apparently successful in excluding the Social Democratic trade union and substituting for it the more amenable Deutschnationale Handlungsgehilfenverband.[70] When in October 1925 a workers' uprising occurred, aimed at improving wages, which due to the stabilization of the currency had fallen to a very low level, the Alpine's management succeeded in undermining the position of the Social Democratic trade union. Initially, the Christian trade unions benefited from this move,[71] but in May 1928 the Heimwehr-Gewerkschaft, the so-called Independent Trade Union (UG), was founded under the aegis of the Alpine,[72] which was then organized on an all-Austrian level.[73] It rejected every form of class struggle and endeavoured to establish a corporate society. In 1929 it registered its first successes at the works council elections in some Alpine works.[74] At the works council elections in the Donawitz main works Independents and Social Democrats received the same number of places in 1929.[75] The pressure then increased further against the Alpine workers who did not belong to the Independents.[76] At the works council elections in Donawitz in 1931 the Social Democrats were prevented from putting up candidates, while the Christian Socialists withdrew theirs. Thus the Independents received all the mandates.[77] The shift in the relationship of forces within the works councils of the Alpine was reflected in the worsening of some aspects of working conditions. However, it cannot be maintained with certainty that the free trade unions would have been more successful in view of the general economic decline and in face of the management's attitude.

After two years without contracts – a collective agreement was in force with the Metal Workers Union (Metallarbeiterverband) up to 1927 – a collective agreement came into operation on 1 May 1929 which had been negotiated between the management and the Independents, to which Work Rules were attached. Working hours, holidays, overtime, wage conditions and works discipline were altered to the detriment of the workers.[78]

At the beginning of 1931 the Alpine endeavoured to dissociate itself from the collective-contractual obligations to its workers. The immediate reason for this was the management's declaration that due to economic necessity wages would have to be reduced by 12 to 15 per cent. In order to annul the entire system of collectively agreed rules the whole workforce was dismissed and workers who were needed were to be employed on the basis of individual contracts according to wage rates and working conditions offered by the company.[79]

So as to induce the government to issue measures favourable to the Alpine, the Member of Parliament for the Heimwehrpartei 'Heimatblock', who also was a co-founder and chairman of the Independent Union, and the chairman of the works council in the Donawitz foundry, Josef Lengauer, put an urgent question to the Federal Chancellor on 27 December 1930.[80] Though the Social Democrats sharply attacked the management of the Alpine in the ensuing debate and revealed Lengauer's position and that of his parliamentary party as hypocritical, the proposal put to the government for passing a bill which would give official approval to the closure of large works was supported by the 'Heimatblock' and thus was passed by a majority.[81] A few weeks later, on 23 January 1931 – at a time when the Alpine and Graz-Köflacher works had begun to initiate the above-mentioned wage reductions – a further urgent question was addressed to the government by a group of 'Heimatblock' Members of Parliament, amongst them works council chairman Lengauer, regarding the promised measures to alleviate the wages- and market crisis in the Austrian mining industry.[82] During the debate it was the Christian Social Democratic speaker Leskovar who correctly described the situation when he said that the clamour of the

'Heimatblock' Members of Parliament about the Alpine's measures against its workers was a mere sham, since it was the growth of the Independent Trade Union itself which had broken the resistance of the Upper Styrian workers and thus had made a social-reactionary offensive possible.[83]

Whatever the reason may have been, either – as was maintained by some[84] – because of the limited success of the workforce, or because of the evident sympathies of the Alpine's management with the National Socialists, the Independent Trade Union's influence declined. At works council elections in the various Alpine plants in 1933 the results were unfavourable for them. On the 29 July 1933 it was decided by the National Socialist works councils from the Upper Styrian region to found a 'Deutsche Arbeitergewerkschaft' which stood under the protection of high-ranking employees of the Alpine and the firm Böhler.[85] A disagreement had occurred between the Alpine and the Independents,[86] which even led to the expulsion of Lengauer from the works.[87] It is difficult to say to what extent the efforts of the Alpine's management which were started in 1934 were successful in engaging 'patriotically loyal workers'.[88]

The trade union policy of the Alpine was certainly political. The management influenced the character of state intervention and its application. Without wanting to overrate the personal factor, it still has to be pointed out that in the Alpine all decision-making was concentrated in the hands of one man – the general manager Anton Apold who had held this post since 1922.[89] He was one of the most important supporters of the Styrian Heimwehr from the very beginning[90] and soon came forward as an early vigorous supporter for the Anschluss to Germany. Evidence for this can be found in his co-operation with the Central Committee for Questions of the Expansion of the Economic Region (Zentralausschuss für Fragen der Erweiterung des Wirtschaftsgebietes) in 1928.[91] In 1930 Apold's candidacy for the presidency of the Österreichische Bundesbahn was considered, which if it had succeeded would have made the Alpine one of the most important employers in the Austrian economy. However, this move induced other industrialists to protest sharply against such a concentration of power.[92] When Apold's candidacy was abandoned, he strongly opposed the economic policy of the bourgeois government under the Federal Chancellor Schober. In May 1930 he condemned the excessive burden of taxes and social expenditure in the economy during both a meeting of the financial commission of the Alpine and the general meeting of 'Eisenhütte Österreich', an Austrian subsidiary organization of the Verein deutscher Eisenhüttenleute. He addressed these criticisms to gatherings of German big industrialists – the Alpine's board of directors consisted to a large part of such representatives at that time. He sharply attacked the investment loan acquired by Schober from abroad, pointed to the danger of transition from private enterprise to state socialism and on one occasion even went so far as to call Austria a 'rubbish state'.[93] The federal government protested in an official declaration against Apold's speeches;[94] the Association of Austrian Banks and Bankers[95] also did not wish to be identified with Apold; while the Central Association of Industry endeavoured to minimize the conflict through a neutral interpretation of Apold's statements.[96]

Obviously as a protest against Apold's attitude and against the growing German majority on the board of directors of the Alpine, the company's president Kux of the Niederösterreichische-Escompte Gesellschaft resigned from his post several months later (July 1930). Because the Austrian government refused to send a government commissioner to a general meeting of the Alpine in Berlin, a new appointment[97] was delayed. Finally, Albert Vögler was elected as president. The new government under Chancellor Dollfuss co-operated with the Alpine through various measures,[98] so that the opposition press spoke of an agrarian-industrial course.[99] But tensions increased between the Alpine and the rest of the Austrian industry so that, in the end, the Alpine withdrew from the Central Association of Industry in January 1933.[100]

At least from the time of Hitler's seizure of power in Germany in January 1933 German influence on the Alpine moved in conformity with National Socialist policy towards Austria.[101] This assertion can be substantiated as follows: when a strike broke out in the West Styrian coalmines of the Alpine in August 1933, a spontaneous reaction to economic hardship, a cause on which both the Social Democrats and National Socialists agreed,[102] it was used or even supported by the management in order to undermine the government.[103] As a result the cuts introduced in the mining industry on 1 April 1933 were rescinded by government order and a government commissioner was appointed.[104] The government did not take any further steps against the Alpine management. On the contrary they endeavoured to secure a promise of continuous production in the works during negotiations with Apold and Vögler in November 1933.[105] This willingness of the state to co-operate led Apold to prevent anything which could disturb this friendly relationship.[106] Though the Alpine appeared outwardly loyal, internally the National Socialists received full support.[107]

When during the Nazi Putsch of 25 July 1934 armed clashes took place in Alpine works the government thought the time had come to call the management to account. It now regarded the Alpine as 'the centre of the National Socialist movement in Austria',[108] and Apold's efforts to make excuses were unsuccessful.[109] A government commissioner was appointed to supervise the whole enterprise, one director (Dr Zahlbruckner) was arrested, and the general manager Apold was asked to pay damages of 350,000 schillings.[110] Both of them were given leave of absence – of course with full pay.[111] At that time the Federal Government endeavoured to change the ownership of the company in the Alpine: austrification was considered and Italian as well as French interests came into play.[112] But nothing came of all of this. From 1934 until the beginning of 1936 Ing. Josef Oberegger –

incidentally, one of the co-founders of the Independent Union – managed the Alpine as government commissioner together with director Herz who remained in his post, while president Vögler ignored the new management whenever possible.[113] During 1936 the tension lessened between the Austrian and the German governments which was also reflected in changes in the management of the Alpine.

A three-member executive committee was appointed consisting of the National Socialist Dr Maindl, Ing. Oberegger and Benno Fleischmann, who had been the head clerk up to that time. After a longish struggle over the chairmanship of the board of directors Dr Hans Malzacher was appointed general manager in accordance with Vögler's wishes on 15 February 1938. During his management period the integration of the Alpine into the German economy and its merger with the Reichswerke Hermann Göring took place.[114]

Notes

1. See H. Mejzlik, *Probleme der alpenländischen Eisenindustrie. Vor und nach der im Jahre 1881 stattgefundenen Fusionierung in die Österreichisch-Alpine Montangesellschaft* (Vienna, 1971); also *Die Österreichisch-Alpine Montangesellschaft 1881–1931* (Vienna, 1931).

2. As described in the following analysis published immediately after the war: G. Stolper, 'Unsere wirtschaftliche Zukunft', *Österreichischer Volkswirt* (hereafter *ÖVW*), 30 Nov. 1918.

3. This point is developed in my essay 'Die österreichischen Handelskammern und der Anschluss an Deutschland', in *Das Juliabkommen 1936* (Vienna, 1977), 299–324; see also the literature cited in n. 1.

4. Unfortunately the archive of the Alpine does not appear to have survived.

5. 'Die Bilanzen', supplement to *ÖVW*, 5 Apr. 1919.

6. R. Gerlich, 'Sozialisierung in der Ersten Republik' (unpublished dissertation, Vienna, 1975), 376f.

7. Bills 165 and 166, supplement to the Stenographischen Protokollen der Konstituierenden Nationalversammlung der Republik Österreich.

8. 'Übernahme des Donawitzer Werkes der Alpine Montangesellschaft durch die Arbeiter', *Neue Freie Presse* (hereafter *NFP*), 9 Apr. 1919; 'Die Sozialisierung der Alpine Montangesellschaft', *Arbeiter-Zeitung* (hereafter *AZ*), 10 Apr. 1919.

9. 'Die Bilanzen', supplement to *ÖVW*, 5 Apr. 1919.

10. Gerlich, *op. cit.*, 378f., where the share price is estimated as either 300 or 500 K. The *NFP* (18 Sept. 1919) writes in terms of a nadir of 600 K.

11. See also 'Eine sprunghafte Steigerung der Alpine Montanaktien', *NFP*, 26 June 1919; 'Die Bewegung der Alpinen Montanaktien', *NFP*, 19 Aug. 1919; 'Die Alpine-Hausse', *ÖVW*, 23 Aug. 1919.

12. 'Börsenorgien', *AZ*, 20 Aug. 1919; 'Schumpeters Antwort', *AZ*, 22 Aug. 1919; 'Der lachende Dritte', *AZ*, 3 Oct. 1919; 'Schumpeter, Kola und Karpeles', *AZ*, 17 Oct. 1919.

13. Österreichisches Staatsarchiv, Allgemeines Verwaltungsarchiv (hereafter AVA), Bundeskanzleramt, Präsidium, Korrespondenz Renner, Karton 65a. Undated letter, Schumpeter to Chancellor Renner. There is no room here for a discussion of the views of the individual Social Democrats, nor those of Schumpeter.

14. 'Übernahme der neuen Alpine-Aktien durch den Staat', *NFP*, 4 Nov. 1919. 'Der Staat nimmt die neuen Aktien der Alpinen in Anspruch', *AZ*, 6 Nov. 1919.

15. 'Einspruch der italienischen Aktionäre gegen die Beanspruchung der neuen Alpinen Aktien durch den Staat', *NFP*, 7 Dec. 1919.

16. 'Der Verkauf der Aktien der Alpinen Montangesellschaft', *AZ*, 15 May 1920.

17. See for example, 'Hugo Stinnes in Steiermark', *Kölnische Zeitung*, 30 Mar. 1921.
18. 'Verkauf von 200,000 Alpinen Montanaktien an die Stinnes-Gruppe', *NFP*, 15 Mar. 1921.
19. Thyssen-Archive, P7.Bd7(174); Aktenvermerk der Herren Dr Cordes/Dr Husemann vom 23.VIII.1945 betreffend die Beteiligung der Vereinigten Stahlwerke AG bzw. ab 1936 der Stahlverein GmbH an der Österreichisch-Alpine Montangesellschaft.
20. *Ibid.*; see also 'Ein neuer Grossaktionär der Alpinen' *AZ*, 10 July 1926.
21. Thyssen-Archive, P7, Bd1–7, *passim*.
22. AVA; Bundesministerium für Handel und Verkehr, Präsidium, Karton 736, Sammelakt Alpine. See also 'Nochmals der Fall Alpine', *ÖVW*, 30 June 1923.
23. AVA; Bundesministerium für Handel und Verkehr, Z1. 93.216/1934, Sign, 581a. AVA, Nachlass Renner, Karton 6: letter, Renner to F. Somary, 2 Feb. 1931 concerning the take-over of the shares of the Alpine by the Arbeiterbank.
24. 'Alpine Montangesellschaft', *ÖVW*, 3 Mar. 1928.
25. *Ibid.*
26. 'Österreichisch Alpine Montangesellschaft, Die Bilanzen', supplement to *ÖVW*, 5 Apr. 1919 and 17 April 1919. See also 'Alpine Montangesellschaft', *NFP*, 21 Jan. 1919; 'Alpine Montangesellschaft', *NFP*, 30 July 1919.
27. 'Österreichisch Alpine Montangesellschaft, Die Bilanzen', supplement to *ÖVW*, 5 Apr. 1919.
28. 'Österreichisch Alpine Montangesellschaft, Die Bilanzen', supplement to *ÖVW*, 30 Apr. 1921.
29. 'Österreichisch Alpine Montangesellschaft, Die Bilanzen', supplement to *ÖVW*, 5 Apr. 1922.
30. 'Österreichisch Alpine Montangesellschaft, Die Bilanzen', supplement to *ÖVW*, 6 Mar. 1923.
31. 'Österreichisch Alpine Montangesellschaft, Die Bilanzen', supplement to *ÖVW*, 7 June 1924.
32. 'Österreichisch Alpine Montangesellschaft, Die Bilanzen', supplement to *ÖVW*, 18 July 1925.
33. *Ibid.*
34. 'Österreichisch Alpine Montangesellschaft, Die Bilanzen', supplement to *ÖVW*, 3 July 1926.
35. 'Österreichisch Alpine Montangesellschaft, Die Bilanzen', supplement to *ÖVW*, 18 July 1925.
36. 'Österreichisch Alpine Montangesellschaft, Die Bilanzen', supplement to *ÖVW*, 12 May 1928. Widely discussed by F. Busson, 'Die sozialpolitische Entwicklung in den Betrieben der Österreichisch-Alpinen Montangesellschaft', in *Die Österreichisch-Alpine Montangesellschaft 1881–1931* (Vienna, 1931), 133–93.
37. 'Österreichisch Alpine Montangesellschaft, Die Bilanzen', supplement to *ÖVW*, 4 Apr. 1929.
38. 'Österreichisch Alpine Montangesellschaft, Die Bilanzen', supplement to *ÖVW*, 31 May 1930.
39. 'Österreichisch Alpine Montangesellschaft, Die Bilanzen', supplement to *ÖVW*, 20 June 1931.
40. 'Österreichisch Alpine Montangesellschaft, Die Bilanzen', supplement to *ÖVW*, 4 June 1932; 'Österreichisch Alpine Montangesellschaft, Die Bilanzen', supplement to *ÖWV*, 4 June 1933.
41. 'Alpine Montangesellschaft, Die Bilanzen', supplement to *OVW* Notizen, 28 Sept. 1935.
42. 'Österreichisch Alpine Montangesellschaft, Die Bilanzen', supplement to *ÖVW*, 11 Apr. 1936; 'Österreichisch Alpine Montangesellschaft, Die Bilanzen', supplement to *ÖVW*, 30 June 1934.
43. 'Österreichisch Alpine Montangesellschaft, Die Bilanzen', supplement to *ÖVW*, 3 July 1937.
44. 'Alpine Montan an der Jahreswende, Die Bilanzen', supplement to *ÖVW*, 25 Dec. 1937.
45. 'Österreichisch Alpine Montangesellschaft, Die Bilanzen', supplement to *ÖVW*, 23 Apr. 1938.
46. The proportion of total sales exported ranged between 60 and 70 per cent. See 'Österreichisch Alpine Montangesellschaft, Die Bilanzen', supplement to *ÖVW*, 3 July 1926.
47. Übereinkommen (Österreich-Tschechoslowakei), AVA,

Christlichsoziale Partei, Klub, Karton 13, Industrie, Industrieförderung. See also 'Eisenkartell', *ÖVW*, 1 Nov. 1924.

48. 'Alpine Montangesellschaft', in AVA, Bundesministerium für Handel und Verkehr, Präsidium, Karton 736, Sammelakt Alpine, 2.

49. *Ibid.*, 3: 'Österreichisch Alpine Montangesellschaft, Die Bilanzen', supplement to *ÖVW*, 4 June 1927; B. Kautsky, 'Volkswirtschaft Arbeit und Wirtschaft', *Rundschau*, 1 Jan. 1927.

50. A detailed analysis of these problems is not possible here.

51. Stenographische Protokolle über die Sitzungen des Nationalrates (IV. Gesetzgebungsperiod) der Republik Österreich, 32. Sitzung, 19 May 1931, S.894.

52. D. Doering, 'Deutsch-österreichische Aussenhandelsverflechtung während der Weltwirtschaftskrise', in H. Mommsen *et al.* (eds.), *Industrielles System und politische Entwicklung in der Weimarer Republik* (Düsseldorf, 1974), 514–30.

53. *Ibid.*, 526.

54. See 'Alpine Montangesellschaft', *ÖVW*, 23 Apr. 1927.

55. 'Die Aufhebung der Eisenzölle und die Eisenpreise', *NFP*, 1 June 1919.

56. 'Die Alpine gegen die österreichische Volkswirtschaft', *Reichspost*, 23 Apr. 1921; 'Eine Aktion der Industrie gegen die Wiedereinführung der Eisenzölle', *NFP*, 8 May 1921; 'Die Enquete über die Eisenzölle', *NFP*, 12 June 1921. See also the discussion about the iron tariff in the journal of the Hauptverband der Industrie Österreichs: 'Die Frage des Eisenzolles', *Die Industrie*, 30 Apr. 1921; 'Zur Frage des Eisenzolles', *ibid.*, 7 May 1921; 'Eisenzölle', *ibid.*, 14 May 1921.

57. 'Der Eisenzoll', *ÖVW*, 15 Aug. 1925.

58. 'Ein Erpressungsversuch des Kapitals' *AZ*, 30 May 1924. See also AVA, Bundesministeriums für Handel und Verkehr, Zl. 90.029/1926, Sign. 585a.

59. Stenographische Protokolle über die Sitzungen des Nationalrates (II. Gesetzgebungsperiode), 155; Sitzung, 28 July 1926, 3753–3781. The second new tariff was opposed by the Social Democrats.

60. Agreement between the Alpine and the metalworking employers' associations,

Vienna, 1926. Certain export subsidies already existed for manufacturing industry. ('Intervention des Bundes-Kanzlers bei der Österreichischen Alpinen Montangesellschaft', *NFP*, 16 Feb. 1924).

61. 'Revision des Avi-Abkommens', *ÖVW*, 24 Dec. 1927; 'Alpine Montangesellschaft', *ÖVW*, 29 June 1929; 'Apold und der Hauptverband', *ÖVW*, 28 Jan. 1933; 'Avi-Vereinbarung. Die Bilanzen', supplement to *ÖVW*, Notizen, 12 Feb. 1938.

62. 'Arbeit und Wirtschaft', *Rundschau*, 15 July 1931.

63. AVA, Sozialministerium, Sozialpolit. Sektion, Zl. 31.128/1919; letter from Alpine to the Staatsamt für soziale verwaltung, 30 Oct. 1919.

64. *Ibid.*, Zl. 11.564/1921.

65. Zwanzger, a Social Democrat member of the Nationalrat, for the workers (*ibid.*, Zl. 15.623/1921) and a representative of the Bund der Industrieangestellten for the white collar employees (Zl. 15.193/1921).

66. 'Die Alpine Montangesellschaft auf dem Kriegspfad', *AZ*, 27 Dec. 1921.

67. See also the following papers in Sozialpolitische Sektion des Sozialministeriums (AVA), Zl 32.402/1922; 19.257/1923; 43.164/1924; 22.733/1925; 66.094/1927; 3.737/1928.

68. 'Die Schwarze Liste', *AZ*, 20 Feb. 1925.

69. 'Streik der Angestellten bei der Alpinen Montangesellschaft', *NFP*, 1 Mar. 1921; 'Beendigung des Streiks bei der Alpinen Montangesellschaft', *NFP*, 12 Mar. 1921.

70. J. Deutsch, *Geschichte der österreichischen Gewerkschaftsbewegung*, II (Vienna, 1932), 263.

71. 'Streik bei der Alpinen', *ÖVW*, 3 Oct. 1925; 'Streiks', *ÖVW*, 24 Oct. 1925. See F. Klenner, *Die österreichischen Gewerkschaften*, I, 689.

72. 'Was ist die U.G.?', *Freiheit*, 5 and 6 Dec. 1929. See also Busson, *op. cit.*, 186ff.

73. 'Hauptversammlung der Unabhängigen Gewerkschaft', *Freiheit*, 30 Jan. 1929.

74. Busson, *op. cit.*, 186ff.

75. 'Konstituierung des Donawitzer Betriebsrates', *NFP*, 3 Apr. 1929.

76. See the pamphlet *Antiterror* (Vienna, 1930).

77. 'Die Sozialdemokraten verlieren in Donawitz sämtliche Betriebsrats-mandate', *Deutsch-österreichische Tageszeitung*, 16 Mar. 1931; 'Brutaler Alpine Terror in Donawitz', *AZ*, 7 May 1931.

78. AVA, Sozialpolitische Sektion des Sozialministeriums, Zl. 32.132/1929 in 96.776/1930.

79. 'Arbeiterpolitik der Alpine Montangesellschaft', *ÖVW*, 24 Jan. 1931.

80. Stenographische Protokolle über die Sitzungen des Nationalrates (IV. Gesetzgebungsperiode), 7. Sitzung, 27 Dec. 1930, 138; 'Alpine Montangesellschaft', *ÖVW*, 3 Jan. 1931.

81. Stenographische Protokolle über die Sitzungen des Nationalrates (IV. Gesetzbegungsperiode), 7. Sitzung, 27 Dec. 1930, 153–9; 'Gesetz gegen Betriebsstillegungen', *ÖVW*, 3 Jan. 1931.

82. Stenographische Protokolle über die Sitzungen des Nationalrates (IV. Gesetzgebungsperiode), 8. Sitzung, 13 Jan. 1931, 185.

83. Quoted in 'Alpine züchtet Revolution', *ÖVW*, 31 Jan. 1931.

84. B. F. Pauley, *Hahnenschwanz und Hakenkreuz* (Vienna, 1972), 86.

85. Klenner, *op. cit.*, II, 978ff.

86. AVA, Bundesministerium für Handel und Verkehr, Zl. 96.817/1933 in 96.573/1933, Sign. 585a; letter from Lengauer to Minister of Commerce, 26 Apr. 1933.

87. AVA, Bundesministerium für Handel und Verkehr, Präsidium, Karton 736, Sammelakt Alpine; 'Werksverbot für Lengauer.

88. See AVA, Bundesministerium für Handel und Verkehr, Zl.91.660/1934, Sign, 585a.

89. 'Über die Ersetzung des bisherigen Generaldirektors Rothballer durch Apold', *ÖVW*, 2 Feb. 1922.

90. As in Pauley, *op. cit.*, 160.

91. This committee was composed of representatives of the Chambers of Commerce and employers' associations. For further published material see the sources cited in n. 3, 303–5.

92. 'Warum die Wirtschaft Apold ablehnt', *Extrablatt*, 20 Feb. 1930.

93. 'Dr Apold über die österreichische Wirtschaftspolitik', *NFP*, 26 May 1930. 'Herr Apold ist unzufrieden', *AZ*, 25 May 1930; 'Der Dreckstaat der Heimatschützler', *AZ*, 29 June 1930; 'Apold und die österreichische Volkswirtschaft', *ÖVW*, 7 June 1930; 'Alpine Montangesellschaft', *ÖVW*, 21 June 1930; 'Apold hat recht', *ÖVW*, 5 July 1930.

94. 'Die Regierung gegen Apold', *AZ*, 28 May 1930.

95. 'Der Bankenverband über die Investitionsanleihe', *Neues Wiener Tagblatt*, 29 May 1930.

96. 'Die Industrie zu den Reden Apolds', *NFP*, 31 May 1930; 'Resolution der Präsidentenkonferenz', *Die Industrie*, 6 June 1930.

97. 'Alpine Montangesellschaft', *ÖVW*, 2 Aug. 1930.

98. These consisted of measures relating to fuel, tariffs and commercial policy.

99. 'Gegensätz im Unternehmerlager', *AZ*, 16 Dec. 1932.

100. 'Apold und Hauptverband', *ÖVW*, 28 Jan. 1933.

101. See Pauley, *op. cit.*, 160.

102. 'Die Probe auf das Exempel', *AZ*, 15 Sept. 1933; 'Streik bei der Alpine', *ÖVW*, 23 Sept. 1933; 'Volksaufstand gegen die Dollfuss-Hunger-Diktatur', *Völkischer Beobachter* (Munich), 1 Sept. 1933.

103. There is no room here for a wider examination of the degree of 'spontaneity' and the factors responsible. See also Apold's correspondence with Handelsminister Stockinger as well as various police reports: AVA, Bundesministerium für Handel und Verkehr, Präsidium, Karton 736, Sammelakt Alpine.

104. AVA, Ministerratsprotokolle, Nr. 989, 22 Sept. 1933, Punkt 28. 'Regierungskommisär, *ÖVW*, 23 Sept. 1933.

105. AVA, Ministerratsprotokolle, Nr. 909, 1 Dec. 1933, Punkt 7, and Nr. 910, 7 Dec. 1933, Punkt 14.

106. Memorandum of the Directors' Conference at the Aumühl Works, 5 Jan. 1934, Kindberg (copy), AVA, Bundesministerium für Handel und Verkehr, Präsidium, Karton 736, Sammelakt Alpine.

107. *Ibid.*, See the interpretation of the events leading to the July *putsch* in the region where the Alpine works was situated in

'Vorgeschichte der Alpineangelegenheit'.

108. AVA, Bundesminister Neustädter-Stürmer in Punkt 12 of 959 Ministerratssitzung on 30 July 1934.

109. AVA, Bundesministerium für Handel und Verkehr, Präsidium, Karton 736, Sammelakt Alpine; numerous letters by Apold.

110. AVA, Ministerratsprotokolle, Nr. 959, 30 July 1934, Punkt 12; Nr. 961, 7 Aug. 1934, Punkt 11. 'Alpine unter politischer Kontrolle', *ÖVW*, 11 Aug. 1934; 'Apolds Schadengutmachung', *ÖVW*, 18 Aug. 1934.

111. AVA, Bundesministerium für Handel und Verkehr, Präsidium, Karton 736, Sammelakt Alpine: Report on the situation of the Alpine, 3 Dec. 1934.

112. AVA, Ministerratsprotokolle, Nr. 960, 3 Aug. 1934, Punkt 8, und Nr. 962, 17 Aug. 1934, Punkt 12.

113. See sources cited in n. 110, and on the dismissal see AVA, Bundesministerium für Handel und Verkehr, ZL. 162, 313/1936. Sign. 269.

114. Thyssen Archive, p.7, vol. IV (173): statements of witnesses Dr Hans Malzacher, Dipl. Ing. Richard Krön, Dr Erwin Daub, all dated 7 Jan. 1954; and sworn testimony of Dr Hans Malzacher, 20 Jan 1950.

COMMENTARY *Eduard März*

I shall concentrate on a few of the issues raised – mainly economic ones, as P. G. Fischer has well covered the political issues. The Alpine Montan, it must be emphasized, was the most important industrial enterprise in the Austrian inter-war economy. Along with the Prague Iron Company and the Vítkovice Mining and Foundry Works, the Alpine dominated iron and steel production during the closing years of the Habsburg Monarchy. Unlike the other two major producers, the Alpine after 1918 remained an Austrian enterprise, but it had a major weakness as it was now cut off from its coal and coke base in Czechoslovakia. This problem of securing the necessary coke during the immediate post-war years even had an effect on the capital ownership of the Alpine. Very soon the question of nationalization of the works arose as part of the programme of the Social Democrats. This was part of a general policy of the state taking over Austria's key industries. P. G. Fischer may have underestimated the strength of the Social Democrats, particularly given the Hungarian revolution, and so the nationalization of the Alpine could perhaps be put more accurately as 'touch and go'.

The nationalization programme was in fact foiled by Joseph Schumpeter.[1] Shortly before his resignation as Finance Minister he wrote to Chancellor Renner admitting that he had known of the buying of Alpine shares by the Italian group. The transaction was providing the Austrian Treasury with much-needed foreign exchange for the purchase of food and coal imports. Schumpeter was informed by his agent that he was buying shares of the Alpine and the Finance Minister made only a token protest despite the implications for the nationalization policy.

The second point I wish to make is that the Alpine shares did not remain for very long in the hands of the Italian Fiat group. The Italians were unable to supply the Alpine Works with the coal that it so desperately needed. The Germans were in a position to supply this vital raw material, and soon the Stinnes group took over the Alpine, lock, stock and barrel. I want to stress that Germany at that time had not mounted a general offensive strategy of take-over. There was no German counter-offensive mounted against Western attempts to take-over Austrian industry during the years immediately after the First World War. Some aspects of German policy within Austria require further comment. First, the Alpine was restricted in terms of sales to the Austrian market and Eastern markets, and therefore sales policy was directed from the Düsseldorf headquarters of the German concern. Second, whereas before the war the Alpine had a very diversified product range, after the German take-over the output was limited to certain products, to crude iron and cast iron, with finishing being carried out at Düsseldorf. Third, top management came to be centralized in Düsseldorf, and Apold acted as a Roman Consul in occupied territory.

Politically the bilateral relationship between the Alpine and Düsseldorf was a disaster for Austria. Economically the experience, as I have already indicated, was unfortunate. It should be stressed that the burden of the depression was transferred as far as possible on to the shoulders of the Austrian people. With the slump in product sales stemming from the depression the Alpine was given a very thin slice of this now sharply contracted market. In 1932 and 1933 blast furnaces were completely shut down as a result. Austria's present experience of multi-national enterprises does not quite resemble that of the 1920s and 1930s. Austria is no longer in any way an underdeveloped country and has a number of devices with which to defend itself against policies harmful to its economy.

Notes

1. C. A. Gulick, *Austria from Hapsburg to Hitler*, I, *Labor's Workshop of Democracy* (San Francisco, 1948, repr. 1980), 139–42; E. März, *Österreichische Bankpolitik in der Zeit der grossen Wende 1913–1923* (Vienna, 1981), 337–40.

11. Göring's 'Multi-national Empire'[1]

R. J. Overy

The growth of Göring's 'multi-national' business empire was not in the strict sense a business venture. Though it closely resembled the increasing concentration of private heavy industry in Germany during the 1930s, the resemblance disguised certain basic differences. The expansion of Göring's industrial interests was a function of both the internal Nazi power struggle and the development of the wartime economy of occupied Europe. In the first place Göring's growing role in the economy reflected Hitler's conviction that war preparations could only be guaranteed if controlled by leaders whom he could trust to carry out Nazi programmes. In addition Göring's role was a reflection of the growing struggle between more conservative financial and business circles – represented by Schacht and the less nazified elements of the Ruhr elite – and the Nazi state whose military and international ambitions demanded a greater control over economic policy and industrial development.[2] This conflict took place against the background of the more parochial struggle between rival Nazi potentates for influence in party and state.

Göring's economic empire was to be a rival to the social empire of Ley on the one hand, and the security empire of Himmler on the other. In 1936 Göring's political position was clearly compromised by his failure to retain police powers and his subordination in military affairs to Blomberg and in economic affairs to Schacht. The Four Year Plan, together with the prospect of more general plenipotentiary rule over economic life, altered the political balance once again in Göring's favour. By 1939 both Blomberg and Schacht were gone. When war broke out Hitler confirmed Göring in his key role in mobilizing resources, expanded the Four Year Plan and charged his deputy with the 'special assignment of adapting [the economy] to the needs of war'.[3] Under these instructions Göring with great energy took over the direction of the conquered European areas through either direct exploitation of existing resources in the native economies or the looting of stocks and equipment for use in the Reich. The Four Year Plan and the Reichswerke 'Hermann Göring' were the organizational and industrial agencies respectively for carrying out such exploitation. Both agencies were able to penetrate the economies of captured and allied areas though in competition with both private industry and other state agencies. The process adopted for such penetration was the setting up of a vast multi-national state concern based on the Reichswerke which through a variety of devices, some legal, some not, was able to expand in the economy of the New Order as fast and as far as Göring's fiat could go. The concern was only finally modified by the Speer reforms of 1942 and the growing administrative indolence and political isolation of the Reichsmarschall himself.

Because of the strong political content in the establishment and expansion of the Reichswerke an interpretation simply on business grounds is unsatisfactory. Göring insisted from the start that purely economic considerations were unimportant. Political and racial-economic considerations took precedence, even over Göring's own greed. The Reichswerke were not acquired for Göring's personal use nor did Göring in any sense 'own' the concern. That is not to say that Göring did not personally profit from the enterprises. In a number of well-documented cases payments were made direct to Göring's account from the profits of the concern either as a regular contribution or to clear temporarily embarassing debts.[4] This was a by-product of the concern. It was run and organized by managers and bureaucrats working within the structure of the Four Year Plan, in particular Körner, Keppler, Kehrl, Pleiger and Voss.[5] A second important point that has to be remembered is that the expansion of the firm outside Germany was not a purely wartime phenomenon, prompted by the necessity of war. Far from it, for the decision to involve Austria pre-dated the Anschluss and the Reichswerke had already begun to acquire interests in Central Europe before Munich as part of the growing Nazi economic offensive in the area. War obviously accelerated the programme and also encouraged short-term investment and product policies to cope with military demands, but the long-term strategy of concern-building had been established already and was intended to continue in peacetime. One final consideration should be borne in mind. The legal form of the Reichswerke and its subsidiaries was essentially the same as that of private companies except in the rather special case of the trusteeship set up in Russia. It is as a result sometimes tempting to see the works as a 'private' concern, a Second World War 'Stinnes Empire'. Yet Göring was only the agent of the Reich and the German 'Volk', holding the concern on a condition of trust through which the political and economic programme of Nazi imperialism could be actively underpinned by direct state ownership of the means of production. It represented one of the major steps towards restricting private capitalism and substituting a 'völkisch' industrial economy.[6]

It is not the purpose of this paper to discuss at any length the details surrounding the founding and early growth of the Reichswerke. By mid-1938 the company had a share capital of 400m RM and had either acquired or set up a number of related businesses in the Salzgitter Watenstedt area with long-term plans for the development of low-grade iron ores and iron and steel production.[7]

The progressive realization of Hitler's foreign policy aims from March 1938 onwards gave Göring considerable opportunities to extend the scope of the Reichswerke. This task was eased considerably as for most of the period up to the invasion of Russia Göring had a special role to play in consolidating the territories falling to Reich control. In Austria Göring acted as Hitler's deputy and as head of the economy. After the war had broken out he was able to obtain from Hitler the promise that he alone was responsible for economic questions in the New Order. For the invasion of Russia Göring got further powers from Hitler to strengthen his position in the jurisdictional jungle that had begun to develop in the East.[8]

Göring and his deputies were usually in a position to have first choice when arranging exploitation and were able to negotiate with foreign governments from a position of strength. In the case of countries allied to Germany very much less might have been gained for the Reichswerke had Göring not had the opportunity to work through the highest government and foreign office channels. In conquered areas a different pattern of expansion developed based on either direct confiscation or forced sales. Direct seizure of industrial property came as a result of either the aryanization drive or through conquest.[9] In the latter case state-owned firms in Poland and Russia were regarded as the spoils of war to be disposed of by the victor as he saw fit. In one instance – the confiscation of Fritz Thyssen's industrial holdings – the state used the law of 1934 which gave the power to expropriate the property of communists. Direct seizure like that was the most important source of growth of the Reichswerke. The system of forced sales was also widely practised, together with currency and exchange control manipulation. Sometimes this took the form of direct terror. Count Louis Rothschild was imprisoned after the Anschluss and freed only in return for his substantial industrial holdings. Even major German trusts could be compelled to sell. Political pressure was brought to bear on the Vereingte Stahlwerke for the sale of shares in the Alpine Montangesellschaft. Similar pressure was exerted in Czechoslovakia for the sale of shares in the Škodovy závody (Škoda Works) and the Československá zbrojovka akc. spol. (Czech Armaments Works) at Brno, all of which were bought on the open market though at a very favourable price. In fact several devices were used to buy shares at well below their market value, allowing a greater expansion of German financial participation than would have been possible in peacetime.[10] In addition to the exercise of *force majeure* there was expansion generated from within by either the creation of new capital or the founding of new firms. In such situations it was possible to expand the share capital of foreign firms through Reich loans and so turn a minority into a majority holding.

It is important to emphasize here the crucial role played in the course of expansion by the German banks. The Dresdner Bank in particular was largely responsible for actually acquiring or holding shares which were then transferred to the Reichswerke, the government paying a commission to the bank for its agency work. Karl Rasche of the Dresdner Bank, a committed Nazi, was the official responsible for carrying on negotiations between other banks and businesses with Körner, head of the Reichswerke.[11] In a few cases the banks became shareholders themselves. Göring's political position also gave him access to other banks. The Bank der deutschen Luftfahrt was set up to organize finance for aircraft firms and contractors and through this agency Göring was able to acquire influence in enterprises in which the bank had invested. In fact when the armaments sector of the concern was taken from his direct control in 1942 the air bank continued to provide some of the finance and a direct line back to Göring.[12] His position as Prime Minister of Prussia also gave him advantages in using the holdings of the Preussische Staatsbank. In this way he was able to acquire an interest in the Société des Mines de Bor owned by the Banque Mirabeau which the Prussian bank took over, as well as in other Prussian state holdings.[13]

The chronology of expansion more or less followed the course of territorial and military expansion. Göring had expressed a personal interest in gaining control over Austrian iron resources in 1937.[14] A few days after the Anschluss both Göring and Pleiger began to plan the exploitation of Austrian ores and the possibility of acquiring an interest in the Österreichisch-Alpine Montangesellschaft. The majority holding was in the hands of the Vereinigte Stahlwerke (VS) and to all intents and purposes apparently safeguarded for the Reich. Nevertheless the Reichswerke took over a 13 per cent stake in Alpine Montangesellschaft through the purchase of shares held by the Industrie-Kredit Bank in Vienna and continued a campaign for the following six months to compel VS to hand over control to the Reichswerke.[15] One reason for the campaign was the need to guarantee ore supplies for the first of the large Tochtergesellschaften founded at Linz, the Reichswerke AG für Erzbergbau-und Eisenhütten 'Herman Göring', Linz. Its foundation in Linz was not coincidental. For Hitler the area had a special significance. Göring promised to make this company the greatest industrial concern in the world as a compliment to the Führer. There was also the more practical problem that VS control of the Erzberg would not necessarily guarantee a large enough flow of ore for war purposes. Instead the ore might be used for private Ruhr firms anxious to expand exports, policies over which conflict had already arisen between the Ruhr leaders and the Nazis.[16] Reichswerke control of the Erzberg and the Linz complex would ensure that political and ideological considerations would be a governing factor. In March 1939 VS gave up the fight and over 70 per cent of the control in the Alpine company passed to the Reichswerke. VS personnel left the board of directors of both their old business and the new foundation at Linz and in June 1939 the name of the company was changed to Alpine Montan AG 'Hermann Göring' Linz.[17] By this time the Reichswerke had penetrated into the rest of the Austrian iron and steel industry and into end-production in order to exploit the locational advantages and to spread the area of war production.

Most of the additional Austrian firms were acquired through the Reich holding company Vereinigte Industrie-Unternehmungen Aktiengesellschaft

(VIAG) which had acquired the shares in turn from the Österreichische Creditanstalt-Wierner Bankverein when Austrian financial institutions were absorbed into the Reich. The shareholdings passed on to the Reichswerke were in many cases only minority holdings. Nevertheless through manipulation it proved possible either to acquire more shares or to effect virtual control through political influence. In armaments and engineering the Reichswerke acquired control over the Maschinen-und Waggonbau-Fabriks-AG, the Grazer Maschinen-und Waggonbau-AG, Paukerwerke AG and the large vehicle and armaments producer Steyr-Daimler-Puch AG.[18] The degree of holding in each company is not clear. In the case of Steyr-Daimler-Puch there was clear ownership by the middle of the war but ownership and control were not interdependent. With this concern it seems likely that its share capital was raised over the period to cope with war orders and that since the additional share capital was provided by the Reichswerke control gradually developed into ownership as well, a device commonly used elsewhere. Through the same VIAG source the Göring concern was able to acquire large holdings in the rest of the Austrian iron, steel and mining industry. The Steirische Gusstahlwerke, AG was taken over completely and large minority holdings acquired in the Feinstahlwerke Traisen AG vorm. Fischer and Veitscher Magnesitwerke-AG. A number of small coal workings were also taken over.[19] In addition to this some completely new firms were founded: the Eisenwerke Oberdonau GmbH for arms production, set up jointly with the high command of the army and the Wohnungsbau AG der Reichswerke 'Hermann Göring' Linz which, together with the takeover of the construction firm Bau AG 'Negrelli', gave the works a stake in the Austrian building trade.[20] The process of vertical integration was completed with the take-over of the Erste Donau-Dampfschiffahrts-Gesellschaft from the Alpine-Montan company and the setting up jointly with the Bayerische Lloyd of the Süddeutsche Donaudampfschiffahrts GmbH.[21] Within the space of a few months the Reichswerke had changed from being one of the smaller iron and steel corporations to a large concern controlling a whole production sector in Austria from raw material production through armaments manufacture to sales and distribution. Moreover, the close interlocking of the industrial and commercial structure of Central Europe, and in particular the German Austrian links with the old Habsburg areas, gave the Reichswerke claims on a large outer circle of smaller firms in which the larger acquisitions had had a stake. By 1944 the Reichswerke 'Montanblock' alone had a controlling interest in 33 firms with a total share capital of 226.1m RM.[22]

The successful penetration of the Austrian economy prepared the way for the expansion into the rest of Central Europe and even gave the Reichswerke ownership of companies in Latin America and South Africa.[23] Actually before the occupation of Sudetenland and rump Czechoslovakia, the growing German control in Austria led automatically to an increased claim on other economies, in particular on the Czechoslovak holdings of the major Jewish families in Vienna which fell to the Reichswerke in the course of 1938 and 1939.

The pre-war acquisitions made certain changes inevitable in terms of the structure of the enterprise. The good iron ores of Austria and the hard coal and lignite deposits from both Austria and Czechoslovakia made the original Salzgitter project to a certain extent redundant. In order to safeguard internal economic resources for long-term Nazi plans, Central Europe provided a much more secure base for 'autarky'. The building up of metalworking capacity, particularly the production of armaments, had not been the initial intention. Such a move had the advantage that it gave guaranteed markets for the industrial raw materials produced by the concern, especially for over-priced Salzgitter/Watenstedt iron and steel, and gave Hitler and Göring the opportunity to produce a large Nazi-controlled armaments sector, free from interference from the Ruhr and open to manipulation directly in the interests of the developing imperialism. Acquisition by the Göring concern made possible a speedier integration into the war economy and cut through all the delaying negotiations and business arrangements that might have resulted from the more haphazard intervention of private concerns. Certainly the advantages to be won from the Czechoslovak economy were exploited rapidly and systematically, though not always efficiently, by the Reichswerke through its control of all the main sectors of Czechoslovak heavy industry.

The Sudetenland provided Göring with the first real opportunity for acquiring large deposits of coal, though in this case it was lignite rather than hard coal. More than half the lignite mines of the area were consolidated into a single company under the combined control of VIAG and the Reichswerke called the Sudetenländische Bergbau AG, Brüx (Most). Some mines were seized as Czech state holdings. Others were the proceeds of the 'aryanization' of the holdings of the Petschek concern in Prague, of Ignac Petschek of Ústí n. L. and Weinmann of Ústí n. L.[24] As the capital of the lignite concern expanded from initially 50m RM to 140m RM the share of the Reichswerke rose to 78 per cent.[25] On the basis of the lignite and in support of the Four Year Plan programme for synthetic oil production the largest planned synthetic oil plant was set up at Brüx. Originally established under the Four Year Plan and run by the trustee company Mineralölbau GmbH, it was converted by Göring into a massive oil plant under the direct control of the Reichswerke as trustee for the Reich. In October 1939 the Sudetenländische Treibstoffwerke AG was established as a Tochtergesellschaft with 250m RM capital.[26] Again the availability of the raw material and the advantage of distance from Allied bombers probably played a part in the decision. IG Farben was, perhaps rather surprisingly, not given control over the plant, a fact that caused some concern as to whether the Reichswerke was intending to expand into chemicals production too.[27] It did mean, however, that

Göring's direct control over resources in the conquered Czech Lands was all-embracing.

Czech heavy industry was concentrated around the big armament firms of Škoda and the Czech Armaments Works, Brno, and the iron and steel complexes of Poldina huť, Vítkovicke horní a hutní těžířstvo [Vítkovice Mining and Foundry Works], Báňská a hutní společnost [Mining and Metallurgic Co.] and Pražská železářská společnost [Prague Iron Co.]. In the case of the last of these, control was already exercised before 1939 by Mannesmann.[28] In the case of all the remainder the Reichswerke became the predominant influence between 1939 and 1940. Initially the German government maintained the industrial and banking structure as superficially still Czech and concentrated on giving large arms orders, particularly for aircraft and aircraft components, to tie Czech firms more closely to the Reich.[29] This was to a certain extent the result of the fact that much foreign capital was still involved in Czech industry – British capital at Vítkovice, French capital in the Mining and Metallurgic Company – and until war was declared the German government could only rely on negotiation to achieve control.[30] It was also the case that many Czech firms continued to work with their new German masters on the basis, among others, that responsibility lay first towards the shareholders. In many cases a German controlling interest simply replaced, or was superimposed upon, a French or British interest.[31]

Much of the capital of the large concerns lay, however, either with the Czech state or with the large Czech banks. It was the acquisition of these state shares, coupled with the Germanization of the banking system, that supplied the Göring concern with its Czech shareholdings. Through the offices of Kehrl of the Four Year Plan Organization and Rasche of the Dresdner Bank, acting on the direct orders of Göring, the Česká eskomptní banka úvěrní ústav [Bohemian Discount Bank and Society of Credit] and the Česká banka Union [Bohemian Union-Bank] bought substantial holdings in the following companies:

	% of base capital
První brněnská strojírenská společnost (First Brno Engineering Co.)	37.6
Poldina huť	35
Czech Armament works	49
Škoda-Works	9
Mining and Metallurgic Co.	23

The German Finance Ministry reported in October 1939 that 'the Reich Ministry of Economics intends soon to apply for approval . . . in order that the Hermann Göring Works [holding] should take over these investments'.[32] By December the Dresdner Bank was in a position to offer the Göring concern 130,528 shares in Czech Armaments works and 62,426 Škoda shares where only 12,960 had been available in June; very probably 62,000 shares of those now available had been taken up by the Czech state in 1937.[33] The advantage of acquiring a large share in the capital of the Czech Armanent Works was the fact that this enterprise in turn controlled the largest single block of Škoda shares. After acquiring other Czech firms the Reichswerke actively owned 64 per cent of the Armament Works shares and controlled in a syndicate the remaining 36 per cent, thus automatically acquiring an additional 30.5 per cent of the Škoda shares. By acquiring the shares of Omnipol, a Škoda subsidiary, this participation was raised to 54.5 per cent. Through influence in the banking system actual control was exercised over 63.6 per cent of all Škoda shares by October 1940 (see table 11.1).[34] By the

Table 11.1. SHAREHOLDING IN ŠKODA-WORKS AND ČESKOSLOVENSKÁ ZBROJOVKA, OCTOBER 1940.

(a) Škoda-Works (687,500 shares)		(b) Československá zbrojovka (300,000	
Reichswerke	59,448	shares)	
controlled by Reichswerke		Reichswerke	130,528
through syndicate		*controlled by Reichswerke*	
Československá zbrojovka	210,000	*through syndicate*	
Omnipol	105,000	Škoda-Works	61,312
Česká eskomptní banka a úvěrní		Česká estomptní banka a úvěrní	
ústav	20,850	ústav	15,600
Anglo-československá banka	20,000	Anglo-československá banka	15,000
Živnostenská banka	18,000	Agrární banka	8,229
Agrární banka	4,150	Ferdinandova severní dráha	22,223
		Explosia a.s. pro prumysl	
	437,448	výbušnin	17,375
		Kooperativa	10,973
		Živnostenská banka	15,600
			296,840

same date the Reichswerke had also acquired a 49.9 per cent holding in the First Brno Engineering Co.[35] Once the position had been clarified German managers were installed under the general direction of Voss and Albert Göring.[36] Until the reform of the Reichswerke structure in 1942–3 control was exercised over product policy, commercial and financial affairs, in much the same way as it had been exercised by Schneider-Creusot before 1938.[37]

Penetration of the Czech iron, steel and mining sector was as thorough as that in armaments. The Reichswerke acquired only a minority holding in the Mining and Metallurgic Co. Sufficient shares were bought up in the Poldina huť to give the Reichswerke a 56 per cent stake and to bring it into the Göring fold.[38] The largest complex was the Vítkovice Works, owned mainly by the Rothschilds of Vienna and London. It was to this complex that Hitler paid particular attention when planning the exploitation of the Czech Lands.

During the mid-1930s the Rothschilds, in order to improve the competitive situation against Germany, acquired the minority holdings in Vítkovice and then transferred control over the whole business to the Rothschild London-based company, Alliance Assurance. Even though Louis Rothschild was forced to pay for his life with all the remaining Rothschild assets in Austria and Czechoslovakia, the Vítkovice Works was now a British company and could not be expropriated.[39] The works were, nevertheless, occupied at once when rump Czechoslovakia was seized, and handed over for administration to the Reichswerke which continued to exercise control until the end of the war. Negotiations continued during 1939 with the Rothschilds in Paris for the sale of the company which, through conquest, was already compelled to work for the German war economy. Agreement was finally reached in July 1939 for the purchase of the works for the sum of £2.9m but the transaction was postponed by war.[40]

The acquisition of the iron and steel sector complemented that in armaments. Poldina hut and Vítkovice both provided high-grade steel for army production and continued to supply them for tank production both at Škoda and Linz throughout the war. Vítkovice also had contacts in Slovakia, an area which Göring hoped would be a potential territory for armaments expansion within the structure of the Four Year Plan. Although not much came of the scheme, except for an agreement on aircraft production, what industry there was in Slovakia was attached to the Reichswerke through its controlling interests elsewhere.[41] The take-over of the coal and rail company Ferdinands-Nordbahn through the Dresdner Bank, together with some smaller coal mines, completed the integration of holdings in Czechoslovakia and between the Czech and Austrian holdings.[42] Figure 11.1 shows the extent of such penetration by 1940–1. In Czechoslovakia the Reichswerke controlled approximately 50–60 per cent of Czech heavy industry by value; in Austria slightly less.[43]

Just as the earlier Austrian invasion opened up the way to penetrate into Czechoslovakia, so the occupation of that country opened the way for expansion into the rest of central Europe, particularly into Poland, Hungary and Romania. In all these areas actual ownership of assets by the Reichswerke was much smaller, though its influence was considerable. In the case of Poland this was partly due to the seizure policy that followed the invasion. In the case of Romania influence was exercised through enforced 'co-operation' between the Reichswerke and Romanian heavy industry.

After the outbreak of war Göring turned his attention to the need to secure German dominance in central Europe both to safeguard the German war economy and to avoid the problems, particularly with food supplies, experienced during the First World War. Göring's directive in August 1940 made it clear that Göring wanted personal control over the extension of German firms into the industry of Central Europe to the advantage of the Reichswerke.[44] This authority gave a guarantee of material control in a world of competing Nazi empires in which possession was nine-tenths of the law. While a strategy was being prepared for the eventual integration of the Hungarian and Romanian economies into the Nazi European economy, the invasion of Poland returned large areas of pre-1914 German Poland back to the Reich. Unlike the case of the occupation of Austria and Czechoslovakia, Göring was faced with the problem that many of the industrial enterprises seized from Poland had traditional contacts with large German firms. In fact the word commonly used to describe the return of Silesian industry was *Repatriierung*, echoing the view of private heavy industry that its old claims should be satisfied.[45] Göring's main interest was in hard coal which, despite the acquisitions in other areas, was still in short supply for the entire concern. Pleiger had already managed an exchange of holdings between the Reichswerke and the Ruhr to secure a larger coal base, but this was clearly not enough for a concern the size of the Göring works, anxious to consolidate its raw material base.[46] In late 1939 Göring demanded that his appointee in Upper Silesia, Max Winkler, arrange the transfer of the coal mines to the Reichswerke. Many of the mines were owned by the Polish state but were now held in trusteeship by the Haupttreuhandstelle Ost (HTO) for the Reich under the watchful eye of the army. It was agreed that the Reich should, in effect, pay itself for the mines to make the transaction appear 'legal', and a transfer of 200m RM was affected from the Bergwerkeverwaltung Oberschlesien GmbH der Reichswerke 'Hermann Göring', to whom the money was loaned, to the HTO and thence back to the Reich. As with many other concerns the Reichswerke held the mines on trust for the *Volk*.[47] Through this device it had succeeded in gaining control over coal deposits that provided nearly 60 per cent of all the Göring works' hard coal requirements by 1944 and constituted some 25 per cent of all Silesian production. In addition the Reichswerke had established sizeable participations in a number of allied industries despite the existence of competing claims.[48]

It was only in the iron, steel and armaments sector that there was relatively less success. The army entrusted the Reichswerke with operating firms within the General Government that had been owned by Vítkovice and Poldina hut.[49] Most of the large Silesian steelworks were acquired by trustees from Ruhr industry. Other smaller firms were taken over in the Warsaw area though usually through the activities of a subsidiary as, for example, the acquisition of the Radom and Warsaw factories of the Polish State Armaments Works. Even this takeover had to be ratified by the OKH authorities which were able to exercise much greater control over the Polish economy than in areas where Göring had been able to dominate the civilian takever.[50] This position only altered in 1943 with a decision to increase arms production in the General Government, a task with which the Reichswerke was again associated.[51] Interestingly, the experience in Poland prompted Göring to get Hitler to decide beforehand who would have the power in economic affairs in the war with Russia. Hitler decided in favour of Göring, who was thus able to act as the arbiter in distributing economic resources after the invasion and attach to the Reichswerke the major portions of the Ukrainian and Donets Basin industrial region.[52]

Göring's idea was to create a monopoly organization of all captured industry which became automatically the property of the Reich. The Berg-und Hüttenwerkgesellschaft OstmbH (BHO) was set up for this purpose and on 1 September 1941 it took over control, under Pleiger, of the mining installations at Kriwoj-Rog and Nikopol. On 1 March 1942 it took over the coal workings of the Donets Basin and the industrial complex at Dniepropetrovsk where, through a programme of heavy investment and the moving of tools, equipment and engineers from the Reich, a revival of coal, manganese and steel output was achieved.[53] During 1943 a system of *Patenschaften* was created through which Pleiger and Körner were able to force Ruhr firms to take over the running of a particular Russian steelworks for the duration of the war. It was always stressed that this did not imply that the Reich had abandoned its own claims and the Reichswerke distributed the operating franchises under its direct supervision. This was complied with reluctantly by the more radical elements of the party in the East and only in order to satisfy Hitler's demand for expediency in getting the experts in the Reich to exploit Russian and East European industry before it was too late.[54] It is hard to see Göring's ambitions in Russia as simply expedient. Expansion in Russia was both a natural extension of state industrial penetration elsewhere and also a better guarantee that the party should have a decisive say in the political and economic reconstruction of the area after the war.

By the end of 1941 Göring had achieved his promise of creating the largest economic enterprise in Europe. Only Romania remained as a Central European country with a significant industrial base that had not been successfully penetrated by Göring. The 1939 economic treaty negotiated by Göring had certainly created the framework for co-operation. However, until 1941 the Romanian government was determined to keep as much control over its own industry as possible in order to prevent German penetration, particularly after the outbreak of war when the Reich regarded Allied oil and industrial holdings in Romania as forfeit enemy property.[55] A way in had been provided, however, through the Reichswerke take-over of Czechoslovak industry. The Czech Armament Works had been a minority shareholder in both the Reşiţa (Uzinele de Fier şi Domeniile din Reşiţa Societate Anonimă) iron and steel complex and the Copşa Mică şi Cugir mines. Although the shares had been deposited with the Westminster Bank in London, which subequently refused to release them, Göring was able to bring pressure to bear on the Romanian government to produce duplicate shares. These were duly produced in November 1939. The transaction was completed on 24 January 1940 giving the Reichswerke an 8 per cent stake in Reşiţa (soon raised to 13 per cent) and a 19 per cent stake in Copşa Mică. In July 1940

Company names

Czech	German	English
	Sudetenländische Treibstoffwerke AG,	Sudetenland Fuel Works Ltd,
Poldina huť, Kladno	Poldihütte	Poldi Works, Kladno
Vítkovické horní a hutní těžířstvo, Ostrava	Witkowitzer Bergbau und Eisenhütten Gewerkschaft	Vítkovice Mining and Foundry Works, Ostrava
Škodovy závody, Plzeň	Škodawerke	Škoda-Works, Plzeň
Československá zbrojovka akc. spol., Brno	Brünner Waffenwerke	Czechoslovak Armaments Works, Brno
První brněnská strojírenská společnost, Brno	Erste Brünner Maschinen-Fabriks GmbH	First Brno Engineering Co., Brno
Ferdinandova severní dráha, Moravská Ostrava	Ferdinands Nordbahn	Ferdinand Northern Railway, Ostrava
	Sudetenländische Bergbau AG	Sudetenland Mining Co. Ltd, Most
	Motan Kohlen- und Kokshandel AG	Coal and Coke Trading Co. Ltd
Kamenouhelné doly a.s., Lany-Rakovnice	Lana-Rakowitzer Steinkohlen AG	Lany-Rakovnice Collieries Ltd
	Ruda Bergbau und Hüttenbetriebe AG	Ruda Mining and Metallurgic Works Ltd , Slovakia
Akciová společnost železářských a ocelářských závodů Prakovce, Slovakia	Eisen und Stahlwerke zu Prakovce AG	Iron and Steel Works at Prakovce Ltd , Slovakia
	Prager Feilenfabrik AG	Prague Files Factory Ltd
Továrna na železné zboží v Čenkově akc. spol., Prague	Tschenkauer Eisen-und Stahlwarenfabriken AG	Iron and Steel Wares Factories Ltd , Čenkov
Západočeský báňský akciový spolek, Prague	Westböhmischer Bergbau-Aktien-Verein	West Bohemian Joint-Stock Mining Association, Prague
Krompašské závody na med' úč. spol., Slovakia	Krompacher Kupferwerke AG	Krompachy Copper Works Ltd , Slovakia
Báňská a hutní společnost, Prague	Berg- und Hüttenwerksgesellschaft	Mining and Metallurgic Co.
Julius Rütgers KG, Moravská Ostrava	Julius Rütgers KG	Julius Rütgers KG, Moravská Ostrava

Reichswerke AG 'Hermann Göring'

Austria	% held	Czechoslovakia	% held
Reichswerke AG Alpine Montanbetriebe	96	Sudetenländische Treibstoffwerke AG	100
Eisenwerke Oberdonau GmbH, Linz	100	Poldina huť, Kladno	56
Steyr-Daimler-Puch AG	81	Vítkovické horní a hutní těžířstvo, Ostrava	
Steirische-Gusstahl AG	100	Škodovy závody, Plzeň	63
Simmeringer Maschinen- und Waggonbau	54	Československá zbrojovka akc. spol., Brno	99
Eisenwerke AG Krieglach	75	První brněnská strojírenská společnost, Brno	49
Pauker-Werke	100		
Stahl und Temperguss AG	80	Ferdinandova severní dráha, Moravská Ostrava	53
Grazer Waggon- und Maschinen-Fabriken AG	100	Sudetenländische Bergbau AG, Brüx	78
Kärntnersche Eisen und Stahlwerks GmbH	100	Montan Kohlen- und Kokshandel AG	83
		Kamenouhelné doly a.s., Lany-Rakovnice	100
Eisen und Stahl AG Wien	100		
Johann Einicher Eisenhandels	75	Ruda Bergbau und Hüttenbetriebe AG, Slovakia	100
Eisen Handels- und Industrie AG	67	Akciová společnost železářských a ocelářských závodů Prakovce, Slovakia	100
Erste Donau Dampschiffahrtsge- sellschaft mbH	97	Prager Feilenfabrik AG	100
Graz-Koflacher Eisenbahn und Bergbauges.	80	Továrna na železné zboží v Čenkově ack. spol., Prague	100
Wohnungsbau AG der Reichswerke	100	Západočeský báňský akciový spolek, Prague	57
Stahlbau GmbH der Reichswerke	100	Krompašské závody na med' úč. spol., Slovakia	99
Steirische Bergbau- und Eisenbahn AG	91		
Bau AG 'Negrelli'	100	51 smaller firms	
Fanto AG	100		

(minority holdings)

Báňská a hutní společnost, Prague	23
Julius Rütgers KG, Moravská Ostrava	32

n.a. not available

29 smaller firms

(minority holdings)

Feinstahlwerke Traisen AG	n.a.
Veitscher Magnesitwerke AG	n.a.

*Only the major firms are listed. There were many subsidiaries. The names by which they were known in German during the war have been used.

Figure 11.1. Main firms under Reichswerke control in Austria and Czechoslovakia, 1940–1.

three seats on the board of directors at Reşiţa went to the Reichswerke, while the anti-semitic campaign forced the resignation of the Jewish general manager, Max Ausschnitt.[56] In January 1940 the Reichswerke turned to the other major industrial complex in Romania, the Malaxa works. A 'Technischer-Hilfsvertrag' (technical assistance agreement) was signed with the company under which arrangement experts were attached to Malaxa to tie it more closely to the German economic strategy in the area.[57] It was not possible to do more until the overthrow of King Carol because of Romanian resistance. Göring was able to reach agreement with Antonescu to expand Reichswerke influence in both Reşiţa and Malaxa. In the case of the latter Malaxa himself was put on trial on profiteering charges and the entire complex taken over by the Romanian state, 50 per cent through confiscation, 50 per cent at a price fixed by the government.[58] In March Germany demanded 'the participation of German industries in the management of Romanian heavy industry – considered from the Reich's point of view'.[59] Negotiations continued throughout 1941 and in the autumn a new company was formed called the Rumänisch-Deutsche AG für Eisenindustrie und Handel (Rogifer) in which the capital was divided unequally between the Reichswerke and the Romanian state. The firm operated the Reşiţa and Malaxa works and overall control in technical, financial and commercial questions passed to the Reichswerke. With this transfer the German company also gained interests in other large firms such as the Astra car and arms works at Braşov.[60] As in Austria, Czechoslovakia and Russia the Reichswerke acquired control over almost all the iron and steel output in Romania and maintained this control until it was forced to abandon and destroy the installations by the advance of the Russian armies.

The intervention in Romania also provided Göring with the opportunity to extend his influence over the foreign oil industry. Such an interest stemmed from the priorities under the Four Year Plan but before 1941 had not resulted in any plans to extend formal control over oil companies except in the founding of the Sudetenland factory utilizing Reichswerke lignite. At the end of 1940 Göring suddenly appointed Dr Neubacher of the Four Year Plan office as Bevollmächtigter für Erdölangelegenheiten im Südosten and set up a holding company, the Kontinentale Öl AG 'to take over companies belonging to enemy and neutral powers in the countries occupied by Germany'. The company was formally constituted on 27 March 1941 with a capital of 80m RM, 30m provided by the state which had the sole voting rights in the company.[61] There had already been some penetration of Romanian oil through Czech acquisitions. The First Brno Engineering Company had a large share in Petrol Block AG which came under Reichswerke influence in 1940.[62] Austrian, French and Dutch holdings were taken under the administration of Kontinentale Öl and there were plans for the company in Russia, where both Hitler and Göring were determined that oil resources would remain permanently Reich properties operated by firms owned by the

Reich.[63] Nevertheless it seems likely that the oil interests lay at the periphery of the industrial empire created around the Göring concern. Indeed within two years any hope of utilizing Russian oil resources had disappeared for good as the Reichswerke was forced to retreat westwards with the German armies, contracting, as it had previously expanded, with the path of war. In April 1944 the Economics Ministry wrote to Göring recommending the winding up of his Ostgesellschaften whose personnel had now dwindled to a mere 90.[64] By the end of the war there only remained that part of the German core of the concern that had been left standing in the bombing.

When the period of expansion virtually came to an end in 1941 an unwieldy and untidy industrial colossus had been carved from the spoils of Central Europe. Because so much had been acquired so quickly, and under the conditions of war, the need arose for a reorganization of the original structure of the company. Initially the organization had developed through the Reichswerke AG für Erzbergbau und Eisenhütte 'Hermann Göring'. When the capital of the company was raised from 5 to 400m RM in 1938, 265m RM was taken over by the state, the remainder by other private or state agencies which had no voting rights in the company. A new holding company was formed in 1939 – the Reichswerke AG 'Hermann Göring' – and most of the non-state participation was taken over at the same time by the government.[65] This organization was kept until January 1941 when, under pressure from the scale and nature of the acquisitions since 1939, the company was broken up into three major blocks, still under the control of the central holding company in Berlin but divided according to the nature of the economic activity. The largest block was the Montanblock made up of the iron, steel and mining interests. The second block was an armaments sector organized under the Reichswerke AG für Waffen-und Maschinenbau 'Hermann Göring'. The final block was a small shipping sector under the Reichswerke AG für Binnenschiffahrt 'Hermann Göring'. Subsidiary companies and companies in which a controlling interest was held were grouped roughly according to product into one or other of the blocks.[66] Figure 11.2 shows the structure of the firm in 1941 and its links with other sectors. The most important of these were the linkages with the oil industry, with the holdings of the old Prussian state, through Göring's position as Prime Minister of Prussia, and with the aircraft economy in which Göring had also established a substantial state-owned sector.[67] The concern itself was made up primarily of businesses either wholly owned by the state or with a majority state holding, though some with a minority holding were included where effective control was exercised through the Reichswerke. Because of Göring's insistence on expansion at all costs there had been little attempt either to concentrate or rationalize the concern. It soon became clear that unless something was done the concern would become hidebound in its efforts to cope with what Pleiger called its 'inorganic growth'. In 1942 the discussions with Göring on organization finally led to a decision to divide the concern up by removing the

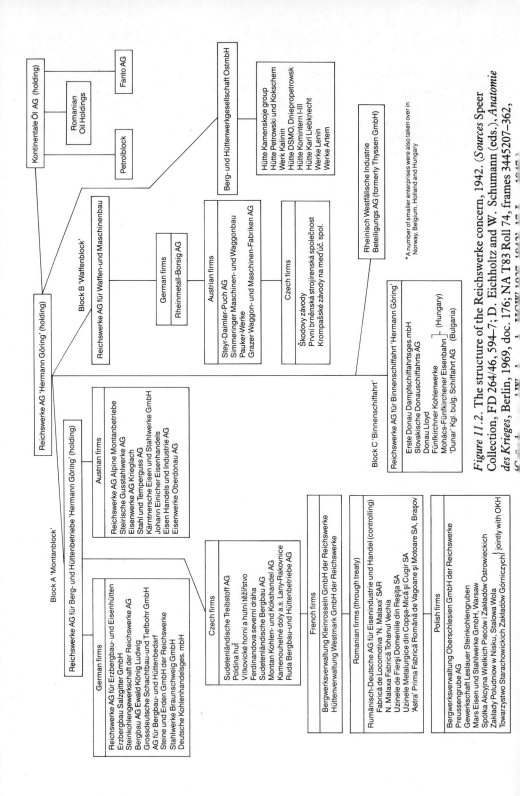

Figure 11.2. The structure of the Reichswerke concern, 1942. (*Sources* Speer Collection, FD 264/46, 594–7; D. Eichholtz and W. Schumann (eds.), *Anatomie des Krieges*, Berlin, 1969, doc. 176; NA T83 Roll 74, frames 3445207–362,

Kontinentale Öl AG (holding)
Petrolblock
Romanian Oil Holdings
Fanto AG

Reichswerke AG 'Hermann Göring' (holding)

Block B 'Waffenblock'
Reichswerke AG für Waffen- und Maschinenbau

German firms
Rheinmetall-Borsig AG

Austrian firms
Steyr-Daimler-Puch AG
Simmeringer Maschinen- und Waggonbau
Pauker-Werke
Grazer Waggon- und Maschinen-Fabriken AG

Czech firms
Škodovy závody
První brněnská strojírenská společnost
Krompašské závody na med'uč. spol.

Rheinisch Westfälische Industrie Beteiligungs AG (formerly Thyssen GmbH)

Berg- und Hüttenwerkgesellschaft OstmbH
Hütte Kamenskoje group
Hütte Petrowski und Kokschem
Werk Kalinin
Hütte DSMO, Dniepropetrowsk
Hütte Kominterm I-III
Hütte Karl Liebknecht
Werke Lenin
Werke Artem

* A number of smaller enterprises were also taken over in Norway, Belgium, Holland and Hungary

Block A 'Montanblock'
Reichswerke AG für Berg- und Hüttenbetriebe 'Hermann Göring' (holding)

German firms
Reichswerke AG für Erzbergbau- und Eisenhütten
Erzbergbau Salzgitter GmbH
Steinkohlengewerkschaft der Reichswerke AG
Bergbau AG Ewald König Ludwig
Grossdeutsche Schachtbau und Tiefbohr GmbH
AG für Bergbau- und Hüttenbedarf
Steine und Erden GmbH der Reichswerke
Stahlwerke Braunschweig GmbH
Deutsche Kohlenhandelsges. mbH

Austrian firms
Reichswerke AG Alpine Montanbetriebe
Steirische Gusstahlwerke AG
Eisenwerke AG Krieglach
Stahl und Temperguss AG
Kärntnersche Eisen und Stahlwerk GmbH
Johann Einicher Eisenhandels
Eisen Handels und Industrie AG
Eisenwerke Oberdonau AG

Czech firms
Sudetenländische Treibstoff AG
Poldina hut'
Vítkovické horni a hutni těžířstvo
Ferdinandova severni dráha
Sudetenländische Bergbau AG
Montan Kohlen- und Kokshandel AG
Kamenouhelné doly a.s. Lany-Rakovnice
Ruda Bergbau- und Hüttenbetriebe AG

French firms
Bergwerksverwaltung Kleinrosseln GmbH der Reichswerke
Hüttenverwaltung Westmark GmbH der Reichswerke

Romanian firms (through treaty)
Rumänisch-Deutsche AG für Eisenindustrie und Handel (controlling)
Fabricà de Locomotive 'N. Malaxà SAR
N. Malaxa Fabricà Tohanul Vechia
Uzinele de Fierşi Domeniile din Reşita SA
Uzinele Metalurgice din Copşa-Mică şi Cugir SA
'Astra' Prima Fabricà Română de Vagoane şi Motoare SA, Braşov

Polish firms
Bergwerksverwaltung Oberschlesien GmbH der Reichswerke
Preussengrube AG
Gewerkschaft Leslauer Steinkohlengruben
Mars Eisen und Stahlwerke GmbH, Warsaw
Spółka Akcyjna Wielkich Pieców i Zakładów Ostrowieckich
Zakłady Południow w Nisku, Stalowa Wola
Towarzystwo Starachowickich Zakładów Górniczych } jointly with OKH

Block C 'Binnenschiffahrt'
Reichswerke AG für Binnenschiffahrt 'Hermann Göring'
Erste Donau Dampfschiffahrtsges.mbH
Slowakische Donauschiffahrts AG
Donau Lloyd
Fünfkirchner Kohlenwerke
Mohács-Fünfkirchener Eisenbahn } (Hungary)
'Dunar' Kgl. bulg. Schifahrt AG (Bulgaria)

Waffenblock from the control of the Reichswerke and, while not abandoning state involvement, placing the manufacturing firms under the leadership of the new production rings set up by Todt and Speer.[68] Göring still insisted on maintaining some links with the armaments sector, appointing his adjutant General Bodenschatz as a liaison officer between them.[69] Effective control over the sector had passed, however, from Göring back to Speer and private industry. The main armaments firms in Czechoslovakia were formed into the Waffenunion Škoda-Brünn and different parts of the concerns brought under the control of the production rings organized in the Reich.[70] The Göring concern was left in control of the Montanblock, which on its own still constituted the largest of its kind in Europe.

One factor that bound together the various parts of the organization was the duplication of personnel in the management of the major branches of the concern. The two most important figures were Paul Körner, Göring's deputy in charge of the Four Year Plan, and Paul Pleiger, the general manager of the Salzgitter-Watenstedt complex. Until Körner was forced to resign through Hitler's insistence in 1943 that Reichstag deputies should not hold business positions, he was the chairman of the entire concern and of its major subsidiaries. Pleiger, who was also general manager of the iron and steel holding company, became his successor.[71] In addition both men were normally appointed as either honorary chairman or director of the major subsidiaries. There were other appointees who similarly worked on the boards of numerous of the Reichswerke businesses: Dr Wilhelm Voss, prominent in the take-over of banking and industry in Czechoslovakia and mainly concerned with the processing side of the concern; Hellmuth Roehnert, general manager of Rheinmetall-Borsig and later general manager of the Junkers aircraft combine, whose main responsibility was with the armaments works; Karl Rasche, the Dresdner Bank representative of the Reichswerke; Paul Rheinländer, one of the first directors of the concern and deputy for Pleiger. Both Voss and Roehnert had wide responsibilities for the commercial expansion into Austria and Czechoslovakia and the latter took over general direction of the Waffenblock when its constitution was changed in 1942. Pleiger had begun to extend his own responsibility for management into the conquered areas in 1939 but was gradually excluded from Austria by the ambitions of Malzacher, manager of the Donawitz holdings, and from Czechoslovakia by Voss.[72] Göring himself maintained a close link with the various parts of the concern by appointing Bodenschatz as a director of its more important components. While actual production management was decentralized, the central direction of the concern was concentrated in the hands of a relatively small group which, through contact with the Four Year Plan office, the banks and the armed forces was in a good position to direct the affairs of the concern in the wider framework of the political and economic demands of war. The structure for policy-making depended on the nature of the decision required. Göring reserved for himself 'all questions of principle as well as matter of special importance'.[73] He took little interest in routine but kept himself informed about the activities of the concern and its links with other state agencies through his own Forschungsamt, both a research and security organization.[74] Anything to do with administration, information auditing, budgetary policy and minor personnel questions was carried out by Körner. Decisions about participation in small enterprises was also left to Körner in co-operation with the appropriate ministries.[75] The main boards and committees met fairly regularly but the huge size of the concern left much of the day-to-day business in the hands of the production management staff at the individual businesses. The independent juridicial status enjoyed by the different firms encouraged the decentralization still further. It was in order to restore the balance between local initiative and central control that the reorganization of 1941 took place.[76] The main task of the central controlling body was to achieve greater co-operation and efficiency by 'setting up production programmes in co-ordination, technical experience, joint support between companies, regulating the position of markets, division of market areas among the companies, price regulations'.[77]

The concern was usually financed directly through the Reich Finance Ministry on behalf of the state and only occasionally through other state agencies such as the Bank der deutschen Luftfahrt which played an important part in financing projects for enterprises producing Luftwaffe material.[78] Some of the finance was found from the occupied territories themselves though no records survive of the relative importance of this method of funding. Many of the assets of the concern were, of course, the product of direct seizure and confiscation and required little or no state investment except to keep them in operation. Moreover, it was policy to encourage firms working for the state war effort to plough profits back into their businesses to relieve the burden on the state. By 1944 the main branches of the concern had advances from the state of more than 1,500m RM, 763m outside the Reich.[79] More is known about the size and distribution of capital employed in the concern, though only for the Montanblock in the period of the split after 1942. The small shipping sector had assets of 89m RM and lay largely outside the Reich.[80] The distribution of capital assets by area together with the net worth of the concern are given in table 11.2. The parent company was heavily dependent on sectors outside the Reich which provided 67 per cent of the fixed assets and 70 per cent of the net assets of the concern. Pleiger estimated that the total capital employed in the concern by the end of 1944 was 4,375m RM excluding the holdings in Poland and Lorraine, which suggests that a final figure in excess of 5,000m RM would represent the Reichswerke at its fullest extent, more than six times larger than the largest concern in pre-war Germany.[81]

Most of the labour of the concern was drawn from outside the Reich as well. The figures for labour employed in the concern are set out in table 11.3. Figures for 'German' workers in the plants usually included Austrians and

Table 11.2. CAPITAL ASSETS, LIABILITIES AND NET VALUE OF PRINCIPAL REICHSWERKE PLANTS BY AREA 1943–4 (mill. RM)*

	Fixed capital[†]	Investments in affiliates	Accounts due from affiliates
Pre-war Germany	1,038,910	210,093	148,098
Austria	355,068	42,341	338,033
Czechoslovakia	1,361,493	55,088	123,900
Poland[‡]	368,446	45,304	31,357
France	34,800[§]	22,834	24,848
Total	3,158,717	375,660	666,236

	Other current assets	Total assets	as %
Pre-war Germany	329,103	1,726,204	32.0
Austria	157,851	893,293	16.6
Czechoslovakia	551,275	2,091,756	38.8
Poland	53,591	498,698	9.3
France	96,350	178,832	3.3
Total	1,188,170	5,388,783	100.0

	Total liabilities	Net worth	as %
Pre-war Germany	1,052,721	672,802	29.9
Austria	583,491	309,802	13.8
Czechoslovakia	1,257,695	835,061	37.1
Poland	99,235	399,463	17.7
France	194,662	34,128	1.5
Total	3,187,804	2,250,937	100.0

* Statements for individual firms were published between September 1942 and September 1944.
† Properties, plants, construction in progress less depreciation.
‡ Excluding steel mills operated on behalf of OKH.
§ French statements include only capital added after acquisition by Reichswerke.

Source: USSBS Special Report 3, 54a.

Sudeten Germans, so that the proportion of workers from the old Reich area was smaller than the aggregate figures suggest. Table 11.3(b) gives the geographical distribution of labour in the concern, showing that 76.5 per cent of the entire workforce was employed outside the Reich. Some, of course, would have been Germans working as skilled or managerial cadres at foreign enterprises. But employment within Germany was also mixed, as more and

Table 11.3. DISTRIBUTION OF LABOUR IN PRINCIPAL
REICHSWERKE PLANTS, 1941–4.

(a) Employment in main plants 1941–4

	Germans*	%	Foreign	%	POWs	%	Total
Dec. 1941	176,339	57.6	121,822	39.7	8,262	2.7	306,423
June 1942	175,554	55.3	133,210	41.9	8,867	2.8	317,631
Dec. 1942	179,544	51.1	151,289	43.2	20,177	5.7	350,640
June 1943	182,807	49.0	166,045	44.5	23,952	6.5	372,804
Dec. 1943	172,192	42.3	180,394	44.2	54,788	13.5	407,374
June 1944	172,186	41.3	188,979	45.3	55,312	13.4	416,477
Dec. 1944	158,285	42.5	168,845	45.2	46,271	12.3	373,401

* Includes *Volksdeutsche* from Austria and Sudetenland.

(b) Distribution by area, June 1944

	Workers	POWs	Total	%
Germany	77,442	15,469	92,911	22.3
Austria	48,096	6,797	54,893	13.2
France	27,617	4,909	32,526	7.8
Czechoslovakia	120,840	12,904	133,744	32.1
Poland	82,403	15,191	97,594	23.4
Others	4,765	42	4,807	1.2
Total in Occupied area	283,721	39,843	323,564	77.7
Grand total	361,163	55,312	416,475	100.0

Source: USSBS Special Report 3, 66–8.

more forced labour was brought into the Reich from occupied Europe. There
is not much evidence of labour or capital shortages for the concern. Capital
had to be argued for at the Reich Finance Ministry and the Economics
Ministry, although this situation was eased by placing officials sympathetic to
the Reichswerke in key positions.[82] If anything, there was a tendency to
over-manning in the less efficient enterprises where production was kept
going at all costs regardless of the best economic interest of the concern.
Productivity declined sharply in the German plants over the war years and it
is likely that under the constant pressure of war the same thing occurred at
those in Occupied Europe. In the competition for capacity and labour
resources the Reichswerke was well placed to resist intrusions into its own
sphere of influence and to hoard its own labour.

Despite the problem of evidence, it is possible to draw some conclusions
about the way in which the concern operated, both in terms of product and

investment policies, and in terms of its competitive relationship with other concerns. Decisions on investment were largely coloured by the order of priority established for war production. New investment was concentrated in those areas where the greatest gains were to be expected, in particular in Silesia, the Sudetenland and in the Ukraine. Here supplies of coal, which proved to be a substantial bottle-neck during the war, were expanded rapidly for the war effort.[83] In other sectors, notably iron and steel, some of the increase in production was the result of the fuller utilization of existing capacity. There is no doubt, however, that substantial investment was undertaken by the Reichswerke in its foreign holdings. In the Steyr-Daimler-Puch works some 328m RM were invested between 1938 and 1943.[84] On taking over control of Škoda investment plans were laid for spending 200m crowns in 1940 alone.[85] Such investment was an obvious necessity if the newly acquired industrial booty was going to be fully utilized for the war effort, though at times, as in Romania, much was promised in the way of investment and little given.[86] Although it had been intended that some investment would come from ploughed-back profits, the Montanblock ran at a loss from 1939 to 1943, as is shown in table 11.4. To this should be added

Table 11.4. NET ANNUAL LOSS OF 'MONTANBLOCK', 1939–43 (RM).

1939	5,420,063
1940	11,732,302
1941	6,362,544
1942	8,630,556
1943	4,268,000

an estimated net loss of 75m RM in the French companies operated by the Reichswerke from 1941 to 1944.[87] There were profits made in the large Czech firms, particularly Vítkovice and Poldina huť, and these were used to offset the losses in other enterprises. Losses were sustained partly because of the massive investment programme called for in establishing new firms and refurbishing old ones, partly because of high operating costs (including the more expensive Salzgitter iron ore and iron), and partly through poorly utilized capacity together with the impact of bombing, which reduced the efficiency of the plants considerably. Reluctance to work for the German war effort must also have been a factor. In 1941 Rheinmetall-Borsig calculated that sales in the German plants came to 9,900 RM per head per year, but in Škoda the figure was only 6,000 RM and at Brno only 5,500 RM.[88]

Despite losses the gross sales of the concern continued to expand rapidly over the course of the war (see table 11.5). Again the concern was very heavily dependent for its sales on enterprises outside the Reich. This remained true of production also. The pattern of production followed the

Table 11.5. COMBINED SALES OF THE REICHSWERKE 'MONTANBLOCK', 1941–4 (mill. RM).

	1941	1942	1943	1944
Pre-war Germany	364,294	584,190	683,250	698,604
Alpine group	156,039	205,122	327,067	371,496
Lorraine steel	122,423	131,244	157,638	87,888
Lorraine coal	12,511	29,615	39,386	29,280
Silesian group	242,746	306,923	348,382	344,292
Vítkovice	230,950	235,857	253,917	267,804
Nordbahn, Prague	45,594	59,416	63,907	55,224
Poldina huť	98,360	101,140	117,828	140,364
Sudeten oil	1,999	33,687	139,708	89,736
Sudeten coal	106,485	121,427	148,814	145,056
Polish steel	75,780	89,254	119,043	80,328
Others	33,876	32,132	34,006	31,932
Grand total	1,491,057	1,930,007	2,432,946	2,342,004

Source: USSBS Special Paper 3, 60.

lines originally intended. Control over the supplies of iron ore led to control over iron and steel production and back into coal production. Railway industries, armaments and shipping were added both to utilize the iron and steel and to ship the materials and finished products in Central Europe. The geographical breakdown of the distribution of production in table 11.6 shows the extent to which the concern depended for most of its iron and steel and coal capacity on the occupied areas. There is insufficient evidence to show the pattern of sales between enterprises in the concern or the flow of trade across pre-war frontiers. In Austria, Czechoslovakia and Romania a considerable amount of the production was used within the country of origin and not sent to the Reich.[89] This was due on the one hand to the existence of an armaments sector in the Occupied economies that was used and expanded with the needs of war, and on the other to the gradual dispersal of production into bomb-safe areas.

Unlike a capitalist multi-national concern, the Reichswerke had to worry little about its operating costs and not at all about its shareholders.[90] Since it was a wartime situation the only sanction was that the concern should be run as efficiently as possible to guarantee maximum output at a reasonable cost. It was clearly a policy of the directors, particularly Pleiger, to increase efficiency by introducing the best available production methods wherever possible. Any attempt to concentration was caught between Göring's insistence that output should be expanded as far as possible even where the long-term effects of such increases might be damaging and Pleiger's own desire to keep the Reichswerke extended to its fullest capacity for fear of its competitors.[91]

Table 11.6. DISTRIBUTION OF REICHSWERKE PRODUCTION BY PRODUCT AND AREA, 1941–4 (in %).

	1941	1942	1943	1944
Iron ore				
Pre-war Germany	58.1	59.1	59.9	60.1
Austria	41.9	37.5	36.3	37.4
Slovakia		3.4	3.8	
Pig iron				
Pre-war Germany	24.8	26.8	27.4	31.7
Austria	20.9	21.0	21.9	24.6
Czechoslovakia	24.4	21.2	18.9	20.7
France	29.9	29.5	30.3	22.1
Poland		1.5	1.5	0.9
Crude steel				
Pre-war Germany	17.1	22.1	21.4	26.8
Austria	17.0	13.5	13.8	14.9
Czechoslovakia	33.6	27.8	26.0	28.6
France	32.3	32.6	34.5	27.3
Poland		4.0	4.3	2.4
Rolling mill products				
Pre-war Germany	20.3	23.8	19.2	25.2
Austria	12.7	13.0	14.4	16.0
Czechoslovakia	32.1	27.8	28.1	31.6
France	34.9	36.5	33.4	24.5
Poland		3.9	4.9	2.7
Bitumous coal				
Pre-war Germany	25.7	22.0	20.3	19.3
Czechoslovakia	17.3	17.4	19.4	19.2
France	1.6	4.9	5.5	4.3
Poland (incl. Silesia)	55.4	55.7	54.8	57.2
Metallurgical coke				
Pre-war Germany	48.6	46.8	45.8	45.4
Czechoslovakia	27.4	26.0	26.0	28.3
Austria		3.9	6.8	7.7
France	6.4	6.9	6.5	3.6
Poland (and Silesia)	17.6	16.4	14.9	15.0
Lignite coal				
Pre-war Germany	20.7	19.8	18.2	18.0
Austria	10.4	9.6	8.8	9.2
Czechoslovakia	68.9	70.6	73.0	72.8

Source: USSBS Special Report 3, 72–3.

A satisfactory relationship between efficiency and output was never fully developed because of the wider political problems involved. Thus little attempt was made to close down inefficient plants or to transfer resources between plants. The allocation of quotas was simply an exercise in wartime economics rather than a strictly economic calculation. The planning of what industry to keep and what to close down was reserved for peacetime.[92] Such a policy was bound to lead to a more wasteful production in the long run. In Austria and Czechoslovakia the Reichswerke operated a near monopoly in heavy industry (except chemicals) and had the opportunity to run and expand the most efficient units; instead it continued to run them all and indeed set about constructing new units from scratch. However necessary from a business-political point of view this tended to spread resources of labour, machinery and managerial expertise more thinly than was compatible with achieving the highest level of exploitation. The Reichswerke might have achieved more if it had been run along the lines of a private trust rather than a state arsenal. Even attempts to make the Reichswerke accept more rational operating methods often miscalculated the extent of dislocation elsewhere. When Hitler insisted that 'experts' from private industry be brought into Russian iron and steel production to help Göring the Ruhr firms did so only with great reluctance as it meant taking skilled men and materials away from the Reich, which would reduce the ability of the efficient Ruhr firms to produce at their optimum.[93]

Part of the explanation for this failure to take the greatest possible advantages of the Reichswerke capacity lay in the fact that competition provided much less incentive than for the private trusts. What competition there was tended to be a jurisdictional and political struggle between private economic groups and the state and Nazi officials, a struggle that usually favoured the Reichswerke. It was necessary, however, to conform to some of the pressures of the market. Some of the coal, iron and steel was sold to private manufacturers and had to be roughly competitive with private production to conform to the structure of costs in government armaments contracts. In the case of iron production at Linz, for example, the state gave a subsidy of 20 RM a ton to cover the difference in production costs between that plant and those of the Reich.[94] On the whole the economic conditions of wartime disguised much of the competition between the private and state concerns. Many of the decisions were made within the broader context of war requirements and increasingly the controls exercised over private firms became indistinguishable from those in state concerns. Where competition did survive, however, it was in terms of who should do the controlling. In some cases the Reichswerke was able to acquire a special position. When, on the other hand, the Reichsvereinigung Eisen was controlled by the Ruhr, relations with the Reichswerke were unsatisfactory.[95] Such competition was felt most keenly in the occupied territories themselves where the Reichswerke specifically excluded private firms or controlled entry and where

Göring was involved in a long series of rivalries with the Labour Front, the SS and the armed forces.[96] The existence of such potential rivalry (it was not always clear that private firms were threatening to forestall Göring) confirmed both Göring and Hitler in the appropriateness of using a giant state concern to expel British and French capital from Eastern Europe, to safeguard the spoils of war and prepare the ground for the New Order in peacetime Europe.

Notes

1. The main source for the material used in the preparation of this paper was the collection of German documents from the Second World War in the Imperial War Museum, London, The most useful collection was that of *Privatfirmen* papers, in particular the partial collection for the Reichswerke 'Hermann Göring', the Rheinmetall-Borsig papers and the files of Steyr-Daimler-Puch. I have also used the records of the Speer Ministry (available on microfilm), the German Air Ministry (also on microfilm) and the Nuremberg Trials. The Strategic Bombing Surveys also proved invaluable. I am at present working on a more general study of the Reichswerke both in Germany and occupied Europe. This present paper represents the fruits of that work in one particular area, the setting up of the Reichswerke concern as it affected Central and Eastern Europe. I have deliberately not included a discussion of Western Europe and Scandinavia although any more general study would have to include them both.

2. A. E. Simpson, *Hjalmar Schacht in Perspective* (The Hague, 1969), 111–25; H. Schacht, *Account Settled* (1949), 98–103; A. S. Milward, 'Fascism and the Economy', in W. Laqueur (ed.), *Fascism: a Reader's Guide* (1976), 432–5.

3. *Trials of the War Criminals before the Nuremberg Military Tribunal* (hereafter cited as *TWC*) (Washington, 14 vols.), XII, 575 Doc. NI-125. For a more general discussion of the Four Year Plan see B. Carroll, *Design for Total War* (The Hague, 1968), 142–50; D. Petzina, *Autarkiepolitik im Dritten Reich* (Stuttgart, 1968); Simpson, *op cit.*, 132–59.

4. *TWC*, XIII, Doc. NID;15575, letter from Pleiger to Göring 5 Dec. 1941 and Pleiger to Körner 5 Dec. 1941. In this case a sum of 3m RM was sent to Göring for his personal use out of the profits of Vítkovice and Poldina huť in Czechoslovakia.

5. Paul Körner was deputy for Göring in the Four Year Plan and chairman of the Reichswerke until 1943. Wilhelm Keppler was Göring's personal economic adviser and one of the main business supporters of the party. He was made Reich commissioner in Vienna in 1938. Hans Kehrl was an industrial manager who worked in the Economics Ministry. He was brought into the Four Year Plan to help run the raw material department, rising to high office in the war economic structure under Speer as head of the *Planungsamt*. Paul Pleiger, son of a miner, became a small Ruhr industrialist and an economic adviser to the Nazis after 1933. He was head of the original Salzgitter works and became chairman of the Reichswerke in 1943. Wilhelm Voss, who helped run the state auditing company Deutsche Revision und Treuhand AG, became a leading figure on the commercial and legal side of the Reichswerke, eventually running the main weapons sector of the concern after 1941.

6. R. Brady, *Business as a System of Power* (New York, 1943) 3, 49–50, who described the Reichswerke as 'a privatized regrouping of industrial properties previously owned by the Reich'; F. Neumann, *Behemoth* (1942), 299; Petzina, *op. cit.*, 105–6. For a contemporary view see E. Schrewe, 'Die Entwicklung der Betriebsgrössen in der gewerblichen Wirtschaft', *Zeitschrift für gesamte Staatswissenschaft*, CII (1942).

7. M. Riedel, *Eisen und Kohle für das Dritte Reich* (Göttingen, 1973), 155–232.

8. *Nazi Conspiracy and Aggression* (hereafter cited as *NCA*) (8 vols., Washington,

1946), VII, 543–7, Doc. EC-485 'conference under the Chairmanship of the Reichsmarshal on October 1 1940 about the economic exploitation of the occupied territories'.

9. *TWC*, XIII, 670 Doc. NID-13436, 'Arisierungsbericht' Böhmische Escompte Bank, 6 Aug 1941.

10. A good example was the purchase of Werk Radom in Poland whose book value in 1940 had been 33m zł. By fixing an arbitrary exchange rate, calculating notional sums for depreciation and by subtracting the assets seized as booty at the time of the invasion, the final agreed purchase price was only 7m RM instead of the 16m RM it would have been in 1939. See Speer Collection FD 787/46, 'Werke in Warschau und Radom', 13 Aug. 1943.

11. *TWC*, XIII, 666–7, Doc. NID-13927; letter from Kehrl to Rasche, 18 Apr. 1940, 'concerning repayment to the Desdner Bank of the purchase price of Czech industrial shares'; letter from Reichswerke to Kehrl giving details of a commission of 200,000 RM paid to the Dresdner Bank for agency work. K. Lachmann 'The Hermann Göring Works', *Social Research*, VIII (1941), 33.

12. Speer Collection, FD 787/46, Steyr-Daimler-Puch records, description of firm, 15 Sept. 1943.

13. Royal Institute of International Affairs, *Hitler's Europe* (1954), 206.

14. *TWC*, XII, 468–9 Doc. NI-09, Minutes of a discussion of the work group on iron and steel production, 17 Mar. 1937. Göring was reported as saying: 'it is important that the soil of Austria is reckoned as a part of Germany in case of war. Such deposits as can be acquired in Austria must be attended to in order to increase our supply capacity'.

15. Riedel, *op. cit.*, 234–42.

16. W. Carr, *Arms, Autarky and Aggression* (1972), 62–3.

17. Riedel, *op. cit.*, 242–3; *Der deutsche Volkswirt*, XIII (1938/9), 1091–2.

18. Lachmann, *op. cit.*, 30–1.

19. Speer Collection, FD 264/46, 594–7, 'Konzern Verzeichnis HGW Montanblock' (hereafter cited as 'Konzern Verzeichnis'); Riedel, *op. cit.*, 241.

20. Eisenwerke Oberdonau was set up jointly with OKH to undertake army production. See Speer Collection, Reel 63, FD 3742/45 File 1, letter from OKH to Eisenwerke Oberdonau GmbH 'betr. Finanzierung des weiteren Ausbaues der Eisenwerke Oberdonau', 1 Apr. 1944. The firm was under the full management of the Reichswerke.

21. *Der deutsche Volkswirt*, XIII (1938/9), 405; Lachmann, *op. cit.*, 31.

22. 'Konzern Verzeichnis', 594–7.

23. Acquisition of Steirische Gusstahlwerke gave ownership of three marketing companies in Brazil, Argentina and Uruguay and of Steel and Machinery Supplies (Pty) Ltd, Johannesburg, with a capital of £1,000.

24. United States Strategic Bombing Survey Special Paper No. 3, *The Effects of Strategic Bombing upon the Operations of the Herman Goering Works during World War II* (Washington, 1946/7), 42; *Conditions in Occupied Territories (5): the Penetration of German Capital into Europe* (1942), 10–11.

25. Lachmann, *op. cit.*, 32; 'Konzern Verzeichnis', 596.

26. W. Birkenfeld, *Der synthetische Treibstoff 1933–1945* (Göttingen, 1963), 135–7.

27. National Archives (hereafter cited as NA), Washington DC, Microcopy T83 Roll 74, frame 3445163–4, IG Farben volkswirtschaftliche Abteilung 'Konzernaufbau und Entwicklung der Reichswerke AG für Erzbergbau and Eisenhütten "Hermann Göring", 19 Oct. 1939.

28. A. Teichova, *An Economic Background to Munich* (1974), 123–7.

29. NA Microcopy T177 Roll 3, frame 3684568, Wirtschaftsinspektion Prag to RLM, 30 Sept. 1939; Bundesarchiv (BA) RL 3 3, Folder 1, report from Udet to Göring 'Problem der Rüstungsindustrie Dez. 1939'.

30. Teichova, *op. cit.*, 82–3, 118.

31. NA Microcopy T 83 Roll 77, frames 3449351–5, Jahresabschluss der Brünn-Königsfelder Maschinen-und Waggonbau-Fabriks AG für den 31.12.1939 Prüfungsbericht der Treuarbeit; *TWC*, XIII, 710, Rasche Defence Exhibit 3.

32. *TWC*, XIII, 657, Doc. NID-939, letter from Böhmische Escompte Bank to

Kehrl, 12 June 1939; 667, Doc. NID-13927, letter from Reichswerke to Kehrl, 26 Mar. 1940; 668, letter from Reichswerke to Kehrl (n.d.).

33. *Ibid.*

34. NA Microcopy T83 Roll 77, frame 3449313, 'Verteilung des Aktienbesitzes von Skodawerke und Brünner Waffenwerke, 6.11.1940'; frame 3449318–20, 'Abschrift betr. Beteiligung des Reichs an der Aktiengesellschaft vormals Skodawerke in Pilsen', Oct. 1940.

35. NA Microcopy T83 Roll 77, frame 3449356, report from Reichsfinanzministerium 'betr. Erste Brünner Maschinen-Fabriks-Ges.', 10 Sept. 1940.

36. K. Lachmann, 'More on the Hermann Göring Works', *Social Research*, IX (1942), 397; *Conditions in Occupied Territories*, 11.

37. Teichova, *op. cit.*, 193–245 for details on Škoda-Works before 1939.

38. 'Konzern Verzeichnis', 596; *TWC*, XIII, 662–4 Doc. NID-15640 (see n. 32).

39. F. Morton, *The Rothschilds* (1962), 224–6; Teichova, *op. cit.*, 82–3.

40. *Ibid.*, 91–2. A full managing contract was finally drawn up between Vítkovice and the Reichswerke in December 1942. See *TWC*, Transcripts Case XI, vol. 231, 14883.

41. BA/RL3 243, report from RLM agent at Firma Letov 17 Aug. 1942 concerning discussions with the Slovakian Luftwaffe; *Conditions in Occupied Territories*, 12. In Slovakia Vítkovice controlled the 'Ruda' Bergbau-und Hüttenbetriebe AG, Bratislava and the Krompacher Kupferwerke AG.

42. USSBS Special Paper 3, 42; 'Konzern Verzeichnis', 596.

43. These figures can only be approximations. In Czechoslovakia the Göring Werke clearly had an interest in the mining and metallurgy sector of approximately 60–70 per cent of its total value. In metalworking the proportion was probably closer to 40 per cent. The estimates are based on figures in Teichova, *op. cit.*, 87; 'Konzern Verzeichnis', 594–7; and NA Microcopy T83 Roll 74, frames 3445174–7. Because all the details of minority participations are not available such estimates are probably conservative.

44. *NCA*, VII, 310, Doc. collection EC-137, letter from Göring to Wehrwirtschaft-und Rüstungsamt on 'German influence with foreign enterprises', 9 Aug. 1940, in which he wrote that 'One of the goals of the German economic policy is the increase of the German influence with foreign enterprises'.

45. D. Eichholtz, *Geschichte der deutschen Kriegswirtschaft 1939–1945* (Berlin, 1969), 185–6 and 294–338 (document collection 'Ruhr-Montankonzerne').

46. Riedel, *op. cit.*, 275–6.

47. *TWC*, XIII, 742–5, Doc. Koerner 177 'Affidavid of Max Winkler, Director of Main Trustee Office East, 7.5.1948'; 749, Doc. NI-598; R. Jeske, 'Zur Annexion der polnischen Wojewodschaft Schlesien durch Hitler-Deutschland im Zweiten Weltkrieg' *Zeitschrift für Geschichtswissenschaft*, V (1957), 1073–5, 1087.

48. USSBS Special Report 3, 42, 73; Riedel, *op. cit.*, 301–2. The following firms had substantial Reichswerke participation by 1944:

Bergbau-Elektrizitäts-AG, Kattowitz
Kokerei-Vereinigung GmbH, Katowitz
Oberschlesische Hydrierwerke AG, Blechhammer
Schlesische Elektrizität -und Gas AG, Gleiwitz
Schlesisch-Sandomir'sche Schiffahrtsges.mbh. Krakau
Sprengstoffwerke Oberschlesien GmbH, Katowitz
Vereinigte Holzindustrie Ost GmbH, Kattowitz
(*Source:* 'Konzern Verzeichnis', 595.)

49. USSBS, Special Report 3, 42–3; Riedel, *op. cit.*, 300. The firms were Ostrowiecer Hochöfen-und Werke AG, Werk Starachowice (through Vítkovice) and Werk Stalowa Wola (through Poldina huť).

50. Speer Collection, FD 787/46, Protokoll über die am 13.8.1943 abgehaltene Sitzung des Aufsichtsrates der Steyr-Daimler-Puch, Beilage 3 'Werke in Warschau und Radom'.

51. Speer Collection, Reel 63, FD 3742/45 File 1, Staatssekretär Regierung des Generalgouvernements to Speer, 30 Nov.

1943 'betr. Einsatz polnischer Betriebe in der Rüstungswirtschaft'.

52. BA/RL3 18, File 1, Kurzbericht 31, 21 Sept. 1941, 1–2; *TWC*, XIII 847, Doc. EC207 'Decree of the Führer concerning the Economy of the Newly Occupied Eastern Territories of 29 June 1941'.

53. *TWC*, XIII 892–5, Doc. NI-5261, letter from Körner enclosing minutes of a meeting on 31 Mar. 1943 of the Verwaltungsrat of BHO; D. Eichholtz and W. Schumann (eds.), *Anatomie des Krieges* (Berlin, 1969), Dok. 176 'Rundschreiben der Wirtschaftsgruppe Eisenschaffende Industrie vom 21 August 1941'. The following firms came under the direct trusteeship of the Reichswerke in 1943:
Hütte Kamenskoje group
Hütte Petrowski und Kokschem, Werk Kalinin, in Dnjepropetrowsk
Hütte DSMO in Dnjepropetrowsk
Hütte Komintern I-III in Dnjepropetrowsk-Nishnedneprowsk
Hütte Karl Liebknecht in Dnjepropetrowsk-Nishnedneprowsk
Werke Lenin in Dnjepropetrowsk
Werk Artem in Dnjepropetrowsk-Nishnedeprowsk

54. A. Dallin, *German Rule in Russia* (1957), 385–8; Eichholtz and Schumann (eds.); *op. cit.*, 411–12, Dok. 217 (Grundsätze für die Führung von Patenschaftsbetrieben der BHO von 3 November 1942'.

55. E. Campus, 'Die Hitlerfaschistische Infiltration Rumäniens 1939–40', *Zeitschrift für Geschichtswissenschaft*, V (1957); N. N. Constantinescu, 'L'Exploitation et le pillage de l'économie roumaine par l'Allemagne hitlérienne dans la période 1939–1944', *Revue roumaine d'histoire*, III (1964).

56. P. Marguerat, *Le IIIᵉ Reich et le pétrole roumain 1938–1940* (Leiden, 1977), 180; Lachmann, 'Hermann Göring Works', 34; *Conditions in Occupied Territories*, 29. Two of the directors of the company were Albert Göring and Guido Schmidt. The latter had been installed by Göring as general director of the Linz complex in return for his help in the period of the Anschluss.

57. A. Hillgruber, *Hitler, König Carol and Marschall Antonescu* (Wiesbaden, 1954), 156.

58. Lachmann, 'More on the Hermann Göring Works', 396–7; Constantinescu, *op. cit.*, 112.

59. *Ibid.*, 110. The demands were made through the Reich envoy, Neubacher.

60. *Ibid.*, 112; *Conditions in Occupied Territories*, 29. Reichswerke participation was 75m lei out of a total of 3m lei.

61. M. Pearton, *Oil and the Roumanian State* (1971), 231; Hillgruber, *op. cit.*, 157; British Intelligence Objectives Sub-Committee (BIOS) Final Report 513 *Notes on the Organisation of the German Petroleum Industry during the War*, 7.

62. *Conditions in Occupied Territories*, 29.

63. Eichholtz and Schumann (eds.), *op. cit.*, Dok. 190, 'Protokoll der Sitzung des Aufsichtsrats der Kontinentale ÖI AG am 13 Januar 1942'; *TWC*, XIII, 863, Doc. NI-440, Körner to economic authorities, 20 Nov. 1941, enclosing a memorandum 'on the essential results of the discussion of economic policy and economic organisation in the recently occupied eastern territories'; Pearton, *op. cit.*, 231.

64. Speer Collection, Reel 63, FD 3742/45 File 1, Reichswirtschaftsministerium to Göring, 15 May 1944.

65. Riedel, *op cit.*, 231–2; *TWC*, Transcripts of Case XI, vol. 231, 14839.

66. USSBS Special Paper 3, 43–4; *TWC*, Transcripts of Case XI, vol. 231, 14845–14855; W. Huppert, 'Konzern-Organisation', *Der deutsche Volkswirt*, XVI (1941/2), 844–6.

67. R. J. Overy, *German Aircraft Production 1939–1942* (Ph.D. thesis, University of Cambridge), 117–125, for details on the state sector of the aircraft industry.

68. *TWC*, Transcripts of Case XI, vol. 231, 14843, 14859–62. The exact timing of the change is unclear. Steyr-Daimler-Puch, for example, officially left the Reichswerke only in 1943 and Voss continued to act as its chairman until replaced by Roehnert in March 1943. See Speer Collection, FD 785/46, Satzung der Steyr-Daimler-Puch AG; FD 787/46 letter from Roehnert to Göring, 26 Feb. 1943.

69. Speer Collection, FD 787/46 Protokoll über die am 13 August 1943 abgehaltene

Sitzung des Aufsichtsrates der Steyr-Daimler-Puch AG, 3–4.

70. *TWC*, Transcripts of Case XI, vol. 231, 14875.

71. *TWC*, XIII, 893, Doc. NI-5261.

72. *TWC*, Transcripts of Case XI, vol. 231, 14859, 14871, 14877, 14893–4. There are numerous references in the documents to individual directors but unfortunately very few complete lists of directors. Certainly in many foreign firms both Germans and native businessmen served side by side on the boards of directors.

73. *TWC*, XIII, 745 Doc. Koerner 177. Although this statement was made in Körner's defence and could thus be interpreted as an attempt to shift responsibility onto Göring, there is enough evidence from contemporary documents of Göring's personal concern to supervise major decision-making to confirm that this was indeed the process. See, for example, Speer Collection, FD 787/46 Protokoll, 13 Aug. 1943, 9.

74. *TWC*, Transcripts of Case XI, vol. 231, 14842–3.

75. For example, Speer Collection, FD 783/46 letter from Roehnert to Thomas, 3 Jan. 1942 'betr. Verkauf der Beteiligung der Rheinmetall-Borsig AG an die Basch-Jaeger-Lüdenscheider Metallwerke AG, Lüdenscheid'; letter from Roehnert to Wessig, 23 July 1941; letter from Voss to Roehnert, 26 July 1941.

76. Pleiger confirmed this situation at his trial. Pleiger had in fact produced a memorandum on the inorganic growth of the combine on 21 Apr. 1940 and sent it to Göring. See *TWC*, Transcripts of Case XI, vol. 231, 14843–8.

77. *Ibid.*, 14847.

78. *Conditions in Occupied Territories*, 7, 12.

79. USSBS Special Paper 3, 54a, table 8, 'Summary of Assets, Liabilities and Net Worth of Principal Subsidiaries of the Hermann Göring Group'.

80. *Ibid.*, 55.

81. Lachmann, 'More on the Hermann Göring Works', 396; USSBS Special Paper 3, 54–5; Riedel, *op. cit.*, 359; *Conditions in Occupied Territories*, 5.

82. The Reich Finance Minister himself looked favourably on the Reichswerke. See S. von Krosigk, *Staatsbankrott* (Stuttgart, 1974), 233–4. Pleiger's

associate Gabel was appointed Chef der Bergbauabteilung in the Economics Ministry at the same time that Funk replaced Schacht. Both these men reduced the resistance of the Economics Ministry to Göring's activities. See Riedel, *op. cit.*, 231–2.

83. *Ibid.*, 303. A total investment of 120m RM was made between April 1940 and December 1944 to raise output from 55,000 to 120,000 tons per day.

84. Speer Collection, FD 787/46 Protokoll über die am 8 September 1944 abgehaltene Sitzung des Aufsichtsrates der Steyr-Daimler-Puch. The investment was made up as follows:

improvements   52m RM
new projects   212m RM
subsidiary   56m RM
state loans   8m RM

See also *TWC*, Transcripts of Case XI, vol. 231, 14895–6.

85. NA Microcopy T83 Roll 77, frame 3449320, Abschrift betr. Beteiligung des Reiches an der Aktiengesellschaft vormals Skodawerke in Pilsen, Okt. 1940.

86. Constantinecu, *op. cit.*, 111–12.

87. USSBS Special Paper 3, 57–9. Alpine was run without loss for the first time in 1944.

88. Speer Collection, FD 717/46, Rheinmetall-Borsig 'Bericht über die Entwicklung im Jahr 1941', 20 Apr. 1942, 3.

89. USSBS Special Paper 3, 60.

90. *TWC*, Transcripts of Case XI, vol. 231, 14863–4. Pleiger claimed that 'the interests of the Reich in its capacity as shareholder were first of all safeguarded by the Reich Ministry of Economics and . . . later on . . . the Plenipotentiary of the Four Year Plan managed this responsibility'.

91. Göring, for example, wanted to expand output of ore from the Erzberg, against the advice of his deputies, to 20,000 tons per day when the original plan had called for 10,000 tons. Similarly Hitler's demand for an expansion of steel output in 1943 forced Göring to insist upon huge but unmanageable increases in production from the Linz plant whatever the cost elsewhere.

92. Royal Institute of International Affairs, *Hitler's Europe*, 194ff.

93. Dallin, *op. cit.*, 384–5; Riedel, *op. cit.*, 323–4.
94. USSBS Special Paper 3, 61. Pleiger calculated that the difference in the level of production costs between the Austrian and German part of the concern was 20 per cent in 1938.
95. Riedel, *op. cit.*, 279ff.; Eichholtz and Schumman (eds.), *op. cit.*, 451, Dok. 251, 'Bericht von W. Schieber (Leiter des Rüstungslieferungsamtes) für A. Speer,
23.6.1944'. Pleiger himself claimed that his point of view was 'what is healthful for competition is dangerous to the Hermann Göring Works'. See *TWC*, Transcripts of Case XI, vòl. 231, 14842.
96. *NCA*, VII, 310–11 Doc. EC-137, EC-485; E. Georg, *Die wirtschaftlichen Unternehmungen der SS* (Stuttgart, 1963), 52; Lachmann, 'The Hermann Göring Works', 29.

COMMENTARY *Waclaw Długoborski*

The 'Reichswerke Hermann Göring' concern is correctly seen as a typically 'fascist' enterprise, its fascist nature being clearly discernible in the purposes for which it was founded, in its expansion tactics, and in its system of management. The first two factors have been discussed by economists and historians. R. J. Overy has broken new ground in dealing with the third, comparing the economic functioning of the Reichswerke with that of the other, older German mining-metallurgical concerns, whose origins and growth were not solely attributable to the Nazi system and its territorial expansion.

Overy rightly stresses that in the case of the Reichswerke 'an interpretation simply on business grounds is unsatisfactory' and also that, in the words of Göring, 'purely economic considerations were unimportant'. I should like to propose a broader examination of this point, returning to the discussion of the 'economic mentality' of Hitler and the Nazi party elite, and the objectives they set out to achieve in their internal and external policies.[1] As for Hitler himself, it was not so much that he under-estimated the importance of economic problems but rather that he envisaged their solution by non-economic means. His method in this matter – as in many others – was to rely on an escalation of compulsion and force, starting with administrative injunctions and prohibitions, through political and military pressure, up to armed aggression, plunder and terror. The economic concepts of Hermann Göring were in a similar category. Already before the Machtübernahme, within the narrow circle of the top party executive it was he who: (1) maintained continuous close contact with the representatives of heavy industry, extracting financial aid for the NSDAP from this source; (2) represented the interests and attitudes of the Nazi party in economic matters; and (3) categorically rejected 'socialist daydreams' in all discussions on the

NSDAP economic programme, standing out for an uncompromisingly pragmatic policy, i.e. in accordance with the economic needs of the large industrial concerns.[2]

Broadly speaking these needs, particularly in the case of the mining-metallurgical concerns, were increased assistance from the authoritarian, hence strong and active, state apparatus. This was designed to stabilize the market situation by allocating government contracts, including armaments, and to reinforce the position of German industry in foreign markets by political pressures. Simultaneously administrative coercion (suppression of workers' class-orientated organizations, curtailing the mobility of the workers, etc.) kept the labour market subservient to the needs of the industrialists, enabling the freezing of wages and hence the stabilization or reduction of production costs. These generally known facts are quoted merely to stress that other industrial concerns, operating in the same sector as Reichswerke Hermann Göring, were ready to profit from, and actually did profit from, the administrative-political exogenic means of economic coercion offered first by the Nazi party, and then by the Nazi state. It is noteworthy that during the Second World War they were quick to take advantage of the opportunities created by the Nazi state for expropriation/theft of the production potential of the Occupied countries plus compulsory exploitation of their labour force. It is conjectural whether this was simply profiting from the situation created by Nazi aggression and annexation, or if these concerns were directly involved in creating these opportunities, in developing and implementing the Nazi economic and social policies in the Occupied countries, or even actually in the inception of these annexation plans. Certainly German heavy industry juntas had, much earlier, proved their abilities in such undertakings, the traditions going back to the Wilhelmine period. It is also instructive to note the remarkable similarity between the concepts of the Deutsches Institut für Technische Arbeitsschulung (DINTA) set up by the Rhineland-Westphalia concerns in the early 1920s, and the corresponding points of the NSDAP programme. As regards social policy, DINTA postulated the introduction of compulsory labour service (*Arbeitsdienst*), endeavoured to inculcate in workers the spirit of *Betriebsgemeinschaft* or *Werksgemeinschaft* (virtually identical with the Nazi *Volksgemeinschaft* ideology), and proposed that industrial plants should be organized and managed on the *Führerprinzip*.[3]

Considered in this context, the creation of the Reichswerke concern and its operations may be regarded as a blatant and extreme instance of certain practices already well established in German industry. Arguments as to whether some of the German industrialists and managers were particularly susceptible to Nazi ideas and methods, or whether the Nazis adopted the already developed concepts of these industrialists may be dismissed as a tautological exercise. However, not to discern the differences between Reichswerke and the private heavy industry concerns would be oversimplification. R. J. Overy has distinguished and analysed these differences. I should like to broaden and deepen that analysis.

For the privately owned German iron and steel concerns, seeking aid from the state and reaching for exogenic means of operation, particularly in external expansion (new locations in under-developed countries, export of products and import of raw materials), was an economic necessity. Difficulties encountered in the switch from war to peacetime production between 1918 and 1923, lost time in the race for technical advance, and the lack of capital reserves severely handicapped them in competition with the heavy industry of the U.S.A., England and to a certain degree even France and Belgium. These difficulties were still evident during both the 1929–33 crisis period and the post-crisis recovery. After 1933, the Third Reich tried to overcome these difficulties by politico-military or politico-economic pressure, or again, as in the case of Bulgaria, Hungary and Spain, by appealing to common political aims and ideology. Where rivalry was purely economic, German capital still felt itself to be unfairly handicapped, even in the Balkan countries, which at that time were considered the 'informal German Empire'. This was admitted, in November 1939, by the 'Mitteleuropäischer Wirtschaftstag', representing the expansionist circles of German monopolist capital, when it recommended the prenetration 'dort wo bereits deutsche Aufträge nach dem Südosten gegangen sind [referring to import of industrial raw materials], die Bezahlung durch deutsche Lieferungen und im Notfalle durch Beteiligung an deutschen Unternehmungen im Südosten (Versuch, etwa Aktien dortiger Neugründungen unterzubringen)', and also recommended the widening of 'Beteiligungen an bestehenden industriellen Unternehmungen, [nur dann] wenn wir das nicht in Devisen, sondern durch Sachgütereinlagen können'.[4] When they could not, however, get away without currency payment, as was the case when increasing their holdings in the industry of Romania, France or Belgium, the more traditional methods of expansion were utilized, only resorting to a show of superior power in certain particular transactions. Reichswerke, on the other hand, based its expansion plans primarily on direct expropriation, paying a merely symbolic purchase price, in the case of Poland payable on the account of Haupttreuhandstelle-Ost. It would be interesting to calculate what percentage of the Reichswerke production potential was acquired by 'aryanization', the expropriation of state property in the occupied territories, or confiscation of Allied (French and English) property as took place in Austria, Czechoslovakia (though here purchase was made in some cases) and Poland, and what percentage of this potential came into the hands of the concern by more or less normal purchase, as in Romania and probably in France. From table 11.2 it may be seen that in the year 1943–4 the total net assets in the first three countries represented 68.5 per cent of the Reichswerke assets; and this calculation does not take into account industrial plants in the occupied territories of the U.S.S.R., at that time already abandoned by the Germans.

This method of annexation and restructuring could be most freely and broadly applied in East Central and Eastern Europe. In South-East Europe expansion was hindered either by the policy of maintaining the economic sovereignty of the satellite states, as in Hungary and Romania (in my opinion Overy over-estimates the role and influence of Reichswerke in Romania) or again, as in conquered and occupied Greece and Yugoslovia, where it was essential to avoid friction with Italian interests and also those of other German concerns, primarily Krupp's, who after 1941 had come into possession of the deposits of bauxite, chrome and iron ores. In Western and Northern Europe the economic policy of the Third Reich envisaged co-operation with the heavy industry potentates of the Occupied countries, to win friends rather than to seize by force. It is noteworthy that state-owned assets, the most 'convenient' for Nazi appropriation, accounted for only a small proportion of the whole in the industry of Belgium, Holland, occupied France and Norway. It was different in Poland, where the state owned at least 50 per cent of Upper Silesian industrial potential; and even more so in the Soviet Union, where in effect the whole economic potential of the country was state-owned, thus facilitating German efforts to adapt the economic structure of the Occupied territories totally to their purposes. In Poland their task was less easy in the Occupied part (i.e. the General-Gouvernement), while in the annexed territory, particularly in Upper Silesia, the Reichs-werke's moves to take over the most important mining and metallurgical plants met with opposition from concerns from the western, German parts of this province (and not 'trustees from the Ruhr industry') who were anxious to regain the property lost in 1921 or 1937. Here, indeed, the Reichswerke had to admit defeat in certain cases – 'Giesches Erben wollen wieder erben', – said Göring ironically in September 1939.[5] Eastwards of Upper Silesia, in the Dąbrowa Basin, which before 1914 had belonged to Russia, Reichswerke managed to grab the largest plants, above all the coal mines. This was the reason for the large share of 'Polish' parts of the concern in its total coal production (57.2 per cent in 1944: see table 11.6), while that in other production sectors was insignificant. The setting up and development of the Upper Silesian section of the Reichswerke itself (Bergwerksverwaltung Oberschlesien GmbH der Reichswerke Hermann Göring), and the history of the individual mines and steelworks seized by the Reichswerke during the Second World War, has not yet been adequately researched although there is no lack of source material in Polish archives. The same applies to the Czechoslovak section of Reichswerke. I feel that investigation of this problem would be of value both to document the overall activities of the Reichswerke concern and to elucidate the methods employed by the Third Reich to exploit the countries of East Central Europe.

Notes

1. Cf. J. D. Heyl, 'Hitler's economic thought: A reappraisal', *Central European History*, VI (1973), 83–96; H. A. Turner Jr, 'Hitler's Einstellung zu Wirtschaft und Gesellschaft vor 1933', *Geschichte und Gesellschaft*, II (1976), 89–117.
2. O. Wagener in H. A. Turner Jr (ed.), *Hitler aus nächster Nähe. Aufzeichnungen eines Vertrauten 1929–1932* (Frankfurt/Main and Berlin 1979), 226–9 and 441–3.
3. G. Albrecht, 'Arbeitsgemeinschaft, Betriebsgemeinschaft, Werksgemeinschaft', *Jahrbücher für Nationalökonomie und Statistik*, III/73 (1928), I, 530ff.
4. Cf. Bundesarchiv/Militärarchiv (Freiburg i.Br.), Wi I/167, 138–9.
5. Quoted in W. Długoborski and C. Madajczk, 'Ausbeutungssysteme in den besetzten Gebieten Polens und der UdSSR', in J. Forstmeier and H. E. Volkmann (eds.), *Kriegswirtschaft und Rüstung 1939–1945* (Düsseldorf, 1977).

COMMENTARY *Robert Waller*

I would firstly like to make it clear that I have not undertaken a specific study of the Reichswerke 'Hermann Göring', and that I am only able to comment on R. J. Overy's paper insofar as the activities of this large combine cross the path of my own individual research field.[1] I wish to discuss Overy's paper partly in the form of an explanation as to why a case study of the Reichswerke ought to be approached by researchers in a fundamentally different vein than, for example, the activities of other multi-national enterprises which have already been discussed here, and partly also in the form of a reply to some points specifically raised by Overy.

First, the Reichswerke was not a business enterprise whose primary goal in the 'classical sense' was to seek to maximize its profits at all times, or indeed even to obtain its optimum scale of output. This, of course, arises from the fact that the enterprise was a state-owned one, and also because Germany's economic preparation for war – in which the Reichswerke figures prominently – made profit and efficiency considerations of the combine purely secondary. This was made apparent from the time of the very foundation of the concern in 1937, when the ostensible economic purpose of the setting-up of the combine – which was to open up and exploit Germany's low-grade iron ore deposits in the Salzgitter region – was viewed by Germany's more conservative financial and business circles as a hazardous and probably unprofitable business venture. It is quite likely therefore that the majority of the various organic parts comprising the total structure of the Reichswerke operated constantly under conditions of diminishing returns and hence higher average costs, because the main criteria governing the business practices of the concern was simply in the short term to produce as much as it possibly could with available resources. Moreover, such business ventures of the Reichswerke that were indeed unprofitable were undertaken at the same time in the full knowledge that the concern had the full backing of the financial resources of the state. In a similar vein, the constant quest by the Reichswerke for subsidiaries in the wake of Germany's territorial expansion after 1938 was not undertaken in the light of pure profit considerations, but rather out of the economic necessities brought on by Germany's preparations for war. To end my first point, therefore, the researcher should not expect to find and indeed often will not find rational behaviour in the business practices of the Reichswerke.

Second, the unprecedented speed of both vertical and horizontal expansion of the Reichswerke calls into question problems relating to its organizational structure. In the space of just four years – from the time of its foundation in 1937 to the peak year of its growth in 1941 – the Reichswerke rose to become one of the three largest business empires in Europe, mainly due to the acquisition of foreign subsidiaries. Even if, therefore, the objective of the Reichswerke's business managers was to instil as much efficiency into the concern as possible, time would clearly have prohibited its accomplishment. In short, whether in the production, marketing, or managerial sectors of the entire combine, a higher degree of optimum utilization of factors of production or techniques of production could not have made themselves available in so short a period of time.

Third, as Overy's paper rightly stresses, the foundation of the Reichswerke had very clear political overtones. Its foundation was in part a response to the disinclination of private capital interests to undertake the exploitation of the low-grade Salzgitter ores, which was strongly desired by Germany's economic leaders, on the one hand, while on the other hand the Reichswerke was intended to rival and replace German private capital interests in the exploitation of Germany's own economic resources as well as those of the annexed and occupied territories. In this context also the Reichswerke was intended by Germany's economic leaders to act as a spearhead in the creation of an economic New Order in Europe in accordance not with the profit motivations of private capital, but with Nazi political, racial and economic conceptions. In this respect, it is indeed surprising that hitherto the Reichswerke has been somewhat overlooked and even exempted from the historical literature concerning the relationship between the Nazi party and private capitalism. Yet it surely cannot be without significance to a discussion of their relationship that the Reichswerke enjoyed a clear privileged position in acquiring industrial subsidiaries in the wake of Germany's territorial expansion after 1938, and which at the same time was very strongly envied by the interests of German private capital.[2] In the cases of Austria and Czechoslovakia respectively it was clear that the most important industrial concerns in the heavy industry of these territories were earmarked for acquisition by the Reichswerke by Germany's economic leaders, even before the actual political events leading to the German annexation of these lands, so that there occurred little or no competition from other German concerns for them.[3] In the Protectorate of Bohemia and Moravia, where the Reichswerke gained control of more than 50 per cent of coal production and more than 75 per cent of steel production, as well as the Škoda armaments combine, such figures clearly sustain the view that the Reichswerke 'took over heavy industry in the Protectorate'.[4] To conclude my third point, I would like to refer to a file memorandum of the Reich Ministry of Finance dated 28 October 1939, concerning German share purchases in the armament, engineering and iron and steel industries of the Protectorate of Bohemia and Moravia, and in which the privileged position occupied by the Reichswerke in acquiring subsidiaries as well as its function as a spearhead in the creation of an economic New Order is made abundantly clear:

> The Reich Ministry of Economics ordered investment purchases already before the occupation of the Protectorate by German troops. The motive was based on ethnic policy as well as economic policy considerations. It is desired to preserve and to strengthen Germanism in the Bohemian-Moravian economy, and thus to have the Protectorate economy shaped according to the Greater German pattern. In the view of the Reich Ministry of Economics, this task could not be left to private enterprise.[5]

In emphasizing to a high degree the political role of the Reichswerke, however, the danger exists that something is detracted away from its vital economic functions. It is in this respect, above all, that I would like to end my discussion by drawing R. J. Overy's attention to a possible lack of emphasis in his paper. For instance, he writes (p. 270):

> Because of the strong political content in the establishment of the Reichswerke an interpretation simply on business grounds is unsatisfactory. Göring insisted from the start that purely economic considerations were unimportant. Political and racial-economic (*volkswirtschaftlich*) considerations took precedence, even over Göring's own greed.

I have not attempted to undermine Overy's arguments concerning the political considerations surrounding the establishment of the Reichswerke. Indeed, in my own foregoing arguments I have tried to strengthen them. However, I cannot agree with his statement, or even Göring's statement for that matter (which I do not take literally), that purely economic considerations were unimportant or did not play a role in the foundation of the Reichswerke in 1937. This is not the place to instigate a discussion of Germany's economic policy at this time. However, we must stress that Germany was striving to achieve certain levels of armament readiness and economic autarky, and in these endeavours it was intended by Germany's economic leaders to acquire additional territories and economic resources to achieve their goals. Moreover, Germany was already encountering serious bottlenecks in production and supply of factors of production in 1937–8, and Germany's export opportunities were also rapidly receding at this time. I would like to suggest, therefore, that the foundation of the Reichswerke in 1937 bears a direct correlation to the decision taken by Germany's leaders to commence the expansion of Germany's production possibility frontiers. In this respect, it is no coincidence that the economic planning of the Reichswerke to acquire large industrial subsidiaries in Austria and Czechoslovakia pre-dated actual political events. Hence, in preparing the expansionist direction of the Reichswerke in Bohemian and Moravian heavy industry *before* the German occupation of these territories, Göring had his eyes cast not only on the armaments-producing capacity of Bohemian and Moravian heavy industry to serve the needs of the Wehrmacht, but also towards the high export orientation of Czechoslovak industry, which in this respect included also the Škoda-Works. This was revealed when on the very day of the foundation of the Protectorate on 16 March 1939 decreed by Hitler, Göring in his capacity as Plenipotentiary of the Four Year Plan issued a further decree authorizing that all current export contracts placed with Protectorate firms must at all costs be fulfilled out of the 'well-known Devisen reasons' pertaining to the Germany economy at that time.[6] When Hans Kehrl wrote in September 1940 that already in the economy of the Protectorate 'the last available capacities were utilized to meet the tremendous requirements of Greater Germany', he was referring in this context chiefly to the newly-acquired Reichswerke subsidiaries – Škoda-Works, Vítkovice Mining and Foundry Works, Czechoslovak Armament Works, etc. – all of which he had personally been active in acquiring for the Reichswerke.[7] Seldom before or since could a single business enterprise have been so closely identified with the political and economic aims of a régime.

Notes

1. This comprises the contribution made by the raw material wealth and industry of the former Austrian and Czechoslovak Republics to the German war economy 1938–45 (for a Ph.D. thesis). As the results of my research thus far reveal, the activities of the Reichswerke 'Hermann Göring' figure prominently in the German exploitation of these territories in the period after 1938.

2. Karl Rasche of the Dresdner Bank confided in a letter dated 23 Dec. 1943 to Gritzbach, Goering's Chief of Staff, that his personal activity in acquiring subsidiaries for the Reichswerke in Czechoslovakia had always been condemned by other industrial concerns: *Report on the Investigation of the Dresdner Bank*, 100, in *Trials of the War Criminals before the Nuremberg Military Tribunal (TWC)*, Case XI.

3. Hence, even in the interval between the Munich Agreement and the German occupation of Bohemia and Moravia, Göring handed commissions to Hans Kehrl of the Reich Ministry of Economics and Karl Rasche of the Dresdner Bank – who subsequently became known among Czechoslovak business circles as the notorious Kehrl-Rasche group commissioned to acquire Czechoslovak heavy industry for the Reich – to establish German influence in the industry of Bohemia and Moravia for the Reichswerke. Thus, in February 1939, a month prior to the invasion of Bohemia and Moravia, the Dresdner Bank, acting as trustee for the Reichswerke, purchased from the Bohemian Discount Bank, Prague, substantial minority holdings in the Poldi Works (Poldina huť), Prague, a high-grade steel works, and in the First Brno Engineering Company (První brněnská

strojírenská společnost), Brno: *ibid.*, 100.
It is further to be noted that in those
sectors of Czechoslovaki industry where
the Reichswerke largely did not
participate, such as in the chemical
industry, there did occur fierce
competition between other Reich concerns
for Czechoslovak enterprises. In this
respect, the IG Farbenindustrie concern
encountered fierce competition from other
Reich chemical concerns in its plans to
acquire the leading Czechoslovak chemical
plants.

4. *Prosecution Final Brief on Criminal Responsibility of the Defendant Kehrl*: in *TWC*, Case XI.
5. *TWC*, no. 10, XIII, 665, Doc. NID-15640, Case XI.
6. Bundesarchiv-Militaerarchiv Freiburg, RW 46/2. (Bestand RW 46: *Nachgeordnete Dienststellen des Wehrwitschafts- und Ruestungsamtes bei Staeben des Heeres und fuer besondere Aufgaben*).
7. *TWC*, Kehrl Doc. 119: Case XI, Doc. Book IIA.

Part Four

Western Capital and the Commercial Banks of East Central Europe

12. Aspects of Western Equity Investment in the Banking Systems of East Central Europe*

P. L. Cottrell

> 'I cannot but think that although Austria has been dismembered as the result of the War she will remain the financial centre of Eastern Europe and the head for all economic purposes of the neighbouring countries.' *Montagu Norman, 16 June 1921*

By the mid-1920s nearly all of the major banks of East Central Europe[1] had substantial proportions of their equity capital held by foreigners, primarily Americans, Belgians, Dutch, English, French and Germans. This was almost a complete reversal of the situation in 1914 when most of the great Viennese banks had been largely domestically owned and controlled. The purpose of this paper is to trace in general terms the process of Western penetration into the financial sector of East Central Europe, thereby providing an introduction to the case studies which form the rest of the papers in this section. However, although the object is to provide a background for the other studies, particular consideration will be paid to the English and French take-overs of the Anglo-Österreichische Bank and the Österreichische Länderbank in which both state and private interests played a role. Given these objectives, the 1920s will be the focus of study, but some attention, albeit brief and cursory, will be paid to the 1929–33 slump and the 1930s.

PRE-1914 FOREIGN INVESTMENT IN EAST CENTRAL EUROPE

Austria-Hungary had imported capital, sometimes on a substantial scale, throughout the nineteenth century. The need to acquire foreign financial resources had become more urgent during the decade or so before the First World War when a growing import surplus began to develop. At the end of 1913 the Dual Monarchy's total foreign indebtedness amounted approximately to 9,760m crowns and the debt servicing burden so imposed was only slightly alleviated by Austro-Hungarian investment in the Balkans.[2] It is difficult to establish with any degree of precision the identity of the principal long-term creditors of the Dual Monarchy, with for example estimates of total French private and public investment in Austria-Hungary in 1914 ranging from 2,090m crowns to 6,190m crowns.[3] Informed opinion at the end of the 1930s pointed to British investment in Austria-Hungary in 1914 totalling 191.8m crowns, with German investment amounting to 3,520m crowns.[4] A slightly different picture emerges if only securities admitted under the Innsbruck Convention are considered – Austrian and Hungarian state bonds and securities of the state railway company. French holdings on this basis amounted to £35m, German £27.6m, and British £6.8m. Germany, probably the largest long-term creditor of the Dual Monarchy in 1914, was its most important trading partner. The Imperial Reich supplied 39.3 per cent of Austro-Hungarian imports in 1912 and took 39 per cent of the Dual Monarchy's exports, but these shares are inflated by transit trade, in particular Austro-Hungarian goods imported and exported via Hamburg and Bremen. Although British financial interests in the Danube region in the 1900s were relatively small in comparison with both her investments else-where[5] and those in East Central Europe of France and Germany, Britain was in 1912 the third largest supplier of imports into the Dual Monarchy and provided her largest export market after Germany. However, France was only the seventh largest supplier of imports, with a share of the Austro-Hungarian market half that of Britain, and was the eighth largest export market; for although Paris was, until 1890, a large purchaser of Austrian government securities and the largest market for Hungarian state securities, the growing political tension between West and Central Europe during the next quarter of a century led to the decline of French financial interests in the Dual Monarchy. The Austro-Hungarian share of the French foreign invest-ment portfolio almost halved, falling from about 8.9 per cent in 1900 to 4.8 per cent by the outbreak of the First World War. As Europe gradually divided into two hostile camps during the 'belle époque', Austrian securities were tacitly refused admission to the Paris Bourse, a ban which was extended to Hungarian paper after the Bosnian crisis of 1908–9. This government veto was opposed by the French banks, which had considerable interests in the Danube Basin, but it was maintained with only a few exceptions, such as the admission of securities of the Allgemeine österreichische Boden-Credit-Anstalt in 1912. Various efforts by Viennese diplomats to raise the ban were totally unsuccessful.[6]

Most pre-1918 foreign investment in the Dual Monarchy consisted of state and transport securities. Foreign holdings of Austrian industrial shares in 1901 amounted to only 12 per cent, rising to 20 per cent in the case of financial institutions, most of which consisted of the shares and bonds of the quasi-central bank and of agricultural mortgage credit banks. The French, for instance, held between 50,000 and 60,000 shares of the Boden-Credit-Anstalt in 1919, about a quarter of this bank's capital, while the Crédit Lyonnais had bought 50m fr of its 4 per cent bonds during the years immediately before the war.[7] There were apparently very little foreign holdings in the case of the domestic industrial 'mobilier' banks, especially those which operated in the Czech Lands.[8] English interests in the Anglo-Österreichische Bank had waned considerably after 1875, although it did have a London branch with an English director on its committee in 1914.[9] The only major exception may have been been the Länderbank. This had been established in 1880 by the Union Générale, whose chief director, Eugene Bontoux, had been the *directeur-général* of the Rothschild controlled Südbahn. French investors held about 70,000 out of 200,000 of this bank's shares in 1904 and after two new share issues undertaken by the Société Générale in 1905 and 1910, French holdings amounted to about 170,000 shares out of 325,000 in 1914, an investment of between 80 and 90m fr. at market prices.[10] However, during the opening decades of the twentieth century, the foreign links of the great Viennese banks, where they existed, were with German institutions – a reflection of the orientation of the Dual Monarchy's international economic intercourse – and these ties were to be greatly reinforced by the First World War.

RELIEF AND RECONSTRUCTION, 1918–22

East Central Europe, in fact all of Europe east of the Rhine and north of the Alps, was in chaos at the end of the First World War. The Dual Monarchy together with the western portion of the former Russian Empire had become a patchwork of new nation states, often delimited by arbitrary boundaries and divided by mutual antipathy. International economic intercourse had almost broken down in a vast region where basic food supplies were inadequate, the production of manufactured goods was at very low levels, and consequently the population, racked by war and civil turmoil, was close to starvation. Inflation, which had got under way during the war, now took on fresh momentum. In the midst of all this dislocation, representatives of institutions and companies of allied and neutral countries arrived in the capitals of the successor states with lists of desirable assets to be bought at knock-down prices. One of the main attractions was the great Viennese banks with their interests not only in the Danube Basin but throughout the Balkans, Poland and parts of the Ottoman Empire. A holding in one of these major financial institutions could provide a key to a major economic region.

The motives for the post-war western penetration of East Central Europe were mixed. There was considerable interest, both private and public, in the reconstruction of the region but for varying reasons. Its economic rehabilitation was a necessary corollary to the diplomatic and military *cordon sanitaire* which was being erected around Germany. There were continuing fears of a *Mitteleuropa*, given fresh grounds by Austria's attempts to establish either a political or an economic union with Germany. In December 1918 Stolper proposed to unify the German and Austrian currencies and the introduction of a pan-german mark was a way of both breaking down the growing isolation of the now enfeebled Viennese banks and maintaining their links with German institutions.[11] The rapid post-war expansion of western interests was, moreover, a way of earmarking the East Central European market and forestalling any German export drive to this region which would come about with a recovery of the German economy. The October Revolution of 1917 together with the post-war revolutions in Central Europe led to different motives for political and economic intervention as many western diplomats and politicians now considered that it was necessary to construct a bulwark against any Bolshevik contagion in eastern Europe. Further, the removal of Russia from the capitalist world economy left a vacuum which could be filled, in part at least, by the substitute markets of the Danube Basin and the Balkans. The process of intervention and penetration took many forms. Part of the aims were fulfilled by economic clauses in the Versailles system of treaties which prevented the union of Austria with Germany and assisted the passage of western capital and goods into the region. Reconstruction throughout Europe was begun through a series of relief deliveries and loans, mainly provided by American organizations, which amounted to $1,517m during the post-armistice period. Austria, Czechoslovakia and Hungary received $210m in post-war relief loans while paying $63m for relief goods.[12] Relief, although paraded as a humanitarian measure, required staffing and supervision and relief officials were seen by some as disguised asset and concession hunters, preparing the path for western penetration.[13]

Allied policy towards eastern and Central Europe was not monolithic. Political aims varied and there was intense rivalry between the various allied powers for assets in this area. Italy and Italian companies were very early into the field in an effort to secure gains not only in the former Süd-Tyrol but also in the new Austria, the Balkans, and parts of the Near East. The attempts of representatives, both public and private, of individual nations turned the 'relief' period not simply into a carpetbagging spree but a highly intensive competitive situation – so much so that it could be turned to advantage by the 'despoiled' through playing one rival bidder off against another. The degree of concerted action between private companies and state departments also varied. In the case of France, there was a high degree of cohesion between the Quai d'Orsay and the Ministry of Finance on the one hand and private concerns on the other. This was less apparent with regard to England where the Foreign Office did not have anything like the same tradition of using the capital market as an instrument for the implementation of foreign policy. There were certainly different attitudes in London and Paris concerning East Central Europe but Montagu Norman may have been overstating the contrast to some extent when he wrote in November 1921: 'The quarrels in Austria between the protagonists of the French on the one side and of the British on the other have been very unfortunate and of course all spring from the fundamentally different standpoints of the two countries. Our basis is economic, the French basis is political, and nowhere is the distinction more clearly seen than in Austria.'[14]

The Governor of the Bank of England was writing at the time when the relief period had more or less come to an end and a reconstruction period was just getting underway, the prime aim of which was monetary stabilization. Austrian reconstruction was to be bedevilled by inter-allied differences. The need for financial assistance to be given to the new Republic had been agreed at the time of the signing of the Treaty of St Germain and was first discussed at the London conference in March 1921, but a reconstruction loan was not floated until after a further two years had elapsed. The Bank of England had drawn up a scheme of assistance during the summer of 1921 which involved a substantial 'neutral' participation in order that it should be administered from an economic rather than a political standpoint. Italy stood out against the scheme, considering that she had primary rights over Austria. Being unwilling to contribute to a loan, Italy would only assist through postponing her liens on food and reparation debts if the U.S.A. followed a similar course and if she obtained a place on any Control Commission. This effective blocking allowed some German economic penetration of Austria, in particular by the Stinnes group which took over some parts of heavy industry and hydro-electricity generation.[15] However, the bogey of German capital acquisitions, whatever the occasional alarms, was never a real threat in the 1920s. Generally the German economy was not in a position to export capital, itself requiring substantial inflows of financial resources.

The continuation of wartime controls over the export of capital in England and France until 1925 and 1928 respectively did provide a mechanism which could be used to bring private initiatives into line with official policy. Controls in France reinforced the already existing ties between the capital market and the Quai d'Orsay. Official supervision of capital issues was an entirely new procedure for the City of London but it did have a foundation in the consultations between the Bank of England and the issuing houses which had got underway just before the outbreak of the war. Post-war British policy in this area was implemented through 'moral suasion' and sanctions were very much a weapon of the last resort. By 1924 all general restrictions on overseas lending with regard to the type of borrower and the term of lending had been lifted but the practice of consultation continued. The aim of policy had changed by 1924 from supporting domestic reconstruction to maintaining the foreign exchanges. The Dominions received better treatment than entirely foreign borrowers but the recognition that Britain was 'overlending' led to official attempts to fend off even potential Imperial issues. 'The old full freedom of the market' was finally restored in November 1925 but the authorities kept a watching brief and found the 2 per cent Stamp Duty on bearer bonds a useful check on foreign issues as well as a source of revenue. In practice British controls were by no means watertight; consultation only applied to issues of £1m or more, while British residents could purchase securities on foreign primary and secondary financial markets,[16] and this was precisely the type of 'non-official' investment which took place in East Central Europe.

The motives for acquiring East Central European securities and other even less liquid investments varied over a period of time. The post-war depreciation of local currencies did lead to a speculative inflow of funds in the expectation of a capital gain arising when stabilization was achieved at or near pre-war parities. Generally such profits were never realized but the acceleratio of inflation into hyper-inflation provided a different market opportunity – 'bear' operations. Such short-term activities, while of considerable importance in the monetary and economic history of the region, are not our concern here; rather, long-term strategic investments in the Viennese great banks and their affiliates.

The western acquisition of sizeable proportions of the equity capitals of the banks of East Central Europe was often the result of bi-lateral rather than unilateral negotiations. In the case of Czechoslovakia, which had a different political standing amongst the Entente powers from Austria and Hungary, Prague bankers approached Paris for capital almost before the war was over. In April 1919 Beneš forwarded to the Quai d'Orsay a letter from Tůma, the director-general of the Pražská úvěrní banka [Prague Credit Bank]. The Prague banker maintained that about half of Bohemian property was in German hands and that there was a second, economic battle to be fought whose outcome would be more certain if French banks provided the resources with which to enlarge the capital base of a Czechoslovak bank.[17] The consequent negotiations took some time, for initially the French minister in the new republic doubted whether the moment was yet opportune for such an involvement.[18] By the autumn theses qualms had been dispelled and consequently when the Prague Credit Bank increased its capital from 50m Kč to 75m Kč, a group headed by the Société Générale took up 80 per cent of the new shares. The other members of the western consortium were the Banque de Paris et de Pay Bas ('Paribas'), Gunzberg et Cie, the Crédit Mobilier, and the Rotterdamsche Bankvereiniging.[19] Although being the bride rather than the suitor in this instance, France was unable to lay down the most advantageous terms for her finance, it being noted in September 1923, when the Crédit Mobilier applied for an official quotation for the bank's shares, that French representation on the bank's management was not in proportion to French participation in its capital.[20] One problem here was Czechoslovak nationalism. In a similar case, when the Banque de l'Union parisienne attempted to set up a link with the Živnostenská banka through taking up 50,000 new shares of the Czechoslovak bank, Barève, its director, found that it was impossible to secure a French directorship as only Czechoslovaks were admitted to the board.[21]

It was not only the Czechoslovaks that applied to the West for finance. Viennese bank officials came to Geneva and Zurich, useful half-way neutral meeting places, and then London and Paris to secure capital for new share issues caused by post-war enfeeblement and inflation. The branch and filial systems of the Viennese banks were in danger of being dismembered as a result of nationalism in the successor states in the same way as the Dual Monarchy had been broken up in 1918 and 1919. A western share participation would not only provide much-needed capital but also could bring with it the necessary countervailing power required to ensure that the Viennese concern at least retained an influential interest in the branches and filials from which it was now cut off by new boundaries. In addition to problems brought about by the new national structure of East Central Europe, some of the biggest Viennese banks were heavily burdened by pre-war debts in London and Paris which had to be settled at pre-war parities, a problem which grew each day with the continuing depreciation of the Austrian crown. An agreement, alliance, or some form of understanding with a western institution was a possible useful device for ensuring a more favourable consideration of the problem. Weiner, a director of the Boden-Credit-Anstalt, went to Geneva in the spring of 1919 to open discussions with the French. He pointed out that although the servicing of the bank's French-held securities had been suspended during the war, the bank had in reserve the necessary francs. It had acquired an interest in the Banque Générale de Bulgarie [General Bank of Bulgaria] through the Pesti Magyar Kereskedelmi Bank [Hungarian Commercial Bank of Pest] and the Austrian and Hungarian institutions were holding the shares earmarked for French shareholders in the Bulgarian bank which they were prepared to transfer to any interested French group. Weiner's most pressing problem may have been the future of the Czechoslovak industrial companies in which the bank had an interest but which he thought could be transferred to a new financial concern formed by the Boden-Credit-Anstalt in conjunction with French capital. This he considered to be a way of safeguarding common interests. The Austrian underlined the need for rapid decisions by pointing out that Italians, English and Americans were already engaged in talks in Vienna with a view to acquiring interests in Austrian banks and their affiliates. Weiner threw in for good measure the opinion that Austrian financial circles favoured a Danubian confederation but that the attitude of the successor states and of the Entente was driving Austria into the arms of the Germans.[22]

Similar approaches came from d'Adler, a director of the Wiener Bank-Verein, a former director of the Société Générale and a francophile with a French wife, who played a considerable role in smoothing the way for the French acquisition of assets in Austria, elsewhere in Central Europe, and in the Balkans. In early 1920 he was involved in the acquisition of the Orient-Bahn, was attempting to sell the 20 Czechoslovak branches of the Wiener Bank-Verein to the Banque de l'Union parisienne (having known Villar for some time), and was responsible for the sale of the Banque Balkanique to the same French *banque d'affaires*. His general objective was to establish in the successor states tripartite ownership and control of the Wiener Bank-Verein's interests in the form of continuing Austrian participation, a local participation, and a foreign protective – preferably French – participation.[23]

Generally the involvement of western capital in the banks of East Central Europe was on the lines indicated above, but in two instances, the Anglo-Österreichische Bank and the Länderbank, the banks were completely transformed into English and French institutions, losing their nationality in the process.

THE LÄNDERBANK AND THE ANGLO-AUSTRIAN BANK, 1918–22

French 'official' interest in the acquisition of a Viennese bank developed during the spring of 1919. The Quai d'Orsay had become concerned about the take-over of Austrian and German interests in both western and eastern Europe by the British and the Americans. This led to M. Schwob being asked to undertake an investigation into the acquisition by Czechoslovaks, Italians, Americans and Swiss of German and Austrian holdings in Romanian companies through the Viennese Bourse.[24] Most of Schwob's subsequent report was based upon conversations with d'Adler. It was wide-ranging but focused upon a possible French take-over of the Länderbank, a move favoured by the bank's general manager, Rotter, with whom T. Jenesco, the former President of the Romanian Council, had begun discussions on behalf of an English group. The acquisition of the bank would bring with it control of six others – the Banca de Credit Român [Romanian Credit Bank], the Srpska kreditni banka [Serbian Credit Bank], the Galizische Volksbank für Landwirtschaft u. Handel, the Hrvatska eskomptna banka [Croatian Discount Bank], the Deutsche Effecten und Wechsel Bank, and the Magyar leszámitoló és pénzváltó-bank [Hungarian Discount and Exchange Bank]. In Schwob's words: 'Ce serait, dans l'esprit de M. Rotter, le contrôle absolu de France dans toute l'Europe centrale et orientale, contrôle financier, contrôle industriel et commercial, du fait des nombreuses sociétés et entreprises commenditées par les Banques susmentionées ou en dépendant.'

Schwob's despatch from Bucharest was followed up by a study of transforming the Länderbank into the Banque Française des Pays de l'Europe Centrale.[25] The resulting written report began by pointing out that any major profitable intervention by French enterprise in Central Europe required a financial instrument for its execution. Echoing a study made in 1917 of French investment in the Ottoman Empire,[26] it rejected the pre-war practice of simply financing domestic banks as this did not guarantee any permanent profitable influence and occasionally had unwittingly assisted other foreign, sometimes prejudicial, intervention. One solution was the formation of a completely new bank under French control, but this was rejected because of the lack of time. Accordingly the 'francization' of an existing institution was recommended, the obvious choice being the Länderbank, a French creation in which there had been a sizeable pre-war French participation and which had had in 1914 three Parisian directors. This recommendation was supported by a recapitulation of the bank's banking filials in the successor states to which was added a list of its main industrial interests which included a sugar works in Bohemia, timber concerns in Bucovina and Transylvania, coal mines, engineering and electrical works, agricultural machine building concerns, and explosive and chemical works.[27] In the view of the study, the best way of proceeding was for the bank to become a French concern but with an increased capital, a proposal approved by its board. The 'francization' of the Länderbank was supported by the French ministers in Austria and Czechoslovakia and the Austrian and Czechoslovak governments.[28] Possibly its greatest attraction was that it would not require any export of capital, the necessary new funds going to its Paris branch, the bank's future headquarters. It would seem that the study was drawn up by Captain de Sèze at the Quai d'Orsay and initially the Banque de l'Union parisienne was approached to execute it.[29]

Contact had been made with Rotter in June 1919 in order to validate the bank's balance sheet while the bank's French directors were brought into the discussions. It would appear that the Banque de l'Union parisienne quickly withdrew from the scheme, possibly because of its other growing commitments in East Central Europe, but other French banks were soon brought in as replacements to head any syndicate for the issue of new capital and Rotter was asked to adjourn any other negotiations regarding the bank.[30] At the beginning of July 1919 the Quai d'Orsay informed the Rue de Rivoli of the project. The need to safeguard French interests was pointed out to the Ministry of Finance while the situation of the bank's Paris branch was described. The credit side of its balance sheet was in difficulties because of the depreciation of Central European and Balkan currencies, the fall in Austrian securities, and events in Russia. The branch was highly illiquid and it was impossible to replenish it from Vienna because of the depreciation of the crown against the franc. The new capital required was going to be injected by consolidating the branch's engagements in the form of preference shares. The letter concluded by stating that: 'La possession par la France d'instrument financier puissant dont l'activité a été surtout dirigée vers le développement industriel et dont les succursales, les filiales, et les participations s'étendent sur tous les nouveaux États de l'Europe Centrale et des pays voisins me semble présenter des avantages politiques appréciables qui m'engagent à considérer avec faveur la réalisation du projet.[31] The Ministry of Foreign Affairs' initiative in this area led subsequently to some friction between it and the Ministry of Finance, especially when it called a meeting of Parisian banks in the autumn of 1919 to discuss the 'francization' project.[32] As a result of these discussions 'Paribas', together with Jacques Gunzberg et

Cie and the Banque Industrielle de Chine, agreed to act as a placing syndicate for the 40m fr. of preference shares to be issued for the transformed Länderbank.[33]

Although the basic outlines of the scheme had been settled by the end of 1919, there were a considerable number of problems which had to be overcome before it could be realized. The bank's Paris branch had been sequestered and it had considerable pre-war sterling liabilities outstanding as a result of the activities of its London branch, which were now mainly in the hands of the Bank of England. Growing Czechoslovak nationalism threatened any large-scale activities by a non-domestic bank in the new republic. Lastly, the change in the bank's nationality required the passage of legislation through the Austrian Parliament where pan-german opponents would be able to delay and obstruct it. In addition, totally unforeseen problems arose which contributed to delaying the project's successful completion until January 1922.

First, the bank's French tax position had to be considered: this was a perplexing problem, complicated by wartime events and decisions and compounded by the subsequent depreciation of the crown. Seven different ways of transforming the Länderbank were reviewed of which the most advantageous in terms of limiting fiscal liability was also that which carried the greatest political advantages, namely outright 'francization'.[34] Other difficulties were less easy to resolve. One of the main reasons for establishing the bank in its new form was to allow the French to head off 'allied' rivals in the economic penetration of the lower Danube and the Balkans. The Quai d'Orsay telegraphed the French Minister of Bucharest at the beginning of 1920 requesting him to bring pressure to bear in order to suspend the Romanian government's sequestration of the Romanian Credit Bank, pointing out that: 'La conservation de l'influence de la Banque des Pays de l'Europe Central [the revamped Länderbank] est une des conditions categoriques du plan de réorganisation en cours dont la réalisation favouriserait les relations franco-roumaines.'[35] The problems surrounding the Romanian Credit Bank soon proved to be more than a matter for inter-governmental negotiations as it was discovered that the Länderbank had sold at least a large part of its holding (11,071 ordinary shares and 206 founders' shares) to a Belgian, Gustave Chandoir, in July 1916.[36] Actually the plan to take over the Länderbank went from one crisis to another during 1920 and 1921. The various difficulties which confronted the Quai d'Orsay and the syndicate of Parisian banks will be considered separately but it is important to understand that the diplomats and bankers were not able to deal with them in this manner and that one problem often aggravated or provoked another.

At the beginning of the sugar campaign of 1920, the Czechoslovak government through the Bank Office announced that it was altering the method by which the harvest was financed. It was only through the intervention of the French minister at Prague, who stressed the imminent 'francization' of the Länderbank, that the preponderant role of the bank in the Czechoslovak sugar industry was maintained. As with its participation in the Romanian Credit Bank, this aspect of the bank's business was 'un des attaits de sa réorganisation et un élément d'influence très utile dans la vie economique de l'Europe Centrale.'[37] This preliminary skirmish with Czechoslovak nationalism was followed in the summer of 1921 by a direct threat to the bank's future in the republic as a result of the passage of the nostrification laws. It was met by turning the Czechoslovak branches into an autonomous concern – Banka pro obchod a prumysl dříve 'Länderbanka' [the Bank for Commerce and Industry formerly Länderbank] – with a capital of 80m Kč. This was subscribed by the Agrární banka [Agrarian Bank] (25 per cent) and the Länderbank (75 per cent). French influence was to be maintained through the bank's presidency and a number of directorships. It would appear that this solution to this problem was the work of officials of 'Paribas' who then enlisted the aid of the Quai d'Orsay to implement it.[38]

Second, along with the growing problems of dealing with the Czechoslovak government, a settlement had to be reached with the Länderbank's English creditors, principally the Bank of England, while lastly a bill to change the bank's nationality had to go through the Austrian Parliament. An agreement had been made with the Bank of England by April 1921 which basically ranked the payment of the bank's sterling liabilities after the distribution of both its ordinary and preference dividend and managerial commissions.[39] This was extraordinarily advantageous to the French, a factor which made the French promoters very anxious when they encountered both delays in getting the Länderbank bill passed and difficulties in keeping the financing syndicate intact. The agreement was due to expire on 31 December 1921, and it was very doubtful whether a similar settlement would be obtained a second time,[40] the Governor of the Bank of England indicating by late October 1921 that he now had some regrets in granting such favourable terms. At the same time 'Paribas' was experiencing problems in maintaining the composition of the financing syndicate which had been joined early in 1921 by the Banque française pour le Commerce et l'Industrie and the Crédit Mobilier. In April the Banque Industrielle de Chine decided to renounce its quarter share and the other banks gave notice to 'Paribas' that if another partner was not secured by 1 May then they would resign from the syndicate. The French were extremely worried that the failure to raise the deficiency of 10m fr. on the Paris market, caused by the withdrawal of the Banque Industrielle de Chine, would create a bad impression, especially in London, and jeopardize other Central European operations.[41] 'Paribas' asked for government assistance but initially was unable to find other backers. This impasse continued even after the Länderbank bill had been passed and did raise the possibility of having to negotiate a fresh agreement with the Bank of England.[42] Even in December 1921 12m fr. were still required and the financing gap was finally bridged by bringing in the Agrarian Bank and the Bank for Commerce and Industry which had taken over the Czechoslovak branches of the Länderbank. As only the French were to have the voting rights attached to the new preference shares, these were held by the French members of the syndicate until the securities were sold on the Paris market. This compromise solution received the blessing of the Quai d'Orsay.[43]

The other major obstacle which endangered the execution of the scheme to transform the Länderbank into a French concern was the attitude of the Austrian Parliament. Initially irritating delays caused by the Pan-German party had by the spring of 1921 become a major barrier to further progress. This opposition led to the French and English joining forces, at least publicly. The English were undertaking a parallel scheme to anglicize the Anglo-Österreichische Bank, which also required Austrian legislation, but which was looked upon more favourably by the opposition parties in the Federal Parliament.[44] The Austrian Chancellor and Minister of Finance had expressed, at least in London, their willingness to see the legislation through while the English and French governments stressed that the two bank bills were important elements in their collaboration with the Republic.[45] Either this diplomatic manoeuvre was insufficient or, and more likely, the Austrian government could not exert enough pressure, and consequently parliamentary obstruction continued throughout the summer of 1921.[46] By September it appeared that the 'Anglobank' bill would pass while the Länderbank bill would fail.[47] The French were now beginning to distrust their English partners, gallic disquiet being provoked by discussions undertaken by an English representative in Vienna who appeared to be willing to ditch the Länderbank bill in order to allow the Anglobank bill, with which it had been linked, to succeed in the forthcoming session of the Austrian Parliament.[48] French suspicions appeared to be substantiated in October when the Austrian Chancellor showed the French Minister in Vienna a letter supposedly written by Spencer-Smith, a director of the Bank of England. This possible *canard* stated that the enactment of the Anglobank law was a condition *sine qua non* of Bank of England financial support for Austria and indicated that there was no need for the fortunes of the bill to continue to be wedded to that of its French twin.[49] By the autumn of 1921, such manoeuvrings, real or otherwise, were considered unnecessary by the Austrian Chancellor although he thought that the publication of the confidential communication, apparently from Spencer-Smith, would prevent the passage of both bills. The French took the revelation by the Austrian Chancellor seriously and the French Ambassador was asked to find out what he could in London. The French distrusted Montagu Norman, a factor which continued throughout the 1920s, while the Austrians may have been attempting to play the French off against the English, perhaps to make headway with the reconstruction credits that they needed so badly. As far as the English were concerned it was the French who were their own worst enemies by insisting on such harsh terms in the Länderbank bill.[50] The incident, whatever its foundations, had no effect as within a week of the meeting between the Austrian Chancellor and the

French Minister, the two bills to transfer the registered offices of both the Länderbank and the Anglo-Österreichische Bank to foreign soil became law.[51] The necessary extraordinary general meeting of the shareholders of the Länderbank to modify its statutes in view of its change of nationality and new internal structure was held on 28 January 1922,[52] some three years after the project had been launched.

The transformations of the Anglo-Österreichische Bank and the Länderbank into English and French institutions were not typical of the penetration of western capital into the banking system of East Central Europe, which was generally a private process. But the preceding negotiations do reveal some of the aims of both French and English business and governments in this region during the period of relief and reconstruction.

WESTERN EQUITY CAPITAL IN THE 1920s – THE BODEN-CREDIT-ANSTALT

Stabilization was formally achieved in East Central Europe during the first half of the 1920s. The Czechoslovak crown settled around a parity of 8 Swiss centimes during 1920 and 1921 but then appreciated considerably at the beginning of the following year as a result of an influx of funds – refugee capital fleeing from inflation and dislocation elsewhere in Central Europe. Rašín, the conservative Czech finance minister, tried to maintain the crown at its artificially appreciated value of 16 Swiss centimes with the support of foreign reserves but at the cost of domestic deflation. The stabilization of the German and Austrian currencies in 1924 was followed by a repatriation of funds and it proved difficult to sustain the Czechoslovak crown at 15.3 Swiss centimes, its level at the end of 1923. Foreign exchange controls were reintroduced in Czechoslovakia in 1924 and maintained until 1928.[53] Both Austria and Hungary achieved monetary stabilization with the assistance of the Financial Committee of the League of Nations which involved the flotation of foreign loans and the supervision of the domestic economy by a Commissioner-General.[54] Although the spectre of hyper-inflation had been banished from the Danubian region by 1925, the economies of the area were still generally weak as post-war relief, reconstruction and external financial expertise made little headway in solving their structural weaknesses. Only Czechoslovakia, which had within its borders the industrial heartland of the old Dual Monarchy – Bohemia and Moravia – moved forward positively. Rates of economic progress in the region in the 1920s look impressive with Gross Domestic Product in Czechoslovakia rising at 6.0 per cent per annum, Austrian Gross National Product increasing at 5.3 per cent per annum, and Hungarian Net National Product growing at 4.7 per cent, but this was from the very low base of 1920,[55] hardly a normal year. The furthering of economic growth and the establishment of modern industrial economies, the overt or implicit aim of government policies, required substantial financial resources, usually from external sources. Additionally in the cases of both Austria and Hungary, capital inflows were required to finance balance of payments deficits which averaged 75,000m sch. and 353.3m gold Pg. per annum respectively during the second half of the 1920s. The demand for funds was met in a wide variety of ways but of concern here is further western equity investment in the banking system. As in the preceding section, the problem will be examined through a case study to illustrate the needs for further capital and the methods adopted to find it. The example taken is the Viennese bank – the Boden-Credit-Anstalt.

Following the Geneva protocols which marked the first step in Austrian stabilization, financial activity within the Federal Republic was generally flat after a hectic stock exchange boom in 1923 which had been fuelled by the realization that security prices had lagged during the inflation period. The more or less moribund state of the new issue market after 1923 caused industrial firms to turn to their bankers for accommodation and the banks attempted to meet this demand for funds by obtaining finance in a variety of ways. Most well known is the use of acceptance credits drawn on London, Paris and New York, but at the same time the bankers did attempt to enlarge their capital bases. Also the banking system began to contract in size through a series of failures and amalgamations to a level closer to that warranted by an Austria shorn of its empire. Austrian financial interests elsewhere in East Central Europe continued but demands for funds from Prague, Budapest and other previous satellite centres now increasingly by-passed Vienna.

The process of bank concentration, which had as its corollary the concentration of the ownership of industrial shares, until nearly the end of the decade mainly affected the 'middle' banks of Vienna and the provincial banks, which did have some grave effects upon smaller manufacturing and trading firms. In 1924 the Allgemeine Depositen-Bank failed and the second banking crisis of the decade was sparked off by the closure in 1926 of the Centralbank der deutschen Sparkassen, an institution which had acted as a clearing house for the smaller savings banks. This process of financial collapse contributed to industrial malaise and by 1928 about 10 per cent of all Austrian limited companies ('AGs') were in liquidation and activity on the Bourse remained slack until the autumn of the ensuing year. Failure and bankruptcy, however, also yielded opportunities for the apparently strong and these were seized by the management of the Boden-Credit-Anstalt.

Although events were shaped by the play of economic forces, the particular form of their outcome in Austria in the 1920s was often the consequence of the character of the persons concerned in addition to the interaction between economics and politics, both domestic and international. The Boden-Credit-Anstalt was headed by the energetic but grandiose Dr Sieghart whose aim was to complete the transformation of this former agricultural mortgage bank into a full industrial 'mobilier'. He was allied to the Christian Social Party, fought a battle of prestige with Bosel (the guiding spirit behind the Union-Bank), and was prepared to go to great lengths to secure his ends. His bank increased its capital practically every year during the inflation period and in so doing drew upon foreign, western, funds. It had a French participation dating from before the war, while the Mutuelle Solvay, together with two Dutch banks – the Amsterdamsche Bank and Lippmann, Rosenthal – appear to have had interests in it dating from the Armistice if not before. Sieghart began to look, almost tout, for further foreign resources during the autumn of 1920. He had established contacts with the London market through playing a major role in the transfer of a sizeable packet of shares of the Erste Donau-Dampfschiffahrts-Gesellschaft to English shipping interests.[56] Sieghart informed the British chargé d'affaires at Vienna that he preferred an English participation and was in touch with a number of London banks including Hambros. American advances had been declined as they involved the loss of control of the bank while Sieghart would not consider an Italian participation because of the Süd-Tyrol question, although an Italian insurance company – Assicurazioni Generali – did subsequently take up Boden-Credit-Anstalt shares. Sieghart's 'experience with the French was not such as to encourage him to receive their advances favourably. They would, he anticipated, if admitted to participation, endeavour to establish a much closer control of the bank than Austrian interests in it would care for.'[57] In London Sieghart announced that:

> any co-operation with the Boden-Credit-Anstalt means an entrance into the most important industries and companies of Central Europe. In view of the fact that the Boden-Credit-Anstalt is closely attached to all these companies through share-participation and long and intimate commercial relations, it is clear that a partnership with the Boden-Credit-Anstalt would likewise be equal to a certain influence upon all these undertakings. The leading persons of the Boden-Credit-Anstalt would be quite ready to consider seriously such co-operation with, or participation of a prominent English group.[58]

Paris was also on the itinerary and here an agreement was reached over the bank's outstanding obligations arising from the war period.[59]

It is not clear whether Sieghart's tour in the autumn and winter of 1920–1 led immediately to any new English or French involvement in the bank, but in 1922 and 1923 J. Schroeder & Co. of London acquired an interest which initially was probably small. However, during the winter of 1922–3 when the bank increased its capital by an issue of a million shares, about half were taken by Schroeders in conjunction with J. P. Morgan & Co. and possibly Baring Brothers. The cost to the western syndicate was thought to be £70,000 but a £400,000 trade credit may also have been involved – the stated aim of the new issue being to raise capital to facilitate the financing of Central European imports.[60] Schroeders also had interests in the Hungarian Commercial Bank of Pest. Both the Austrian and the Hungarian banks had participations in Yugoslavian institutions, which in the case of the Boden-Credit-Anstalt were in conjunction with the Mutuelle Solvay.

In the spring of 1924 the Boden-Credit-Anstalt applied to have its equity capital quoted officially on the Paris Bourse. Initially this request was refused, since with the franc exchange crisis there was a total ban on the admission of foreign securities, but in May approval was given.[61] At the same time Eugène Schneider went on to the board of the Boden-Credit-Anstalt at the request of François-Marsal, the Minister of Finance.[62] Schneider had been associated with the Austrian bank since the beginning of the decade through the French industrialist's acquisition of at least part of the bank's interest in the Báňská a hutní společnost [Mining and Metallurgic Co.]. During the following year Sieghart tried the American market for funds through his now established contact with Schroeders and Morgans. This resulted in an issue of $2.4m 8 per cent mortgage bonds made by the European Mortgage and Investment Corporation backed by the Schroeder Banking Corporation and Lee, Higginson. The flotation was followed in 1926 by the joint formation of the American, British & Continental Trust in partnership with Schroeders, Blith, Witter, and the Hungarian Commercial Bank of Pest.

During the second half of the 1920s Sieghart tried to enlarge his bank through the acquisition of weakened 'middle' and provincial banks – taking over in 1926 the Allgemeine Verkehrsbank and in 1927 the Union-Bank which had formerly been controlled by his arch-rival Bosel. The Verkehrsbank was bought initially with the support of the Schoeller group of companies, which banked with the Boden-Credit-Anstalt, and the industrialist E. Hardmeyer.[63] The acquisition of the Union-Bank was a bigger operation and eventually led to an almost desperate search for foreign funds. It was carried out by relieving the Postsparkasse of its embarrassing holding of 3m shares in the Union-Bank, the total share capital of which numbered 4m. This transaction resulted subsequently in the Austrian state, via the Postsparkasse, holding possibly as many as 167,000 shares in the Boden-Credit-Anstalt.[64] It was to be one embarrassment replacing another. The take-over of the Union-Bank gave the Boden-Credit-Anstalt 3,500 shares in the Veitscher Magnesitwerke-Actien-Gesellschaft; a further 7,000 were acquired in January 1929 in conjunction with the Union de Banques Suisses and the Banque de Commerce de Bâle which gave the Austrian bank control of this important metallurgical company. The other major shareholder was Schneider-Creusot with 7,000 shares.[65]

Initially Sieghart's take-over of the Union-Bank caused some difficulties in France. The Crédit Mobilier was a minority shareholder, having bought 50,000 in 1923, as was the Banque Claivin of Lille.[66] These complications were smoothed over by direct negotiations in Vienna but more difficult was the raising of the necessary resources to finance the acquisition. The

Boden-Credit-Anstalt's capital was increased from 30m sch. to 45m sch. by the creation of 300,000 new 50 sch. shares which Sieghart then attempted to place abroad. In April 1927 the Union Européenne industrielle et financière applied for official permission to acquire 60,000 of these shares at a discount of 6 fr. a share on the current Paris quotation.[67] It would appear that the Banque de l'Union parisienne, Schneider's banking partner in the Union Européenne, subsequently acquired these securities. The substantial increase in the Boden-Credit-Anstalt's capital proved to be insufficient because at the bank's general meeting in May 1927 a further increase was announced, raising the bank's capital to 55m sch. through the issue of 200,000 new shares at a price of 105 sch.[68] At the same time parts of the portfolios of the Verkehrs and Union banks were transferred to the Maatschappij vor Beheer which had been established by the Boden-Credit-Anstalt's Dutch partners – the Amsterdamsche Bank and Lippmann, Rosenthal – in conjunction with English and Swiss houses who provided the Austrian bank with an advance of 9m florins at 9.75 per cent. It is also highly likely that other packets of shares that the Boden-Credit-Anstalt had acquired went into the portfolio of the American, British and Continental Trust formed the previous year.

Despite these injections of capital the bank continued to require liquidity to sustain its operations and those of its client industrial firms and an air of near-despair now becomes evident as Sieghart continued to peddle shares around the capital markets of Western Europe. In November 1927 he gave a short-term option on 50,000 to Louis Hirsch, an *arbitrageur*.[69] Subsequently in the summer of 1928 a director of the Crédit Lyonnais, while in Vienna, was offered up to 175,000, a packet which Sieghart was simultaneously trying to place in London. The Austrian banker explained that he preferred the shares to go to Paris but their introduction was barred by the authorities, and the real reason for approaching the French bank would appear to have been a refusal in London. Sieghart then tried Berlin where he discussed the possibility of the German government secretly purchasing shares in his bank in order to increase German influence within Austria.[70] By the end of the decade some of the Boden-Credit-Anstalt's foreign backers wished to withdraw, which compounded the bank's financing problems. At the beginning of 1929 Sieghart returned to Paris to speak directly to the Quai d'Orsay in order to find funds to replace those of Schroeders and the Mutuelle Solvay.

Sieghart's search for funds in any quarter during the early months of 1929 came at a time when further mergers, now involving the 'great' banks, were being either rumoured or planned in Vienna. Directors of the Niederöster-reichische Escompte-Gesellschaft, in which there was a large French interest, were considering the desirability of a fusion with the Österreichische Credit-Anstalt für Handel u. Gewerbe which in 1926 had taken over the Austrian interests of the Anglo-Austrian. Since 1927 Sieghart had been trying to take over the Vienna branch of the Banque des Pays de l'Europe Centrale, a proposal firmly rejected by both the French Ministry of Finance and the

Managing Director of 'Paribas'. The matter was brought up again early in 1929. Such a merger, whatever France's attitude, would have caused further ripples in the strong undercurrents that were developing in Austrian politics. As has already been indicated Sieghart was a conservative whereas one of the Banque des Pays de l'Europe Centrale's most important customers was the Municipality of Vienna, controlled by the Socialists.[71] As in 1927 the acquisition of the Vienna branch of the Banque des Pays de l'Europe Centrale by the Boden-Credit-Anstalt was firmly opposed by the board of 'Paribas'.[72] Rebuffed in this direction, Sieghart then tried to bring off a marriage with the Wiener Bank-Verein.[73]

Further banking concentration was supported by some of the officials of the Österreichische National Bank [Austrian National Bank]. It was also seen as desirable by some of the foreign shareholders, as was the case with the proposed merger between the Niederösterreichische Escompte-Gesellschaft with the Credit-Anstalt which was backed by the Banque de Bruxelles. This particular scheme appears to have faltered as a result of the opposition of de Krassny, the effective head of the Niederösterreichische Escompte-Gesell-schaft. He, like Sieghart, preferred an amalgamation with the Vienna branch of the Banque de Pays de l'Europe Centrale[74] but such a plan, as with an issue of Niederösterreichische Escompte-Gesellschaft shares on the Paris market, was out of the question following the failure of the Boden-Credit-Anstalt in October 1929.

The immediate cause of the collapse of the Boden-Credit-Anstalt was political instability within Austria. The growing friction between the Heim-wehr and the Schutzbund led in September 1929 to a domestic withdrawal of funds from the Austrian banks and their conversion into dollars, causing the National Bank to lose over £1.5m of devisen during the month. This foreign exchange drain, coupled with a retreat of foreign short-term capital and rising interest rates at other financial centres, led the National Bank to increase its discount rate from $7\frac{1}{2}$ to $8\frac{1}{2}$ per cent on 28 September. The political crisis was calmed by the formation of the Schober cabinet but the run on deposits and the refusal of the National Bank to continue to discount paper for the Boden-Credit-Anstalt in excess of its quota resulted in the bank closing its doors. It was known that the bank was in a weak position but it had been expected, before the events of September, to 'weather its troubles'.[75] The bank was highly illiquid with three concerns – the Steyrwerke, the Erste Donau-Dampfschiffahrtsgesellschaft, and Mautner – having in aggregate at least 218m sch. in advances. The other main interests of the bank were Fanto AG and Staatseisenbahngesellschaft.[76] Any 'knock on' effects within the Austrian banking system were nipped in the bud by the fusion of the defunct Boden-Credit-Anstalt with the Credit-Anstalt brought about by the govern-ment, itself an indirect major shareholder in the former. The terms of the merger were severe, with four 50 sch. shares of the Boden-Credit-Anstalt being exchanged for one 40 sch. share of the Credit-Anstalt, a loss on nominal values of 80 per cent which brought forth protests from the foreign shareholders involved, especially the smaller ones.

It is difficult to establish who were the main holders of the Boden-Credit-Anstalt's shares in the autumn of 1929. Information collected by the Bank of England but admitted to be rumour pointed to the Postsparkasse having 30 per cent, the bank itself 30 per cent, a position thought possible as it had been buying its own shares to sustain their price, and foreign and Austrian shareholders 40 per cent. French calculations – an estimate made within the Ministry of Finance – indicated a total possible French holding of 80,000,[77] although 780,000 were quoted on the Paris market. One French stockbroker thought that 100,000 was more likely.[78]

Possibly only Czechoslovak bankers together with Schroeders and Mutuelle Solvay had been able to read accurately for some time the true underlying situation of the Boden-Credit-Anstalt. The Austrian bank in 1918 had made an alliance with the Živnostenská banka in order to cover the position of its interests within the Czechoslovak Republic. However, from 1928 the Živnostenská tried to disengage itself from its Austrian partner and in January 1929 terminated the agreement, a decision which took effect from the following June. At the same time the Czechoslovak bank had acquired the shares in Czechoslovak companies which the Boden-Credit-Anstalt held and which had been controlled for the most part during the 1920s on a joint basis.[79]

The experience of the failure of the Boden-Credit-Anstalt soured foreign attitudes towards Central European banking, especially Austrian; words such as 'swindled' were to be used later. The events of the autumn of 1929 were to be repeated on a far grander scale in the late spring and summer of 1931 when the Credit-Anstalt collapsed, an event partly caused by its take-over of the Boden-Credit-Anstalt. The autumn of 1929 in Vienna was actually an overture to a major long-lasting crisis in East Central Europe, which unlike that of 1929 could not be quickly dampened down by domestic initiatives, and which involved European and American bankers, central bankers, diplomats and governments, and supra-national bodies such as the Financial Committee of the League of Nations and the newly established Bank of International Settlements. There were many aspects of the crisis, by no means all financial, but one important element was the size of the Credit-Anstalt's industrial holdings throughout Austria and East Central Europe, augmented by its previous acquisitions of the Anglo-Austrian Bank and the Boden-Credit-Anstalt.

The events of the summer of 1931 have been described, discussed and analysed many times before in both general and particular terms. Some aspects of the collapse of the Credit-Anstalt will be discussed elsewhere in the this volume. Equally as grave was the position of most of the other remaining Viennese banks. Understandably their directorates and managements tried to take advantage of the almost moribund state of the Credit-Anstalt. One aim of the so-called Weiner scheme for the reconstruction of the Credit-Anstalt was that the Wiener Bank-Verein together with the Niederösterreichische Escompte-Gesellschaft and possibly with the Vienna branch of the Banque des Pays de l'Europe Centrale would acquire the 'sound banking assets' of the Credit-Anstalt in order to increase their liquidity as well as expanding the volume of their business. This scheme, like others, proved to be impracticable, not least because it did not appreciate the true position of the foundered Rothschild bank.[80] With this avenue blocked, others were re-explored. In October 1932 Krassny again suggested a merger between the Niederösterreichische Escompte-Gesellschaft and the Vienna branch of the Banque des Pays de l'Europe Centrale.[81] However, the general position of the banks was now well beyond such remedies, even if foreign investors had been prepared to continue in partnership with Austrian bankers.

The Wiener Bank-Verein in August 1932 was forced to write off 33m sch. of its existing capital and raise 23m sch. in new priority shares. The Austrian National Bank was a party to this reconstruction scheme and took 10m sch. of the new shares while the balance came from some of the Wiener Bank-Verein's foreign associates – the Deutsche Bank, the Société Générale de Belgique and the Banque Belge pour l'Étranger. The Viennese bank had been able to repay about half of its foreign currency short-term loans but had been badly affected by the fall in its schilling deposits which had dropped from 80m to 50m between its 1930 and 1931 accounts. The crisis was a further factor in the retreat of Austrian interests in East Central Europe; two of the bank's Austrian branches were closed while those in Czechoslovakia, Yugoslavia, Romania and Poland became entirely autonomous banks.[82]

During 1933 both the Wiener Bank-Verein and the Niederösterreichische Escompte-Gesellschaft failed to cover their expenses. Their position had been eased to a degree by a new subsidiary of the National Bank – the Gesellschaft für Revision und treuhändige Verwaltung – which had been established in March and which had taken over obligations totalling 140m sch. This accommodation proved to be insufficient and by the end of the year a possible amalgamation was being explored. These negotiations foundered upon personal animosity and the possible implications of a successful merger upon the position of the Credit-Anstalt.[83] The impasse was resolved in July 1934 by the Credit-Anstalt taking over the Wiener Bank-Verein and 70m sch. of the assets and liabilities of the Niederösterreichische Escompte-Gesellschaft. The consequent necessary increase in the Credit-Anstalt's capital – 25m sch. – was subscribed by the National Bank. The remaining 'rump' of the Niederösterreichische Escompte-Gesellschaft was transformed into the Österreichische Industrie-Credit AG, the capital of which – 9.9m sch. – was taken up by the National Bank.[84] The foreign shareholders in the two banks were faced with a loss of the whole of their participations, an outcome which was made more galling by their agreement under some pressure two months earlier to exchange standstill assets for shares in the two banks. Hambros, a participant in the Niederösterreichische Escompte-Gesellschaft from the mid-1920s, had taken up 1.5m sch. of shares.[85] The state-managed consolidation of the Austrian banking system in 1934 resulted in only three banks with foreign participations continuing to operate in the Republic during the second half of the decade – the Vienna branch of the Banque des Pays de l'Europe Centrale, the Merkur Bank controlled by German interests, and the Austrian branches of the Czechoslovak Živnostenská banka.

Austrian developments during the inter-war period were perhaps the most extreme but they were mirrored in both Czechoslovakia and Hungary. In these two states there were inflation-fuelled new issue booms following the Armistice. The Czech promotion spree between 1919 and 1921, during which new issues rose from 270m Kč to 1,000m Kč, was halted by deflation caused by Rašín's conservative and possibly misguided monetary policy. The course of domestic political events in Hungary delayed the onset of a new issue boom until early 1920 but it then continued till 1922, hardly checked by the government's attempts to control it via the Hungarian Institute of Banking Corporations from November 1920. During the course of 1921 603 joint stock companies with an aggregate capital of 1,804m crowns were established in Hungary and, unlike in neighbouring states, most of the subscribed funds came from domestic sources. The Czechoslovak deflation which ran on until the second half of 1923 had serious repercussions upon industrial firms and the banks with which they were associated. Bank advances, which perhaps had been too freely given and had been granted on political rather than commercial criteria, were rendered illiquid and losses mounted upon them until the second half of the decade. Consequently three small banks suspended payments in 1923, the Česká průmysolvá a hospodářská banka ran into serious difficulties in February 1925, and at that time two other banks were making serious losses. The Czechoslovak economy recovered during the second half of the 1920s, especially from 1928, but the condition of some of its banks remained fragile, susceptible to any shock. In 1930 the Anglo-československá banka [Anglo-Czechoslovak Bank], the Česká komerční banka, and the Prague Credit Bank were merged and received government financial aid totalling 310m Kč., followed by a further 286m Kč. in 1932.[86] However, unlike Austria where foreign participations in the banks were extinguished in capital reconstruction schemes, overseas interests in major Czechoslovak financial institutions continued throughout the 1930s with 15 per cent of the total capital of all joint stock banks being foreign-owned on 31 December 1937.[87] The much greater weight of agriculture within the Hungarian economy led to some divergence in the experience and fortunes of its financial sector. The increasing failure of foreign loans to be fully subscribed in 1928 was one factor contributing to growing economic difficulties in 1929 and the collapse of one land mortgage bank during the year.[88]

The economic and financial development of the three constituent national economies of East Central Europe during the 1920s and the early 1930s did take different courses but there was something of a common strand. This consisted of an inflationary boom during the early 1920s when production facilities were expanded, often with the injection of foreign financial resources either directly or via the domestic banking system. But the various processes of stabilization pursued then generally produced a hiatus in expansion and growth which was only resumed during the second half of the decade as a result of foreign stimuli – either the expansion of export markets and/or an inflow of further financial resources. The contraction in international economic intercourse at the end of the decade was one factor responsible for domestic stagnation and financial stringency, possibly producing a crisis. A contributory factor to banking problems was the delayed contraction of the financial sector, it being larger than that warranted by the size of the real sector. Such imbalances were not simply the result of post-war territorial changes and subsequent economic nationalism but also of physical expansion as well as financial during the inflationary period, with the latter being characterized by the continuance of illiquid loans. Domestic financial problems during the second half of the 1920s were masked by a further inflow of funds from western institutions in a variety of forms – equity participations, bond issues, the acquisition of securities by investment trusts and holding companies, and acceptance credits, often attracted by apparent stabilization. These resources were often employed with complete disregard of their maturity for the medium- and long-term support of industrial firms.

EXPECTATIONS AND EXPERIENCE

One of the major themes treated here has been the tracing of the process of the penetration of western capital into the domestic banking systems of East Central Europe. This has been illustrated by some case studies while an overall view is provided by the list of participations, bank by bank, contained in the appendix. Some explanation has been given for the undertaking of this investment in both general and particular terms. This concluding section returns to the problem of motivation but once again it will be treated by a case study – the Anglo-Austrian Bank.

This institution was very much the English twin of the Länderbank. The anglicization of the Anglo-Österreichische Bank in 1922 has been accounted for by the British government's attempts from 1916 to foster overseas banking in Europe on a German model, together with the Bank of England's desire to liquidate its £1,665,000 claim on the bank dating from the outbreak of the First World War coupled with Montagu Norman's particular European plans.[89] The formation of the Anglo-Austrian, like others which sprang from the Runciman speech and the Farringdon Committee, was very much an experiment. Some 'Anglo-European' banks had been established in the 1860s and the 1870s but in 1914 the main spheres of interest of British corporate overseas banks lay in the Near East and South America. There were only ten branches of British 'international' banks in Europe in 1910.[90] There was some reluctance after the war to move into what was literally a foreign area – as was commented in 1921 with regard to an attempt to obtain British capital by the Živnostenská banka two years earlier: 'the mission failed . . . chiefly . . . owing to the lack of confidence of the English bankers in Central Europe, and to their ignorance of the possibilities and even the whereabouts of Czechoslovakia.'[91] This was hardly conducive to a successful investment in the area but understandable given the balance of pre-1914 British investments. Another problem was the degree of specialization within the English financial sector, and it is noticeable that the absence of 'mixed' and 'investment' banks led to twinned placements in the case of some Britsh investments in the region in the 1920s as with the joint participation of the National Provincial and Lazards in the Credit-Anstalt and Lloyds and Hambros in the Niederösterreichische Escompte-Gesellschaft.

A pioneer such as the Anglo-Austrian was bound to run into difficulties and could hardly be expected to match up quickly with the type of bank which it was expected to emulate. However, the problems caused by having to 'learn by doing' were joined by a host of others. 'Learning by doing' or 'the English amateur approach' not only applied to the bank's senior British directors but also to its expatriate staff. One was a chemistry graduate, who like many of his colleagues was fresh from Oxford. They constituted the *Kindergarten* and had to learn the ropes and sometimes the native language from the local staff.[92] The bank's continuing strong physical and personal links with Vienna proved to be a handicap in some of the successor states. Its branches in Czechoslovakia, as with those of the Länderbank, had been transformed into a semi-autonomous concern, but the competition that it threatened was resented by the Živnostenská banka. This was echoed in the Czechoslovak Ministry of Finance with which the native bank had special connections despite, or possibly because of, Beneš's personal role in the formation of the Anglo-Czechoslovak Bank. Some of the hostility may have stemmed from the failure of the Czechoslovaks to obtain the privileged position in the London market which they had expected to come with this institutional tie. The presence of Viennese on the bank's board was another drawback, although this was soon remedied.[93] Spencer-Smith, a director of the new banks and the Bank of England, wrote to Montagu Norman:

I spent four days in Prague on my way here, and am going back there probably next week, as Beneš was away and I haven't quite been able to settle matters there. We are having some trouble because the Czechs accuse us of giving the Austrians too much influence and making the Czech influence nominal only. As there is some truth in this, especially in appearance, I am taking steps to settle the matter in such a way that the Czechs will see that we intend to adhere strictly to the spirit as well as the letter of the arrangement I originally made with Beneš.[94]

The bank began operations separated from its Czechoslovak branches but policy with regard to its other branches in the successor states was by no means clear. This confusion may have resulted from the time and energy consumed by negotiations first in Vienna, protracted by the pan-germanist opposition to the Länderbank, and second in Prague arising from the nostrification laws. The Austrian directors opposed any further fragmentation, especially the separation of the Budapest branch. However, Young, one of the English directors, was feeling his way forward to a total break-up, cutting out intermediate control from Vienna, followed by mergers with local banks. Possibly the pieces were to be finally knitted together again by 'ultimate amalgamation'.[95] On the one hand the bank lacked a clear organizational structure, and on the other it recommenced business more or less at the beginning of the hiatus following the onset of the stabilization process. Young, the English representative at Vienna, was pessimistic, writing in November 1922: 'For the moment the outlook in Austria itself is almost cheerful; the krone is stabilised, and the plan of reform required by the Delegates of the League of Nations has been carried through Parliament. But none the less I must admit that I feel no confidence for the future . . . I do not see any policy for the Bank in Central Europe except caution almost amounting to inaction.'[96] Similarly, but for different reasons, the immediate future in Czechoslovakia appeared difficult – 'We are going to make some considerable losses in Prague owing to the process of deflation and the consequent crisis.'[97]

Some Central European banking practices proved to be puzzling to both the bank's English staff and the Foreign Office's local representatives. Phillpotts, the commercial attaché in Vienna, visited the Austrian Ministry of Finance in connection with the strained relations between the Anglo-Austrian Bank and one of its customers, the Österreichisch-Alpine Montangesellschaft [Alpine Montan Co.]. The attaché stated in his subsequent report that 'In a discussion about the merits of a majority syndicate being given special advantages when new shares are issued the Minister said that he understands that this would not be possible in England but conditions here were different, owing to the lack of capital. The privilege given to these syndicates sometimes enables the Government to prevent the control of an important company or bank falling into undesirable hands, foreign or otherwise.'[98] This point had arisen from the method chosen to increase the capital of the Alpine Montan Co. The Anglo-Austrian in February 1923 had lent £0.25m to the steel company, in the process acquiring a seat on its board and concluding an agreement that it was to manage any future capital issues. However, the bank was not kept informed of the company's policy which appears to have been strongly influenced by Camillo Castiglioni of the Allgemeine Depositenbank who represented the interests of the controlling Stinnes group and Italian shareholders. The Alpine through Castiglioni acquired the Bismarkhütte AG and the Katowitzer AG für Bergbau und

Eisenhüttenbetrieb in Silesia as a source of coke, apparently from the Flick concern via the Rhein-Elbe Union. However, the necessary increase in capital was to be managed by the Niederösterreichische Escompte-Gesell-schaft which was acquiring half of the new issue for its syndicate at a discount of 50 per cent on the market price. Anglo-Austrian directors suspected that the real vendors of the Silesian concerns were Stinnes and Castiglioni and that there would be no surplus coke available from them for the Alpine. Their anger at being duped was increased by an offer of £15,000 in hush money to come from the profits of the issuing syndicate. This was declined and the Anglo-Austrian's representative withdrew from the Alpine's board.[99]

By early 1925 some of the English directors were taking an extremely pessimistic view of Austrian prospects, an outlook shared by members of the Foreign Office. M. W. Lampson wrote to Akers Douglas at Vienna asking for a comprehensive report, suitable if required to go to the Cabinet, explaining that he was 'seriously perturbed at the way things are developing in Austria' and asking if some form of Zollverein with either Germany or the Little Entente was feasible.[100] At the same time directors of the Anglo-Austrian approached French Ministries to explore the possibility of a merger of the Austrian branches of the Anglo-Austrian with the Vienna branch of the Banque des Pays de l'Europe Centrale. The case made covered a variety of points. It was argued that Austria had too many banks and although contraction had got underway, the remaining stronger banks needed to reduce their expenses. Second, as the crown was now stabilized, it was no longer necessary to have the respective banks' capitals denominated in a foreign currency, as was shown by the experience of the Anglo-Czechoslovak Bank and the Bank for Commerce and Industry. Bark, the director most involved in the negotiations, concluded that the bank resulting from the merger would be the largest in Vienna with first-class connections in both London and Paris, while adding that a French majority shareholding in the new concern was acceptable.[101]

The French viewed this approach from a political aspect rather than a commercial one and possibly they were right to do so, given some of the lines on which Foreign Office policy was developing. In any case the dividend record of the Anglo-Austrian since 1922 was hardly distinguished, especially in comparison with the Banque des Pays de l'Europe Centrale. The Quai d'Orsay thought that they perceived behind the proposal the machinations of Montagu Norman, who was considered to be highly favourable to the union of Austria with Germany and was thought to be closing the London, and possibly the New York, market to Austrian issues as part of a pro-German policy. No allowance was given that this action might be part of the necessary preparations for Britain to return to the gold standard. The French did agree that the Austrian economic situation was precarious and that an economic *entente* between the successor states was necessary but gave priority to supplying Austria with capital in order to expand the industrial base, particularly water power, and so reduce unemployment. The French declined the proposition, Finaly of 'Paribas' having turned to the Quai d'Orsay as the proper arbiter of the question.[102]

After a year the English found a solution for their problems in another quarter – marriage with the Credit-Anstalt. The extra-Austrian assets of the Anglo-Austrian Bank were acquired by a new concern, the Anglo-International Bank, which also took over the British Trade Corporation. This followed the sale of the Italian branches of the Anglo-Austrian bank to the Banca Italo-Britannica in January 1926. One result of the financial agreement behind the transfer of the Austrian branches to the Rothschild bank in July 1926 was that the Bank of England indirectly became a shareholder in the Credit-Anstalt. The English instead of easing themselves out of Central European engagements had unwittingly become more involved. The Anglo-International acquired the Anglo-Austrian's interests in the Anglo-Czechoslovak Bank and the Croatian Discount Bank.[103] The winding up of the Anglo-Austrian, as it was called by the Foreign Office, badly affected the prestige of the Anglo-Czechoslovak Bank which was burdened by a considerable number of bad debts.[104] Six months after the conclusion of the Austrian transfer, Bark went to Prague to sell the Anglo-International's holding in the Anglo-Czechoslovak Bank. The shares were first offered to the government which had originally intended to participate in the venture. Eventually only part of the holding was sold, the Anglo-International retaining a 30 per cent participation,[105] and despite the attitude of the Czechoslovak government German-Bohemian capital in the form of the Petschek group came into the bank.

Unlike the Banque des Pays de l'Europe Centrale group of French interests in East Central Europe, the Anglo-Austrian proved to be substantially a failure; even disengagement was impossible. A large number of factors account for this outcome, not least unfamiliarity with the area and its business practices. However, even continental bankers more used to the 'mixed' approach could at times be found out of their depth. As Van Hengel pointedly stressed to its foreign creditors in November 1932: 'It must be understood that the Credit-Anstalt is not a bank. It still carries on a larger banking business than any other bank in Austria, but this, compared to its total business is relatively small, and has contracted with the decrease in banking turnover all the world over. The Credit-Anstalt is chiefly a holding company, most of whose holdings are industrial and in a very weak state.'[106]

Appendix: *Indications of 'Western' Investments in the Banking Systems of East Central Europe in the 1920s*

Information on participations has been drawn from English and French official sources – Foreign Office papers, Archive of the Ministry of Foreign Affairs, Paris, and the Archive of the Ministry of the Economy-Ministry of the Budget, Paris. This, in turn, was drawn from a wide variety of sources – rumour, newspaper reports, and applications to export capital – so it is by no means exact.

AUSTRIA

ALLGEMEINE ÖSTERREICHISCHE BODEN-CREDIT-ANSTALT

Date	No. of shares bought	Purchaser
?1919/20	?140,000	Mutuelle Solvay
?1919/20	?	Amsterdamsche Bank, Lippmann, Rosenthal
1922 end	'small parcel'	J. Henry Schroeder
?1922/3	?100,000	Assicurazioni Generale, Trieste
Apr. 1923	new share issue – 1m, of which:	
	500,000	to existing shareholders
	?500,000	to syndicate
	of which 220,000	taken by Schroeders
	balance	J. P. Morgan and possibly Baring Brothers
Apr. 1927	new share issue – 300,000, of which:	
	60,000	to Union Européenne industrielle et financière

Jointly established investment trusts, holding companies, and bond issues:

1925	$2.4m 8% mortgage bonds	issued by Schroeders Banking Corp. and Lee, Higginson & Co. via European Mortgage & Investment Corp., Boston

Date		
1926	American, British & Continental Trust	jointly established with Schroeders and Blith, Witter
1927	Maatschappij vor Beheer u. Effekten	established by Amsterdamsche Bank; Lippmann, Rosenthal; and 'English and Swiss houses' ? took over holdings in the Fanto petrol group

Österreichische Credit-Anstalt für Handel u. Gewerbe

Date	No. of shares bought	Purchaser
1920	125,000	Kuhn Loeb and Guaranty Trust Corp. of New York
1921	issues of 250,000 new shares, of which: 50,000	taken by syndicate led by Hope & Co. and Nederlandsche Handels Maatschappij
July 1923	'important parcel'	National Provincial Bank and Lazards, London
1927	'important parcel' (?100,000)	Prudential Assurance Co., London
end 1927	new issue of 400,000	Goldmann Sachs & Co.; Strupp & Co.; Ames, Emerich & Co.; International Acceptance Bank. (Issued on Wall Street in form of certificates of 8 shares each.)
June 1928	'participation'	Union Européenne industrielle et financière

Jointly established banks, investment trusts, holding companies and bond issues:

1919	Amstelbank, Amsterdam capital 8m florins	Rothschild group took 50% of shares; co-founders – Nederlandsche Handels Maatschappij; Hope & Co.
1922	Bank für Auswärtigen Handel, Berlin; capital 250m marks	co-founder – Česká eskomptní banka a úvěrní ústav [Bohemian Discount Bank and Society of Credit]
mid-1928	'Dutch company of Credit and Finance'; capital 12m florins	co-founders – Rothschild & Sons, Warburgs, and 'Swiss and American houses'
1930	Continentale Gesellschaft für Bank u. Industriewerte established in Basle	took over Austrian and foreign securities of the Credit-Anstalt and the defunct Boden-Credit-Anstalt

Acquisitions

1926	Austrian interests of Anglo-Austrian Bank
1929	Boden-Credit-Anstalt

Dispersements

Adriatic coast filials to Banca Commerciale, Trieste

Lublin and Lwów filials to Bank Dyskontowy Warszawski [Warsaw Discount Bank]

Sudeten branches to Česká eskomptní banka a úvěrní ústav [Bohemian Discount Bank and Society of Credit]

Ljubljana branch to independent company

NIEDERÖSTERREICHISCHE ESCOMPTE-GESELLSCHAFT

Date	No. of shares bought	Purchaser
1921	new issue of 250m crowns	
	185,000 shares	Crédit Liègeois
	125,000 shares	Banque de Bruxelles, which took up shares in new issues in 1922 and 1923
end 1921	?250,000	Comptoir d'Escompte, Geneva and associates
June 1923	'Parcel'	Union Européenne industrielle et
	?100,000 shares	financière
Nov. 1923	?150,000 shares	Hambros and Lloyds Bank, London
Mar. 1925	'important parcel'	Banque de Bruxelles for King of the Belgians
Feb. 1926	'important parcel'	W. A. Harriman, New York
?1928	'important parcel'	Berliner Handelsgesellschaft

Jointly established holding company:

Mar. 1927	Central European Investing Co.; capital $4m.	W. A. Harriman; Comptoir d'Escompte, Geneva; Banque de Bruxelles; Union Européenne industrielle et financière

Dispersements

Czech interests to Česká eskomptní banka a úvěrní ústav [Bohemian Discount Bank and Society of Credit] (see also Credit-Anstalt)

WIENER BANK-VEREIN

Date	No. of shares bought	Purchaser
		Deutsche Bank held a participation from 1889 which by 1929 was 5% of the equity capital
1920	150,000	to Société Générale de Belgique and Banque Belge pour l'Étranger; this group took up their 'rights proportion' of new issues made in 1921, 1922, 1923 and 1927
1922	??	Banque de Commerce de Bâle
1925	parcel of shares	placed in the U.S.A. by Gutmanns
July 1927	capital increased from 50 to 55m sch.: 500,000 shares	taken by Dillon Read & Co.; blocked in the U.S.A. for two years; part transferred to United States and Foreign Securities Corp.

Dispersements

Czechoslovak interests to Všeobecná česká bankovní jednota [General Bohemian Bank Union] in which the Wiener Bank-Verein and the Sociéte Générale de Belgique group held a participation; similar association in the case of the Opšte jugoslovensko bankarsko društvo a.d. (1927).

AUSTRIA – 'MIDDLE BANKS'

BANK & WECHSELSTUBEN-ACTIEN-GESELLSCHAFT 'MERCUR'

Date	No. of shares bought	Purchaser
1902 on		participation in new issues held by Darmstädter u. National Bank in conjunction with Banque de Commerce de Bâle and l'Union des Banques Suisses
1920, 1921, 1922, 1928		post-war new issue syndicates headed by Darmstädter; Simon, Hirschland u. Sohn, Essen, a member
1921	100,000	Incasso Bank, Amsterdam
1923	participation, c. 10%	Hallgarten & Co. and E. F. Hutton & Co., New York
1928		Hallgarten & Co. member of placing syndicate for new issue which increased the bank's capital from 12 to 20m sch.

The possibility of establishing an investment trust for the 'Mercur' was investigated in 1928 by the Darmstädter in conjunction with the Schweizer Credit Gesellschaft and the Union Financière de Genève.

CZECHOSLOVAKIA*

Anglo-československá banka (Anglo-Czechoslovak Bank)

Date	No. of shares bought	Purchaser
1922	100%	Anglo-Austrian Bank which in 1926 became the Anglo-International Bank
Oct. 1927	30%	Anglo-International Bank
	25%	Czechoslovak State
	25%	Czechoslovak Agricultural Co-operatives
	20%	Petschek-Schicht-Lichtenstein group
1929	?6.25%/12.5%	Samuel & Co., London
	?6.25%/12.5%	Harriman, New York
1930	merged with the Pražská úvěrní banka [Prague Credit Bank]	

Česká eskomptní banka a úvěrní ústav [Bohemian Discount Bank and Society of Credit]

[Took over Czechoslovak interests of the Credit-Anstalt and Niederösterreichische Escompte-Gesellschaft. The latter held a majority of shares at the bank's inception.]

Date	No. of shares bought	Purchaser
1920	capital increased from 48m to 100m Kč	
	?	Banque de Bruxelles;
	?	Warburg & Co., Hamburg;
	?	International Acceptance Bank, New York
1923	?	Kleinwort & Sons
?1928/9	'parcel'	taken by W. A. Harriman and the International Acceptance Bank

NB. It was thought that in 1929 55% of the bank's shares were held by Živnostenská banka.

* See A. Teichova, *An Economic Background to Munich* (1974).

ČESKÁ BANKA UNION [BOHEMIAN UNION BANK]

Date	No. of shares bought	Purchaser
1920 new issue of 200,000 shares of which:		
	120,000	taken by Banca Commerciale Italiana, Lazard Frères, Paris
?1924		?Castiglioni's holding (Depositenbank) taken up by Banca Commerciale Italiana
1926	'large parcel'	at least part of Banca Commerciale holding and some Czechoslovak holdings transferred via Helbert Wagg to Prudential Assurance Co.
Jan. 1929	merged with Všeobecna česká bankovní jednota	

Všeobecná česká bankovní jednota [General Bohemian Bank Union] was established in 1922 to take over Czechoslovak interests of the Wiener Bank-Verein; capital subscribed by Société Générale de Belgique, Banque Belge pour l'Étranger and Wiener Bank-Verein. In the merger with Bohemian Union Bank the Banca Commerciale's shares were transferred to the Wiener Bank-Verein and its Belgian associates, thus retaining a 22.5 per cent interest in the bank.

PRAŽSKÁ ÚVĚRNÍ BANKA [PRAGUE CREDIT BANK]

Date	No. of shares bought	Purchaser
1919	nominal capital increased from 50m to 100m Kč 1st tranche of 25m Kč	
	20%	Czechoslovak sources
	80%	Société Générale, J. Gunzberg et Cie, 'Paribas', Crédit Mobilier, Rotterdamsche Bankvereinigung
1923	2nd tranche of 25m Kč	? Crédit Mobilier J. Gunzberg et Cie
[by 1927		Société Générale interest totally eliminated]

HUNGARY

ANGOL-MAGYAR BANK RÉSZVÉNYTÁRSASÁG [BRITISH AND HUNGARIAN BANK]

[reformation of the Hungarian Trading Bank; started with a capital of 120m K.]

Date	No. of shares bought	Purchaser
May 1920	capital increased by 100m K; 250,000 new shares	taken by Marconi Wireless Co. Ltd (British interest 42½%)
1927	capital increased from 18m to 31m Pg; 120,000 new shares	taken by British Overseas Bank and Helbert Wagg & Co.
1929	new issue of 12m Pg, of which 8m	taken by Helbert Wagg & Co.

Jointly established companies, bond issues:

1927	$1.5m 7½% bonds	issued through Ames Emerich & Co., New York
1928	£100,000 mortgage bonds	London market
Oct. 1920	British Danubian Trading Co. capital £100,000, of which 50 per cent	taken by British interests; jointly established with G. Isaacs to develop the trading interests of the Bank

PESTI MAGYAR KERESKEDELMI BANK [HUNGARIAN COMMERCIAL BANK OF PEST]

Date	No. of shares bought	Purchaser
1920	41,666	placed in Switzerland
[1923	300,000 shares issued in all]	
1925	capital increased from 800,000m to 1,000,000m K new issue of 100,000	all taken by Schroeders for an international syndicate of English, American, Dutch and Swiss houses; blocked for several years

Jointly established investment trusts, holding companies, and bond issues:

| 1926 | American, British & Continental Trust | jointly founded with Boden-Credit-Anstalt and J. M. Schroeder & Co., New York |
| Oct. 1930 | 15m Swiss francs mortgage bonds | |

Connections with Disconto Gesellschaft, Commerz u. Privat Bank, Banque Generale de Bulgarie, Crédit Foncier Franco-Bulgarie.

Affiliated with Bank Handlowy w Waszawie, Bank Malopolski.

MAGYAR ÁLTALÁNOS HITELBANK [HUNGARIAN GENERAL CREDIT BANK]*

Date	*No. of shares bought*	*Purchaser*
1920	new issue; 200,000	to Union Européenne industrielle et financière, thus obtaining 25% interest
1922	new issue: 50,000	to Union Européenne industrielle et financière
[1923	1,050,000 shares issued in all]	
?1923/5	new issue:	
	50,000	to Rothschild, with whom the Bank was closely linked
	100,000	Mendelssohn
	200,000	French syndicate
[1925	total issued 1,200,000 shares of which 300,000 thought to be held by French group and c.120,000 by Rothschilds, Vienna]	
1926	new issue: 'considerable parcel'	to Schneider et Cie, l'Union Européenne industrielle et financière, Banque de l'Union parisienne, Rothschilds, Vienna, Credit-Anstalt, Lazard Bros., London, International Acceptance Bank, Hallgarten & Co., New York, Industrial Finance & Investment Corp., London, Kleinwort & Co., London, Mendelssohn, Berlin, Warburg, Hamburg
late 1920s	'parcel'	acquired by National Provincial Bank

Jointly established banks:

1928	Sté de Banque pour le Commerce et l'Industrie de Paris: capital 5m fr.	formed with l'Union Européenne industrielle et financière, Credit-Anstalt, Amstelbank, and Hungarian Bank of Discount and Exchange
1929	increase of capital to 30m fr.	taken by previous syndicate together with Banque de l'Union parisienne, Anglo-Czechoslovak Bank, Bohemian Discount Bank and Society of Credit, and Živnostenská banka

Relations with M. Samuel & Co., Disconto Gesellschaft, and S. Bleichröder.

★ See also Chapters 13 and 15 below.

MAGYAR OLASZ BANK RÉSZVÉNYTÁRSASÁG [HUNGARIAN-ITALIAN BANK]

[Established-owned by Banca Commerciale Italiana.]

Bond issues

Date	No.	
?	$1.75m 7½% bonds	E. M. Rollins & Sons, New York
?1927	$1m 7½% bonds	
Oct. 1928	$2.7m 7½% bonds	
Nov. 1929	$2m 7½% bonds	with Banca Commerciale Italiana

MAGYAR JELZÁLOG HITELBANK [LAND MORTGAGE BANK OF THE KINGDOM OF HUNGARY]

Bond issues

Date	No.	
1924	?	issue on French market
Jan. 1926	£1m 7½% bonds	syndicate headed by Hambros and Anglo-Austrian Bank; £0.14m taken by Royal Hungarian Postal Savings Bank and National Bank of Hungary
?1926	£3m	syndicate of Hambros, Anglo-International Bank, Haes & Sons
?1927	$1.8m 7½% bonds	

Bond issues

Date	No.	Purchaser
?1927	£0.5m 7½% bonds	
Jan. 1928	£0.5m 7½% bonds	
Sept. 1928	$3m 7½% bonds	
Sept. 1929	£0,66m 7½% bonds	Hambros with Anglo-International Bank

Notes

* This paper, very much a preliminary essay or rather foray, is based upon some of the material gathered during research work generously financed by the S.S.R.C. Considerable help and assistance has been given by three part-time research assistants – Ms E. Boross, Dr E. Kandler and Mr R. Waller, attached to the project 'Multinational Companies in Central East Europe, 1919–1939' directed by Professor Alice Teichova and the author. In this instance, the views expressed in this paper are those of the author alone, not because of any internecine divisions but rather as a consequence of pressure of time and commitments.

1. Austria, Czechoslovakia, and Hungary for the purposes of this paper.
2. A. Basch, *The Danube Basin and the German Economic Sphere* (1944), 8–10.
3. R. E. Cameron, *France and the Economic Development of Europe* (Princeton, N.J., 1961), 420.
4. Calculated from Royal Institute of International Affairs, *The Problem of International Investments* (1937); see also H. Feis, *Europe the World's Banker 1870–1914* (repr. New York, 1965), 23, 51, 74.
5. British holdings of Austro-Hungarian securities constituted about 0.0004 per cent of the British foreign investment portfolio in 1914.
6. Feis, *op. cit.*, 202–8.
7. Ministry of Foreign Affairs Archive, Paris (henceforth MAE); Europe 1918–1929, Autriche (henceforth Autriche) 137, 'Notes prises au cours d'une conversation avec M. Alexander Weiner, Directeur du Crédit Foncier d'Autriche lors de sa visite à Genève', 3 Mar. 1919, f. 7.
8. R. L. Rudolph, *Banking and Industrialisation in Austria-Hungary* (1976), 174–5.

9. P. L. Cottrell, 'London financiers and Austria 1863–1875: the Anglo-Austrian Bank', *Business History*, XI (1969); *Stock Exchange Year Book* (1914).
10. MAE, Autriche 142, 'Note sur la Francisation de la Banque des Pays Autrichiens', f.66.
11. *Ibid.*, Autriche 137, 'Project d'un Mitteleurope financier', note submitted by A. E. Sayous, 5 Dec. 1918, Lausanne, fos. 3–4.
12. For a brief survey, see League of Nations, Economic, Financial and Transit Department, *Relief Deliveries and Loans 1919–1923* (Geneva, 1943).
13. Ministry of the Economy-Ministry of the Budget, Economic and Financial Archives, Paris (henceforth ME), F^{30} 614, 'Note remise par M. Marcel Schwob', 22 May 1919.
14. Quoted in H. Clay, *Lord Norman* (1957), 184–5.
15. Bank of England Papers, London (henceforth BoE), W. R. Laverack, 'Outline of the General Scheme for the Rehabilitation of Austria with special reference to the part played by the Bank of England'.
16. The above is drawn from D. E. Moggridge, *British Monetary Policy 1924–1931. The Norman Conquest of $4.86* (1972), 201–19. See also J. M. Atkin, 'Official regulation of British overseas investment, 1914–1931', *EcHR*, 2nd ser., XXIII (1970).
17. MAE, Tchecoslovaquie 79, Beneš to Kammerer, 11 Apr. 1919, f. 7.
18. *Ibid.*, Ministry of Finance to Ministry of Foreign Affairs, 8 May 1919, f. 18.
19. *Ibid.*, Beneš to Pichou, 1 Nov. 1919, f. 55; Prevost, chargé d'affaires, The Hague, to Ministry of Foreign Affairs, 20 Sept. 1919, f. 62.

20. *Ibid.*, Ministry of Foreign Affairs to Ministry of Finance, 22 Sept. 1923, f. 155.
21. *Ibid.*, Banque de l'Union parisienne to Ministry of Finance, Direction du Mouvement Général des Fonds, 23 Mar. 1920, f.85.
22. MAE, Autriche 137, 'Notes prises au course d'une conversation avec M. Alexandre Weiner, Directeur du Crédit Foncier d'Autriche lors de sa visite à Genève, 3 Mar. 1919, fos. 7–9.
23. *Ibid.*, 'Visite de M. d'Adler', 2 Jan 1920, fos. 172–7.
24. ME, F^{30} 614, 'Note remise par M. Marcel Schwob', 22 May 1919.
25. *Ibid.*, 'pour M de Fabry: "Projet de Transformation de la Banque I.R.P. des Pays Autrichiens en Banque Francaise des Pays de l'Europe Centrale"'; undated but written at the earliest in May 1919. There is also a copy, but with its full supporting documentation, in MAE, Autriche 142, fos. 44–73.
26. MAE, Serie Y, Internationale 1918–1940, 242: Maurice Bompard, 'Rapport sur la Fortune Française en Turquie et dans les états Balkaniques', Paris, 21 Sept. 1917.
27. The Länderbank held:
    1,808 shares of the Banque de Croatie, Agram
    7,500 Banque de Crédit Serbe
    5,700 Banque Hongroise d'Escompte et de Change, Budapest
    9,800 Banque de Crédit Roumain, Bucharest
    4,975 Boden-Credit-Anstalt
    5,000 Zentral Boden Credit Anstalt
    Its main industrial interests were Dynamit Nobel, Fabriques de produits émaillés et metalliques Austria, Fonderies R. Ph. Waagner, Usines Siemens-Schukert, Constructions Mécanique de Brünn, Fabriques de Machines agricoles Hofherr-Schrantz-Clayton-Shuttleworth, Raffineries de sucre de Schönpriessen, Union des Fabriques de Sucre de Moravie, Fabrique de ciments de Perlmoos, Fabrique d'allumettes 'Solo', Charbonnages de Trifail, Sté de Carborundum and Sté pour l'industrie du bois 'Bukowine': MAE, Autriche 142, Documents Annexes au Projet de Transformation . . ., fos. 78–9.
28. *Ibid.*, Heidler, Czechoslovak Minister of Industry and Commerce to Rotter, 28 Aug. 1919, fos. 102–3.
29. *Ibid.*, note to M. Celier, Paris, 4 July 1919, fos. 81–3.
30. *Ibid.*, telegrams, Minstry of Foreign Affairs to Allize, French Minister at Vienna, fos. 63, 64, 88, 89.
31. *Ibid.*, Ministry of Foreign Affairs to Ministry of Finance (Direction du Mouvement Général des Fonds), No. 1687, 'Transformation de la Banque des Pays Autrichiens', 12 July 1919, fos. 90–2.
32. *Ibid.*, Ministry of Finance to Ministry of Foreign Affairs, No. 16,056, 'Rapports avec les banquiers', 21 Oct. 1919, f. 118.
33. *Ibid.*, letter from 'Paribas' to the Minister of Foreign Affairs, 6 Nov. 1919, fos. 127–9.
34. *Ibid.*, Le Conseiller d'État, Directeur Général to the Ministry of Finance (Direction du Mouvement Général des Fonds), No. 17, 730, 30 Dec. 1919, fos. 159–61.
35. *Ibid.*, telegram, Ministry of Foreign Affairs to French Minister, Bucharest, 17 Jan. 1920, f. 163.
36. *Ibid.*, letter from 'Paribas' *et al.*, to the Minister of Foreign Affairs, 27 Jan. 1920, f. 166.
37. MAE, Autriche 143, undated, unheaded note, ?early summer 1920.
38. *Ibid.*, letter, 'Paribas' to the Ministry of Foreign Affairs, Direction des Affaires Politiques et Commerciales (Service Financier), 13 June 1921, fos. 83–4. See also Ministry of Foreign Affairs to Couget, French Minister at Prague, 20 June 1921, f. 94, and Couget to Ministry of Foreign Affairs, 25 Aug. 1921, f. 112.
39. *Ibid.*, 'Note sur la "Länderbank"', fos. 76–7'.
40. *Ibid.*, 'Aide-Memoire', 27 Oct. 1921, fos. 161–3; 'Memorandum', 27 Oct. 1921, fos. 164–5.
41. *Ibid.*, 'Note sur la Länderbank', 7 Apr. 1921, fos. 77–8.
42. *Ibid.*, 'Memorandum', 27 Oct. 1921, fos. 164–5.
43. *Ibid.*, 'Paribas' *et al.* to the President of the Council, 6 Dec. 1921; fos. 166–7; see also fos. 171–3. The French members of the syndicate were 'Paribas', the Crédit

346   *P. L. Cottrell*

Mobilier, Banque Française pour le Commerce et l'Industrie, and J. Gunzberg et Cie.

44. A. Teichova, 'Versailles and the expansion of the Bank of England into Central Europe', in N. Horn and J. Kocka (eds.), *Law and the Formation of the Big Enterprises in the 19th and Early 20th Centuries* (Göttingen, 1979).

45. MAE, Autriche 143; 'Note sur la Länderbank', 7 Apr. 1921, f. 77.

46. *Ibid.*, Lefevre Pontalis, French Minister at Vienna to the Ministry of Foreign Affairs, 18 July 1921, fos. 103–4.

47. *Ibid.*, Pontalis to the Ministry of Foreign Affairs, 7 Sept. 1921, fos. 117.

48. *Ibid.*, Ministry of Foreign Affairs to Comte de Saint-Aulaire, Ambassador in London, 22 Sept. 1921, f. 132.

49. *Ibid.*, Telegram from Pontalis, Vienna, 2 Oct. 1921.

50. BoE, W. R. Laverack, 'Outline of the General Scheme for the Rehabilitation of Austria with special reference to the part played by the Bank of England'.

51. MAE, Autriche 143, 'Memorandum', 27 Oct. 1921, f. 164.

52. *Ibid.*, Österreichische Länderbank, Ausserordentliche Generalversammlung, 28 Jan. 1922, f. 174 *et seq.*

53. See Z. P. Pryor, 'Czechoslovak economic development in the inter-war period', in V. S. Mamatey and R. Luza, *A History of the Czechoslovak Republic 1918–1948* (1973), 195–7.

54. See League of Nations, *Financial Reconstruction of Austria; idem, Financial Reconstruction of Hungary.*

55. On a base of 1913 the rates are Czechoslovakia 2.7 per cent Austria 0.5 per cent and Hungary 1.6 per cent; see Z. P. Pryor, 'Czechoslovak fiscal policies in the Great Depression', *EcHR*, 2nd ser., XXXII (1979).

56. MAE, Autriche 137, Pontalis, French Minister at Vienna to Ministry of Foreign Affairs, 18 Aug. 1920, f. 216.

57. Public Record Office, London (henceforth PRO), FO 371 4653.

58. *Ibid.*

59. MAE, Autriche 141, f. 17.

60. Me, F30 628, Ministry of Foreign Affairs to Ministry of Finance, 14 Dec. 1922.

61. *Ibid.*, 'Rapport au Ministre', 20 May 1924.

62. *Ibid.*, F30 629, François Marsal to E. Schneider, 29 Apr. 1924.

63. *Ibid.*, F30 628, French Minister at Vienna to Ministry of Foreign Affairs, 27 Mar. 1926.

64. MAE, Autriche 139, French Minister at Vienna to Ministry of Foreign Affairs, 27 Mar. 1929, f. 123.

65. ME, F30 627, French Minister at Vienna to Ministry of Foreign Affairs, 24 Jan. 1929.

66. MAE, Autriche 139, Chargé d'Affairs, Vienna to Ministry of Foreign Affairs, 6 Feb. 1929, fos. 46–7.

67. *Ibid.*, Autriche 141, l'Union Européenne to M. le Président de la Commission de la Commission du Contrôle de l'Exportation des Capitaux, Ministry of Finance, 8 Apr. 1927. The total sum involved was 4.6m fr.

68. ME, F30 627, 'Note pour le Ministre', 11 Oct. 1929.

69. MAE, Autriche 141, 'Note pour Monsieur de Beaumarchais', 7 Nov. 1927, f. 119.

70. E. W. Bennett, *Germany and the Diplomacy of the Financial Crisis, 1931* (Cambridge, Mass., 1962), 42, 102.

71. MAE, Autriche 139, French Minister at Vienna to Ministry of Foreign Affairs, 29 Jan. 1929, fos. 110–3.

72. *Ibid.*, telegram to French Ministry, Vienna, 19 Mar. 1929, f. 125.

73. ME, F30 627, French Minister at Vienna to Ministry of Foreign Affairs.

74. MAE, Autriche 139, Ministry of Foreign Affairs to French Minister at Vienna, 21 Nov. 1929, f. 195.

75. BoE, 'Austria at the time of the Boden Credit Anstalt Affair, 30 Jan. 1930'.

76. *Ibid.*, 'Boden-Credit-Anstalt, 14 Oct. 1929'.

77. ME, F30 627, 'Note pour le Ministre', Paris, 11 Oct. 1929.

78. *Ibid.*, F30 628, 'Credit-Anstalt', 12 May 1931.

79. *Ibid.*, F30 627, French Commercial Attaché at Prague to the Minister of Commerce and Industry, 10 Oct. 1929.

80. BoE, 47/1, Rost van Tonningen to Niemeyer, 18 Dec. 1931.

81. ME, F30 627, Ministry of Finance to Ministry of Foreign Affairs, 11 Oct. 1932.

82. PRO, FO 371 15891, Memorandum from Sir Eric Phipps, Head of the British Legation at Vienna, 11 Nov. 1932.

83. *Ibid.*, FO 371 16629; *ibid.*, 18366.
84. *Ibid.*, FO 371 19483.
85. *Ibid.*, FO 371 18842 R 1813; *ibid.*, R 2420; *ibid.*, R 2637; FO 371 19483.
86. Most of the above paragraph is drawn from Annual Reports compiled by British Legations in Budapest and Prague and published in FO 371 series.
87. A. Teichova, *An Economic Background to Munich* (1974), 342.
88. PRO, FO 371 13666.
89. In addition to Teichova, *loc. cit.*, see also A. S. J. Baster, *The International Banks* (1935), 193–202.
90. *Ibid.*, 245.
91. PRO, FO 371 5830, Annual Report on Czechoslovakia for 1920.
92. Interview with Sir Eric Berthoud, 2 Aug. 1979.
93. PRO, FO 371 8584, Annual Report on Czechoslovakia for 1922.
94. BoE, Spencer-Smith to M. Norman, 4 Dec. 1922.
95. *Ibid.*, G. M. Young to Spencer-Smith.
96. *Ibid.*, G. M. Young to the Executive Committee, Anglo-Austrian Bank, London, 28 Nov. 1922.
97. *Ibid.*, Spencer-Smith to M. Norman, 4 Dec. 1922.
98. PRO FO 371 8552.
99. *Ibid.*
100. PRO FO 120 1009 2064/1.
101. ME F^{30} 627, P. Bark to Minister of Finance, Paris, 2 Feb. 1925.
102. MAE, Autriche 138, Note. Visite de M. Finaly à M. Seydoux, 26 Mar. 1925.
103. PRO FO 371 12078; *ibid.*, 11213.
104. PRO FO 371 11226.
105. PRO FO 371 12097.
106. ME B12655. Report by Van Hengel to the Foreign Creditors of the Austrian Credit-Anstalt, 19 Nov. 1932.

COMMENTARY   *M. Lévy-Leboyer*

After this very able and solid paper, I shall limit myself to a few comments which I hope will be taken as stemming simply from common sense.

The presentation deals with the penetration of western capital into banking in Austria, Hungary and Czechoslovakia after the First World War and so I think we should address to ourselves three questions. The first concerns scope: how important or unimportant was the flow of capital into this region? The second has to do with motivations. Why did the French, English, Swiss or Dutch enter the field? Were they rational or not? And last, what was the cost and benefit, either for the bankers, for the firms to which they belonged, and for the community at large?

So, first, the problem of scope. Cottrell has been careful to bring out the pre-war situation to give a proper perspective: he mentioned the fact that in 1914 France held £35m in state bonds and railway securities, which was equivalent to the total held by the British and German investors together. But it is also fair to be reminded that French investments in this area dated back from the mid-nineteenth-century, and that bankers and railway promoters, who had been responsible for this venture, had long been superseded by newcomers. In fact, after the foundation in 1880 of the Länderbank the French ceased issuing Austrian bonds on the Paris market for many reasons which have been dealt with earlier; so that, in spite of their past stake in the region, Cottrell rightly recalled that one may wonder what experience they really had in the region. The general impression is that they had lost contact and skills and were facing an entirely new situation, often under the lead of Foreign Affairs officials. One may wonder whether what has often been presented as a continuous drive might not turn out to be a fresh departure. It would be interesting to know – as the free export of capital did not regain legal status until the later part of the 1920s in England and France – what was the amount of western capital genuinely invested in East European banks in 1931. Are we not somewhat mistaken in bringing together the pre-1880s experience and the post-1919 one? Cottrell's list of take-overs shows that the French were very slow to break in, and rather modest on the whole; there was the case of Schneider and the Union Européenne, but otherwise they were out of the picture in most of the on-going ventures. So, are we justified in stressing traditions? And, furthermore, are not we simplifying the picture by assuming that any export of capital is made at the initiative of the exporter or rather of the banks in the capital-exporting countries?

This brings us to the second point. Why was capital being exported to this region? And were motivations similar all through the period under review? There were four main stages or types of movement detectable. First, immediately after the war – at least this was the case in Germany – foreigners bought notes and other assets on the assumption that pre-war parities would be regained. Then, in 1923–4 refugee capital poured from Germany into Czechoslovakia, but this was a very short-lived interlude. Eventually, when money was stabilized, speculation in the exchange market and also in the security market regained some momentum, because stocks had lagged in price behind commodities and services during the inflation period. And last, capital was imported – normally on a wider and safer scale, to cover the deficit with foreign countries and develop new capacities – with the revival of the various economies. So capital investments into the industrial and the banking sectors should have assumed wider proportions after 1925 than during the post-war instability period. Facts, however, do not fit with this pattern: the main take-overs, those of the Länderbank and of the Anglo-Austrian Bank, were completed by 1921–2, i.e. in the first period; and, contrary to what could be expected, after 1926, English and American bankers tried and often succeeded in disposing of their new holdings, either by selling bank participations or by setting up trust funds to be marketed in Amsterdam or New York. Is the explanation a political one? Was capital penetration – possibly against Western bankers' reluctance – one of the means used to build up a *cordon sanitaire* around Germany or a barrier against Russian expansion? As a matter of fact – and Dr Cottrell seems very convincing – economic factors were the prime forces. Western bankers had to bear the pressure of Beneš and the Prague bankers in their drive for nostrification of the Czechoslovak banking system in 1921, and that of the

Austrian banks in their search for fresh capital in order to make up for illiquid assets and accumulated foreign debts at the end of the war. The initiative came from the East. This goes a long way to explain the difficulties that were met when Paris bankers had to build up the syndicate of banks that took over the Länderbank, or the failure of the Živnostenská banka in London in 1921, or the English disinvestment move of the late 1920s, etc. Attitudes were similar in the second stage, after 1926. Capital was imported, but at short term and at very high rates, so that the whole system was vulnerable to interest rate differentials, in particular between Vienna and New York. It was a logical outcome of this situation that the Boden-Credit-Anstalt failed in September 1929, at the very moment of the Wall Street crash, or that the Wiener Bank-Verein was compelled to submit to onerous capital manipulations in the post-crisis period of reconstruction. In short, factors and motivations that can be used to give account of the pre-war and the post-war experience are hardly comparable: capital movements present a continuous thread, but in a completely different environment.

The last point – that of the cost and benefit – is not so easy to deal with, although its importance is not to be doubted. Who benefited from these capital movements? Was it the individuals, the firms or the capital-importing countries? Obviously the bankers themselves were not neutral. Although Dr Cottrell points out one case where the representatives of the Anglo-Austrian Bank were offered (and refused) bribes, were there other instances of similar behaviour on the part of eastern and western banks? Second, what were the returns for the banks? Were they looking for commissions and/or for capital gains? When the Alpine Montan had to buy the Bismarckhütte and the Kattowitzer Bergbau AG, in Silesia, it is said that the company issued new stock and sold part of it at 50 per cent below par to one of its bankers: was this a normal procedure? and if so, did this stock-taking pay in the long run? All students of banking history are well aware that such information is difficult to assess. But one would wish for a better evaluation of the risks involved by the banks and of their true rewards. At a more macro-economic level, a final point worth considering is that of the social profit, if any. It has been argued in many instances that foreign debts turned out to be a heavy penalty for the various countries in Eastern Europe once the depression of the 1930s set in; it is partly not to repeat the mistakes of the 1920s that direct investments have replaced purely financial ventures. But the question of the positive contribution of foreign investments – in the banking sector as well as in the industrial and service sectors – remains open. One could argue that the point raised goes beyond the scope of Cottrell's paper. But answering it would certainly contribute to a better understanding of the financial relations between East and West Europe and of course of the working of the inter-war economy.

COMMENTARY B. Michel

I would first like to stress that this is a very rich paper, opening many paths and closing absolutely none for further research. I cannot follow all the paths that Dr Cottrell has opened, but I would like to make four points.

First, in reading the diplomats' commentaries one receives the impression of such an enormous amount of foreign capital flooding into Eastern and Central Europe that it would be surprising if this flood had not enveloped the banks. But I do not think that the diplomats' view is quite correct because in fact the local banks of Central Europe were not drowned by this flood of capital. On the contrary, it seems to me that there was no domination by the two western powers, France and England, over the banks of Central Europe. Consequently I think that Cottrell is right when at the beginning of the paper he writes: 'By the mid-1920s nearly all the major banks of East Central Europe had substantial proportions of their equity capital held by foreigners'. He was very cautious and was right to say 'nearly all' and 'a substantial proportion', because, of course, we must not think in terms of an enormous change involving the banks of Central Europe losing control of their own capital. I find, for instance, that many of the important banks in some countries came under only very slight control by France or England. All the Czechoslovak banks, in my opinion, were quite free from western influence. For instance, the Živnostenská banka always had a very independent position because its leader, Jaroslav Preiss, maintained his own strategy and was not willing to have to make concessions to anyone. Many other banks were also extremely strong; for instance, the Agrární banka [Agrarian Bank] was exporting capital and was relatively free from foreign influence. So caution has to be exercised, at least with respect to the Czechoslovak banks. Further, it seems to me that in Romania and Poland the influence of foreign capital was also not so important as some writers have sometimes maintained. The crux of the problem is that the agreements between the French banks and the Austrian or Czechoslovak banks were not imposed by the French but rather were negotiated. If the French banks had their own strategy, so did the Austrian or the Czechoslovak banks. They were using foreign capital as a means of realizing their own ends. Each party was trying to use the other and it was not such an unequal struggle as we might imagine. The Austrian case cited can be somewhat misleading, for if the Anglo-Austrian Bank was so openly English and the Banque de Pays de l'Europe Centrale was so openly French, it is because they needed the British or the French flag to cover their interests in Central Europe. They feared nationalization or confiscation in the successor states. Otherwise, foreign influence was generally concealed in order not to be so obvious. (One of my assistants, Miss Nicole Piétri, has been working on the problem of Austria after the First World War and has been studying the help given by the League of Nations to the Austrian economy; she has also looked at the case of the Banque de Pays de l'Europe

Centrale. Her opinion is that the French influence was strongly desired by the Austrians and that it was on a relatively equal basis.)

The second question is the problem of continuity and change. Of course, the diplomats at that time were primarily struck by the changes, and the changes, of course, were obvious. The break-up of the Central and East European economic area was, as Herbert Matis has pointed out, not so clear or so simple, but it certainly was very striking for foreigners. However, I want to point mainly to the continuity of the policy of the banks. This is very clear with the Czechoslovak banks, which continued to pursue, after the First World War, the policy they had been following during the first years of the twentieth century. Here the continuity is absolute. In the case of Austria, of course, continuity could not be sustained to the same degree because the post-war change was enormous for the Austrian banks. But it is clear, for instance, that the foreign capital flowed through various channels which already existed. For instance, French capital came to Austria through Sieghart and d'Adler, bankers who had been collaborating closely with the French banks before the First World War: as it was impossible before 1914, officially, to invest French capital in Austria and Hungary itself, they had invested together in the Balkan countries. This continuity is most important, but sometimes the French banks created a continuity which did not really exist. I will take only one example here: the question of the French capital in the Länderbank before the First World War. Like Cottrell, I have read in the archive of the Quai d'Orsay a report of a French official in which he stated that the French owned half the capital of the Länderbank before the First World War; but this is absolutely impossible. It was only a strategem. I have seen the lists of the shareholders who attended the annual meetings before the First World War and the number of the French shareholders was extremely small. I can find two explanations for this. The French banks wanted to give the impression to the French diplomats that the change was not so great and that they were only pursuing the same policies. Or it may be that the French had been buying many shares on the free market in 1919 and that they wanted this capital to be considered as 'old' French capital so that the new states would not protest. In that case we have to be very careful and consequently these documents on foreign capital after the First World War have to be very criticially evaluated.

The third question concerns the economic point of view. I think that the great problem for historians, especially in the 1920s, is to see the connection between investment policy and economic trends in Central Europe, which were not the same as in France or England. Timing in the Danube region was quite different. The periodization of these economic trends is not very clear in most books because even the diplomats' reports, or the banking reports at that time, very often used the word 'crisis' in a misleading way. They used the word 'crisis' for widely varying situations. For instance, during the inflation period there was of course a sort of 'crisis', but afterwards, when the inflation ended, there was not a crisis but the opposite, as the economy was recovering. However, small firms collapsed then because they had only been supported by inflation. Very often when the reports state that crises were developing again, it was actually quite the opposite. For instance, in Czechoslovakia there were some economic problems caused by the deflationary policies of Dr Rašín. Rašín is very often considered as conservative, but I am not sure that this was the case since he did not want to preserve the existing situation; on the contrary he wanted to create a very strong Czechoslovak currency in order to make Prague the centre of banking in Central Europe and replace Vienna. So the actual situation was quite contrary to the reports; it was a kind of revolutionary endeavour. For instance, Cottrell quotes the reports of Young in November 1922, saying: 'We are going to make some considerable losses in Prague owing to the process of deflation and the consequent crisis.' What type of losses are these? If you look at current business, of course some money is being lost; but if you look at the prices of the shares on the Stock Exchange the picture is totally different. When it is considered that the English banks had frequently been buying companies when money was at a very low price, they were not making a loss at all because the value of their capital in all cases was increasing. Losses on current business had to be balanced with some enormous gains on the other side. As M. Lévy-Leboyer has already said, we have to consider the differences between short-term investment and borrowing, and long-term investment. Austria's problem, even before the First World War, was that her economy always required short-term money. It was not so much a problem of long-term but of short-term investment. If in Austria and Czechoslovakia in 1926 or 1927 some banks were in difficulties, then it was part of the economic recovery after the inflations. The smaller institutions could not find money so the bigger ones acquired them because they were big enough to receive money from outside. Further, we must not forget that at that time the real price of capital after the inflation fell to a very low point and it was a very opportune moment to buy.

Now I want to make just one further point: the problem of the connection between politics and economics is not so simple as that stated by Montagu Norman: 'Our basis is economic, the French basis is political.' Both English and French investments were both economic and political. Whatever the case we cannot understand why it was precisely the Anglo-Austrian Bank, which was supposed to have been created on an economic basis, which collapsed and the French Banque de Pays de l'Europe Centrale, which was supposedly created on political grounds, which prospered. It should have been the opposite.

Lastly, I would like to draw attention to the fact that many of the contributors to this volume – especially Dr Cottrell – have referred to 'Czechoslovak nationalism'; it is not enough, however, to speak of 'nationalism'. We must also consider the economic and social aspects of Czech policy.

In my opinion the problem is not so much nationalism – of course, a strong Czechoslovak nationalism did exist, but it was rather the important weight of the Czechoslovak state, which was very reliant on private firms. We must not forget the strong personality of the Finance Ministers in Czechoslovakia from Dr Rašín in the 1920s to Dr Engliš at the beginning of the 1930s; consequently we have to consider what was only nationalism and what was economic policy. Most of the successor states were pursuing very strictly controlled economic policies and this was true especially of Poland; it was true to a lesser degree of Romania, but it was especially true of Czechoslovakia.

13. The Hungarian General Credit Bank in the 1920s

G. Ránki

In Hungary, as in most European countries where capitalism developed later, efforts towards social, political and institutional modernization occurred against a background of a relatively underdeveloped economy. They began first during the 1848 Revolution and second after the Compromise of 1867. From the late 1860s the Hungarian economy began to change, an important step forward, and one of the most important causative factors was the substantial investment activities of the Viennese banks whose position had been strengthened by the consolidation of the country. Before 1867 there had been only a few dozen savings banks and one land bank in Hungary. However, during the speculative boom which raged between 1867 and 1873 hundreds of joint stock banks were incorporated. The formation of these institutions was assisted by foreign capital and a number of them were large, having considerable resources. One of these very large banks was the Magyar Általános Hitelbank [Hungarian General Credit Bank] which was established in 1868 with funds supplied by the local commercial community but particularly by the Viennese Rothschilds and the Credit-Anstalt. The Credit-Anstalt, which had been set up in 1855, was the Rothschilds' most important response to contemporary financial demands – to the need for a form of *crédit mobilier* bank as first established in France by the Pereire brothers. The Hungarian General Credit Bank was conceived in the same terms as its French predecessor. From its formation the bank concentrated Hungary's extraordinarily scarce supplies of capital, was a major intermediary in the inward flow of foreign capital into the economy and, by creating, promoting and aiding big enterprise, supported the native but weak entrepreneurial class.

Unlike most of the other pioneering big banks, the Hungarian General Credit Bank survived the economic crisis of 1873. This was due primarily to the support of both the extraordinarily strong Credit-Anstalt and the House of Rothschild. In 1871 the bank had come to an agreement with the Credit-Anstalt under which the latter closed its Budapest branch for an annual payment of 244,500 K. The Credit-Anstalt continued to share in a certain percentage of the business transacted in Hungary but provided the Hungarian General Credit Bank with a substantial current balance, a rediscount credit, and a reserve line of cash.[1]

During its first years the bank's main business besides normal daily transactions was in the field of railway investment and the provision of government loans. In 1873 it obtained a virtual monopoly of Hungarian state finances as a result of pressure from the Rothschilds. Its main interest in industrial banking was the short-term profits which could be obtained from promotions rather than the revenue arising from permanent associations with industrial companies. However, from the 1880s the bank's range of activities was enlarged and began to include trading in products such as coal, sugar, salt and tobacco. This led to a greater involvement with a number of industrial undertakings and accordingly the bank's business came more and more to resemble the pattern of German 'mixed' banking. It was not only the first Hungarian bank to take on this form of business but was also the financial institution that had the greatest influence on industry. During the 1880s it played a role in either forming or converting into joint stock companies eight major industrial enterprises. The bank did this mainly with the assistance of foreign – principally Austrian – capital. Through organizing the finances of the major enterprises, the bank acquired a significant interest in a number of branches of industrial activity, machine building and sugar especially.

The Hungarian General Credit Bank's position was further strengthened by the close ties that it developed in the 1890s with some German banks, in particular with Mendelssohns, Bleichröders and the Disconto Gesellschaft. At the same time it established a network of affiliated banks – institutions in which it had either a direct or indirect interest. In 1900 these connections consisted of three banks and savings banks, but by 1912 the network of filials had grown to 15 banks directly dependent upon it and 13 banks indirectly connected to it. The Hungarian General Credit Bank in 1900 had a nominal capital of 48m K. By 1913 it was 80m K while its net turnover and capital assets were approaching 500m K, or 1,400m K if its affiliates are included. This group, which had the Hungarian General Credit Bank at the centre, controlled nearly 20 per cent of the capital assets of all Hungarian banks.

There are two major aspects to the relationship of financial institutions to Hungarian development during the early twentieth century. The first is that the banks, especially the Hungarian General Credit Bank, played a vital role in the formation of various cartels and associated commercial organizations. Second, the big banks' involvement with Hungarian economic change became even greater. In various ways they took advantage of the accelerating process of industrialization through establishing large industrial companies, building up close links with a number of the leading growing industries, and through either forming enterprises or managing them. In 1913 the Hungarian General Credit Bank group controlled over 63 industrial enterprises which had an aggregate nominal capital of 233m K – 16 per cent of the total nominal capitalization of all Hungarian industrial joint stock companies. The bank had a particularly important influence over the following industries: mining, sugar, engineering, electrical engineering and oil refining.

The co-operation of the bank with the Rothschilds and the Credit-Anstalt continued into the twentieth century, especially with respect to the flotation of all important Hungarian government loans. The Rothschild group included two Viennese joint stock banks and two German institutions – Bleichröders and the Disconto Gesellschaft. The syndicate shares of this group are of some interest: the Rothschilds and the Credit-Anstalt always had a larger share than the Hungarian General Credit Bank, while the Boden-Credit-Anstalt participated on equal terms with the Hungarian bank and the two German banks played a smaller role.

Although the Hungarian General Credit Bank had a considerable amount of domestic capital at its command, particularly in the form of deposited savings, a substantial part of its capital liabilities and consequently its influence came from the Credit-Anstalt and other members of the Rothschild group. However, the balance of power between the Viennese banks and the Budapest institution altered. An agreement of 1 January 1906 which dealt with co-operation with the Credit-Anstalt was more favourable to the Hungarian bank than that of the 1870s which it replaced. Under the new terms the Hungarian General Credit Bank obtained higher limits on the facilities provided to it by the Credit-Anstalt, while conversely the 'royalty' paid to Vienna was lowered. Further, henceforth it was to be offered a share of 20 per cent of business undertaken by the Credit-Anstalt while it reciprocated by granting the Vienna bank a share of 35 per cent of its industrial transactions.[2]

The Hungarian General Credit Bank became the central institution of the Hungarian economy. There was only one other bank of comparable size and importance – the Pesti Magyar Kereskedelmi Bank [the Hungarian Commercial Bank of Pest]. In terms of type and function, the Hungarian General Credit Bank closely resembled the German 'mixed' bank, playing a far greater role both directly and centrally in the economy than the more traditional banks of the Atlantic periphery of Europe. It was an example *par excellence* of the intertwining of bank and industrial capital which Hilferding in *Finance Capital* showed to be a new development of the twentieth century.[3]

Two other aspects of the role performed by the Hungarian General Credit Bank before 1914 deserve attention. First, the Hungarian banking sector had a prime role in the accumulation and distribution of capital, probably because of the country's state of economic development. If any of the indicators of the development of the financial sector, established by Goldsmith, are applied to the Hungarian situation, then all, like the ratio of bank assets to money in circulation,[4] support this conclusion. Banking capital played a predominant role in capital formation, while at a certain level, growth through 'self-financing' was relatively slower. Second, the provision of long-term bank finance through rolled-over credits was a very common form of financing: it led to the establishment of industrial concerns under the direction of the accommodating bank.

The situation after the First World War – the break-up of the Austro-Hungarian Monarchy and the reduction of Hungary to a third of its former size by the terms of the Treaty of Trianon – led to a totally new framework and a new set of conditions for the development of the Hungarian economy. This entirely new situation meant that the domestic and international financial position of the Hungarian General Credit Bank required revision. The post-war political changes alone raised a number of questions. The territorial shifts caused uncertainties over part of the bank's assets, particularly those held by branches, affiliates and interests which were now situated in alienated areas. War and post-war inflation rapidly eroded the real value of the substantial current and savings deposits placed with the bank. A radically new business policy was required to salvage them. During the 1900s the bank had gained greater independence from the Rothschild group and the Credit-Anstalt, but the war and its effects had further loosened these ties with Vienna. This deprived the bank of its main foreign financial support, especially as Vienna had lost its former position as the money market for Danubian and Balkan Europe.

The capitalist groups that were to be dominant during the 1920s soon made their presence and position felt. In 1920 the French attempted to obtain a position of tutelage over Hungary's main economic assets – the railways, the iron industry and the banks. It would distort the structure of this essay to undertake here a discussion of the comprehensive French plans designed to achieve this goal.[5] For present purposes it is sufficient to point out that the initial negotiations were concerned with the Hungarian railway network, the iron industry and the proposed river port at Budapest. In return for rights in these areas, Count Armand de Saint-Sauveur, who led the negotiations on behalf of the French, promised to make Budapest the centre of the activities of the Schneider group in south-eastern Europe. On 25 May the Hungarian Council of Ministers gave this French company an option on the railway system and the proposed new harbour, suggesting that Baron Adolf Ullman, the vice-president of the Hungarian General Credit Bank, be one of the Hungarian delegates at the subsequent negotiations.[6] Unfortunately, there is no clear indication of when the Hungarian General Credit Bank itself started to be an object for these negotiations.

On 29 May the French declared that the option given by the Hungarian government was inadequate and went on to state that their first requirement was an interest in the Hungarian General Credit Bank. The discussions in Paris over this matter were conducted on behalf of the Hungarian General Credit Bank by Baron Paul Kornfeld, one of its directors, while the French delegate, Fouchet, remained in Budapest to exert pressure on the government to ensure that it would accede to the French demands.[7] The source material is conflicting, with some indicating that the discussions had been held in April in Paris, but at the end of May it is clear that the directors of the Hungarian General Credit Bank were having second thoughts, and for political rather than economic reasons. French pressure increased, with Paléologue, the secrétaire-général at the Quai d'Orsay, stating in a memorandum of 15 June that the French acquisition of a participation in the Credit Bank was a *sine qua non* for the continuance of the general negotiations.[8] The affair was eventually discussed by the Hungarian Council of Ministers on 16 June. This body came down in favour of the transaction, influenced by both the political considerations and the undertaking that the French group would 'transact all our business in Central Europe and the Balkans through the Credit Bank'.[9] At the insistence of the Hungarian General Credit Bank, the Hungarian government sent the bank a letter stating explicitly that the bank was giving shares to the French as an act of patriotic duty at the government's request.[10]

Actually, French plans for massive involvement with the Hungarian economy were much greater but were never fulfilled. English competition restricted the range of opportunities open to the French, who at the same time could not and did not pay the political price asked by the Hungarian government for dominance over its country's economy. This was the revision of the Treaty of Trianon. However, the French did obtain a very large equity holding in the Hungarian General Credit Bank, the nation's most important financial institution.

The Credit Bank issued 300,000 new shares of which only a third were taken by its existing shareholders, while the balance – 200,000 – went to the Union Européenne industrielle et financière.[11] This was a unique French holding company which had been formed by the Schneider industrial concern in conjunction with the Banque de l'Union parisienne and others.[12] As inflation was forcing the bank to increase its share capital every year, what is of interest is not the actual sums involved but rather the ratios in which the shares were taken. These are summarized in a short memorandum produced by the bank when it increased its capital in 1923. The shares taken by members of the underwriting syndicate for the 1923 issue were in the following proportions:[13]

	%
Union Européenne	25
Rothschilds, Vienna	8
Credit-Anstalt	8
Boden-Credit-Anstalt	3
Disconto Gesellschaft, Berlin	3.5
Mendelssohns, Berlin	2.5
Bleichröders, Berlin	2

It would appear that blocks of the bank's shares were generally held in the same proportions, with consequently strong French (25 per cent) and Viennese (19 per cent) interests and a relatively less significant German holding. Hungarians did hold 48 per cent of the bank's shares but these were dispersed in the form of small packets. However, the bank remained controlled by Hungarians who transacted its business and took the real and important decisions, subject to the approval of the Parisian and Viennese groups. Each of these alien interests had representatives on the bank's board and on its executive committee, a body which had been created in parallel to the board by the bank's managing directors.[14] The Parisian group was represented by Pierre Cheysson, the Viennese by Ludwig Neurath.

As has been shown, the Germans held considerably fewer shares than the other foreign groups interested in the Hungarian General Credit Bank. But the influence of Mendelssohns became somewhat stronger during the 1920s. This came about initially as a consequence of the Hungarian General Credit Bank acquiring the Elsö Magyar Iparbank [the First Hungarian Industrial Bank] in which the Mendelssohns were a major shareholder.[15] More important was the growth of the Mendelssohn interest arising from its participation in the annual increases of the Hungarian bank's capital during the inflation period. The Hungarian General Credit Bank decided to increase its nominal capital from 550m K to 825m K by creating a further 587,500 shares. Mendelssohns offered to take up over 500,000 of these new shares, provided that they were given four seats on the bank's board and one on its executive committee.[16] The consequent negotiations were protracted and inconclusive with the result that the bank had to temper its aim and make do with a smaller increase in its nominal capital. This restricted issue of new shares was taken up by the bank's existing shareholders and one newcomer – Lazard Brothers of London. The bank's directorate were dissatisfied with what they regarded as an interim solution to the problem of the inflationary erosion of the bank's capital base and therefore agreed to raise further the bank's capital from 690m K to 920m K. No option on these new shares was given to existing shareholders and instead they were taken by the International Acceptance Bank, the International Finance and Investment Company, and Kleinwort & Sons operating in conjunction with Mendelssohns. This new foreign group took up the parcel of new shares in the following respective proportions: 37.5 per cent, 37.5 per cent and 25 per cent. According to the bank's management minutes, the Parisian and Viennese shareholders did not object to this transaction.[17] In 1926 József Tivadar Salamon, a representative of the Berlin group, joined the bank's executive committee and Lord Churston became a director on behalf of the English group.[18]

The power structure, in its essentials, remained unaltered from 1926 until the outbreak of the Second World War. It consisted of a strong French interest, a smaller but influential Austrian involvement, and a German presence which could not be ignored. The bank's leadership throughout the period remained in the hands of a triumvirate consisting of Dr Tibor von Scitovsky, Baron György Ullman and Baron Paul Kornfeld, but it was heavily dependent on both the French and Austrian groups when determining the bank's commercial and fiscal policy.

What were the business activities of the Hungarian General Credit Bank? What role did the bank play in international business? A major influence on the bank's business was its strong and well-established connection with the Hungarian Treasury. The bank had signed its first contract with the Ministry of Finance in 1873 by which it became the 'commissioned buyer and seller of bonds, bank notes, and coins of all kinds both within the country and abroad'. This contract was renewed with some slight revisions in 1886, 1901 and again in 1915. Following the war a new agreement was made which reiterated that the Hungarian General Credit Bank was the state's banker but included a number of new clauses. Under these the bank agreed to take over 15m K of treasury notes which had been issued by the Ministry of Finance and was given an option on any further issues. Branches of the bank would redeem government bonds at a commission of 1 per cent. 'In recognition of its five decades of service' the bank was given an option on all future government loans and an undertaking that it would be given priority if other banks should tender on equally favourable terms.[19] That the Hungarian General Credit Bank set great store on its position as the banker for the state is shown by the two following transactions.

On 14 December 1926 the Credit Bank's board of directors sent a strictly confidential letter to Mendelssohns informing them that the Hungarian Ministry of Finance was about to issue through it three months interest bearing bonds. They offered this paper to Mendelssohns at 0.5 per cent discount provided that the Berlin bank agreed first to renew the bonds until 1 November 1927 and second to guarantee the exchange rate on the New York, London and Amsterdam markets. If further bonds were issued, then Mendelssohns were to have an option on either half of the issue or, if the rate of interest was increased, a third. In his reply Mendelssohn stated that the terms were certainly not advantageous but he realized 'dass sie vielmehr darauf sehen muss sich der ungarischen Regierung wirklich zu erweisen, um die Monopolstellung, die sie in Bezug auf die Diskontierung von Kassenscheinen vor dem Kriege halte, wieder zu erlangen.'[20]

After the renewal of the agreement concerning the position of the Hungarian General Credit Bank as banker to the state, Scitovsky, its chief director, wrote a memorandum reporting on his visit to London. He had accompanied János Bud, the Finance Minister, and had had the opportunity to 'document our appointment as state banker'. Besides members of the staff of the Bank of England, Bud had visited merely one of Rothschilds' directors 'wishing thereby to indicate that he considered the House of Rothschild to be the institution for the flotation of Hungarian bonds'.[21] The consolidation of its connection with the Ministry of Finance was of the greatest importance for the Hungarian General Credit Bank which was having to fight off severe competition from the other substantial Hungarian financial institution, the Hungarian Commercial Bank of Pest.

In 1926 the Hungarian General Credit Bank was able to acquire the right to manage the issue of a long-term state loan amounting to £2.25m at 7.5 per cent. The bond issue was contracted out at 88.5 to an English underwriting group consisting of N. M. Rothschild & Sons, Baring Brothers Co. Ltd and J. Henry Schröder.[22] The Commercial Bank of Pest, which worked mainly with American houses such as Speyers, protested and took steps to give weight to its opposition. The rivalry continued with the financing of Hungarian electrification.

Budapest's new electrical generating station became the next bone of contention in the competition between the two banks. After press reports of offers for the contract from an American-Belgian group with which the Commercial Bank was associated, the British Ambassador at Budapest wrote to the Hungarian Foreign Minister asking that the government make no decision until Talbot, an Englishman, had been to Hungary to make a tender.[23] The Talbot concern had the full support of the British government; according to press reports, Chamberlain had spoken to Prime Minister Bethlen on its behalf.[24] The Hungarian government did intervene with Lajos Walko, the Minister of Commerce, replying to the British Ambassador: 'I have duly called upon the Lord Mayor of Budapest to use his official influence to assure that the municipal authorities, competent to decide on the American offer to develop the capital's electrical works, suspend their judgement until the promised British offer is made.'[25] The negotiations began in 1926. They were soon made more complex by the intrusion of a consortium consisting of the Hungarian General Credit Bank with the Magyar Általános Köszénbánya Rt [Hungarian General Coal Mines Ltd] which proposed that the generating station be located at Tatabánya rather than Várpalota, a site owned by Salgótarjáni Köszénbánya Rt [Salgótarján Coal Mines Ltd]. To ensure its success, this consortium both put pressure on the Salgótarján company by threatening to break up the coal cartel and used its influence with Prime Minister Bethlen. The effect of these tactics was clear. The executive committee of the Hungarian General Coal Mines Co. subsequently noted that the government 'had taken a very decided stand on the issue, with the Prime Minister intervening on behalf of our company'.[26] Miksa Hermann, the new Minister of Commerce, wrote in December 1926 'that he had to agree that Tatabánya too had by all means to be involved in solving the electrification problem'. The government then asked the Hungarian General Credit Bank to submit a tender.[27] Accordingly the Credit Bank won this round with the Minister of Commerce notifying the Budapest Council in November 1927 that the new power plant was to be at Bánhida, near Tatabánya.[28]

In November 1927, at the same time that the decision over the site was made, the leading directors of the Hungarian General Credit Bank – Tibor von Scitovsky its managing director and György Ullman – went to London with János Bud, the Finance Minister, to settle the final details of the necessary supporting loans.[29] The Talbot loan was floated in London on 9 May 1928. Backed by the British Treasury, the loan was for £3.3m nominal (92m Pg) and the first tranche of £1m was issued at 97, giving an overall yield of 4.5 per cent. The second tranche of £2.3m had a lower issue price of 93 and therefore bore a correspondingly higher yield of 6.5 per cent. However, Hungarian creditworthiness had improved as a result of changes in both the domestic and international money markets so that the terms of this loan were better than previous foreign loans floated in the 1920s.[30] Part of the loan was issued under the terms of the British Trade Facilities Act which aimed at improving British exports, and consequently 40 per cent of the proceeds of the loan had to finance orders placed in the U.K. The Hungarian General Credit Bank obtained a commission of 0.25 per cent for its role as an intermediary in the flotation of the loan, while one of its industrial associates Ganz-Féle Villamossági Rt [Ganz Electric Co. Ltd] – together with Hungarian General Coal Mines, was to take part in building the plant.[31]

The second transaction which illustrates the Hungarian General Credit Bank's close relationship with the government was connected with the 'Swedish Match loan' negotiated by Rothschilds shortly after the Talbot loan. The origins of this issue were the efforts of the Kreuger company, which held a near-monopoly of European match production, to extend its influence to Hungary. After lengthy negotiation the Hungarian government came to an agreement with this Swedish company, conscious of its own need to raise funds with which to compensate owners who had lost land as a result of the reforms carried out in the early 1920s. (Actually the Hungarian reform had only affected a mere 4 per cent of the total land area.) The loan of $36m offered by the Svenska Tändsticks Aktiebolaget was to be paid over in three equal instalments. Rothschilds, which had been kept fully informed on the terms of the loan by the Hungarian General Credit Bank, agreed to make advance payments at a discount on the future loan proceeds. The secret and intricate nature of these complex negotiations when they finally became generally known led to serious attacks in the press.[32]

The Hungarian General Credit Bank had very close ties with the London Rothschild bank. On 13 March 1928 the Credit Bank, acting on behalf of the 'Hermes', Magyar Általános Váltóüzlet Rt ['Hermes' General Hungarian Exchange Office Co. Ltd] of Budapest and the Union Européenne, made a contract with Thurn & Sons Ltd for the sale of 175,000 of its own shares – 21 per cent of its issued capital. The shares of 50 Pg each were bought at £2 17s. 4d. (£2.87) each[33] and Thurn & Sons agreed to deposit the acquired shares with Rothschilds. A further indication of the intimate link that the Hungarian bank had with Rothschilds was that the latter was the most important of the hundred or so financial institutions which provided the

Hungarian General Credit Bank with credits. It had a credit margin of $3m with both the Parisian and the Viennese Rothschild banks and one of £0.7m with the London house.[34]

The extraordinarily widespread international contacts of the Hungarian General Credit Bank were responsible for the bank becoming Hungary's most important investment institution. As a result of its very close ties with a particular group of the leading European big banks, the Hungarian bank participated in both establishing and increasing the capitals of an extraordinarily large number of joint stock companies. There is no point in listing the very great number of non-Hungarian companies with which the Hungarian General Credit Bank became associated in this way as it generally had only an insignificant shareholding in them – 0.5 to 1 per cent. Generally it was its English, French and German partners which provided such opportunities for the Hungarian General Credit Bank to participate profitably in various promotional and underwriting syndicates. For instance, the minutes of the meeting of the bank's managing directors of 25 April 1929 show that one item of that particular day's agenda was the purchase of shares in the Monks Investment Trust of London, the Schweizerische Bankverein, the Vorarlberger Illwerke, the Banque de l'Union parisienne, the Živnostenská banka of Prague, and the Česká eskomptní banka a úvěrní ústav [Bohemian Discount Bank and Society of Credit].[35] The Hungarian General Credit Bank had also played a part in raising the capital of the Credit-Anstalt, the Deutsche Bank, the Dresdner Bank, and other comparable European financial institutions.

The Hungarian General Credit Bank not only profited from its very extensive range of international contacts through receiving participants in syndicates for extra-Hungarian affairs, but also through acting as a procurer of funds for Hungarian undertakings and not simply government loans. At the beginning of the 1920s when the rivalry between English and French capitalists over the Hungarian communications network began, the English managed to acquire control over shipping on the Danube through the co-operation of the Hungarian Credit Bank. The River Syndicate was formed in London in March 1920 and most of its nominal capital of £10,000 was provided by Furness, Withy & Co. The Hungarian General Credit Bank through an agreement of 19 April 1920 passed over to the River Syndicate 144,000 £2 shares of the Magyar Királyi Folyam-és Tengerhajózási Rt [Royal Hungarian River and Ocean Shipping Co. Ltd]. By the terms of this agreement the shipping company received a government subsidy for 20 years, but it also stipulated that it was to remain a Hungarian concern. The English company was to have two seats on its board of directors for five years after which it would have the right to appoint a quarter of the directors.[36]

The Hungarian General Credit Bank played a role in expanding the industrial base of the native economy that it served. In the case of the newly established textile industry, the bank operated in conjunction with foreign capital and established in 1921 the large plant of Hazai Fésüsfonó és

Szövögyár Rt [Home Worsted Mill Co. Ltd] with the assistance of the Elberfelder Textilwerke. Two years later the bank formed the Magyaróvári Müselyemgyár [Hungarian Synthetic Fabrics Factory] in partnership with the Disconto Gesellschaft and the Kunstseidefabrik Schweitzingen GmbH.[37] Similarly an international holding company was established in Switzerland to exploit the bauxite deposits in Transdanubia which were considerable by European standards. This company was owned on the one hand, by the German Vereinigte Aluminiumwerke, the Ottavi Minen und Eisenbahn Gesellschaft and Blankart & Cie, Zurich, and on the other by a Hungarian group led by the Credit Bank.

Electrification in Hungary began in earnest after the First World War when the introduction of high voltage distribution technology allowed the possibility of supplying current over great distances. The Hungarian General Credit Bank, with its close association with the country's biggest mining company – Hungarian General Coal Mines Ltd – had a direct interest in the electrification of those regions which could be supplied by the coal company's own power plant, which ran on its own poor quality fuel. Consequently the bank together with the coal company formed the Villamosági Tröszt [Electricity Trust] to further electrification in Budapest and its immediate environs. The trust's capital of 35m Pg (£1.5m) was subscribed in equal shares by the Belgian trust Société Financière des Transports et d'Enterprises Industrielles (SOFINA), the Gesellschaft für Elektrische Unternehmung of Berlin, and the Hungarian General Credit Bank.[38]

Since the bank had the most important international connections of all Hungary's domestic financial institutions, it became the major intermediary in the flow of foreign loans into Hungarian business in the 1920s. Its ties with the Rothschild houses in Berlin and Vienna gave it contacts with many other German banks, while it enjoyed a certain degree of support from the French Schneider concern. However, for political reasons, French loans to Hungary dwindled to practically nothing from the mid-1920s.[39] The bank's monopoly of government business together with the foreign capital that it attracted was all the more impressive because of the debilitating inflation of the first half of the decade which had annihilated the domestic economy's store of savings and circulating capital. This resulted in levels of both internal capital accumulation and reserves considerably lower than before the war. But as the lack of capital became even more acute, so agriculture and industry needed more in both relative and absolute terms. It was the machine building industry that was central to the industrial interests of the Hungarian General Credit Bank. However, the demands of general technology apart, engineering required even greater investment and a restructured Hungarian market.

Until 1913 the bank had had a business policy of deliberate expansion coupled with centralization which can be most clearly seen in the establishment of a wide network of affiliated banks. Its strategy towards industrial clients had been to supply existing firms with credit and gradually draw them under the bank's influence by converting such establishments into joint stock companies, acquiring part of their share capital in the process. The bank had also taken part in the formation of entirely new companies.

The process of affiliation continued in the 1920s. In 1923 the bank bought the shares of the relatively important First Hungarian Industrial Bank from Bloch & Co. of Berlin.[40] During the second half of the decade small local banks and savings banks were acquired and transformed into branches of the Hungarian General Credit Bank. The chronology of this process was as follows: the acquisition of the Szekszárd branch of the Tolna Megyei Takarék és Hitelbank Rt [Tolna County Savings and Credit Bank] in the spring of 1926, the Agrár Takarékpénztár Rt [Agrarian Savings Bank of Eger] in the summer of 1926, and the Mikolci Hitelintézet [Mikolci Credit Bank] in the autumn of the same year. In 1927 the Hungarian General Credit Bank drew both the Soproni Hitelbank Rt [Sopron Credit Bank] and the Általános Hitelbank és Tararékpénztár [General Credit and Savings Bank] of Székesfehérvár into its group.[41] This form of expansion and concentration came to a halt with the growing financial crisis at the end of the decade. Affiliates which were alientated as a result of Hungary's post-Trianon borders did remain largely under the control of the Budapest bank through the co-operation of Czechoslovak, Romanian and Yugoslavian banks but for the present purposes of this discussion have not been included.

In 1929 there were 18 banks and savings banks within the sphere of influence of the Hungarian General Credit Bank and they had an aggregate nominal capital of 9.45m Pg. The Credit Bank's own nominal capital amounted to 41.4m Pg and so its combined group accounted for over 15 per cent of the total nominal equity capitalization of the Hungarian banking system – some 339.48m Pg.

With regard to industrial firms linked to the bank, in 1929 the Hungarian General Credit Bank had some control over 75 such firms, the aggregate nominal capital of which was 254.5m Pg – 28 per cent of the total nominal capitalization of all Hungarian industrial joint stock companies (900m Pg). Apart from its traditional interests in coal mining (especially through the Hungarian General Coal Mine Co.), machine building and the sugar industry, after the war the bank acquired a significant interest in textiles and the electrical industry. Generally Hungarian industry experienced serious difficulties in the 1920s and therefore it is not surprising that the Credit Bank invested only in the electrical industry and textiles, the two industrial branches where there was definite growth. As has been mentioned previously, the Credit Bank was instrumental in obtaining foreign capital to aid the foundation of the Electricity Trust. This worked in conjunction with the Hungarian General Coal Mine Co. to develop the capital and technologically intensive electrical engineering sector and supply industries so that they were capable of establishing a network of local power stations. The less capital-intensive textile industry enjoyed a fantastic boom with production tripling by 1929, caused by the restriction of Austrian competition resulting from the domestic policy of import substitution. The Hungarian General Credit Bank either directly initiated or participated in the creation of a number of important new textile factories.

Generally the Hungarian General Credit Bank acquired its industrial holdings either by buying up shares held by foreign investors – for instance the joint take-over with the Credit-Anstalt of the Amstelbank's interest in the Vulkán Gépgyár Rt [Vulkan Machine Factory Ltd][42] – or through taking shares when it increased the capital of a company. This latter policy is exemplified by the Magyar Pamutipar Rt [Hungarian Cotton Industry Ltd], Magnezit Ipar Rt [Magnesite Industry Ltd] and Borsodi Szénbányák Rt [Borsod Coal Mines Ltd].[43] The final step in a company becoming a part of the Hungarian General Credit Bank group was usually through involvement in the merging of a number of smaller companies into one which rationalized the business structure of an industry. Two examples are illustrative of this process – the amalgamation of the Köbányai Polgári Serfözö Rt [Köbánya Civic Brewery Ltd] with the Szent István Tápszer Müvek Rt [Saint Stephen Food Co. Ltd] and the combining of the Linum Fonóipar Rt [Linum Spinning Mill Ltd] with the factories of Taussig Samuel és Fiai [Samuel Taussig & Sons] at Győr.[44] The sugar factory at Selyp was acquired by a rather unusual method. This very large plant was owned by a long-established merchant family whose wealth had enabled them to remain unfettered by ties with any of the big banks. With post-war inflation, the family moved into banking but then made losses. These were covered initially by a £20,000 loan but in 1926 the family's debts exceeded their capital resources by 50 per cent and its company became bankrupt. The Hungarian General Credit Bank offered to refloat the company, and mortgaged the 8,000-acre rural estate together with the urban land held by the company in Budapest – but on the condition that the Selyp plant, a competitor of its own sugar concerns, was handed over.[45]

Initially the bank would supply its clients with various types of credit – trade loans, discounts and overdrafts – which could be renewed provided a stable relationship developed. Undoubtedly the nature of a company's relationship to a bank made a considerable difference to the supply of credit and capital available to it. The actual character of the bank/client relationship varied very considerably in the case of the industrial customers of the Hungarian General Credit Bank. These variations occurred not only because of differences in the size of the companies but also because of the great variety in the agreements by which companies became a part of the group of the bank. For instance, the Hungarian General Coal Mines Co., which had a nominal capital of nearly 50m Pg, had very close business ties with the bank. The company's electrical and building materials divisions made a number of joint transactions with the bank. The bank managed the company's finances and held its current account. However, the bank did not have a decisive voice in the management of the coal company's affairs. The company's managing director, Jenő Vida, was on the bank's board and it was very much the case of a business group working in tandem with a bank rather than the subordination of industry's interests to a bank.

The situation was entirely different with regard to Hungarian Cotton Industry Ltd, one of the most important textile factories. It had come into the bank's sphere of interest in 1907 when the bank had acquired half of the company's shares. A third remained with the Szurday family which had founded and managed the factory, and they generally continued to control the company. The Hungarian General Credit Bank provided the company with loans of the order of a few million crowns and received a share of its profits through its equity interest. During the textile boom of the 1920s the factory was expanded and reconstructed. This was financed by the bank to the extent of 7m Pg ($1.5m). Anticipated rebuilding costs were exceeded and the factory began to experience financial difficulties which led the Hungarian General Credit Bank to attempt to have a greater influence over its management than previously. Szurday, despite severe disagreements, continued to hold sway even at the end of the 1920s. It was not until the mid-1930s, when the differences between Szurday and the bank had become very grave indeed, that the bank began to take part directly in the company's management. In 1935 Szurday signed an agreement with the bank under which he became effectively an employee of the company. He remained the managing director but was now a subordinate of the bank, since it had the right to instal a vice managing director if it thought necessary. Szurday was to engage in no other business activity other than directing the company. In 1937 he resigned and staff of the Hungarian General Credit Bank took control.[46]

With respect to smaller companies, the bank naturally had a greater influence, as is illustrated by the case of the Debreceni Kefegyár [Debrecen Brush Factory]. This was a medium-sized plant which exported a considerable part of its output. In 1923 the bank obtained 40 per cent of the company's shares and demanded that it should nominate six out of the ten members of the company's board, have priority over existing shareholders, and become the company's sole creditor. At the end of the 1920s the Hungarian General Credit Bank established an industrial department overseen by the bank's managing director. From 1930 onwards it was he who took the Debrecen Brush Factory's investment and business policy decisions. The situation was tantamount to exercising complete control over the company; in effect the bank made all decisions concerning the company's structure, marketing and all its other activities, with the factory's owner merely carrying out the tasks set him by the bank. This experience was common to a number of smaller companies like the Debreceni Faipari Vállalat [Debrecen Woodworking Co.], another medium-sized establishment.[47]

A new strand to the bank's activities developed during the 1920s. Before the war, the Hungarian General Credit Bank had not provided long-term credits to agriculture but it did have close ties with the Magyar Földhitelintézet [Hungarian Land Credit Institute] which specialized in this market. In 1925 the Credit Bank obtained permission from the Ministry of Finance to grant agricultural loans by way of mortgages. These were to be funded through the issue of dollar or sterling debentures on Western capital markets. The necessary modifications were made to the bank's charter which specified a loan period of 35 years with interest at 8.8 per cent. Land could thus be mortgaged up to 20 per cent of its estimated value – calculated to be equivalent to either 50 times the net income or $25 per 'hold'.[48]

Table 13.1. THE DISTRIBUTION OF MORTGAGE LOANS, 31 Dec. 1929.*

Value ($)	No. of loans	as % of all loans
−1,000	163	2.7
1,000–3,000	143	6.8
3,000–5,000	28	2.9
5,000–10,000	27	5.6
10,000–20,000	23	8.7
20,000–50,000	13	11.1
50,000–100,000	6	10.7
+100,000	3	51.5

* Hungarian National Archives, Credit Bank Secretariat, Fasc. 251/15.

The Magyar Pénzintézetek Jelzálogkibocsátó Szövetkezete [Hungarian Banks' Debenture Bond Association] was formed in conjunction with the European Mortgage and Investment Co. of Boston.[49] Mortgage loans rapidly developed thereafter together with the corresponding foreign debenture issues. Among the first eight recipients of loans through mortgages were Archduke Joseph Habsburg, Count Gyula Batthyany and Count Miklós Degenfeld Schönburg.[50]

In 1926 $1.6m of loans secured by mortgage of land were raised; in 1927, $1.9m together with $0.45m on real estate; followed in 1928 by the issue of $2.5m of debenture bonds. By the spring of 1929 when mortgages on land amounted to $7m and on real estate $0.9m, the company found itself in serious difficulties. Half of the debenture bonds that had been issued had remained in the association's own portfolio.[51] At the end of the year Hungary's nine big banks in conjunction with the two land banks issued a mortgage loan of 421m Pg ($84m), of which the Credit Bank's share was 42.7m Pg.[52] Most of the mortgage loans made in the second half of the 1920s went to the great landowning aristocrats.

During 1928 mortgage loans amounting to $2.5m were made, of which $1.25m was taken by Archduke Louis Charles, $0.35m by Count János Zichy, $0.15m by Count Rafael Zichy, $0.04m by Archduke Friedrich Habsburg, $0.055m by Archduke Albert Habsburg and $0.05m by Count János Majláth. A further 20 per cent of the total went to four other big landowners with the result that no more than $30,000 went to all the other borrowers on mortgage.[53]

'Les banques au sens strict et la monnaie de banque ne sont que des instruments, accessoires de la croissance economique,' wrote Lévy-Leboyer.[54] In this sense the part played by the Credit Bank was inseparable from the economic growth of the 1920s which was, without a doubt, considerably slower than that of the pre-war years. But Jean Bouvier's formulation is, perhaps, more apt:

> Banque et crédit sont des éléments fonctionnels de la croissance economique. Mais leur jeu est toujours demeuré ambigu. D'une part, ils sont sous la fondamentale dépendence du degré de développement économique; d'autre part, ils conservent dans ces limites mêmes, une certaine dose d'autonomie par rapport au développement; ils disposent, pour ainsi dire, d'une certaine marge de liberté, qui leur laisse la possibilité de jouer le rôle de moteur – ou le rôle de frein – dans le développement économique.[55]

Did the bank have such a relative autonomy; and if so, what did it consist in? Did the Credit Bank function as a brake or as a motor to the period's economic development? There can be no doubt that in Hungary's pre-war economic development, banks were more likely to act as a motor. In this sense, Hungary's economic development was much more along the lines of Gerschenkron's Western European model than what he describes as the Eastern European model, and which he maintains (in our opinion, mistakenly) that Hungary, too, followed. In the inter-war years, however, we can hardly speak of the banks having been motors, though they not only kept, but even consolidated, their central position.

The Credit Bank continued to be a 'mixed' bank. It was an investment bank, but one which also functioned as a deposit bank, while its affiliated small provincial banks made it a veritable banking network. The Credit Bank thus was able both to mobilize a part of the domestically accumulated small capital, and, by virtue of its international connections, to transact big business.

Given the country's diminished capital reserves, the Credit Bank's foreign investments were mostly small, formal affairs. It had managed to keep some of its old Balkan interests, for the most part with the help of French or German capital. The Credit Bank managed to keep hold of branches in areas that the Treaty of Trianon had given to Hungary's neighbours either through enlisting the support of western capital, or, more frequently, by giving local capitalists an interest in them. After the war the Credit Bank was able to turn its depleted resources more thoroughly to the service of the Hungarian economy. But these resources were depleted.

Table 13.2. DATA FROM THE CREDIT BANK'S BALANCE SHEET* (in Pg m)

Year	Nominal capital	Reserve capital	Stocks & bonds	Bills of exchange	Debts	Deposits, credits	Profit
1913	92.8	6.7	48.1	199.3	394.4	436.4	14.4
1925	41.4	20.4	41.7	56.3	82.0	125.8	3.3
1926	41.4	20.5	40.6	81.6	127.6	194.3	5.3
1927	41.4	21.1	42.2	102.9	184.8	296.7	6.9
1928	41.4	21.1	53.0	110.2	197.7	343.5	7.5
1929	41.4	22.4	54.4	106.5	199.1	346.0	7.5

* *Nagy Magyar Compass* (*Big Hungarian Compass*), I, Mihály Della Vadella (ed.), (Budapest, 1930–1).

In view of the fact that the nominal value of the national income was between 4.3 billion and 5.4 billion Pg, we can safely conclude that the role the banks – especially the Credit Bank – played in the country's economic life continued to be a vital one. We might even say that its role was greater than its strength, for as soon as the international money and loan market was shaken, in 1931, when the Viennese Credit-Anstalt collapsed, the Credit Bank, too, was on the verge of bankruptcy.

Notes

1. Hungarian National Archives, Credit Bank Secretariat, Fasc. Z51/56.
2. *Ibid.*, data based on the agreements signed on 27 Feb. 1871 and 1 Jan. 1906.
3. For the Credit Bank's pre-1914 activities, see Vilmos Sándor, *Nagyipari fejlődés Magyarországon* [*The Development of Big Industry in Hungary*] (Budapest, 1954); I. T. Berend – G. Ránki, *Magyarország gyáripara 1900–1914* [*Hungary's manufacturing industry 1900–1914*] (Budapest, 1955); and B. Michel, *Banques et banquiers en Autriche au debut du 20e siècle* (Paris, 1976).
4. R. W. Goldsmith, *Facteurs determinants de la structure financiere* (Paris, 1966), and L. Katus' chapter in the *History of Hungary*, VII (Budapest, 1977).
5. The reports in the archives of the French Foreign Ministry show that the idea originated in the Quai d'Orsay rather than

with the Schneider group. 'En mai 1920 a la demande du Gouvernement francais M. M. Schneider et cie sont entres en rapport avec le Gouvernement hongrois et les banques hongroises sur un programme propose.' Ministère des Affaires Étrangères (henceforth MAE) Europe Hongrie, 84/116. Note from 10 Mar. 1923. According to a note dated 7 July 1920 French policy wished to counterbalance English expansion. British interests had already seized control of Danube shipping: MAE Europe 1918–1929, Hongrie, 85.
6. *Papers and Documents Relating to the Foreign Relations of Hungary*, I (1938), 361. J. Bouvier, in *Un Siècle de Banque Française* (Paris, 1973), sees France's plans in South-East Europe as an attempt to compensate for the lost Russian market.

7. M. Ormos, 'Francia-magyar tárgyalások 1920-ban' ['Franco-Hungarian negotiations in 1920'], *Századok* [*Centuries*] (1975), 5–6.

   According to information found in the German archives, French capital tried to obtain a share in the Commercial Bank as well: German Foreign Ministry E 460 034, 23 Aug. 1920. Traces of negotiations are to be found in Paris as well: MAE Europe 78/86, 1 Sept. 1920 and 14 Sept. 1920. See also the report of Mr Athlesten Johnson from the British High Commission in Budapest, 22 July 1922: according to this the French group obtained 25 per cent of the Hitelbank's shares. They asked for 6 seats out of 26 on the Board: PRO F0371, C2633.

8. Magda Ádám, 'Duna konföderació vagy kisantant' ['Danubian confederation or little entente'], *Történelmi Szemle* [*Historical Review*] (1977), 3–4.

9. Elek Karsai, *Számjeltávirat valamennyi magyar királyi követségnek* [*coded Telegram to all Royal Hungarian Embassies*] (Budapest, 1969), 23.

10. Dezső Nemes, *Az ellenforradalom története Magyarországon 1919–1921* [*The History of the counter-revolution in Hungary* 1919–1921] (Budapest, 1962), 321.

    On the basis of the unanimous decision brought today by the Council of Ministers, I have, honoured Sir, the fortune to inform you of the following: The royal Hungarian government knows that the Parisian Union Européenne industrielle et financière, with the knowledge and consent of the French government, desired the Hungarian General Credit Bank to increase its nominal capital, and to permit the above-mentioned Parisian firm – more precisely, the major French group with an interest in it – to take over a considerable portion of the newly issued shares, in order that it might, in the future, take part in the building up of the Hungarian economy. The royal Hungarian government has also considered the fact that you, honoured Sir, considering only your own business interests, would not, at least at this time, accept this offer. In view of the fact, however, that the French government – which is willing to give Hungary political and economic support of historic significance – has made the French capitalists' participation in the Hungarian General Credit Bank as described above one of the indispensable conditions of this support, the royal Hungarian government, recalling, honoured Sir, your merits as a patriot, gives emphatic expression to its desire that you, honoured Sir, take steps to bring about the above-described transaction.

11. Hungarian National Archives, Credit Bank Board of Directors, Fasc. Z50/26; directors' report of 6 May 1921.

12. See Bouvier, *Un Siècle de Banque Française*; and *idem, Initiation au vocabulaire et aux mecanismes économiques contemporaines* (Paris, 1969), 185.

13. Hungarian National Archives, Credit Bank, Fasc. Z51/9/18.

14. *Ibid.*, Credit Bank Board of Directors, Fasc. Z50/26; Meeting of the Board of Directors, 6 May 1921.

15. *Ibid.*, Credit Bank.

16. *Ibid.*, Fasc. Z50/29; meeting of the Board of Directors, 4 July.

17. *Ibid.*, Fasc. Z50/29; meeting of the Board of Directors, 30 Dec. 1925. See also MAE Europe, 78/46. The French Ministry of Finance immediately approved the French participation.

18. Hungarian National Archives, Credit Bank, Fasc. 30; meeting of the Board of Governors, 29 May and 20 Nov. 1926.

19. For the contract made with the Treasury, see: Hungarian National Archives, Credit Bank Secretariat, Fasc. Z51/56, esp. the contract dated 1 Jan. 1928.

20. *Ibid.*, Fasc. 251/14.

21. *Ibid.*, Fasc. Z50; meeting of the Board of Directors of 19 Nov. 1927.

22. Hungarian National Archives, Foreign Ministry Economic Policy Department, 1926/253; and Credit Bank Secretariat, Fasc. Z51/14.

23. Hungarian National Archives, Foreign Ministry Economic Policy Department, Reserved documents 117/adm., 1926; the Ambassador's letter of 9 Dec. 1925.

24. *Pesti Tőzsde* [Pest Stock Exchange], 13 May 1926.

25. Hungarian National Archives, Foreign Ministry Economic Policy Department, Reserved documents 117/adm., 1926.

26. Hungarian National Archives, Hungarian General Coal Mining Co., Fasc. 61; Executive Committee meeting, 28 June 1927.
27. *Ibid.*, Fasc. 61, Executive Committee meeting, 17 Dec. 1926.
28. Hungarian National Archives, Salgótarján Coal Mines, Fasc. 193; the Talbot affair.
29. Hungarian National Archives, Credit Bank, Fasc. 21, Minutes of the meeting of the Board of Directors, 19 Nov. 1927.
30. *Magyar Kereskedők Lapja [Hungarian Merchants' Journal]*, 19 Feb. 1927. Hungarian National Archives, Minutes of the meeting of the Council of Ministers, 18 Feb. 1927.
31. Hungarian National Archives, Credit Bank, Fasc. 22, Minutes of the meeting of the Board of Directors, 14 May 1928.
32. *Ibid.*, Credit Bank Secretariat, Fasc. Z51/14.
33. *Ibid.*, Fasc. Z51/57.
34. *Ibid.*, Credit Bank Board of Directors, Fasc. Z50/28.
35. *Ibid.*, Fasc. Z50/34. They shared in the two previous increases of capital that the Union Européenne had carried out, the first time with a profit of 11,000 fr., the second time with a profit of 6,000 fr.
36. *Ibid.*, Credit Bank Secretariat, Fasc. Z51/5 and 11. At the end of the 1930s, of the company's 8.82m Pg worth of nominal capital held in 588,000 shares, 250,000 were in English hands, 146,000 were owned by the Hungarian Treasury, and 125,000 by the syndicate headed by the Credit Bank. The remaining shares were free.
37. I. T. Berend and G. Ránki, *Magyarország gazdasága 1919–29 [Hungary's Economy 1919–29]* (Budapest, 1963), 103.
38. Hungarian National Archives, Credit Bank Board of Directors, Fasc. Z50/23, 30, 34.
39. The French government took no part in the League of Nations loans for political reasons. Bouvier, on the other hand, emphasizes the fact that the French capital export in the 1920s was considerably smaller than the volume exported before 1913. Bouvier, *Un Siècle de Banque Française*, 265.
40. Hungarian National Archives, Credit Bank Secretariat, Fasc. Z51/56.
41. Calculations based on: Berend and Ránki, *op. cit.*, 214 and 223.
42. Hungarian National Archives, Credit Bank Board of Directors, Fasc. Z50/27; Meeting of 6 Sept. 1923.
43. *Ibid.*, Fasc. Z50/77, meeting of 5 Apr. 1922; Fasc. Z50/26, meeting of 11 June 1921; Fasc. Z50/26, meeting of 13 July 1922.
44. *Ibid.*, Fasc. Z50/30, meeting of 22 Nov. 1926.
45. *Ibid.*, Fasc. Z50/30, meeting of 29 May 1926.
46. P. Hanák and K. Hanák, *A Magyar Pamutipar története [The History of the Hungarian Cotton Industry]* (Budapest, 1964).
47. G. Ránki (ed.), *Debrecen iparanak története [The History of Industry in Debrecen]* (Debrecen, 1976). Lajos Timár's study, based on the factory documents found in the Debrecen Archives, is the one that treats the companies' relations with the Credit Bank.
48. Hungarian National Archives, Credit Bank Secretariat, Fasc. Z51/15.
49. *Ibid.*, Credit Bank Board of Directors, Fasc. Z50/29, meeting of 14 May 1925.
50. *Ibid.*, Fasc. Z50/30, Board meeting of 10 April 1926.
51. *Ibid.*, Fasc. Z50/34, Board meeting of 25 April 1929.
52. *Ibid.*, Credit Bank Secretariat, Fasc. Z51/15.
53. *Ibid.*
54. M. Lévy-Leboyer, 'Le Role historique de la monnaie de banque', *Annales* (1968), no. 1, 8.
55. Bouvier, *Un Siécle de Banque Française*, 33.

COMMENTARY *P. L. Cottrell*

There are three issues that I would like to raise with regard to György Ránki's admirable analysis of the role of the Hungarian General Credit Bank in the 1920s. One stems directly from the paper while the other two deal with more general points. However, I would like to preface my few remarks by pointing out that in the case of Hungary, one is dealing with a less industrialized section of the Danubian region. How does a very late developer with a very large agricultural sector break through this hump of backwardness? The aspect that has to be addressed here is the question of the construction of conduits which would channel savings, either domestic or foreign, to those entrepreneurial groups within Hungarian society which were prepared to undertake industrial investment.

First, Ránki seems to suggest a time division in the role played by the Hungarian General Credit Bank before and after the First World War. His view is that before 1914 the domestic investment banks did act as dynamos of change, fostering industrialization by facilitating capital formation. However, he perceives the banks playing a far weaker and more passive role in the 1920s. So, had the banks in Trianon Hungary been replaced by other agents of change in the development of industrialization? Did the state itself come forward as the facilitating agent of modernization? Certainly Hungarian governments from the 1880s had tried to pursue policies which would force the pace of industrialization.

Second, as Ránki shows, foreign capital did play a role in the transformation of the Hungarian economy. However, both Hungarian historians and some documentary sources, such as the files of the British Foreign Office officials and reports prepared for the OKW [Oberkommando der Wehrmacht – Supreme Command of the Armed Forces] in the early 1940s, show that foreign capital did not make much of an inroad into the inter-war Hungarian industrial sector. The inflationary boom of the early 1920s was a period of quite marked company formation but without much reliance on foreign sources of funds. The foreign inflow of funds that did take place during the 1920s occurred largely after stabilization and went mainly into fixed interest loans for agriculture, not industrial equities.

Third, and an issue which links with much of the earlier discussion, is that of the Hungarian General Credit Bank as an example of the centrifugal and centripetal forces operating within the Habsburg economy. The bank had been established by the Rothschilds, it was the Credit-Anstalt's twin in Budapest, but the survey of the relations between the two given by Ránki would suggest a weakening of the tie before 1914 and almost complete independence after 1918. Accordingly this would seem to provide evidence in terms of banking relationships of steady disintegration within the Habsburg economy, a process which accelerated from the beginning of the twentieth century.

14. The Interests of the Union Européenne in Central Europe

C. Beaud

The Union Européenne industrielle et financière (UEIF), formed on 22 April 1920, had as its two major shareholders the Banque de l'Union parisienne (BUP) and the major industrial concern of Schneider et Cie. This holding company had been established to control the assets acquired by Eugène Schneider at the end of the war in the ruins of Austria–Hungary. In 1920 these consisted primarily of two major Czechoslovakian industrial investments – the Škodovy závody [Škoda-Works] and the former Austrian enterprise Berg- und Hütten Werksgesellschaft [Báňská a hutní společnost; the Mining and Metallurgic Co.], a major extractive and manufacturing enterprise in the Těšín basin. In addition there were a number of minor interests, namely the Société Anonyme française de Huta Bankowa and shareholdings in Austrian and Hungarian banks. The most important of the latter was an interest in the Magyar Általános Hitelbank [Hungarian General Credit Bank] which allowed control over this bank's group of participations throughout Danubian Europe. The origins of the creation of this industrial and financial empire lay in the convergence of the interests of three separate parties – the Schneider-BUP group, the French state, and the successor states to Austria–Hungary, particularly Czechoslovakia.

As Teichova has shown,[1] one important dynamic force was the new Czechoslovak government. Beneš, the Czechoslovak Minister of Foreign Affairs, made good use of his visit to Paris in the spring of 1919 to encourage both the French government and representatives of the Schneider concern to become involved with his country's economy. Although political motives were important in the establishment of the 'Little Entente', economic and financial factors also played a part. In 1919 the largest Czechoslovak enterprises were still dependent upon Austrian capital and management. The rapid application of 'nostrification' policies in 1919 created difficulties for such companies, particularly Škoda. This enterprise was in disarray as a result of the expulsion of Baron Skoda and the introduction of inexperienced Czechoslovak management, and of the daunting problem of conversion from military to largely civil production. In the Těšín basin, where the new national boundaries were still not established, the nationalization[2] of mining and metallurgical companies, such as Berg- und Hütten, was proceeding far more cautiously and partially. The extremely bitter dispute with the large group of Polish miners had diverted attention from the 'Austrian problem'. However, this did not mean that the old imperial presence in the form of domination by either Viennese finance, in particular the Allgemeine österreichische Boden-Credit-Anstalt, or Günther, the competent but domineering general manager of Berg- und Hütten, was going to remain indefinitely. Consequently in order to carry out its policies of nostrification and reconstruction of the economy in a state that was small, cramped and economically isolated, the Czechoslovak government required foreign, but friendly, financial and managerial assistance.

Other countries were in a better position than France to provide the help that was required. A secret note of 19 August 1919 written by A. Fournier, the bold general manager of Schneider et Cie, to Eugène Schneider justified the need for urgent decisions on the basis of their mutual apprehensions regarding Italian and American designs on Škoda. Similarly a note of March 1920, one of the background papers to the establishment of UEIF, referred to the numerous American and English missions clearly backed by government support and assisted by the strong position of their respective currencies on the foreign exchange market. Although the Italians did not carry much industrial and financial weight, post-war impoverished France was not in a position to match the strength of Anglo-American financial resources. While there was always the possibility of an Anglo-Saxon credit, the still fragile Czechoslovakia could not expect to obtain from either the Italians or the Anglo-Saxons the political and military support that was likely to be forthcoming from France. Put another way, it was logical to prepare the ground for a future Franco-Czechoslovak alliance through establishing joint economic interests. It is very likely that this is how Beneš saw the situation. There was no difficulty in either swaying the Czechoslovaks who would have to make particular decisions – such as Šimonek, the new president of Škoda – to favour French initiatives, or applying pressure on the major Austrian shareholders such as Baron von Škoda, the Boden-Credit-Anstalt, and the Archduke Frederick to liquidate most, if not all, of their Czechoslovak holdings.

Was it very difficult to obtain French support? The sympathy and support within government circles for an industrial policy which would strengthen France's diplomatic position in Central Europe can be well documented. Typical is a note of March 1920 in which it is stated that 'the French Government has encouraged financial and industrial groups to look after established positions, especially in countries which are traditionally sympathetic to France and which have need to be defended ... Nothing would better assure French influence in these areas than the permanent involvement of French capital in undertakings which dominate the industrial life of these nations.' Although there is no trace in the Schneider archive of contact with the government in 1919, there can be no doubt that this steel-maker was not in the least reluctant with respect to this major policy of international economic expansion. It is certain that General Pelle's visit to Prague prepared the way for the Champigneul mission mounted by Schneider to examine the Škoda proposal in August 1919. In the secret note mentioned above, Fournier acquainted Schneider with the 'cordial welcome' of both the Czechoslovak government and the French mission and concluded that majority control should be grasped as quickly as possible.

It should not be thought that Schneider was only carrying out a policy that had been developed by French and Czechoslovak governments. Although in 1919, E. Schneider and A. Fournier played a major role in the Czechoslovak adventure, they were not seeking a quick and easy return because Škoda and Berg- und Hütten were not acquired cheaply.

The costs of the acquisitions made in 1919 and 1920 were about a third higher than the stock exchange valuation which then fell substantially during the crisis of 1921. If there was a temptation to take advantage of the enormous possibilities of French expansion in Europe in 1919, it was counterbalanced by substantial economic and social risks stemming from Bolshevik contagion or merely the socialist thrust in Czechoslovakia. Several years of continuing effort were required to consolidate the investments and make them financially profitable.

Schneider's policy fitted into an overall strategy worked out from the beginning of the twentieth century. Because of the limits to the firm's growth both at its Le Creusot nucleus and in the French hexagon where new but dispersed axes of development had multiplied, a double objective was established. This comprised a financial orientation for the concern coupled with the international expansion of its interests. UEIF was a continuation of the concern's Russian initiative which had been overseen by Fournier, its financial director. Unlike BUP the troublesome Russian experience had been less of a lesson for Schneider as the concern had suffered only minor losses since it had staked its technology rather than capital. In the view of Schneider and the other French representatives involved in the new affair, Škoda was to be the arsenal of the Little Entente, replacing or even complementing Putilov. This position was taken up because French economists, until 1921, considered the Bolshevik régime to be on the verge of collapse. A note of March 1920 envisaged the realization, from bases in Central Europe, of 'programmes sketched out before the war in Central and Southern Russia which had been interrupted by the hostilities and the Bolshevik Revolution'. Schneider's financial department wrote in October 1921 in terms stressing that 'the Škoda-Works will be the best agents for the reconstruction of Russian industry when this can be accomplished; their technical and commercial links with the Schneider plants are of the right kind to allow them to open up the markets of eastern Europe.'

With respect to the industrial advantages which would accrue from the control of Škoda, Fournier was content to present them as a postscript to his note of August 1919. Without taking into account the evident contradictions, this control would permit:

'1. Close collaboration with respect to cast steel;
2. A privileged position for the reconstruction of sugar refineries;
3. The development of our eastern position and our opportunities to sell raw
   materials and manufactures.'

Schneider's personality involved international aims and so it is probable
that the highly debatable advantages listed in this postscript, such as the
search for immediate profit, were secondary. With the position of power that
Schneider had achieved, it is highly likely that he desired to play a part, in
some way, in increasing France's greatness. It was the time of the 'Bloc
national' when the superior and further interests of the nation overrode the
short-term economic goals of a firm.

Moreoever, this new policy of international expansion had the backing of
far greater financial resources in 1919 than in 1912. Although already high in
1914, the gross profits declared by Schneider et Cie continued to rise,
reaching a maximum of 40 per cent at the end and immediately after the war.
During the three accounting years covering the period 1918 to 1920, the
firm's distributed dividends equalled its nominal capital while the annual
commissions paid to directors amounted to more than 1m fr. Central Europe
therefore represented the investment region for these war profits, barring the
period taken to acquire the two great Czechoslovak companies for about 50m
fr followed by their resale to the UEIF at cost price. Although the payment of
war profit duties was nominally a heavy burden, actually it was spread over
several years and the real cost was greatly reduced by inflation. Further, by
1919 Schneider had managed to bring BUP and its group back into his fold,
despite the substantial losses that the bank had suffered in Russia. Before
participating in UEIF, BUP contributed to the acquisition of the major East
Central European assets through supplying credits. In this way Schneider
obtained control over Škoda and Berg- und Hütten by 1919. It was in
character that he straight away concentrated his efforts upon the two most
important industrial entities in Central Europe, on the metallurgical industries which he understood.

From its formation in April 1920 the general policy of UEIF reflected on
the one hand the internal struggles of opinion between the Schneider group
and BUP and its associates, and on the other the changes in French policy.
Like French diplomacy, the policy of the holding company swung between
two poles – one consisting of Czechoslovak industry, the other being a new
financial Hungarian position but involving Hungarian revisionism. During
the spring of 1920, Paléologue, the Secrétaire-général at the Quai d'Orsay,
favoured a Danubian Confederation 'co-ordinated' by Hungary and accordingly seemed to respond to the wishes of the Hungarian government of
Regent Horthy. This led in April 1920 to the opening of negotiations between
the Quai d'Orsay, the Comte de Saint-Sauveur (Schneider's brother-in-law),
Dr C. Halmos who was the Hungarian government's representative in Paris,
and representatives of Hungarian economic interests, in particular Baron

Adolf Ullmann, Vice President of the Hungarian General Credit Bank, the most important investment bank in Budapest. On 14 April Halmos wrote to de Saint-Sauveur, saying that he had 'authority to inform him that all the business proposals discussed could easily be completed with groups put forward by the French government, with your firm having first place, but subject to a general settlement'. It is clear that the Hungarian government considered that the negotiations would take the form of wheeling and dealing. A very large and deep penetration by French business interests into a great variety of companies, both state and privately owned, was to be the price paid for a 'general settlement' – a political agreement. A meeting took place on 23 April chaired by Halmos at which Hungarian financiers and financial representatives from Schneiders studied 'various enterprises to be taken over by' the French firm. At that time Schneider was interested in private industrial companies like the Villamossági Tröszt [Electricity Trust], the two companies Ganz-Féle Villamossági Rt [Ganz Electric Co. Ltd] and Ganz és társa-Danubius gép-, waggon és hajógyár részvénytársaság [Ganz & Company-Danubius machine railway-carriage manufacturing and shipbuilding Co. Ltd], and the Magyar Általános Köszénbánya Rt [Hungarian General Coal Mines Ltd]. It was only at the end of the meeting that Baron Ullman put forward the idea 'of a French participation in the Credit Bank which controlled some 250 industrial and commercial companies'.

In a confidential letter of 26 April to Paléologue, Halmos was more pressing: 'During the next week I will be able to deliver to the French group with which I have been negotiating options in the name of the Hungarian government. I fully appreciate that the French government is not able to intervene in Hungarian affairs without defending very important French interests. But you must understand Mr Ambassador that I can not make definite engagements unless the political questions are also resolved.' Included in the letter were proposals to form the basis of a general agreement and so 'break the vicious circle'. When the Hungarian requirements for a general political accord with France are read, and then the economic proposals, the lack of a definite course in French diplomacy over the following months is understandable. That a copy of this letter with its enclosure can be found in the Schneider archives proves beyond all doubt the existence of a close relationship between Schneider and Paléologue. But it also shows that although the Secrétaire-général at the Quai d'Orsay strongly favoured a rapprochement with Hungary, he wanted Schneider to understand that such excessive political conditions could not be accepted, even in exchange for substantial economic concessions.

The clear impression is gained that Paléologue was above all searching for a way through this diplomatic maze, giving the Hungarians some hope of French support without making too firm a commitment before a precise settlement, so sparing Hungary's neighbours – France's allies. The aim became that of obtaining limited economic interests in Hungary in exchange for moderate political support. Actually during the following months the UEIF's involvement with Hungarian industrial companies did not assume any concrete form but the visit in the summer of 1920 of de Saint-Sauveur and Bavière (the latter acting for BUP) led to a minority shareholding of 14 per cent in the Hungarian General Credit Bank. While BUP, which obtained a parallel minority holding in its own name, appears to have been attracted to this investment, Schneider became more reserved over the Hungarian situation. Nevertheless in August 1920 Fournier, although fully aware of the contradictions between the Hungarian option and the consolidation of the positions in Czechoslovakia, showed that the Hungarian bank was capable of becoming a turntable for a wide-scale policy throughout Danubian Europe.

In January 1921 Paléologue left the Quai d'Orsay to join the board of the UEIF. When in the spring of 1921, Berthelot, the new Secrétaire-général at the Quai d'Orsay, definitely turned towards the Little Entente and a pro-Hungarian policy no longer even received moderate support from Briand, there was the same conflict at the centre of UEIF. Schneider hesitated over any further involvements in Hungary and claimed that he was taken up with 'purely industrial matters'. The jilting of Hungary by French diplomacy in October 1921 had the effect of steering the UEIF towards Czechoslovakia. Thereafter the holding company's interests in the Hungarian General Credit Bank and in several of the bank's minor affiliates were of a very low level. UEIF merely collected a few dividends and provided some minimal services for which it complained that it was not paid. Its Prague 'friends' now gained the upper hand over those in Budapest.

By the end of 1921 UEIF had not only been established and consolidated; in addition the principal features of the structure of its network in Central Europe had been formed.[3]

UEIF was faced with a considerable task from its inception. Before looking at the company's activities, the organization and management of this French inter-war multi-national should first be established.

With respect to the internal structure of this holding company and the relationships between the interest groups which it combined, one major question emerges. How was Schneider able to control one of the most important industrial and financial empires of the period with only an investment in it of less than 14 per cent?

Schneider's antipathy towards the limited company form of organization was overcome by the advantages of prevailing legislation and the particular structure of a holding company which allowed the control of several powerful companies while tying up only a minimum of capital. A note of March 1920, part of the preparations for the formation of UEIF, clearly indicates the double objective of the projected enterprise:

'1. To ensure the effective control of interests acquired and resold to the Holding Company and the maintenance of that control;

2. The acquisition of a large number of important enterprises without rendering too much capital illiquid; so therefore placing with the public the largest possible number of shares of the Holding Company but without losing control over it.'

Schneider was able to dominate UEIF as a consequence of two, then current, practices (see the schematic structure of UEIF, fig. 14.1). First was the differentiation between the rights carried by the two types of shares issued. The A shares, enabling a holder to have a preference dividend, were registered, and above all carried a plural vote, 10 votes per A share held, whereas the B shares, which were issued frequently in a bearer form, had only a single vote, but because of their nature were not difficult to sell to the public. The A shares accounted for only 10 per cent of the capital of UEIF but their holders held more than a majority of the total voting rights at general meetings of the company. With a holding of 52.3 per cent of the A shares of UEIF, an interest which had cost less than 4m fr, Schneider held 27.5 per cent of the voting rights in the concern. Second was the practice of freezing the ownership of the A shares to the members of a syndicate. This consisted of three groups – Schneider, BUP and Empain – to which were reserved all the A shares and which then blocked them, as the A shares could not be subsequently resold to any outside interest without the authorization of the board of UEIF. By having the majority of votes this syndicate controlled UEIF and Schneider dominated this blocking syndicate through holding the majority of the A shares. In the case of the B shares, which actually constituted 90 per cent of the capital of the holding company, it was only a matter of the blocking syndicate retaining a small proportion, selling the rest to small shareholders. The Crédit Lyonnais, which initially subscribed for more than 13 per cent of the B shares, liquidated its interest completely which had been expected by the founders of UEIF. The constituents of the blocking syndicate reduced their own holdings of B shares through a selling syndicate managed by BUP. This procedure disposed of about a third of the B shares but only in face of some difficulty and at little profit because of the crisis of the early 1920s. The Belgian Empain group, consisting of the Longueville enterprise and the Banque industrielle, retained less than 11 per cent of the shares. Although an ally of Schneider it was overshadowed by the French industrialist, the predominant figure of the period.

The BUP group could only play second fiddle. Along with its associates, the banks with which it had close working relationships, and the Société Générale de Belgique, BUP held much the greatest proportion of the capital of UEIF – nearly 30 per cent as opposed to the 28 per cent held by the Schneider group. However, by having a little less than a third of the A shares, the bank was in a subordinate position. Like the earlier Russian venture, it was eclipsed by the forces of large industry. The bank came increasingly to play the role of the milchcow, a position which largely explains the growing tensions and difficulties of the Schneider-BUP alliance.

Union Européenne industrielle et financière

Holding company formed on 22 Apr. 1920

Capital 75 m.fr. in 150,000 share of 500 fr; 15,000 blocking A shares and 135,000 B shares

	A shares %	B shares at formation %	B shares end of 1921 %
Schneider group of which:	52.3	34.7	25.3
Framerican		19.2	14.3
BUP group	34.8	35.6	28.9
Empain group	12.8	16.3	10.9
Crédit Lyonnais		13.3	
Shares sold by BUP syndicate			34.8

1
Škoda Works

1919: capital 144 m.Kč in 450,000 share of 320 Kč Factories at Plzeň: metallurgy and mechanical construction

Steel works subsidiary company at Hrádek (near Plzeň – 55% controlled by Škoda)

Participation of UEIF in 1920: 229,567 shares bought by Schneider at 104,6 fr. each, i.e. 51% of the capital + 42,800 to the blocking syndicate (32,000 of which to Huta Bankowa) + 5,400 to the Živnostenská banka

In 1921 following purchases on the stock exchange UEIF controlled 52.3% of the capital of Škoda

2
United Engineering Construction Plants Co. Ltd.

1919: Capital raised from 25 to 50 m.Kč by the creation of 125,000 shares reserved for Škoda which controlled more than 50% of the capital

4 mechanical construction works at:
Smíchov (suburb of Prague)
Plzeň
Doudlevec (near Plzeň)
Hradec-Králové

1922: Amalgamation of United Plants with Škoda which increased its capital by 156,250 shares, UEIF subscribing 78,125

3
Berg- und Hüttenwerksgesellschaft

The Austrian company became the Czech company Báňská a hutní společnost

1920: Capital 50 m.Kč in 125,000 shares

UEIF controlled 24% of the capital and 48.4% with the blocking syndicate: Boden-Credit-Anstalt, Huta Bankowa and the American group Equitable Trust Co.

1921: Participation of UEIF in increase of capital from 50 to 76 m.Kč

4

Participation of UEIF as member of group of French steel manufacturers in an Austrian company, the Veitscher Magnesit Werke at Vienna, for the exploitation of magnesite products

The participation of the group of French steel manufacturers, initially a minority holding in 1919-1920, gradually became a majority one; the VMW controlled 70% of MIAG (Magnesit Industrie AG) at Bratislava which owned three magnesia plants, two in Slovakia and one in Hungary

5

UEIF participation of 4% in 1923 in the Niederösterreichische Escompte-Gesellschaft.

Principal installations in Czechoslovakia in the Těšín region:
coal mines in Ostrava-Karviná
steelworks at Třinec
sheet metal rolling mills at Karlova Huť
in Slovakia: iron mines at Maria metallurgic works and at Bindt
in Poland: foundry at Węgierska Górka, run as Polish company

Subsidiary companies in Russia:
Steel Foundry Co. of Donetz (with iron mines at Krivoi-Rog)
Participation of Huta Bankowa in Škoda and in Báňská a hutní společnost

6
Huta Bankowa Co. (Poland)

French company, the capital of which was raised in 1920 from 23 to 80 m.fr. by the issue of 114,000 shares of 500 fr. 22,000 of which, i.e. 13.7% of the capital, were subscribed by Schneider then transferred to UEIF.

Iron mines and metal works at Drombrowa

Subsidiary companies in Poland:
Count Renard Coalmining Co.
Metallurgical industries company in Russia
Franco-Russian Mining Co.

Subsidiary companies in Russia:

7

Small participation by UEIF in the Polish Financial Union formed in 1928 under the aegis of the Banque belge pour l'Étranger, a subsidiary of the Société générale de Belgique

8
Hungarian General Credit Bank

1920: capital raised from 160 to 280 m.CH in 700,000 shares of 400 CH

Participation of UEIF with 100,000 shares, i.e. 14.3% of the capital, and BUP with 100,000 shares

Participation of UEIF in increases of capital in the Croatian General Credit Bank as well as in three timber companies reorganized in a Swiss Holding Co., the Lignum Trust
Hungarian General Timber Co.
Ehrlich Hungarian General Co. Ltd.
Yugoslavian Forestry Co. Ltd of Zagreb

9
'STEG' participation in 1920-21

Participation of 10% taken by UEIF in the syndicate formed by the Cie française du Levant for the purchase of Staats-Eisenbahn-Gesellschaft (STEG) locomotives and their resale to the Romanian government.

Warsaw · POLAND · Cracow · Dombrowa · Brno · Těšín · CZECHOSLOVAKIA · Prague · Plzeň · GERMANY · Vienna · AUSTRIA · Budapest · HUNGARY · Zagreb · ITALY

Figure 14.1. The network of the Union Européenne industrielle et financière (UEIF).

The Schneider group was organized in the best possible way to dominate the holding company at the least possible cost. Only Schneider et Cie held the 52.3 per cent of the A shares, whereas the B capital was generously offered to its associates, in particular the Framerican Industrial Development Company, which was none other than Schneider et Cie's exclusive agent in the United States. At the end of 1921 Framerican still held nearly 15 per cent of the B shares while Schneider et Cie had got rid of as many as it could so that only 9 per cent were in its name. Accordingly with only 13.5 per cent of the capital of UEIF – worth about 10m fr. – Schneider controlled nearly a third of the votes in the holding company, dominating it as a result of both the organization of his own group and that of the blocking syndicate.

UEIF endeavoured to establish an all-embracing network, like a spider's web, to cover Central Europe (see fig. 14.1). However, was it possible to reintroduce an element of unity surmounting the hostile boundaries which now partitioned the region both politically and economically?

The two set pieces of the organization were its Czechoslovak dependencies – the Škoda Works, its subsidiaries, the Spojené strojírny akciová společnost dříve Škoda, Ruston, Bromovský a Ringhoffer [United Engineering Construction Plants Co. Ltd] fully taken over by Škoda in 1922, and the Mining and Metallurgic Co. which formed a balanced vertically integrated production group comparable to that of Schneider et Cie in France (see fig. 14.2). UEIF held 50 per cent of this Czechoslovakian industrial grouping. In 1921 the French holding company held directly more than 52 per cent of Škoda but only 25 per cent of the shares of the Mining and Metallurgic Company. However, in the case of the latter, UEIF's influence held sway over 48 per cent of the shares as a result of a blocking syndicate composed of the Polish Huta Bankowa concern, the Boden-Credit-Anstalt (the last remnants of Austrian domination), and an American group headed by the Equitable Trust Company. The latter consisted of representatives of Pennsylvanian metallurgical interests which at the end of the war had strenuously attempted to gain a foothold in Central Europe. In particular it had managed to become the liquidator of the interests of Archduke Frederick who had a substantial stake in the Mining and Metallurgic Co. This transatlantic offensive petered out after acquiring a mere 6 per cent holding in the Mining and Metallurgical Co. In December 1920 an attempt by this group to obtain a stake in UEIF which was searching for more capital proved entirely fruitless. Schneider must have distrusted the birth of a rival imperialism.

The use of a blocking syndicate reinforced UEIF's domination over Škoda and gave it greater foundations in the case of the Mining and Metallurgic Co. At the same time UEIF strove to create a system of interdependence between these two companies and others in which it had an interest. The activities of the French Huta Bankowa company, formed before 1914 by St Etienne and Lyon interests, stretched initially across a broad area from the Silesian coalfield to the Krivoi-Rog iron basin. Schneider's subscription to a share

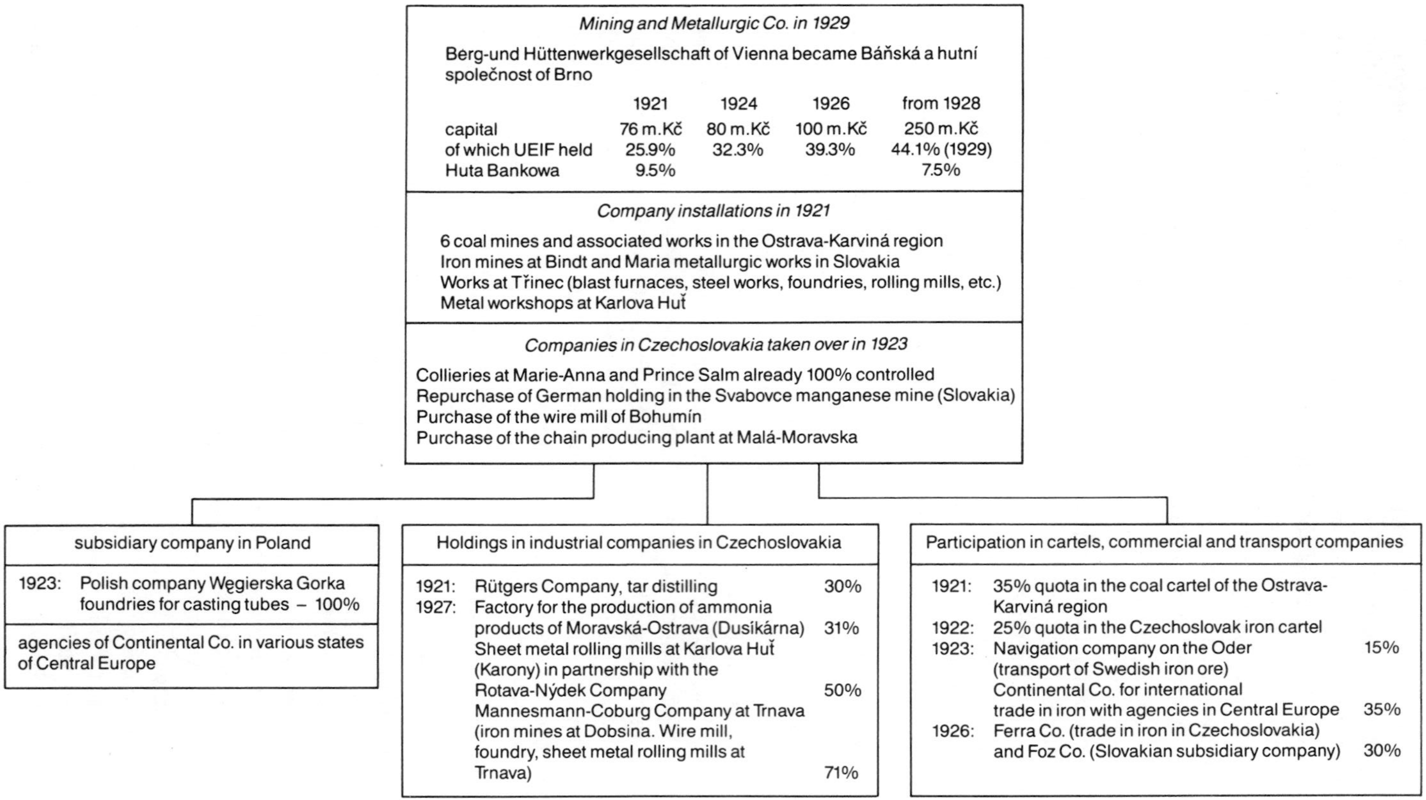

Mining and Metallurgic Co. in 1929

Berg- und Hüttenwerkgesellschaft of Vienna became Báňská a hutní společnost of Brno

	1921	1924	1926	from 1928
capital	76 m.Kč	80 m.Kč	100 m.Kč	250 m.Kč (1929)
of which UEIF held	25.9%	32.3%	39.3%	44.1% (1929)
Huta Bankowa	9.5%			7.5%

Company installations in 1921

6 coal mines and associated works in the Ostrava-Karviná region
Iron mines at Bindt and Maria metallurgic works in Slovakia
Works at Třinec (blast furnaces, steel works, foundries, rolling mills, etc.)
Metal workshops at Karlova Huť

Companies in Czechoslovakia taken over in 1923

Collieries at Marie-Anna and Prince Salm already 100% controlled
Repurchase of German holding in the Svabovce manganese mine (Slovakia)
Purchase of the wire mill of Bohumín
Purchase of the chain producing plant at Malá-Moravska

Participation in cartels, commercial and transport companies

1921:	35% quota in the coal cartel of the Ostrava-Karviná region	
1922:	25% quota in the Czechoslovak iron cartel	
1923:	Navigation company on the Oder (transport of Swedish iron ore)	15%
	Continental Co. for international trade in iron with agencies in Central Europe	35%
1926:	Ferra Co. (trade in iron in Czechoslovakia) and Foz Co. (Slovakian subsidiary company)	35% / 30%

Holdings in industrial companies in Czechoslovakia

1921:	Rütgers Company, tar distilling	30%
1927:	Factory for the production of ammonia products of Moravská-Ostrava (Dusíkárna)	31%
	Sheet metal rolling mills at Karlova Huť (Karony) in partnership with the Rotava-Nýdek Company	50%
	Mannesmann-Coburg Company at Trnava (iron mines at Dobšina. Wire mill, foundry, sheet metal rolling mills at Trnava)	71%

subsidiary company in Poland

1923: Polish company Węgierska Gorka foundries for casting tubes – 100%

agencies of Continental Co. in various states of Central Europe

Figure 14.2. The structure of the Mining and Metallurgic Co., 1937. (*Source* Schema of the Mining and Metallurgic Co., 1937 by A. Teichova in 'Munich 1938', Colloquium on Munich, Paris 1978.)

issue which enlarged this company's capital gave the UEIF a minority interest of 14 per cent. In return the Huta Bankowa concern was invited to participate in both the Škoda syndicate, which was of no real importance, and the arrangement for the shares of the Mining and Metallurgic Co. which was the objective of the UEIF and absolutely necessary for its interests. These consisted of an attempt to build a bridge crossing the disputed frontier between Poland and Czechoslovakia, but the development of the Polish situation, and likewise the Hungarian, by heightening the tension between the successor states, very quickly put a brake on this initiative. Actually the fundamental interests of the UEIF in Czechoslovakia formed not only a springboard but also an obstacle to the expansion of its influence to neighbouring countries. In this context it is significant that the only direct participation of relative importance undertaken by the UEIF in Poland was an investment in a French company which had its registered office in Paris. This was not completed until 1928 when a small interest was taken in the Union financière polonaise which was controlled by the Banque belge pour l'Étranger, a subsidiary of the Société Générale de Belgique. The Węgierska Gorka foundry, the only plant of the Mining and Metallurgic Co. to remain on Polish territory until 1939, had to be separated from its Czechoslovak business nucleus and be transformed into a Polish company.

The extensions of French influence in Poland had therefore to take place by different devices – through the growing and direct interests of Schneider et Cie which was heavily involved in major construction work at the port of Gdynia and the important Silesia-Baltic railway line. In 1931 Schneider and the Banque des Pays du Nord, control of which had been taken by the iron and steel concern in 1929, formed the Cie Franco-Polonaise de Chemins de Fer to undertake the concession from the Polish state to build the railway line. The French group, along with the Bank Gospodarstwa Krajowego of Warsaw, held the majority of shares of the railway concession company but although Schneider dominated, UEIF with only 200 shares out of 8,000 merely had a foothold in the enterprise. In areas where the activities of UEIF became very delicate as a consequence of its substantial involvement with Czechoslovakia, Schneider worked through the intermediary of its banking subsidiary.[4]

Corresponding with the hardly successful attempts to establish links between similar industries in Poland and Czechoslovakia, there were efforts to increase the more discreet financial interconnections. The bank-industry connections in Central Europe corresponded with the French financial relations of the Schneider group with the group composed of BUP and the Société Générale de Belgique. The UEIF strove to maintain, even reinforce, banking connections with Vienna, the old nerve centre of the Austro-Hungarian Empire. The Boden-Credit-Anstalt continued to be the principal bank for the Mining and Metallurgic Co., although it was now a Franco-Czechoslovak enterprise, as the price for its participation in the syndicate which blocked the shares of the company. But the agreement made in 1923 to take a 4 per cent participation in Niederösterreichische Escompte-Gesellschaft was based upon all the former banking connections in Austria, Czechoslovakia and Hungary; the Niederösterreichische Escompte-Gesellschaft accordingly had to be satisfied with any, and probably small-scale, operations of UEIF in Austria. Actually very quickly the bank-industry relations tended to contract within the Czechoslovak framework. UEIF must have distrusted Škoda's substantial dependence upon the Živnostenská banka of Prague. It was not the small participation of the institution in Škoda which allowed its director Dr Preiss to be so forcible on the industrial company's board but rather the bank's connections with the Czechoslovak government and the very substantial credits that it had given to the company. Preiss, on becoming vice-president of the Mining and Metallurgic Co., strove to diminish the Austrian position within this other major enterprise. With respect to UEIF's banking participations in Hungary and Croatia, these gave neither control of the banks themselves nor any major influence over their numerous subsidiaries. For obvious reasons there was no question of the interests of UEIF in Czechoslovakia and Hungary leading to the formation of an economic community consisting of the two countries. At the very most French influence in the Hungarian General Credit Bank formed a façade behind which could be maintained the network subsidiaries situated in the former Hungarian territories now part of Romania and Yugoslavia.

It has to be acknowledged that the efforts of UEIF to reconstruct a certain economic unity in Central Europe ran up against virulent nationalism.

It is now necessary to establish clearly the form of the relations between UEIF and the enterprises that it controlled in Central Europe, especially those in Czechoslovakia. Did UEIF have sufficient resources either to guide or to aid its subsidiaries? Doubts arise when the skeletal numbers of personnel attached to the holding company during its first years are considered. The general policy was worked out at monthly meetings of the board chaired and dominated by Schneider. Under the board and the mainspring of the working of the system was the administrateur-délégué, initially Colonel Weyl, but from 1922 P. Cheysson, inspecteur des finances. The latter had only a small staff – a secrétaire-général, a chief accountant with first one and then two assistants, a secretary and an office boy. A little later the establishment of UEIF was completed with the appointment of de Saint Paul, Škoda's former representative in France, as head of the commercial service. In 1928 a sugar refineries office was detached from the commercial service headed by the engineer Pernot who had displayed such aggressive behaviour that little by little he displaced the ageing de Saint Paul before replacing him.

Gradually the staff of the holding company filled out, to the extent that during the crisis the question of reducing personnel costs arose. There was an increasing concentration of power from 1929. The large board lost much of its influence to a management committee consisting of Schneider, the dominating force, and a general manager who replaced the post of administrateur-délégué. This new position was potentially very powerful and it was used to the full by the dynamic mining engineer A. Lepercq.

Actually, and especially until 1929, many of the staff requirements of UEIF were fulfilled by Schneider et Cie which also seconded, when required, skilled personnel, technicians, and accountants who either visited or were permanently based in Czechoslovakia. Moreover, it was necessary to establish links with the subsidiaries. In the case of UEIF's minor interests in Poland and Hungary, it was represented only by directors who were unable to affect decisively the policies of these companies. On company boards in Czechoslovakia as a result of legislation there had to be a balance between local and French representatives. Although apparently at odds with its ownership, Schneider was only the vice-president of Škoda and further there was a relative Czechoslovak preponderance in the company's administration, but this was due to the post-war nostrification of the concern and the importance attached to it by the state. In contrast Schneider reigned as president at the Mining and Metallurgic Co. where the French had very easily replaced Austro-German domination. However it proved difficult to displace Günther, the general manager, but he did become successively the administrateur-délégué and consulting engineer. When Lepercq became the administrateur-délégué he controlled the new general management of Kruliš-Randa.

At the same time French permanent management structures were established following temporary missions like those of Champigneul at Škoda, Lavigne at the Mining and Metallurgic Co., the tour of Schneider and the administrateur-délégué in May and June 1920, and the technical surveys of Caillet, the sub-manager at Le Creusot. These post-war missions were undertaken to study the position on the spot and prepare reorganization and production plans. But in order to oversee their fulfilment, it seemed necessary to put alongside the general managers of Škoda and the Mining and Metallurgic Co. 'a very small yet highly qualified French group'. By September 1920 a delegation was at work at Škoda with a technical assistant for the director of the Plzeň works and an administrative and financial assistant for Hanuš, the general manager in Prague. This latter post was held by Charles Rochette and his work was so appreciated by Hanuš that he appointed Rochette first as the inspecteur-général of Škoda and the United Works, and then the principal director at the Škoda Works. At the Mining and Metallurgic Co. after Günther had been expelled and replaced by general manager Kruliš-Randa, the latter was flanked by Lavigne, a French assistant, who planned for a mixed Franco-Czechoslovak management like the composition of the company's board. Finally, after giving the task of liaison between Paris and the subsidiaries to Colonel Lapebie of Schneider's top management, UEIF established a permanent office in Prague managed by Rochette.

Did these ever closer ties produce a relationship of either domination, involving unfair advantage, or even-handed collaboration? It is clear that during the 1920s the UEIF was the dominant force. Faced with the problems of reconversion which in 1920 were increased by the crisis, the leaders of UEIF felt the pressing need to impose their men, their objectives, and their commercial interests.

The technical delgation at Škoda was first accepted and then appreciated locally but it had been imposed on the enterprise along with a reorganization programme by Schneider who had spoken as the master at a meeting at Plzeň in May 1920. At that time 'general manager Hanuš recalled that he had asked Champigneul on several occasions to request Schneiders to send a number of their trusted staff in order not only to ease mutual relationships but also to avoid misunderstandings arising from the divergence of views'. The UEIF asked its seconded staff to respect 'legitimate national sensitivities' and to establish themselves locally 'through force of character and level of expertise' rather than by the authority of their official position. However, with the difficulties of the early 1920s, it was necessary not only to advise but also to ensure that the local general management carried out the programmes prepared in Paris.

A letter of 3 December 1920 written by Colonel Weyl to Šimonek, the president of Škoda, provides evidence of an initial tendency to exploit financially the subsidiary companies. After listing several examples of the efforts made by UEIF on behalf of Škoda, Weyl insisted, despite Šimonek's reluctance, that Škoda came to an agreement over the charges for these services. Defending himself against any charges of 'bargaining' and any 'criticism', Weyl presented 'a plan for a letter to be sent to the Union Européenne'. After a bitter confrontation, a settlement was made in April 1920 whereby Škoda paid a fixed commission of 0.75 per cent of its foreign turnover in exchange for representation in France, the French colonies, Belgium, Spain and Portugal. This commission together with that extracted from the Mining and Metallurgic Co. constituted by far the largest part of UEIF's earnings until 1922. Lepercq, the general manager, understood the risks and the excesses involved in these methods. In rough drafts of letters to Schneider sketched out in 1936, Lepercq considered that the 'agreements' went well beyond currently accepted practice in the relations between a mother company and its subsidiaries. After having accepted either a moratorium or a suspension of commission payments during the Great Depression, Lepercq took the initiative to introduce reforms and replaced the fixed commission on turnover by a much less burdensome schedule of varying charges which corresponded more exactly with the services provided by UEIF.

Once the balance between charges and profits became more comparable with other combines and there was a likelihood of a progressive return to profitability, then the correspondence between Prague and Paris was increasingly marked by cordiality and open collaboration. This was particularly the case between Lepercq and the president-general manager Loewenstein and his successor Hromádko. 'Munich' and the collapse of UEIF brought about a real split for the Czechoslovaks as well as the French. It was then necessary from 1920 for the personal relationships, in terms of mutual understanding between the French and Czechoslovak executives, to be gradually established so that the position of the mother company towards its subsidiaries changed from domination to friendly collaboration.

The policy of UEIF towards its subsidiaries, especially those in Czechoslovakia, during the 1920s now has to be considered. The report of Schneider and the administrateur-délégué's visit of June 1920 to Czechoslovakia reveals the importance of the task that had to be accomplished: 'The aim to be realized is not simply that of a financial holding, it is above all an industrial effort, an endeavour of organization and management'. The network of subsidiaries was powerful but it required careful guidance not only financially but also in technical, commercial and administrative areas. This management task was made a more sensitive problem by the need to take into account the particular position of each firm and the shaping it required.

The surviving papers of UIEF give the impression that the strategy for the combine was established in Paris by the board. It was passed to Prague or Brno by either the administrateur-délégué or Colonel Lapebie, the liaison manager, and it was then carried out under the close control of the French teams, set up initially at Škoda but then also at the Mining and Metallurgic Co. It would seem that the local general managements of the two enterprises were left little room for their own initiative. However, UEIF did undertake important functions for its subsidiaries. Once the UEIF became responsible for the future of the companies that it controlled, then it made use of all of its power, resources and connections, both French and international, in order initially to rectify the position of the plants and then to increase their profitability and develop their strength.

Immediately after the war the strategy was to meet the demands of a situation which was fundamentally different to that pertaining either before or during the war. It was not only a matter of reorientating Škoda's output towards civilian products, it was also necessary to take account of the political and economic fragmentation of Europe and the great difficulties involved in both obtaining supplies and trading with neighbouring countries which were jealous of their independence. UEIF, soon after it had acquired its subsidiaries, was faced with not only the normal problems of readaptation but also the difficulties stemming from the economic crisis of 1921–2 and the inflation which particularly affected Austria and Czechoslovakia along with Germany in Central Europe. This conjunction of events called for the greatest reduction of costs, the improvement of productivity, and in general terms better management. The extent of the losses sustained by Škoda in 1918 and 1919 together with the collapse of the stock exchange prices of the shares of the subsidiary companies in 1921, which in the case of the Mining and Metallurgic Co. involved a fall of 40 per cent from the quotation at which the company had been acquired, formed a very worrying situation for UEIF. It was these events which were responsible for the weak role played by Czechoslovak management in the debate over the major decisions that had to be made and the almost dictatorial nature of the safeguarding measures which were imposed.

Although the new political boundaries prevented the UEIF from drawing together its scattered nuclei, the company was a unifying element in Central Europe and a link between this region and France. Actually UEIF was responsible for increasing the number of 'political' or diplomatic representations made on behalf of its subsidiaries. Accordingly the Union Européenne enabled its 'filials' to benefit from France's then dominant position and this great influence involved not only the French government but also had effect in the states which were friendly with France but antagonistic towards one another.

It was in this context that the Hungarian General Credit Bank saw an advantage in having French participation in its equity capital even after Paléologue's initiative had failed. It was the easiest method by which the bank could maintain its old Romanian, Croatian and Slovakian dependencies – its network of subsidiaries and investments – although it entailed reappearing in these areas through the intervention of a French company. The 8,000 shares of the Hrvatska sveopća kreditna banka dioničarsko društvo [Croatian General Bank] classified by UEIF as its own investment had actually been paid for by the Hungarian bank – the Union being the most acceptable façade in Yugoslavia. Similarly the involvement of UEIF in the increase of the capital of the Jugoslavenska sumska industrija [Yugoslavian Forestry Co. Ltd] of Zagreb allowed the continuation of Hungarian interests. In return the Credit Bank assisted in the negotiations with the Hungarian government over the repatriation of the shares held by Škoda in the Raab cannon works, an enterprise in which the Hungarian state was the majority shareholder. (This example also shows the strong wish of Škoda to disengage itself from Hungarian commitments.) The 10 per cent participation held by UEIF by October 1920 in the contract linking the Cie française du Levant with STEG (Privilegirte österreichisch-ungarische Staats-Eisenbahn-Gesellschaft) for the purchase of STEG locomotives and their resale to Romania was part of a very complicated transaction. In the first instance, it allowed the supply, and export, to Hungary of the necessary coal and coke following the approaches of UEIF to the Mining and Metallurgic Co. and the Czechoslovak government. UEIF hoped that this would lead to an order from the Cie française du Levant for locomotives from Škoda. At the depth of the crisis of the early

1920s – March 1921 – a Romanian order for 100 locomotives was forthcoming. This outcome was particularly important as at that time locomotives accounted for more than half of Škoda's turnover. In 1921 it would have been difficult to have foreseen the subsequent payment problems that arose from deliveries to Romania.

In the same way, using its own position and that of France, UEIF made many approaches to settle on a favourable basis the credits that Škoda had given before and during the war to Turkey, Austria and China. The Chinese bonds affair was connected with orders placed before 1914, but unfulfilled, and it absorbed several years of effort before even a rickety settlement was achieved. Colonel Weyl spoke in December 1920 of the drawing up of a note asking for the support of the French government to aid Rosenthal's representations in China.

The most important task of all was that of reorganizing the Czechoslovakian subsidiaries, especially Škoda, because until 1922 UEIF did not have much influence over the Austrian management of the Mining and Metallurgic Co. The critical step taken in the reshaping of the Czechoslovak subsidiaries was the visit of Schneider in May–June 1920. This was not a trip to note the situation but involved presenting and imposing the main strands of the reorganization programme which would alter the nature of the products produced by the firm. Further, it had to prepare the ground for the arrival of the seconded French executives who from September would control the realization of the plan. In return Hanuš, the general manager of Škoda, visited Paris and Le Creusot in June–July 1920 and was interested in a wide variety of Schneider products which were suitable for production at Plzeň. But this mission to the West was simply a courtesy and above all formal.

The reorganization of both Škoda's structure and its product range was urgently required in order to improve the company's competitiveness. UEIF strove to establish a greater degree of interdependence between its Czechoslovak subsidiaries. After reducing Škoda's dependence upon the Vítkovické horní a hutní těžířstvo [Vítkovice Mining and Foundry Works] for supplies of metal products by June 1920, UEIF established Škoda as a privileged client of the Akciové železárny a ocelárny v Hrádku [Iron and Steel Co. in Hrádek] which actually was a subsidiary of both Škoda and the Mining and Metallurgic Co. After initially pressing for a greater specialization in the products produced by Škoda and its subsidiary, the United Plants, UEIF in 1922 insisted that there should be either an amalgamation or the complete take-over of the United Plants by Škoda. The aim of this restructuring was to reduce the administrative staff and offices which were considered to be far too large. However, it was very difficult, if not impossible, to solve the problem of the vast number of blue collar workers because of the resistance of the trade unions and the opposition of the Czechoslovak government to all large-scale lay-offs. The greatest necessity was to re-establish discipline and increase the use of workshop capacity through the application of the new programme. It was agreed at Škoda to diminish the plant's traditional dependence upon armament production by developing new product ranges including machine tools, agricultural machinery (tractors and cream separators) but especially locomotives. The latter product line had been established by the beginning of 1920, before the formation of UEIF, but perhaps on Schneider's advice. The United Plants were to specialize in both plant for sugar refineries and electrical equipment.

Certain of the new products introduced by the plan required technical agreements between Škoda and Schneiders. It was planned in December 1920 to form a company with Schneider et Cie and UEIF which was to produce tractors to the design of the Italian engineer Pavesi. Škoda was to have the exclusive right to produce them for Central and Eastern Europe in its new automobile workshops. An agreement was reached in April 1921 by which Schneider locotractors were to be made in the same workshops. A month previously the Doudlevec workshops of the United Plants had been entrusted with the production of electric motors of the Schneider type. Finally in May 1921 the talks led to an agreement whereby better use would be made of the Škoda steel foundry through the production of railway material in both steel and manganese.

UEIF was able to assist Škoda's entry into the French market which had been greatly expanded by reconstruction requirements and this opportunity compensated for the reduction in the size of the nearer markets in Central and Eastern Europe. Following from this, UEIF became Škoda's commercial representative in France and Belgium, their colonies, Spain and Portugal through an agreement made in April 1921. The previous representation agreement between Škoda and de Saint Paul was replaced by a contract by which de Saint Paul headed the commercial services of UEIF. It was for this representation and other various, but less clear, services that Škoda had to pay to the UEIF a fixed commission of 0.75 per cent of its foreign turnover. It should be pointed out that the size of this commission seemed justified during the very difficult post-war period not only by the number of activities undertaken on Škoda's behalf but also by the commercial results in France. Škoda recorded total orders of more than 1,000m Kč in 1921, of which 531m originated in Czechoslovakia and 346m came from France. In order to obtain such results, UEIF was prepared to support its subsidiaries on the French market at the cost of local producers represented on the Comité des Forges. In May 1921 French orders for Škoda foundry products ceased following the increase in the French tariff. However, it was hoped that business would resume with the Franco-Czechoslovak commercial convention of 28 April, the shaping of which had probably been determined by UEIF.

However the interdependence of UEIF and its subsidiaries did not include competition with the products of the dominant company, Schneider et Cie. Consequently the commercial representation agreement did not cover munitions and sugar refining equipment which were the subject of particular understandings made in 1922 embracing both technical and commercial areas.

In the case of artillery, the understanding reached by Schneider and Škoda in May 1922 had the object of reducing technical multiplication and achieving commercial harmony by the division of the costs of obtaining orders and sharing the orders themselves between the two enterprises. The market division delineated was very clearly to Schneiders' advantage since it 'reserved' to the French firm France, Belgium, Spain and Latin America except Mexico. Škoda had to be content with its home market and Austria, Romania and Mexico. Representation was divided between Schneider and Škoda in non-reserved countries but any orders from this area were apportioned in the ratio 75 : 25 to Schneiders' favour. Technical agreements were appended to the commercial understanding. Each producer was to have at its disposal the materials and papers of both and it was intended to divide future research and development studies. With the narrowing of the market in artillery and the earmarking of the largest part of what remained to the Le Havre workshops of Schneiders, it can be readily appreciated why it was so urgent to undertake the conversion programme at Škoda, switching the firm to the production of civilian goods.

With the advantages that Schneiders had extracted in the military field, it was able to provide something of a counter-balance in the production of sugar refining plant, the biggest demand for which in the 1920s came from France and Belgium. Schneiders, alone, were unable to meet all the orders, especially those from Sommier, and by passing on a part to the United Plants it was possible to establish a monopoly for Schneiders-Škoda over the reconstruction of the sugar refineries in the north of France. The agreements of 1922, never understood by either party, planned a division of production destined for the following countries – France, Belgium, the Belgian colonies, Spain, Portugal and the extra-European Spanish and Portuguese speaking areas. These agreements were modified in 1928 to the advantage of Škoda's profitability. Škoda now became solely responsible for seeking and undertaking orders for any customer outside France and the French colonies but was to use the marque 'Schneider-Škoda'. However, Schneiders were to receive a commission of 1 per cent on the volume of orders received by Škoda from countries which under the 1922 agreement had been set aside for the French firm. Further, Škoda was to pay a 2.5 per cent commission on French orders which were relayed east.

This new understanding over orders for sugar refining plant coincided with a new commercial representation contract for Škoda. By letters exchanged in June 1928 UEIF retained only the general representation rights in France together with the responsibility for the sales of sugar refining, distilling and chemical plant in Belgium, the Belgian colonies, Spain and to Parisian firms in Egypt. The marketing of this equipment was the responsibility of a special sugar refineries office managed by engineer Pernot who subsequently in 1930 became the consulting engineer to the Cie sucrière marocaine, which was controlled by Schneider and became part of UEIF in 1932.

The major preoccupation of UEIF was unquestionably the financial difficulties of the companies that it controlled, but this was the most difficult problem to surmount. Škoda was the biggest headache.

In addition to its immediate post-war losses, there were risks arising from the inflation, the slowness of its customers in paying for orders – a problem which grew worse with the economic crisis of the early 1920s – and the continuing and difficult task of resolving the question of the old Turkish, Austrian and Chinese credits.

Was UEIF able to help its subsidiaries to overcome their difficulties? Recognizing its responsibilities and fully aware of the interdependence of its interests, UEIF put its maximum effort into this area. However it had to meet this challenge precisely when its own financial resources were very restricted. UEIF immediately dealt with the problem of fluctuating exchange rates. By 1920 it had assumed the exchange risk in the settlement of French orders for sugar refining equipment passed by Schneiders to the United Plants. These payments were made in francs, often late, and UEIF bought exchange when the rate was favourable to assure their cover in Czechoslovak crowns. UEIF followed the same practice in 1921 for the payment of locomotive orders for the Cie française du Levant. Actually this procedure generated profits and the balance sheet of UEIF showed a net gain of 1m fr from foreign exchange operations.

Much the greatest burden was the growing difficulties of the finance departments of Škoda and the United Plants. There can be no doubt that UEIF endeavoured to obtain a better financial position within its subsidiaries and comment has already been made regarding its insistence on a progressive reduction of production costs. UEIF intervened continually to increase and accelerate payments due from French orders for sugar refining equipment and for supplies to the Czechoslovak state. The Prague government in 1920 accepted price increases amounting to 285m Kč. Its negotiations with the Turkish and Hungarian governments were largely successful. However, it proved very difficult to obtain payment for the locomotives which Romania had ordered through the Cie française du Levant. The outcome was that the French company and Škoda had to be content with taking Romanian loan bonds for part of the deliveries.

Despite these efforts, the bank overdrafts of the subsidiaries, especially with the Živnostenská banka, continued to mount until the beginning of 1920 although the UEIF had provided growing advances. By August 1920 the French holding company had granted loans totalling 30m Kč to the United Plants to offset the effect of delays in payments for sugar refining equipment. By October this facility had increased to 41.5m Kč. The largest by far were

Škoda's needs. As its bank overdraft progressively increased, the Živnostenská banka stiffened its security requirements, making it a condition that the bank took over the firm's accounting and imposing a general mortgage. Consequently there was a risk that the Plzeň enterprise would become completely dependent upon the Prague bank. In order to avoid this dangerous situation, UEIF in June 1920 provided an advance of 65.5m Kč (19.5m fr.) in exchange for a six months' option on the 125,000 shares of United Plants held by Škoda. The minutes of the relevant board meeting of UEIF put on record evidence of the degree of interdependence that was felt: 'We are happy to seize this opportunity to show our friends in Prague, by the speed of our action, that we intend not only to take the profits which stem from our relationship but also that we are prepared to assume the burdens involved, the first of which is to lend our support, as much and as effectively as possible'. Yet for all that the advance was merely a straw in the wind. It only reduced the overdraft with the Živnostenská banka for a short while and by November it had once more become dangerously large. At the end of a discussion with the administrateur-délégué of UEIF, Dr Preiss proposed to increase to 120m Kč the amount of credit that the bank was providing but subject to new conditions. These were that Škoda merged with the United Plants and its capital be increased to 250m Kč. Colonel Weyl pointed out that conditions were not opportune for such an increase of capital which led the director of the Živnostenská banka to air the possibility of a resort to an obligatory loan.

By the end of 1921 the financial position of UEIF was severely endangered by the liquidity and debt problems of its subsidiaries. On 31 December 1921 the cost of UEIF's participations – 78.5m fr. – exceeded its registered capital. The various advances that it had made in Czechoslovak crowns had risen to nearly 33m fr while the credit that the UEIF for its part had obtained, mainly from BUP, amounted to 37m fr. It was a situation which could have led to UEIF becoming dependent upon BUP and was similar to the relationship of Škoda with the Živnostenská banka. UEIF's financial resources were minimal just at the time when it was necessary both to plan, at short notice, an increase in Škoda's capital, a policy forced by the take-over of United Plants, and to extend the financial aid that it was giving its subsidiary. It was not possible either to increase the capital of UEIF or to float an obligatory loan for Škoda on the Paris capital market. Consequently UEIF was reduced to appealing to the Anglo-Saxons for credit. Soundings made on the American market regarding the placing of either Škoda or UEIF bonds had produced no result by December 1920. The proposal by the American group headed by the Equitable Trust Company to take a participation in UEIF was considered to be 'a delicate question of national and international policy' and it seemed that it would not receive 'official authorization in France and Czechoslovakia'. The only avenue that remained was an approach to the British banks. However, it was not until July 1923 after long negotiations that Škoda was

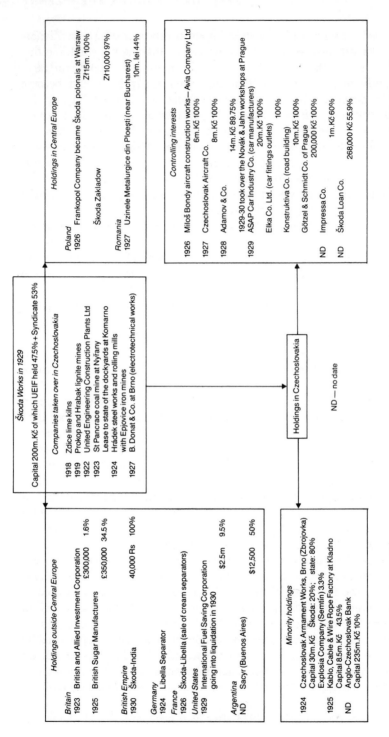

Figure 14.3. The structure of the Škoda-Works, 1929. (*Source* A. Teichova, 'Munich 1938, une réappreciation économique', *Revue des études slaves*, Paris, LII. 1–2, 1979, 153–68.)

able to raise through the British and Allied Investment Corporation an obligatory loan of £1m at 8 per cent secured by a first mortgage on all the business premises of the company. This loan was repaid in April 1926 but was replaced by a new tranche of £2.5m of $7\frac{1}{2}$ per cent stock. In turn this was redeemed but with an issue of £5m 6 per cent bonds made jointly on the London and Paris markets in 1930.

Accordingly Škoda was only able to bring foreign sleeping partners into UEIF once its own profitability had recovered. It was UEIF itself, at the cost of important sacrifices and by assuming risks, that had enabled the Czechoslovak company to turn the corner. Moroever, when this flow of British capital reached Czechoslovakia, it was no longer a question of these resources being absorbed solely in mopping up short-term debts and increasing working capital. This finance permitted a spectacular expansion of the Škoda-Works, increasing not only its own business but also that of its own network of subsidiaries (see fig. 14.3). This growth took place without any major financial strain for either Škoda or UEIF which until the onset of the Great Depression received substantial profits from its empire.[5]

Notes

1. A. Teichova, *An Economic Background to Munich. International Business and Czechoslovakia 1918–1938* (1974).
2. In the French documents, the term 'nationalisation' is used in the same sense as 'nostrification': that is to say the transformation of Austrian companies into Czechoslovak companies. This 'nationalisation' has to be distinguished from certain proposals concerned with the 'socialisation' of the mines in 1922.
3. It is only possible to note here that 1926 was marked by a new field of expansion in the Mosel region caused by the penetration of the Union Européenne into the powerful Belgo-Luxembourgeois ARBED group, but this third and last offensive was not as successful in terms of what had been achieved in Hungary and South-East Europe in 1920.

4. The activities of Schneider in Poland and the Franco-Polish Railway Company merit a separate study. The weakness of the participations of Škoda and the Mining and Metallurgic Co. is significant. It is necessary to take account at one and the same time of the size of the capital of the controlled companies and the participation of the mother-company. The influence of the Union did not extend much beyond Czechoslovakia either directly or through the intermediation of the branch companies of its own subsidiaries.
5. The Union Européenne's capital was raised from 75m fr. to 100m in 1924, to 112.5m in 1926, and to 140m in 1928. Škoda's capital moved from 144m Kč to 194m in 1922 and to 200m in 1924.

15. The Interests of the Banque de l'Union parisienne in Czechoslovakia, Hungary and the Balkans, 1919–30*

Eric Bussière

Before the First World War it was quite normal for a French investment bank (*Banque d'affaire*) to invest abroad. The Banque de l'Union parisienne (BUP) had undertaken this type of business since its formation in 1904. This was most clearly shown through its direct participations in enterprises. A geographical analysis of the composition of the bank's share portfolio in 1914 shows that it had interests throughout the world and although its holdings in Central Europe and the Balkans were considerable it was not the bank's most important single area of investment.

Table 15.1. ZONES OF ACTIVITY, 1 JAN. 1914 (% age of share portfolio).

Region	%
France	28.19
French colonies	4.32
Central Europe and the Balkans	11.99
Russia	13.74
South America	27.44
Other foreign investments	14.32

Between 1919 and 1930 the geographical composition of the bank's investments changed. On the one hand, Russia no longer played any role and South America became a privileged area for American interests, while on the other, Central Europe and the Balkans progressively became more important, so that by 1928 it was the largest single foreign region, as table 15.2 shows.

Table 15.2. BUP ZONES OF ACTIVITY (% age of share portfolio), 1919–31.

Year as on 1 Jan.	France	Colonies	South America	Central Europe & Balkans	Others
1919	31.65	10.75	24.87	14.38	18.35
1921	37.45	9.61	15.34	16.03	21.57
1925	29.64	16.97	15.55	18.15	19.71
1928	27.72	16.77	7.64	15.18	32.69
1931	38.72	17.61	3.65	26.90	13.16

BUP's activities in Central Europe and the Balkans were closely inter-twined. They were components of the same wave of capital exports that went to this part of Europe after the war to aid reconstruction at the political, monetary and economic level. It was aimed at reducing German influence, to the advantage of the Allies, who were themselves now rivals. Moreover, the economic links between all these countries were mirrored in BUP's complex banking and industrial network. However, between 1919 and 1930 BUP's interest in Central Europe and the Balkans took on two different forms. First, after the war there was intervention in heavy industry and banking in Czechoslovakia and Hungary through the medium of the Union Européenne industrielle et financière (UEIF) which had been established in collaboration with the firm Schneider & Cie. Second, there was investment in the Balkans, principally in banks in which BUP had had interests before 1914. These two different forms of investment activity will now be considered.

1. BUP, SCHNEIDER AND THE UNION EUROPÉENNE INDUSTRIELLE ET FINANCIÈRE IN CENTRAL EUROPE

The origins of the Union Européenne industrielle et financière

Schneider's activities in Czechoslovakia after 1919 led to BUP's interest in Central Europe. Schneider had been associated with the Škodovy závody (Škoda-Works) since before the war. In September 1919 an option was obtained on the whole of an increase of the Czechoslovakian company's capital, namely 225,000 320 Kč shares at 400 Kč each, which raised Škoda's capital from 72m to 144m Kč. At the same time Schneider bought 40,000 shares from Baron von Škoda and 9,725 shares on the Vienna stock exchange. As a result, Schneider now held 274,725 shares, 61 per cent of Škoda's capital. After April 1919 Schneider provided for an improvement in existing facilities, the construction of new plant and the partial alteration of the armament workshop to locomotive construction. An important armament component was still maintained, allowing Schneider & Cie to meet any shortfall in capacity caused by the reorganization of the Creusot works. Lastly, Schneider & Cie now acted as the French selling agency for sugar-refining equipment produced by one of Škoda's subsidiaries.

At about the same time, probably in January 1920,[7] Schneider got a foothold in the Österreichische Berg- und Hüttenwerks Gesellschaft, now called the Báňská a hutní společnost [Mining and Metallurgic Co.]. Schneiders bought 32,989 shares and then subscribed 10,000 out of an issue of 12,500 which increased the company's capital from 45 to 50m Kč. In addition Archduke Frederic transferred to Schneider the voting rights on the 7,500 shares that he held. Finally, an agreement with the Allgemeine österreichische Boden-Credit-Anstalt gave Schneider control over a further 10,000 shares, and the result of all these transactions was to give the French industrial concern, through its total holding of 60,500 out of 125,000 shares, absolute control of the metallurgical company. Then Schneider & Cie exchanged a part of its Škoda shareholding for 22,000 shares of the Société des Forges et Acières de Huta Bankowa, situated in Poland. The total cost of all these operations, after a number of resales, amounted to 51,4m fr. in March 1920. It was important for the necessary financial resources to be found as quickly as possible because the increase in Škoda's capital, through which Schneider was to assume control of the company, had to take place during the last quarter of 1921. In conjunction with BUP, with which Schneider had many common business interests in France, an investment company was formed. This was to take from either Schneider or BUP any majority shareholdings which they possessed or might possess and would manage these interests.

On 21 April 1920 the Union Européenne industrielle et financière (UEIF) was founded with a capital of 75m fr divided into 15,000 A shares which had 10 votes at company general meetings and 135,000 B shares which only had a single vote. Schneider and BUP held the A and B shares in conjunction with the Empain Group (Forges et Acières de la Longueville).

UEIF: original subscribers

	A shares	B shares
Schneider and its associates	7,848	61,132
BUP and its associates	5,232	54,088
Empain	1,320	1,760

The UEIF board consisted of E. Schneider (president), Neuflize, A. Fournier, and Champigneul all representing Schneider & Cie, Lucien Villars (vice-president of UEIF and president of BUP), Ch. Sergent (president of BUP from 1923), L. Lion and C. Mallet for BUP. Also on the Board were Cheysson and Maurice Paléologue, Secrétaire-général of the Ministry of Foreign Affairs, which indicates that Schneider and BUP played an active role in the formation of the foreign policy of the French government. Actually UEIF, although an investment company, had to expand its activities to embrace commercial representation in France of the enterprises which it controlled and to develop their connections with French industry, and as a result contributed to the reinforcement of French influence in Central Europe.

It can be seen that UEIF, from its formation, veered towards an industrial policy formulated by Schneider which held the largest number of shares carrying a multiple vote (A shares). Was the role of BUP to be merely the supplier of the necessary capital for the implementation of this policy through slowly selling the UEIF B shares on the French capital market? Or was UEIF rather to be the vehicle for a policy of joint participation in banks and industry as it had been maintained at a Directors' Committee of BUP on 6

April 1920, when it had been stated that 'the formation of a company whose object was the continuing active control of various industries and financial businesses which the group had or might acquire' ('création d'une société ayant pour objet de s'assurer de façon active et durable le controle que le groupe s'est acquis, ou pourrait acquérir au moyen de participations dans differentes affaires industrielles et financières')? With the second assumption, investments by UEIF would have had to be complemented by a policy of banking or financial participations, an activity more compatible with BUP than Schneider. This policy was indeed tested.

BUP, Schneider and Central European banks

A. THE BANKERS OF ŠKODA AND THE MINING AND METALLURGIC CO.

In October 1919, BUP was contacted by the Česká průmyslová a hospodářská banka, Prague, whose president, Josef Šimonek, was also the president of Škoda. He proposed to strengthen the relations between the two banks by BUP taking part in several increases in the Czechoslovak bank's capital. Until 1919 the Česká průmyslová a hospodářská banka had not been a major bank, but it now hoped to acquire the 16 Czechoslovak branches of the Wiener Bank-Verein which would considerably increase its influence. At the same time the Živnostenská banka got in touch with BUP, offering it a 5 per cent participation in its capital which would give BUP two seats on the bank's board. BUP, probably in agreement with Schneider, considered promoting a regrouping between the two Czechoslovak banks which had approached it. The Česká průmyslová a hospodářská banka was no longer of a sufficient size to ensure the financing of Škoda's cash flow and in 1919 Schneider had ceded 5,400 Škoda shares to the Živnostenská banka with a view to a rapprochement.

Then at the beginning of March 1920 a double understanding was reached between the Česká průmyslová a hospodářská banka and the Živnostenská banka (Šimonek having joined the board of the latter) and between the Živnostenská banka and BUP, which had bought 50,000 of the latter's shares as well as granting it credits totalling $7\frac{1}{2}$m fr. However, the second part of these agreements was never fulfilled. A fall in the stock market quotation of the Živnostenská banka prevented it from obtaining the share price which it wanted. The deal, although only postponed provisionally, never took place. BUP was the main loser; on the one hand it had lost the opportunity of counterbalancing Schneider's influence in Czechoslovak affairs, on the other there was no contact between it and the Boden-Credit-Anstalt. It was E. Schneider who joined the board of the Boden-Credit-Anstalt.

B. INTERVENTION IN THE MAGYAR ÁLTÁLANOS HITELBANK

Shortly after its formation the UEIF group was able to take over a significant proportion of the capital of the Magyar Áltálanos Hitelbank [the Hungarian

General Credit Bank]. This participation was a consequence of the Hungarian policy pursued by Millerand and particularly by Maurice Paléologue, Secrétaire général at the French Ministry of Foreign Affairs at the beginning of 1920. In exchange for a 'pro-Hungarian policy aimed at reversing certain injustices in the Peace treaty, an objective which was to be realized with the aid of France', France asked for financial and economic concessions from the Hungarian government.

A syndicate consisting of Schneider & Cie, BUP, the Banque de Paris et de Pays-Bas (Paribas) and Gunzberg et Cie was put in contact with some leading Hungarians by the Ministry of Foreign Affairs, from whom a six-months option was obtained on the Hungarian State Railway together with the state workshops at Budapest. At the same time UEIF took up two-thirds of an increase in the capital of the Hungarian General Credit Bank. The new capital of the bank was to be 280m K, with the French group holding 200,000 shares out of a total of 700,000. In June 1920 UEIF and the Hungarian General Credit Bank decided to offer one another mutual participations in affairs in which they were interested in Central Europe and the Balkans. The reorganization of the Hungarian railways was a possible market opportunity for Škoda. The participation in the Hungarian General Credit Bank was more important for BUP than for Schneider and could be seen as bringing about a counterbalancing of forces within UEIF. Further, it created direct links with one of the principal shareholders in the Banque Balkanique (in Bulgaria), a concern in which BUP was interested. Finally BUP and UEIF, through the Hungarian General Credit Bank, came into contact with the Österreichische Credit-Anstalt für Handel und Gewerbe of Vienna. UEIF retained 100,000 out of the 200,000 shares. The other 100,000 shares of the Hungarian General Credit Bank were taken up by a marketing syndicate consisting of BUP (two-thirds) and UEIF (one-third). BUP retained 20,000 shares for itself, a decision which indicated that it was to play a direct role in the Hungarian General Credit Bank. In August 1920, P. Cheysson, L. Lion, A. de Saint-Sauveur and E. Weyl were elected to the board of the Hungarian bank.

France's pro-Hungarian policy did not last; in September 1920 Paléologue was replaced by Philippe Berthelot as the Secrétaire-général at the Ministry of Foreign Affairs and negotiations with Hungary were immediately suspended. This created difficulties between the French group and the Hungarian government. The railway option was not taken up. Similarly Cheysson was unable effectively to represent French interests at the Hungarian General Credit Bank's headquarters and could not exercise any control over the bank or its policy. These difficulties and the abandonment of the Hungarian railway project seem to have resulted in the industrial element in UEIF not wishing to expand further their interest in the Hungarian General Credit Bank; consequently on 5 April 1922 when the bank's capital was increased from 280 to 420m K, a move necessitated by inflation, Baron Paul Kornfeld, director of the Hungarian General Credit Bank, told BUP that UEIF was not going to subscribe for 50,000 new shares which it would be offered and asked BUP what it intended.

For BUP, collaboration with the Hungarian General Credit Bank was desirable for a number of reasons. The common interests of BUP and the Hungarian General Credit Bank in Bulgaria have already been discussed; similarly in Romania BUP would have liked to have seen the Transylvanian branches of the Hungarian General Credit Bank taken over by the Banca Commercială Română, a concern in which BUP predominated in 1922. Moreover, it seems that BUP's Central European interests could have been furthered with the aid of the Hungarian General Credit Bank, as on 5 April 1922 when Baron Kornfeld proposed that BUP take up a participation in the Bank dla Handlu i Przemyslu w. Warsawie.

The industrial and banking interests which made up UEIF were in conflict at the beginning of 1922. However, an agreement between the two partners led to UEIF finally subscribing to the new shares in the Hungarian General Credit Bank which had been reserved for it, at the beginning of 1923, a move in BUP's interest.

C. INTERVENTION IN THE NIEDERÖSTERREICHISCHE ESCOMPTE-GESELLSCHAFT

In May 1923 an opportunity arose for Union Européenne to take an interest in the Österreichisch-Alpine Montangesellschaft, an important Austrian metallurgical company, which amongst its holdings controlled two large Upper Silesian undertakings, the Bismarckhütte AG and the Königshütte.

In 1923 the Austrian company's capital consisted of $1\frac{1}{2}$m 200 K shares, of which 900,000 were held by Stinnes. In May 1923 the Alpine Montan planned to double its capital, an operation of which the Austrian government approved, but with the condition that Stinnes lost his majority holding. An arrangement was planned by which Stinnes would retain 750,000 shares after the increase in capital, the Niederösterreichische Escompte-Gesellschaft would have 1,250,000 shares and the remainder would be shared amongst the bank's clientèle with a large packet of shares going to UEIF. This proposal had some interest for the French holding company, as it provided a way of extending its influence in Austria. But in order to obtain a stronger influence in Alpine Montan, UEIF tried to get a foothold directly in the Niederösterreichische Escompte-Gesellschaft. At a directors' meeting of the UEIF on 11 June 1923, Cheysson disclosed that he had received an option on 100,000 shares of the Niederösterreichische Escompte-Gesellschaft. The option expired that day. The Austrian bank would give its financial co-operation in Central Europe to UEIF in exchange for the industrial co-operation of Schneider. BUP had not been informed either of the joint discussions or of the option. UEIF's intervention in the Niederösterreichische Escompte-Gesellschaft ran counter to its interest in the Hungarian General Credit Bank and it risked creating difficulties with the Credit-Anstalt and the Rothschilds, which were closely allied to the Hungarian General Credit Bank. Moreover, as has been shown, it was more in BUP's interest than in Schneider's to maintain good relations with the Hungarian bank.

Once again the French industrial and banking interests involved in the UEIF were in conflict over the policy to be pursued. Schneiders were using UEIF for exclusively industrial aims and consequently there was no room for a banking policy formulated by BUP. As a result UEIF was slipping gradually out of BUP's hands. The decision over the Niederösterreichische Escompte-Gesellschaft brought things to a head. On 11 June 1923, after having protested against the acquisition of this participation, BUP's representatives on the Board of UEIF refused to take part in the vote. After this a policy to be followed in concert by BUP and Schneider in Central Europe was made difficult, if not impossible, although in 1924 BUP, in conjunction with UEIF, did participate in the foundation of both the Hungarian National Bank and the Société Européenne de l'Ammoniaque, which had the licences from Air Liquide to manufacture synthetic ammonia in Central Europe.

From 1925 BUP ceased to have a direct interest in UEIF's Central European policy. The bank was no longer regularly informed of the development of UEIF business interests. The break with Schneider in Central Europe was echoed by others elsewhere, especially in France. After 1925 BUP merely serviced the shares of UEIF. In June 1930, however, the bank did manage the issue of the French tranche of the Škoda debenture loan. But we are no longer concerned here with major financial policy in Central Europe. However, one common interest of UEIF and BUP continued, to which the latter attached a certain importance – the Hungarian General Credit Bank.

BUP and the Hungarian General Credit Bank

In January 1923, the French group held 28.57 per cent of this Hungarian bank's shares; UEIF held 152,250 shares, BUP had 32,750 and the rest were in the hands of various associates of BUP. The bank's capital was increased from 420 to 489m K in May 1923 and during the following November it was further increased to 550m K. In the autumn the group headed by BUP held 156,674 shares of which 37,656 were held by BUP alone and the UEIF had 172,233 shares. The French group accordingly made up the largest single shareholding block, having almost a quarter of the Hungarian Bank's shares.

The raging inflation in Hungary necessitated in June 1923 a new increase in capital and it was decided to raise it to 690m K. The lack of capital in Hungary meant that it had to be imported. The Germans were able to take up a position in the Hungarian General Credit Bank as a result of this further share issue, an outcome which troubled the French Foreign Ministry. The French group then had to react to the Ministry's request to counterbalance the German initiative. The issue of 350,000 new shares was guaranteed by a syndicate headed by Rothschilds of Vienna and was made up of an Austrian Group: 50,000 shares (Rothschild); a German group: 100,000 shares

(Mendelssohn); and a French group: 200,000 shares. The French group consisted of Deutsch de la Meurthe (20,000 shares), Rothschild, Paris (50,000 shares), BUP (32,000 shares), Schneider (6,200 shares) and UEIF (101,600 shares).

It is difficult to understand why BUP continued to increase its holding in the Hungarian General Credit Bank, especially in December 1925 when a further increase in capital was required and the Hungarian General Credit Bank decided to approach an Anglo-American group. However, BUP did decide to limit its total participation to 60,000 shares. The UEIF, for its part, subscribed for only 4,900 new shares. So at the end of 1926 French interests amounted to no more than 15.2 per cent of the bank's capital of 920m K. But it appears that the American group which underwrote the increase in capital did not maintain their relations with the Hungarian General Credit Bank. The shares taken up by this group gradually appeared on European capital markets, so much so that the French interest in 1927 amounted to 20.8 per cent of the bank's capital.

Despite this BUP and UEIF no longer acted with the Hungarian General Credit Bank in Hungarian business proposals. BUP merely allowed the Hungarian General Credit Bank an acceptance credit of 10m fr. between September 1929 and 1930. Economic conditions became difficult in 1929 and in 1930 necessitated a fresh appeal for foreign funds. The Hungarian General Credit Bank approached a group headed by Lazards of London. This time the UEIF withdrew from the Board of the Hungarian General Credit Bank and BUP did not substantially increase its holding in the bank.

BUP's continuing participation in the Hungarian General Credit Bank can only be explained fully within the context of the relationships existing in the partnership of the Hungarian General Credit Bank with the Credit-Anstalt in the Balkans and not by solely looking at profitable Hungarian business affairs.

2. BUP's ACTIVITY IN THE BALKANS

BUP's interest in the Balkans centred on three banks: the Banca Commercială Română, in Bucharest, the Banque Balkanique in Sofia, and the Banque d'Athènes. These institutions, as E. Baldy commented in 1922, underpinned any business proposals in their respective countries. But from 1919 one of BUP's principal concerns was the preservation of its influence in this region in the face of either a possible return of German interests or the Anglo-Americans.

BUP's banking links
A. POST-WAR REORGANIZATION AND STABILIZATION, 1918–28

In 1906 BUP had taken part in the foundation of the Banca Commercială Română along with Belgian, Austrian (Wiener Bank-Verein) and Romanian (Chrissoveloni, Economos) interests. The bank's business was hampered by

Romania's entry into the war on the Allied side, and the country's occupation by Austrian and German troops. In 1919 the bank was reorganized. Two main problems had to be overcome: the position of its Austrian shareholders (Wiener Bank-Verein) and maintaining the bank's existence in the face of its heavy indebtedness to French banks at a time when the lei had fallen heavily against the franc.

The problem of the Wiener Bank-Verein's holding was crystallized by the Romanian government which threatened to sequester the Banca Commercială Română if the Austrian influence was not eliminated. BUP was in favour of removing Austrians from the Romanian bank's board and was responsible for turning down several propositions which, although favourable for the Banca Commercială Română, would have allowed the Wiener Bank-Verein to maintain its position. BUP found a solution to the problem of the Banca Commercială Română's foreign indebtedness; in March 1921 it obtained a moratorium on the bank's debts from its French creditors which was to last until 1924, when it had to repay a loan, indexed to the franc, which had been made to the Romanian state. In this way BUP was able to reinforce its position within the Banca Commercială Română and consolidate the French management position (Boutry was nominated to head the Committee of Direction). At the same time, BUP, at the end of 1921, brought about a raprochement with the liberal group which, in Romania, dominated finance (the Banca Românêscâ) and politics (the Ion brothers and Vintila Bratiano). Between 1924 and 1927 BUP further increased its position by substantial participations in share issues made to increase the capital of the Banca Commercială Română. These resulted in BUP holding about 35 per cent of the bank's shares.

Since 1908 BUP had been involved in the Banque Balkanique. This was the principal Bulgarian bank in 1914. However, during the war BUP lost contact with the bank and in 1917 Austro-Hungarian interests in it were increased when the Credit-Anstalt and the Hungarian General Credit Bank took up shares. BUP was also involved in the Crédit Foncier Franco-Bulgare along with 'Paribas' and other French, Bulgarian and Austro-Hungarian groups. At the end of the war BUP quickly secured its position in the Banque Balkanique and increased its shareholding by an agreement with the Hungarian General Credit Bank/Credit-Anstalt group and the Wiener Bank-Verein. BUP's influence over the Banque Balkanique was reflected in its dominant position on the Bank's executive committee. This dominance was also bolstered when the Société Générale de Belgique obtained a seat on the Board. (The Société Générale de Belgique had taken an important position in the Wiener Bank-Verein). BUP's controlling position was confirmed in July 1923 when it guaranteed, together with the Wiener Bank-Verein, an increase in the capital of the Banque Balkanique from 20 to 30m lei and obtained for itself a large number of the shares. However, the Crédit Foncier Franco-Bulgare remained moribund until 1928 when it had to be reorganized.

In Greece, on the other hand, between 1918 and 1928 the Banque d'Athènes was working well and BUP was able to maintain its rather distant control without having to increase its capital investment.

B. THE CONSOLIDATION OF BUP'S INVESTMENTS

In France the renewed freedom to export capital from 1928 allowed BUP to buttress its foreign interests. This happened in Greece where BUP substantially increased its holding in the Banque d'Athènes between 1929 and 1930; and more important changes took place in both Bulgaria and Romania.

In Bulgaria the position of the Banque Balkanique got progressively worse between 1922 and 1928 because of lack of support from foreign investment. An initial reconstruction took place at the beginning of 1928, after which BUP held 38 per cent of the bank's shares. Then in November 1928 the Banque Balkanique was merged with the Banque Franco-Belge de Bulgarie to form the Banque Franco-Belge et Balkanique. The Banque Franco-Belge de Bulgarie was a filial of the Banque Belge pour l'Étranger, a member of the Société Générale de Belgique Group. Through the merger BUP and the Société Générale de Belgique regrouped their forces in Bulgaria in a bank which had a capital of 150m leva. Moreover, a secret voting agreement was drawn up between BUP and the Banque Belge pour l'Étranger in order to counter the Austro-Hungarian group. However, the Crédit Foncier's situation was beyond hope. BUP and the Société Générale de Belgique (which had interests in the Franco-Bulgare through the Banque d'Outremer) proposed a rapproachement with an Anglo-American group (Blair-Chase and Lazard Brothers) but this was refused by the French Ministry of Finance. This group then set up one new bank, the Banque Hypothecaire de Bulgarie, which quickly prospered. Consequently it was in vain that the shareholders of the Franco-Bulgare sought a merger between the two banks in 1930.

In Romania BUP, with the Société Générale de Belgique, organized the absorption of the Romanian filials of the Banque Belge pour l'Étranger by the Banca Commercială Română. Previously, in June 1928, BUP had removed the former Romanian shareholders (Chrissoveloni) by buying their shares. The take-over of the filials of the Banque Belge pour l'Étranger led to the capital of the Banca Commercială Română being raised to 300m lei. By 1930 the Banca Commercială Română was probably the most active Romanian bank.

Between 1928 and 1930 there was a concerted drive by BUP and the Société Générale de Belgique which has been described. This collaboration led to the formation in 1930 of the Banque Française d'Acceptation, with Charles Sergent as president and in which the Société Générale de Belgique and its associates held 20 per cent of the shares.

Other activities in the Balkans

According to E. Baldy, the foreign filials of investment banks were only a stepping stone for other business deals abroad. How did BUP operate in the Balkans during the 1920s?

A. STATE LOANS

In Romania, BUP was able to manage state loans on several occasions. On 20 August 1923, Boutry, representing BUP in Romania, negotiated a government loan of 250m fr which was to finance the purchasing of industrial plant and material. This loan was not sanctioned by the French Ministry of Finance. In December 1925 BUP tried again, this time with an American group, but once again without success. Between 1927 and 1929 a Romanian loan was negotiated but 'Paribas' rather than BUP headed the syndicate.

B. INDUSTRIAL AND OTHER BUSINESS

BUP's investments in concerns other than banks in the Balkans were very limited between 1919 and 1928. However, there was one exception: BUP's important participation in the Compagnie Financière Belge des Pétroles Société Anonyme (Petrofina), which drew most of its petrol from Romania. But this involvement was more a consequence of the development of the French petrol industry than the bank's policy of investment in Central Europe and the Balkans.

The removal of controls on the export of capital in 1928 allowed a more vigorous policy to be pursued; but this was not the case in Bulgaria where BUP's filials were experiencing difficulties. However, in Greece in June 1930 BUP along with the Banque d'Athènes established the Banque Hypothécaire Franco-Hellenique with a capital of 50m drachmas. BUP closely controlled it through a Committee of Management located in Paris. The mortgage bank made good progress and in 1932 it was the most important of this type of institution backed by foreign capital in Greece.

However, Romania was the most important area for BUP between 1928 and 1930 with participations in mining companies, a major sugar refinery and in the Crédit Foncier Agricole de Roumanie. BUP's largest industrial concern in Romania was the Compagnie Financière d'Exploitations Hydro-electriques Société Anonyme (Hydrofina), formed in July 1928. Hydrofina, an investment company with a capital of 150m Belgian fr., held the shares of a number of Romanian electricity companies – the thermal power station of Gura Ocnitei (which supplied electricity to the Romanian filiales of Petrofina), 'Lignitul' Societate anonimă minieră, 'Electrica' Societate Română pe Acţiuni, and above all the Jalomita Societate anonimă Română which was establishing a hydro-electric station on the river of the same name. The main shareholders were Belgian (Société Générale de Belgique, Banque d'Anvers, Electrobel), French (BUP, Demachy, Cie D'Enterprises Electromecaniques) and Austrian (Brown Boveri, Niederösterreichische Escompte-Gesellschaft). C. Sergent became president and the company's shares were serviced by BUP. But the technical direction of the business went to Electrobel which managed the building of the Jalomita works and shared out the equipment orders between Belgian, French and Austrian suppliers.

From the very beginning differences developed between the Austrians and other suppliers of electrical equipment. Once more this resulted in a Franco-Belgian alignment between BUP and the Société Générale de Belgique. Then difficulties also occurred between the Jalomita company and the Romanian authorities over the conditions for supplying electricity to Bucharest, which Boutry, BUP's agent in Romania, was unable to resolve. At the same time the volume of credit furnished by the banks to finance the works mounted rapidly, so that at the end of 1931 BUP, which was in difficulties, had to make a partial withdrawal.

During the 1920s there were two periods and two types of investment undertaken by BUP in Central Europe and the Balkans. First, an established form corresponding to the outline given by Baldy – banking filials through which business was conducted in economically under-developed countries at a high rate of interest. BUP tried to hold to this approach until 1928 and continued with it, but with difficulties, between 1928 and 1930 especially in the Balkans. Second, a mixed approach, a partnership of bank and industry with a powerful industrialist, Schneider, who aimed to take over rapidly the key points of Czechoslovak heavy industry. On one side there was a banking policy of an old form, on the other a policy with an industrial involvement which was completely new for BUP.

This double policy was carried out until 1928 with limited resources because of the difficulties in obtaining the authority to export capital. All that could be done in the Balkans was to keep the door open, while in Central Europe expenses had to be controlled closely; as Cheysson, director of UEIF, wrote to BUP at the end of 1920: 'Il ne convient pas d'éparpiller son effort sur de très nombreuses petites affaires ... mais de se réserver pour les plus importantes'. After 1928 the attempt to return to pre-war levels of capital exports was very quickly brought to a halt by the crisis.

Notes

*. This paper is based upon the archives of
the Banque de l'Union parisienne.

COMMENTARY on chapters 14 and 15
François Crouzet

On the whole, I do not have any serious criticism of these papers to put forward and I shall mostly stress some points which seem to me of special interest.

The first is Claude Beaud's interpretation of the intervention by Schneider – the driving force in the UEIF – in Central Europe after the First World War. He sees this move – quite rightly – as part of a grand strategy of French international economic expansion. Indeed, this fits well with recent research, especially by Jacques Bariety and Georges Soutou. They have shown that both during the war and after until 1924, French political leaders, and also a number of top businessmen, had definite plans to substitute France for Germany as the dominant economic power on the Continent. In a word, they were much more 'imperialist' than has hitherto been accepted in France (but this was suspected in England, for instance by J. M. Keynes). That such plans were foolish and unrealistic does not alter the fact that they existed and that a serious attempt was made to carry them out. The take-over by Schneider, relayed by the UEIF, of Škoda, the Mining and Metallurgic Co. and other companies is one of the few successful moves in that large-scale economic offensive by France.

From this point of view, we can understand better the motivations for Eugène Schneider's involvement; he was neither a mere tool of the French government, nor an operator looking for a 'fast buck'. Though his policy fits into a long-term strategy which had been elaborated before the war and is in some respects an extension of his earlier Russian venture, I am prepared to accept Beaud's excellent suggestions: Schneider's main ambition was to contribute to the great task of building up French power and influence in Central Europe, even to the detriment of his own firm's short-term financial interests.

Another interesting point is the financial structure of the UEIF and the methods by which the Schneider group succeeded in controlling effectively a large empire with the minimum outlay and immobilization of capital. Of course, such practices – preferred shares with plural-voting, which are kept by the founders of a holding, the syndicating of such shares' blocks, etc. – were common at the time in holding companies. But we have here an elegant, almost classical, example of 'domination by the cheapest way possible', as Beaud puts it; and also, one can add, an honest one, without the sharp practice and crooked manipulations, which have marred the record of many holding companies.

Anyhow, both Beaud and Bussière emphasize that Schneider dominated UEIF and that the BUP played second fiddle only. The marriage between investment banking and heavy industry, which had been concluded when UEIF was founded, was not a happy one; the industrial component got the better of the banking one. Not only did Schneider own the majority of A shares, but it was the driving force in UEIF. Bussière shows how BUP, discontented with its subordinate role, tried to react on several occasions, but without success, and eventually after 1925 lost interest in UEIF, over which it had lost any real influence. If the French government's flirtation with Hungarian revisionism in 1920 was favourable to the banking interests in UEIF, its return to its Czechoslovakian friend in 1921 gave the upper hand to Schneider.

All this is surprising to addicts of stages theories; we all believe and teach that finance capitalism had once and for all superseded industrial capitalism and brought industry under its dominance by the early twentieth century. It would be interesting to discover other examples of the inverse relationship which is obvious within UEIF; indeed, some such instances have been mentioned by several speakers this morning.

My final comments will deal with the problem which Beaud discusses in the last part of his paper, and which Bussière also mentions: the consequences of French investment and of French management leadership for the firms which were involved in East Central Europe and for that region's economy. On the latter problem, Beaud is rather pessimistic: UEIF did not contribute to the economic integration of an area which the war – and the peace – had left 'balkanized'; and, because the bulk of its interests were in Czechoslovakia, it was not of much use, for obvious political reasons, in furthering French economic influence in other countries. On the other hand, if I may parody a well-known *cliché*, Beaud inclines to think that what was good for Schneider was good for Škoda, for Czechoslovakia and for East Central Europe as a whole. But he puts forward some strong evidence to support this optimistic view: if overall strategy was decided in Paris and its enforcement supervised by French agents, if the sharing of markets was at first to the advantage of Schneider, the French firm gave to its Central European subsidiaries a good deal of financial and technical support, thanks to which they survived the difficult post-war years and eventually prospered. I hope that, in another study, Beaud will examine how UEIF and Schneider benefited from the expansion which Škoda achieved after 1923.

The name of Aimée Lepercq crops up several times in Beaud's paper; he was an interesting character, who would be worth studying; a top executive and businessman of the inter-war period, he was active in the Resistance during the German occupation of France and became Minister of Finance in De Gaulle's first government in 1944, but he was killed a few weeks later in a road accident. He had been instrumental in making a success – up to Munich – of Schneider's investment and involvement in Czechoslovakia. But my feeling is that such successes were exceptional among French economic ventures in East Central Europe and the Balkans. I hope I am not betraying Bussière's views in saying that his paper shows that the BUP did not achieve much altogether, except perhaps in Romania. The conventional wisdom is that the French bid to obtain a dominant economic position in the area and supersede Germany was bound to fail, not only because the French financial position was weak up to 1926 and the French industrial basis not powerful enough for such an undertaking, but also because, unlike Germany, France had an economy which was not complementary to that of the Danubian and Balkan countries. Almost self-sufficient for food, she could not offer them markets for their farm products, and she was not able, like Nazi Germany, to barter cameras for pigs.

I shall conclude with a question, which seems to me relevant to the general theme of this conference. In his classical *Growth and Stagnation in the European Economy*, I. Svennilson suggested that the inflow of western capital during the 1920s into the area which concerns us was not large enough; the result was slow industrialization and high tariff walls. I wonder what the experts think presently of this hypothesis?

16. The Reconstruction of the Credit-Anstalt

Dieter Stiefel

'*If even the Credit-Anstalt cannot be relied on,
everything in Austria must be rotten.*'[1]

The banking history of Austria in the twentieth century has three main
turning points: the first after 1918, when, following the First World War and
the resulting inflation, the banks had to start business again with much less
capital and in a more difficult business atmosphere. The second was the
difficulties arising out of the Credit-Anstalt crisis of the 1930s when the
Austrian banking system, which still had an international dimension, was
reduced more and more to a national basis. This affected their business
activity as well as the raising of capital. By 1934 there was only one big bank
remaining in Austria, the Credit-Anstalt, following its take-over of the
Boden-Credit-Anstalt, the Wiener Bank-Verein and part of the business of
the Niederösterreichische-Escompte-Gesellschaft. With 51 per cent of the
shares the state became the principal shareholder. The third turning point,
after the Second World War, followed the changes which took place during
the 'Ostmark' period. After 1945 the main Austrian banks were nationalized
and thus became almost completely Austrian-orientated. It is a direct
consequence of this historical development that banking in Austria is now
almost completely nationalized.

This paper will concentrate on the financial developments of the 1930s,
when international banking in Austria broke down and was replaced by
national banking. It will show how Austria lost its traditional role of an
intermediary in the eastern and south-eastern states of Europe owing to the
withdrawal of western capital. This process of withdrawal or liquidation,
which will be called 'Austrification' here, is characterized by a remarkable
conflict between private and government institutions. On the one side there
were the foreign creditors of the Credit-Anstalt united into the 'Austrian
Credit Anstalt International Committee' in London, led by Lionel Rothschild. This was a completely private creditors' committee composed of
roughly 130 banks from all over the world, which managed to gain the
support of the British and French governments, the Bank of England,
Banque de France, the Bank for International Settlements (BIS) and also the
League of Nations. On the other side was not so much the Credit-Anstalt

itself, which stayed mostly in the background, but the Austrian government, which negotiated for the bank and finally stood guarantee for it. The Austrian National Bank provided the Austrian state with the necessary financial means, but apart from this, tried to maintain an impartial position. In order to discuss the political complications it is necessary to look at the position and structure of the Credit-Anstalt before 1930.

INTERNATIONAL BANKING IN AUSTRIA

Until 1930 the Credit-Anstalt was an international business. It is possible to describe the Viennese banks during the Habsburg Monarchy as being already multi-national banks, although the political borders between nations were not yet established. They were multi-national banks in a multi-national monarchy. But, even towards the end of the Monarchy, some of the Viennese banks tried to introduce a more national character into their provincial branches in Prague and Budapest. With the fall of the Monarchy, multi-national became international. On the one hand, Viennese banks lost some of their influence in the successor states, but still retained a substantial financial position, which even expanded in the 1920s.

Table 16.1. CREDIT-ANSTALT HOLDINGS, 1930.

Successor states and traditional sphere of influence

	Number of holdings
Czechoslovakia	26
Poland	9
Hungary	4
Yugoslavia	4
Romania	4
Bulgaria	4

The Credit-Anstalt had interests in 11 banks and 40 industrial enterprises in these new national economies, mainly sugar, iron, textiles and oil companies. In addition it had a few holdings in the west, which, however, were very closely associated with its eastern interests, and so about a third of the 158 business ventures with the Credit-Anstalt's sphere were outside Austria. Even these equity interests do not show the complete extent of the Credit-Anstalt's business activities. The Credit-Anstalt also exercised its influence through the provision of industrial credit. About 40 per cent of the loans and advances of the Credit-Anstalt were to businesses outside Austria. Thus in 1931 the foreign assets of the Credit-Anstalt consisted of 28.8m sch. in shares and 393m sch. in debtor accounts.[2]

But even 40 per cent of its business activity being foreign does not necessarily prove that the Credit-Anstalt was an international enterprise.

However, foreign participations were also present in the bank's share capital, on its supervisory board and in its borrowed capital. The Viennese Roth-schilds had certainly no more than a third of the bank's shares, while another third was held by English interests – the Bank of England and the Anglo-International Bank in London, which had received 375,000 shares in return for the assets of the Anglo-Austrian Bank acquired in 1926, and the Prudential Insurance Company, which had bought 100,000 shares as a capital investment. Another 125,000 shares had been bought by American banks – Kuhn, Loeb and Co. and the Guarantee Trust Company of New York in 1920. The rest of the share capital was probably in the hands of small shareholders.[3] The foreign influence in the bank is further shown in its presence on the bank's managerial bodies. The day to day management was purely Austrian, but on the supervisory board there were 29 Austrians and 22 foreigners – 11 Czechoslovaks, 3 Britons, 2 Dutchmen, 2 Frenchmen, 1 Hungarian, 1 Yugoslav, 1 Belgian, 1 American and 1 German. There is a similar picture with regard to the bank's borrowed capital, of which roughly a third was foreign, mainly British and American. 'The extensive short term credits given to the Vienna banks by lenders in London, Paris, Amsterdam, New York and elsewhere . . . really form the economic life-blood of this country.'[4]

The Credit-Anstalt was therefore a financial institution based in Vienna, which had an important part of its business in Austria and which was overseen by an Austrian management. But about 50 per cent or more of its shares were in foreign hands, a large number of foreigners sat on its supervisory board, about a third of its borrowed funds came from other countries and at least 40 per cent of its business activities were outside Austria. The Viennese banks were sometimes criticized for not acting patriotically – not in Austrian interests. But this was hardly possible. In the Credit-Anstalt one did not think 'Austrian', one thought 'international', or at least 'Central European'.

This international bank collapsed in 1931. The causes for this were numerous. They were partly due to an ill-conceived business policy, but lay mainly in the disintegration of the Habsburg Monarchy after the First World War. The principal banks of Vienna tried to ignore the break-up of the Monarchy in their business policy, but in the long run their funds were insufficient to sustain this myopia. They managed to continue their policy of retaining their traditional sphere of influence for a further period of 10 to 15 years after the breakdown of the Empire, but then they broke down too. The economic disintegration of the successor states went yet another step further. The second cause lay in the structure of the Austrian banking system itself. The Credit-Anstalt was as much an industrial holding company as a bank. It held shares and gave industrial credit, which were very closely related to one another. As the great depression began, a lot of its credits were frozen and share values dropped. But the Central European capital market after 1918 was such that even leading financial institutions had great difficulty in obtaining long-term credit. The expansion policy of the Credit-Anstalt in the 1920s was financed mostly by short-term (3 month) home and foreign deposits.

THE ECONOMIC ATTITUDE OF THE AUSTRIAN GOVERNMENT

What could an Austrian government of 1931, which was still Liberal and dreamed of *laissez-faire*, undertake, when faced with the Credit-Anstalt crisis? After all, the Credit-Anstalt was the largest enterprise of the country with a balance practically the same as that of the Austrian state budget. This government acted against its principles and intervened on behalf of the bank. On Friday 8 May, the Credit-Anstalt declared its catastrophic losses to the government and this led to negotiations which lasted the whole weekend, and produced a reconstruction plan largely backed by the state. On Monday 11 May this plan, together with the news of the losses of the Credit-Anstalt, was made public. Why did the Austrian government act in this way? A way which the socialists described as 'Privatization of profits and socialization of losses?'[5] The basic argument, which was supplied by the Credit-Anstalt itself, was that Austrian industry was largely dependent on this banking institution. The estimated proportion of the amount of Austrian industry which relied on the bank ranged from 60 to 80 per cent. The true figure was considerably smaller. An investigation by the Ministry of Finance concluded 'That the number of industries really dependent on the Credit-Anstalt seems to lie somewhere between 13.75 per cent and 68.75 per cent, but probably nearer the 13.75 per cent.'[6] Of all Austrian limited companies (by capital), 68.75 per cent did their business through the Credit-Anstalt; and 13.75 per cent of all Austrian limited companies were so deeply in debt to the Credit-Anstalt that they would collapse with the bank. The Austrian government feared the complete breakdown of the Austrian economy with the closure of the bank. Consequently a government which pursued an economic policy of *laissez-faire* was forced to intervene. It raced to the financial rescue like a 'knight in shining armour'.[7]

The question remains why the Austrian government, which was mainly interested in the industries which were dependent on the Credit-Anstalt, did not let the bank go bankrupt and instead directly support the industries. This would have been cheaper in the long run, but current Austrian state intervention policy would not go that far. Supporting the Credit-Anstalt was seen as an exception to the rule, and the government would retreat as soon as possible. Intervention in individual industry would have meant a permanent presence and influence in private business by the state, and that was neither possible nor acceptable. The ruling Christian-Social party stated quite categorically: 'The state has no intention whatsoever of remaining a partner of the Credit-Anstalt. At the first opportunity the state will get rid of its shares.'[8] Reisch, the president of the Austrian National Bank, wanted to place most of the shares on the French, English or German markets in order to prevent nationalization.[9] The Committee of the Guarantor States, when asked to give its permission to an Austrian 150m sch. treasury bond scheme, imposed a condition that the independence of the industries, which were now indirectly under Austrian governmental control, would not be impaired and that the shares should be sold within three years.[10] And the Austrian Bundeskanzler declared to the Financial Committee of the League of Nations: 'The government will not interfere in the commercial administration of the Credit-Anstalt . . .'[11] The state could temporarily intervene in an economic fulcrum, like the banks, but did not want to intervene in the whole economic machine. The state's reconstruction plan was a direct result of these conflicting attitudes.

First Reconstruction Plan – Law 14 May 1931

Losses: 139.6m sch.

Financial aid

State	100m sch.
National Bank	30m sch.
Rothschild	30m sch.
Shareholders	30m sch.

Cover of losses		New capital	Capital share (%)
State	41.4m sch.	58.6m sch.	33
Open Reserves	33.6m sch.		
Devaluation of shares 25%	29.4m sch.		
Rothschild	16.7m sch.	13.2m sch.	7.4
National Bank	12.4m sch.	17.6m sch.	10
	139.6m sch.	89.4m sch.	50.4
Remaining share capital		88.1m sch	49.6
New share capital		177.5m sch.	100

The shareholders were treated surprisingly gently in this plan. Although share capital is the risk capital of a limited company, the shares were only devalued by 25 per cent, whereas the state was to contribute 100m sch. and carry the greatest part of the losses. In return the state received shares to the value of only 58.6m sch. This rather peculiar arrangement had a very simple explanation. Because of the attitude described above, the government wanted to avoid becoming the principal shareholder of the bank. Had the share capital been devalued to 25m sch. as the bank's losses implied and had the state payment been fully taken into consideration, the state would have become a shareholder with 65 per cent of the bank's equity. In order to avoid this, the state accepted just a third of the shares, thus having, together with the National Bank, 43 per cent. In addition the government wanted to take into consideration 'that the most notable and the greatest proportion of the shares are in foreign countries'. In order to maintain Austrian financial credibility, the state wanted to avoid foreign investors suffering any great losses, in exchange for which the government hoped to receive active financial support from abroad.[12] 'In our present situation, it is of greatest importance', stated the Austrian Minister of Finance, Weidenhoffer, 'that international confidence in the Austrian economy should be maintained at least to the same extent as in the past, to help us to overcome the approaching difficulties with an influx of capital.'[13] The Austrian government 'put on its velvet gloves to pray to the Rothschilds to appeal to their connections abroad'.[14]

Such was the attitude of the Austrian government during the first days of the Credit-Anstalt crisis – characterized by a conflicting attitude towards its own policy and certain illusions as to the reaction of the foreign investors.

THE POSITION OF THE AUSTRIAN CREDIT-ANSTALT INTERNATIONAL COMMITTEE

In 1930 the Credit-Anstalt had a balance sheet amounting to 1,885m sch. The greatest part of its assets were debtors (1,382m sch.) while the largest liability was creditors (1,359m sch.). Approximately 500m sch. of the Credit-Anstalt's creditors came from about 130 foreign banks. In May 1931 these banks started to get together and formed the 'Austrian Credit-Anstalt International Committee' with Lionel Rothschild as chairman. Their goal was to withdraw from the Credit-Anstalt as painlessly as possible without investing new capital which the Austrian government was anticipating. Rothschild himself declared that 'a new financial support by international capital seemed to him to be inexpedient',[15] and the British Treasury stated: 'The Bank of England was quite clear that there was no possibility of further foreign money being put into the Credit-Anstalt, as the Austrian government had suggested . . .'[16]

The Committee's problem was that of bringing such a large number of banks to agree to one common plan of action. Even with such a clear goal of a painless withdrawal from the Credit-Anstalt there were still many serious disagreements. The American banks, for example, had discounted their drafts, consequently getting into financial difficulties, and therefore took a much firmer standpoint than, for example, the British. At this time it even appeared that the Americans wanted to split away from the European banks and go their own way. Despite this lack of unity, the Committee developed into an extremely influential organization. One of the reasons for this was that the Credit-Anstalt had had really substantial financial connections in the west. 'These 130 banks are the biggest and the best banks between America and France. The Credit-Anstalt had really first class creditors in contrast to the debtors',[17] commented the *Neue Freie Presse*. But the main reason was that the Committee was led by a number of highly influential bankers, for example, Sir Robert Kindersley, one of the directors of the Bank of England and member of the Financial Committee of the League of Nations, and Lionel Rothschild, who considered himself to be more a financial diplomat than a banker. Thus the Committee gained an influence and a position far above that of a normal private creditors' association.

THE NEGOTIATIONS BETWEEN THE AUSTRIAN GOVERNMENT AND THE AUSTRIAN CREDIT-ANSTALT INTERNATIONAL COMMITTEE

As far as the Austrian government was concerned the Credit-Anstalt crisis ended with their brave reconstruction measures. They had helped to cover the losses and also to restore the capital of the Credit-Anstalt. All further details were left to the bank itself. The management was not changed, no conditions were set for further business activity, there was no restriction on payment and no control of foreign exchange.

However, these measures were not sufficient. Withdrawals from the Credit-Anstalt reached proportions of a run although this was always denied and played down in Austria.[18] The bank lost nearly all its domestic and a part of its foreign short-term funds. 216.1m sch. were lost in the first two days of the crisis and by 30 June losses had reached 518.7m sch.[19] At the same time domestic withdrawals were being changed into foreign exchange because a devaluation of the Austrian Schilling was expected. The Credit-Anstalt financed these withdrawals through discounting drafts with the National Bank, of which only a very small part were trade bills and the bulk were finance bills, which were only accepted by the National Bank with the permission of the Austrian government. In this way the Austrian state had not only become the principal shareholder, but also had, through the National Bank, become the principal creditor. Therefore the government had to try to restore confidence in the bank and at least prevent the foreign creditors from withdrawing their money. The Austrian government consequently started to negotiate with the Austrian Credit-Anstalt International Committee.

Austria's weakness was the state of national finance. At the time of the reconstruction plan the Austrian government had no money in the treasury. The great depression had already left its mark on the national revenue. In 1930 the tax revenue was considerably less than expected and consequently budgetary restraints were planned for 1931. Unemployment benefit was to be restricted and state investments were not only reduced but practically stopped.[20] Owing to this situation the Minister of Finance did not have 100m sch. available for the Credit-Anstalt. The government therefore intended to float 150m sch. of three-year treasury bonds abroad. Meanwhile the reconstruction plan was being partly prefinanced by other Austrian banks. The Austrian shortage of capital was also the weak point in their political conflict with France. But it was not only France which looked at this financial problem within a political framework. Austria itself tried to float the bonds in France, in an attempt to sustain the German Austrian Customs Union plan. The Austrian negotiators turned to Berlin and London.[21] Curtius, the German Foreign Minister, promised to help his Austrian colleague Schober to get a 100m sch. loan from the German banks and representatives of the Austrian Ministry of Finance and the Credit-Anstalt negotiated in Berlin.[22] Just how confused the situation was is shown by a conversation between the French Ambassador in Vienna and the Austrian Bundeskanzler Ender at a reception. The ambassador stated that a member of the Banque de France and the French Ministry of Finance would be coming to Vienna. 'Ender seemed somewhat taken aback and told Clauzel [the French Ambassador] that two members of the Credit-Anstalt had just left for Paris, so that the presence of these high French officials was perhaps hardly necessary. After some time had passed, Ender, who had meanwhile consulted Schober, returned, and, looking rather flustered, whispered to Clauzel that the Credit-Anstalt officials had gone to Berlin and not to Paris!'[23] But the German Reich gave only vague promises of support and England declared it was only willing to contribute to the loan under the leadership of the French banks. Accordingly Paris became the only possible capital market left for Austria. But the Austrian negotiators dithered so long over the political necessity to withdraw from the German Austrian Customs Union plan that they finally achieved nothing, not even with France. The treasury bond idea came to naught.

Owing to both the great depression and the losses of the Credit-Anstalt, the state's financial situation and the condition of the Schilling became precarious and consequently a much larger foreign credit of about 500m sch. was thought to be necessary. Meanwhile a form of interim financing had to be found at all costs, in order to stabilize the Schilling and to prevent a general moratorium. In this critical situation the Bank for International Settlements, supported by 12 national banks, furnished the Austrian National Bank with a credit of 100m schillings.[24] But one of the conditions that the BIS insisted upon was a governmental guarantee for the Credit-Anstalt in order to stabilize the financial situation in Austria.[25] The foreign creditors demanded this security too and would only then agree to leave their money in the bank.

This produced the historic moment – when the Austrian state stood guarantor for the Credit-Anstalt. The original intention had been to provide the Credit-Anstalt with new capital. 'The Minister of Finance was empowered to use the state guarantee as a means of stimulation to bring in new money for the reconstruction and current business of the Credit-Anstalt.

Following public panic, the necessity to calm the investors and to satisfy the creditors, the bank became guaranteed "from head to foot" by the state. Far more than had been intended.'[26] The Minister of Finance had originally intended to guarantee only new investments, but in order not to lose the old investments these were also covered by the guarantee. At first the Minister of Finance was very circumspect in his use of the guarantee, but as a result of the negotiations with the foreign creditors and the insistence of the Austrian National Bank the guarantee was finally extended to all Credit-Anstalt liabilities.[27] The background of this general guarantee was the belief held by the Austrian government that it would lead to the foreign creditors putting new money into the Credit-Anstalt.[28] The state expected at least 500m sch., but the general use of the guarantee had not originally been planned and was to prove disadvantageous. In 1931 the Austrian government stood guarantor for 1,200m sch., with a state budget of only 1,800m sch.

This was a remarkable success for the foreign creditors. The weakness in their negotiating position had been the problem of claiming money from an insolvent bank. The liquidation of the Credit-Anstalt in the middle of a world depression would have led to catastrophic losses. Their only chance was to continue business and slowly dispose of the Credit-Anstalt's assets. They therefore had to find someone to take over responsibility for the Credit-Anstalt, continue its business, bear the resulting losses and accept their claims. They found someone, the Austrian state, and were able to transform their illiquid claims against the bank into guaranteed claims. In this way they greatly improved their position. The *Neue Freie Presse* stated: 'It is now a fact that there has been a complete change of roles since the beginning of the crisis. The conditions, by which a creditors' association will be formed, are imposed by foreigners. The foreigners lay down the conditions for the issue of the government treasury bonds and they are investigating the bank. Their negotiations are not, however, with the management of this institution, but the state and the National Bank. . . . In any case the foreign creditors' position is now much better than they ever dreamed.'[29] The reason for the improvement in the foreign creditors' position was the political conflict between Austria and France, the pressure from the BIS and the threat by the foreign creditors 'that unless the Austrian state gave the guarantee for the foreign creditors of the Credit-Anstalt immediately . . . the credit of the government and of the country would be done for permanently.'[30] But the deciding factor for the foreign creditors' position was the support of the Bank of England.

On 14 June 1931, Sir Robert Kindersley, member of the board of directors of the Bank of England and president of Lazards bank, London, came to Vienna as the negotiator for the foreign creditors of the Credit-Anstalt, accompanied by J. H. Gannon, representative of the Chase National Bank of the City of New York, which in addition to the London Rothschilds was one of the most important creditors. Their original intention had been simply to put forward their private claims, but they soon saw that their problem could only be dealt with in connection with the whole Austrian financial problem. As a result of the Credit-Anstalt crisis there was a constant outflow of foreign exchange and the position of the Schilling became critical. Austria was near to declaring a general moratorium. The foreign financiers tried their best to change the mind of the Austrian government and National Bank. They immediately contacted Montagu Norman, Governor of the Bank of England. The general fear was that the Austrian moratorium would result in similar difficulties for other Central European currencies.[31] Late in the night of 14 June the Bank of England, therefore, agreed to give the Austrian National Bank a short term (7 days) credit of 150m sch. as an advance on the planned treasury bond issue.[32] The political role of this financial aid has always been a point of argument. The Governor of the Bank of England was certainly not known for his love of France. He considered the political pressure of France on Germany and Austria to be false, because of the critical position of many European currencies at this time. It must, however, be stated that the Foreign Office was not informed of the Bank of England's action and was presented with a *fait accompli*.[33]

After the situation had been temporarily saved with the help of Sir Robert Kindersley, the Austrian government was willing to meet the terms of the foreign creditors. The Minister of Finance signed the Austrian state guarantee for all the foreign liabilities. Two hours later the government resigned. Now the National Bank insisted upon the remaining Austrian liabilities also being covered by the guarantee.[34] Thus the Austrian state stood guarantee for all the liabilities of the Credit-Anstalt.

The new Austrian government now had to try to get a long-term foreign loan in order finally to resolve the Austrian financial situation. But it took another year to obtain it in the form of the Lausanne loan. The main reason that it took so long was the state guarantee from which the government had expected so much. As long as there was an unlimited guarantee, the principal foreign financial centres were not willing to lend money to the Austrian state and even in the Financial Committee of the League of Nations 'no majority could be found, which would be willing to allow the issue of new credit to a country like Austria which maintains an unlimited guarantee.'[35] It was now up to the Austrian government to fix the level of their financial obligations and to come to an agreement with the foreign creditors about the repayments.

The situation was simple. The Austrian government wanted to cancel the guarantee and get rid of its obligations. The foreign creditors would be compensated by the foreign assets of the Credit-Anstalt, shares and future profits. But the foreign creditors saw only the guarantee and insisted upon their financial demands being met in cash and foreign exchange without any further restriction or conditions, either from the Credit-Anstalt or by the Austrian state.[36] However, in the following negotiations the foreign creditors were forced to recognize that the Austrian state was not capable of meeting its obligations. Whereas 150m sch. from the Bank of England had been enough to rescue Austria from a currency crisis in 1931, a payment of 500m sch. was absolutely impossible in 1932.[37] The negotiations seemed endless. The degree to which the creditors were willing to make concessions and the government's estimate of Austria's paying capacity were poles apart. But the English, French and League of Nations' support for the foreign creditors increased in relation to the length of the negotiations. Rost van Tonningen, the representative of the League in Austria, tried to push the government to an agreement.[38] Sir Otto Niemeyer, director of the Bank of England, wrote in a letter to the Banque de France: 'The Creditors, however, say, and I think naturally, that they must be sure that they have the support of the League. I feel that we should give them this support, both through Rost and directly ourselves', and recommended: 'That we may use the influence of the Financial Committee cojointly with that of the creditors'.[39] France and England also officially urged the Austrian government more than once to clear up the disagreeable Credit-Anstalt problem once and for all and to come to an agreement with the foreign creditors. The British Ambassador in Vienna was at last instructed to work together with the French Ambassador on the Credit-Anstalt question.[40] The League of Nations finally made formally clear to Austria the necessity to come to an agreement as quickly as possible. An agreement with the foreign creditors was laid down as a condition in Article 6 of the loan protocol of 16 July 1932.[41] The pressure on

---

SECOND RECONSTRUCTION PLAN: Agreement between the Government of the Federation of Austria and the Austrian Credit Anstalt International Committee 11 Jan. 1933 Agreement between the Government of the Federation of Austria and the Austrian National Bank 18 Aug. 1932

1. Credit-Anstalt debts

691m sch. by discount of drafts to the National Bank
420m sch. to the foreign creditors

2. Measures concerning domestic debts

177.5m sch. to 1m sch., devaluation of share capital
571m sch. Credit-Anstalt drafts taken by the Austrian state
71m sch. preference shares for the Austrian state

3. Measures concerning foreign debts

70m sch. preference shares for the foreign creditors
140m sch. foreign assets of the Credit-Anstalt given to the foreign creditors, foundation of a Foreign Assets Company in Monaco (Gesco)
210m sch. remaining debts (live claims) to be paid by the Austrian state

4. Terms of payment

16.5m sch. annuities for 20 years – actual value (4.5%) 210m sch., or
27m sch. annuities for 7 years – actual value (4.5%) 140m sch.

the Austrian government and the superior position of the foreign creditors was finally so great that the British and French ambassadors in Vienna recommended that governmental pressure should not only be put on Austria but also on the Creditors Committee to make more concessions.[42] At last in January 1933, after long and often dramatic negotiations in Vienna and London during which it sometimes appeared as if the European and American banks would separate and go their own ways,[43] an agreement was reached.

In Austria this agreement was considered to be a major success because it brought Austrian financial insecurity to an end and cleared up the general financial situation. But above all the agreement was important for the Credit-Anstalt. It was the basis for the reconstruction of the bank, but on a much more modest plane than before. First, the old shares were devalued to the sum of 1m sch., and the state became the principal shareholder with 51 per cent. The majority of the Credit-Anstalt's previous liabilities to the National Bank were taken over by the Austrian state. Second, the foreign creditors accepted new preference shares of the Credit-Anstalt and its foreign assets as part payment of their demands. Half of the foreign assets of the Credit-Anstalt were to be slowly disposed of by a newly founded company in Monaco (Gesco). The other half were taken over by the state in the form of annuities. The foreign creditors were willing to agree to a reduction equal to one-third of the remaining debts (live claims) if the repayments were made over seven years. Also interesting was the creation of a new body in the Credit-Anstalt, the Executive Committee, which consisted of five members, three to be appointed by the Austrian government and two by the foreign creditors. Within the reconstructed Credit-Anstalt this Committee represented the interests of the principal shareholders, the Austrian state and the foreign creditors. Thus a body was created whose position was somewhere between the board of directors and the supervisory board. It was to justify its existence completely. Together with the new general director, the Dutchman van Hengel, who had been appointed and was paid not only by Austria but also the foreign creditors,[44] the newly formed Executive Committee was responsible for the near completion of the reconstruction of the Credit-Anstalt by 1938.

The Credit-Anstalt crisis seemed to be over. Actually it was to a great extent for the bank, but not for the Austrian government. In 1934 Austria should have paid the first annuity to the foreign creditors. It was, however, in such financial difficulties that the government asked to be allowed to postpone payment for one year and then, in 1935, for yet another year. Thus the first payment should have been finally due in March 1936, but then the Austrian government refused to pay anything at all. The Minister of Finance declared that the financial situation had improved to the degree that by extreme cuts in public spending the budget could be balanced, but not to the degree by which they state could take on an additional and completely sacrificial unproductive burden for private foreign interests, without compensation.[45] Austria declared that it was unwilling and unable to pay, but the foreign creditors had included a clause to cover the possibility of payment inability in the agreement of 1933 under which the League of Nations was to determine the extent to which Austria was unable to pay. Since economic development in Austria had shown a definite improvement from 1934 to 1935, it was very difficult for them to make a 'plea of poverty'[46] in Geneva. The League's decision was expected to be in favour of the foreign creditors. For this reason on 26 January 1936 the Austrian Minister of Finance, Draxler, boarded a train and, accompanied by the president of the National Bank, set off for London. Three days later they had achieved a very favourable agreement for Austria.

AGREEMENT BETWEEN THE GOVERNMENT OF THE FEDERATION OF AUSTRIA AND THE AUSTRIAN CREDIT-ANSTALT INTERNATIONAL COMMITTEE 29 JAN. 1936

1. Redemption of foreign debts

60m sch. payment immediately in cash and foreign exchange
2m sch. annuities in foreign exchange for 20 years

2. Financing

The 60m sch. will be prefinanced in schillings by the Credit-Anstalt, the Austrian state pays annuities of 3m sch. to the Credit-Anstalt for 40 years.

3. Actual value

(4.5%) 77.8m sch.

With one great financial effort the Austrian government had achieved a reduction of its Credit-Anstalt debts from 140m sch. to 77.8m sch. Even then the funds in schilling had come from the Credit-Anstalt. Thus the Credit-Anstalt crisis was finally over. The general guarantee had already been lifted in 1934 and in 1936 the General Director of the Credit-Anstalt was, once again, an Austrian.

'AUSTRIFICATION', THE CONSEQUENCE OF THE CREDIT-ANSTALT CRISIS

The consequences of the Credit-Anstalt crisis can be described as Austrification, in banking business and borrowed capital, as well as in the economic policy of the Austrian government. The first reconstruction and the state guarantee were measures which had been taken to retain the internationality of the Credit-Anstalt. For this reason the Austrian government did not want to take a permanent interest in the Credit-Anstalt and was satisfied with a minority share in order to protect its interests. This was why the state categorically refused to interfere in the Credit-Anstalt's business and intended to dispose of its shares as soon as possible. This attitude explains the measures taken by the Austrian government.

This attitude eventually changed, but only after the unexpectedly high losses of the Credit-Anstalt, the increasing lack of interest of the foreign financiers, and the hesitant support of the Schilling by other countries which had only been achieved by political concessions until the Lausanne loan. The second reconstruction plan was, consequently, quite different. It lifted the unlimited state guarantee, the Austrian state took over the majority of the Credit-Anstalt's losses and increased its shares to 51 per cent. More than a few percentage points lay between the first plan's minority share agreement and the 51 per cent of the second plan. Between the two plans lay the admittance by the Austrian government of the failure to maintain the internationality of the Credit-Anstalt and the decision to dominate the bank in the interest of Austrian industry and economy.

This change explains the Austrian government's uncompromising attitude in 1935–6 towards the foreign creditors, which was so different from that of 1931. Austria was able to adopt such a firm attitude because it was obvious that there was little to expect from abroad. In 1931 Austria had expected the foreign creditors to invest new capital in the Credit-Anstalt to put it back on its feet, but in 1932 it was clear that they were only interested in withdrawing from the Credit-Anstalt with as few losses as possible. The result of the Credit-Anstalt crisis was, generally speaking, a loss of capital in an economy which was traditionally poor in capital. The major part of the Lausanne loan had to be used to at least partly reduce the losses of capital and foreign exchange incurred by the Credit-Anstalt crisis. The final agreement with the foreign creditors in 1936 demanded once again the immediate payment of 60m sch. in foreign exchange. The Credit-Anstalt losses finally reached about 1,000m sch. The state took over about 70 per cent of these losses and received in return 51 per cent of the reconstructed Credit-Anstalt, a bank which had a business volume of 635m sch. in 1932, in contrast to 1,400m sch. in 1929 and even 1,885m sch. in 1930. The foreign deposits which had once played such an important role in the bank now practically disappeared and the Credit-Anstalt foreign assets, liabilities and shares were mostly passed on to the foreign assets company Gesco in Monaco. Thus the Credit-Anstalt became a nationally orientated Austrian bank and lost its traditional role of mediator between western capital and Central and East European investment. All this could also be said of the whole Austrian banking system. In 1934 the Wiener Bank-Verein and the Niederösterreichische Escompte-Gesellschaft, the last remaining large Austrian banks, had to face losses of 48.8m sch. and 77.3m sch.[47] On this occasion the Austrian government did not give a guarantee. Instead, it merged the two banks with the Credit-Anstalt, which now became the one and only large bank of Austria. From then on the Austrian banking system was to a large extent under government control. This merger brought new foreign interests to the Credit-Anstalt which, however, were small compared with those of the bank in the 1920s. At the time of the merger Viennese international banking was a thing of the past. The international enterprise became a national bank, with mainly domestic and only modest foreign interests. This showed itself in the business policy of the bank in disposing of foreign assets and reconstructing the industries dependent upon the bank by rationalization and cancellation of debts. Foreign capital, in particular British and American, had been withdrawn from the Austrian banks. The question remains of who took over the financial positions which the Austrian banks had given up. It seems that some successor states tried to buy back the shares of their industries. One example is the Prague bank, the Živnostenska banka, which tried to get Czechoslovak shares from the Credit-Anstalt.[48] Thus in the 1930s not only political but also economic nationalism advanced a step further, a development which for Austria was closely related to the Credit-Anstalt crisis.

Notes

1. Public Record Office London (PRO), FO 371/15150/02382. Phipps to Henderson, Vienna, 15 May 1931.
2. Finanzarchiv Vienna (FA), 77.685/32, memo. Van Hengel, 19 Nov. 1932.
3. PRO, FO 371/15150/02382, Phipps to Foreign Office, Vienna, 15 May 1931.
4. *Ibid.*
5. *Neue Freie Presse*, Vienna (*NFP*), 12 May 1931.
6. FA 32.757/32. Auskunft des Departement 15 zur Verwendung im Ministerrat am 7.8.1931.
7. Erkärung Finanzminister Weidenhoffer vor dem Parlament Stenographische Protokolle des Österreichischen Nationalrats, 29 Sitzung, 13 May 1931, s. 837.
8. *Reichspost*, Vienna, 13 May 1931.
9. Archives Économiques et Financières Paris (ME) F 30/628, Compte Clauzel, Ministre de la République Française en Autriche à M. le Ministre des Affaires Étrangères, Vienna, 27 May 1931.
10. ME F 30/1847, Report by Rist on his mission to Vienna, 31 May–24 June 1931.
11. PRO, FO 371/15154/02435, letter of Rost van Tonningen, Vienna, 3 Nov. 1931.
12. PRO, FO 371/15150/02382, Sir Eric Phipps to Arthur Henderson, Vienna, 16 June 1931.
13. Stenographische Protokolle des Österreichischen Nationalrats, s. 838,

Finanzminister Weidenhoffer, 13 May 1931.
14. PRO, FO 371/15151/02402, Sir Eric Phipps to Froeng Office, 17 June 1931.
15. FA 88.760/31.
16. PRO, FO C/3616/61/3, Sir F. Leith Ross (Treasury) to Sir R. Vansittart.
17. *NFP*, 20 Dec. 1931.
18. *NFP*, 12 and 13 May 1931.
19. ME F 30/1847, Report by Rist of his mission to Vienna, 31 May–24 June 1931.
20. D. Stiefel, 'Konjunkturelle Entwicklung und struktureller Wandel der österreichischen Wirtschaft in der Zwischenkriegszeit', Institut für höhere Studien Wien', Forschungsbericht Nr. 135 (Nov. 1978), 47.
21. ME F 30/628, Note au sujet de la Credit Anstalt, Paris, 26 May 1931. See also E. W. Bennet, *Germany and the Diplomacy of the Financial Crisis, 1931* (Cambridge, Mass., 1962).
22. ME F 30/628, Compte Clauzel au Ministre des Affaires Étrangères, Vienna, 27 May 1931.
23. PRO, FO 371/15150/02382, Sir Eric Phipps to Orme G. Sargent (FO), Vienna, 27 May 1931.
24. ME F 30/1847, Report by Rist of his mission to Vienna, 31 May–24 June 1931.
25. PRO, FO C/2616/61/3, Sir Leith Ross (Treasury) to Sir R. Vansittart, London, 27 May 1931.

26. *NFP*, 9 Feb. 1932.
27. 'Erklärung Dr. Enders über die Credit Anstalt', *NFP*, Vienna, 14 May 1932.
28. *NFP*, 28 May 1931.
29. *ibid.*, *Economist*, 14 May 1931.
30. PRO, FO 371/15150/02382, Sir Eric Phipps to Arthur Henderson, Vienna, 16 June 1931.
31. ME F 30/1847; Report by Rist of his mission to Vienna, 31 May–24 June 1931.
32. ME F 30/624, Compte Clauzel à Briand, Ministre des Affaires Étrangères, Vienna, 17 June 1931. PRO, FO 371/15150/02382, Sir Leith Ross to Orme G. Sargent, London, 17 June 1931.
33. PRO, FO 371/15150, Orme G. Sargent to Hadow, London, 24 Aug. 1931.
34. ME F 30/624, Compte Clauzel à Briand, Ministre des Affaires Étrangères, Vienna, 10 July 1931.
35. ME F 30/629, Ministre de la République Française en Autriche à Ministre des Affaires Étrangères, Vienna, 23 Nov. 1932.
36. ME F 30/629, Ministre des Affaires Étrangères à Ministre des Finances, Paris, 26 June 1932.
37. ME F 30/629, Ministre des Affaires Etrangères à Ministres des Finances, Paris, 6 Sept. 1932.
38. PRO, FO 371/15891/024499, London, 4 Nov. 1932.
39. ME F 30/629m Sir Otto Niemeyer to le Compte de Chalendar, London, Bank of England, 19 Nov. 1931.
40. ME F 30/629, Ministre de la République Française à Londre à Ministre des Finances, London, 29 July 1932.
41. ME F 30/629, Ministre de Affaires Étrangères à Ministre des Finances, Paris, 23 July 1932 and 7 Nov. 1932. See also G. Klingenstein, *Die Anleihe von Lausanne, Ein Beitrag zur Geschichte der Ersten Republik in den Jahren 1931–1934* (Vienna, 1965).
42. ME F 30/629, Compte Clauzel à Herriot, Ministre des Affaires Étrangères, Vienna 27 July 1932 and Ministre des Affaires Étrangères à Ministre des Finances, Paris, 12 Nov. 1932
43. ME F 30/629, Ministre des Affaires Étrangères à Ministre des Finances, Paris, 28 June 1932, and Roger Combon à Diplomatie Paris, 29 July 1932.
44. ME F 30/629, Meeting of the Creditors of the Credit Anstalt, 15 March 1932.
45. ME F 30/629, Ministre de la République Française en Autriche à Ministre des Affaires Étrangères, Vienna, 24 July 1935.
46. ME F 30/645, Remarques sur la Situation financière en Autriche, Paris, 19 Dec. 1935, and Ministre de France en Autriche à M. le Ministre des Affaires Étrangères, Vienna, 3 Feb. 1938.
47. FA 33.198/34.
48. FA 21.186/34 Kaufangebote an die Gesco. See also A. Teichova, *An Economic Background to Munich: International Business and Czechoslovakia (1974)*.

COMMENTARY   *Eduard März and Fritz Weber*

Dieter Stiefel's paper on the crisis of the Credit-Anstalt, which we consider an excellent piece of work, deals with three closely interrelated issues: first, with the causes of the crisis which culminated in the spectacular breakdown of the institution in the summer of 1931; second, with the policies designed to resolve the crisis, which were worked out in the course of protracted and complex negotiations by the Austrian government and the consortium of creditors; and third, with the altered role of the Credit-Anstalt in Austrian and Central European economic affairs after the resolution of the crisis.

In our comments we shall focus attention primarily on the first part of Dr Stiefel's paper, on the events leading up to the crisis of 1931. Stiefel considers the Credit-Anstalt as a multi-nationally oriented banking institute from the very inception of its remarkable career. We should prefer to say that the Credit-Anstalt was an institute of the *crédit mobilier* type of banking which first operated within the confines of a multi-national empire. Even after 1867, when the Habsburg Monarchy turned into the Austro–Hungarian Empire, a customs union was established which permitted the institution to carry on its banking affairs within a monogeneous legal and monetary milieu. It is true that in the last two decades before the First World War both the Hungarians and the Czechs made considerable efforts to establish an indigenous banking system, but the indications are that this did not seriously interfere with the operations of the Credit-Anstalt. Thus, it seems hardly appropriate to characterize the bank as multi-national before the dissolution of the Empire.

It is clear, however, that the situation changed fundamentally after the break-up of the Monarchy. Now the bulk of the assets and liabilities of the Credit-Anstalt were spread over seven so-called 'successor states', *viz.* Austria, Hungary and Czechoslovakia, which were cut out of the 'full cloth' of the Monarchy, and Italy, Yugoslavia, Romania and Poland, which received considerable chunks of the defunct Empire. Outside the former frontiers of Austria–Hungary the holdings of the Credit-Anstalt amounted to a *quantité négligeable*. Conversely, foreign shareholders held but a tiny fraction (about 4%) of the capital of the bank prior to the disappearance of the great realm.

The dominant interests in the bank, which were the Austrian house of the Rothschilds and its Austrian business confederates, such as the banking house of the Gomperz and other financial groups, were now confronted with a most difficult choice: they could ignore the cataclysmic political changes and attempt to continue business as usual, or they could make a clean break with the past and confine their operations to the new minute Austrian Republic. There were some voices which commanded respect, such as that of Alexander Spitzmueller – a former general manager of the Credit-Anstalt, who had later served as the head of the Treasury of a wartime government – who pleaded for a rigorous course of retreat from all former parts of the Empire and for a policy of concentration on the critical industrial needs of the new Austria: in Stiefel's words, there were voices in favour of 'Austrification' at an early date in the life of the Republic.

It must be admitted, however, that such voices were few and far between. Most financial experts, both inside and outside the bank, came out resolutely on behalf of continuing the traditional policy of the Credit-Anstalt, i.e. to cater for the financial needs of *all* territories formerly belonging to the Monarchy. One of the most prominent advocates of such a course was Professor Joseph A. Schumpeter, who served as Minister of Finances of the Austrian Republic in the crucial year of 1919. Schumpeter, who was opposed to the then generally favoured course of union with Germany, championed close economic co-operation among the newly created Danubian states. If economic frontiers were not to be a logical corollary of political frontiers, as he somewhat optimistically assumed, then an economic scenario could indeed have emerged from the wreckage of the war which was not too dissimilar from the erstwhile Austro–Hungarian customs union. These happy assumptions were shared by the spokesmen of the Credit-Anstalt, notably Dr Paul Hemmerschlag, director of the bank and a financial expert of international repute.

It is hardly necessary to say that the actual course of events in no way corresponded to these optimistic predictions. The peace treaties of St Germain en Laye and of Trianon, it is true, contained provisions for preferential customs treaties between the main Danubian states, but neither Czechoslovakia nor Hungary, for different reasons to be sure, seriously contemplated the conclusion of a preferential treaty with Austria. Hungary was hell-bent on a course of forced industrialization behind protective customs duties, and Czechoslovakia was fearful lest Vienna established its former financial predominance with the help of one stratagem or another. When the Beneš government after year-long procrastinations seriously considered an economic rapprochement with Austria, Germany had become strong enough to block it by threatening retaliatory measures.

The post-war world, especially its variant in the Danubian Basin, was indeed radically different from the familiar liberal or *laissez-faire* model. It abounded with protective tariffs, administrative trade barriers, foreign exchange restrictions and all sorts of other devices designed to strangle international trade. Since economic growth was exceedingly slow, industry remained depressed, and banking of the *crédit mobilier* type, insofar as it was possible at all, had to face risks of an unprecedented nature. It was under these auspices that the Credit-Anstalt resumed its old 'missionary' task of nourishing industrial activity by providing long-term credit – chiefly through the vehicle of 'credit on current account'.

Naturally, the Credit-Anstalt had hardly the wherewithal to do so, considering its greatly diminished capital resources. Despite the stupendous nominal profits harvested during the war, the bank had emerged at the end with a considerably weakened financial structure. Since it was by far the most important Austrian industrial holding company, its weakened constitution was but a reflection of the shaky state of many of the industrial enterprises tied to the bank through the links of credit or capital relationships. After the war another wave of severe capital losses set in, when the whole and extremely profitable network of branches in the successor states had to be sold to the leading domestic banks on terms none too favourable to the Credit-Anstalt. Again, a good deal of its industrial holdings had to be relinquished to either national or western – predominantly French or British – interests. Even in their Austrian backyard, Austrian banks had to abandon control over some of their most highly valued industrial assets.

But there was an even deeper underlying reason why the Credit-Anstalt and the other great commercial banks were constitutionally unable to continue their traditional role in the Danubian Basin on the slim capital basis available to them after the war. Prior to 1914 the balance on foreign accounts of the Monarchy had become unfavourable, but there was genuine hope, entertained by some of the most acute contemporary observers, that the situation would sooner or later be redressed as a result of the rapid industrialization of both the Austrian and Hungarian parts of the Empire.

After 1918 the balance of payments problem became the most acute economic weakness of the new Austria, resulting mainly from its inability to provide sufficient fuel for its industry and adequate food for its population. Moreover, Austrian industry was confronted with highly restrictive trade policies on the part of the now independent Danubian states. Naturally, the Austrian commercial banks could draw little comfort, never mind material sustenance, from the depressed state of the industries with which they had such intimate relationships.

It was hardly conceivable that the Credit-Anstalt could have persevered in its traditional function – of the *crédit mobilier* bank for the whole of the Danubian Basin – without broadening its capital base substantially. This it could do in no other way than by soliciting support among western financial interests. The house of Rothschild, still the dominant influence of the Anstalt, proved instrumental in bringing about the much desired close partnership between the Credit-Anstalt and some of the most formidable financial groups of the West. Stiefel has given us the essentials of the story.

The institution under consideration might well have succeeded in this venture of multi-national banking – of *genuine* multi-national banking, we may add – had it not been for the extremely adverse economic climate of the 1920s. But apart from these objective negative influences, which ought not to be discounted too easily, there were plenty of subjective factors which contributed to the eventual downfall of the bank. As for the objective influences, nothing can be said here which would not have an extremely familiar ring. Let us just be mindful of an observation of the British economic historian Aldcroft that the Western and Central European economic performance was particularly weak during the 1920s, and that the British, German and Austrian economies provided some of the worst examples of a particularly dark chapter of recent economic history.

What were the most striking negative aspects of Austrian banking policy in that period? We have already commented on the highly dubious initial decision of carrying on banking business for the whole of the Danubian area in the traditional way. As Stiefel has shown, the Credit-Anstalt derived some of its strength from western financial interests which had taken over a strong minority shareholding in the capital of the bank. This infusion of foreign blood, important as it was, would not have sufficed to maintain the bank as a major source of credit for its numerous clientèle widely dispersed throughout the successor states.

However, if the Anstalt had returned to its pre-war policy of carefully selecting its major clients, and concentrating its – now greatly diminished – strength on a limited number of industrial ventures, multi-national banking on a moderate scale might have proved feasible, even in the new environment. The Wiener Bank-Verein, another of the great Viennese commercial banks, could have served as a model, since this institution never undertook a major industrial venture single-handed, but succeeded in forming international syndicates, thus carefully limiting its stake in each major foreign as well as domestic investment transaction. Perhaps, the 'lone-wolf approach' of the Credit-Anstalt would not have proved fatal, had it not been for two further major errors in its management.

The first of these errors was the decision to take over – even though involuntarily, i.e. under heavy pressure from the government – in 1929 the colossal financial corpse of the Boden-Credit-Anstalt, whose illiquidity resulted primarily from the frozen industrial accounts. The management of the Credit-Anstalt should have perceived this as the proverbial writing on the wall, and either refused to take on the burden of the bankrupt Boden-Credit-Anstalt, or compelled the Austrian government to compensate it far more generously than it actually did for jumping into the breach. Perhaps this was the last opportunity for the Credit-Anstalt to prevent the coming catastrophe by putting its cards on the table in its negotiations with the government.

Perhaps the greater of the two errors was the policy of borrowing substantial funds in the West in order to channel them to the East. Stiefel has shown the extent of the short-term commitment of the bank to western creditors. As the 1920s progressed it must have become increasingly apparent to the management of the Credit-Anstalt that a good deal of its commercial credit to eastern customers had become irrecoverable, and that even part of the interest service could only be maintained in consequence of new loans provided by the bank. Long before the collapse of the Boden-Credit-Anstalt there were plenty of signals counselling the Anstalt to embark on a policy of slow but systematic retreat. But perhaps the management of the bank preferred to behave like good old Micawber, in the hope that something might eventually turn up. What did turn up in the end was the severest crisis in the history of European capitalism, a consummation hardly, and certainly not devoutly, hoped for by Neurath and his crew.

Given the economic conditions of the 1920s, once the fatal decision was taken to conduct multi-national banking on a large scale, and in an environment not particularly congenial to it, the calamitous outcome, if not the enormous extent of the calamity, was perhaps inevitable. The Credit-Anstalt, shorn of its age-old aura as the most eminent bank of Imperial Austria, might not have been quite so successful in attracting western funds, had it not been for the house of Rothschild, now openly – and quite visibly – identifying itself with the fortunes of the bank.

In 1920 Louis von Rothschild, the last scion of the Austrian house of the

Rothschilds, assumed the presidency of the Credit-Anstalt after, we may presume, considerable prodding from other members of the board of directors. Although the Rothschilds had always exercised considerable influence over the affairs of the Credit-Anstalt, none of them had ever aspired to the highest office during the long history of the bank. Their reluctance to identify themselves too openly with Austria's most important banking institute had its roots, no doubt, in their perception that the Credit-Anstalt should not be considered by the public as the extended arm of one of the most powerful private financial houses of Europe. To our knowledge, none of the numerous critics of the bank has ever raised the charge that the Rothschilds had taken advantage of their dominant position to manipulate the Credit-Anstalt on behalf of their special interests.

The decision to elevate Louis von Rothschild to the presidency was undoubtedly taken to underline the fact that the Credit-Anstalt, even in the new – so drastically altered – political setting, had the full backing of the renowned private banking house. This was quite obviously designed to enhance the reputation of the bank *vis-à-vis* the West, and to attract desperately needed capital funds from diverse western sources. Nevertheless, Louis von Rothschild, at that time a comparatively young man, was ill-advised to depart from the traditional policy of his house of reticence and cautious reserve, and to ally himself quite openly with the Credit-Anstalt, whose future destiny must have appeared, even if viewed through rose-coloured glasses, as quite uncertain.

In subsequent years, the young Rothschild paid little attention to the affairs of the Anstalt. He devoted himself primarily to his many artistic and philanthropic interests, and spent a good deal of time outside Vienna in pursuit of his passion for hunting. It was perhaps symptomatic of this state of affairs that at the time of the Boden-Credit-Anstalt crisis Louis von Rothschild could not be found for several days, since he had ventured into the forests of a thickly wooded part of Austria, and had left no notice of how and where he could be found.

In these circumstances Ludwig Neurath, the general manager of the bank, a man of great organizing ability but with little insight into the complex economic problems besetting Central Europe, was free to pursue business pretty much as he saw fit. Since he was certain that the general course of the bank, i.e. to channel western funds into eastern investment outlets, was correct, if only it were adamantly followed through, he encouraged firms to pay out dividends, even if they had to borrow money from the Credit-Anstalt to do so. Increasingly, new credits were extended to firms which were hardly able to repay interests on their outstanding debt. It seems fair, however, to add that inside Austria Neurath and his crew were under considerable pressure from the government to prop up crumbling businesses so as to relieve a steadily worsening economic situation. No doubt, government and business, as well as union representatives, shared to some extent in the moral guilt of the Credit-Anstalt of insisting on a business policy which seemed increasingly at variance with the underlying reality.

It seems fair to ask also why the creditors of the Credit-Anstalt, who had a fair share of respresentatives on the board, exercised such perfunctory control over the affairs of the bank. Surely, they should have been able long before the full impact of the crisis to perceive that something was going very wrong. No doubt, the answer to this question is to be found in the magic name of Rothschild, which enabled the bank to obtain western funds without the inconvenience of having to put up with rigorous controls. We may add that some of the western banks which so readily gave aid and comfort to the Anstalt, especially in the latter part of the 1920s, seemed quite anxious to provide short-term funds on the highly convenient terms (or so it seemed at that time) which were offered to them by the Austrian institution. Thus the name of Rothschild as well as the lure of 'easy money' may have accounted for the carelessness with which western entanglement in Central European banking proceeded apace during the 1920s.

We should like to add a short postscript on the issue of nationalization which arose out of the remedial measures taken by the government after the full eruption of the crisis. As Stiefel has shown, the conservative government which was confronted with the failure of the Credit-Anstalt had at first not the slightest intention to acquire a majority of the shares, and was eventually compelled to do so after it had grasped the full dimensions of the crisis. Yet, even after becoming the majority shareholder of the bank, the government did not consider it as a newly won instrument of its economic policy, but rather as a liability to be relinquished at the first suitable moment. No such opportunity arose during the remaining years of the First Republic, and after the occupation of Austria by the Nazis the Credit-Anstalt was taken over, lock, stock and barrel, by Germany's biggest bank, the Deutsche Bank.

After the seven years of German domination were over, a sizeable part of Austrian industry and the three major commercial banks, including the Credit-Anstalt, were nationalized by an Act of Parliament in 1946. It is not our intention to probe here into the complex set of motives which underlay the Nationalization Act of 1946. Suffice it to say that the Credit-Anstalt, together with its still not inconsiderable industrial combine, was declared public property and put under the nominal control of the Minister of Finance, but otherwise was permitted to act according to the rationale of the free market. The main, if not the only, function of the public authority has consisted thus far in the naming of the chief officers of the bank. Thus the nationalization of Austrian banking can only be understood against the background of the history of the First Republic and of the period of Nazi domination.

Index *to authors cited in the text*

Index *to banks and firms*

Subject index

European Economic Community (E.E.C.), 73
exchange control, 87, 126, 130, 147, 154, 198, 202, 271, 321
explosives, 23, 155–7; German manufactures of, 156; South American market for, 156

facility, transportation, 3, 11
factory, 3, 11
fats processing industry: in Czechoslovakia, 37, 40; in Germany, 14, 16, 28
fabricated metals industry, 4
Feilchenfeld, O., 111
Fellinger, 186
fibres, 26
films, 26
Finaly, 334
financial sector, 99
firm, British definition, 17, 18
firm, multi-unit industrial, 3, 24, 25; in Czechoslovakia, 40; in the United States, 4–11
firms, American, 12; British machinery, 22; German food, 16; German machinery, 17; growth rates of, 32
firms, large, 32; in America, 16, 23; in Britain, 22, 24, 32; in Czechoslovakia, 37, 40; in Germany, 12, 16, 23; in the food industry, 25
firms, manufacturing, in the United States, 10
firms, shipbuilding, in the United States, 8
firms, textile, 25
First World War, 8, 25, 52, 57, 58, 60, 70, 78, 85, 104, 106, 107, 112, 144, 145, 148, 173, 176, 182, 188, 196, 209, 211, 234, 250, 255, 309, 310, 311, 357; effects of, on Austria-Hungary, 73–4, 76, 145, 155
Fleischmann, Benno, 263
Flick, Frederic, 232, 237, 238, 241, 242, 333
flour, 22
food companies, British, 19, 22; large, 28
food industry, 24, 26, 27, 28; in Austria, 57, 61; in Britain, 19, 20, 22; in Czechoslovakia, 41
  in Germany, 14, 15
    foreign subsidiary enterprises in, 16
  in the United States, 9, 10, 23
    multi-unit firms in, 7
  large firms in, 25
foreign capital: definition, 227–8, 247; economic and political consequences of, 229; in East Central Europe, 74, 347–8
Fouchet, 358
Fournier, A., 376, 377, 380, 401
FRANCE, 3, 33, 53, 78, 89, 92, 93, 145, 152, 176, 182; acquisition of assets in East Central Europe, 315–16; and Austria, 422, 423; and Czechoslovakia, 376–7; capital in Czechoslovak banks, 314; capital in Czechoslovak industry, 275; capital in Hungary, 358–9, 365; capital in Poland, 231, 235, 247, 385; Comité des Forges, 392; controls over capital exports, 313, 408
  government, 415
    policy towards foreign investment, 376
    investment in Austria-Hungary, 310, 347–8; match monopoly, 217
  Ministry of Finance, 312, 327, 422
    and Austrian banks, 325, 422; 'francization' of the Länderbank, 317
  Ministry of Foreign Affairs (Quai d'Orsay), 312, 314, 333, 351
    and the capital market, 312, 313; and Hungary, 359, 378–80, 401–4; and western

penetration of East Central Europe, 316, 348; discussions with Dr Sieghart, 325; 'francization' of the Länderbank, 317
  post-war attitudes towards Russia, 377; state-business relations, 312, 313, 401; tariffs, 392; trade with Austria-Hungary, 310
François-Marsal, 324
Franke, Dr, 175
Frankfurt, 140, 141
Freistadt, 121
von Friedländer-Fould, Frederic, 232
Frýštat, 121
furniture industry, 4; in Austria, 80; in Britain, 20; in Germany, 13; in the United States, 9
Fürth, Bernard, 211, 213, 214
Fürth, Dr Ernest, 212, 220, 222, 223

von Gahlen, Hugo, 111
Galicia, 80, 90
Gannon, J. H., 423
gas industry, in Czechoslovakia, 40
gasoline, 25
Gdańsk, 244
Geisenheimer, Paul, 234
Geneva, 314; protocols, 322
German-Austria: see Austria
German-Austrian Customs Union, 186, 422
German-French dyestuffs agreement (1927), 150
Germans, 74; in Poland, 234, 248
GERMANY, 3, 4, 11–17, 17, 18, 20, 22, 23, 24, 25, 27, 28, 35, 53, 78, 145, 156, 184, 210; and Upper Silesia, 234–6; banks in Poland, 243, 244; bilateral trade, 154
  capital, 80
    direct, in Austria, 93; in Austrian banks, 92; in Poland, 228, 229, 230, 244, 247, 248, 249
  chemical industry, 12, 13, 14, 17, 20, 22, 148, 149, 204
    markets of, 148
  credit banks, 230, 232, 242, 243, 244; credits to Polish companies, 237; Deutsche Stiftung, 244; Deutsches Institut für Technische Arbeitsschulung, 299; 'Drang nach Südosten', 203; Economics Ministry, 283; economic war against Poland, 236, 249; export subsidies, 155; Finance Ministry, 286; foreign economic policy, 140; Foreign Office (Auswärtiges Amt), 132, 244; foreign trade controls, 143, 203; French occupation, 107; government administration, 141; government orders to Czechoslovak industry, 275; government secret purchase of the shares of the Boden-Credit-Anstalt, 325; Grossraumwirtschaft, 153, 199, 220; Hauptreuhandstelle-Ost, 250, 278, 300; Hugenberg economic policy, 186; imperialism, 234, 249; inflation, 173; influence in the Alpine Montan Co., 262; investment in Austria-Hungary, 310; match monopoly, 217, 219; Mitteleuropäischer Wirtschaftstag, 143, 155, 186, 188, 300; monetary stabilization, 321
  National Socialist government, 117, 130, 131, 202
    autarky, 274; controlled armaments sector, 274; economic coercion, 299; economic offensive in Central Europe, 270; imperialism, 270; integration of Hungary and Romania, 278; internal power struggle, 269; programmes, 269, 274
  'New Plan', 130; penetration into Central and

investment goods industry, in Austria, 61
iron and steel industry, 23, 24, 28; cartels in, 81; European market for, 81; in Austria, 44, 58, 60, 81; in Britain, 20; in Czechoslovakia, 36, 37, 81; in Poland, 230, 232, 233, 234, 238; in the United States, multi-unit firms in, 7
iron industry: in Austria-Hungary, 34, 45, 58, 78; in Bohemia and Moravia, 45, 78
iron ore: Austrian, 253, 272, 274; for Mannesmannröhren-Werke, 104; Styrian, 78, 79
Italy, 31, 75, 88, 90, 106, 107, 152; Austrian policy, 313, 315; nostrification, 92

jams, 22
Jenesco, T., 185, 316
jute industry: in Austria, 44; in Czechoslovakia, 37

Katowice, 80, 232, 237, 241, 244
Kehrl, 270, 275
Keppler, 270
kerosene, 25
Kiedrón, Jozef, 237
Kiel, 141
Kindersley, Sir Robert, 421, 423, 424
Kladno, 116, 120, 199, 201, 253
Klesper, Otto, 108, 111, 112, 116, 117, 127
Kola, R., 92
Komotau, 103, 105, 107, 108, 109, 110, 111, 112, 116, 120, 127, 132
Korfanty, Wojciech, 232, 241
Körner, Paul, 270, 272, 279, 285, 286
Kornfeld, Baron Paul, 358, 361, 403, 404
Köttgen, Dr, 175
Kraków, 89, 231
Krassny, 326, 328
Kreuger, Ivar, 209, 211, 212, 213, 214, 215, 217, 218, 220, 221, 222, 223
Krieglach, 83
Kruliš-Randa, 387
Kriwoj-Rog, 279, 383
Kux, 262

laboratory, research, 3, 27
labour, unskilled, 25
labour-intensive industries, 271; in the United States, 9
Lahn, river, 104
Lampson, M. W., 333
Landore, 103, 105
Lapebie, Colonel, 387, 389
Latvia, match monopoly, 218
Lavigne, 387
lead, Polish, 230, 233, 234, 235, 238
League of Nations, 415, 425, 427; administration of the Saar, 107; Financial Committee, 327, 419, 421, 424; loan to Austria, 217, 321, 350; loan to Hungary, 217, 321
leather industry: in Britain, 20; in Germany, 13; in the United States, 9
Lengauer, Josef, 260, 261
Lepercq, Aimée, 387, 388, 389, 412
Leskovar, 260
Levant, 214, 216
Leverkusen, 140
Ley, social empire of, 269
lignite, 274
limited liability, 32
Linz, 272
Lion, L., 401, 403

Little Entente, 161, 182, 186, 197, 199, 375, 377, 386
Łódź, 227
Loewenstein, 389
London, 89, 97, 107, 211; capital market, 313–14; and Austrian banks, 314, 323
Ludwigshafen, 141
lumber industry: in Britain, 20; in Germany, 13; in the United States, 9
Lwów, 88, 89, 231

machine industry, 24, 26, 27, 28; in Austria, 44, 64, 82, 83; in Austria-Hungary, 34; in Britain, 19, 20, 22; in Germany, 12, 13, 14, 15, 20; in Poland, 234; in the United States, 9, 10, 12
Magyars, 74
Maindl, Dr, 263
Majláth, Count János, 370
Mallet, C., 401
Malzacher, Dr Hans, 263, 285
management strategy, financial, Austrian, 82
management structure, 15, 32; in East Central Europe, 45
manager, 3, 24, 27; administrative, 45; corporate, 28, 45; industrial, 28; in the successor states, 45; production, 27; technical, 45
Mannesmann, Max, 103
Mannesmann, Reinhard, 103
manufacturing, 27
manufacturing and mining, in Germany, 12
manufacturing companies, British, 17
margarine, 22, 25
Marcus, H., 111
market: Austro-Hungarian, 33, 35; domestic American, 23; European iron and steel, 81; for branded goods, 28; nitrogen, 151–3
　　urban:
　　　British, 23; German, 16, 23
　　world, for chemicals, 148–9
marketing, 9, 20, 22, 25, 27, 32; German, 16
marketing departments for industrial chemicals, 26
mass-production, 17, 23, 27; in Czechoslovakia, 37–8; in the United States, 8
mathematics, 45
meat packing industry, 27; in the United States, 8
mechanical engineering, 24; in Czechoslovakia, 36
mechanics, 45
mechanization, in Austria, 65
Merano, 88
metals industry, 24, 25, 27; in Austria, 64, 82, 83; in Britain, 19, 20, 22; in Czechoslovakia, 37; in Germany, 12, 13, 15, 20; in the United States, 9, 10, 12
matches, 209, 211; British market, 210
middlemen, German, 35
Milan, 106
Millerand, 403
mimeograph machines, 17
mines, 3, 10; Austrian, 82
Mining and Foundries Employers Association, 111
mining and metallurgical industries, in East Central Europe, 45
mining companies: Austrian, 82, 82–3; British, 17
mining industry, 28; in Austria, 58, 59, 60, 82–3; in Britain, 22; in Germany, 14